SEVENTH EDITION

A Short History of Western Civilization

Volume 1: To 1776

JOHN B. HARRISON
Late Professor Emeritus of History
Michigan State University

RICHARD E. SULLIVAN
Michigan State University

DENNIS SHERMAN
John Jay College of Criminal Justice
City University of New York

McGraw-Hill Publishing Company

New York   St. Louis   San Francisco   Auckland   Bogotá   Caracas   Hamburg
Lisbon   London   Madrid   Mexico   Milan   Montreal   New Delhi
Oklahoma City   Paris   San Juan   São Paulo   Singapore   Sydney   Tokyo   Toronto

to Mary, Vivian, and Pat

The present overwhelms our forgotten selves;
but we are what we were,
with only a frosting of changes
—D.S.

A Short History of Western Civilization
Vol I: To 1776

3 4 5 6 7 8 9 0   **DOH DOH**   9 4 3 2 1 0

ISBN 0-07-557084-X

This book was set in Palatino by Ruttle Shaw & Wetherill, Inc.
The editors were Christopher J. Rogers and Eleanor Castellano;
the designer was Wanda Siedlecka.
Printed by R. R. DONNELLEY & SONS, Harrisonburg, Virginia

Credits for Part Opening Photos
Part One: Ralph Mandol/DPI; *Part Two:* Alison Frantz; *Part Three:* Anderson/Giraudon; *Part Four:* The British Museum; *Part Five:* Epreuve D'Archives/Rapho-Photo Researchers; *Part Six;* The British Museum; *Part Seven:* The Granger Collection.

Credits for Maps
The maps were executed by Jean Paul Tremblay, Francis & Shaw, Inc., Dyno Lowenstein, and Vantage Art, Inc.

Cover Photo Credit
The conquest of England by the Normans: Death of the Brothers of King Harold. Detail of the Bayeux Tapestry. ("Tappiserie de Bayeux," with special permission of the City of Bayeux.)

Library of Congress Cataloging-in-Publication Data

Harrison, John Baugham.
  A short history of Western civilization / John B. Harrison,
Richard E. Sullivan, Dennis Sherman. — 7th ed.
    p.   cm.
  Includes bibliographies and index.
  Contents: v. 1. To 1776 — v. 2. Since 1600.
  ISBN 0-07-557084-X — ISBN 0-07-557088-2
  1. Civilization, Occidental—History.   I. Sullivan, Richard
Eugene, (date).   II. Sherman, Dennis.   III. Title
CB245.H32   1990
909'.09821—dc20   89-35195

ABOUT THE AUTHORS

John B. Harrison was born in Lawrenceville, Virginia, and grew up in Rich Square, North Carolina. He received his B.A. and M.A. at the University of North Carolina, and his Ph.D. at the University of Wisconsin. He also studied at the Sorbonne. He taught history at Lees Junior College, Jackson, Kentucky, the University of Wisconsin extension, Ohio Northern University, and Michigan State University where he was Professor Emeritus of History. He was Visiting Professor at the University of North Carolina, 1963–1964. Professor Harrison was a member of the American Historical Association and the Society for French Historical Studies. During seven trips to Europe he visited twenty-one countries. He has also traveled in the Far and the Middle East, Africa, and Latin America. He is the author of *This Age of Global Strife* (1952), and of a number of articles and book reviews.

Richard E. Sullivan was born and raised near Doniphan, Nebraska. He received a B.A. degree from the University of Nebraska in 1942, and an M.A. degree and a Ph.D. degree from the University of Illinois in 1947 and 1949 respectively. His doctorate was earned in the field of medieval history. He has taught history at Northeast Missouri State Teachers' College (1949–1954) and at Michigan State University (1954 until his retirement in 1989). While at Michigan State University he has served as chairman of the Department of History (1967–1970), Dean of the College of Arts and Letters (1970–1979), and Associate Provost (1984–1987). Professor Sullivan held a Fulbright Research Fellowship and a John Simon Guggenheim Fellowship to Belgium in 1961–1962. He is the author of *Coronation of Charlemagne* (1959), *Heirs of the Roman Empire* (1960), and *Aix-la-Chapelle in the Age of Charlemagne* (1963). His articles have appeared in many scholarly journals.

Dennis Sherman is Professor of History at John Jay College of Criminal Justice, the City University of New York. He received his B.A. (1962) and J.D. (1965) from the University of California at Berkeley and his Ph.D. (1970) from the University of Michigan. He was Visiting Professor at the University of Paris (1978–1979, and 1985). He received the Ford Foundation Prize Fellowship (1968–1969, 1969–1970), a fellowship from the Council for Research on Economic History (1971–1972), and fellowships from the National Endowment for the Humanities (1973–1976). His publications include *Western Civilization: Images and Interpretations* (1987), a series of introductions in the Garland Library of War and Peace, and several articles and reviews on nineteenth-century French economic and social history in American and European journals.

CONTENTS

Where Historians Disagree

Maps

Chart

PREFACE

In this seventh edition of A SHORT HISTORY OF WESTERN CIVILIZATION, we have attempted to achieve the right mix of continuity and change. Those features that made the sixth and previous editions so successful have been retained. We have kept our account brief enough so it offers readers a realistic opportunity to absorb a meaningful overview of the essentials of the history of Western civilization. The scope of the book is not limited to European history; brief treatments of other parts of the world, such as the United States, and non-Western civilizations as they have come to interact with the Western world, are included to put Western civilization into a broader context. The book continues to be organized into sixty chapters, a structure that fits well with most academic calendars. Introductory and retrospective essays at the beginning and the end of each of the twelve units of the book provide a broad summarizing perspective on major historical eras. The interpretative essays featuring points on which historians disagree are designed to encourage readers to develop a healthy skepticism toward accepted generalizations about the past and to learn to ask questions about the meaning of historical investigation. The large number of maps and illustrations highlight and complement the written text. The suggested reading lists offer alternatives for deeper study of topics covered in each chapter. The instructor's manual is a tool available to assist in making full use of this book.

Several important changes have been made in this edition to improve the quality and appeal of the book. There has been an additional infusion of social history and women's history into the text, continuing the changes already made in this direction in the sixth edition. The addition of this material reflects a growing consensus in modern scholarship that such matters need greater attention in order to portray past human experience fully and accurately. Parts of the book have been reorganized, particularly those chapters covering the early modern and modern eras. There have been extensive revisions of the text to include the most recent historical scholarship and, in some cases, new sections have been written. Sixteen pages of color plates have been added, and a large number of illustrations are new to this edition. Most of the maps have been revised and clarified. Five additional "Where Historians Disagree" essays have been added. A new introductory essay on historiography has been written for this edition. The suggested readings have been completely revised and updated.

As in previous editions, our goal is to produce a high-quality, clearly written, useful, and flexible account of Western civilization. We are indebted to numerous teachers and students who have aided us in this effort. We hope this book can serve as the basis for an effective survey of the history of Western civilization, a subject that remains essential for any understanding of who we are and what of significance is happening in the present.

We would like to thank the following reviewers for their many helpful comments and suggestions: Richard L. Bates, Villanova University; Mirian J. Levy, University of Hartford; and David C. Riede, The University of Akron.

RICHARD E. SULLIVAN
DENNIS SHERMAN

HISTORY AND THE HISTORIAN

As our readers undertake to expand their knowledge and understanding of the past, we ask them to reflect for a moment on what history is and on how the historian works. These are perplexing questions. At the heart of the problem is the fact that history has a dual meaning. On the one hand, history is everything that has happened in the past: all that an almost infinite number of humans beings did and thought over the millions of years of human existence. On the other hand, history is the reconstruction of these already completed activities and thoughts undertaken by explorers—called historians—who can only be outsiders trying to discover what happened, to explain why something occurred as it did, and to ascertain why such occurrences are in some way meaningful. The gap between what happened in the past and what historians are able to discover about what actually occurred is immense. Our readers can perhaps sense this gap by comparing all the things that must have happened to each of them with what they can accurately reconstruct about all the events of their own lives. As a consequence of the distance between the two meanings of history, the examination of the past goes on continually, and the reconstruction constantly changes as explorers of the past discover more about what happened and as they change their interpretations of why and how humans acted and thought as they did in the past.

There is no law that dictates that the limitless past should be explored, described, and understood. But people continue to find that exercise irresistible. Many have found and still find the past inherently interesting, just as is gazing at stars or watching birds. Others have been and still are convinced that learning about the past has an important social function. It can inform us about who and what we are as human beings. It can shed light on the contemporary situation, either by providing an understanding of how things came to be what they are or by supplying analogies that help us comprehend our situation and formulate solutions to issues that face our society. Societies have especially prized history as an instrument for socializing their members (particularly the young), that is, for teaching them how to behave and to think in ways that are appropriate to their cultural environment. In writing this book, we have assumed that both of these perspectives are equally valid. We firmly believe that gaining knowledge and insight into the past not only is interesting but also is constructively useful to the collective well-being of any society.

In their explorations of the past historians differ in many ways, but most agree that there is a common, basic methodology suited to the task facing them, that is, reconstructing the past. Fundamental to that methodology is the formulation by the historian of a question or a hypothesis about what happened in the past. Obviously, the range of such questions and hypotheses is infinite; as a consequence, historical studies are richly and unpredictably varied. In many ways the vitality of historical studies depends on the imagination and the ingenuity of historians in formulating the problems they wish to study. Once having defined a "subject," the historian starts searching for sources that will provide information about that subject. Of crucial importance are what historians call primary sources, which are surviving pieces of evidence produced by human beings who were directedly involved in the activity under investigation or by those in a position to know what happened. Primary sources exist in many forms. Most important are written documents of a variety of kinds in which observers of past events recorded what happened. But other kinds of primary sources can help the historian find out what happened, including buildings, art works, maps, pottery, tools, clothing, and oral traditions. Primary documents do not necessarily speak to the historian in clear and unmistakable terms. Historians must apply critical techniques to them in order to evaluate them and to extract information from them. That criticism can be external, aimed at such things as uncovering forgeries and errors; or it can be internal, aimed at resolving such matters as the motives that moved someone to produce the source or the meaning intended by the creator. In addition to primary sources, historians must also take into account what are called secondary sources. They are the works of other historians and scholars who have examined the same general subject and the same segment of time. Secondary sources must also be critically evaluated.

When historians have completed their search for sources and have extracted from them whatever information they can relative to the question or hypothesis with which they began, they then must present in comprehensible form the results of their research. This is a formidable task. In oversimplified terms it involves a series of choices: what sources to emphasize; how those sources relate to the problem under investigation; what data is not relevant; how to organize information in order to convey a meaningful explanation of what happened; and what literary devices to use in order to permit others to understand what happened in the past. This process can never be totally objective, for historians inevitably decide these issues in terms of their own perspective and their own values about the human condition. As a consequence, many prefer to call the reconstruction of the past an art rather than a science.

Although it is impossible to provide a neat formulation of how history is finally presented, in a rough way historians tend to reflect one of two perspectives in their treatment of the past. Some, representing a humanistic orientation, see the past in terms of unique actions and events that are studied for their intrinsic value and for the insights they provide about the human situation in a particular historical setting. These historians tend to present the past in narrative form, telling a story that unfolds in a chronological order with each succeeding episode somehow related to and conditioned by what went before. Others, reflecting a social science orientation, look for patterns in human thought and behavior over time. They tend to focus on repetitive commonalities rather than uniqueness, on comparisons rather than chronology, and on the universal relevance of the past rather than the unique, nonrepetitive nature of the past's specific episodes. These historians tend to write history in an analytic style, focusing on explanations, causes, and relationships. In this book, both perspectives will be used.

Given the vastness and the complexity of the past, historians cannot deal with all of history at once. To meet this problem, they have adopted several conventions that permit more effective and meaningful reconstruction. One means is to divide the past into periods, each of which has common features allowing it to be treated as an entity. An example of such a periodization scheme is the one applied to the history of Western civilization. The six-thousand-year span involved in that history is typically divided into four periods: the ancient period; the Middle Ages; the early modern period; and the modern period. As will be illustrated in this book, these larger periods are divided into subperiods. Historians often disagree on periodization schemes, and the boundaries between periods shift considerably. A second way to break up history into manageable segments is to focus attention on topics; sometimes these topics are broad, such as the Reformation, and sometimes they are narrow, such as the consequences of World War I. A third way of segmenting the past is to focus on geographical areas. In this book the area treated is extensive: In geographical terms Western civilization embraces what is today Europe, the Mediterranean basin where Western civilization originated, those areas of the world where offshoots of Western civilization have been established, and areas where there existed non-Western civilizations that were significantly affected by the Western world. Historians often focus on smaller areas: nations, regions or cities. The choice made by historians about how to break up the entire past into manageable units has an important bearing on the way the past is treated.

Historical research and writing are decisively affected by the judgments made by historians as to what aspect of human activity is most important in shaping and explaining the collective destinies of past societies. For example, some argue that political factors are crucial in forming societies, while others insist that economic conditions are decisive. Such formulations have produced several widely recognized categories of history: political history, economic history, social history, intellectual history, religious history, and cultural history. Each of these categories produces its unique version of the past and its unique manner of explaining the historical process. Such categorization also invites some historians to undertake a synthesis that will produce a version of the past embracing all aspects of human activity. The effort to synthesize has played an important part in the writing of this book.

Historians constitute a scholarly community in which knowledge, interpretations, interests, and concepts are shared. As a result, schools of historical thought develop, usually derived from shared assumptions about the fundamental characteristics of human development. An example is one of the best-known schools of thought in the twentieth century, the Marxist school. Proponents of this school argue that modes of economic producton are the determinant force in historical development. Each mode of production serves as a dynamic force creating its own unique political, social, religious, and cultural structures. And each contains within it conflicting class interests that provide the impetus for change and that determine the direction of change. Such schools encourage a collective approach to the past guided by a shared angle of attack and by a common mode of interpretation. They also tend to produce generalized explanations of the past. The constraints implicit in almost any school of historical thought cause most historians to withhold commitment to a particular school. But the existence of such schools often plays a role in shaping the way uncommitted historians approach major historical developments. In this book an effort has been made to represent various interpretations and to emphasize those that seem most useful in explaining a particular situation in the past.

Over the generations there have been numerous changes in what is most challenging both to historians and to their audiences. In recent years three broad developments have been particularly influential. Efforts have been made to integrate some of the results of these developments into this text.

First, there has been a broadening and growing importance of social history. Social historians increasingly emphasize looking at the past "from the bottom up" by studying the everyday experiences and attitudes of "ordinary" people or sub-ordinated groups rather than concentrating on political leaders, elite groups, and great thinkers. To recount the history of these heretofore "silent" people and to assess its significance, social historians have had to ask new questions and to make innovative use of sources often overlooked by traditional historians, such as parish registers, gravestone inscriptions, police reports, manorial records, folk tales, and popular art. Their efforts have greatly enriched our knowledge and understanding of the past in its entirety.

The second development is often termed "the new history" (although, like many elements of social history, its roots go back several decades). The new history has been shaped by the methods and the theoretical constructs formulated by social scientists. For example, historians have applied to the past the methods and the findings of demographers to expand knowledge of changes in population size, age groups, birth rates, age of marriage, fertility rates, family size, and death rates. Other historians have used the methods and findings of modern psychology to expand their understanding of the past. Psychohistorians emphasize emotional factors in explaining individual and group behavior in all kinds of historical situations, including such often-overlooked topics as child rearing, family relations, charismatic leadership, and death. Many historians practicing the new history rely on comparative and quantitative analysis to support their conclusions. Increasingly this approach involves the use of computers and statistical analysis of data pertaining to such things as voting patterns, price fluctuations, and population changes.

A third development has been the growing interest in women's history. Traditionally history has been written from the male perspective and has focused primarily on the thoughts and behavior of men. Women's history attempts to correct this neglect of women in history and the distortions that inevitably result. It focuses on women's experiences and on the roles women played in a large number and variety of historical developments. It also tries to alert us to gender bias in the way historical questions are posed, evidence is evaluated, and history is written.

Perhaps all of these considerations will suggest what is most important: The writing of history involves numerous choices, judgments, and compromises. The history one studies or writes depends on what questions are posed. Historians usually want to know more than only what happened, more than only the facts. They want to know how something of importance happened, why it happened, and why it is significant. They must create some reasoned order out of the chaos of past acts and thoughts. All of these considerations shape how they use historical facts and determine what they make of those facts. It may be true that history defined as all that has happened over the ages is a closed book in which nothing changes. But history defined as reconstructing that past is always in the process of change. Not only are new events happening every day and forgotten events of the past constantly being discovered, but the way we look at and interpret the past also changes as our interests, perspectives, and interpretative modes change. In this book, we have attempted to reflect this dynamic quality of history by making revisions that reflect our changing views and those of our colleagues engaged in exploring the past.

PART ONE

THE ANCIENT NEAR EAST, 4000–300 B.C.

This book will seek to explain the evolution of Western civilization by describing the numerous ingredients that combined over a long period of time to shape its basic features. While the emergence of civilized life on this planet occurred over immense ages, the crucial "roots" from which Western civilization developed began to grow about six thousand years ago in a particular area of the world known as the Near East.

This first section of the book will concentrate on developments occurring in the Near East over a long era stretching from about 4000 B.C. to 300 B.C. After a few introductory remarks concerning the long era of human history that preceded the emergence of civilization in the Near East, we shall focus on the amazing activity that unfolded in two river valley systems in the Near East: the Tigris-Euphrates in Mesopotamia and the Nile in Egypt. For it was in the challenging environment of these river valleys that human communities developed the first complex patterns of institutions, techniques, and ideas that can be called "civilizations." What was achieved in this setting established the foundations upon which Western civilization was to grow. Beyond characterizing the main features of the early civilizations of Mesopotamia and Egypt, we must consider the beginnings of a process as important to the history of the Western world as was the original creation of civilized life—namely, the beginning of the expansion of the river valley civilizations into a large area of northeast Africa and southwest Asia. Not only did this process permit new peoples to raise the level of their existence, but it also created a cultural setting in which they made their own unique contributions to the broadening stream of civilization. Until at least 500 B.C. the peoples of the Near East were on the forefront of the civilized world. This creative population fashioned a priceless heritage that was later exploited by other peoples participating in the shaping of Western civilization.

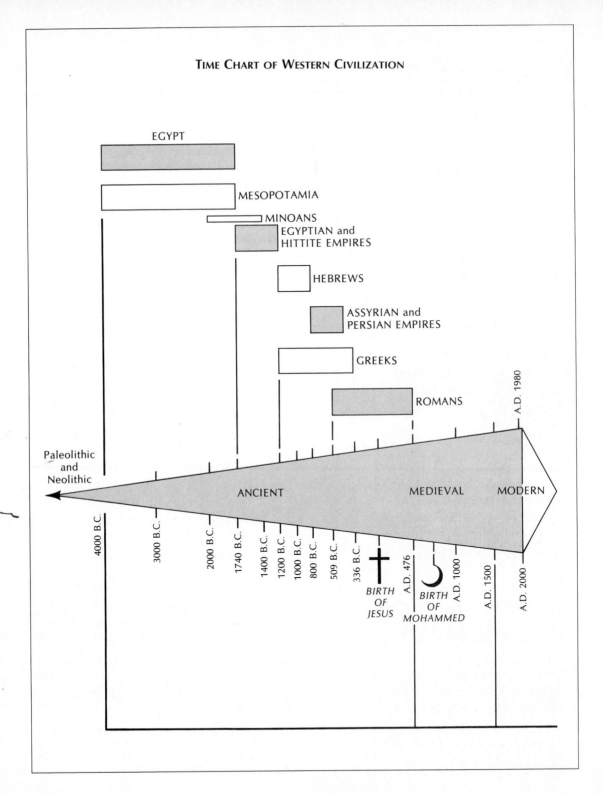

Time Chart of Western Civilization

EGYPT

MESOPOTAMIA

MINOANS

EGYPTIAN and
HITTITE EMPIRES

HEBREWS

ASSYRIAN and
PERSIAN EMPIRES

GREEKS

ROMANS

A.D. 1980

Paleolithic
and
Neolithic

ANCIENT

MEDIEVAL

MODERN

4000 B.C.

3000 B.C.

2000 B.C.

1740 B.C.

1400 B.C.

1200 B.C.

1000 B.C.

800 B.C.

509 B.C.

336 B.C.

BIRTH
OF
JESUS

A.D. 476

BIRTH
OF
MOHAMMED

A.D. 1000

A.D. 1500

A.D. 2000

CHAPTER 1

The River Valley Civilizations: Mesopotamia and Egypt, 4000–1750 B.C.

FIGURE 1.1 A Divine Ruler The statue of Menkure (an Egyptian pharaoh of the Fourth Dynasty) and his queen conveys the majesty and power that surrounded the rulers of the early river valley societies of the Near East. The ability of such rulers to organize human effort on a large scale was crucial in establishing control over the rich river valleys that provided the material base for the first civilizations. This statue also illustrates the basic characteristics of Egyptian sculpture—rigid posture, stylized clothing, a personal touch revealed in the faces of even the majestic god-kings and their consorts. (Museum of Fine Arts, Boston)

Somewhere just before 3000 B.C. there occurred a decisive turning point in the long history of human beings. The change was marked by the creation of the first higher civilizations based on urban societies. The scene of this accomplishment was a unique one: the special environment existing in the Tigris-Euphrates Valley in Mesopotamia and the Nile Valley in Egypt. The establishment of higher civilization in these areas created the foundations upon which all the subsequent history of Western civilization was built.

1. THE PREHISTORIC BACKGROUND

The emergence of higher civilizations in the Near Eastern river valleys was made possible by complex developments during an immensely long prehistoric period of human preparation—perhaps five hundred times longer than the time span shown on the chart on page 2. Our knowledge of what happened during this prehistoric period is fragmentary, and there is disagreement on how to interpret what is known. In simple terms these vast ages involved three interrelated processes: geological developments, which created the topography and the climate of the earth; biological developments, which produced the human species as well as other creatures and plants; and cultural developments, through which human beings created techniques and practices that allowed them to enhance their capabilities of survival and improvement in a constantly changing physical and biological environment.

On the basis of a meager collection of skeletal remains found scattered over the earth, it appears that the existence of humanlike creatures (hominids) must be extended back at least 3 million years. It was only about forty thousand years ago that the human species (conventionally designated as *homo sapiens,* meaning "thinking man") assumed its present physical form, perhaps first in East Africa or southwest Asia. Over the long period separating primitive hominids from *homo sapiens,* most of it dominated by conditions created by four successive ice ages, something happened biologically to create special creatures endowed with physical traits that provided them with advantages over other creatures sharing the earth. Especially important were an upright position, stereoscopic vision, a large and complex brain, a voice mechanism that made verbal communication possible, and a unique hand structure that permitted the manipulation of objects.

No less important in preparing for the emergence of higher civilization was the capacity of humans to create objects and techniques that reinforced their biological capabilities and increased their adaptability in their struggle to control the environment in ways beneficial to them. In large part, this ability to create and transmit *culture* was a consequence of the superiority of their brain. The reconstruction of prehistoric cultural development, derived largely from artifacts discovered and interpreted by archaeologists, is as complex and as open to debate as is the biological history of the human species. Despite these difficulties, certain broad lines of development are evident.

Across prehistoric times human cultural activity was most clearly demonstrated in the making of stone tools. For this reason the prehistoric age has been called the Stone Age. Surviving stone tools indicate that during 99 percent of all human prehistory men and women lived as hunters and food gatherers. Although this culture varied in detail from place to place around the globe, it involved certain basic features that permit us to give it a common name—*Paleolithic* (Old Stone Age) culture. Paleolithic peoples lived in small groups dispersed at considerable distance from each other. They were perpetual wanderers, their lives controlled by the movements of animals and the growth patterns of plants upon which survival depended. They sheltered themselves temporarily in caves, holes covered with animal skins, or fragile tents made of skins or branches. At best, their existence was precarious, as is evident from the complete disappearance of some branches of the hominid species, and improvement in the human condition was slow.

But no matter how slowly and painfully, Paleolithic peoples did advance their culture. They developed increasingly complex and effective techniques for making a greater variety of stone tools, eventually complemented by implements made from bone, horn, and wood. These improved tools made them more efficient killers of even the largest and fiercest animals. They accumulated and transmitted a growing store of knowledge about animals and plants that allowed succeeding generations to hunt and gather food more effectively. They learned how to use fire to warm themselves, prepare their food more easily, and scare away predatory animals. Especially important was their ability to shape social structures permitting group activities. The family, perhaps rooted in the demands of child rearing, appears to have been a basic social unit. Several families, perhaps related by kinship ties, joined forces to create a hunting pack that was more effective because of cooperation. Social and economic functions based on gender developed within these groups. The efforts of male hunters were complemented by equally vital activities carried out by female plant gatherers, fire keepers, and child raisers. Interactions within these communities necessitated spoken languages, a prime instrument not only in promoting effective group action but also in passing on knowledge about animals, plants, weather, and toolmaking. Scanty bits of evidence indicate the existence of religious life centered on a belief in the existence, in all things, of spirits susceptible to human manipulation and perhaps in life after death. The cave paintings found at Altamira in Spain and Lascaux in France—as well as crudely shaped human figures, decorated hunting weapons, and jewelry scattered wherever Paleolithic groups passed—suggest an urge and a capacity to express ideas and feelings about the world and to enhance life with created beauty. All of these elements of evolving Paleolithic society leave no doubt that by the time *homo sapiens* had occupied large portions of the globe forty or fifty thousand years ago, the human species had progressed far in establishing mastery over the world and in utilizing its biological and cultural resources to sustain human life with some degree of security.

A culture based on hunting and food gathering had limitations, perhaps too narrow to contain expanding human capabilities. Ultimately, Paleolithic culture gave way to a new pattern of life that changed the human condition in a fundamental way. This great transformation involved the domestication of plants and animals, which allowed human societies to rely on agriculture to provide the material basis for society. This change marked an essential step along the path to higher civilization. The most recent results of archaeological research into human cultural development on a world scale make it almost certain that the change from a hunting and food-gathering to a farming culture first occurred in a relatively limited area of southwest Asia defined by the upper boundary of the Fertile Crescent (as traced on Map 1.1). Not too much later, as time is measured on the scale of human prehistory, agricultural life appeared in most other areas of the world, sometimes borrowed from the original inventors and other times "invented" anew.

The archaeological evidence collected over the past fifty years from many sites in the area where agriculture first appeared suggests that the "revolution" came gradually and was accompanied by much experimentation. The transition period, extending from about 9000 to 6000 B.C. and coinciding in a rough way with the end of the last period of glaciation, has been called the *Mesolithic* (Middle Stone) age. The experimentation occurred in an ecosystem that had a unique combination of features: moderate but regular rainfall; large numbers of wild sheep, goats, cattle, and swine; rich stands of wild cereals, legumes, and plants with oil-bearing seeds; a substantial population sustained by a well-established Paleolithic culture. Perhaps there was a slight change in the climate associated with the retreat of the glaciers that produced conditions favorable to grass-eating animals and cereal plants. And perhaps population pressure prompted people to put their extensive knowledge of plants and animals to new uses. In any case, behavior patterns began to change in Mesolithic times. People stayed longer in one place. Some groups gave increasing attention to the control and selective killing of animal herds, utilizing the harvest of wild grasses to supplement their meat supply. Others concentrated more heavily on the management of wild plants, depending secondarily on hunting. As these practices continued, certain wild animals—sheep, goats, cattle, and pigs—and certain wild plants—especially wheat and barley—were modified genetically to the point where they flourished best under human care. When that happened, human beings were in a position to abandon hunting and food gathering

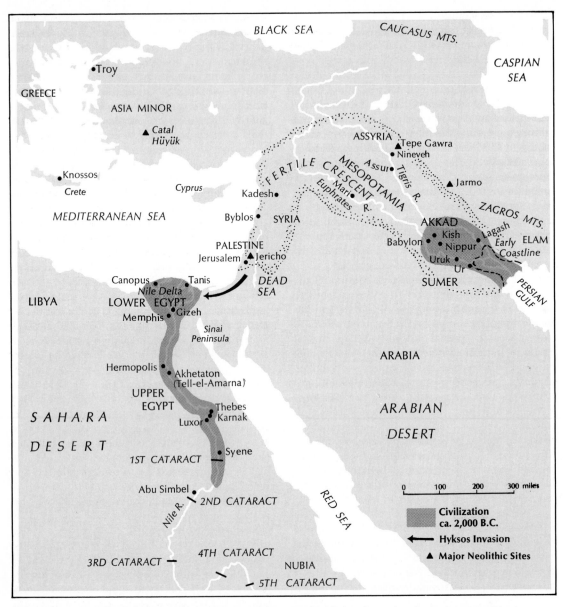

Map 1.1 **EARLY MESOPOTAMIA AND ANCIENT EGYPT** This map highlights the rather limited geographical areas in which higher civilization first appeared. Compared with the vast stretches of territory surrounding them, the areas nourished by the waters of the Tigris-Euphrates and the Nile rivers were small. But what was accomplished there was indeed revolutionary.

in favor of agriculture.

The emergence of agriculture as the basis of life opened what is called the *Neolithic* (New Stone) age. Its revolutionary impact is evident in the remains of several sites excavated in recent years, especially Jericho in Palestine, Halicar and Catal Hüyük in modern Turkey, and Jarmo and Tepe Gawra in modern Iraq (see Map 1.1). People settled permanently in villages, some of which supported populations of several hundred. They built substantial baked-mud houses, featuring not only living quarters but also storage facilities, household shrines, and even burial places. Such public facilities as temples, walls, and wells appeared. Human activity, shared by men and women alike, focused on regular planting and harvesting of wheat, barley, legumes, and fruits, and on the care of domesticated animals, valuable not only for meat but also for milk, cheese, hides, and wool. This new mode of life called for a new kit of stone tools, especially hoes and sickles. Before Neolithic culture progressed far, people were beginning to complement stone tools with copper instruments, heralding a coming age of metals that would make stone tools obsolete. Pottery and basket weaving developed to provide storage for food, and the weaving of fibers emerged to create a new range of clothing.

Besides its new technological features, Neolithic culture had significant new social characteristics. Settled agricultural life demanded greater specialization of labor, which allowed more highly developed skills and better products. Such specialization appears to have given women a greater variety of opportunities to contribute to the village economy; however, the demands of child rearing still limited the extent of that involvement and perhaps increased women's economic dependence on males. Settled life made it possible to accumulate wealth in the form of stored grain and animal herds. This wealth provided the basis of exchange for products that a particular village was unable to provide for itself, thus creating trade, which is clearly evident in the spread of pottery made in a specific area to widely scattered places across the Near East. Increased wealth also made the successful peasant village the target of outsiders, requiring collective action to defend the village. And wealth based on land and animal ownership generated quarrels that posed a threat to internal order in the village. A major consequence of problems related to trade, defense, and adjudication of quarrels was the development of a more complex system of village governance. This system usually took the form of a tribal structure in which several kinship groups or clans acting through family heads selected a village chief who joined the family elders in making and carrying out collective decisions to meet common problems.

Neolithic villagers also had to expand their mental skills to cope with their new situation. The demands of farming called for more complex calculations, extended planning, and disciplined behavior than did hunting and food gathering. Different moral standards were required to fit situations arising from closer contacts with larger numbers of people and from ownership of things. Religion, increasingly centered on the worship of the forces of nature believed to control the fertility of plants and animals, challenged Neolithic villagers with concepts far more complex than those associated with animal spirits. The art created in places such as Catal Hüyük clearly reflects expanding human consciousness. The increasing complexities surrounding religion also led villagers to place greater trust in religious experts—priests—and to dedicate more energy and wealth to winning the favor of the spirits who nourished the crops and animal herds and protected the village. The responsibilities of directing the government of the village and of conducting religious life began to bestow on those involved in these functions a special place of prominence and power in village life, creating the basis for a class system. The evidence strongly suggests that males monopolized these leadership roles as well as family life. Perhaps the emergence of agricultural life created a social system and a set of values that cast women in a position of dependence and inferiority that would be difficult to eradicate. However, it is worth noting that the female figure was a prime symbol used in Neolithic religious cults to represent the regenerative powers of nature. This symbolism suggests a high respect, perhaps even awe, for femininity as a potent force in shaping and controlling human destiny.

2. MESOPOTAMIAN CIVILIZATION: POLITICAL, ECONOMIC, AND SOCIAL LIFE

From a global perspective the development of agriculture had put the peoples of southwestern Asia in the forefront of human activity by about 6000 B.C. Recent studies of the development of some of the area's peasant villages between 6000 and 4000 B.C. suggest some potential for further evolution, but nothing indicates that any of them were capable of developing into complex cities. Urban civilization was created by farmers who learned how to master the more demanding environment existing in the Tigris-Euphrates Valley, a relatively small territory extending about three hundred miles northwest from where the rivers flowed into the Persian Gulf (see Map 1.1).

This flat alluvial plain, called Mesopotamia (a word of Greek origin meaning "between the rivers"), presented both opportunity and challenge to Neolithic peoples on its fringes. As a result of constant silting caused by the annual flooding of the rivers, the soil was immensely rich. Those same floods, brought about by melting snows in the Caucasus Mountains where the Tigris and the Euphrates had their sources, provided a dependable water supply to an area almost devoid of rainfall. However, the potential gifts of Mesopotamia were not easily possessed. The somewhat irregular floods were destructive unless they were controlled, and the rich soil was nonproductive unless the postflood swamps could be drained and cleared of swamp vegetation. And even then the soil was useless unless it could be watered during the arid growing season. Mesopotamia was lacking in many natural resources, especially stone, timber, and minerals. Unless its occupants could organize trading ventures extending over considerable distances, only the most primitive level of culture could be sustained. Finally, Mesopotamia lacked any natural barriers to restrain the raids of peoples living to the east, north, and west.

While agriculture slowly evolved around the fringes of Mesopotamia during the Mesolithic age, that land remained relatively backward. Eventually, perhaps just before 4000 B.C., peasant villages did appear in the river valley. Sometime after about 3500 B.C. these Neolithic villages began to be overshadowed by larger, more complex, and richer communities. Although the evidence is far from clear, this leap forward appears to have involved more than an inevitable evolution from simple village to complex urban culture. The change was due to a burst of creativity that allowed the formation of larger human communities capable of planning, constructing, and maintaining effective irrigation systems. Systematic irrigation permitted the successful exploitation of the full productive potential of Mesopotamia. Perhaps that achievement was the work of the Sumerians, invaders who settled in south Mesopotamia in a land eventually named Sumer. They succeeded in organizing relatively large and complex communities dependent on an irrigation-based agricultural system. By 3100 B.C. several rich and populous city-states had developed in Sumer, including Ur, Lagash, Uruk, and Umma. Each consisted of two elements: a densely populated urban center defined by walls, impressive temples and palaces, and teeming residential areas occupied by people engaged in pursuits other than farming; and a considerable stretch of irrigated farmland carved out of the chaotic river valley environment by an elaborate system of dikes, canals, and reservoirs and then systematically cultivated by a tightly controlled peasant population. The Sumerian accomplishment soon served as a model for another group of intruders who occupied the area just north of Sumer. These were the Akkadians, a Semitic-speaking people from the Arabian Desert, who developed several thriving city-states in northern Mesopotamia. For at least seven centuries, from about 3100 to 2400 B.C., these independent city-states enjoyed remarkable stability and prosperity.

The key to their success was an effective system of government capable of controlling a large population engaged in a variety of mutually supportive activities. From an early date responsibility for decision making rested in the hands of a single human leader. Perhaps initially that power was held by a high priest (*ensi*), but eventually a secular king (*lugal*) exercising military force came to dominate. In either case authority was grounded primarily in religious belief. The Sumerians believed that each city-state had been originally created by a god or a goddess. The city and its surrounding lands belonged to the divine founder, and its citizens were the founder's slaves. The *ensi* or the *lugal* was the agent through whom the will of the divine owner was carried out. He based his activities in a temple-palace that served as the center of the community. From there flowed divine orders coordinating the numerous activities required to exploit the resources belonging to the patron deity. The efforts of the rulers to control the total population were greatly aided by the development of writing, which allowed the keeping of careful records of what was produced and what was due. Back to the temple-palace came a huge income used to sustain the divine city. Around the temple-palace and supported by this income clustered a wide array of specialists who served to carry out the ruler's orders. They included priests and priestesses, record keepers, engineers, architects, sculptors, traders, artisans, soldiers, and tax collectors. The combined creative efforts of these specialists, whose livelihood derived largely from surplus agricultural productivity made possible by the carefully planned and controlled irrigation system, provided the essential features of civilized urban life existing on a plane far beyond life in Neolithic villages. But none of this would have been possible without an effective political system; higher civilization depended more on the relationships among humans than it did on relationships between humans and the natural environment, as had been the case in Paleolithic and Neolithic cultures.

Although the independent city-state pattern of government dominated Mesopotamia between 3100 and 2400 B.C., political problems emerged that eventually brought changes. The wealth of the city-states led to constant attacks from outsiders, undeterred by any natural barriers shielding Mesopotamia. Equally unsettling were conflicts among the city-states, usually caused by the quest for additional land to support increasing populations and more elaborate urban life. The solution was eventually found in the establishment of *empires* built by conquest and ruled by powerful kings who developed new techniques for keeping peace and order among peoples of diverse backgrounds.

The first attempts at shaping empires were made by strong kings from prominent Sumerian cities who used military force to establish mastery over other cities, but these "empires" were short-lived. Ultimately, the Semites were more successful in uniting Mesopotamia. The first great empire builder was Sargon I (ca. 2370–2315 B.C.) from Akkad. He led his Semitic warriors in campaigns that not only subdued the city-states of Sumer but also extended Akkadian dominance into the Zagros Mountains, Assyria, and Syria. Sargon's empire was sustained by his descendants until about 2200 B.C., but then it collapsed under the combined pressure of internal resistance and external attacks.

For an interval after the collapse of the Akkadian Empire, the Sumerian city-states again enjoyed independence and leadership in Mesopotamia. But soon a new empire-building people, the Amorites, overshadowed them. They were a Semitic-speaking people who entered Mesopotamia from the Arabian Desert about 2000 B.C. Their day of glory came with Hammurabi, ruler of the city-state of Babylon. His reign (ca. 1792–1750 B.C.) was distinguished by a series of conquests that once again created a large empire stretching in a great arc from the Persian Gulf to the Mediterranean Sea. From the great city of Babylon Hammurabi asserted control over a large population and spread the fruits of Mesopotamian civilization to many different peoples. For all its brilliance, the Amorite Empire was relatively short-lived. Shortly after 1700 B.C. outside attackers began to batter its frontiers until eventually the Kassites conquered Mesopotamia; their rule led to a long period of political obscurity.

Hammurabi's career exemplifies the new ideas and practices of government introduced by the empire builders who dominated Mesopotamia between 2400 and 1700 B.C. These contributions, aimed chiefly at using political power to create common bonds among diverse peoples, proved to be among the most important of all Mesopotamian contributions to civilization. One technique used by Hammurabi to unify the peoples over whom he ruled was to impress on them their total dependence on the power of their one ruler. This technique called for a conscious effort to exalt the person of the king as the sole source of earthly power. To heighten his visibility, Hammurabi made his court at Babylon the setting for a vast display of wealth toward which his subjects from "the Four Quarters of the World" could turn for their well-being. He sought to create a common religion in his empire, based on the worship of Marduk, once the patron god of the city of Babylon but now presented as the divine lord of all the other deities and of the earth. Hammurabi proclaimed himself as Marduk's sole agent, alone capable of bringing divine favor to his subjects. But his power was more than appearance. He maintained a well-organized army ready to curb threats to peace in the empire. He established a centralized bureaucracy in Babylon consisting of specialized departments devoted to administration. This central government kept careful watch over governors sent out to administer local units into which the empire was divided and to collect taxes, raise troops, and administer justice.

One of Hammurabi's most significant measures to solidify and unify his empire was his law code. He claimed it was handed down to him from the deities "to destroy the wicked and the evil, so that the strong may not oppress the weak" (see Figure 1.2). Although a modern reader of Hammurabi's law code is taken aback by the brutal punishments imposed on lawbreakers, the code is better characterized by its commonsense, humane approach to basic human problems: protection for women, children, and slaves; fairness in commercial exchange; protection of property; standard procedures for adjudicating disputes; debt relief for victims of flood and drought. It reflected an enlightened concept of justice that drew people of all kinds to accept the rule of a king trying to provide common rules governing the behavior of his subjects.

For its material base Mesopotamian civilization depended largely on a carefully organized and controlled agricultural system. Although there were some technological advances in agriculture, especially the introduction of bronze tools and wheeled ploughs, farming depended chiefly on the traditional crops and animals of Neolithic times. The chief difference was the larger productive capacity of the fertile, irrigated fields of Mesopotamia. The prime agricultural unit was a large farm, usually owned by a member of the aristocracy and tilled by tenants and slaves working un-

FIGURE 1.2 An Ancient Lawgiver This relief, showing Hammurabi receiving a code of laws from a deity, was carved at the top of a stone cylinder upon which were inscribed the provisions of the law written in cuneiform script. Sumerian artists were especially adept in relief carving, an art form that would have an illustrious history. (Giraudon)

der careful supervision of the owner or his agents, whose decisions in turn were guided by directives flowing from the ruler and his agents. Every city supported a large number of skilled artisans who made a variety of fine products consumed in the city or distributed far and wide across the Near East by enterprising merchants in return for the raw materials lacking in Mesopotamia.

The political and economic order in Mesopotamia provided the basis for a more diverse and structured social system than was typical of Neolithic peasant villages. At the summit of society stood an aristocracy made up of priests, landowners, and royal officials who derived their high status from their close association with the ruler and their involvement in the governance of society. This aristocracy benefited most from Mesopotamia's material wealth and created a glittering life for itself. Merchants and artisans enjoyed a prosperous and relatively free life, often closely attached to aristocrats as clients. Each city-state had a large population of urban laborers who performed the menial tasks required to run the city and the households of the powerful. The bulk of the population consisted of farmers, living in villages outside the urban center and devoting themselves to agricultural routines from which they derived meager rewards. Slavery existed but was not a dominant feature of Mesopotamian life. The relationships among various social classes, as well as the rights and responsibilities of each, were carefully defined by law.

At all levels of Mesopotamian society the family was a basic institution. Marriages were arranged by family agreements, and the husband and father exercised almost absolute control over the wife and children. As a consequence, women played a limited role in societal decision making. However, the law did recognize that they had certain rights, especially to the dowries provided them by their fathers at the time of marriage. Surviving records indicate that women often inherited their husbands' property and were engaged in economic ventures of many kinds. Aristocratic women certainly shared in the luxuries that accompanied their husbands' social status. The wives and children of artisans and farmers were actively engaged in the work of the heads of households—and they shared the meager returns for their efforts. As a whole, Mesopotamian society was stable and seldom troubled by social strife and tension.

3. MESOPOTAMIAN CULTURAL LIFE

The emergence of higher civilization in Mesopotamia was marked not only by the advances in government, economy, and social structure just described but also by impressive developments in cultural life—in religion, literature, the arts, and the sciences. By and large, the Sumerians were the prime creators of Mesopotamian culture. The Semites were usually imitators of the Sumerians. The result of this relationship was a common culture based on Sumerian models that ultimately embraced all of Mesopotamia.

A prime force shaping Mesopotamian cultural life was religion. The Mesopotamian religion was *polytheistic,* based on a worship of many deities believed to live in all things and to cause everything to happen. Especially awesome were the spirits that controlled the forces of nature: gods and goddesses of the sky, air, water, sun, moon, storms. One or another of these deities was usually accepted as founder and ruler of each city-state. Particularly appealing to ordinary people who lived close to the soil was the goddess of fertility, called Inanna by the Sumerians and Ishtar by the Semites, whose munificent power renewed nature every spring, usually with the help of a male lover. Sharing the universe with these great gods and goddesses were legions of lesser spirits, each of whom could bring blessings or misfortunes, great or small, to men and women in all stations of life. The Mesopotamians spent considerable intellectual energy trying to define the powers of these deities, their origins, and their relationships to one another and to the human community. The result was a rich and intriguing mythology that had a powerful influence on later religious thinking.

The lot assigned to human beings in the god-dominated universe was not an easy one. They were viewed as slaves of the deities, bound to suffer whatever the angry, vengeful, unpredictable gods and goddesses wished. Especially heavy was the burden of trying to please the deities. To do so required the building of splendid temples where the deities could live, supporting priests and priestesses to attend the divine needs, offering endless prayers and gifts, organizing expensive public festivals, and spending endless efforts to discover the intentions of the gods and goddesses as these might be revealed in the movement of the stars, dreams, and the shapes of the entrails of animals. Not only did the great deities need to be kept pleased, but so did all the lesser spirits to whom honor and tribute were paid at countless shrines in homes, fields, and city streets.

Life was an endless ritual aimed at pleasing a multitude of unpredictable spirits. In return the Mesopotamians expected the material gifts the deities had to offer—the safety and material prosperity of the city-state, the family, and the individual. Most men and women were never sure that the all-powerful gods and goddesses would smile on them. A tone of pessimism and fatalism permeated their view of life. Their religion was lacking in any ethical dimensions that taught that good behavior and good deeds were pleasing to the divine powers. Nor did the Mesopotamians entertain any hope for a happy life after death; the dead passed on to a "land of no return" somewhere underground "where dust is their feed, clay their substance; where they see no light and dwell in darkness." Without a chance to please the deities through good behavior nor a hope for a happy afterlife, perhaps there was little choice but fear of the deities and pessimism about the human lot.

The urge to know and to please the gods and goddesses inspired an impressive literature made possible by the development of a writing system—one of the great inventions in history. The Sumerians were the first to develop writing. In its earliest form their writing consisted of pictures (pictograms) used primarily to record what was due to the deities in terms of cattle and grain. Gradually pictograms evolved into symbols representing sounds that could be combined into words that could express chains of thought of various kinds. For the recording of such thoughts these symbols were pressed onto soft clay tablets with a wedge-shaped stylus and then the tablets were baked; thus the writing is called *cuneiform* (from a Latin word meaning "wedge"). Eventually the Sumerian system of writing was adapted to the Semitic language of the Akkadians, which by Sargon I's time was replacing Sumerian writing in Mesopotamia. However, for centuries learned people continued to study Sumerian texts much as modern scholars learn ancient Greek, Latin, and Hebrew. Thus, much Sumerian literature survived as a model to be followed by other peoples.

While writing in Mesopotamia served a major function in keeping records of a large array of ordinary activities, talented individuals learned to use it for creative purposes. The most impressive literary productions were religious epics, of which the *Creation Epic* and the *Epic of Gilgamesh* are examples. The *Creation Epic* describes how Marduk won supremacy over the spirit world and created earth and human beings, a feat that earned him universal worship in the time of Hammurabi. The *Epic of Gilgamesh* recounts the fruitless struggle of a legendary king of Uruk, Gilgamesh, to find immortality. The Mesopotamians also wrote hymns, chronicles of the deeds of great rulers, and letters. The literary forms, themes, and styles developed by Mesopotamian writers not only enriched their own culture but also asserted an important influence on the literature of later peoples, as is evident in Mesopotamian influences reflected in the Hebrew Old Testament, written a thousand or more years later.

From the beginnings of their civilization, the Mesopotamians showed impressive skills and creativity in the visual arts. The need to provide their deities with suitable dwellings stimulated monumental architecture and produced impressive mud brick temple complexes as the central feature of every city. The crowning feature of the temple complex was the temple tower, called a *ziggurat*, designed as a series of terraces one on top of another, each successive layer smaller than the one below. A sanctuary remote from the world was placed atop the final terrace. Around the ziggurat there usually developed an elaborate complex of lesser shrines, offices, priestly dwellings, storehouses, and workshops, all comprising a sacred precinct where the deities could be served. Hardly less elaborate were the palaces where the kings and their courts lived. The palace at Mari, an important city in the Amorite Empire, covered six acres and contained more than two hundred fifty rooms. Mesopotamian architects knew how to use columns, domes, arches, and vaults, but the lack of stone as a building material limited their ability to exploit these forms fully.

The Mesopotamians were also skilled sculptors. Most three-dimensional statues portray the deities and famous kings. Sculptors took some pains to give a distinctive character to the faces of their subjects but concerned themselves little with a realistic rendering of the human body. Their work, strongly influenced by geometrical forms, is solid, stiff, and motionless (see Color Plate 1).

More realistic and animated scenes were created by sculptors working in low relief to depict historic events or divine exploits (see Figure 1.2). The most exquisite carving was done by seal makers who wrought miniaturized scenes in stone used to press an identifying mark onto documents written in clay. The same deft skill is illustrated in jewelry, metalwork, and decorated pottery.

Chiefly as a result of their efforts to cope with divine forces and with the rivers, the Mesopotamians produced a body of knowledge that can be called science. They devised a system of time reckoning based on cycles of the sun and the moon. They developed a standard system of weights and measures almost universally used by Hammurabi's time. Their numbering system combined a decimal system with units of sixty. They were able to perform the basic functions of arithmetic and geometry. A body of medical knowledge, mixing observations and religious lore, was developed. As a result of the travels of merchants and soldiers, the Mesopotamians amassed a considerable store of geographical information. Inspired by an urge to foretell the future, the Mesopotamians gathered accurate information about the movement of the stars. Although the Mesopotamians were seldom concerned with gathering knowledge about nature for its own sake, the information they did compile about nature in the course of meeting practical problems was stored up for the use of later peoples, particularly the Greeks, as the basis for theoretical science.

4. EGYPT: POLITICAL, ECONOMIC, AND SOCIAL LIFE

Not long after urban civilization took shape in Mesopotamia, a similar leap forward occurred in Egypt. Although bits of archaeological evidence found in Egypt suggest the presence of Mesopotamian influences there at the moment of transition to higher civilization, the basic developments in the Nile Valley were native and the resultant pattern of civilization was unique.

Just as in Mesopotamia, the advent of higher civilization in Egypt hinged on meeting the challenge posed by a river valley environment. The Nile has its source in the mountains of equatorial Africa (see Map 1.1). From there it flows northward past a series of rapids (cataracts) to trace a narrow, cliff-lined trough seldom more than ten miles wide through bleak deserts almost devoid of rainfall. As it nears the Mediterranean, the river fans out into a series of channels to create the Delta, a triangle of rich land about one hundred twenty miles on each side. The annual floods of the Nile come with predictable regularity to create what the Egyptians called the "black land" of the narrow valley and the Delta, which they contrasted with the dreaded "red land" of the desert. However, the Nile floods had to be controlled and their waters distributed across the "black land" during the rainless growing season before the productive potential of the valley could be realized.

During many centuries prior to the emergence of higher civilization in the Nile Valley, Neolithic agricultural life existed across much of North Africa. However, only somewhere between 5000 and 4500 B.C. did some of these farmers begin to establish their villages on the fringes of the Nile Valley. During the next thousand years these peoples developed the technical and organizational skills that permitted them to move into the valley and to establish irrigation systems capable of controlling the floods and utilizing the immensely rich soil as a basis of village life. By a process that is ill understood, these villages in time were joined together to form small kingdoms.

The era dominated by these small kingdoms, called the Predynastic Age, ended suddenly about 3100 B.C., when Egypt was united under a single ruler, later given the title *pharaoh*. Egyptian tradition ascribed this feat to Menes, who founded the first dynasty of pharaohs (a dynasty was a group of rulers from a single family who followed one another as pharaoh) and opened an era called the Old Kingdom (3100–2200 B.C.). Six dynasties ruled during this long era, the most glorious being the Third and Fourth dynasties. From their capital at Memphis, these pharaohs asserted a beneficial authority that brought peace, prosperity, and the fruits of higher civilization to the entire valley. Egypt benefited especially from freedom from outside attacks, a boon afforded by the formidable natural barriers guarding the Nile Valley: the cataracts, the deserts, the Mediterranean Sea. The massive pyramids built at Gizeh by the powerful pharaohs of the Fourth Dynasty—Menkure, Kephren, and Khufu (Cheops)—mirror the immense wealth of a society unified in exploiting the Nile and the great power of the rulers who directed this collective effort.

The key to this success was the political system that had taken shape by the time of the Third Dynasty. Its central feature was the absolute power of the pharaoh, who was considered to be a god sired by the sun god Ra and destined to eternal life. The pharaoh owned Egypt and its people. Every person was his servant, subject to his unchallengeable orders. Despite their lofty status, most of the pharaohs of the Old Kingdom were active statesmen, well trained for their role and constantly occupied in overseeing the irrigation system, giving justice, directing building programs, and sponsoring trade. They exercised their power through a highly developed administrative system centered at Memphis. Egypt was divided into smaller administrative units, called *nomes,* each controlled by royal officials held closely accountable by the central government for carrying out the pharaoh's orders in the villages of each nome.

During the Sixth Dynasty this highly effective system faltered. Egypt entered a period of anarchy called the First Intermediate Period (2200–2050 B.C.). The pharaohs of this era (Seventh through Tenth dynasties) were shadowy, ineffectual figures. Political power fell into the hands of local rulers whose pursuit of their own interests led to internal wars, lawlessness, injustice, and economic depression.

About 2050 B.C., the princes of Thebes, previously an insignificant city far to the south in the valley, undertook to reunify Egypt. After a fierce struggle, these princes (designated as the Eleventh Dynasty) succeeded and began what is known as the period of the Middle Kingdom (2050–1750 B.C.). Reunited Egypt reached a new peak during the Twelfth Dynasty, especially during the rule of Amenemhet I and Senusret. They consciously restored many of the political institutions and practices characteristic of the Old Kingdom—the divine power of the pharaoh, the centralized bureaucracy, the provincial administration—and labored successfully to revive and even to expand the economic system. Although the main features of the traditional political order were restored, there was a change in the spirit guiding the government of the Middle Kingdom. Less emphasis was placed on the divine power and majesty of the pharaoh and more on the quality of his government. A major concern of the pharaohs was to ensure that *ma'at* prevailed. In Egyptian thought *ma'at* was the principle of right order, justice, and harmony that should prevail throughout the universe, including the human community. During the Middle Kingdom the pharaohs assumed a special responsibility for providing justice, protection, and respect for all of their subjects, including the poor and the powerless who had been badly abused by the powerful during the First Intermediate Period. The concern that *ma'at* should prevail for all society gave the government of the Middle Kingdom a quality not often seen in the history of the ancient Near East.

After about three centuries of orderly government and prosperity, a new period of disturbance brought the Middle Kingdom to an end. A variety of internal problems were aggravated by a threat that Egypt had heretofore not faced: outside invasion. About 1750 B.C. a people called the Hyksos moved into the Delta area from Asia. Once established on Egyptian soil, Hyksos rulers proclaimed themselves pharaohs. Their presence led to divisions within Egypt and to violence and lawlessness. This interlude, called the Second Intermediate Period (1750–1580 B.C.), set the stage for another recovery and a new era of glory in Egypt to be discussed later.

In their fundamental features the economic and social institutions of the Old and Middle kingdoms were strikingly similar to those of Mesopotamia. A carefully controlled agricultural system provided the prime source of wealth in Egypt. The backbone of this system was a numerous peasant population, living in small villages and devoting their lives to the endless round of labor required to maintain the irrigation system and to plant and harvest the crops of wheat, barley, flax, vegetables, and fruit. To these responsibilities was added the burden of extra labor on the immense building programs organized by the pharaohs and their agents and friends. The economy was enriched by the efforts of artisans and merchants who produced or acquired by exchange the luxury goods desired by the powerful and rich in society. Both artisans and traders often worked directly for the pharaohs, the rich officials of his court, the numerous priests, and the powerful provincial nobility.

Egyptian society was dominated by a relatively small aristocracy. At its summit stood the pharaoh and his family, enjoying command over all elements of society and control over the total wealth of the state. The rest of the aristocracy consisted of those to whom the pharaoh chose to extend high status and reward with wealth. Especially influential were the priests who managed the religious system and the officials who assisted the pharaoh in governing Egypt. A mark of aristocratic life was wealth, which its privileged holders spent to create a life of luxury and display.

Despite the efforts of the good pharaohs the lower classes were sometimes exploited and oppressed; their laments constitute a major theme in literature. Yet the surviving evidence, much of it in the form of pictorial representations of the lower classes adorning the tombs of the pharaohs and their nobles, suggests social harmony in Egypt. The scenes depicting peasants and artisans at work and play convey a sense of contentment and even joy. There is very little evidence of the oppression of particular groups in society. Slavery played only a minor role in Egypt during the Old and Middle kingdoms. Women appear to have suffered no special social disability, even though they were subjected to control by fathers and husbands. The consorts of the mighty pharaohs were extended high respect by their divine husbands (see Figure 1.1) and by society in general. Noble women shared most aspects of aristocratic life, especially its material wealth. They owned property and played an important role as priestesses serving the chief deities of Egypt. Lower-class women joined their husbands in working in the fields and played a key role in sustaining the economy. In general, Egyptian society was stable and secure. Most people apparently felt that *ma'at* prevailed to reward a happy, confident society.

5. EGYPTIAN CULTURAL LIFE

The efforts associated with conquering the Nile and exploiting its riches were accompanied by bril-liant and sustained cultural activities. To this day, the early Egyptian cultural achievement impresses the world as one of the major creative bursts in human history.

Egyptian culture was an outgrowth of powerful religious forces that shaped every aspect of Egyptian society. The fifth-century B.C. Greek historian Herodotus concluded that the Egyptians were the most religious of all peoples. From at least some perspectives that seems to be true. Certainly few peoples honored more gods and goddesses; the deities worshiped by the Egyptians numbered in the thousands. These spirits were portrayed in a confusing array of forms—as humans, animals, birds, plants, abstractions, and mixtures of any of these forms. They lived everywhere, roaming freely across the skies and the earth; they were always present wherever and whenever humans were at work or at play. And their influence on human affairs was decisive. While the Egyptians never developed a very precise definition of the nature or the powers of the divine forces, they generally conceived their deities as benevolent toward humans, easy to live with, and not to be feared.

Over the centuries the Egyptians did come to agree that certain deities possessed special powers and deserved universal worship. This mythology accorded special prominence to deities associated with rulers victorious in earthly wars. For example, the falcon god Horus worshiped by Menes, the unifier of Egypt, became a major public deity of the Old Kingdom; likewise, Amon, a minor deity at Thebes, became a powerful national god after the princes of Thebes rose to power as pharaohs during the Middle Kingdom. Two deities ultimately emerged as the most powerful divine forces in Egyptian religion: Ra, the sun god whose worship reflected the power of nature in shaping the good life of the Nile Valley; and Osiris, the god who had the power to grant a happy life after death. But even as gods like Ra and Osiris came to be accepted by all Egyptians, never were the innumerable local deities eliminated as important forces in human affairs.

Another indication of the validity of Herodotus' statement was the energy expended by the Egyptians to please their deities and win their favors. An elaborate set of ritual practices was established early in Egyptian history and changed

FIGURE 1.3   Judgment Day   This Egyptian funerary papyrus from the tomb of a princess shows some of the steps in the transition to afterlife. In the center, the gods weigh her heart in a balance against the figure of the Goddess of Truth. Any flaw in her life would result in a loss of eternal happiness. (The Metropolitan Museum of Art)

little over the centuries. To the pharaoh belonged prime responsibility for bringing the favor of his fellow gods and goddesses upon his land and his people; no small part of the activities of a typical pharaoh was devoted to religious worship. He was aided by a numerous and powerful priesthood. In the many temples that dotted the land priests and priestesses conducted an elaborate round of rituals to please the deities with food, gifts, song, prayer, and dance. A considerable portion of public income was devoted to these activities. Acts of worship and sacrifice also took place in homes, villages, and city shrines. A rich array of magical practices evolved to attract the attention of the deities and to drive away evil spirits. Much of this religious activity was intended to win the material rewards that the gods and goddesses had to offer—abundant harvests, good health, security, happy times.

Besides earthly benefits, the divine powers held another precious gift for deserving Egyptians—a happy life after death. From early times,

Egyptians believed that every person had a *ka*, a double for his or her body that lived on after death in close association with the divine spirits. The *ka* had to be supplied with what it needed for a happy afterlife. In early Egyptian history a key to caring for the *ka* centered on mummification of the body so that its spirit could continue to live in it. A tomb that would last forever was built to house the mummy and its *ka*. Elaborate arrangements were made to ensure that the spirit would have food, drink, luxuries, company—everything it had enjoyed during life—to make immortal life tolerable. Perhaps only the pharaoh could afford such equipment, but he was willing to build and provision tombs for his wives, his children, his officials, and his friends so that they could continue to be his companions as all enjoyed eternal life.

Although the fate of the *ka* of ordinary people in early Egypt is not clear, the expectation of gaining immortality was gradually democratized and universalized. Perhaps the critical moment in this development came during the First Intermediate

Period as a reaction against the materialism and greed of the ruling class of the Old Kingdom. The broadened concept of immortality found its focus in the worship of Osiris, which by the Middle Kingdom had assumed a central place in religious life and was embodied in a touching myth. Osiris, a god associated with life forces and the Nile, was murdered by his wicked brother, Seth, who dismembered his body and scattered it over the earth. Isis the wife of Osiris, patiently gathered the pieces, whereupon Osiris returned to life. Thereafter, he had the power to raise everyone from death to life. When any Egyptian died, Osiris placed his or her heart on one pan of a balance and a feather on the other. If the heart was heavy with evil, it outweighed the feather and the dead person was judged unfit for a happy hereafter and tossed to a ferocious beast. If it was buoyant with good, its bearer was allowed to live forever in a heavenly place much like the earthly Nile Valley (see Figure 1.3).

A central feature of this concept of immortal life was the idea of moral worth attached to each person. Osiris was concerned with goodness in evaluating people's fitness for eternal life, not with their wealth and social status. In developing a moral dimension to life, the Egyptians introduced a concept unknown in Mesopotamia, but one that would have a rich history. One must be cautious, however, in assessing the impact of moral concerns on Egyptian society. People continued to provide for the material welfare of the dead, although from the Middle Kingdom onward the emphasis was less on the grandeur of the tomb and more on its decoration with a record in pictures and writing that would convince Osiris that its occupant had lived a "good" life; and in time, many busied themselves devising clever formulas to conceal their moral shortcomings.

Out of the immense effort to understand, please, and thank the divine forces there emerged an impressive literature. Egyptian literature in the proper sense was preceded by the development of a system of writing, called *hieroglyphic*, which made its appearance about 3200 B.C. Like cuneiform writing, it began as pictograms out of which evolved symbols representing sounds that could be combined into words. The first use of writing was probably in record keeping and letter writing

connected with the pharaoh's court, but it was not long before more artistic uses were found for writing skills. Much early writing has survived on pyramid walls in the form of hymns, prayers, magical incantations, mythology, and accounts of the deeds of the occupant of the pyramid, all intended to send a message to the divine forces. Besides the pyramid texts other forms of literature survive, set down either on stone or papyrus (a writing material made from the pulp of the papyrus plant pressed into flat sheets). The Egyptians apparently enjoyed collections of maxims and wise sayings, often presented in the form of instructions given by father to son or teacher to pupil. Poetry, often expressing disgust with worldly affairs, was composed. Especially appealing were tales of fancy and romance recounting the adventures of travelers, sailors, and soldiers. On the whole Egyptian literature was confident in mood, more varied and versatile than Mesopotamian literature, but less profound.

The visual arts reflect the character and quality of the Egyptian genius most clearly. In all its forms, Egyptian art mirrors what may be the keystone of Egyptian civilization: the ability of a creative people to work for long ages with set forms and subjects without loss of freshness and vitality. Their artists created for eternity with confidence that the existing order was right and worth sustaining.

Architecture was the queen of all the arts, most of the other forms serving to adorn great buildings. Architects worked with bricks, reeds, and timber, but the most monumental work was in stone, of which there was a plentiful supply in Egypt. The first flowering of architecture came early in the Old Kingdom period and was devoted chiefly to tomb building, which reached its apogee with the construction of the pyramids. The pyramid of Khufu, built about 2600 B.C., still stands as one of the major construction feats of all time. Built on a cliff overlooking the Nile, it measured 755 feet on each side and was 480 feet high. It contained over 2 million blocks of stone, each of which was precut in quarries many miles away and floated down the Nile to the building site, a procedure that required careful planning, skilled engineering, and a huge expenditure of labor. Surrounding the pyramid was a complex of temples and tombs for Khufu's dead family and friends. A roadway led down to the valley where there was another building complex intended to house the priests, officials, and laborers who carried on the many services required to care for the spirit living in the pyramid tomb. Pyramid building continued for many centuries, but later architects never equaled those of the Old Kingdom. Shifting concepts of life after death militated against such massive structures. By the end of the Old Kingdom temples and palaces commanded more attention. The basic temple style, established very early, was the hypostyle hall. Such structures consisted of a high-ceilinged central hall flanked by side halls, each covered with a roof set on columns shorter than those of the central hall. Builders achieved splendid artistic effects by modeling their columns after plants—the palm tree, the lotus plant, the papyrus plant, the reed. Within the temple, numerous chambers were grouped to create a sanctuary where the god or goddess to whom the temple was dedicated could live (see Color Plate 2). Before the temple was an open court surrounded by a columned portico and entered by a massive gate. Scanty surviving evidence indicates that the palaces built for pharaohs and nobles were as splendid as the temples and probably utilized the same basic architectural forms.

Egypt's sculptors matched architects in skill. At a very early date sculptural styles became fixed and changed little over most of Egypt's history. The chief subjects of three-dimensional works were the deities, the pharaohs, their families, and their companions, most such statues being intended to adorn tombs and temples. Human forms were usually massive, stiff, unemotional portrayals following fixed proportions. But the faces were another matter; here the sculptor tried to show feeling and purpose: the power of a god or goddess, the majesty of a pharaoh, the devotion of a royal servant (see Figure 1.1). The artist was not concerned with realistic portrayal of an individual but with projecting a quality embodied in and exemplified by the subject.

Sculptors were also skilled at relief work. Most relief work was carved on the walls of tombs and temples and was intended to record the lives and the deeds of those commemorated (see Figures 2.1 and 2.2). As a consequence, Egyptian reliefs contain a remarkably rich record of everyday life at all levels of society. However, sculptors seldom tried to be realistic. They let the space available determine the size and shape of their figures, and they often used conventional designs to represent objects. Human figures are distorted, the feet and faces usually shown in profile while the main trunk of the body faces the viewer. Many of the reliefs were painted to heighten the effect. Painting, most of which survives in tombs, bears striking similarity to relief work in terms of subject and form.

The Egyptians made advances in technology and science that rivaled the work of the Mesopotamians. They recorded information about the movement of the stars, from which they developed an accurate time-reckoning system based on the annual appearance of the star Sirius and a calendar of twelve thirty-day months plus five days added at the end of each year. They developed a system of numbers that permitted them to perform basic arithmetic functions and to calculate areas and volumes. They accumulated considerable information about the properties of metals and about plant and animal life. In medicine they developed surgical techniques and learned to use a wide range of drugs. Their understanding of anatomy was extensive, undoubtedly a result of observations made in the process of mummifying the dead. However, like the Mesopotamians, the Egyptians had little interest in pursuing knowledge about nature for its own sake. Once they found a practical solution for a problem of engineering, metallurgy, medicine, or discovering the intention of the deities, they sought no further.

SUGGESTED READING

Overview of the Ancient Near East to ca. 330 B.C.

William W. Hallo and W. K. Simpson, *The Ancient Near East: A History* (1971).

Jean Bottéro et al., *The Near East: The Early Civilizations,* trans. R. F. Tannenbaum (1967).

Either of these two books will provide an excellent overview.

Prehistory

Frank E. Poirier, *Understanding Human Evolution* (1987).

Richard E. Leakey, *The Making of Mankind* (1981).

John E. Pfeiffer, *The Emergence of Humankind,* 4th ed. (1985).

Each of these three works provides provocative treatments of the much disputed problem of human origins.

Brian M. Fagan, *People of the Earth: An Introduction to World Prehistory,* 4th ed. (1983). An excellent treatment of prehistoric culture.

Frances Dahlberg, ed., *Woman, the Gatherer* (1981). Informative essays on the role of women in prehistoric society.

Mesopotamia

H. W. F. Saggs, *The Greatness That Was Babylon; A Survey of the Ancient Civilization of the Tigris-Euphrates Valley* (1969). An excellent survey covering all aspects of Mesopotamian history.

H. W. F. Saggs, *Everyday Life in Babylonia and Assyria* (1965). Rich in material on how people lived in ancient Mesopotamia.

Thorkild Jacobsen, *The Treasures of Darkness: A History of Mesopotamian Religion* (1976). An excellent introduction.

Anton Moortgat, *The Art of Ancient Mesopotamia; The Classical Art of the Near East,* trans. Judith Filson (1969).

André Parrot, *Sumer. The Dawn of Art,* trans. Stuart Gilbert and James Emmons (1961).

Either of these beautifully illustrated volumes will provide a good introduction to Mesopotamian art.

Egypt

Cyril Aldred, *The Egyptians,* rev. and enl. ed. (1984).

Barbara Mertz, *Temples, Tombs, and Hieroglyphs: A Popular History of Egypt,* rev. ed. (1978).

Either of these two works will provide an excellent guide to the development of Egyptian civilization.

B. D. Trigger, ed., *Ancient Egypt: A Social History* (1983). Studies by various experts on aspects of Egyptian social history.

Barbara Mertz, *Red Land, Black Land: Daily Life in Ancient Egypt,* rev. ed. (1978).

John Romer, *People of the Nile: Everyday Life in Ancient Egypt* (1982).

These two works are rich in details about how people lived in ancient Egypt.

Erik Hornung, *Conceptions of the Gods in Ancient Egypt: The One and the Many,* trans. John Baines (1982).

A. Rosalie David, *The Ancient Egyptians: Religious Beliefs and Practices* (1982).

Either of these works will help the reader understand the complexities of ancient Egyptian religion.

Kurt Lange and Max Hirmer, *Egypt: Architecture, Sculpture, Painting in Three Thousand Years,* 4th ed., trans. Judith Filson and Barbara Taylor (1968).

W. Stevenson Smith and William Kelly Simpson, *Art and Architecture of Ancient Egypt,* 2nd ed. (1981).

Either of these two works, both well-illustrated, will provide a sense of the basic characteristics of Egyptian art.

CHAPTER 2

The Diffusion of Near Eastern Civilization, 1750–800 B.C.

FIGURE 2.1 Egyptian Imperialism This scene, from the temple of Karnak, shows the pharaoh Thutmose III (1504—1450 B.C.) grasping Egypt's enemies by the hair prior to striking them to show Egypt's mastery over them. This scene captures the spirit of Egyptian imperialism during the period of the New Kingdom. Such relief carvings occupied a major place in Egyptian artistic activity. (Hirmer Fotoarchiv)

By about 1750 B.C. the Near Eastern world reached a turning point. The higher civilizations produced in the unique environment of the river valleys had matured fully. Well before 1750 B.C. the influence of Mesopotamian and Egyptian civilizations had begun to spread beyond their original settings. During the period 1750–800 B.C. the process of cultural diffusion quickened and became a central theme of Near Eastern history. Not only did new peoples come to share higher civilization, but also many of them made important contributions that enriched the basic patterns of civilized life.

1. DIFFUSION AND THE MOVEMENT OF PEOPLES

Cultural diffusion in this period was a complex process. Ideas, products, and techniques were carried out from the established centers of civilization by traders, soldiers, and diplomats. Imitation of the superior ways of the river valley civilizations by people long settled on their fringes was common. As cultural patterns spread, they were adapted and modified to fit new settings and situations. Especially important as a catalytic force was the movement of peoples into and around the civilized zones to upset the existing order and to create new political entities eager to share the benefits of civilized life.

Two peoples were especially significant in creating conditions that lead to cultural diffusion. One was the Semitic-speaking inhabitants of the Arabian Desert, with whom we are already familiar as intruders into Mesopotamia. After 1800 B.C. these seminomadic desert dwellers continued to pour out of the desert to play a prime role in the history of northern Mesopotamia, Syria, Palestine, and Egypt.

The other people were the Indo-Europeans (sometimes called Aryans). Beginning about 2000 B.C. they fanned outward from their ancient homeland, perhaps north of the Caspian Sea. Their impact was felt over a broad area embracing central Europe, Italy, Greece, the Aegean area, the Near East, Iran, and India. They spoke a language that was new to the Near East and from which later evolved Sanskrit, Latin, Greek, Persian, and most modern European languages. Their general cultural level was more primitive than that of most Near Eastern peoples. However, their superior weapons and military organization allowed them to establish political dominance. Their first settlements in the Near East extended from the upper Tigris-Euphrates valleys westward across much of Asia Minor. Initially they established small principalities led by petty warlords. Eventually, some of these principalities coalesced and expanded by conquering native populations to create larger kingdoms. Among the more prominent were the Kassites, the Hittites, and the Mitanni, all destined to play important roles in the Near East during the period under review. In the process of establishing themselves, these newcomers absorbed and spread major elements of the established civilizations, especially those of Mesopotamia.

2. THE EGYPTIAN AND HITTITE EMPIRES, 1750–1200 B.C.

We have already noted the impact of some of these migrants on Mesopotamia and Egypt. Shortly after 1600 B.C. Indo-European Hittites and Kassites played a major role in dismembering the Amorite Empire founded by Hammurabi. The Kassites were able to establish their political domination over Mesopotamia. They ruled there for nearly four centuries, a period during which Mesopotamia played a secondary role in Near Eastern political life but continued to assert a major cultural influence over many peoples beyond Mesopotamia. To the north of Mesopotamia Indo-European warlords established dominance over an area embracing the upper Tigris-Euphrates valleys and north Syria to create the kingdom of the Mitanni, which flourished from about 1550 to 1350 B.C. Also about 1750 B.C. the Hyksos, predominantly Semitic wanderers from the Palestine area, intruded into Egypt. Although they never succeeded in extending their direct rule beyond the Delta region, they were a factor in causing the chaos in Egypt that characterized the Second Intermediate Period (ca. 1750–1580 B.C.). However, their presence did result in developments that cast Egypt into a new role in Near Eastern history.

The main result of the Hyksos' presence in

Egypt was the emergence of a feeling that foreigners were the cause of Egypt's troubles. That feeling manifested itself in efforts to expel the Hyksos, an enterprise in which many princes aspiring to power became engaged. Eventually, the rulers of Thebes emerged as leaders in this war of liberation. The expulsion of the Hyksos was finally achieved by Ahmose I (1558–1533 B.C.), the founder of the Eighteenth Dynasty. His triumph again placed Egypt under a single ruler and opened a third period of glory in Egyptian history, called the New Kingdom or Empire (1558–1200 B.C.).

During the first century of the Eighteenth Dynasty Egypt was ruled by a succession of able pharaohs. One of the ablest was a woman, Hatshepsut, who is portrayed in a surviving statue with a false beard, suggesting an artist uncomfortable about a woman ruler. These able rulers devoted their energies to restoring internal peace, "cleansing" the land of the taint of foreign rule, and reestablishing order in administration, agriculture, trade, religion, and artistic and intellectual life. In all of these pursuits traditional patterns were highly respected so that the restored system closely resembled that of the Old and Middle kingdoms.

However, a new factor played an increasingly important role: a more aggressive posture toward the outside world. Rooted originally in a haunting fear of a reoccurrence of invasions like that of the Hyksos, this attitude ripened into full-scale imperialism. The first pharaohs of the Eighteenth Dynasty reflected the fear of outside attacks by creating a standing army and by conducting raids against Nubia to the south and into Palestine and Syria, the original homeland of the Hyksos. These raids not only built Egypt's confidence in its strength but also created elements in society with a vested interest in expansionism, especially the military forces and the priesthood. Eventually, during the reign of Thutmose III (1504–1450 B.C.) defensive raiding turned into imperialism (see Figure 2.1). Thutmose led a series of campaigns into Nubia, Libya, and Syria-Palestine that established Egyptian dominance. This expansion brought the Egyptians into contact with other Near Eastern powers, especially the Mitanni, who were rivals for control of Syria-Palestine (see Map 2.1). These confrontations resulted in active diplomatic efforts that made Egypt's might felt beyond the areas of actual conquest. The Mitanni, the Kassites, and the Assyrians all sought peace with Egypt. For a century Thutmose's successors pursued his policy and made Egypt the dominant power in the Near East.

Successful imperialism brought Egypt a new period of magnificence. Added to the wealth produced by the carefully managed agricultural system was a vast income from tribute exacted from foreign subjects and from greatly expanded trading connections embracing the Sudan, Mesopotamia, Asia Minor, Crete, and the Aegean world. Artistic life blossomed, expressing itself with special brilliance in the magnificent temples built at Luxor and Karnak in honor of Amon-Ra, the chief national god (see Color Plate 2). The influences of Egyptian art styles, literary models, pottery and metal-working techniques, and religious practices were felt throughout the Near East with a force unknown prior to the period of the empire.

But imperialism also brought problems. The burden of controlling conquered peoples required a standing army, the maintenance of garrisons abroad, periodic campaigns to display strength, and complex diplomatic efforts. All of this put a heavy demand on Egypt's resources. A major consequence was an increasing regimentation of Egypt's native populace and a growing reliance on slavery in the service of the state. The concerns of empire distracted the attention of the pharaohs from the welfare of their subjects and created opportunities for oppression by grasping officials, especially the powerful priests of Amon-Ra. New ideas brought to Egypt by foreigners raised questions about the validity of traditional beliefs and practices.

Beginning about 1400 B.C., these problems, complicated by developments outside Egypt, put the New Kingdom to a severe test. The emerging crisis found its focus in the increasing rebelliousness of the dependent princes of Syria-Palestine whose loyalty was a keystone to Egypt's imperial structure. These princes were encouraged to resist Egypt by an aggressive, formidable external foe, the Hittites, whose power base was located in Asia Minor. Of all the "new" people who emerged from the Indo-European invasions, the Hittites enjoyed the greatest success. Their history began in about 1800 B.C., when invading Indo-European warlords imposed their rule on the natives of eastern and central Asia Minor and formed a series of small kingdoms. By about 1600 B.C., several of these kingdoms were united to form a single Hittite kingdom with its capital at Hattusas (modern Boghazköy). The Hittites developed an advanced culture, derived in large part from their borrowing and adaptation of Mesopotamian models. While always reflecting their Mesopotamian origins, Hittite political institutions, religion, literature, art, and technology possessed distinctive features that displayed the creative powers of this ''new'' people. Their dominance in Asia Minor marked a significant expansion of the area of higher civilization.

Once firmly established in Asia Minor and fortified by their expanding level of material wealth and culture, the Hittites were able to assert a decisive influence in Near Eastern affairs. They forced one of Egypt's chief allies, the Mitanni, into their sphere of influence and eventually destroyed that kingdom. By 1400 B.C. they were actively engaged in encouraging and supporting rebellion among Egypt's client principalities in Syria and Palestine. Hittite power reached its zenith under King Suppiluliumas (1375–1355 B.C.), who threatened to oust Egypt from its Asian holdings (see Map 2.1).

In the face of the mounting threat to its empire, Egypt was distracted by an internal crisis brought on by a religious reform instituted by Amenhotep IV (1379–1362 B.C.) with the help of his queen, Nefertiti. Although his motives have been much debated, it appears that this enigmatic pharaoh acted for both political and religious reasons: to reestablish the pharaoh's absolute supremacy in the face of threats offered by such powerfully entrenched groups as the military establishment, the royal officials, and especially the priests of Amon-Ra and to revitalize a traditional religious system encrusted with contradictory beliefs and overelaborate rituals based on crude materialism. In any case, Amenhotep IV proclaimed a new religion based on the worship of the god Aton, depicted as the source of all life who was represented to humanity in the form of the sun disc giving off rays that sustained all existence (see Figure 2.2). To dramatize his break with the old order, Amen-

FIGURE 2.2 An Egyptian Religious Reformer This scene shows Akhnaton with his wife, Nefertiti, and one of their daughters making an offering to the new deity, Aton, promoted by Akhnaton. The new deity is represented by the sun disc pouring its fruitful rays on the worshipers, who in turn would bestow such benefits on the pharaoh's subjects. The artistic style reflected in this carving is more naturalistic than the traditional Egyptian artistic canon (compare with Figures 1.1, 1.3, and 2.1). (The Metropolitan Museum of Art)

hotep IV changed his name to Akhnaton (''It pleases Aton'') and abandoned the old capital at Thebes for a new one named Akhetaton (modern

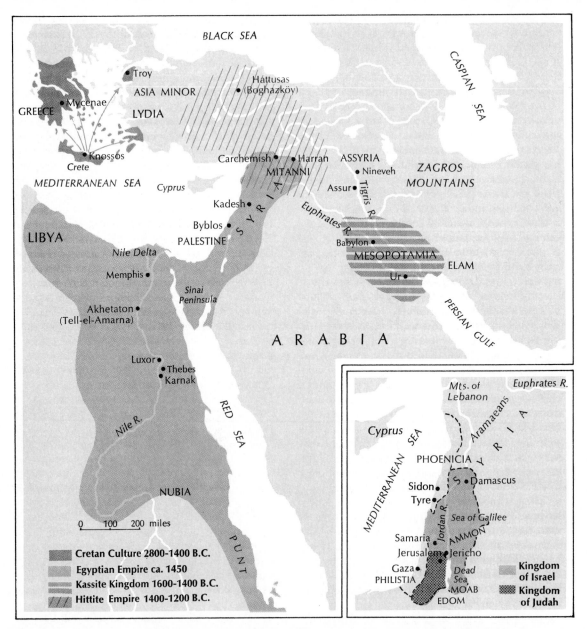

Map 2.1 **THE ANCIENT NEAR EAST, CA. 1450 B.C.** This map illustrates the main centers of political power during the period 1600–1200 B.C. The ambitions of the rulers of the major states led to considerable conflict, especially in Syria and Palestine, where Egyptian and Hittite interests clashed. The map also indicates how extensively the ways of civilized life had spread beyond the original centers of civilization in the river valleys.

Tell el Amarna). The worship of the old deities was forbidden, their temples destroyed, and their priests demoted. New rituals and a new art style, fresh and naturalistic, developed to honor and portray Aton. Some have argued that Akhnaton sought to establish monotheism, that is, a religion based on the worship of a single, universal deity; but close scrutiny of the record does not support this view. Rather, he probably intended to establish Aton as the supreme god to be worshiped and honored by the pharaoh while the Egyptians would worship the god-pharaoh. Many other uncertainties surround what kind of religious system Akhnaton had in mind. Together they raise the intriguing possibility that he intended a religious system that would rid Egyptian society of its restrictive traditionalism, rooted in the old religious order, and equip the Egyptians to take the lead in exploiting the cosmopolitan currents circulating in the Near East in this era of the mixing and mingling of cultures.

However, such questions are moot, for Akhnaton's reforms were stillborn. His proclamation of a new religion raised a storm of protest, led by the priests of Amon-Ra, which for a decade consumed the energy of society. Even before his death Akhnaton's foes had forced him to abandon his reforms. Under his successor, his son-in-law Tutankhamon, the forces of reaction rapidly restored the old order. The restoration of the cult of Amon-Ra is reflected not only in Tutankhamon's name but also in the cult objects found in his tomb, one of the most magnificent reflections of traditional Egyptian art and thought that has survived. Among other things, "King Tut" made a concerted effort to eradicate all signs of Aton worship and all memory of its chief proponent, Akhnaton.

The disturbances associated with Akhnaton's attempted reform and with the efforts to undo it weakened Egypt's capability to defend its empire. Hittite aggression in Syria and Palestine, accompanied by defections of local princes, temporarily ended Egyptian control in that area. Eventually, under the early rulers of the Nineteenth Dynasty, especially Seti and Rameses II, the Egyptians were able to regroup their military forces and to redress the balance in Syria and Palestine after a bitter struggle with the Hittites. The costly and indecisive struggle between these two powers ended about 1270 B.C., when they reached a peace settlement that assigned each a sphere of influence in that embattled area. For an interval both Egyptians and Hittites regained their former vitality as the leading powers of the era.

However, both empires were approaching the end of their greatness; their incessant struggles had sapped their strength. Decisive in determining their end was a new wave of Indo-European invaders, especially formidable because they possessed iron weapons, who spilled over Asia Minor, the Aegean Sea area, and the waterways of the eastern Mediterranean. Their assaults were abetted by new movements of Semitic nomads from the Arabian Desert. The Hittite Empire was completely destroyed about 1200 B.C. Attacks by Nubians, Libyans, and the mysterious "People of the Sea," seafaring marauders probably from Asia Minor, forced the Egyptians back into their old boundaries and for a time established foreigners as pharaohs. These setbacks greatly weakened Egypt internally and reduced its capacity to influence the course of Near Eastern history.

3. THE MINOAN WORLD

The age of diffusion witnessed the development of a vital civilization on the island of Crete, which played an especially important role in history because it provided a link between the ancient Near East and the world to the west—especially Greece. Modern historians have called this civilization Minoan, after Minos, a legendary Cretan king. Minoan civilization owed a great deal to influences from the Near East, but the Cretans put their own unique stamp on their borrowings to give their civilization its own character. A crucial factor in shaping Minoan civilization was the ability of the Cretans to enhance the limited resources of the island by utilizing the seas to reach sources of wealth, ideas, and techniques that stimulated and enriched their society.

By about 6000 B.C. a Neolithic farming culture had been established on Crete. For many centuries thereafter Neolithic farmers shared a simple pattern of culture with other people living in Greece, the Aegean Islands, and Asia Minor. Gradually, over that period the Cretans developed skills in pottery making and metalwork; especially important was the introduction of bronze technology from Asia Minor about 3000 B.C. And the Cretans learned to sail the seas to establish contacts with the advanced civilizations of Egypt and Asia and to gain access to markets and raw materials in the area around the Aegean. By about 2000 B.C. their developing technical skills, increasing wealth, and expanding contacts resulted in the emergence of several full-fledged urban centers, including Knossos, Phaistos, and Mallia. Each was ruled by a king whose magnificent palace was the center of civilized life. Minoan civilization reached its peak between about 1700 and 1450 B.C. During this period Knossos outstripped the other cities of Crete, asserting cultural leadership that provided a common pattern of life on the island and perhaps even establishing a loose political control. Not only did Knossos dominate Crete, but the city's influence was felt over a wide circle of the eastern Mediterranean and the Aegean seas, chiefly through trading ventures. Then between 1500 and 1450 B.C. a disaster struck the Minoan world, destroying many cities, crops, and fleets. Perhaps this catastrophe was a consequence of a devastating volcano on the island of Thera, north of Crete. At about the same time Crete suffered at the hands of invaders from Greece called Mycenaeans. Knossos continued for an interval as a center from which the invaders ruled the island, but shortly after 1400 B.C. it too was destroyed, perhaps as a result of a revolt against the outsiders. Minoan civilization had run its course.

Our knowledge of the major features of Minoan civilization is derived chiefly from archaeological evidence produced by excavations of city sites, especially Knossos. The Minoans did develop their own writing system, called Linear A by modern scholars, but it has not yet been deciphered. About 1450 B.C. that system was replaced by another, called Linear B, which has been deciphered and proved to be based on an early form of the Greek language. It probably represents an adaptation of Minoan writing by the Mycenaean invaders from Greece. The surviving documents in Linear B are chiefly economic records and provide only limited information about Minoan society.

At the height of Minoan civilization Crete was governed by several kings, each controlling a particular city and its surrounding territory. The king of Knossos exercised some form of authority over the other kingdoms, but that overlordship was based on consent rather than force. The fact that Minoan cities were unwalled indicates that the kingdoms lived without serious conflict or great expenditure for arms. The power of Minoan kings rested on strong religious sanctions and on wealth derived from control of the agricultural system and from overseas trade. Royal administration was conducted by a highly developed bureaucracy especially skilled at orderly record keeping. A wealthy and influential nobility made up chiefly of landowners grouped itself around the kings to uphold royal authority.

The Minoan economy was based on a productive agricultural system devoted to the cultivation of grain, olives, grapes, and vegetables and to the raising of livestock, especially sheep. But trade and industry produced the additional wealth necessary to support an advanced urban civilization. Highly skilled artisans laboring in the workshops of the royal palace or in their own shops produced a wide variety of goods that adorned the lives of the rulers, their officials, and the wealthy landowners and merchants. Especially skilled were Minoan potters and metalworkers. Enterprising merchants, sometimes serving the kings and sometimes working on their own, carried Minoan manufactured products over the seas to a wide area around the Mediterranean, including not only the major Near Eastern centers of civilization but also the less developed peoples of the Aegean world. These merchants brought back a variety of raw materials and manufactured goods. The wealth produced by this vigorous economy allowed the Minoan upper class to live in luxurious, well-furnished houses and enjoy fine clothing and abundant jewelry. Upper-class women shared freely in the social life of the palaces and aristocratic households. Every royal city had a considerable population of laborers who performed all kinds of work needed to sustain city life. The rural population clustered in villages where they labored under the supervision of royal officials and powerful landowners. There was little slavery in Minoan society.

The Minoans worshiped a variety of gods and

goddesses, most of them representing the forces of nature. Especially prominent was the goddess of fertility, whose life-giving powers were evoked by all classes of people. A major function of the king was conducting religious services to win the favor of the deities for his entire community, a responsibility that was carried out regularly in each palace. The worship of the gods and goddesses was less elaborate than were the religious practices of Mesopotamia and Egypt. The Minoans built no great temples; they worshiped at simple shrines in private houses, on hills, in groves and caves, and near springs. Priests and priestesses were maintained at the palace to serve the deities, but they played only a limited role in shaping Minoan life and culture. Prominent place in religious ceremonies was given to animal sacrifice, gift giving, dancing, and bull leaping—a dangerous feat in which young men and women vaulted over the horns of a charging bull to do a handstand on its back before dismounting over its rear quarters (see Figure 2.3). The pictorial representations of these rituals suggest a religious life that was joyful and lighthearted, little marked by fear and gloom. There was a belief in afterlife and some attention was given to the care of the dead, but never on the scale that occurred in Egypt.

The genius of the Minoans expressed itself most fully in the visual arts. Their highly developed architectural skills were lavished on palaces and private dwellings rather than on temples and tombs. The immense palace at Knossos reflected a technical mastery of a variety of architectural forms and a fine sense of scale. Many of the multistoried palaces and private dwellings were equipped with a piped water supply, skillfully constructed drainage systems, and indoor toilets. Palaces and houses were decorated with paintings and carvings that focused on nature and human activity. Especially skilled were elaborate frescoes portraying processions of young men and women bearing gifts to the gods and goddesses. Animals, fish, and birds were also favorite subjects of carvers and painters. Minoan decorated pottery reflects a fine sense of form and a love of color. In all its forms Minoan art is mobile, free of stylization, intense, and energetic. It reflects a civilization that was worldly, lacking in fear, eager for change, and pleasure loving. Although strongly

FIGURE 2.3 Minoan Sports This bronze figure dating from the sixteenth century B.C. portrays a favorite Minoan sporting activity—vaulting over a charging bull. Both young men and young women participated in this dangerous game. The artist's ability to convey a feeling of movement on the part of both the leaper and the animal is reflective of much of Minoan art. (The British Museum)

influenced by Mesopotamian and Egyptian models, Minoan civilization contrasts sharply with both; it points not east but west toward a world yet to come—especially to Greece.

4. ERA OF SMALL NATIONS, 1200–800 B.C.: PHOENICIANS AND ARAMEANS

The collapse of the Hittite and Egyptian empires about 1200 B.C., coupled with the decline of Minoan power, left the Near East without a dominant power center for about four centuries. Several small groups seized the opportunity to establish their independence. As these peoples struggled to establish and maintain themselves, they borrowed heavily from the older civilizations. As a result, cultural diffusion continued as a major feature of Near Eastern history.

Two peoples stand out especially as borrowers and disseminators: the Phoenicians and the Arameans. Both were Semitic in origin, the products of the numerous migrations from the Arabian Desert that had been in progress for many centuries before 1200 B.C. These migrants were repeatedly conquered and strongly influenced by Mesopotamians, Egyptians, and Hittites. Consequently, by 1200 B.C. they were already highly civilized peoples; when Egyptian and Hittite power collapsed, they were able to establish political independence. The Phoenicians, located in the narrow coastal area between the Mediterranean Sea and the mountains of Lebanon, developed a number of independent city-states, chief of which were Byblos, Tyre, and Sidon. The Arameans were located east of the Lebanon Mountains between the northern fringes of the Arabian Desert and the Euphrates River. They were organized into a number of small kingdoms centered around Damascus, Kadesh, and Palmyra (see Map 2.1). For about four centuries these city-states and kingdoms were among the chief states in the Near East. Their independence was finally crushed by the Assyrians in the eighth century B.C., as we shall see in the next chapter.

The Phoenicians and the Arameans derived most of their wealth from trade. The Phoenicians took to the seas and established a virtual monopoly on trade in the Mediterranean, chiefly as successors of Minoan traders. Their merchants carried manufactured goods from the entire Near East to the less developed peoples of Greece, Italy, North Africa, Spain, and southern France and brought back the raw materials of these areas. From these traders many peoples to the west got their first taste of higher civilization. The Phoenicians not only traded but also established colonies, notably the North African city of Carthage, destined to become an important center of civilization after 800 B.C. The Arameans were overland traders, exploiting the trade routes that linked Egypt, Mesopotamia, Asia Minor, and points beyond. Both Phoenicians and Arameans reaped a rich reward from their commerce, allowing them to live well and to support a wide range of cultural activities. Neither people was particularly creative in learning and the arts. However, the Phoenicians did perfect an alphabet that later served as a model for the written languages of the Mediterranean basin, and the Aramean language became the chief spoken language of much of the Near East.

5. ERA OF SMALL NATIONS, 1200–800 B.C.: THE HEBREWS

One people emerging into prominence for the first time in this era of small nations had a particularly enduring impact on the history of Western civilization. These were the Hebrews, who left a magnificent literary record of their own version of their history in their Bible, now generally referred to as the Old Testament. This complex document, composed over many centuries by many authors out of a mixture of historical traditions, folklore, legal enactments, moral exhortations, and prophecies, confronts the modern historian with formidable problems. However, the main lines of the story it tells, coupled with supporting evidence from non-Hebrew literary sources and from archaeology, provide a fairly accurate account of the history of the Hebrews during the period with which we are now concerned.

The surviving evidence suggests that the Hebrews were originally nomads, part of the extensive migration of Semite peoples that played a crucial role in the age of diffusion. Early Hebrew history centered on a search for a place to settle. During this age of the patriarchs, as the Old Testament calls it, small tribal groups based on kinship ties left their early places of settlement on the fringes of Mesopotamia and, under the leadership of family heads such as Abraham, Isaac, and Jacob, migrated around the southern fringes of the Fertile Crescent to the area of Palestine. Perhaps this migration began about 1800 B.C., roughly in the time of Hammurabi, and took place over a relatively long period. In the area of Palestine the nomadic Hebrew herders encountered and began to clash with more advanced agricultural societies, especially the Canaanites. This interaction set in motion a slow transition from pastoral to settled agricultural life. An important feature of Hebrew tribal life was a religion rooted in a fierce allegiance among tribal members to a deity who gave special protection to the tribe and interacted with it through its patriarch. Among such deities was Yahweh, the god of Abraham.

Not all of the wandering Hebrews remained in the Palestine area. Some made their way to Egypt, perhaps as part of the Hyksos invasion or as hostages taken during Egyptian expansion into the

Syria-Palestine area during the Eighteenth Dynasty. Assigned lands in the Delta region (the biblical land of Goshen), these foreigners prospered for a time, and some, like Joseph, even found favor at the pharaoh's court, suggesting that the Hebrews accommodated to the higher civilization of the Egyptians. Eventually, however, there arose a pharaoh "who knew not Joseph" and whose mistreatment led to a decisive event in Hebrew history—the Exodus, which probably occurred during the reign of Pharaoh Rameses II (1292–1235 B.C.).

The circumstances surrounding the escape from bondage in Egypt and subsequent period of wandering in the deserts of the Sinai Peninsula pose difficult problems for the historian. However, it seems indisputable that a religious experience occurred that marked a decisive stage in Hebrew history and gave fundamental shape to the religious consciousness of that people. Under the leadership of Moses, the Hebrews of the Exodus came to believe that they as a people had become special partners of Yahweh, who at least some had worshiped during the age of the patriarchs. Master of history and of nature, as he had demonstrated through the events of the Exodus, Yahweh made a *covenant*, or mutual contract, with Moses' people: He selected them as his people and promised to care for them under all circumstances. In return, they pledged to honor him as their only god and to follow his law, set down in the Bible as the Ten Commandments, in the conduct of their collective existence. These fundamental concepts, which thereafter remained central to the Hebrew religion, transformed Moses' "mixed multitude" of tribal groups into "a holy nation," the Israelites, whose unity was rooted in their unique relationship with their god who would brook no rivals.

The people of the covenant now renewed their search for their Promised Land. Their object became Palestine, an area where considerable instability existed in the wake of the collapse of the Egyptian and Hittite empires (see Map 2.1). The Old Testament provides a somewhat simplified account of the Israelite occupation of Palestine, beginning when Joshua led a loose confederation of twelve Hebrew tribes to an initial triumph over the Canaanite city of Jericho about 1200 B.C., fol-

lowed by a succession of victories over the Canaanites that ultimately assured Hebrew control. According to that story, the chief hindrance to success was the unfaithfulness of the Israelites to their convenant with Yahweh, who punished them by allowing their enemies to defeat them. In reality, the Hebrew occupation of Palestine was a complex, drawn-out process involving more than military engagements. To be sure, the Canaanites were formidable foes but not the only ones. Repeatedly the Hebrews had to contend with outsiders equally intent on occupying Palestine, a threat that often necessitated cooperation between Hebrews and Canaanites and to gradual assimilation of the two peoples. The Hebrew effort was impeded by tribal jealousies, especially as the tribal structure became more firmly established and each tribe sought to establish its identity on a territorial basis. These complex situations produced crisis after crisis, sometimes dramatically resolved by charismatic leaders, called "judges," who persuaded the Hebrews to act in unity at least temporarily; such leaders included Gideon, Samson, and Samuel. As the Hebrew occupation proceeded, the newcomers were slowly transformed into farmers, adopting in the process many features of Canaanite culture; this transformation often challenged traditional values and practices and sometimes divided the Hebrews.

After about a hundred and fifty years of struggle and change, the Hebrews were close to dominance. Then they were almost destroyed by the Philistines, warlike newcomers armed with iron weapons who settled along the south Palestine coast after being rebuffed in their attempt to enter Egypt. By about 1050 B.C. the Philistines had made major inroads into Palestine and seemed on the verge of overpowering the Hebrews. The threat of disaster led to a momentous step: an agreement among the Hebrew tribes—forged in large part through the efforts of the most famous of the judges, Samuel—to place themselves under a single king, thereby creating a political "nation."

The unified Hebrew nation lasted for about a century (1020–930 B.C.), embracing the reigns of Saul, David, and Solomon, who collectively brought the Hebrews to the high point of their history in ancient times. These kings were able to organize military resources that expelled the Philistines from Palestine and then subdued not only the Canaanites but also many small principalities on the borders of Palestine, allowing the unified Hebrew kingdom to assume a place as a leading power in an era of small nations. A centralized government was established at Jerusalem, which, especially under Solomon, took on the basic features of a typical Near Eastern absolute monarchy with powers to tax, to impose forced labor, and to spend lavishly on public buildings, support of the arts, and an impressive royal court. The kingdom was greatly enriched by royal economic policies that helped Hebrew traders take advantage of Palestine's strategic location on international trade routes. Solomon was particularly effective in creating an extensive network of diplomatic ties in the Near East that enhanced the prestige of the kingdom and brought its ruling elements into contact with the increasingly cosmopolitan world of the Near East; visible evidence of these contacts was provided not only by Solomon's many foreign wives but also by foreign influences on the arts and on life styles increasingly prevalent among the Hebrews.

Amidst the tribulations and the successes experienced by the Hebrews between 1200 and 930 B.C., their religion—Judaism—continued to develop. The struggles to occupy Canaan and to resist the Philistines brought constant reminders, especially from the aforementioned judges, to remain loyal to the covenant with Yahweh. The success under the early monarchs appeared to vindicate Yahweh's concern for his people and thus keep his worship central in Hebrew life. In fact, the institution of a monarchy, which was believed to be sanctioned in a special way by Yahweh, marked an important step in creating a truly national religion. A prime symbol of this national religion was the establishment by David and Solomon of Jerusalem as the cult center of the Hebrew people, featuring Solomon's splendid temple housing the Ark of the Covenant, a wooden chest containing the commandments Yahweh had given to his people in the time of Moses. The system of law originally set forth in the Ten Commandments was greatly expanded to serve as a common bond among the Hebrews and to relate their new lives as farmers and urban dwellers to basic religious principles rooted in the covenant.

A more complex set of religious practices shaped by an emerging priesthood took on increasing importance in the collective lives of the Hebrews. Despite the repeated outcries in the Old Testament against the dangers of outside religious ideas and practices, the changes in law and worship involved the assimilation of elements from non-Hebrew sources into Judaism. Especially influential was the religion of the Canaanites, based on familiar Near Eastern fertility deities, especially the often-condemned Baal, and on cult practices associated with the agricultural seasons. This process of assimilation sustained constant tension in Hebrew religious life but ultimately resulted in an enriched and flexible common religion attuned to the more advanced level of civilization attained by the Hebrews during the period reaching from the first attempts to occupy their promised land to the culmination of their national history under Solomon.

Even while Solomon reigned in all his glory, deep-seated discontents threatened the unity of the Hebrew kingdom. Among the major causes of this discontent were the autocratic methods of the kings, growing economic and social inequality, rural-urban rivalry, and concerns over foreign religious usages in the rituals of the temple and the royal court. Immediately after Solomon's death these discontents resulted in a division of the kingdom. Dissidents in the northern part of the kingdom refused to recognize his son as king and formed a new kingdom called Israel, with its center at Samaria. The remnant of the previously united kingdom, called Judah, continued under kings descended from the house of David. Each of these nations had a stormy internal history, marked by social and religious conflict. Ultimately, neither was able to survive outside aggression. In 722 B.C. Israel was conquered by the Assyrians and many of its people were carried off into captivity. Judah survived until 586 B.C., when the Chaldeans captured Jerusalem, destroyed the Temple, and took large numbers of Hebrews to Babylon as captives. Although the Persian ruler Cyrus (ca. 560–530 B.C.) allowed those victims of the Babylonian captivity who wished to do so to return to Jerusalem and aided them in restoring the Temple, the political independence of the ancient Israelites had ended. An important consequence of this troubled course of events was the dispersion of many Hebrews across much of the Near East, marking the beginnings of the Diaspora, the scattering of Hebrews into new settings where their religion would undergo new challenges and where they could assert an important influence on the non-Hebrews among whom they lived.

As Hebrew political power eroded and then vanished in the centuries after 900 B.C., Judaism took on new depth. During the period of the divided kingdoms and foreign conquests, religion became the sole force that sustained a sense of commonalty and uniqueness among the Hebrews. Although constantly challenged by the lures offered by non-Hebrew religions, the Hebrew priesthood fashioned a sober, austere cult that cut away much of the magic and superstition surrounding other Near Eastern religions; observance of these practices became a mark of belonging to Yahweh's special community. Much more significant was the reformulation of the traditional concepts of Judaism by a series of powerful religious leaders known as *prophets*. Several of them rank among the world's greatest spiritual leaders: Elijah, Amos, Isaiah, Jeremiah, Ezekiel, the anonymous second Isaiah. Although their careers spanned four centuries and each spoke a unique message appropriate to his own time, these remarkable figures collectively explored with deep spiritual insight many of the essential elements of religious experience. The message of all of them was rooted in a shared conviction, based on their reading of history and their interpretation of their own times, that the Hebrews were guilty of abandoning their covenant with Yahweh. Their mission was to call Yahweh's errant and hardhearted people back to that covenant. In the course of reinterpreting the essence of that covenant, they expanded and clarified certain fundamental concepts that became the essence of Judaism.

First, the prophets proclaimed a true monotheism. They insisted that Yahweh was the only god in the universe and denied that any other deities existed. To give any sign of recognition to any other deity except Yahweh was the greatest of all sacrileges.

Second, the prophets proclaimed a radically new concept of Yahweh's nature. Yahweh was the creator of all things, existing outside of time and nature. Unlike other gods worshiped in the Near East, he was not in nature; he created it and controlled it, making the worship of natural forces idolatry. He was a god of justice, acting according to law instead of whim. He was omnipotent, ruling the entire universe and causing everything in the past, present, and future to happen. He was a god with a plan for the universe and for humanity, a plan that would be worked out in history. He was a god of righteousness, pleased by those who did good, vengeful toward those who did evil. He was a caring god, "merciful and gracious, long-suffering, and abundant in goodness and truth," always watchful over his entire creation.

Third, the prophets projected a new vision of the essence of human nature. As Yahweh's special creatures, human beings were created to become godlike. This end could be achieved only by moral perfection, which involved a choice between good and evil. Human beings were basically moral beings, each endowed with the freedom and the capacity to choose the good. They were not Yahweh's slaves, for whom he cared not and upon whom he might vent his wrath at his whim; rather, each was his child who could earn divine mercy and love and favor by righteousness. Men and women were individuals capable of choosing how they would respond to Yahweh's call, of determining what kind of humans they wished to be. This moral freedom imposed a burden, but it opened avenues of human aspiration and endeavor largely absent in the other religious systems in the ancient Near East.

Fourth, the prophets proclaimed a new basis for defining the conduct of each individual toward others and of a community toward the individuals who were its members. Just as Yahweh treated men and women with righteousness and justice, so also must individuals treat all others according to these same principles. Likewise, the community of Yahweh's followers must conduct its collective actions to promote righteousness and justice. The principles of social righteousness and justice were set forth in a code of law (the Torah) that all were obliged to observe if they were to be counted among those faithful to Yahweh. As that law evolved, it provided detailed regulations for all aspects of individual and communal life. Although some aspects of Hebraic law may seem less than enlightened to today's world, it is firm in its insistence that every individual was worthy of respect and compassionate treatment. Some of the prophets put special stress on the obligation of the rich and the powerful to show mercy, charity, and compassion to the weak and the unfortunate. The ethical dimension of early Judaism was one of its most unique features.

Finally, the prophets reasserted that the Hebrews—the followers of Yahweh—were the people chosen to carry out Yahweh's plan for his creation. No matter what disasters might befall them, they would ultimately emerge victorious over the other peoples of the earth, and through them the one god would eventually be worshiped by all. In the face of the disasters that befell the Hebrews after Solomon, the prophets put special emphasis on Yahweh's eventual intention to send a Messiah to lead the Hebrews to victory. While awaiting their deliverer, the Hebrews must hold fast to their allegiance to Yahweh, maintain their religious ties with one another, and resist the temptation to follow false gods.

As the last centuries of Near Eastern monopoly on higher civilizations unfolded, Yahweh's promise delivered by the prophet Jeremiah seemed unlikely to be realized: "They shall all know me from the least of them to the greatest . . . ; for I will forgive their iniquity and I will remember their sin no more." By about 500 B.C. the Jewish community consisted of a small number of the faithful living around Jerusalem under Persian domination and often at odds with one another. Many of their religious compatriots were scattered around the Near East; they too were under foreign domination and hard-pressed to maintain their ancient faith. The bulk of the population of the Near East remained untouched by the religion shaped by the Hebrews over several centuries; these people preferred their traditional nature deities, their elaborate mythologies, and their complex rituals devoted to winning divine favors. Despite its modest impact on the ancient Near East, Judaism would ultimately have a major impact on history. The Hebrews had written one of the great chapters in the spiritual and moral history of humanity, and the message would not go unnoticed.

SUGGESTED READING

Egyptian and Hittite Empires

P. H. Newby, *Warrior Pharaohs. The Rise and Fall of the Egyptian Empire* (1980). A full treatment of the history of the New Kingdom.

Donald B. Redford, *Akhenaten: The Heretic King* (1984). An excellent study of an enigmatic figure.

T. G. H. James, *Pharaoh's People: Scenes from Life in Imperial Egypt* (1984). Excellent social history of the New Kingdom.

J. G. Macqueen, *The Hittites and Their Contemporaries in Asia Minor*, rev. and enl. ed. (1986).

Johannes Lehmann, *The Hittites. People of a Thousand Gods*, trans. J. Maxwell Brownjohn (1975).
Either title will provide an excellent survey of Hittite history.

Ekrem Akurgal, *The Art of the Hittites*, trans. Constance McNab (1962). A well-illustrated study.

Minoans and Phoenicians

R. F. Willetts, *The Civilization of Ancient Crete* (1977).

Arthur Cotterell, *The Minoan World* (1979).
Either of these two titles will provide a full introduction to Minoan history and civilization.

Reynold Higgins, *Minoan and Mycenaean Art*, rev. ed. (1981). A sound study that is enriched by excellent illustrations.

Gerhard Herm, *The Phoenicians: The Purple Empire of the Ancient World*, trans. Caroline Hillier (1975).

Raymond Weill, *Phoenicia and Western Asia to the Macedonian Conquest*, trans. Ernest F. Row (1980).

Sabatino Moscati, *The World of the Phoenicians*, trans. Alastair Hamilton (1968).
Any of these three titles will help the reader to understand the role of the Phoenicians in the ancient world.

Hebrews

John Bright, *A History of Israel,* 3rd ed. (1981).

Michael Grant, *The History of Ancient Israel* (1984).

J. Maxwell Miller and John H. Hayes, *A History of Ancient Israel and Judah* (1986).

Three fine histories of ancient Israel; the Miller and Hayes book provides the fullest treatment.

Bernhard W. Anderson, *Understanding the Old Testament,* 4th ed. (1986). A well-done attempt to weave together history, literary criticism, archaeology, and biblical theology in order to show how Judaism developed.

G. W. Anderson, *The History and Religion of Israel* (1966). A helpful treatment of the evolution of ancient Judaism.

Roland de Vaux, *Ancient Israel: Its Life and Institutions,* 2 vols. (1961). Rich in details about ancient Hebrew society.

CHAPTER 3

The Great Empires: Assyria and Persia, 800–300 B.C.

FIGURE 3.1 **A Near Eastern Empire Builder** This portrayal of the Assyrian ruler Sargon II (721–705 B.C.) conveys a sense of power—even arrogant power—that was typical of the rulers of the great Near East empires from ca. 800 to 300 B.C. One can well believe that this man was capable of dominating "the four rims of the world," as Assyrian and Persian empire builders claimed to do. (Hirmer Fotoarchiv)

During the ninth century B.C. significant changes began to occur in the Near East to herald a new era characterized by the formation for the first time of vast empires unifying almost the entire area enjoying the benefits of higher civilization under a single political regime. The ground for this development had been prepared during the previous millennium. The diffusion of the river valley cultures had provided large numbers of diverse peoples with common techniques, religious practices, and literary and art styles. Expanding trade connections had knit distant communities together with common economic interests. Shared cultural, religious, and economic interests invited attempts at political consolidations, and adventuresome leaders appeared to respond to the opportunity.

1. THE ASSYRIAN EMPIRE

The first people to unify almost the entire Near East were the Assyrians. They were a people of Semitic origin who migrated from the Arabian Desert as early as 3000 B.C. and established a homeland on the plateau astride the upper Tigris River, a land that lacked natural barriers and was open to repeated attacks. During the ensuing centuries the Assyrians were powerfully influenced by Mesopotamian civilization; at times, such as under Sargon I and Hammurabi, they were incorporated politically into the empires based in the lower Tigris-Euphrates Valley. The era from 1750 to 1000 B.C. was especially testing for the Assyrians. They were constantly assaulted by Kassites, Hittites, Mitanni, Semitic nomads from the Arabian Desert, and barbarians from the east and north. The hardy farmers of Assyria met this challenge by developing one of the best military forces in the Near East, especially after they adopted the new iron weapons and the horse-drawn war chariots introduced into the Near East shortly before 1000 B.C.

Eventually the fear for the safety of their ancestral homeland, coupled with the absence of any major political powers in the Near East during the era of small nations, provoked the Assyrians to undertake preventive wars against potential enemies. During the ninth century several surrounding nations felt the force of these raids—the Hebrews, the Phoenicians, the Arameans, the Mesopotamians, the mountaineers living to the north and east of Assyria, and the nomads of the northern Arabian Desert. None was able to resist the well-armed Assyrian infantrymen, archers, and charioteers, ably backed by siege equipment and skilled engineers. The effectiveness of the military machine was increased by a deliberate policy of terrorism waged against those defeated by the Assyrians. So awesome did the Assyrians become that many people preferred to "embrace the feet" of the attackers rather than resist (see Figure 3.2).

These raids showed the Assyrians that they could not only defend but also enrich themselves by exacting tribute from their victims. This prospect eventually changed defensive raids into conquest and the establishment of permanent control over Assyria's enemies. The founder of the Assyrian Empire was Tiglath-pileser III (745–727 B.C.), who began the policy of imposing permanent control over conquered peoples. He and a successor, Sargon II (721–705 B.C.), led the Assyrian armies on a series of expeditions that destroyed the chief political powers from Mesopotamia northward and westward to Syria and Palestine. Assyrian governors were imposed on most of the conquered peoples, although a few minor kingdoms, such as Judah, were allowed to exist as tribute-paying clients of Assyria. The central administration of Assyria was enlarged to supervise tribute collection, and effective means of communication were devised to keep the royal court informed of affairs throughout the empire. The army stood ready to crush all signs of resistance; it continued its policy of terrorism, even resorting to the large-scale deportation of conquered peoples, as was the case with a large part of the population of the kingdom of Israel. Once this base of power was established, rulers such as Sennacherib (705–681 B.C.), Esarhaddon (681–669 B.C.), and Ashurbanipal (669–626 B.C.) devoted their energies to dealing with outsiders who insisted on interfering with Assyrian rule. Egypt was forced to accept Assyrian overlordship, and Assyrian influence was extended into Asia Minor, the Zagros Mountains region, Iran, the northern Arabian Desert, and the highland region north of the Assyrian homeland. By 650 B.C. almost the entire civilized Near East stood subject to a single

FIGURE 3.2 Embracing the Feet of an Assyrian King This carving from an Assyrian royal palace represents Jehu, King of Israel, bowing before his Assyrian conqueror, King Shalmaneser III. It conveys the awe that Assyrian rulers struck in the victims of their conquest. (The Granger Collection)

master, the great king of Assyria, "ruler of the four rims of the world" (see Map 3.1). The arrogant visages of these mighty kings still stare out at us from the remarkable stone busts and reliefs wrought by Assyrian artists to celebrate their deeds (see Figure 3.1); all of them left boastful accounts of their exploits in building the first genuinely ecumenical empire in the Near East.

However, the Assyrian Empire was not as strong as its size and heavy-handed rule suggested. Its brutal treatment of subject peoples aroused their irreconcilable hatred, nowhere better reflected than in the writings of some of the Hebrew prophets. Constant warfare depleted Assyria's human resources and eventually forced its rulers to rely on less efficient levies from conquered subjects. Internal discontent arose, often stemming from dissatisfaction over the distribution of tribute. Worst of all, the Assyrians encountered the plague of all empire builders—enemies beyond the frontiers, aroused by threat of absorption and greed for the riches of the empire. During the reign of Ashurbanipal these problems began to weaken Assyrian power, and troubles mounted rapidly after his death in 626 B.C. The Egyptians

successfully revolted and then stirred up trouble among Assyrian subjects in Syria and Palestine. A Semitic group, the Chaldeans, raised the standard of revolt in southern Mesopotamia, a threat so serious that the Assyrians were forced to commit most of their resources to quelling it. Then the Medes, a people living east of the Zagros Mountains who had learned a great deal by imitating Assyrian military techniques, struck out of the east. In 612 B.C. they and the Chaldeans destroyed the Assyrian capital at Nineveh. Assyrian power collapsed almost immediately, leaving the empire at the mercy of its many foes, who hastened to partition it.

No one in the Near East lamented Assyria's passing. The Hebrew prophet Nahum spoke for all the world: "All who hear the news of you clap their hands at your downfall." However, the Assyrians' bad reputation should not conceal their contributions to history. They broke ground in trying to create a single state out of many different peoples. Their attempt to erect a centralized monarchy was to be imitated by others. The Assyrians wiped out many artificial political boundaries that kept small groups at sword's point. At least briefly

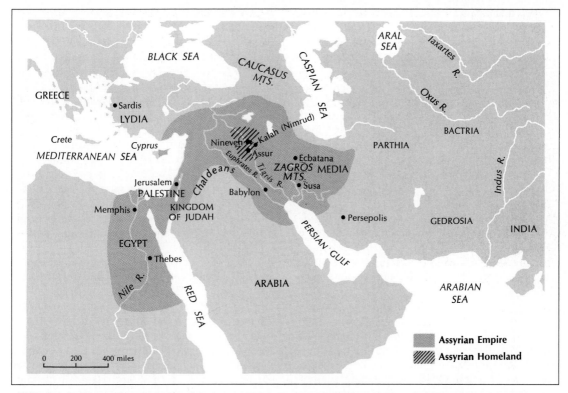

Map 3.1 THE ASSYRIAN EMPIRE, CA. 662 B.C. This map shows the extent of the Assyrian Empire just before its collapse. Some idea of its size is illustrated by the fact that it was more than one thousand miles from its capital at Nineveh to Thebes in Egypt—roughly as far as Washington, D.C., is from Omaha, Nebraska. Its size should be compared with that of the earlier empires of the Egyptians and the Hittites (see Map 2.1). A better appreciation of the Assyrian Empire can be gained by making an effort to account for the different peoples we have studied who were included in it.

they imposed a beneficial, albeit burdensome, peace on the Near East, protecting it for nearly three centuries against barbarians who might have destroyed its civilization had they succeeded in seizing control.

Economically, the Assyrian regime had significant effects. The Assyrians themselves added very little to Near Eastern economy, but they encouraged trade and assisted it by breaking down barriers impeding the movement of goods. They encouraged the spread of a common spoken language across their empire, greatly facilitating the exchange of goods and ideas. Through their ef-

forts goods flowed freely over much of the Near East, and technical skills became more widely disseminated.

In cultural activities the Assyrians also made a notable contribution. Their efforts were not creative, but their imitations resulted in the continuation of cultural activity. Their contributions can be seen best in architecture and sculpture. Assyrian kings were avid builders, constructing the great cities of Assur, Kalah (modern Nimrud), and Nineveh as monuments of their power and glory. In these cities earlier Mesopotamian architectural styles were followed closely and thus kept alive.

Temples and palaces were decorated with massive sculptured pieces and with excellent stone reliefs. The vigorous application of traditions from the past gave the Near East a new era of artistic glory. To the tradition they honored, Assyrian artists often gave a unique quality. Especially impressive were the carved friezes done in relief to decorate the walls of royal palaces. This narrative art put together a succession of carved panels to tell in realistic detail the story of a military campaign or a hunting expedition (see Figure 3.2).

In literature the Assyrians devoted a great deal of effort to collecting older works in Sumerian and Akkadian. One of Assyria's kings, Ashurbanipal III, built a huge library at Nineveh as a repository for thousands of copies of cuneiform tablets. Aside from administrative and economic records, most of the writing in Assyrian was a rerendering of earlier literary works, especially the religious epics and creation stories so dear to the Mesopotamians. The Assyrians did show some originality in compiling annals that vividly recounted the events surrounding the innumerable military campaigns of the kings, thereby making a contribution to the art of historical writing.

Assyrian religion was likewise strongly colored by borrowings from Mesopotamia. The great state god of Assyria, Assur, resembled the Amorite Marduk. Assyrian rituals, prayers, and priesthoods are almost indistinguishable from those of the earlier Mesopotamians. Despite the derived character of their religion, there is considerable evidence that the Assyrians were deeply religious. Perhaps even their imperialism was motivated by a genuine desire to assert Assur's dominion over other gods. In many reliefs Assur is shown hovering over the field of battle, ready to take up arms to assure the victory of the king doing battle in Assur's cause. In all these ways the Assyrians kept alive some of the most precious cultural traditions in the Near East.

2. SUCCESSORS OF ASSYRIA, 612–550 B.C.

In the wake of Assyria's sudden collapse several states entered a spirited competition to carve up the empire. Some of these rivals even aspired to replace the Assyrians as masters of the Near East.

One of the competitors was Egypt. After a long period of weakness following the end of the Egyptian Empire about 1200 B.C. (see Chapter 2), foreign rule by the Assyrians again goaded the Egyptians to unify under a single pharaoh, Psammetichus (663–609 B.C.), founder of the Twenty-sixth Dynasty. Egypt again enjoyed a brief period of internal order, prosperity, and international prestige, especially in the Syria-Palestine area. But the Egyptians were incapable of sustaining a role as a great power. The pharaohs had to rely on foreign mercenaries (chiefly Greeks) to provide a military force; these forces were a constant source of internal trouble. A backward-looking spirit dominated thought and expression. A reactionary priesthood used religion as a force to resist change. Old age had gripped Egyptian society. In 525 B.C. the Persians were able to conquer Egypt without much difficulty.

In Asia Minor the small kingdom of Lydia, which first emerged after the fall of the Hittites, benefited from the fall of Assyria. Its rulers, the most famous of which was Croesus (560–546 B.C.), were able to establish control over most of Asia Minor, including several important Greek city-states on the Aegean seacoast. Despite the considerable prosperity of Lydia, it was unable to resist the Persians, who conquered the kingdom in 546 B.C.

Still another participant in the dismemberment of the Assyrian Empire was Media. Based in northern Iran, the Medes had long been restless dependents on Assyria, but they had raised their level of life considerably by borrowing from their oppressors. Eventually they played a major military role in destroying Assyria. After Assyria's fall, they established control of a vast area extending from Iran westward toward Asia Minor. However, the Median kingdom was badly organized. Eventually a vassal prince, Cyrus of Persia, deposed of the Median king and laid claim to the Median realm.

The most spectacular of all Assyria's successors was the kingdom of the Chaldeans, a Semitic people who had established themselves in southern Mesopotamia prior to its conquest by the Assyrians. Their revolt against the Assyrians played a major role in Assyria's downfall. After Assyria's defeat, the Chaldeans established a kingdom based in Mesopotamia. Under the one great Chaldean king, Nebuchadnezzar II (605–562 B.C.), Syria and Palestine were conquered. Among the victims of Chaldean expansion was the tiny kingdom of Judah. Jerusalem and its Temple were destroyed, and many Hebrews were deported to Babylon as captives. Nebuchadnezzar's reign was marked by a conscious effort to cast the Chaldeans in the role of restorers of ancient Mesopotamian civilization; the result was a notable cultural renaissance. The jewel of this revival was his rebuilding of Babylon as his capital. Its massive walls, beautiful temples and palaces, fabulous hanging gardens, impressive sculpture and painting made it one of the most splendid of ancient cities. Even the redoubtable Hebrew prophet Jeremiah, amid his lamentations over the Babylonian captivity of his people, had to admit that "Babylon was a golden cup in the hands of Yahweh." A religious revival in this period restored the worship of ancient Mesopotamian deities, above all Marduk, as a major feature of the civilization of "New Babylonia." However, despite its outward brilliance, the Chaldean Empire lacked military and economic strength. Under Nebuchadnezzar's weak successors, it proved an easy victim of the Persians in 539 B.C.

3. THE PERSIAN EMPIRE, 550–328 B.C.

As is obvious from the review of the competition for the Assyrian Empire, the final victory belonged to the Persians. They were of Indo-European origin, their ancestors having settled shortly after 2000 B.C. in the barren southern part of Iran as simple farmers and herders. For centuries they maintained their political independence. However, during this period civilizing influences penetrated Persia, especially from Assyria, so that the Persians were drawn into the orbit of the higher civilization of the Near East. They did retain significant aspects of their old Indo-European culture, especially in religion and language. In the late seventh century they were forced to accept the overlordship of the Medes, who were closely akin to them in language and culture. About 560

B.C. a Persian prince, Cyrus, overthrew the Median king and proclaimed himself "king of the Medes and the Persians."

With Cyrus' accession to power the Persians began a period of rapid expansion. Cyrus (ca. 560–530 B.C.) was the most successful conqueror. He seized control of Asia Minor by overpowering Lydia. Then he subdued various peoples living to the east, pushing the boundaries of his empire to the frontiers of India, where there existed another highly developed civilization based in the Indus River valley. In 540 B.C. he attacked the Chaldean kingdom and annexed Mesopotamia, Syria, and Palestine. His successor, Cambyses (530–522 B.C.), overran Egypt. Darius I, "the Great" (522–486 B.C.), extended Persian power into Europe by conquering territory in Thrace, but his attempt to subdue the Greeks failed, as we shall see later (see Chapter 5). He also established Persian control over the Indus Valley. When Darius died in 486 B.C., the Persians controlled one of the largest empires ever created (see Map 3.2).

The first Persian rulers were not only successful conquerors but also skilled statesmen whose decisions in the face of the complex problems presented by so large an empire laid the basis for sound government. Cyrus established one basic principle undergirding Persian rule: tolerance toward defeated peoples and respect for their cultural uniqueness. After he overthrew the Median king to launch the Persian rise to power, he drew the Median aristocracy into his regime as participants in his administration and military force. His policy of tolerance was illustrated in an especially dramatic way by his treatment of the Hebrews. Immediately after conquering the Chaldean state, he allowed the Hebrew captives in Babylon to return to Jerusalem, helped them to rebuild the Temple, and encouraged them to reconstitute their religious community. For this generous act the Hebrews hailed Cyrus as Yahweh's "shepherd." Such actions convinced most peoples in the Near East that the Persians did not intend to continue the brutal policies of the Assyrians and made Persian dominance more acceptable.

Darius was the most effective political leader of his dynasty, called the Achaemenids. Borrowing and adapting old ideas and practices in statecraft, he laid the basis for a highly effective po-

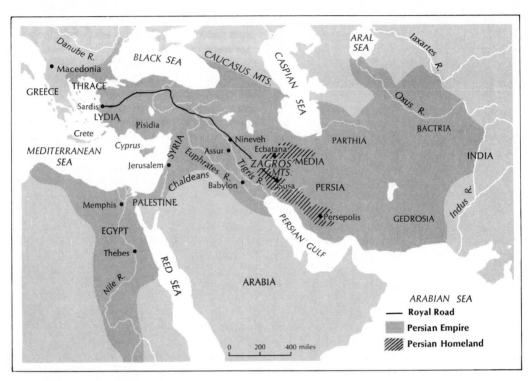

Map 3.2 **THE PERSIAN EMPIRE, CA. 500 B.C.** At its peak the Persian Empire embraced a vast territory, varied in terrain and climate and occupied by a complex mixture of peoples. In area the Persian Empire was approximately the size of the continental United States. The Persians were able to overcome some of these vast distances by building an excellent road system that fanned out from the capital cities of Susa and Persepolis to key cities across the empire. One of the most famous was the Royal Road, which extended from Susa to Sardis, a distance of about sixteen hundred miles. The Persians developed a system of regular outposts along this road and teams of mounted couriers who, by working in relays, could carry a message from Susa to Sardis in as little as a week.

litical system, often imitated by later empire builders. Like his Near Eastern predecessors, he claimed absolute power with authority to make laws, to judge, and to command obedience and service from his subjects. Court life at his capital cities of Ecbatana, Susa, and Persepolis involved an elaborate etiquette designed to impress everyone that he was indeed "The Great King" (see Figure 3.3). He developed a highly skilled bureaucracy staffed by officials, usually of Median or Persian origin, who represented an elite fanatically devoted to maintaining Persian power.

Darius' most notable innovation lay in the techniques he devised for extending his authority

to all parts of his vast empire. He divided the empire into twenty large districts, called *satrapies*, some of which coincided with the boundaries of the kingdoms conquered by the Persians. Over each he appointed a governor, called a *satrap*, usually a Persian and often a member of the royal family, who was given sufficient power to control local affairs. The satraps were removable at the will of the great king and were held strictly accountable for the administration of their districts. Periodically, Darius sent out inspectors to investigate local administration and report to the central government. Contingents of the imperial army under trusted commanders were garrisoned in

Figure 3.3   The "King of Kings" at Work   This relief from the royal palace at Persepolis shows Darius receiving a commander of the royal guard. Behind the king stands his son, Xerxes. (Oriental Institute, University of Chicago)

strategic spots both to support the satraps and to curb their ambitions. An excellent road system and a postal service were developed, permitting rapid communications between the satrapies and the central government. Careful records were maintained by the central government as a means of holding each satrap accountable. By these methods Darius managed to create twenty semi-independent governments, each capable of reacting to situations that were unique to each locality but all guided by common policies shaped by the great king and his high officials seeking to maintain unity amidst diversity.

In the final analysis, Darius' power rested on his armed forces. The Persian army was built around the Immortals, a loyal, disciplined corps of about ten thousand professionals recruited from the Medes and the Persians. When occasion demanded, this elite force was reinforced with contingents mobilized in vast numbers from the subject population of the empire. Although such mass armies could be gathered, armed, and supplied only slowly and although they were hard to control in battle, their sheer numbers made them awe inspiring. The Persians also commanded impressive naval forces, composed largely of hired

Phoenician and Greek ships and crews.

Darius' imperial system endured about one hundred fifty years. The history of the Persian Empire after his death was marked by few events that require our attention. There were numerous wars with outsiders in defense of the empire's immensely long frontiers; the Persians seldom won decisively, but neither did they lose much territory. Rebellions occurred frequently within the empire, but usually they were smashed by the superior power of the great king. The Persians played a major role in the diplomacy of the period, often using their money to build alliances with foreign powers and to manipulate relations among these outsiders; Persian diplomacy was especially significant in the Greek world during the fifth and fourth centuries B.C. Despite its status as a great power, Persian strength gradually eroded during the fourth century. Some of the later kings were deficient in political abilities. Their court became corrupt and torn by intrigue involving royal wives and children, officials, and friends. Ambitious satraps constantly attempted to overthrow the rulers, often putting themselves forward as champions of subject peoples and usually generous in their promises of rewards for those who joined them against the king. A gradual decline in the efficiency and the loyalty of the royal bureaucracy and the armed forces impeded the ability of the kings to control the satraps. By the middle of the fourth century B.C., all that was needed to destroy the Persian Empire was a strong attack from the outside. That attack was soon forthcoming from a powerful Greek/Macedonian army led by Alexander the Great, who was driven in part by an urge to destroy the Persian menace that had haunted the Greek world since the time of Darius the Great. In a brief, brilliant campaign Alexander was able to destroy the Persian power and to take possession of its territory.

The Persians, emerging suddenly from the fringes of the civilized world to master the Near East and confronted constantly with the heavy burdens of holding their huge empire together, devoted most of their talents to administrative, military, and diplomatic affairs. As a consequence, their unique contributions to the cultural development of the Near East were limited. In general, they played a role similar to that of the Assyrians, borrowing from the cultural resources that already existed and synthesizing these borrowings in a way that would create a culture meaningful to a variety of peoples. They continued to utilize already developed languages, especially Aramean, for administrative purposes, although they were able to produce highly sophisticated literary works in their own language. Their kings were lavish in their patronage of art, the results showing chiefly in the royal palaces built at Ecbatana, Susa, and Persepolis. They continued the practice of commissioning artists to render in stone reliefs pictorial records of royal exploits. The kings and their satraps welcomed to their capitals individuals from all over the empire who were schooled in the literary and scientific traditions of the past; as a result, the Persians helped substantially in keeping these traditions alive to serve the cause of learning and expression among later peoples, especially the Greeks, who came to the Persian Empire in large numbers following Alexander's conquests. The tolerant attitude of the Persian masters toward the many different cultural elements embraced in their empire encouraged local cultural activity.

The Persians did make one outstanding contribution to Near Eastern civilization in the form of a new religion, Zoroastrianism. This religion was rooted in beliefs held by the Persians before they became masters of the Near East. Early Persian religion centered around the worship of many deities who represented forces of nature, especially a god of the sky and a god of fire. A complicated ritual, including sacrifices, magic, and prayer, developed as a means of winning the favors of the deities. Priests, called Magi, played a prominent role in directing religious life among the early Persians.

It was into this religious setting that Zoroaster (Zarathustra in Persian) came as a reformer. Although the details of his life are vague and clouded by legend, it appears that he lived about 600 B.C., before the emergence of Persia as master of the Near East. According to tradition, he prepared himself for his ministry by a long period of contemplation in the desert, finally receiving a revelation to guide him to the truth. He then returned to the world to seek converts to his beliefs. At first he enjoyed little success and even suffered persecution, but eventually he began to win adherents, and his religion was implanted in Persian society before the Persians began their rise to dominance.

Zoroaster's exact teachings are as elusive as are the details of his life. His message was eventually set forth in a sacred book called *Zend-Avesta*, but it was compiled over many centuries and contains a confusing array of interpretations and refinements of Zoroaster's original teachings. As a consequence, it is difficult to reconstruct what Zoroaster thought and said. It seems certain that he cast his new message in terms of a protest against existing Persian religion, especially its polytheism and its ritualistic formalism. At its core was a unique concept of the nature of the universe, one based on a principle of dualism. On the one hand, there was the god Ahura Mazda (Lord of Wisdom), the all-powerful, all-pervading lord of creation. This good and benevolent spirit presides over all creation, emanating and personifying such qualities as justice, pure thought, integrity, good intentions, and virtue. But the good Ahura Mazda is opposed by the diabolical Ahriman, an evil force seeking to blot out justice, light, wisdom, and good. The warfare between Ahura Mazda and Ahriman, good and evil, going on since the beginning of the world, provides the dynamic force in the universe. Eventually, in a final day of judgment, Ahura Mazda will prevail; but in the meantime, the conflict will rage, extending into every soul and demanding that each individual elect whether to serve good or evil. On the final day of reckoning, those who have chosen good will be rewarded with eternal happiness, while those who have elected the way of Ahriman will be condemned to eternal misery.

By postulating the struggle between good and evil as fundamental in the cosmic order, Zoroaster made the basic obligation of each human being clear. Only good conduct would win favor in the eyes of Ahura Mazda. The worship of old deities, magic, sacrifices, and priestly ministrations were irrelevant and even constituted a surrender to evil because they diverted attention from doing good. Zoroaster defined a vigorous moral code for his followers, derived in its particulars from the qualities of goodness surrounding Ahura Mazda. Obversely, he set forth a clear concept of sin, rooted in the evil nature of Ahriman. Certainly none of the religions in the world that the Persians were soon to rule, except Judaism, gave such emphasis to ethical issues—and not even Judaism placed the burden of goodness so squarely on each individual. Zoroaster did not associate goodness and righteousness with a particular chosen people or system of law; his message was aimed at all humankind.

Although the record is again confusing, it appears that Zoroaster's religion took firm hold among the Persians and the Medes after the master's death and that it became in some fashion the official religion of the Achaemenid dynasty. However, its acceptance was not universal in the Persian Empire. The general policy of tolerance in the empire permitted other religions to maintain their hold. As time passed, Zoroaster's original message lost its uniqueness. Ritual practices aimed at pleasing Ahura Mazda and warding off Ahriman's evil powers grew increasingly prominent. The role of the Magi again became predominant. Polytheistic concepts crept back into Zoroastriansim. Ahriman was elevated to the status of god, standing equal to Ahura Mazda in the cosmic order. Old Persian deities and hosts of angels and devils reappeared as combatants in the eternal war between good and evil. The concept of the struggle between good and evil tended to associate good with purely spiritual forces and evil with material things. This interpretation of dualism had the effect of belittling the practice of virtue in everyday life and of exalting withdrawal from the world. These developments, tending to make Zoroastrianism like most other Near Eastern religions, blunted its appeal. After the collapse of the Persian Empire, Zoroastrianism declined as a major religious force in the Near East. However, it has survived across twenty-five centuries to the present; its modern adherents, called Parsees, live in Iran and India. Zoroaster's concept of dualism was destined to provide a rich source of spiritual speculation among later religions, especially Christianity.

The sudden end of the Persian Empire at the hands of Greeks and Macedonians must not detract from the importance of the Persians in history. The enlightened and tolerant rule of the Achaemenids built a universal empire in the ancient Near East in which all kinds of people at many levels of civilization were brought together in a viable community. The cosmopolitan environment in that empire permitted local cultures to persist and grow while providing instruments through which all could mix and fertilize each other. In a sense, the resulting amalgam reflected the best the ancient Near East had produced during the thirty-five centuries in which its people stood in the forefront of civilized life.

SUGGESTED READING

Assyrians

H. W. F. Saggs, *The Might That Was Assyria* (1984).
Georges Roux, *Ancient Iraq,* 2nd ed. (1980).
Two well-written treatments of Assyrian history and civilization.
André Parrot, *Arts of Assyria,* trans. Stuart Gilbert and James Emmons (1961). An excellent introduction to all aspects of Assyrian art.

Persians

J. M. Cook, *The Persian Empire* (1983). An effective treatment of Persian history and institutions.
Richard N. Frye, *The History of Ancient Iran* (1983). Surveys Persian history down to the Moslem conquest in the eighth century A.D.

Richard N. Frye, *The Heritage of Persia* (1963). Excellent survey of Persian cultural influence on the larger world.
Mary Boyce, *Zoroastrians: Their Religious Beliefs and Practices* (1984). A brief treatment covering the entire history of Zoroastrianism.
Mary Boyce, *A History of Zoroastrianism,* 2 vols. (1975–1982). A detailed history of early Zoroastrianism.
Roman Ghirshman, *Persia from the Origins to Alexander the Great,* trans. Stuart Gilbert and James Emmons (1964).
Edith Porada, *The Art of Ancient Iran. Pre-Islamic Cultures* (1965).
This and the preceding work provide a full treatment of all aspects of Persian art.

RETROSPECT

When in 330 B.C. Alexander the Great stood in triumph over the body of Darius III, a chapter in world history had ended. The Persians, symbolizing an old order, had given way to a youthful conqueror who represented a vital new order emerging on the western periphery of the Near East. Before shifting our attention to that new setting, a brief epitaph for the ancient Near Eastern world is in order.

For the purposes of this epitaph, let us view the Persians as the last scions of a great family whose origins are rooted in simple Neolithic villages and whose members include all the peoples whose histories have been reviewed in the preceding pages. Over several millennia, especially after 4000 B.C., that family had put together a rich and varied patrimony. They had devised effective systems for extracting sustenance from nature. They had developed impressive techniques for controlling large numbers of people and permitting them to interact with each other. They had learned to enrich lives through a magnificent art and literature. They had interwoven the many

facets of their existence into patterns that gave meaning to their activities and provided them with a sense of direction in a mysterious cosmic order. Their religions provided the integrative, unifying, sense-giving dimension of their civilization. In all these ways the peoples of the ancient Near East had created a priceless storehouse from which future peoples could draw without having to invent higher civilization over again. In one sense, world history is a story of the diffusion of ancient Near Eastern achievements across much of the face of the earth.

Yet, the civilizational pattern of the ancient Near East had limitations. The environment imposed serious constraints, for aside from the river valleys the Near East had limited potential in terms of material resources. Technology imposed another limitation. We must not let the spectacular advances of the last century or two blur a basic fact: Technological advance through most of history has been slow and painful, making difficult all efforts to expand control over nature. The ancient Near East suffered too from the overpowering influence of the river valley peoples. What succeeded so remarkably in early Mesopotamia and early Egypt became the model of civilized life for every people in the Near East. Although they benefited from imitation, those living beyond the valley flood plains became prisoners of modes of life that were creative only in a small geographical setting. Slavish imitation of the river valley pattern of civilization brought people to a certain point— and then stopped them from further advance. Still another limitation on the ancient Near Eastern world was its waste of human resources. It was a world directed by small elites who achieved wonders but who ultimately failed to call forth fresh creative talent. The social structure was too inflexible, too closed, to permit genius to break through from unexpected sources.

However, the greatest constriction on ancient Near Eastern civilization and the ultimate cause of it stagnation lay in the minds of human beings. The world view encased in the great religious systems made it extremely difficult for people to use to full capacity their greatest asset: the power to reason. Instead of freeing them to reflect on the nature and potential of themselves and the things around them, the ancient Near Eastern world view required that people pour their intellectual energies into acts of conformity with the directive forces of the cosmos. Because rationality was smothered, humans failed to discover themselves. They were reaching in this direction, as the Hebrew prophets and Zoroaster testify, but they never broke through the formidable barriers imposed by the assumptions on which their civilization was based. Only someone outside their world still had the freedom to discover what humanity really was. When that discovery was made, the Near Eastern peoples had to surrender the leadership of civilization to others.

Here then is the epitaph of the ancient Near East: It was a world that knew people not well enough.

PART TWO

GRECO-ROMAN CIVILIZATION, 1200 B.C.–A.D. 200

While the civilizations of the Near East were reaching maturity under the political sway of the Assyrians and the Persians, a new civilization was appearing in the lands around the Aegean Sea. It began to emerge about 1200 B.C. and reached its most creative phase in the fifth century B.C. From its Aegean center the new civilization exerted a powerful influence over other peoples. The Greeks themselves propagated their style of life through trading and colonizing ventures that ringed the Mediterranean with their city-states. In the latter part of the fourth century, the Macedonians under the meteoric Alexander the Great joined with the Greeks to burst out of the Aegean basin and overrun the old centers of civilization in the Near East. In the third century B.C. the Romans, just emerging as a world power, became enamored of Hellenic civilization and turned their energies to absorbing and spreading it. The Romans eventually conquered Greece and the Near East but were themselves mastered by the ideas and culture of their victims. The empire that they forged became the setting for a further extension of the Greek pattern of life so that much of western Europe and North Africa fell under Greek influence.

In tracing the complex evolution of Greco-Roman civilization through fourteen or fifteen centuries, one should try to identify in an orderly way the main stages of development and to comprehend the essential ingredients of Greco-Roman civilization. But perhaps most important, one should grasp the extent to which the Greco-Roman world discovered and unleashed a new range of human talents. To many historians, the key to this chapter of human history was the discovery and development of the idea expressed by the Athenian dramatist Sophocles in his *Antigone:* "Many are the wonders of the world, and none so wonderful as Man."

CHAPTER 4

The Origins and Development of the Greek City-State Polity

FIGURE 4.1 The Heart of a Polis The fact that the rocky promontory shown in this photo features the surviving ruins of one of the great artistic achievements in all history should not hide another important consideration: Such physical settings played a prime role all over ancient Greece as focal points that drew people together to form a unique community—the *polis*. That the Athenians chose to invest their wealth and talent in adorning the Acropolis is a reflection of the role that this modest hill played over many centuries as a center of their collective activities. (Hirmer Fotoarchiv)

Greco-Roman civilization originated in a group of small, independent communities located around the Aegean Sea. It is impossible to understand that civilization without grasping the unique nature of these communities. However, none of them sprang full-grown from a void; each was a product of slow growth and long experimentation. This chapter will trace that evolution and show the nature of these communities.

1. THE ENVIRONMENT

Greco-Roman civilization had its origins in the physical environment provided by the Aegean basin. The whole area is blessed with beneficent climate, marked by mild winters and long, dry summers that permit relatively safe travel by sea and allow comfortable life on land without great expenditure on clothing and housing. The topography, especially of Greece proper, is dominated by mountains, valleys, bays, and peninsulas that cut the land into many small pockets of tillable soil and create barriers impeding communication and political unification. The area's resources are not abundant. Tillable soil is limited, poor in quality, subject to erosion, and ill suited to cereal production. Tin, copper, iron, and timber are in short supply. As the Greek historian Herodotus said, "Greece has always poverty as her companion."

But there was an avenue of escape from this restrictive setting: the sea. The Aegean provides excellent harbors and good sailing winds during the summer season. It served as a roadway allowing the Greeks access to a wider world of raw materials and markets and to contacts with other peoples who stimulated and were stimulated by the Greeks.

2. THE MYCENAEAN AND DARK AGES, 2000–800 B.C.: GREEK ORIGINS

The emergence of a unique Greek civilization occurred over a long period of time. Perhaps the first important step was taken when Neolithic culture was introduced to the Aegean area about 6000 B.C. During many ensuing centuries life centered around simple agricultural villages and typical Neolithic institutions. About 2000 B.C. this primitive order was profoundly affected by the intrusion of Indo-Europeans into the area, part of the same movement that disturbed much of the Near East and produced such peoples as the Kassites, the Hittites, and the Persians. The newcomers in Greece imposed their overlordship and their language on the natives, but they adopted from their victims the basic features of agricultural life. For the next four or five centuries, Aegean history centered on the activities of a number of small principalities dominated by aggressive warlords and their armed retainers.

Surviving archaeological evidence indicates that some of these warlords were able to accumulate considerable wealth and that technological skills were advancing rapidly. By about 1500 B.C., the kings of some of the small principalities in southern and central Greece were able to build huge fortress-palaces. The most impressive was located at Mycenae, which has given its name to this phase of early Greek history. The key to the success of these kings appears to have been what they learned from expanding contacts as pirates and traders with the major advanced societies of the Near East and especially with Minoan society in Crete. The rulers of Mycenae and other important cities established well-organized bureaucracies capable of imposing strong economic and political control over the populations living in the areas surrounding their fortress cities. A written form of the Greek language, called Linear B, was perfected to assist kings and their agents in keeping records pertaining to political and economic life.

Mycenaean culture reached its peak about 1300 B.C. As it matured, it moved toward assimilation with the larger pattern of civilization developing across the Near East during the age of cultural diffusion. The art, technology, and religion usages of the Mycenaeans contained features that suggest that the first Greeks were on the way to absorbing the common cultural patterns of the Near East. However, that process was cut short about 1200 B.C. by the decline and then the collapse of Mycenaean culture. The causes are not entirely clear. Perhaps the collapse of Minoan civilization about 1400 B.C. deprived the Mycenaean world of a vital source of inspiration. The disturbances that disrupted the Hittite and Egyptian empires about 1200 B.C. may have severed trade connections so vital to the Mycenaeans. The resulting constraints on the economy of the Mycenaean world caused the warlike kings to turn on each other in search of wealth to sustain their expensive way of life. It was in these troubled times, for instance, that warriors from several Greek kingdoms joined hands to destroy Troy in Asia Minor, a venture immortalized in the poetry of Homer. Whatever the cause, between about 1200 and 1100 B.C. most of the mighty Mycenaean citadels, including Mycenae, were violently destroyed, bringing to an end the first chapter in Greek history.

The collapse of Mycenaean culture led to a period of about four centuries in the Aegean world that modern historians have called a "Dark Age." Information about this period depends largely on archaeological remains, which are scarce and difficult to interpret. Only at the very end of the period does another kind of evidence appear in the form of two literary masterpieces, the *Iliad* and the *Odyssey*, attributed to the poet Homer. Although Homer claims to recount the adventures of heroes living more than four centuries earlier during the Trojan War, he puts these legendary figures in the eighth-century setting he knew. Consequently, his poems provide a picture of the Greek world about 800 B.C.

The scanty evidence leaves no doubt that with the collapse of the Mycenaean world, many aspects of Mycenaean civilization disappeared: the bureaucratic kingdoms, the great palaces, writing, trading, art, technical expertise. Many settled locations disappeared, suggesting a population decline. Life depended on simple farming carried on by the inhabitants of small communities with limited contacts with a larger world. Life around the Aegean had returned to a primitive level.

However, there were developments that established the basis for fresh cultural advance. The Dark Age saw considerable shifting of peoples in the Aegean area. Especially important was the movement of Greeks from the mainland to the Aegean Islands and the coast of Asia Minor, where important contacts with the Near Eastern world were again established. The populating of this entire area with people linked by common cultural traits established the demographic base for future Greek development. The peoples occupying the Aegean basin came to share a common Greek language, although that language had several different dialects. A new writing system, based on the adaptation of the Phoenician alphabet to accommodate the Greek spoken language, was developed to a level that made possible the magnificent Homeric epics. A common pattern of religion, clearly delineated in the Homeric poems, spread among the Greeks. Although the Greek world remained poor, all those living in the Aegean world benefited from technological advances, especially the adoption of iron-age technology and advancing skills in pottery making. Complex processes were working to define a people participating in a common pattern of life; these people would soon call themselves Hellenes, a term that conveyed their sense both of their commonalty and of their uniqueness.

The Dark Age was especially important in shaping political life. The Greek world remained politically fragmented into many petty tribal kingdoms. Over each presided a chieftain who led his people in war, judged their disputes, and represented them before their deities. In marked contrast with the power enjoyed by kings during the Mycenaean Age, the power of these kings was limited by a politically active nobility whose authority was based on patriarchal family ties, loyal personal retainers, and control of the best lands and herds of cattle. The nobles in each kingdom met regularly to share with the king decision making on matters of common interest. Noble power was enhanced by the dominant role aristocrats played in warfare, an activity that contributed in an important way to defining noble values. Peasants and artisans were considered to be free and even participated to a degree in political life through attendance at assemblies, where they shouted their approval or disapproval of decisions made by kings and nobles. By the end of the Dark Age these small political entities—their members united by kinship and personal ties, shared religious life, and active involvement in political decisions—constituted a base from which would emerge the key institution shaping Greek civilization: the city-state, called the *polis* by the Greeks.

3. THE ARCHAIC AGE 800-500 B.C.: DEVELOPMENT OF THE *POLIS*

Shortly after 800 B.C. the Greek world entered a period of rapid development that historians call the "Archaic Age." During the next three centuries changes occurred in all aspects of life to create the basic elements of Greek civilization. Central to that development was the evolution of the *polis*.

The shaping of the *polis* was a complex process, proceeding at a different pace and in different ways from one place to another. However, among the nearly seven hundred city-states that established an independent identity during the Archaic Age there were certain common patterns of development that provide the key to the basic nature of the *polis* (see Map 4.1 for the location of the major city-states). Central to the emergence of each *polis* were processes that created powerful bonds linking the inhabitants of a relatively small geographical area into a community and that expanded the involvement of the "citizens" of each community in civic life. These communal bonds found their focus in a physical center, an urban center. Already at the beginning of the Archaic Age the rudiments of such urban centers were emerging in the petty kingdoms that had been established during the Dark Age. At such centers were the king's residence and often a hilltop fortress, called an *acropolis*, where those from the surrounding countryside could find protection. There temples were built where members of the community could gather to honor their shared deities. The same center served as a meeting place for the noble clan leaders when they gathered from their rural estates to counsel with the king; some even established residences there. A market, called an *agora*, developed in connection with the fortress. As the Archaic Age progressed, the range of activities affecting group life expanded in each urban center, and increasingly the members of each community developed a sense of belonging to and depending on a special group. At the same time there emerged institutional forms that increasingly gave structure to the shared experiences of those belonging to the community. Involvement and participation in the political,

economic, religious, and cultural activities unfolding at each urban center became the central focus in the lives of those belonging to each *polis*.

A major step in shaping the political and social structure of the typical *polis* occurred in all but a few communities during the eighth century B.C. This change involved the replacement of monarchy with a system of government in which authority rested with a council of nobles and the execution of the council's decision was entrusted to elected officials from that same noble class. Aristocratic domination of most city-states persisted until at least 500 B.C. The power of these nobles was based on landed wealth, control over the clan structure that undergirded early Greek society, and dominance of the legal system. Although they were often greedy and always jealous of their authority, the nobles felt a strong attachment to their *polis* and were willing to use their talent and wealth to promote its welfare. Especially crucial was their willingness to take political action to resolve basic problems affecting the entire population. Under their governance the bonds undergirding each *polis* were expanded and strengthened.

Another crucial development in broadening the base of participation in civic life involved the military organization of most city-states. As reflected in the Homeric epics, warfare during the Dark Age had been monopolized by nobles, who alone could afford the horses and equipment needed for cavalry and chariot combat. That system was replaced by a military organization based on the *phalanx*, a massed formation of infantry soldiers, called *hoplites*, armed with shields, breastplates, helmets, swords, and spears. This change brought larger numbers of citizens with modest means into the service of the *polis*, placed a premium on disciplined action in a common cause, and increased the devotion of the new soldiers to the city-state whose safety now depended on them more than on a few noble warriors. Before long these soldiers were demanding a share in making the decisions that determined the activities of the *polis*.

Even more significant in expanding the bonds that attached people to the *polis* were actions taken by aristocratic leaders to cope with major economic and social problems that began to afflict

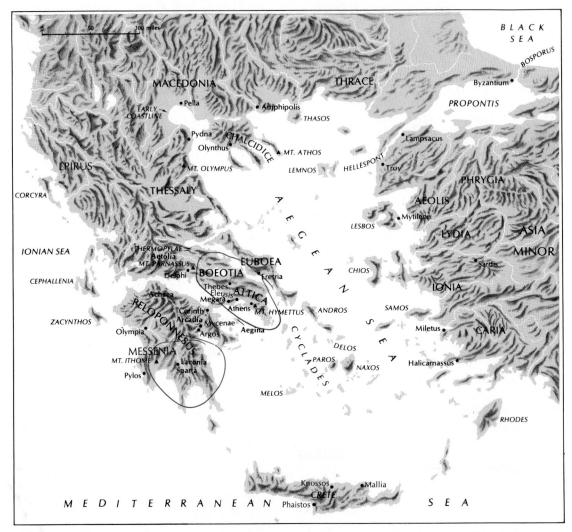

Map 4.1 **EARLY AND CLASSICAL GREECE** This map identifies the major geographical regions of the Aegean world and locates the most important *poleis*—but by no means all of them. It also reflects the proximity of most Greek city-states to the Aegean Sea. The numerous islands in the Aegean and the inlets and bays penetrating the Greek mainland greatly facilitated seafaring.

much of the Greek world during the Archaic Age. The nature and the impact of the crisis are reflected in a poem entitled *Works and Days,* written about 700 B.C. by Hesiod, a wealthy farmer embittered by the growing poverty and injustice of the times. The causes for the crisis were deepseated: growing population, competition for lim-

ited land, and the greediness of what Hesiod called "the land-devouring lords" who controlled each *polis.* The chief victims were small landholders who were being forced into debt, economic dependence on noble landlords, and even slavery, thereby losing their status as citizens of their *polis.*

Despite the fact that the aristocracy was part

of the cause of the problem, aristocratic leaders in most city-states played a key role in finding ways of resolving the crisis. A major solution took the form of organizing overseas settlement. In many city-states noble councils and elected magistrates encouraged or even ordered colonizing ventures, usually led by nobles who recruited impoverished followers to take to the seas in search of new homes. A prime target for such ventures was southern Italy and Sicily, an area so completely Hellenized that it became known as Magna Graecia (Greater Greece). Other Greek settlements were established on the northern shores of the Aegean, in the Hellespont area, around the Black Sea, in southern France, in Spain, in Egypt, and in modern Libya (then called Cyrenaica). In all of these areas the Greeks imposed control over the native populations and established themselves as farmers, traders, and artisans. The new communities were not colonies in the modern sense. Rather, each was an independent *polis* with its own government, citizens, laws, and civic pride. Although many such new city-states maintained contact with the Aegean city-states from which the settlers had originally migrated, the overseas migrations between about 750 to 500 B.C. marked a massive extension of the *polis* and of what the Greeks called Hellas—the area dominated by Greeks and their culture (see Map 4.2).

Equally important in reducing economic pressures in many city-states was a significant expansion of trade and industry. The colonizing undertakings played a key role in the growth of trade and industry by providing access to raw materials and markets for Greek products. The Greeks proved energetic and enterprising in taking advantage of commercial opportunities, and by 500 B.C. they had become the leading traders in the Mediterranean world, rivaled only by Carthage, originally established as a colony by the Phoenicians. Trade spurred manufacturing in many city-states, and Greek artisans proved skillful in making products in high demand, especially pottery. Even the agricultural system changed as a consequence of expanding trade. Enterprising farmers abandoned the raising of grain in favor of grapes, olives, and livestock, from which were derived products that found profitable markets throughout the Mediterranean area. Increasingly, Greek

city-states imported grain, especially from the Black Sea area. For merchants, artisans, and commercial farmers, the center of economic life shifted to the urban marketplace, creating new ties between citizen and *polis*.

The social structure changed under the impact of economic growth. Some aristocrats became involved in trade and industry and developed interests different from those of their more conservative peers whose status and wealth depended on landownership. This development weakened the class solidarity of the aristocracy and made political changes easier. Many individuals from the lower ranks of society were able to amass considerable wealth through trade and industry and became rivals of the landowning aristocracy for power and prestige. Small farmers, lacking the resources needed to engage in the new forms of agriculture and unwilling to become dependents of great landowners, moved to the urban center to become traders, artisans, or hired laborers. This change dissolved ancient family ties, weakened the control of aristocratic clan leaders over the populace, and thrust upon public authorities new burdens in controlling socially displaced groups.

Changing economic and social structures created pressures for political change. In general, aristocratic regimes in each *polis* tried to relieve mounting tensions by instituting "reforms" that did not require surrender of their monopoly on power. They enacted written codes of law that defined more precisely the rights and responsibilities of all citizens and that limited aristocratic dominance over the administration of justice. They granted relief to debtors and protection to small farmers. They devised policies that sought to gain trading advantages for their city-state. They sponsored projects that improved the public facilities of the *polis*. In these "reforms" the aristocrats were motivated in part by self-interest, but they also were moved by a realization that steps must be taken to retain the allegiance and the services of artisans, soldiers, sailors, shopkeepers, and farmers who increasingly made vital contributions to the welfare of the *polis*.

As important as they were in strengthening the *polis*, these "reforms" were not sufficient in many city-states to maintain stability. The growing attachment of individuals of all social levels to the city-state generated demands for greater political participation than the aristocratic masters were willing to grant. Usually force was required to break the nobles' monopoly on power. In many city-states the assault on aristocratic power was spearheaded by individual leaders called *tyrants* by the Greeks. Often of noble origin and ambitious for personal power, these charismatic figures seized control over the *polis* by force and ruled illegally, sometimes with support from the *hoplites* who dominated the military establishment in many city-states. The typical tyrant made no effort to change existing political structure; rather, each sought to dominate it by filling the council and the magistracies with loyal political followers. Once in power the tyrant launched policies that were popular with the common people, especially those dependent on trade and industry. Measures were taken to depose wealthy, highborn nobles from power, to tax their wealth, and to deprive them of their land, which was redistributed to small farmers. Policies pleasing to nonaristocratic elements in society were pursued, including measures to increase trade and industry, huge expenditures on beautification of the city, and more equitable administration of the law.

The duration of tyranny was relatively brief in most city-states, often lasting only during the lifetime of the first tyrant. Since tyrants had seized power illegally, their regimes depended on their individual talents and their popularity. Eventually, the aristocrats who had been their chief victims took the lead in unseating them and in restoring "legitimate" government. But these aristocrats were unable to reestablish their traditional monopoly based on landownership and kinship ties. In those city-states where aristocratic control continued after the overthrow of tyranny, the ruling element was greatly expanded to include men of wealth but without noble heritage. In some cities that had avoided tyranny, leaders of the old nobility understood the course of affairs well enough to open noble ranks and political power to a wider circle. In many city-states the end of tyranny was accompanied by radical changes in the political system that allowed the total citizen body to take control of civic affairs. With all citizens entitled to participate in government, the last knot that would bind them to the *polis* was tied.

4. ATHENS

The history of Athens during the Archaic Age provides a case study illustrating the evolution of a democratic *polis*. During the Mycenaean Age, Athens was a prominent fortress center exercising control over the surrounding area, called Attica. The general decline occurring over most of the Aegean world during the Dark Age resulted in the emergence in Attica of a number of small agricultural villages led by local tribal leaders. Sometime during the early Archaic Age under circumstances still not well understood, these villages coalesced into a single political entity centering on Athens to constitute an embryo *polis* embracing about a thousand square miles—the largest city-state in ancient Greece except for Sparta. The emerging *polis* was ruled by an hereditary king assisted by a council of clan heads called the *Areopagus* and a popular assembly called the *ecclesia*. For political and military purposes, the citizen body was grouped into four tribes, each composed of brotherhoods (called *phratries,* from whence is derived our word *fraternity*), which in turn were made up of several clans. Citizenship was established by admission to a brotherhood and depended on ties with clans. As a consequence, kinship ties played a crucial role in society.

About 750 B.C. monarchy was abolished and an official, called an *archon,* was elected annually to serve as head of the *polis.* Within a short time other archons were established, including a military leader (*polemarch*) and several judges. These magistrates, nine in number, were elected by the *ecclesia,* but only wealthy men of noble birth were eligible. The real power rested in the Areopagus, composed of aristocratic ex-archons who, upon completion of their terms as elective officials, automatically entered lifetime membership in the Areopagus. Combining their political position with their control over the clan structure, this narrow circle of aristocrats completely dominated Athenian life for two centuries after 750 B.C.

However, during those centuries the Athenians experienced mounting tensions, rooted primarily in the deterioration of the economic and social position of small farmers. Under pressures of a growing population, competition for limited land, and increasing emphasis in agricultural pro-

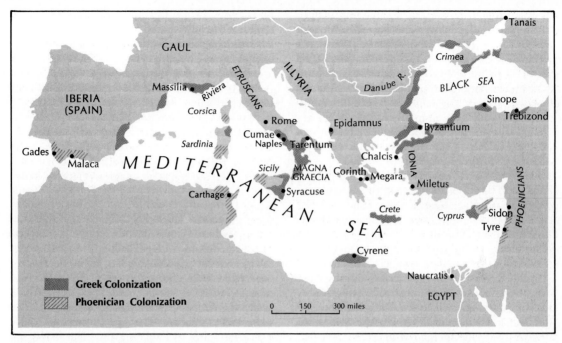

Map 4.2 **GREEK COLONIES ABOUT 500 B.C.** This map shows the major areas of Greek colonization during the period 800–500 B.C. The location of these settlements make it clear that the Greeks were in a position to dominate much of Mediterranean trade by 500 B.C. Their main rivals were Carthage, originally founded by the Phoenicians, and the Etruscans.

duction on olives and livestock, many of them became debtors obligated to turn over a sizable portion of their crops to their noble creditors as debt payment; some were eventually enslaved because they could not pay what they owed. Athens was slow to seek overseas colonies but ultimately directed its efforts toward the Hellespont and Black Sea areas, suggesting that the city suffered serious food shortage. Toward the end of the seventh century B.C. trade and industry began to expand, creating new economic interests not always satisfied with the policies of the dominant aristocrats whose interests were primarily agricultural.

Ultimately, the ruling aristocracy responded to these pressures by introducing reforms. Perhaps they were prodded in this direction by an aborted attempt in 632 B.C. to establish a tyranny. Also by the seventh century Athens had developed a *hoplite* army that brought a wider circle of citizens into a key role in society. In 621 B.C. a reformer named Draco drew up the first written code of law, harsh in its details but significant because it curtailed the power of aristocratic judges and family heads to administer justice in their own interests.

Shortly after, there appeared a more significant reformer, Solon, who was elected archon about 594 B.C. Although an aristocrat, Solon was a man of broad vision and strong patriotism whose concern for injustice in Athens is reflected in surviving fragments of his poetry. Central to Solon's program was his effort to aid the poor and oppressed by a "shaking off of burdens." He struck down the ancient debt laws that permitted landlords to extract exorbitant rents from small farmers who fell into debt and slavery. Many who had fallen into bondage were freed. However, while Solon assured personal freedom to those victimized by debt, he did not return their lost land. He apparently realized that Athens could not remain a city-state totally dependent on agriculture. Thus, he took steps to promote new forms of agriculture, notably olive oil production, which would provide products for export. He was especially concerned with encouraging the growth of trade and industry as a means of providing new opportunities for displaced farmers. Particularly important was his encouragement of the immigration of foreign artisans with skills to upgrade the quality of Athenian manufactured goods and with the ability to teach those skills to Athenians.

Keenly aware of aristrocratic abuse of power, Solon introduced political changes designed to curb such abuses; however, these changes were not intended to deprive the aristocrats of dominance in Athens. As a means of limiting the power exercised by aristocratic families through their domination of the brotherhoods, he reorganized the entire citizen population into four classes, each defined in terms of income derived from land. This classification system greatly weakened the grip of the clans over society by allowing one's political role to be defined without reference to family connections. Eligibility for the chief elective offices—from which individuals passed to life membership in the Areopagus—was confined to the two upper wealth groups, but under the new system involvement in the direction of the *polis* was no longer restricted to the highborn. Solon extensively revised Draco's law code to broaden public control over the administration of justice. He also sought to curb abuses in the administration of justice by making the *Heliaea* instead of the Areopagus the final court of appeal. The *Heliaea* was a large panel of citizens drawn by lot from the membership of the *ecclesia* to serve as a court. The new powers bestowed on it by Solon permitted the citizen body to correct judicial inequities perpetrated in the tribal and brotherhood courts, which were totally controlled by noble family heads. While Solon was certainly no democrat, taken together the changes he introduced marked an important step in breaking aristocratic monopoly of power and expanding the role of the citizen body in public affairs.

Solon's reforms failed to resolve the tensions in Athenian society. The aristocrats split into factions competing fiercely for control of the state. The small farmers who had been given freedom by Solon but no land continued to be depressed and uprooted by changing patterns in agriculture. The growing numbers of merchants and artisans clamored for a larger voice in political decisions affecting economic life. The combined force of these discontented elements paved the way for tyranny in Athens.

Athens' first tyrant was an ambitious nobleman, Pisistratus, who after two unsuccessful attempts finally seized control in 546 B.C. with the help of mercenary troops paid out of his own wealth and the contributions of foreign city-states hostile toward Athens. He held power until his death in 527 B.C., and his sons continued his regime until 510 B.C. Pisistratus and his sons made no changes in the constitutional structure of Athens. They sustained their power by controlling the election of archons, which in turn gave them a powerful hold on the Areopagus. They used harsh means, including confiscation of property and exile, to cow the powerful aristocratic families. Like the policy of all Greek tyrants, their major policy was directed toward building a popular following, chiefly among the small farmers and the emerging merchant and artisan groups. They provided jobs by sponsoring public works projects, promoted Athenian commercial and manufacturing interests by an aggressive foreign policy, tried to ensure an equitable administration of justice, and promoted civic religious life (see Figure 4.2). Their policies increased Athens' wealth and expanded the number of citizens whose welfare depended on the well-being of the entire *polis*.

Despite its broad appeal and its role in promoting the advance of Athens as a leading city-state, tyranny marked only a temporary chapter in Athenian history. Under Pisistratus' sons the regime grew more arbitrary and oppressive. Finally, a coalition of aristocratic families with the support of Spartan military forces drove Hippias into exile in Persia in 510 B.C. Although some of the noble victors hoped to reestablish an aristocratic monopoly on power, their dreams were dashed by another noble faction, led by Cleisthenes, which turned to the citizenry for support of reforms aimed at broadening citizen participation in political life as a means of restoring order.

Assuming leadership in 508 B.C., Cleisthenes took the initiative in instituting basic structural

FIGURE 4.2   Greek Civic Religion   An important part of Greek civic life involved public religious ceremonies, the chief of which was the sacrifice of animals. This pottery painting shows Athenians sacrificing to Apollo, whose statue is shown on the right. The priest is placing the animal parts due the god on the blood-stained altar, while the good meat from the sacrificial animal is held on a spit by a youth; it will be cooked and enjoyed by the sacrificers. The scene reflects the familiarity felt by the Greeks toward their deities. (Museum für Vor und Frühgeschichte, Frankfurt)

changes in the political system. He abolished the political functions of the ancient clans, brotherhoods, and tribes, although he left them certain religious and social roles. To replace the kinship-dominated system, he divided Attica into territorial units, called *demes*. All free males living in a *deme* were registered as hereditary citizens, regardless of family connections. The *demes*, perhaps totaling about one hundred fifty, were grouped together to form thirty second-level organizations, called *trittyes*. Three *trittyes* were then combined to create a *tribe*, of which there was a total of ten. In arranging this basic structure, Cleisthenes provided an ingenious twist aimed at overcoming re-

gionalism and reconciling special economic interests. During the sixth century Attica had become divided into three distinct geographical regions, each with special economic interests: the hill or interior country, dominated by poor farmers; the plain, where the land was most fertile and the great noble families were entrenched; and the shore or city, where merchants, artisans, and urban laborers predominated. Cleisthenes created ten *trittyes* in each of these regions. In shaping the ten tribes, he included one *trittys* from each region in each tribe. As a consequence, each tribe contained a cross section of the entire population, requiring that conflicting interests be conciliated before each tribe could determine its position on major issues affecting the entire *polis*. Each *deme* and tribe was a political unit in its own right, with elected officials, courts, shrines, taxes, and military forces. Each offered wide opportunity for direct participation by the citizenry in local affairs.

Cleisthenes then rearranged the main organs of government to fit the new tribal organization. A Council of Five Hundred, composed of fifty citizens selected by lot from each tribe for an annual term, was created as a prime agency in shaping political life of the *polis*. No one could serve on this council more than twice in a lifetime, thus ensuring that many citizens had an opportunity to participate in this all-important body. The Council of Five Hundred was in essence a steering committee for the citizen body, meeting frequently to supervise many aspects of the administration of the city and to prepare an agenda of issues to be presented to the *ecclesia*, which had the ultimate authority in the government. Made up of all male citizens over eighteen years of age voting by tribe, this body met at least once a month to hear debate on issues presented by the Council of Five Hundred and to vote on a course of action. The citizens were further involved in governing the city by their participation in the popular court, the *Heliaea*, which played an increasing role in the administration of justice. Cleisthenes did not change the Areopagus, although it now lacked the authority to guide crucial decisions, and the elected archons remained the executive officers of the *polis*. The magistrates were elected by the *ecclesia* and were still usually from the wealthy, aristocratic segment of the population, but now they had to win the support of the entire citizen body. Perhaps it was Cleisthenes who introduced a powerful instrument for controlling elective officials and overly ambitious aristocrats by establishing the practice of *ostracism*, through which a majority of the *ecclesia* could declare an individual dangerous to the state and order that person into exile for ten years.

Although Cleisthenes' reforms laid the basis for democratic government in Athens, nearly fifty years were required before the citizenry became accustomed to the full exercise of its power. During that time the aristocratic families continued to dominate the *polis*. Not until the time of Pericles,

the chief political figure from 461 to 429 B.C., did Athenian democracy reach full bloom. During that interval changes were made to encourage greater participation. The chief executive offices were increasingly filled by lot, expanding the chances of ordinary citizens to hold high office. The number of magistrates increased steadily, again allowing a larger number of citizens to take part in public life. Especially significant was the establishment shortly after 500 B.C. of a new elective official, called general (*strategos*), from each tribe to constitute a group of ten military leaders who quickly assumed a key role in directing public affairs. In contrast with the archons, who were eligible for only a one-year term, the generals could be elected year after year if they could command sufficient votes in their tribes. Property qualifications for officeholding tended to disappear. The bastion of aristocratic power, the Areopagus, was gradually stripped of its power. A crucial step in the development of democracy came when Pericles introduced public payment for service in the Council of Five Hundred, the *Heliaea*, the elected magistracies, and the army and navy. This step enabled ordinary citizens to serve the *polis* without sacrificing their livelihood. Gradually, the Council of Five Hundred, the *ecclesia*, and the *Heliaea*, all controlled by the citizens, took over direction of public affairs. Increasingly, they were encouraged to do so by leaders such as Pericles, an aristocrat by birth and wealth who felt no fear in entrusting the final political decisions of Athens to the citizens and who sought to convince them that public life was a dignified, responsible, and rewarding activity owed by all who enjoyed the benefit of living in Athens.

In discussing the nature of democracy in Athens or any other *polis*, we must make one important reservation. Participation in political life was confined to males descended from those enrolled as members of a *deme* in the time of Cleisthenes. Women did not qualify for participation in political life in the *polis*. Neither did large numbers of foreigners, called *metics*, or slaves. In the fifth century B.C. the citizen population of Athens was about forty-five thousand; the entire population of Attica was probably about three hundred fifty thousand. Thus, a minority ruled the democratic Athenian *polis*.

5. SPARTA

The history of another important city-state, Sparta, illustrates a different pattern of development of the *polis* in the Greek world.

Sparta emerged as a city-state during the ninth century B.C. as a result of the coalition of several small agricultural villages clustered around the site of the city. After this union the Spartans slowly established control over an area in the southern Peloponnesus known as Laconia, creating a base for future Spartan prominence. Until about 750 B.C. Sparta's development followed a pattern that differed little from most other city-states during the Archaic Age. But then a significant change began to occur that gave Spartan society a unique character. When the Spartans began to feel the economic stresses that gripped most of the Aegean world in the Archaic Age, their solution was to conquer their neighbors and force them to support Spartan society.

Especially crucial was the conquest of Messenia, a fertile agricultural region west of Sparta. The First Messenian War (ca. 720 B.C.) ended in the annexation of Messenia, whose inhabitants were made servile dependents of Sparta forced to labor as tillers of the soil to support their conquerors. In about 640 B.C. the Messenians revolted, with the encouragement of some of Sparta's enemies in the Peloponnesus. After a desperate struggle lasting twenty years, the revolt was suppressed. During the long struggle with Messenia, which tested the military resources of Sparta to the limit, Spartan society was radically restructured so as to ensure military strength sufficient to maintain control over the city-state's subjects. These reforms were attributed to a single lawgiver, Lycurgus, but probably were carried out by several leaders over several decades in the late seventh and sixth centuries B.C.

A fundamental feature of the new order was the division of the population into rigidly defined classes, each with specific responsibilities in the service of the state. Most important were the *Spartans*, a relatively small portion of the total population who were the real citizens. Numbering about ten thousand males considered to be social equals, the Spartans were required to devote their lives to military service in the interest of exerting control over other elements in the population and defending Sparta against outside enemies. The Lycurgan system prescribed a strict regimen for this group. At birth each male child of a Spartan citizen was inspected for physical fitness. If defective, the state ordered death by exposure. If allowed to live, the child remained with his mother until he was seven. Then he joined other males in barracks life, where all were subjected to rigorous military training until they were twenty. At twenty the Spartan became a regular soldier. He was assigned a piece of state land along with laborers to farm it as a source of his livelihood. He could marry after twenty, but he was not permitted to establish his own household until thirty, when he became an "equal" with full rights to participate in the political life of the *polis*. During these long formative years the social life of each Spartan found its focus in a mess group, a small circle of military companions who shared barracks life and contributed payments derived from their state-assigned land allocations to provide common meals. The values and the relationships formed in these mess groups dominated the life of each male Spartan. All Spartans were required to perform military service until they were sixty years of age. Spartan females were likewise rigorously trained to become wives and mothers. Their training emphasized physical fitness and the development of skills in the household arts. As wives, they often played an important role in managing the family economic resources, but there was no place for them in political life.

A second element of the population of Sparta was made of *perioeci*, often living in towns scattered across Spartan territory. This group represented descendants of peoples subjected by the Spartans when they asserted mastery over Laconia. Although they were required to render military service and pay taxes, they were not subjected to the training regimen required of full Spartans. They served the state chiefly as artisans and traders. They enjoyed some degree of control over local town affairs but were not permitted to take part in the governance of the entire *polis*.

Finally, there were the *helots*, state slaves required to spend their lives as agricultural laborers or household servants toiling to support the full

Spartans
Perioeci
Helots

Spartan citizens who had no occupation except soldiering. The helots were allowed to maintain family life and were permitted to keep enough of what they produced to maintain a simple level of life. However, they were treated brutally by the Spartans, apparently to ensure their service as the mainstay of the Spartan economy. The fear of helot revolt remained a constant factor in Spartan life, so much so that the Spartan state declared war on the helots every year, permitting the killing of a suspected helot troublemaker on the spot. Part of the military training of Spartan youths involved seeking out and murdering allegedly dangerous helots.

This rigid social order was held in place by a governmental system that Lycurgus was credited with shaping but that was derived in large part from earlier political institutions. The government was formally headed by two kings, but the actual power of the co-kings was slight unless they were able to distinguish themselves as military leaders. Real power rested with the *gerousia*, a council made up of the two kings and twenty-eight other men over sixty elected to serve for life. This body formulated all legislation, judged the most important cases, and acted as an advisory body in the administration of the state. Its decisions were subject to approval by an assembly made up of all male Spartans over thirty. Theoretically, the assembly could repudiate any proposed policy, but usually its members, trained from childhood to obey orders, were inclined to accept direction from superiors. The execution of laws was entrusted to a board of five *ephors*, elected annually by the assembly, which conducted foreign affairs, supervised military training, policed the helots, controlled state finances, and organized military operations. When supported by the *gerousia*, the *ephors* were able to exercise almost complete control over Spartan political life, despite the fact that the male citizens possessed the power to check them. In essence, Sparta was ruled by an oligarchy of military commanders.

The Spartan political and social system proved effective. Sparta enjoyed an internal stability that was envied by many other Greeks, and the dedication of Spartan citizens to the service of their *polis* was often praised. While the system was not conducive to intellectual and cultural activities, it made Sparta a dominant force in Greek intercity affairs. By 500 B.C. Sparta had forced most of the other city-states in the Peloponnesus to join the Peloponnesian League, whose members followed Spartan leadership in foreign affairs. The combined forces of Sparta and its allies allowed Sparta to play a major role in Greek history after 500 B.C.

6. THE CHARACTER OF THE *POLIS*

To gain a complete understanding of the nature of the Greek *polis*, one would have to study the institutions of several hundred other city-states that had been formed by 500 B.C., each of which believed its institutions to be as typically "Greek" as those of Athens and Sparta. Such a wide-ranging study would certainly highlight variety in the structure of Greek city-states, but it would also reveal certain shared characteristics of the *polis*.

Greek city-states were all small entities within which residents could interact intimately. In each *polis* life focused on an urban center, where were concentrated political, economic, religious, and cultural activities bearing directly on the lives of all. Each made citizenship a distinctive and precious condition of life. In some fashion or other, citizenship involved those who held it—almost exclusively males with the proper family pedigree—directly and actively in civic life. Such involvement was at once a great privilege and a grave responsibility. As Pericles allegedly put it, "We alone regard a man who takes no interest in public affairs, not as harmless, but as a useless character." The giving of one's talent in the service of the *polis* made the citizen a complete human, drawing of the *polis* made the citizen a complete human, drawing each out of clan, calling, and class into participation in a community enterprise. Active involvement nourished patriotism, a fierce pride in and love for the *polis*. Every *polis* was thus a pressure chamber compelling citizens to discover and exercise their talents in the interests of something larger, more enduring, and more splendid than themselves. As such, the *polis* nourished an intensity of life and a level of human achievement seldom witnessed in the human experience and it bred in each citizen a sense of superiority over non-citizens and foreigners that boded trouble for Greek society.

SUGGESTED READING

General Surveys of Greek History

John V. A. Fine, *The Ancient Greeks: A Critical History* (1983).

M. G. L. Hammond, *A History of Greece to 322 B.C.*, 3rd ed. (1986).

Both of these works will provide a full treatment of Greek history down to the time of the Macedonian conquest.

Early Greece to 500 B.C.

John Chadwick, *The Mycenaean World* (1976). An excellent treatment that reflects the best of recent scholarship.

R. J. Hopper, *The Early Greeks* (1976).

Oswyn Murray, *Early Greece* (1980).

Anthony Snodgrass, *Archaic Greece. The Age of Experiment* (1980).

M. I. Finley, *Early Greece: The Bronze and Archaic Ages*, new ed. (1981).

Any of the above four titles will provide an excellent treatment of a period in Greek history that has received significant new interpretations in recent times.

L. H. Jeffery, *Archaic Greece: The City States c. 700–500 B.C.* (1976). Valuable for the attention paid to city-states other than Athens and Sparta.

Chester G. Starr, *Individual and Community. The Rise of the Polis 800–500 B.C.* (1986). A masterful treatment of the forces that produced the *polis*.

A. H. M. Jones, *Athenian Democracy* (1958). This work will provide the reader with a good grasp of how Athenian democracy worked.

General Surveys of Greek History

W. G. Forrest, *History of Sparta, 950–192 B.C.*, 2nd ed. (1980).

J. T. Hooker, *The Ancient Spartans* (1980).

Two very perceptive treatments of Spartan history.

Economic and Social History

Chester G. Starr, *The Economic and Social Growth of Early Greece, 800–500 B.C.* (1977).

M. M. Austin and P. Vidal-Naquet, *Economic and Social History of Ancient Greece: An Interpretation* (1977).

Either of these two works will provide invaluable information on all aspects of Greek economy. The Austin–Vidal-Naquet work includes original documents illustrating economic development.

John Boardman, *The Greeks Overseas*, rev. ed. (1982). An excellent treatment of a crucial aspect of Greek development.

Sources

Homer, *Iliad and Odyssey* (many translations; among the best are those by Richard Lattimore). Two works that played an essential role in shaping the Greek civic mentality.

Hesiod, *Works and Days*, trans. Richard Lattimore (1959). A picture by a contemporary of the problems that caused stress in the Greek world about 700 B.C.

CHAPTER 5

War, Politics, and the Failure of the Greek City-State Polity

FIGURE 5.1 **Pericles** This statue portrays Pericles under whose leadership the city-state of Athens reached the peak of its power politically, economically and culturally. The key to Pericles' fame rests largely in the faith he had in the Athenian citizen body to decide its own destiny democratically. The artist captures the intelligence, dignity, and political sagacity for which Pericles was honored. (Museo Vaticano/Alinari)

D riven by the energies unleashed in its many city-states, the Greek world enjoyed a Golden Age during the fifth and early fourth centuries B.C. Although each individual *polis* continued to promote the internal well-being of its citizens, another issue grew ever more critical: the problem of relationships among the fiercely patriotic communities, each struggling to strengthen and enrich itself. At the beginning of the fifth century, a threat from the outside demonstrated the need for cooperation, but progressively the city-states surrendered to their parochialism and became embroiled in destructive intercity struggles. In the end they so weakened themselves that they fell easy victims to a powerful external foe.

1. THE PERSIAN WARS, 490–479 B.C.

Prior to 500 B.C. the Greek city-states often warred against one another, but these wars were generally on a limited scale. Nor did any major outsiders threaten the Greeks during the Archaic Age. In fact, there were significant developments promoting cooperation and interdependence among the Greeks. Their common language encouraged a shared culture. Expanding commerce linked the city-states together. Religion was an especially important force promoting pan-Hellenism. It provided a common set of deities, pan-Hellenic festivals—such as the Olympic Games, which drew Greeks together for worship, athletic competitions, and cultural performances honoring their gods and goddesses—and shared shrines, such as the Delphic oracle, where all Greeks came to seek divine guidance. Some progress had even been made in establishing political federations allowing city-states to collaborate without surrendering their autonomy; a prime example was the Peloponnesian League.

The practical need for strong pan-Hellenism was dramatically posed at the beginning of the fifth century by the threat of the Persian Empire. Persian expansion beginning about 550 B.C. had resulted in the conquest of the Lydian kingdom and the subjugation of the Greek city-states of Asia Minor. Although Persian rule was not particularly harsh, the Ionian city-states hated paying tribute and submitting to "tyrants" imposed on them by the Persians. The Persian threat to the entire Greek world increased when Darius invaded Europe in 512 B.C. and established a satrapy in Thrace. Tensions mounted after 499 B.C. as a consequence of a major revolt of the Ionian Greeks. The rebels appealed to their fellow Greeks on the mainland and received support from Athens and Eritrea. Darius eventually crushed the revolt. He apparently decided that Greece must be conquered, moved probably by fear of future Greek intervention in Persian affairs and by ambition to expand his already huge empire. Political scheming among factions within many Greek city-states who saw the Persians as potential allies in the struggles for power and the neutrality proclaimed by several key city-states encouraged Darius to think that the Greek world was ready for conquest.

In 490 B.C. Darius made his move (see Map 5.1 for the Persian campaigns). He sent a fleet and a substantial army across the Aegean, ostensibly to punish Athens and Eritrea for their involvement in the rebellion of the Ionians. After destroying Eritrea, the Persian army landed in eastern Attica, near Marathon. The Greek world had made almost no preparations for the Persian onslaught. Standing alone, the Athenians seemed doomed. But they chose to resist, sending an army to challenge the Persians. Although outnumbered, the Athenian *hoplites*, brilliantly led by Miltiades, defeated the Persians and forced the survivors back to their ships. Miltiades marched his victorious army back to Athens and stood ready to defend the city when the Persian fleet from Marathon appeared there. The Persians elected to return to Asia Minor. Athens celebrated a new breed of heroes whose feats at Marathon rivaled those of the heroes celebrated by Homer.

The Persians were not ready to admit defeat. Although a new attack was delayed ten years by internal troubles, Darius' successor, Xerxes I, was ready by 480 B.C. to mount another assault. In the interval the Greeks made better preparations. In 481 B.C. Sparta took the leadership in organizing a Hellenic League made up of thirty-one city-states willing to pool their military and naval forces under Spartan commanders. Greek armed strength, based on the superb Spartan army, was greatly enhanced by a crucial decision made by Athens. A farsighted leader named Themistocles persuaded the Athenian citizenry to use the income from silver mines recently discovered in Attica to fund a major increase in the Athenian navy, which the Athenians pledged to the support of the Hellenic League. Despite this show of unity, many city-states remained neutral.

Early in 480 B.C. Xerxes began his attack. He chose to trust the Persian cause to a carefully coordinated attack by a huge land army to be supplied by a huge navy. He moved his army across the Hellespont into Europe and advanced slowly around the northern Aegean coast and then southward toward the centers of Greek strength. The Hellenic League made its first stand at Thermopylae, where a narrow pass provided the Greek army a good place to check the huge Persian force and where the narrow sea lanes between the mainland and the island of Euboea could be easily blocked to prevent the Persian fleet from supplying the army. Despite their success in defeating the Persian fleet and the heroic resistance of a Spartan detachment led by King Leonidas, the Greeks were unable to hold at Thermopylae. Having broken through the Greek defenses at Thermopylae, the Persians flooded into central Greece. Athens was captured and burned, although most of its citizens fled to safety.

At this critical point, Themistocles exercised a decisive influence on the course of the war. There was strong pressure in the council of the Hellenic League to withdraw the armies to the Peloponnesus and the fleet to the Gulf of Corinth. Convinced that the fate of the Greeks would be decided at sea, Themistocles combined persuasion with threats of Athens' withdrawal to convince the League to face the Persians in the waters off Attica. In late September 480 B.C., he enticed the Persians into a decisive engagement in the narrow waters between Attica and the island of Salamis. Caught where they could not use their superior naval strength and outmaneuvered by the Greek fleet, the Persians suffered a shattering defeat. Since winter was approaching, Xerxes ordered his fleet back to its bases in Asia Minor and the withdrawal of his army to northern Greece.

In the spring of 479 B.C. Xerxes renewed the campaign by ordering his army southward. The Hellenic League put a major army in the field, anchored by Spartan troops. This force met the Persians at Plataea. Once again the Greek *hoplites* and their phalanx formation proved superior and imposed a major defeat on the larger Persian army. While these events were unfolding, the fleet of the Hellenic League sailed boldly across the Aegean and destroyed the main Persian fleet at Mycale, a victory that triggered a revolt among the Greek city-states of Asia Minor. Xerxes had no choice but to recall his armies from Europe. The jubilant Greeks had saved themselves from what many thought was sure defeat and loss of their independence.

While the Greeks of the Aegean world were throwing back the Persian threat, their fellow Greeks in the West were winning a victory hardly less significant. The struggle here centered on Sicily, where Carthage, a powerful maritime state, was attempting to expand its commercial empire by subduing the Sicilian Greeks. A coalition of Greek city-states, led by Gelon, tyrant of Syracuse, inflicted a decisive defeat on the Carthaginians at the battle of Himera in 480 B.C., ensuring the continued independence of the Greek city-states in Magna Graecia.

2. THE DELIAN LEAGUE AND THE ATHENIAN EMPIRE

Although the Greeks had won a stunning victory in 480–479 B.C., the Persian Empire remained a major power and a real threat. This danger kept alive the spirit of unity among the Greeks. The situation in 479 B.C. demanded that they take the offensive. Leadership for this undertaking passed into new hands. The Spartans, who had led the Hellenic League in the critical days of 480 and 479 B.C., were unwilling to commit their resources to projects remote from the Peloponnesus. Athens now took the lead in summoning a meeting of Greek cities on the island of Delos in 478 B.C. It was quickly agreed to form the Delian League to continue the war against Persia. Policy decisions were to be made by an assembly of League representatives meeting annually; each member city-state would have one vote. Each member pledged to contribute ships and money according to its

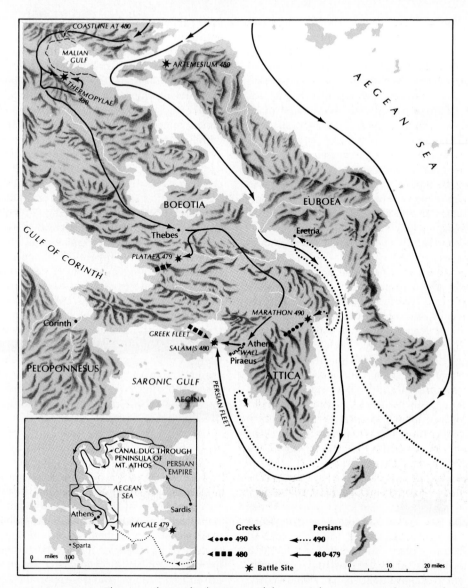

Map 5.1 **THE PERSIAN WARS** The map shows the locations of the crucial engagements between the Greeks and the Persians in the campaigns of 490 B.C. and 480–479 B.C. The inset, showing the long route taken by Xerxes in 480 B.C., may suggest the challenge faced by the Persians in their bid to conquer the Greeks, for they had to engage the Greeks in a constricted setting where the Greeks could make the best use of their resources.

abilities. Athens was charged with making the initial assessments and with commanding the League's forces. No city-state would be required to surrender sovereign control over its internal affairs, thus protecting the principle of autonomy.

The League quickly swung into action. An Athenian, Cimon, was placed in command of its joint forces, which enjoyed immediate success. Within fifteen years, all the Greek city-states in Asia Minor had been freed of Persian rule, while the Aegean and the Hellespont area were cleared of Persian naval power. Athens was obviously the most powerful member of the League, but its leaders conducted themselves with marked restraint in relationships with other members. Cimon's policy was conciliatory even toward nonmembers such as Sparta.

This situation was not destined to last, and Athens was largely responsible for the change. As the danger from Persia receded, some members of the Delian League sought to reduce their contributions and even to withdraw. Athens was unwilling to allow the dissolution of the League. Increasingly, Athenian leaders and citizens came to realize that the League's naval force could be turned to commercial ends that would enrich Athens. Beginning about 465 B.C. Athens began to initiate policies aimed at converting the voluntary Delian League into an empire dominated by Athens, a policy that posed a threat to a basic Greek institution: the autonomous *polis*.

The emergence of Athenian imperialism coincided with the final establishment of democracy in Athens. Pericles was the architect of both developments (see Figure 5.1). From his emergence as leader in Athens in 461 B.C. until his death in 429 B.C., Pericles placed the destiny of the city in the hands of his fellow citizens and constantly urged them to support policies that would ensure Athenian dominance in Greece. They responded by supporting with enthusiasm policies that enhanced Athens' dominance, partly because that course enriched the city-state and partly because imperialism fed the Athenians' pride in the greatness of their *polis*. Emboldened by such support, Pericles launched a two-pronged drive to expand Athenian influence. On the Greek mainland he used every device possible to draw more city-states into the Delian League. He supported re-

volts against nondemocratic governments, tried to entice the members of the Peloponnesian League to abandon Sparta, and used Athenian sea power to bottle up such trading powers as Corinth. Meanwhile, Pericles renewed the assault on Persia, carrying the struggle into the eastern Mediterranean. This effort utilized the money and the armed forces extracted from the Delian League with little regard for the wishes of its members.

This aggressive policy enjoyed considerable success, but eventually Pericles realized that Athens was overextending its power. In 454 B.C. an Athenian effort to liberate Egypt resulted in a major naval defeat, which encouraged revolt within the Delian League. The result was some kind of understanding with the Persians that each would respect the other's sphere of influence: Athens' control of the Aegean and the Greek city-states in Asia Minor and Persia's dominance of the eastern Mediterranean coastal area. Athenian aggressive actions on the Greek mainland raised repeated threats of Spartan retaliation so serious that Pericles finally agreed to the Thirty Years' Truce of 445 B.C. in which Athens agreed to halt its aggression against mainland Greek city-states, especially those belonging to the Peloponnesian League, and Sparta promised to recognize Athenian hegemony over the Delian League.

In the years following 445 B.C. the Athenians concentrated on tightening their control over the Delian League. Eventually about three hundred city-states ringing the Aegean were forced to accept Athenian domination. Athens continued to collect funds from these cities, although the Persian danger no longer existed. This "tribute" was used as Athens wished, chiefly to support the system of pay Pericles introduced for the vastly increased number of citizens who performed public service in Athens and to support the artists and writers who made Athens the "school of Hellas." Athens forced many League members to institute democratic governments resembling the Athenian system. The subject cities were compelled to accept the Athenian money system and Athenian weights and measures, thus ensuring that their economies would be subservient to that of Athens. Athenians were settled on lands confiscated from residents of subject city-states, a policy that relieved Athens of excess population and provided a convenient means of shaping internal affairs in dependent members of the Athenian Empire. By any standard Athens treated these formerly independent city-states as dependents and solely for the benefit of Athens.

The subject city-states benefited in some ways. They shared the fruits of increased commerce and the security resulting from enforced peace. Still, their hatred of Athens grew steadily, primarily for political reasons. Athens had usurped their most valuable possession, their right to exist as independent city-states. The mighty, enlightened democratic gem of Greek civilization had, in the eyes of most Greeks, become an oppressor. The proud, triumphant, even arrogant Athenians made no attempt to compensate for depriving their subjects of their independence. They were not permitted to become citizens of Athens, and they were denied any representation in the Athenian government. Some Athenians raised concerns about the destruction of the liberty of any *polis,* but the Athenian citizenry, aware that the economic welfare of Athens and its citizens depended on imperial power and proud of Athens' glory, overrode these voices. Their prideful, self-serving aggressiveness gradually generated an anti-Athenian feeling throughout much of the Greek world. People began to look toward Sparta as the champion of city-state independence. Such sentiments pointed toward a major clash pitting Greek against Greek and testing the viability of the one institution fundamental to Greek civilization: the *polis.*

3. THE PELOPONNESIAN WAR, 431–404 B.C.

Athens' aggressive efforts to expand its interests across the entire Greek world finally plunged the Greeks into the Peloponnesian War. Its outbreak in 431 B.C. resulted from Athenian actions that threatened the commercial interests of Corinth, an important ally of Sparta. Corinth convinced Sparta that Athens was violating the Thirty Years' Truce. The Spartans, increasingly concerned over the expansion of Athenian influence in mainland Greece, were ready to lead the Peloponnesian League and their other allies against the prideful city-state that threatened freedom in Greece. Ath-

ens was not unwilling to join the issue. Its large fleet and its huge financial resources derived from commerce and tribute appeared sufficient to offset the superior land forces of the Spartan alliance. Pericles was confident that Athens' enemies were incapable of effective action against the real source of Athenian power—the maritime empire (see Map 5.2 for the alignment of forces in 431 B.C.).

The first years of the war were indecisive. Athens refused to commit itself to a land war; Pericles persuaded the Athenians to withdraw within the city's impregnable walls while the fleet roamed the seas to hold together the empire and bring supplies and wealth to Athens. This strategy left the Spartan armies free to ravage the Attic countryside but unable to strike a telling blow either against Athens or its key imperial strongholds. Within a few years this pattern broke down. The Athenian population grew impatient, watching their beloved land ravaged, especially after a plague struck in 430 and 429 B.C., killing at least one-third of the cooped-up population, including Pericles. The restless populace demanded bolder military action. A militant democratic and imperialistic leader, Cleon, responded by leading Athenian armies outside Attica, especially into central Greece and western Peloponnesus, in an effort to wean away crucial Spartan allies. A resourceful Spartan leader, Brasidas, persuaded Sparta to use its military forces to encourage revolt among the subject cities of the Athenian Empire. Brasidas' activities concentrated on the northern Aegean, especially Chalcidice, posing a threat to Athens' route to vital food supplies around the Black Sea. However, before this new phase of the struggle reached a decisive point, both Cleon and Brasidas were killed in 422 B.C. in a battle for control of the key city of Amphipolis. Their deaths gave powerful peace elements in both camps a chance to end the war. In 421 B.C., Athens and Sparta agreed to a Fifty-Year Truce, which restored the situation to what it had been when the struggle began.

The uneasy peace settlement, which had addressed none of the basic issues, lasted only until 415 B.C. Again the Athenians were responsible for the renewal of hostilities. After the death of Pericles, Athenian political life became increasingly unstable. Afflicted by the burdens of war, the citizens were increasingly swayed by ambitious pol-

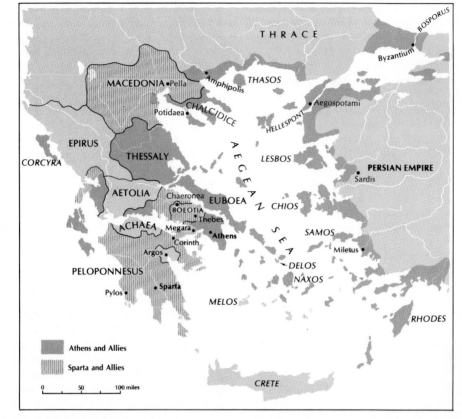

Loss of Power
404 Athens
371 Sparta

Map 5.2 **GREECE, 431 B.C.** This map identifies the members of the two camps engaged in the Peloponnesian War. Particularly noteworthy is the extent to which Athenian strength was concentrated in a circle of city-states under Athens' control ranging around the Aegean Sea, with Sparta's strength located around the outside of that circle.

iticians willing to promise anything in return for power. Such a figure was the flashy, unscrupulous Alcibiades. Playing upon the imperialistic sentiments so strong in Athens, he persuaded the citizenry to undertake a major expedition against the powerful city of Syracuse in Sicily, an important commercial rival of Athens. This ill-conceived venture, badly led by rival politicians, including Alcibiades who deserted to Sparta to avoid serious criminal charges, ended in a disastrous defeat for Athens in 413 B.C. Worse, the attack on Syracuse provoked Sparta and its allies to renew all-out war against Athens.

After 413 B.C. the fortunes of Athens declined steadily. Internal dissension, pitting prodemo-

cratic forces against a growing faction fearful of the consequences of unbridled democracy, hindered decisive action. The Spartans, brilliantly led by Lysander, mounted a powerful attack on Athenian sea power and a skillful campaign to encourage revolt among the city-states of the Athenian Empire. A decisive step in this campaign was the Spartan success in forming an alliance with Persia, whose wealth and naval power played a crucial role in undermining the Athenian Empire. Athens occasionally won an isolated victory, but the net continued to close around the doomed city-state. Finally in 404 B.C. Athens had to surrender. The victors forced Athens to tear down its walls, to destroy all but twelve ships of its once invincible fleet, and to submit to a government of oligarchs backed by a Spartan army stationed in Athens. Although these Thirty Tyrants, as the Athenians called them, were ousted in 403 B.C. and democratic government was restored, Athens would never recover its former power. And Athens was not the only victim of the Peloponnesian War. Its ravages impoverished many Greek city-states, created bitter rivalries among them, bred internal dissension within each *polis,* caused widespread disillusionment and pessimism, and renewed the threat of Persian domination. Thucydides, the historian of the Peloponnesian War, may have been right when he wrote, "No movement ever stirred Hellas more deeply than this [war]."

4. THE TWILIGHT OF THE WORLD OF CITY-STATES, 404–336 B.C.

The years following the Peloponnesian War marked a troubled time in the Greek world. Two interlocking issues dominated this period: the effort of a succession of leading city-states to establish hegemony over the Greeks and the struggle to sustain internal order and vitality within each *polis.* These issues combined to produce almost constant intercity warfare and bitter civil strife, which gradually sapped Greek strength.

In 404 B.C. Sparta appeared to be the predominant power in the Greek world. For the next thirty years it devoted its energies to asserting its hegemony. The key to Spartan policy was the imposition of oligarchic governments on any city-state that could be bullied into submission, including some of Sparta's old allies. This policy badly undermined Sparta's claim to be the defender of city-state independence. In fact, Sparta did not have the strength to control the Greek world. Its narrowly restricted citizen body was declining in numbers, and its rigid social system prevented Sparta from replenishing its citizens from the ranks of the *perioeci* and helots, who remained a constant threat to internal peace. In the final analysis, Sparta was reluctantly forced to depend on Persian assistance to maintain its hegemony at the cost of allowing the Persians to reestablish dominance over the Ionian Greeks. Growing fear and resentment against Sparta led

to the formation of an alliance led by Thebes. Under the brilliant generalship of Thebes' one great statesman, Epaminandos, this alliance smashed Sparta in a single battle in 371 B.C., a defeat that marked the end of Sparta's long history as a major Greek power.

After 371 B.C. Greek history was marked by a succession of claimants to hegemony. Thebes played an important role for a decade, but even with Persian help it was unable to dominate; its power was smashed in a decisive battle in 362 B.C. by an alliance formed by Athens. In the generation after Thebes' defeat Athens sought to reestablish a dominant position, but its efforts were constantly thwarted by rival city-states. All that resulted was a succession of petty wars that wasted human and material resources and asserted a constant strain on internal life in each *polis.* These internal struggles, usually centered on rivalry between democratic and aristocratic factions for control of political life and on issues involving the distribution of declining wealth in each city-state, were often marked by violence. Increasingly, mercenary forces led by ruthless and adventuresome commanders replaced citizen armies and navies; these professionals much preferred war to peace. Some Greeks were aware of the destructive cost of intercity war. They raised eloquent appeals for some kind of union that would curb it in order to create an environment that would allow city-states to restore internal stability. However, political pan-Hellenism was a lost cause. No Greek *polis* was willing to surrender any of its sovereignty to a superior organization—even in the interests of peace. And great philosophers such as Plato and Aristotle, both of whom lived during the fourth century, vigorously insisted that only the traditional self-defining *polis* was fit for the Greeks.

5. MACEDONIAN CONQUEST OF GREECE

Weakened by the incessant warfare and civic strife, the Greeks became increasingly ripe for conquest. The conqueror turned out to be Macedonia. The Macedonians had played only a minor role in Greek history before the fourth century B.C. Its diverse and unruly population long resisted efforts of Macedonian rulers to unify the kingdom. Although Greek influences had penetrated the area, the people remained backward. However, the situation changed rapidly under the rule of Philip II (359–336 B.C.). A gifted, ambitious ruler, Philip II was able to create a disciplined army and to impose an effective internal organization on his kingdom. Assured of a strong power base, Philip II turned his attention toward the Greek world, driven by an urge to gain access to the Aegean Sea and to bring his backward kingdom into closer contact with the Greek civilization he greatly admired.

The intrusion of Macedonian influence into Greece involved a complex play of political forces. Warring Greek city-states could not resist seeking Philip's support. Philip often intrigued in Greek affairs to create opportunities for his involvement. His skilled diplomacy and his adroit use of military force gave him an increasingly decisive role in Greece. Although many warned of the Macedonian "menace," the Greeks were seldom able to join forces to resist. In fact, some Greeks favored Macedonian dominance as a solution for incessant warfare. Eventually Athens, moved both by fear of Macedonian power and by dreams of using the Macedonian threat as a means of re-creating an Athenian Empire, became the focal point of resistance. Under the leadership of the eloquent Demosthenes, always ready with a speech warning his fellow Athenian citizens of the Macedonian danger and damning those in Athens and elsewhere who advocated peace with Macedonia, Athens was able to form a loosely constituted league dedicated to resistance to Macedonian advances into Greece. Although this alliance occasionally offered assistance to those resisting Macedonian influence, such help was usually too little. Philip finally forced the Athenian alliance to commit itself to battle at Chaeronea in 338 B.C., which ended in a crushing defeat that left all of Greece at Philip's mercy.

Philip treated the vanquished Greeks with mildness, but he did act to end the old order. Soon after his victory he called a meeting of all Greek city-states at which they agreed to form the League of Corinth dedicated to the establishment of a common peace. Members of the League were theoretically entitled to independence, but crucial restrictions were imposed on them. No city-state was to make war on another, to interfere with freedom of the seas, or to change its form of government. Such prohibitions obviously greatly restricted the ancient freedom of the *polis*. The League was to be governed by a council of representatives from each city-state, which would meet regularly and decide League actions to keep peace. Each member was obliged to contribute according to its means to a common military force charged with imposing peace. Macedonia was not a member of the League, but Philip did require that the League sign a treaty of alliance with Macedonia. Philip was also designated as *hegemon* (military commander) of the League, thus putting himself in a position to control its activities. At a meeting of the League council in 337 B.C. Philip proposed that its first undertaking should be joining its forces with Macedonia in a war against Persia, but his assassination in 336 B.C. denied him an opportunity to direct this campaign against an ancient foe of the Greeks. Nevertheless, Philip's statesmanship had achieved a notable end: In the League of Corinth he had provided an instrument under Greek control that would allow the warring city-states to impose peace on themselves without sacrificing completely their sovereignty while enjoying the protection of the potent Macedonian army against outsiders.

SUGGESTED READING

Fifth- and Fourth-Century Greece

Simon Hornblower, *The Greek World, 479–323 B.C.* (1983).

J. K. Davies, *Democracy and Classical Greece* (1978).

Either of these two studies will provide a full treatment of Greek history during the fifth and fourth centuries B.C.

A. R. Burn, *Persia and the Greeks: The Defense of the West, c. 546–478 B.C.*, 2nd ed. (1984). A good account of the clash between the Greeks and the Persians.

P. J. Rhodes, *The Athenian Empire* (1985).

Malcolm F. McGregor, *The Athenians and Their Empire* (1987).

Either of these works will help the reader understand Athenian imperialism.

Andrew Lintott, *Violence, Civil Strife, and Revolution in the Classical City, 750–330 B.C.* (1982).

G. E. M. de Ste. Croix, *The Class Struggle in the Ancient Greek World from the Archaic Age to the Arab Conquest* (1981).

Two provocative treatments of a facet of Greek life that was destructive of the *polis*.

R. J. Hopper, *Trade and Industry in Classical Greece* (1979). A work that will throw light on economic conditions in the period under consideration.

J. R. Ellis, *Philip II and Macedonian Imperialism* (1976).

George Cawkwell, *Philip of Macedon* (1978).

Two excellent studies explaining the Macedonian victory over the Greeks.

Sources

Herodotus, *The Histories*, trans. Aubrey de Selincourt (1955).

Thucydides, *The Peloponnesian War*, trans. Rex Warner (1954).

Most of what we know about the fifth century comes from these two great historians; they are essential reading.

CHAPTER 6
Greek Life and Culture

FIGURE 6.1 A Greek Goddess This portrayal of the goddess Athena in mourning suggests the capability of the Greek sculptors to render the human form in an idealized fashion while still injecting feeling into an artistic composition. As the divine protector and patron of the city of Athens, Athena was constantly celebrated in art and literature by the city's artists and writers. She and other deities provided a constant source of inspiration for all forms of cultural creativity. (Acropolis Museum, Athens)

So far our discussion has emphasized the political and economic aspects of the Greek *polis*. However, that institution also had social and cultural dimensions. It provided a milieu where people lived their daily lives. Interactions within its environment stimulated a remarkable achievement in thought and expression. We must now try to summarize that accomplishment, admitting that it would take more than a lifetime of study to fathom the full dimensions of the Greek contribution to thought and expression.

1. DAILY LIFE IN GREECE

The splendid cultural achievements of the Greeks were rooted in the lives of ordinary men and women. Their efforts created the material basis for Greek society; they provided the audiences for creative efforts; and from their ranks came those who produced the literary, artistic, philosophical, and scientific works that constitute the essence of the Greek cultural "miracle."

Most Greeks devoted a significant part of every day to some kind of work related to Greece's diversified economy. In most city-states the bulk of the people earned their living in agriculture. Most farms were small, producing barely enough to sustain a household. There were larger farms managed by aristocratic owners and tilled by tenants and slaves. In the urban center, which was the focal point of each *polis*, large numbers of people worked as traders, artisans, and hired laborers. The scale of operations of retail shops and artisan establishments was small, usually operated by a family household with the help of a slave or two. Only a few enterprises, such as mining and arms making, were large-scale, often utilizing slaves as laborers. As illustrated by the examples of Athens and Sparta, in every city-state a considerable portion of the citizen body lived as employees of the government or as recipients of state-allocated land.

Although most Greeks worked to earn a livelihood, they were not willing to devote all their energies to work; leisure was important. Free time was possible in part because slavery played an important role in the Greek economy. Equally important was the willingness of the Greeks to live simple lives, made easier by Greece's good climate. Their diet was plain: Bread, olive oil, vegetables and fruit, cheese, fish, and wine were the staple items. Houses were modest in size and sparsely furnished. Most men and women dressed in rough-spun tunics and sandals, although the more affluent favored linen garments and at least some jewelry. However, simplicity of tastes and needs was confined chiefly to private life. The Greeks spent heavily to adorn their city-states with costly temples and public buildings, sculpture, and paintings and to support festivals, games, and dramas at whatever price. They took more joy in expending their wealth on their *polis* than on their private comforts.

The basic unit of Greek society was the family. Kinship bonds always played a prime role in determining citizenship, in defining social status, in controlling property, and in determining associations. The nuclear family—husband, wife, children—living in a single household, perhaps served by a slave or two, stood at the base of the kinship group. But these units always maintained significant ties with a considerable circle of relatives. Marriage contracts were arranged by families, often when the prospective partners were very young. The bride's father provided a dowry, which was returned to the bride if the marriage ended. Actual cohabitation of the contracted couple, an occasion for much celebration, usually began when the girl was fifteen or sixteen; the husband was usually older. Children were important in marriage, but there was constant concern with problems resulting from too many mouths to feed; this concern seems to have resulted in modest-sized families. The Greeks practiced various methods of birth control, and they were not averse to exposing unwanted children to death or to giving them up for adoption. Husbands could divorce their wives easily, but it was much more difficult for a woman to end a marriage.

Greek women had a limited place in society. Despite the facts that powerful and active women were enshrined in Greek legends and celebrated in poetry and drama and that powerful goddesses figured significantly in Greek religion, the lives of most women were severely restricted. Greek literature and philosophical writing, most of it produced by men, is filled with portrayals of women as inferior in intelligence and self-control. That view found expression in legal terms. Although wives and daughters of male citizens were recognized and protected under the law, they were always subject to a male. Women could not own property (except in Sparta) or engage in legal transactions and were excluded from political life. The prime role of respectable women was to direct the household, care for young children, and train their daughters for the same role. Women rarely participated in any aspect of public life, except for religious festivals, and they were usually excluded from the social activities of their husbands. Women of poor households did help their husbands run their farms and shops, thus involving themselves at least to some degree in the affairs of the larger society. But most women were literally out of sight, exerting whatever influence they had within the walls of their home. Some evidence suggests that within the household wives enjoyed the respect and the genuine love of their husbands. A few rare women of beauty, intelligence, and social grace became the sexual companions of important citizens and shared with them their social lives. Prostitution was common in the Greek world.

While the household was the center of life for most Greek women, men appear to have spent as little time there as possible. Shortly after the break of day they were out of the house to occupy themselves with their jobs or with the bustling life of the *polis*. Almost from birth males found their lives enmeshed in a variety of social groups whose activities consumed much of their energy. When they were seven or eight, they went forth daily from their homes to begin their education in reading, writing, and physical education under the guidance of private masters. By the fifth century B.C. in a city such as Athens, that education might continue for years, focusing on skills suitable to political activity, especially rhetoric. The sisters of these young men remained at home to be educated in household arts by their mothers or household slaves. At an early age males were enrolled in a *phratry*, a kinship group that sponsored a variety of religious and social activities. As young men grew older, they gravitated to the *gymnasia*, male gathering places devoted to physical education, athletic competition, and endless talk. It was not unusual for a youth to attract the attention of an adult male who served as a role model in introducing young men to the full range of activities of the *polis*. These relationships, forged in a setting that provided little female influence and that often involved homosexuality, played an important role in shaping male values. No less intriguing to the maturing youth were the marketplace, the theater, and the bordello. Often his adult mentor began to involve him in the endless round of private gatherings, called *symposia*, where males met in private houses to eat, drink, and talk—free even from wives and mothers, who withdrew to special female quarters featured in the typical house. By the time his teenage days were ending, a male entered into the responsibilities of citizenship: military service, participation in the popular assembly, office-holding. For the rest of his life these political activities would command an important part of his time and energies. Perhaps shortly after becoming a full-fledged citizen, the typical Greek male married, but already his life was so involved in the affairs of the *polis* and in the social associations to which he was attached that marriage was incidental to his life. Indeed, involvement in the *polis* was more than a political matter; it defined a broad range of activities that engaged its male members completely. And the Greeks were scornful of any man who did not involve himself in that life.

Even a brief look at the essentials of Greek daily life suggests that Greek citizens enjoyed considerable freedom to do what they wished and that many chose to use that freedom to involve themselves intensely in the varied activities of the *polis*. This environment posed challenges that unleashed powerful creative forces. Thus, daily life in the Greek world and the most sophisticated achievements of Greek culture can never be separated.

2. RELIGION

Religion provided a major link between Greek daily life and cultural achievements. Religious concerns permeated every aspect of daily life, and religious beliefs undergirded all forms of cultural expression. The origins of Greek religion are buried in the earliest stages of Greek history. By the time the first systematic statements describing religious beliefs were made—in the writings of Homer and Hesiod early in the Archaic Age—an elaborate mythology and a complex set of rituals already existed.

Greek religion was polytheistic. Among the vast array of divine forces were certain remote and abstract forces—such as fate, death, justice, love—that provided the basic order governing the universe. But most Greek deities were conceived as having human forms and as conducting themselves much as did earthly humans, except that the gods and goddesses were immortal and more powerful than humans. The most conspicuous and attractive deities were the tumultuous family of major gods and goddesses living on Mount Olympus under the authority of Zeus, whose position resembled that of an earthly father of a noble household. To each of these Olympian deities was ascribed a special role: Zeus was the father of the divine family, controller of the forces of nature; Hera, his wife, was protectress of marriage and the family; Athena was goddess of wisdom; Apollo was the bringer of light and patron of arts; Ares was god of war; Aphrodite was goddess of beauty and love; and so on. One or another of these deities was often protector of a city-state, so that the worship of the Olympian pantheon provided the basis for civic religion. Aside from the Olympian deities, the Greeks believed that the universe was filled with lesser spirits—nymphs, satyrs, demons, spirits of departed heroes and ancestors—who meddled constantly for good and bad in human affairs. A rich body of mythology developed to recount the activities of the deities and to describe their relationships with the human community. Learning that mythology was a fundamental aspect of the life of every Greek.

Most Greeks believed that the deities controlled human affairs and therefore that individuals, families, and city-states had to attune their activities to divine will. There were fear-inspiring aspects of Greek religion, but, on the whole, the Greeks viewed their deities as basically benevolent, approachable, and concerned with human well-being. Although the gods and goddesses could be angry and unpredictable, they were too full of life, too "human," to inflict a burden of terror on human beings. If humans learned the ways of the deities, bent to their will, and refrained from a prideful usurpation of their powers, they could expect divine support in gaining good fortune, long life, honor on earth, and success for their *polis*.

The Greeks devoted considerable energy and talent to pleasing their deities. In general, the gods and goddesses were not much concerned with moral behavior; they expected men and women to approach them in tangible ways. Prayers, sacrifices, and gifts were offered according to carefully defined rituals in shrines maintained in each home and by each clan. More impressive were the splendid civic cults, for which great temples were built and maintained at considerable expense to the city-states. Large numbers of people from all walks of life participated in these civic religious activities (see Figure 4.2). On occasion, the entire Greek world joined in honoring the Olympian pantheon; the Olympic Games, held every four years from 776 B.C. on, represented a pan-Hellenic celebration honoring Zeus. Almost every kind of human activity was acceptable as a way of praising the deities—athletic contests, poetry reading, song, dance, dramatic presentations, and gift offering. As a consequence, religious ceremonies were also cultural and social events. There were no elaborate priesthoods in Greece; fathers conducted rituals in households and clan centers, and public officials served as priests for civic ceremonies. The Greeks spent considerable energy seeking advance information about divine intentions: They interpreted dreams, studied the stars, and read the entrails of animals in search of clues. But most of all, they relied on *oracles*, who were especially gifted people through whom the deities spoke. The most famous oracle was at Delphi, where innumerable Greeks went to implore Apollo to send them messages through special priestesses, who would tell them how to solve problems ranging from personal matters to great political issues.

Complementing the mainstream of Greek religious life embodied in the cult of the Olympian deities was another current, represented by the *mystery* religions, which placed greater emphasis on personal and emotional needs. The Greek mystery religions were rooted in the ancient worship of the regenerative forces of nature and were deeply influenced by ideas and practices from the Near East. The mystery cults centered on a belief in a god or goddess who died and then came back to life as a savior for believers properly initiated. Usually these religions emphasized the power of the resurrected deity to give a happy afterlife. The youthful wine-god Dionysus was the center of such a cult. His worship, based on a belief that he had been torn to pieces by evil gods and then reborn (see page 17 for a comparable concept in Egyptian religion), involved his devotees in a highly emotional initiation ceremony and in ecstatic rites involving wild dancing, drinking, and the eating of raw flesh. Another mystery cult, with its center at Eleusis near Athens, developed around the worship of the fertility goddess Demeter and her daughter Persephone, raised from the dead by her mother's efforts. Over time, the mystery cults became more subdued and respectable, as illustrated by the poorly understood movement called Orphism, which modified Dionysus worship by emphasizing the need for an austere, ethical conduct as a way of pleasing Dionysus and winning escape from the material world into a happy hereafter.

Aside from satisfying deep needs among most Greeks, religion provided a framework for intellectual and artistic growth. It encouraged people to try to understand, explain, and please the deities through literature, art, and philosophy. From it artists and thinkers drew inspiration and a basic store of themes out of which they shaped a variety of masterpieces that still awe and intrigue thoughtful people.

3. LITERATURE

Greek literature represents a magnificent outburst of creativity emerging from a substratum of religious themes. It was born in glory with two epic poems attributed to Homer, the *Iliad* and the *Odyssey*, probably set down in the eighth century B.C. Behind them lay a long tradition of oral poetry sung by bards for aristocratic audiences that loved to hear of the deeds of Mycenaean heroes. Homer, who remains a shadowy figure, drew these oral threads together into unified compositions of great artistry and dramatic power. The *Iliad* recounts the

feats of a circle of heroes during a brief period in the war which the Mycenaean Greeks waged against Troy to avenge the theft of a Greek woman, Helen, by Paris, the prince of Troy. Although filled with an array of striking characters, its central figure is Achilles, whose inflated pride and misdirected anger threaten to destroy the Greeks before he is brought to his senses and takes his place as a great warrior able to turn the tide of battle. The *Odyssey* is an adventure story celebrating the clever talents of one of the heroes at Troy, Odysseus, who needs ten years to overcome a variety of obstacles preventing his return from Troy to his homeland and his patient, long-suffering wife, Penelope. Not a little of the appeal of these epics lies in their gripping plots; but they have other dimensions. They create a heroic picture of men and women—but particularly men—endowed with courage, nobility, and a deep love for life. Homer's heroes served as models for noble character and action for all Greeks and for many people in later ages.

For all its richness, the epic tradition could not contain the Greek literary genius. In about 700 B.C. the poet Hesiod wrote his *Works and Days*, a bitter lament about injustice in the world, and his *Theogony*, a summary of Greek mythology. These works pointed to an outburst of lyric poetry in which new forms were developed to express personal reactions to life. Among the best lyricists were Archilochus of Paros, Alcaeus of Mytilene, and above all the poetess Sappho of Lesbos. A woman of aristocratic origins, Sappho composed lyrics celebrating the beauties of nature and describing her erotic feelings toward young women (later ages coined a word for female homosexuality—lesbianism—from the name of Sappho's native island). The nobility and force of Greek lyric poetry were perhaps best exemplified by Pindar of Thebes (ca. 518–441 B.C.), most of whose works took the form of choral songs in honor of victorious athletes at religious festivals. His poems set forth the classic view of aristocratic (in the Greek sense of "the best") qualities.

The burgeoning poetic talent reflected in epic and lyric poetry reached full fruition in the fifth century, with the development of tragic drama, perhaps the greatest literary achievement of the Greeks. Tragedy originated in the dramatic choruses and hymns developed in connection with the worship of the god Dionysus. By the late sixth century B.C., the dramatic element in these rituals was greatly expanded to allow poets to retell the deeds of the deities and heroes enshrined in Greek mythology and to comment on the meaning of these deeds through choral interludes.

This developing dramatic art suddenly burst forth in full maturity during the fifth century in the work of three of the world's greatest tragedians, all living in Athens amidst the flowering of democracy. The first was Aeschylus (525–456 B.C.). He wrote about ninety plays, only seven of which survive. His tragedies spell out with great power the consequences that follow human transgressions of the dictates of the divine powers. His most impressive surviving work is a cycle of three plays called the *Oresteia*, which traces the tragic fate of the family of Agamemnon resulting from its crime of spilling the blood of its own kin. Aeschylus had a genius for making his suffering characters noble and admirable, capable of bearing their burden of punishment with dignity and even with understanding.

Sophocles (495–405 B.C.), a citizen active in Athenian political life, produced a large number of plays, all but seven now lost. His dramas remained closely bound to the traditional themes provided by religion, but his interest is more human, more intent on searching out the psychological effects of suffering on humans who ran afoul of the gods and goddesses. He portrayed suffering as an uplifting and purifying experience. Many would argue that Sophocles' *King Oedipus* is the greatest tragedy ever written. Essentially it is a drama that reveals the measure of the human spirit by showing the response of a heroic individual. Oedipus' fateful act was unknowingly killing his father and marrying his own mother, vile deeds that violated nature's order and for which he had to atone. In presenting Oedipus' discovery of his crime and his acceptance of his fate, Sophocles evokes a powerful celebration of the greatness of human beings.

Euripides (480–406 B.C.) was a dramatist profoundly touched by the growing disillusionment, skepticism, and pessimism of the later fifth century—the generation of the Peloponnesian War. He utilized tragedy as a vehicle for posing profound questions about human values and problems in a way that arouses the suspicion that human powers are limited. His plays, especially *Medea*, represent a search for some understanding of the full nature of human beings, especially their dark and frightening emotional qualities. Again and again he casts doubt on conventional moral values and accepted religious beliefs. But from his incessant probing emerges a picture of humanity that is fuller and subtler—if not nobler—than the portraits by Aeschylus and Sophocles.

Rivaling tragedy in public appeal was comic drama. Like tragedy, it developed out of religious ceremony, especially the ribald songs associated with the worship of Dionysus. By the fifth century, comedy became independent of religious ceremony and was performed as a distinct art intended to inform and entertain audiences by comic treatment of current politics and social affairs. The master of this form was Aristophanes (ca. 445–385 B.C.), a conservative Athenian whose comedies held up for scorn politicians, democratic institutions, artists, and Athenian social mores. Typical is his play *Lysistrata*, based on the efforts of Athenian women to deny their husbands any pleasures with them until the men gave up warfare.

Prose literature long lingered in the shadow of poetry, but during the fifth century B.C. two historians produced works that demonstrated the Greek genius in that mode of expression. The first was Herodotus (ca. 484–425 B.C.), who wrote a history of the wars between the Greeks and Persians. His work is based on information he gathered through his travels and his search of written records. The result is a dramatic, colorful account of the events relating to the struggle between Greeks and Persians that Herodotus believed decided the fate of the Greek world. The second major Greek historian was Thucydides (ca. 460–400 B.C.), whose masterpiece was a *History of the Peloponnesian War*. With great energy he searched out the details of the military campaigns and the political maneuvers associated with the war in which he was personally involved. Out of this evidence he compiled a brilliant account that not only described the course of the war but also revealed the folly, nobility, chicanery, and bravery of which human beings under stress are capable. His presentation leads one to the conclusion that the Athenians lost because of their own choices; humans emerge as responsible for their own destinies. Not only did Herodotus and Thucydides produce great literary works, but they also pioneered a method of reconstructing the past based on the objective search for and verification of evidence. To this day their histories represent the ideal toward which all historians strive: to find the truth about the past and to let it enrich understanding of the present.

4. ART

The Greek genius in art emerged after a long evolution. The art of the Mycenaean Age, strongly influenced by Minoan models, disappeared during the Dark Age. But near the end of that period appeared the first signs of a uniquely Greek art, best illustrated in finely executed pottery decorated first with geometric patterns and then, by the eighth century B.C., with human forms. During the Archaic Age pottery painters, constantly influenced by motifs and techniques from the Near East, established basic themes and conventions for representing humans and animals in action. Sculptors slowly perfected a unique style of portraying the nude male and the draped female. Drawing heavily on mythology for subject matter, these artists increasingly relied on what they saw in their own world to shape their treatment of mythological figures and themes: naked male athletes, reserved and maternal females, real animals. Out of these observations emerged standards defining proportion, balance, and movement. Also during the Archaic Age, architects developed a basic style for temples and other public buildings: a rectangular ground plan whose elevation featured columns surrounding an inner temple chamber and low-pitched roofs. Increasingly these structures were built with the fine stone available in the Greek world. Although emerging architectural forms and techniques were influenced by Near Eastern models, the Greek concern with proportion and balance provided buildings with unique characteristics. Painters, sculptors, and architects received increasing support from the city-state, whose leaders and citizens were interested in beautifying their *polis* and in elaborating civic religions.

By the beginning of the fifth century, the long apprenticeship was over; a burst of creativity produced a golden age in art. Athens became the focal point of artistic excellence. Unquestionably, the city's crowning glory was the complex of buildings constructed on the Acropolis, the hill dominating the *polis*. Under the sponsorship of Pericles and with funds derived from tribute paid by the subject city-states of the Athenian Empire, three major temples were built there during the fifth century: the Parthenon, the Erectheum, and the temple to Victorius Athena. A splendid stairway and gate, called the Propylaea, gave access to the Acropolis, now the center of Athenian civic religion (see Figure 4.1). The Parthenon, portions of which still stand, embodied the basic features of classical Greek architecture. Built in honor of Athena, it is modest in size (228 by 101 feet). Its two inner chambers, serving as shrines, are surrounded by simple, unadorned columns (in a style called Doric), seventeen on each side and eight on each end, which support the roof and create covered colonnades and entry vestibules. Its majesty stems chiefly from its simplicity, its proportions, its unity, and its balance. The total effect derives not only from the logic of its conception but also from subtle technical devices. For example, the middle of every long horizontal line is slightly higher than the ends to avoid the impression of sagging (see Figure 6.2).

The other Acropolis temples and the Propylaea incorporate the same features as the Parthenon, all adjusted to the size of each structure. The only basic departure was the utilization of slightly more slender and ornate columns (in the Ionic style), which add grace and lightness. Similar temples were built in many other cities throughout Greece. The same basic principles were applied to increasing numbers of public buildings—theaters, gymnasiums, market places, meeting halls—constructed in Athens and other city-states.

The Greek style of architecture, especially temples, provided spaces for decoration by sculptors and painters: the walls and interior space of inner chambers, the entablature built above the columns to provide a rest for the roof, the triangular pediments formed at either end of the structure, and the open spaces before the structure. The best Greek sculptors, represented by Phidias (ca. 500–

FIGURE 6.2 The Parthenon This magnificent example of Greek architecture was the chief structure among a complex of temples adorning the Athenian Acropolis (see Figure 4.1). Begun in the Golden Age of Pericles and dedicated to Athena, its distinctive horizontal lines, its stately Doric columns, and its measured proportions typify the classical Greek architectural style. The pediments above the columns and the triangular space created by the roof were filled with sculpture celebrating Greek deities and portraying themes from Greek mythology. (Marburg)

432 B.C.), Polyclitus (ca. 452–412 B.C.), and Praxiteles (ca. 400–320 B.C.), dedicated their talents chiefly to temple decoration. Phidias designed and executed some of the sculpture adorning the Parthenon. His statues in the round, especially the famed statue of Athena in the inner chamber of the Parthenon, have been lost. Around the walls of that same chamber was a continuous frieze of carved reliefs depicting a procession in honor of Athena; it portrays a teeming scene filled with ordinary people and animals shown in various aspects of everyday life. The external entablature and pediments were covered with powerful representations of divine activities drawn from mythology. Polyclitus devoted his talents chiefly to shaping bronze statues of young men (see Color Plate 3—left). Praxiteles created splendid versions of gods and goddesses in human form (see Figure

6.3 and Color Plate 3—right). All of this sculpture focuses on the portrayal of the idealized human body; the figures are dignified, restrained, beautifully proportioned, filled with the potential for action. The effect of viewing them is to catch a vision of the nobility and the power of human beings extracted from the real world in which human beings lived and acted (see Figure 6.1).

Little has survived of Greek painting, except for pottery painting (see Figure 4.2). There is evidence, however, from literary sources that large-scale paintings decorated temples and public buildings. For example, Polygnotus (mid–fifth century) decorated a colonnade in the Athenian *agora*, the area where political meetings and market activities took place, with painted scenes depicting episodes from the Trojan War. It is highly likely that Greek painting reflected the same traits as sculpture: idealization of the human figure, balance, restraint, and dignity.

5. PHILOSOPHY AND SCIENCE

The Greeks leaped furthest beyond the achievements of earlier cultures in the realms of philosophy and science, areas of inquiry they considered interdependent. Until the sixth century B.C., most Greeks were content to accept the explanations provided by mythology to describe the nature of the universe and the place of human beings in it. Then during the sixth century, just when the *polis* was reaching maturity, some thinkers began to move beyond the mythological world view in search of rational explanations of the cosmos that would take into account what was observable in the natural order.

The prime concern of these early speculative thinkers was to find a simple, unifying principle that would describe and explain rationally what constituted the universe and what made it work in order to replace traditional mythological explanations based on arbitrary, irrational factors. This quest gave rise to several schools of thought. One such school developed a materialistic explanation that argued that such obvious elements as fire or water or air were the basic substances out of which all other things emerged through processes innate in the nature of these basic substances. This materialistic approach continued to be explored until Democritus (ca. 460–370 B.C.) propounded an atomic theory, according to which the universe is composed of identical, indivisible particles floating at random; by mere chance these atoms combined into beings and objects and by the same chance decomposed to end existing things. Another school of philosophers rejected materialism and sought the key to the universe in some nonmaterial force. Perhaps the source of this approach was the sixth-century thinker Pythagoras, whose career combined scientific interest with a strong religious bent. He argued that the basis of cosmic order lay in a numerical relationship among its many parts. Equally influential in shaping this school was Heraclitus (flourished ca. 500 B.C.), who insisted that change was the essence of the material world and therefore no simplistic physical

FIGURE 6.3 Hermes with the Infant Dionysus
Most likely the work of the famed sculptor Praxiteles, this statue is an excellent example of Greek artistic canons; the gods are taken as subject matter and portrayed in an idealized human form that emphasizes physical perfection rather than spiritual qualities. (Hirmer Fotoarchiv)

explanation of the universe could have meaning. This whole school of thinkers ultimately concluded that a nonmaterial, changeless being, endowed with perfect intelligence, supplied the creative force of order in the universe.

Although Greek thinkers always remained interested in finding an explanation of the fundamental nature of the universe, about the middle of the fifth century there emerged an increasing interest in the human condition. A diverse group of thinkers, collectively called the Sophists, led the way into this new realm. The Sophists were primarily teachers interested in preparing their pupils for a role in public life. Out of their concern for what should be taught they articulated ideas that gave philosophical inquiry a new emphasis. The Sophists rejected speculative philosophy on the grounds that objective truth was nonexistent, as demonstrated by the contradictory schemes put forward by prior thinkers. In the words of one of the chief Sophists, Protagoras (485–410 B.C.), a famous teacher in Periclean Athens, men and women were the measure of all things. Human reason should be dedicated to a search for the kind of knowledge that would be useful to humans in their quest for a happy, useful life. Such an approach made it obvious to the Sophists that institutions and standards of behavior were human creations, not the results of an unchangeable natural order. On this basis, the Sophists delivered withering attacks on most things accepted as the truth, arguing that truth is relative and encouraging their disciples to live by any rules that proved workable and beneficial. The Sophists as a group were condemned as skeptics and destroyers of morality. But they made the Greek world increasingly aware of fundamental ethical issues and encouraged humans to trust the power of reason as an instrument for improving the human condition. Out of the ferment they caused emerged the greatest Greek thinkers.

One of these was Socrates (ca. 469–399 B.C.), an Athenian famous in his own time as a provocative teacher. He left no writings; he set forth his ideas orally in the Athenian *agora*, where he engaged all comers in debate about philosophical issues. From what his pupils remembered about his teaching, it appears that Socrates believed that objective truth did exist, contrary to the teachings of the Sophists. Human beings were prevented from discovering that truth by their own ignorance. That ignorance could only be dispelled by rigorous, logical self-examination of beliefs. The Socratic method consisted of asking questions un-

til the error of those who claimed to know something was exposed and then leading the mind through further questioning to the truth by way of precise definition and exact logic. Socrates' goal was to get people to understand themselves and to conduct their lives by the light of their reason. Although his gadfly tactics won him an eager following, he eventually encountered trouble. In 399 B.C., amid the bitterness surrounding the Athenian defeat in the Peloponnesian War, he was accused of corrupting the youth and sentenced to die. Although offered an opportunity to escape, he chose to accept the verdict of his fellow citizens rather than abandon his conviction that knowledge alone led to virtue.

Plato (427–347 B.C.) carried on the work of Socrates, his master. He spent most of his career as a teacher in a school in Athens called the Academy, which he founded. His voluminous works, elegantly written in dialogue form, provide a complete although sometimes confusing record of his thought. Plato was a philosophical idealist; his work brought to full maturity the nonmaterialist philosophical tradition dating back to the sixth century. He argued that the fundamental realities in the universe are ideas, or abstract forms, the chief of which is "the good." The so-called realities that humans perceive with their senses are but imperfect reflections of the perfect universal forms. For example, the justice practiced in Athens was only a shadowy reflection of perfect, transcendental justice; a man or a woman is but a pale image of a higher reality, humanity. Plato argued that the human intellect was capable of comprehending the higher reality of forms. Such truth depends on pure reasoning, which allows the mind to reach a level of comprehension beyond what the senses can reveal.

Much of Plato's writing centers on a search for perfect understanding of universal ideas and an effort to make that wisdom and insight applicable to the problems of human existence. His best-known dialogue, *The Republic*, illustrates his idealism, his method, and his earnest concern for the human condition. This work is devoted to governance. Plato assumes that the purpose of the state is to achieve justice, the ideal state being an earthly embodiment of the perfect idea of justice. He concludes that justice consists in each individual doing that for which he or she is best fitted. The ideal state is one in which every person holds that station and does that job for which he or she is qualified. Such a state, Plato argues, must be ruled by a philosopher-king who will be wise enough to know and recognize the talents of his subjects and put these talents to work. A completely socialistic economy controlled by the wise king must be instituted so that all will be rewarded according to their merits and so that competition and greed can be eliminated from society. In short, the perfect society is a dictatorial state guided by those who are wise by virtue of their rational powers. In his other dialogues Plato conducts a comparable search for an understanding of the nature of love, friendship, courage, the soul—in fact, virtually the whole range of those elements that constitute the ultimate reality, perfect good.

Aristotle (384–322 B.C.) was Plato's most brilliant and productive pupil. As a youth, he came to Athens from northern Greece to study at the Academy. After Plato's death, he spent some time in Macedonia as tutor to young Alexander the Great. He then returned to Athens and founded his own school, the Lyceum. His followers were called the Peripatetics because Aristotle often walked about while lecturing.

During his career, Aristotle produced a massive body of philosophical work ranging across the whole spectrum of human knowledge. Perhaps typical of effective teachers in all ages, he had a passion for systematizing and organizing knowledge, so that his works constitute a kind of encyclopedia of the total learning of the ancient world. Imbedded in his massive scholarship, however, is a basic philosophical position. Aristotle was certainly influenced by Platonic idealism, but his approach is basically different. In his seminal *Metaphysics*, he argues that reality consists of a combination of matter and form (or idea). The form makes the object what it is, but it has no reality except when it exists in matter. Every object has some purpose in a larger universal order, and its perfection consists in serving that purpose. Behind the wilderness of individual objects lies an ultimate "cause," a higher force that animates everything. The philosopher's path is from the study of nature toward the formulation of concepts about the entire universe.

In most of his works, many of which deal with scientific subjects, Aristotle pursued the course laid down in the *Metaphysics*. His *Politics* supplies an illustration of his method. On the basis of a study of the history and organization of more than one hundred fifty Greek city-states, he concluded that the state is a natural grouping of human beings for the purpose of promoting virtue. Men and women are political animals; they cannot fulfill their true nature unless they are members of a state. The state as a "form" manifests itself in many different material shapes: monarchy, oligarchy, tyranny, democracy. Aristotle's analysis of these forms clarified the unique consequences for human beings of each type of state. In his *Ethics* Aristotle asked how men and women should conduct their individual lives and argued that happiness is the proper goal of every human action. Men and women are happy, and therefore good, if they control their passions by the use of reason and if they seek a mean between extremes. Aristotle's principal method of seeking truth was inductive—that is, formulating generalizations on the basis of particular pieces of evidence—and he was the most influential exponent of that method among the Greeks. However, he was also the founder of formal logic, a mode of thinking that employs a deductive method of thinking to extract the truth about specific things from general principles. Aristotelian logic would play a dominant role in philosophical inquiry for centuries to come. As the last great thinker of classical Greece, Aristotle was the most comprehensive.

Aristotle's scientific works mark the culmination of a sustained interest in natural science among the Greeks extending back at least two centuries. That interest resulted in significant work in astronomy, physics, botany, zoology, physiology, and geography. Although Greek scientists borrowed extensively from data about the natural world compiled by Mesopotamians and Egyptians, they made significant additions to scientific knowledge by their own observations of natural phenomena. Illustrative of this approach is the work of Hippocrates (460–377 B.C.), a practicing physician to whom is attributed the famous oath still used today defining the responsibilities of a physician. He insisted that nothing could be known about sickness except through observation

WHERE HISTORIANS DISAGREE

The Irrational in Greek Culture

All historians who try to reconstruct the grand sweep of history quickly become aware of a disturbing consequence of their effort: They find themselves distorting the past by concentrating on what is dominant in any era at the expense of those facets that in their judgment are less important. The conventional treatment of Greek culture provides an example. Modern scholars—including the present authors—have emphatically stressed that the crucial factor in Greek thought and expression was rationalism. But is that the whole story? Have we forgotten something in our eagerness to make the Greeks the model of that desirable human trait, reasonableness?

One of the most perceptive modern classicists, E. R. Dodds, has reminded us not to be too hasty on this matter. In his seminal book entitled *The Greeks and the Irrational* (1951) he developed a strong case for the presence of powerful currents of irrationality in Greek culture. He bases his case on a fundamental postulate established by modern anthropologists and psychologists which argues that in the behavior of all people in all ages there is a powerful element of primitive mentality that finds its expression in religion. He asks: "Why should we attribute to the ancient Greeks an immunity from 'primitive' modes of thought which we do not find in any society open to our direct observation?"

Dodds succeeds in demonstrating persuasively that Greek literary and philosophical leaders were always aware of irrational factors governing human conduct and that they expressed their awareness in religious terms. In other terms, he finds that even the most profound Greek thinkers were never quite satisfied to explain human actions solely in terms of rational behavior. He provides massive evidence to show that many Greeks were constantly fearful of psychic intervention in their lives by divine forces capable of polluting them or driving them to madness. Moreover, he argues that the "enlightened" views of the great cultural heroes of the Greek world were looked upon with suspicion and even hostility by most Greeks, who were never free from a deepseated feeling that forces beyond rational comprehension and control governed human behavior.

Dodd's convincing argument forces us to realize that only a few Greek thinkers affirmed that a human being was a rational creature, and in the long run their belief was overpowered by a more primitive conviction that men and women were essentially irrational. When one adds to this the obvious fact that the great mass of Greeks always accepted a religious interpretation of human nature, the generalization about rationalism as a key to Greek culture becomes exceedingly suspect.

Thus it turns out that the historian who stresses rationalism as a major feature of Greek culture is overlooking a factor of immense importance to the Greeks. This sounds dishonest. Yet in fitting the Greeks into the grand sweep of history, their rationalism is of greater significance than their irrationalism. Their consciousness of the rational powers of human beings marked a fresh insight into the human potential, while their awareness of the irrational aspects of human behavior simply provided a common bond with most other societies in history that have tried to cope with the monumental problems of living. What is important is that some Greeks trusted their rational powers as a means of enriching their lives, for they were the ones that made a difference in the history of civilization.

of sick people and through a search for the natural causes of illness. He repudiated the traditional belief that sickness was due to evil spirits; it was a result of natural causes, and the cure for sickness was a natural process that could be controlled. He collected information about the curative power of drugs and about the effects of diet on health. The collective efforts of Greek scientists allow us to credit the Greeks with the invention of the scientific method, which relies on observation as the source of knowledge about nature. Lacking precision instruments, their observations were often imprecise and their interpretations of data erroneous. Moreover, few were interested in using their knowledge for practical purposes. Scientific knowledge was employed chiefly by philosophers seeking to explain the working of the universe.

6. THE GREEK SPIRIT

Any review of the varied achievements of the Greeks in literature, art, philosophy, and science raises at least two basic questions. Are there any common characteristics undergirding Greek culture in its entirety? Did this splendid outburst of creativity in thought and expression affect the lives of ordinary men and women?

To the first question it seems possible to argue that Greek culture in all its aspects reflects certain basic concepts. Greek thought was intensely *humanistic*; it placed human beings at the center of the universe and celebrated their potential for perfection. Greek cultural leaders were confident that the universe existed to sustain human welfare. They were therefore certain that humans were *in harmony with nature* and had no need to struggle against it, to try to escape it, or shrink from it in fear. Greek culture was *rationalistic*; its creators placed trust in the human ability to understand nature and themselves through human intelli-

gence and to act on the basis of rational decisions to resolve human problems. Rationalism emphasized the need to seek *order* and *symmetry* in all things and to act with *restraint* and *balance*. Greek culture was marked by a *spirit of inquiry* that constantly pushed thinkers and artists toward new knowledge and new ways of expressing themselves. Finally, most Greek intellectual and artistic leaders were *civic-oriented,* ready to offer their talents to the service of the community to which they belonged instead of pursuing individual and introspective ends.

Much more difficult to ascertain is the extent to which the basic values expressed in Greek culture shaped the lives of ordinary Greeks. Like most of the nameless peoples in the past, their thoughts and ideals are lost to us. Probably most Greeks, engaged in the routine of daily life, seldom paused to think about what their pattern of civilization meant, just as most modern men and women seldom dwell on this question. But one thing seems certain: An ordinary Greek would have had trouble escaping contact with the cultural achievements we have described. The best of Greek thought on the human condition was made available to all citizens of each *polis* as an intimate dimension of civic life. Poetry reading accompanied religious ceremonies and athletic competitions. The best drama was played out in public theaters. The best philosophers wrangled in the streets, joined their fellow citizens at *symposia*, and taught in the schools. Architects and sculptors devoted their best efforts to civic art. It seems inconceivable that any citizen could have escaped without being touched by some of the values reflected in Greek culture. We must assume that most Greeks found the values and the ideas engrained in Greek culture as attractive and appealing as did innumerable later generations who found in the Greek way a model for civilized life.

SUGGESTED READING

General Cultural Histories

François Chamoux, *The Civilization of Greece,* trans. W. S. Maguinness (1965). A perceptive overview, well illustrated.

John Boardman et al., eds., *The Oxford History of the Classical World* (1986). Excellent studies of varied aspects of Greek civilization.

Social Life

In addition to the social and economic histories cited in Chapter 4, the following works treat selected aspects of Greek social life.

Maurice Pope, *The Ancient Greeks. How They Lived and Worked* (1976).

Robert Flacelière, *Daily Life in Greece in the Time of Pericles,* trans. Peter Green (1965).

M. T. W. Arnheim, *Aristocracy in Greek Society* (1977).

W. K. Lacey, *The Family in Classical Greece* (1984).

Sarah B. Pomeroy, *Goddesses, Whores, Wives, and Slaves: Women in Classical Antiquity* (1975).

Eva Cantarella, *Pandora's Daughters: The Role and Status of Women in Greek and Roman Antiquity,* trans. Maureen B. Fant (1987).

Yvon Garlan, *Slavery in Ancient Greece,* trans. Janet Lloyd (1988).

K. J. Dover, *Greek Homosexuality* (1978).

Religion

Robert Graves, *The Greek Myths* (1955; illustrated edition, 1981). A full description of the myths undergirding Greek religion.

Walter Burkert, *Greek Religion: Archaic and Classical,* trans. John Raffan (1985). A masterful treatment.

Walter Burkert, *Ancient Mystery Cults* (1987). A well-done guide.

Literature

Jacqueline de Romilly, *A Short History of Greek Literature,* trans. Lillian Doherty (1985).

Peter Levi, *A History of Greek Literature* (1985).

Either of these recent works will provide invaluable guides to the main currents of Greek literary history.

Charles Rowan Beye, *Ancient Greek Literature and Society,* 2nd ed., rev. (1988). A stimulating effort to put Greek literature into its social context.

Art

John Boardman, *Greek Art,* new and rev. ed. (1985). An excellent brief treatment.

John Boardman et al., *The Art and Architecture of Ancient Greece* (1967).

Richard Brilliant, *Arts of the Ancient Greeks* (1973).

Jean Charbonneaux et al., *Classical Greek Art (480–330 B.C.),* trans. James Emmons (1972).

These three longer treatments, all beautifully illustrated, provide a rich appreciation of the Greek artistic accomplishment.

J. J. Pollitt, *Art and Experience in Classical Greece* (1972). A good treatment of the social and intellectual foundations of Greek art.

Philosophy and Science

Rex Warner, *Greek Philosophers* (1958).

W. K. C. Guthrie, *Greek Philosophers: From Thales to Aristotle* (1960).

Although old, either of these two works will provide a good introduction to the Greek accomplishment in philosophy.

Jean-Pierre Vernant, *The Origins of Greek Thought* (1982). A challenging introduction.

H. D. Rankin, *Sophists, Socratics, and Cynics* (1983). A balanced treatment of the major schools of philosophy in classical Greece.

G. E. R. Lloyd, *Early Greek Science: Thales to Aristotle* (1970). A thorough assessment of the Greek accomplishments in science.

K. D. White, *Greek and Roman Technology* (1984). A well-done assessment of Greek accomplishments in technology.

Sources

Michael Grant, ed., *Greek Literature: An Anthology in Translation* (1973). A rich sampling. Perhaps it will encourage a reader to read Greek writers in their entirety. Good translations of the works of all the authors mentioned in this chapter are easily available.

CHAPTER 7

Greek Imperialism: The Hellenistic World, 336–31 B.C.

FIGURE 7.1 **Alexander the Great** This Roman copy of an original bust of Alexander the Great (perhaps done by the fourth-century sculptor Lycippus) attempts to capture the strength and the idealism of a great hero of the ancient world. (The Granger Collection)

To many Greeks, the coming of the "barbarian" Macedonians spelled doom. But, as is so often the case when contemporaries judge their own age, they were wrong. The Macedonian conquest set the stage for a new chapter in the history of the Greeks. Under Macedonian leadership, they exploded out of their Aegean-centered world to establish their mastery over a wide circle in Asia and Africa. Their genius and their traditions began to mix with Near Eastern civilizations to produce a new culture that historians have called "Hellenistic."

1. ALEXANDER THE GREAT

The military and political genius of Alexander the Great was chiefly responsible for launching the Greeks on this new phase of their history. Endowed with numerous powers—intelligence, ambition, industry, imagination, physical attractiveness, boldness, an iron will—Alexander has never ceased to fascinate students of history (see Figure 7.1). Although Macedonian by birth, he shared the admiration for Greek culture that prevailed at the court of his father, Philip II, and that was deepened by his education under Aristotle's direction.

Only twenty when his father died, Alexander turned his energies immediately to launching the war against Persia that Philip had planned (see Map 7.1). In 334 B.C. he led his Macedonian-Greek army into Asia Minor in order to attack Persia. Although Persia possessed a huge empire, a rich treasury, and a large army and navy, Alexander was victorious from the beginning. Mindful of the role naval power had played in the long struggle between Greeks and Persians, his first campaigns were aimed at depriving the Persians of control of the coastal cities of Asia Minor and Phoenicia, the chief source of Persian naval power. Shortly after entering Asia Minor, Alexander overpowered a major Persian force at a battle on the Granicus River; this victory assured control of the Greek cities along the east coast of the Aegean Sea. From there he moved into Syria and in 333 B.C. won a brilliant victory at Issus. This victory solidified Alexander's control of Asia Minor and opened the way for his conquest of Syria, Palestine, and Egypt. Then he marched on the center of Persian power in Mesopotamia and in the spring of 331 B.C. destroyed the last major military strength of the Persians at the battle of Gaugamela (Arbela). Following this victory, he occupied the major centers of Persian political power, including the capital city of Persepolis, and hunted down the fugitive King Darius III, who was finally murdered in 330 B.C. by his own officials as Alexander closed in on him.

The conquest of the Persian Empire did not satisfy Alexander's ambition. During the next five years he drove on eastward. Battling vast distances, native resistance, and defection among his own troops, he relentlessly destroyed pockets of resistance led by Persian satraps in the regions of Parthia and Bactria. Then he pushed across the Hindu Kush Mountains into the rich land drained by the Indus River, a venture that brought the Greeks into direct contact with Indian civilization. Beyond the Indus Valley his troops refused to go. Alexander therefore turned back westward through southern Persia and into Mesopotamia, where he fell ill and died in June 323 B.C. at the age of thirty-three.

A career so short and so completely occupied with military campaigns left Alexander little time to face the problems of ruling his vast conquests. Probably he had no definite plans when he launched his campaign, but before he died he had made decisions establishing certain broad policies that guided his successors. He moved toward creating a style of rulership that cast him in the role of divine autocrat who enjoyed the special favor of the deities, a kind of rulership foreign both to Greeks and to Macedonians. He at least toyed with the idea of combining the talents of conquered peoples, especially Persians, with those of the conquerors to create a cosmopolitan elite to control his empire. However, his followers found this policy unacceptable. Eventually he had to take steps to ensure that Greeks and Macedonians would rule his empire. This plan required their migration to Asia and Africa, a move that Alexander sought to make attractive by establishing city-states in which the newcomers would have a special place. However, aside from his conquests, Alexander's accomplishments were few. His main influence on the course of history lay chiefly in

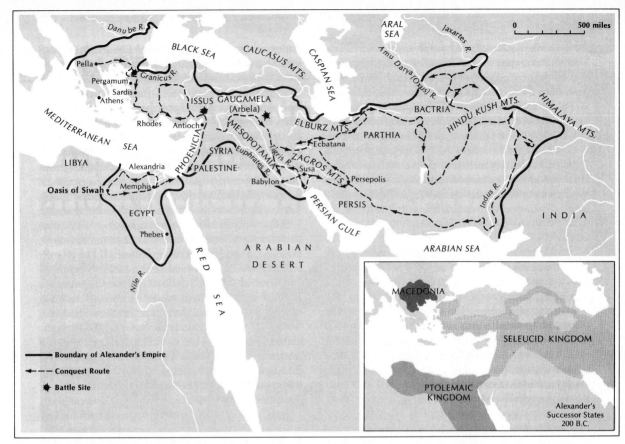

Map 7.1 **ALEXANDER'S EMPIRE, 336–323 B.C.** This map provides a dramatic picture of Alexander's military accomplishment in overpowering the Persian Empire. That the Greeks were able to establish their mastery over this huge territory and impose their pattern of culture on much of it was an amazing achievement. The most intensive Hellenization of Alexander's empire occurred around the eastern end of the Mediterranean from Egypt through Syria and Phoenicia to Asia Minor. But Mesopotamia also felt the powerful force of Greek culture.

his legend: what later generations believed he was trying to do.

2. HELLENISTIC POLITICAL LIFE, 323–31 B.C.

For almost three centuries the consequences of Alexander's conquests dominated the political history of the vast area that fell under his sway. That history was not, however, a simple one. If, as some claimed, Alexander intended to establish a universal empire to be ruled by a philosopher-king

in a way that would bring peace and prosperity to all its people, that was not to be the case. Immediately after his unexpected death, a council of his generals decided to attempt to maintain a united empire under a single ruler. They designated Alexander's incompetent half brother as king, with the understanding that should the child that Alexander's widow, the Bactrian princess Roxanne, was carrying be male, he would share the throne—which is what happened. But this royal pair could provide no effective direction. The generals were soon engaged in a struggle for control. By about 275 B.C. their rivalry had produced a hodgepodge of political entities of various sizes, strengths, and forms of government. By far the most prominent were the major kingdoms established by three of Alexander's companions: Antigonus in Macedonia and the Aegean world; Ptolemy in Egypt; and Seleucus in the vast area stretching from Asia Minor to India (see Map 7.1).

Only the briefest summary of the complex histories of these kingdoms can be undertaken here. Laying claim to the well-established kingdom established by Philip II, the Macedonian kings sustained a fairly effective government during most of the third century B.C. The level of Macedonian economic and cultural life improved, largely due to the continued influx of influences from Greece. Although the Antigonid dynasty always had ambitions to play a major role in the larger Hellenistic world, Macedonian political history centered chiefly on the efforts of the rulers to maintain a hegemony over the Greek city-states and to hold back the barbarians constantly pressing on the northern frontier of Macedonia. These were great burdens, testing the limited human and material resources of Macedonia. Control of the Greek city-states was particularly difficult. Claiming to act in the name of "freedom" for the *polis*, the Greeks constantly intrigued against their masters, often seeking help from outsiders. Macedonian efforts to defuse this resistance by interfering in local city-state political processes and by establishing military garrisons in Greece only sharpened the resistance. And the barbarian assaults never let up. Ultimately, the Macedonian kingdom was incapable of bearing the burden. Shortly before 200 B.C. some of the Greek city-states appealed to Rome for help against what they claimed was Macedonian interference with their freedom. In the ensuing wars, Roman armies conquered both Macedonia and Greece and absorbed them in Rome's expanding empire.

The kingdom established in Egypt by Ptolemy was the most stable Hellenistic state. The Ptolemaic dynasty quickly established an autocratic regime modeled on the ancient Egyptian system of the pharaohs. The key to Ptolemaic power was a bureaucracy and a military force dominated by Greek-Macedonian immigrants. This regime skillfully exploited the native population and the agricultural and commercial resources of Egypt to sustain its power. Internal

stability and wealth permitted the Ptolemies to play an active role in the larger Hellenistic world. They concentrated chiefly on extending their sphere of influence in Syria-Palestine, in Asia Minor, and in the Aegean world. These ambitions involved them in almost constant conflict with other powers in the Hellenistic world, especially the Seleucid kingdom. By the second century B.C. the grip of the Ptolemies on Egypt began to weaken, chiefly because they were forced to rely increasingly on native Egyptians in the army and the bureaucracy and to make concessions limiting their royal income. Growing internal unrest ultimately forced the rulers to seek support from the Romans. Eventually, in 30 B.C., Rome annexed Egypt to its empire.

The Seleucid kingdom had the most troubled history. Its huge size and mixed population provided little basis for unity except what its kings and their Greek-Macedonian followers could impose. Rather quickly the Seleucid rulers lost control over the area east of the Tigris-Euphrates Valley to non-Greeks, who established kingdoms of considerable importance to the future, including Bactria and Parthia. In northern and western Asia Minor local rulers established small but virile kingdoms—Pontus, Bithynia, Cappadocia, Pergamum. Most of the Seleucid political energy was devoted to creating a viable state embracing Mesopotamia, Syria-Palestine, and southeastern Asia Minor. Their authority was based chiefly on military service provided by Greeks and Macedonians established in cities from whence they dominated the native population. Outsiders, especially the Ptolemies, constantly threatened the Seleucids. They also had to contend with native uprisings. For example, a Jewish revolt led by the Maccabees in 167 B.C. was provoked by an effort of the Seleucids to Hellenize the Jews; it resulted in the virtual independence of that long-captive people until they were conquered by the Romans a century later. Ultimately, the Seleucid kingdom was torn to pieces by internal strife and squeezed to death by Parthian pressure from the east and Roman intrusions from the west.

Numerous smaller states shared the political scene with the three major kingdoms. Chief among them were many Greek city-states that remained independent and sought to continue their traditional pattern of governance. A good deal of the political energies of these city-states were devoted to internal affairs, often marked by bitter partisanship and class rivalry. But they also had to concern themselves with the ambitions of other city-states and the threat of the great powers, especially Macedonia. Their fragile independence encouraged many city-states to develop techniques aimed at reducing intercity rivalry and strengthening the religious and cultural ties shared by all Greeks. Especially innovative was the development of effective leagues or federations based on some compromise of total autonomy in the interests of common action emerging from shared political processes. Two particularly important leagues were the Aetolian League embracing several city-states in central Greece and the Achaean League in northern Peloponnesus. Despite their continued existence, the old Greek city-states lost much of their power of self-determination during the Hellenistic Age. Among the smaller states of the era, the most successful were the kingdom of Pergamum in western Asia Minor and the Republic of Rhodes, both of which fared well by capitalizing on commercial activity.

In this world of competing "successor" states that emerged out of Alexander's conquests and Greek-Macedonian domination of the Near East, the conduct of interstate relations took on new intensity and sophistication. As a consequence, the Hellenistic Age marked an important chapter in the history of international relations. Great and small states developed a battery of techniques designed to ensure safety and to gain advantage over others: military force, diplomacy, psychological warfare, internal subversion, economic penetration, arrangements extending privileges to citizens of other states. In a general way, the Hellenistic world moved toward a balance of power aimed at maintaining the status quo. While that balance was constantly in the process of readjustment, it worked fairly well until a major outside power, Rome, moved onto the scene.

The Hellenistic Age witnessed significant developments in terms of political institutions that had an important impact on future history, especially in providing models for the Romans. The very idea of empire itself was important. The Near Eastern world was, of course, familiar with this political concept as a result of the efforts of Amor-

ites, Egyptians, Hittites, Assyrians, and Persians. However, the idea of empire was new to the Greeks, given their enchantment with the microcosmic *polis*. The experiences of the Hellenistic Age put into the Greek vocabulary and mentality the vision of a world state where peoples of many kinds would share a common citizenship and a common destiny. Their concepts of such a political system had an important impact on later political thought.

On a more practical level, the major development in terms of political institutions during the Hellenistic period was the Greek acceptance of the concept of monarchy—an institution that had disappeared from the world of the *polis* as early as the eighth century B.C. During the Hellenistic Age monarchy became the standard form of government among the Greek rulers of the Near East. The system of monarchy practiced by the Greeks was shaped by the traditions of the Near East, but it reflected unique qualities due to Greek influences. In Hellenistic monarchies the king's power was personal. It derived from his feats at arms, his intelligence, his will, and his favor with the deities. By virtue of his personal abilities, he could bestow blessings on his subjects. No constitution or entrenched nobility acted to limit his power. No law other than what he decreed was recognized. Such a concept of royal power clearly reflected the Greek confidence in human ability.

To exercise his vast powers effectively, the king of each Hellenistic kingdom relied on the advice of a circle of "friends" selected because of the king's confidence in their talents and their loyalty. Each ruler developed a well-organized central government featuring a strong army, an elaborate bureaucracy, and an efficient taxation system. Effective military power was the ultimate basis upon which Hellenistic government rested. Greeks and Macedonians filled the chief positions in royal governments and controlled the old structures of local government, which were usually left intact.

The large numbers of Greek and Macedonians who migrated across the Near East to serve Hellenistic kings tended to congregate in cities—some ancient and many newly founded. Into their new abodes the newcomers brought political institutions and practices from their native city-states. As a consequence, assemblies, councils, popular courts, and elected magistrates were established to give the elite outsiders considerable control over their own local affairs. The Greeks and Macedonians in the Near East thus retained their ancient allegiance to the ideal of the small, intimate *polis*, as did their compatriots still living in old Greece. This continued attachment to the ideal of the *polis* detracted from a complete commitment to monarchy. Generally, the Hellenistic kings encouraged and supported the development of such nearly autonomous communities in their kingdoms, chiefly because royal power depended on support from Greeks and Macedonians. However, concerns about retaining their ethnic identity and their elite position in political, social, and cultural life forced all Greeks in the Hellenistic world to turn to the monarchs. As a result, strong, mutually beneficial bonds developed between the monarchs and the Greek-Macedonian city-states of the Near East. The kings could usually count on the support of the local communities and, given their superior resources, were able to impose their will on these communities. Slowly but surely monarchy overshadowed the *polis* as the decisive political force in the Hellenistic world.

3. HELLENISTIC ECONOMIC AND SOCIAL LIFE

Although the Hellenistic era brought prosperity to some areas and to particular groups, on the whole the economic impact of Greek-Macedonian expansion was modest, chiefly because it was not accompanied by changes in the basic structures of production. Agriculture remained the basic source of wealth in the Hellenistic world, but the new masters did not fundamentally change the established system. The conquerors claimed possession of a considerable portion of the agricultural land in their vast empire and imposed on native tenants and increasing numbers of slaves a heavy obligation to till the soil for their benefit. Some Greek owners, including especially the kings seeking revenue, undertook land clearance, new irrigation projects, crop rotation, and the introduction of new crops and equipment; but the resultant increase in production was modest and beneficial to only a few.

An increase in trading activity provided a significant element of prosperity in some areas of the Hellenistic world, especially in a zone embracing the great cities of Egypt, Syria, and Asia Minor. Greek entrepreneurs played a significant role in exploiting the commercial potential of this area and in extending trade connections toward old Greece, Mesopotamia, India, China, and North Africa. Extensive new capital was made available to these entrepreneurs when Alexander confiscated and put into circulation the vast treasury of the Persian kings and the wealth controlled by the Persian aristocracy. Although the Greek and Macedonian newcomers in the Near East spent much of this wealth on luxury goods and the building of new cities, some of it was invested in activities beneficial to commerce: harbors, roads, market facilities, ships, coinage systems, credit and banking operations. Although there was trade in foodstuffs, metals, and timber products, luxury items played a major role in exchange. Hellenistic monarchs, especially the Ptolemies, supported commercial growth to serve political ends and thus created an economic climate favorable to trade.

The Hellenistic economy was marked by significant industrial activity carried on chiefly by native artisans operating small manufacturing establishments. Most manufacturing was devoted to products needed by the populace of each city and thus was highly localized. The surviving evidence suggests that there was no great increase in industrial production and no fundamental change in the organization of manufacturing. Especially noteworthy was the lack of technical progress. Despite some remarkable advances in the level of scientific knowledge, almost no progress was made in applying that knowledge to manufacturing, probably because of the vast supply of cheap native labor and slavery.

Whatever economic expansion there was during the Hellenistic period benefited only a few in society—chiefly the Greek rulers, their political servants, landowners, merchants, artists, and scholars. With the exception of a few natives who adopted Greek ways, most natives were economically exploited. As the Hellenistic era progressed, the gap between the wealthy Greek masters and the poor native farmers, city laborers, and slaves increased. Moreover, economic prosperity was not evenly distributed geographically. Its effects were felt chiefly in the belt extending from Egypt around the eastern end of the Mediterranean into Asia Minor. Increasingly impoverished were the old Greek city-states in the Aegean area, where depopulation and even starvation were not uncommon.

In both the old Greek world and in the vast area conquered by Alexander basic social patterns persisted during the Hellenistic period. In the old Greek city-states family structures and social practices governing daily life remained much as they had been in the fifth century. The chief change involved growing disparities in wealth, hardening class lines, and social tensions breeding conflict and even violence. In "new Hellas" native life was little disturbed by the coming of the Greeks; for most people old masters were merely replaced by new ones. Perhaps the chief new social phenomenon of the period was the implantation into many Near Eastern cities of colonies of Greeks and Macedonians who sought to re-create and perpetuate the social order they brought from their native city-states. But the old social order was difficult to maintain. Wherever Greek migrants settled, they found themselves living among Greeks from many different cities and were constantly confronted by uprooted Greek intellectuals, athletes, soldiers, and merchants seeking their fortunes, a challenge that eroded commitment to local customs based on place of origin. All kinds of opportunities existed to abandon old social ties in order to take advantage of new ways of winning wealth, favor, and high status. Despite their commitment to "Greekness," the contrasts between their way of life and that of the natives eventually modified their patterns of behavior and social values. One aspect of social life so affected involved the status of women. Although still surrounded by legal constraints, many women in the Hellenistic cities of the Near East enjoyed greatly expanded opportunities for education, involvement in cultural and economic life, and even political life—opportunities not available to their ancestors in old Greece.

As the Hellenistic era progressed, the above-noted trends in economic and social life produced a situation that boded ill for the stability of Hellenistic society. Deepening differences in wealth, social strife in the typical Greek *polis*, native re-

sentment against Greek exploitation, and Greek exclusivity generated explosive tensions. The emerging instability represented a serious failure on the part of the Greek masters of the Hellenistic world. In many of the old Greek city-states, intelligent leadership had directed economic and social development toward the improvement of the lot of the deprived, a course that strengthened the entire fabric of society. But the Greek rulers and entrepreneurs of the Hellenistic Age chose to be exploiters, a course that would have a serious cost.

4. HELLENISTIC CULTURE: AN OVERVIEW

The three centuries following Alexander's death marked an important era in cultural history in at least two significant ways. First, that period witnessed the enrichment of the cultural accomplishments of the Greeks. Second, considerable portions of the classical Greek tradition were recast into new forms that became the heritage taken over by non-Greek peoples of later generations. In a sense, much of what survived from ancient Greek culture consists of Hellenistic modifications and adaptations of the Classical Age models.

Hellenistic cultural life was animated by a powerful urge to continue the thought and expression that had developed in Greece during the Classical Age. The Greeks who fought in Alexander's armies and who migrated to populate the cities founded by him and his successors were convinced that they had conquered "barbarians" whose cultural life was not fit for Hellenes. As a consequence, the Greeks felt compelled to take their culture with them into their new world in the Near East and to preserve it in as pure a form as possible. As a result of such feelings, Greek literary, artistic, philosophical, and scientific concepts and forms were implanted across the Near East as the dominant cultural modes.

However, bringing the chief ingredients of Hellenic culture into a new geographical, political, and social setting was not a simple task. In fact, it turned out to be unrealistic, for Hellenic culture began to be transformed almost from the moment of its transplantation. The culturally dominant Greeks found themselves separated from the intimate, tightly knit city-state environment that had originally nourished their culture. They were now widely dispersed in a huge, impersonal world where their destinies were determined by semidivine monarchs and complicated economic forces. In such a milieu some aspects of their old culture appeared to have little relevance. Moreover, the Greeks soon found that the "barbarian" Egyptians, Syrians, Mesopotamians, Persians, and Indians possessed knowledge, techniques, and ideas that were both new and attractive to the conquerors. These tensions and pressures produced an outburst of activity in literature, art, philosophy, and science, which transformed the old modes of thought and expression in ways that broadened and enriched the classical Greek culture.

During the Hellenistic period cities remained the focal points of cultural life. Many of the old city-states of the Aegean area continued to promote active cultural life; Athens in particular enjoyed prominence in philosophical inquiry. However, the most intense cultural activity of the Hellenistic Age was generated in the new Greek centers in the Near East, especially Alexandria, Antioch, and Pergamum. The population of these cities was cosmopolitan, mixing Greeks from throughout the Hellenistic world with the native peoples. The royal governments that controlled these cities and the affluent Greeks who dominated social and economic life were generous patrons, anxious to attract artists, writers, and thinkers to their cities and eager to provide them with the means to pursue their cultural interests. In Alexandria, for example, the Ptolemaic kings spent huge sums to plan and build a city adorned with the best art and architecture that could be created. They built a large library that contained about seven hundred thousand books (actually handwritten papyrus scrolls) and created a research center, called the Museum, where learned scholars were supported so that they could pursue scientific studies. The best talent flocked to these centers and devoted their skills to satisfying the cultural interests of those who patronized them. The cultural activities generated in these "new" cities addressed a much broader world, a different set of interests, and a new range of problems than had the Greek cultural efforts within the small,

independent *polis* of the Aegean world.

The most active period in Hellenistic cultural life centered in the third and early second centuries B.C. As the second century progressed, complex and subtle changes began to blunt the powerful urge to sustain and elaborate the cultural inheritance from the Greek Classical Age. The ethnocentricity of the dominant population of the great cultural centers began to lose its edge as Greeks and natives merged. Patronage declined as royal governments weakened. Perhaps most important, new concerns began to occupy the attention of people in a way that lessened the importance of the rationalistic, humanistic values of Greek culture and heightened the attractiveness of values embraced in religious systems that had their roots in the ancient traditions of the Near East. But before it could be completely overpowered by the resurgence of religious forces, Hellenistic culture had won the admiration of the conquering Romans and thus lived on under Roman patronage.

5. HELLENISTIC CULTURE: LITERATURE AND ART

The literary output of the Hellenistic Age was massive; the names of a thousand Hellenistic writers have survived. The outpouring was due in part to the patronage of wealthy monarchs, their officials, and private individuals and in part to the increased demand for literature by a growing number of literate people. A simplified version of Greek (*koine* Greek) became the common tongue of government, commerce, and learning. Many natives learned the language; for example, the Hebrew Bible was translated into Greek (the Septuagint) in Alexandria in the third and second centuries B.C. for the use of Jews living there. While the writers of the Hellenistic Age were prolific, they were not especially inventive. Mainly they devoted their energies to imitation of the epic and lyric poems, the tragedies and comedies, and the histories of classical Greece. The poets especially were chiefly concerned with style. They often reworked old subject matter in an attempt to achieve stylistic perfection. There were some authors, however, who produced literature that dealt with current situations and appealed to broader audiences than did the "classics"; such literature included novels and biographies.

The Hellenistic Age also produced a multitude of literary scholars who spent their lives reconstructing earlier Greek literary masterpieces, writing commentaries on their meaning, analyzing their grammar, and discussing their stylistic features. This patient scholarly labor played an important role in establishing and preserving the texts of the Greek classics and in elaborating the rules that governed grammar, rhetoric, and literary form. The scholarly establishment provided endless grist for an education system that was expanding in the Hellenistic Age and becoming increasingly literary and formal. Education played a major role in preparing the Greek ruling elite to discharge its duties and to sustain the cultural brand that was, indeed, its mark of superiority.

The artists of the Hellenistic period were no less active than the literary figures. Again classical Greek models exerted a powerful influence, completely overshadowing the artistic traditions of the Near East. Architecture enjoyed a great boom because of the numerous new cities built by the Greeks and filled with the traditional buildings—temples, gymnasiums, theaters, and centers for public business. Although the basic forms remained classic, there was a tendency to stress size and ornateness in these buildings. Most Hellenistic cities were much better planned than the older Greek cities, with emphasis on a rectangular grid layout, wide streets, adequate water supplies, commercial conveniences, and parks. As a result, they were more impressive than predecessors.

Hellenistic sculpture likewise sought to imitate the masters of the Classical Age; in fact, most sculptors did little more than copy classical models. They remained fascinated with the human figure. Sometimes they were able to capture the full spirit of classical style, as is illustrated by the well-known *Winged Victory of Samothrace*, with its idealized, well-proportioned portrayal of the human form. Hellenistic sculptors showed a greater interest in the nude female than had sculptors of classical Greece; their best work in this respect reflected a pleasing combination of idealization of the body and sensuousness, as is evident in the famous *Aphrodite of Melos* (more commonly known

FIGURE 7.2   An Old Woman of the Hellenistic Age
This portrayal of an old market woman of the third or second century B.C. reflects the concern of Hellenistic artists with portraying the real world about them. The work suggests a world that had its share of suffering and hardship. The contrast with the serene, idealized figures portrayed in the sculpture of the Classical Age in Greece is striking. (The Metropolitan Museum of Art, Rogers Fund, 1909)

as the *Venus de Milo*). Hellenistic sculptors produced impressive relief carvings as a part of temple decoration. Although little evidence has survived, it is clear that the classical tradition in painting was continued during the Hellenistic period. Although classical Greek influences dominated the visual arts, Hellenistic art did develop its unique characteristics. Perhaps the most striking development was the increasing realism reflected in sculpture and painting. In place of the classic quest to create idealized perfection, Hellenistic sculptors came down into the streets for their subjects. Children, old people, common laborers, and barbarians occupied their attention, and they gave vent to emotions, seeking to portray action and violence, passion, sorrow, and suffering (see Figure 7.2).

6. HELLENISTIC CULTURE: SCIENCE AND PHILOSOPHY

The most original cultural contributions of the Hellenistic Age were made in science and philosophy, where investigators and thinkers often moved beyond their Hellenic predecessors. Both fields built upon the achievements of classical Greece, but science and philosophy tended to become separate areas of concern. The moment was especially ripe for scientific advance. Earlier Greek philosophers had postulated challenging theories about the natural world and had argued that nature could best be understood by observing its working. Out of this background there emerged during the Hellenistic Age a strong urge to expand the store of knowledge about the natural world and to interpret its meaning. The expansion of the Greeks put them in touch with a huge body of data compiled over many centuries by learned individuals in the Near East. Hellenistic kings and wealthy Greeks were eager to patronize scientists and to provide facilities to make research possible. The result was active scientific inquiry, centered especially at Alexandria, and an impressive expansion of scientific knowledge, especially in view of the lack of instruments making possible precise observations.

Alexander's conquests and the commercial activities that resulted expanded knowledge of and

interest in geography. As a consequence, compilation of geographical knowledge was an important aspect of Hellenistic science. From this new knowledge emerged challenging geographical speculation, illustrated by the work of Eratosthenes (ca. 275–200 B.C.). He calculated the circumference of the earth as 24,662 miles, about 200 miles less than the actual figure. On the basis of his study of tides, he insisted that the Atlantic and Indian oceans were joined and that India could be reached by boat around Africa. He made maps using lines of longitude and latitude and divided the earth into zones still used by geographers. Seleucus (second century B.C.), along with others, studied the tides and came close to relating them to the gravitational force of the moon.

Astronomy likewise attracted attention. The two greatest names were Aristarchus (ca. 310–230 B.C.) and Hipparchus (ca. 185–120 B.C.). Aristarchus insisted that the earth revolved around the sun. Hipparchus denied this premise, working out a geocentric version of the cosmos that involved an intricate array of movements of the sun, moon, and stars around the earth. His system, which took into account what astronomers were then able to observe, won the day and would survive for centuries. He compiled an extensive atlas of the stars and from observation of their movement arrived at an extremely accurate calculation of the solar year. Both these great astronomers tried to calculate the size of the sun and its distance from the earth, but with little success.

Much was also done to advance mathematics. Euclid (323–285 B.C.) compiled a textbook of geometry that remained standard until the twentieth century. Archimedes (287–212 B.C.) calculated the value of pi (the ratio between the circumference and the diameter of a circle). He also devised a system for expressing large numbers, solved the problem of the relative volumes of a cylinder and a sphere, and laid the foundations for calculus. Trigonometry was developed by Hipparchus, and a fundamental work on conic sections was done by Apollonius of Perga (third century B.C.).

Scientific medicine was of great interest to the scholars of this period. Following the lead of Hippocrates, Hellenistic physicians made important progress in anatomy and physiology, chiefly on the basis of careful and systematic observation.

Surgery advanced considerably; so did the use of medicines. Alexandria was especially prominent as a center of medical study, an activity that the Ptolemaic rulers supported even to the extent of supplying the cadavers of prisoners to physicians for dissection.

Hellenistic scientists were also interested in physics, zoology, chemistry, and botany, devoting most of their energies to collecting and classifying data in these areas. Illustrative was the work of Theophrastus (ca. 372–287 B.C.), who compiled descriptive works on botany based on his own observations of plants and their habits. New advances in these fields were limited. However, Archimedes discovered the laws governing floating bodies and developed the theory of the lever.

As Hellenistic science advanced, scientists became increasingly interested in the compilation of encyclopedias intended to summarize knowledge in each scientific field. Euclid's work in geometry has already been noted; other important compilers include Ptolemy (ca. A.D. 85–180) in astronomy and geography, Strabo (ca. 63 B.C.–A.D. 21) in geography, and Galen (A.D. 130–201) in medicine. These encyclopedias served as guides to scientific knowledge at least until the beginning of the great scientific revolution of early modern times.

Hellenistic scientists, like their Hellenic predecessors, had little interest in the practical application of scientific ideas. There were exceptions; Archimedes, for example, developed the windlass, the double pulley, the endless screw for pumping water, and a variety of devices useful in the defense of besieged cities. In fact, virtually the only area where applied technology developed was in the military field. As a consequence, Hellenistic daily life was little affected by the notable advances in science.

Hellenistic philosophy rivaled science in vigor and creativity. The old philosophical interests lived on, as evidenced by the continued activity of Plato's Academy and Aristotle's Lyceum in Athens. However, Hellenistic philosophy was primarily concerned with problems of human conduct and individual destiny, interests that had already attracted the Sophists of the fifth century. This emphasis reflected the stresses felt by Greeks living in a cosmopolitan, impersonal, changing world, which left them seeking reassurance against uncertainty, personal identity, and peace of mind.

The search for individual identity and peace of mind produced several schools of thought that competed loudly and bitterly for public attention. Some attracted popular fancy and aroused ire for their eccentricity and excess. One such group was the Skeptics, who made a principle of doubting everything and who argued that people should live with no concern for truth or values since neither existed. The Cynics were more spectacular; they advocated that society should abandon all its civilized conventions and wealth to return to nature. In search of converts, these disciples of a counterculture took to the streets in filthy rags to deliver diatribes against the establishment and all the amenities of civilized life.

More profound and influential was the teaching of Epicurus (ca. 341–270 B.C.), who taught at Athens. He built his ethical concepts on a materialistic philosophical basis. He argued that the universe consisted of atoms, which by chance formed themselves into beings and things. The deities, if they existed, had nothing to do with this process and therefore need be of no concern to human beings. Death was nothing more than the dissolution of atoms that had come together by accident to bring into being a living creature; thus death need not be feared. Given such a cosmos, human beings should occupy themselves only with happiness and pleasure. Epicurus argued that the path to happiness is not mere physical pleasure but rather those things that bring a peaceful, undisturbed mind. He pleaded with his disciples to withdraw into themselves and avoid excessive wealth, political involvement, superstition, and too great contact with the world. The Epicureans put great confidence in limiting one's association to a narrow circle of intimate friends; "to live in hiding" would shield one from much that could disturb the mind. This philosophy was welcome to many educated people who saw little use struggling in a world where great kings and great wealth determined most things. Although some turned Epicurus' teachings into an excuse for seeking purely physical pleasure, most Epicureans were learned and refined, obedient to public authority, calm, and long-suffering. But they were little given to the active, involved life that was once the ideal for the Greek citizen.

Even more influential in shaping the moral atmosphere of the Hellenistic Age were the Stoics, whose founder, Zeno (336–264 B.C.), taught in Athens while Epicurus was there. Stoicism was based on Zeno's conviction that the material universe of which each human being is an integral part was governed by an unchanging law of nature defined by a Divine Reason. For many Stoics that supreme intelligence was virtually a god who controlled human destiny. Harmony and order would result if the laws of nature were adhered to by all creatures. The course of human beings emerged clearly from such a universal order: They must use their reason to define for themselves a pattern of behavior that would attune them and their actions to the unchanging laws of nature. Such a course would compel all humans to accept the inevitable dictates of the natural order. They must bear all misfortunes with patience since everything that happens has been ordained by an all-knowing providence. All must accept good fortune without pride, since they are not responsible for it. Such submission to the natural order brings tranquility and peace of mind. It ends concern for material things and allows the soul to reach the ideal state—*apatheia* (apathy, absence of feeling). Although in its early stage Stoicism was primarily an individualistic philosophy, it did in time develop a larger dimension that stressed the community of all humans and the need for involvement in public life in order to sustain order and civility, both necessary to peace of mind.

7. HELLENISTIC RELIGION

A major source of ferment in the Hellenistic world was religion. The old civic religions of the Greeks had already been weakened by social stresses within the city-states of the late fifth and fourth centuries and by the assaults of intellectuals. Nonetheless, when the Greeks migrated across the Near East during the Hellenistic period, they sought to transplant and sustain their old beliefs and practices as a part of their "superior" culture. The effort failed. The old deities and the rites in their honor increasingly ceased to answer the basic spiritual needs generated by the changed environ-

FIGURE 7.3 Religious Syncretism This Hellenistic relief illustrates the mixing of religions that was an important aspect of Hellenistic civilization. The seated deity reflects a mixture of Greek and Near Eastern concepts of deity. The priest burning incense in honor of the god is Near Eastern, while the garment of the figure on the right crowning the god is clearly Greek/Macedonian. (Yale University Art Gallery, Duro-Europas Collection)

ment of the Hellenistic world. As a consequence, an important aspect of "Greekness" increasingly suffered eclipse.

To help them in the face of uncertainties and alienation, many Greeks found satisfaction in accepting ideas rooted in the rich religious history of the Near East. These native religious concepts had evolved into well-defined cults, called *mystery religions*, which during the Hellenistic period increasingly won favor among the Greeks at the expense of the old civic religions. Many different mystery religions flourished in the Near East during the Hellenistic period: Isis worship, Mithraism, the Earth Mother cult, Dionysus worship. Whatever their origin, all shared certain fundamental ideas with wide appeal. They centered around the worship of a savior deity, usually identified with the forces of renewal in nature, whose death and resurrection provided eternal life for each individual believer. Those yearning for assurance drew close to that deity by trusting in the deity's saving power, by submitting to a special initiation ceremony, and by participating in emotional rituals, often involving a reenactment of the deity's death and rebirth. Favor with the saving god or goddess depended heavily on the moral conduct of each believer. Since faith in a savior deity, ritual participation, and upright behavior were tests everyone could meet, the mystery religions appealed to men and women of all classes, all levels of wealth, and all ethnic groups. In the cosmopolitan, mobile environment of the Hellenistic world, ideas from various mystery religions constantly mingled. This process, called *syncretism*, pointed toward the emergence of a common faith that not only tended to link Hellenes and native Near Easterners but also created a seedbed out of which would emerge genuinely universal religions (see Figure 7.3).

As the Hellenistic period unfolded, religious attitudes exemplified by the mystery religions increasingly asserted powerful influences over other aspects of thought and expression. Science and philosophy were put to the service of religious thought. Astronomy was transformed into astrology, the "scientist" studying the stars in order to predict the future. The philosopher's effort to learn by rational means the secrets of the cosmic order became an attempt to achieve mystical contact with powerful deities who controlled the universe. This "religionizing" of thought had brought Greek culture and its Hellenistic extension full circle: A culture born out of religion was now being absorbed back into religion. In the process some of the finest achievements of the Greeks were threatened with being twisted out of shape. This transformation was delayed by the emergence of the Romans as champions of Greek culture, but in the long run religious concepts would gain the upper hand, as will be seen in our treatment of the end of Greco-Roman civilization.

The advance of religious values in the Hellenistic world points to a significant dimension of Hellenistic cultural life destined to be an important heritage left to later history. Hellenistic culture was marked by an inner tension. On the one hand, there was a thrust to know the world of people and nature and to understand that world rationally. On the other, there was an equally powerful thrust to retreat from the material world into the spirit world, to abandon thinking in favor of quietude of mind. Although these opposing views sometimes divided the individual mind, in general the first approach was represented by Hellenistic scientists, sculptors, and creative writers, while the second attracted philosophers, literary scholars, and priests. Perhaps the emergence of this polarity in Hellenistic culture was what distinguished it from the Hellenic culture of classical Greece. In any case, the juxtaposition of reason and faith, realism and mysticism, activism and withdrawal at the heart of Hellenistic culture would recur in later chapters of the history of Western civilization as a stimulant to creativity.

SUGGESTED READING

Political History

F. W. Walbank, *The Hellenistic World* (1982).

Michael Grant, *From Alexander to Cleopatra. The Hellenistic World* (1982).

Two challenging syntheses covering all aspects of Hellenistic life.

Robin Lane Fox, *Alexander the Great* (1973). An excellent biography.

Cultural Life

John Ferguson, *The Heritage of Hellenism. The Greek World from 323 B.C. to 31 B.C.* (1973). An excellent overview of the main features of Hellenistic culture.

G. E. R. Lloyd, *Greek Science after Aristotle* (1973). A balanced, readable description of the major accomplishments of Hellenistic science.

A. A. Long, *Hellenistic Philosophy: Stoics, Epicureans, Scep-*

tics (1974). A clear presentation of the teachings of the major Hellenistic schools of philosophy.

Jean Charbonneaux et al. *Hellenistic Art (330–50 B.C.),* trans. Peter Green (1973). A splendidly illustrated treatment of all aspects of Hellenistic art.

John Onions, *Art and Thought in the Hellenistic Age: The Greek World View, 350–50 B.C.* (1979). A challenging effort to interrelate art and thought.

Arnaldo Momigliano, *Alien Wisdom: The Limits of Hellenization* (1975). Discusses how the Greeks dealt with other cultures, especially during the Hellenistic period.

Walter Burkert, *Ancient Mystery Cults* (1987). A good picture of the most powerful religious forces in the Hellenistic world.

Sources

M. M. Austin, *The Hellenistic World from Alexander to the Roman Conquest. A Selection of Ancient Sources in Translation* (1981). A well-selected collection of documents that will help the reader understand many aspects of Hellenistic life as seen and felt by those who lived in that world.

CHAPTER 8

The Rise of Rome to Domination of the Mediterranean World

FIGURE 8.1   A Roman Patrician Honoring His Ancestors   This portrayal of a Roman patrician bearing busts of his ancestors conveys the sobriety, seriousness, and respect for family that characterized the aristocratic citizens who acted through the Senate to lead the Roman Republic to ascendancy in the Mediterranean world. (Alinari/Art Resource)

The powerful impulses toward the establishment of a common culture in the Mediterranean basin, loosed first by the Greek city-states and then by the Hellenistic kingdoms, were picked up toward the end of the third century B.C. by a new power emerging from the West: Rome. The rise of the Romans marked the first appearance of a western Mediterranean people in a decisive role in determining the course of history. It is a story that deserves special consideration because the Romans were equipped with unique talents that allowed them not only to sustain the Hellenic and Hellenistic accomplishments but also to advance civilized life to new levels and to spread its fruits to heretofore primitive peoples.

1. THE ORIGINS OF ROME TO 509 B.C.

The emergence of Rome as the dominant force in the Mediterranean owed much to a combination of geographical factors and the human resources of the Italian peninsula. Aside from its strategic location in the Mediterranean basin, Italy had considerable productive farmland, important mineral deposits, and good timber. Its climate was generally mild and conducive to agricultural production.

The Italian population was formed over a long period out of several different ethnic elements whose diverse patterns of culture fragmented the peninsula into a bewildering array of political entities and institutional systems. An ancient native population developed a Neolithic farming culture perhaps as early as 4000 B.C. Beginning about 2000 B.C., Italy, like many other areas of the Mediterranean basin, experienced successive waves of Indo-European invaders. These newcomers fused with the native population, but they did bring superior technical skills and effective military and political structures, which allowed them to dominate the natives. Their language eventually prevailed over much of Italy, creating the base from which classical Latin emerged.

The still backward Italian population was decisively influenced after about 800 B.C. by the settlement in Italy of two outside peoples bringing with them the more advanced civilization of the eastern Mediterranean world. As we have already seen, the Greeks established numerous city-states in southern Italy and Sicily from whence flowed powerful cultural forces affecting the entire Italian population. Even more important were the Etruscans, probably migrants from Asia Minor, who established a series of cities along the western coast of Italy north of the Tiber River. Although each of these cities remained politically independent, they were bound together by strong economic, religious, and cultural ties that allowed them to dominate the natives. Within a short time after their initial settlement, their influence expanded, so that between 650 and 500 B.C. the Etruscans controlled western Italy from the Po Valley to Naples. During this period they transmitted a wide range of technical skills, agricultural and commercial practices, political techniques, religious ideas and usages, and art forms, which provided many Italians with their first taste of urban civilization and helped prepare them for a larger role in history (see Map 8.1).

Among the most precocious pupils of the Etruscans were some villagers living along the Tiber River about fifteen miles above its mouth. These people later created a colorful legend recounting the founding of their city by Romulus and Remus in 753 B.C. Legend aside, the evidence suggests that Rome began as a settling place for herder-farmers from an area just south of the Tiber known as Latium. Tiny villages were built on a cluster of seven hills lying on the south bank of the Tiber. But nothing about the history of these early villages seemed to suggest future greatness.

Shortly after 600 B.C., the several villages were rather suddenly transformed into a single city-state, probably as a consequence of their seizure by Etruscan warlords who imposed political unity on the villages. A single government under a king was established. Although that government may have incorporated institutions and practices from pre-Etruscan times, it was also decisively influenced by Etruscan political practices. The king was advised by a council of elders, called the Senate, composed of about three hundred men of wealth who drew their authority from their headship of families. The freemen, who constituted the bulk of the citizen body, were given a voice in political affairs by membership in two assemblies. The

Map 8.1 ITALY, 265 B.C. This map shows the main geographical regions into which Italy was divided and indicates the date at which each was brought under Roman domination. As noted in the text, Roman domination did not mean total loss of independence for the peoples of Italy. Many in central Italy became citizens, as is indicated on the map; most of the rest were allies who retained considerable rights of local control as long as they supported Rome's foreign policy and kept the peace.

most ancient was the Assembly of the *curiae,* so called after a grouping of citizens in thirty units called *curiae;* each unit was made up of a number of clans drawn together for military and religious purposes. At a later date, probably during the sixth century B.C., a military reorganization took place that organized that populace into military units called *centuries.* Assignment to a century was based on wealth. This new arrangement led to the formation of the Assembly of Centuries, made up of all citizens eligible for military service. However, both assemblies were severely limited in their power and did little more than approve the decisions of the king and the Senate. The city-state populace was divided into two distinct classes, *patricians* and *plebeians,* with the former exercising a predominant influence over society. Custom prohibited intermarriage between the two classes. Many plebeians were closely tied to patrician families as *clients,* an institution under which a noble *patron* provided legal protection and material assistance to his client, and the client in return performed various services, including following political directions.

Etruscan techniques in trade and industry were adopted by the fledgling Roman city-state, greatly strengthening its primitive economy. An alphabet was derived from Etruscan models, resulting in the rapid development of written Latin. Etruscan architecture and decoration served as models for the temples and public buildings in the burgeoning city. Primitive Latin religious practices took on more sophisticated patterns reflecting Etruscan usages. Rome was rapidly becoming the center of an advanced culture capable of threatening other communities located in Latium.

Despite their debt to the Etruscans, the Romans chafed under their domination. Shortly before 500 B.C. Etruscan power began to be contested by the dependent subjects everywhere in western Italy, while Greeks and Carthaginians vied with Etruscan forces in the larger setting of the western Mediterranean. The challenge was too much for the Etruscans, whose influence in Italy declined rapidly after 500 B.C. In Rome the patricians took the lead in a revolution that dethroned the Etruscan king and established in his place two *consuls* elected annually from patrician ranks to wield the *imperium,* that is, the highest executive authority

of the state. This revolution of 509 B.C. marked the beginning of the Roman Republic, an episode long celebrated by the Romans as the greatest event in their history.

2. ROMAN EXPANSION: THE CONQUEST OF ITALY, 509–265 B.C.

The dominant theme of the first two and one-half centuries of the history of the Roman Republic was Rome's success in establishing dominance over the Italian peninsula (see Map 8.1). Given the fact that in 509 B.C. Rome was only a tiny city-state lost among many other political entities, the Roman victories in themselves represented a remarkable feat. In a larger sense, Roman success created the human and material resources that soon would permit Rome to become a world power.

Rome's expulsion of the Etruscans in 509 B.C. actually weakened the city by depriving it of the powerful support of the Etruscans. For much of the fifth century Rome's survival depended on cooperation with neighboring cities in Latium, which joined Rome to form the Latin League. This League fought a long succession of wars against the Etruscans and the tough mountain peoples trying to gain a foothold in the rich agricultural lands of Latium and Campania. The defensive effort of the League was jeopardized by a Celtic people, the Gauls, who poured into the Po Valley from north of the Alps from whence they raided central Italy; in 390 B.C. they captured and sacked Rome. In the course of their recovery from these attacks, the Romans began to assert pressure on their allies in Latium. Their threat bred fear among the members of the Latin League and caused several of them to rise against Rome in 340 B.C. The "rebels" were subdued within two years, and the League was dissolved, leaving Rome in control of Latium.

From this base, the Romans proceeded to expand their sphere of influence. Between 326 and 290 B.C. they subdued the Samnites, a formidable mountain people living south and east of Rome, who provoked the Romans by challenging them for control of Campania. While engaged in the bitter Samnite Wars, the Romans were attacked from the north by Gauls, Etruscans, and other mountain peoples from north central Italy, but these attacks were thrown back and Roman dominance was gradually established over most of northern Italy lying south of the Po Valley. Hardly had the Samnite Wars ended when Rome was drawn into the affairs of the Greek city-states of southern Italy, chiefly to arbitrate their quarrels. Despite assistance from military adventurers from "old" Greece, the badly divided Italian-Greek city-states could not hold off the Romans. By 265 B.C. Rome had established mastery over all Italy south of the Po Valley and had become a world power— although as yet unproved.

Many forces combined to explain Rome's triumph. The Romans themselves constantly retold the stories of these wars as proof of their superior civic virtues and divine favor. Beneath the legends they created around these struggles there is a core of truth: In these wars the Roman citizens demonstrated bravery, persistence, and self-sacrifice. However, other, more tangible factors played a decisive part in Roman success.

First, the Romans developed a superior military organization. Very early in its history, Rome began to develop a citizen army that required military service of most of the city's population at each soldier's own expense. The effectiveness of this army was greatly enhanced by the development of the *legion* as the basic military formation. The legion was essentially a massed formation of well-armed infantry soldiers, not unlike the Greek phalanx. During the long wars against mountain peoples, the legion formation was modified to create within it small subunits capable of independent action. This modification increased the flexibility of the legion without sacrificing its basic unity and made it a fighting unit that most of Rome's Italian foes were unable to withstand.

A second and even more important factor contributing to Rome's victory in Italy was the innovative policy devised for the treatment of conquered peoples. In its essence this system encouraged conquered people to identify their well-being with Roman success. Rome achieved this end by developing a flexible definition of "belonging" in Rome's spreading network of power. To some conquered peoples, especially those in Latium, Rome extended full rights of citizenship.

The residents of other conquered cities were made what the Romans called "citizens without vote"; these people could not participate in the Roman political process, but they were permitted to trade in Rome and to intermarry with Romans. These cities continued to govern themselves in most matters except foreign affairs, but their half citizens owed to the Roman state the same financial and military obligations as did Roman citizens. Still other communities were made "allies" (*socii*) of Rome, each signing a formal treaty that left it considerable independence in local affairs and imposed on its members the obligation to provide military contingents to serve in Rome's wars. Implicit in these arrangements was the possibility that partial citizenship and ally status would eventually result in full citizenship, especially for those who became Romanized. In many communities that were granted powers of local self-government the Romans gave strong support to continued rule by entrenched aristocracies who found it in their best interests to support Rome. Seeking to provide centers from which conquered territory could be defended, the Romans planted numerous colonies of Roman citizens at various places in Italy. Also, individual Romans were given grants of land upon which they settled at different places in Italy. The presence of Roman colonists and individual settlers became an important factor in the Romanization of Italy. This complex set of arrangements, contrasting so sharply with the way in which other conquerors treated their victims, meant that by 265 B.C. Rome ruled over a loose confederation of Italians, most of whom enjoyed a considerable degree of independence, but all of whom were tied to Rome by virtue of an obligation to serve in its armies, by the hope of achieving full citizenship, and by increasing identification with Roman culture in all its facets. From the Roman point of view this system provided a pool of military resources that ensured Rome's security. But it should be noted that the only way Rome could tap that resource was to engage in war; its Italian subjects paid no tribute. Perhaps this situation served as a major factor promoting imperialism later in Rome's history.

A third element contributing to the conquest of Italy was Rome's ability to adjust its internal political and social structure in a way that promoted allegiance and loyalty among its citizens. When the republic was established in 509 B.C., power fell into the hands of a narrow circle of patricians whose authority rested on birth, wealth, and control of clients. These patricians completely controlled the elective offices, the Senate, and the citizen assemblies. During the next two and a half centuries there ensued what is called the "struggle of the orders." On one side stood the patricians, doggedly determined to maintain their monopoly on power and their exclusive social position. Challenging them were the plebeians, who hardly constituted a homogeneous "class." Some were affluent and ambitious, eager for a share in making political decisions. Most were poor, humble farmers and artisans concerned chiefly with escaping the economic oppression of the patricians and finding more land.

As the struggle of the orders progressed, the patricians grudgingly conceded to the plebeians a larger share in directing the Roman state and took steps to alleviate the most serious economic and social problems facing Rome. Such concessions were often made at moments of crisis created by plebeian leaders; on occasion the plebeians even seceded from the state until their demands were met. Perhaps the ultimate fear of the ruling patricians was that the plebeian soldiers would refuse to serve the state in the wars marking first Rome's struggle for survival and then the conquest of Italy. Whatever the motives and however bitter the struggle, the significant fact was that the dominant patricians did give sufficient ground to prevent civil strife and to avoid alienation of any major segment of the citizen body. As early as 494 B.C., the plebeians gained the right to elect special plebeian officials, called *tribunes*, who were given the power to veto any act of the regularly elected officials that threatened plebeian interests. A new plebeian assembly, called originally the Council of the Plebs and then later the Assembly of Tribes, was instituted to provide a forum where the plebeians could indicate their will to the tribunes. In 450 B.C. plebeian pressure resulted in the famous Twelve Tables, a written codification of ancient legal customs that protected citizens from the arbitrary decisions of patrician judges. A succession of laws gave protection to debtors, permitted marriage between patricians and plebeians, limited

patrician monopoly on the use of public lands, and provided land grants to poor plebeians. One by one the major elective offices were opened to plebeians; particularly important was a law of 367 B.C. that required that one consul be a plebeian, for election to the consulship automatically qualified a Roman citizen for membership in the Senate. Finally, in 287 B.C. the enactments of the Assembly of Tribes were recognized as the ultimate law binding on the entire state, a concession that gave the citizen body final authority.

Viewed from one perspective, the final outcome of the struggle of the orders was the creation of a constitution for the republic that placed the control of the state in the hands of its citizenry— the Roman Senate and the people, as the Romans put it. By 265 B.C. the citizen body theoretically had the final power to decide public policy. They exercised that power through participation in the various assemblies noted above; of these the Assembly of Tribes was the chief instrument for the binding expression of popular will. Aside from the power to make the final laws, the citizens had the power to elect the various magistrates who executed the decisions of the citizens enacted in the assemblies. The Roman executive system was collegiate in form. With minor exceptions, every administrative function was carried out by a board of at least two members of equal rank, each of whom had the power to veto the acts of his colleagues, a system that both constrained rash action by elected officials and led to intricate bargaining in order to achieve any results. The highest executive authority in the state—the *imperium*—was exercised by two consuls charged with the joint management of all civil and military affairs. Next below them were the *praetors*, elected primarily to administer justice but under special circumstances capable of exercising the *imperium*. In time other administrative offices with specialized functions were created to assist in running the increasingly complicated affairs of the expanding republic. Most elective officials were elected for one-year terms. An important exception was the *censor*, chosen every five years to classify the citizens for military service and to judge the moral fitness of citizens for public functions, particularly for membership in the Senate. In times of grave crisis, a *dictator* could be elected for a term of six months with unlimited power to run the state. By law any citizen was eligible for election to these offices, but since there was no pay for service and since electioneering was expensive, few men of humble means aspired to high office and even fewer gained it.

Especially potent in the republican system of government was the Senate, a body of about three hundred men who served for life. Service as consul or praetor automatically qualified a citizen for membership in the Senate, ensuring that it was made up of those with political experience but also that its membership was dominated by the wealthy and the socially prominent. Theoretically, the Senate was an advisory body, counseling the magistrates and the assemblies in making decisions that best served the interests of the state. In fact, its decisions were almost invariably accepted by the assemblies and the magistrates because of the prestige and experience of the senators and because of the influence they asserted on the political process through their numerous clients.

From another perspective the struggle of the orders had resulted in anything but a democratic constitution. During its long course a series of pragmatic compromises had been fashioned that permitted a small circle of wealthy landowners, descendants of a few ancient families, to maintain control of public life in Rome. The members of this circle were convinced that right order in society depended on their collective political wisdom, and thus they acted consciously to control the machinery of government; involvement in the governance of Rome was their career. From the ranks of this circle came most of the elected magistrates, who passed from elected office into the Senate. That body, with its extensive role in decision making, was the bastion of aristocratic control. The power wielders worked as a group to manage the election process and to control the assemblies. Especially effective in achieving these ends was their ability to maintain and to manage their plebeian clients whose support was usually forthcoming in return for public policies that provided economic concessions and protection from oppression under the law. The chief threat to the political power of the patrician families came from enterprising, increasingly wealthy plebeians who sought a share in power. The patricians met this challenge by absorbing these "new men" into their circle, chiefly by opening public offices and Senate membership to them and by linking them to noble families through marriage. This process tended to shift the basis for political power from kinship to wealth, but it in no way weakened control over political life by a small circle of wealthy families, which the Romans increasingly called the *nobiles*, the ruling nobility (see Figure 8.1). By 265 B.C. most Romans were content to entrust the destiny of the city to these *nobiles*. That trust was based on a deep-seated respect in the Roman citizen body for traditional ways of doing things, on a sense that the leadership of the *nobiles* had been effective in enhancing Rome's power and wealth, and on the assurance that the citizens had the means to curb abuses of power. By 265 B.C. this oligarchic system was so powerfully entrenched and so widely accepted that it seemed to many Romans that the ideal form of government had been fashioned. Perhaps the only issues for the future were whether the ruling *nobiles* could remain united in their collective exercise of power and whether they would remain sensitive and responsive to the needs of the citizen body as a whole.

3. OVERSEAS EXPANSION: THE PUNIC WARS, 264–201 B.C.

By 265 B.C. Rome had completed the unification of Italy and had put in place a system of government that seemed effective. Perhaps without yet knowing it, Rome had become a major power because of these developments. During the next century and a half, Roman history was shaped by an expanding involvement in the complex affairs of the entire Mediterranean world, which resulted in a series of victories that made the Romans the rulers of a large empire (see Map 8.2).

Rome's first encounter with a major Mediterranean power was with Carthage. Originally a Phoenician colony, Carthage had established its independence about 800 B.C. In the succeeding centuries, the Carthaginians had built a thriving commercial empire based on colonies located at strategic places around the western Mediterranean. During much of this period, their main ri-

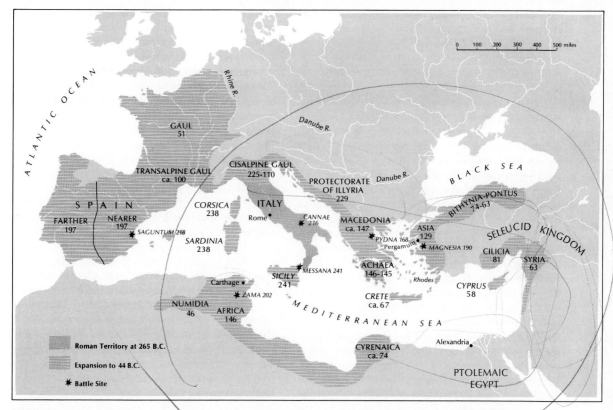

Map 8.2 **THE ROMAN EMPIRE, 265–44 B.C.** As this map shows, Rome's expansion around the Mediterranean came a bit at a time. By the beginning of the second century B.C. the Romans had established their supremacy in the western Mediterranean, chiefly as a consequence of territory annexed following the Punic Wars. Between about 200 and 125 B.C., the Romans established dominance over Macedonia, Greece, and the west coast of Asia Minor. With that power base it was only a matter of time until further expansion occurred both in the East and in the West. The circumstances surrounding Rome's expansion after 133 B.C. will be discussed in later chapters.

vals for commercial supremacy were the Greek city-states of Sicily and southern Italy. Carthaginian relationships with Rome during this period were generally friendly. Eventually their interests clashed over control of Sicily. In 265 B.C., the Carthaginians, who controlled western Sicily, took steps to protect the Greek city-state of Messana against the aggression of another Greek city-state, Syracuse. After some hesitation, the Romans decided to intervene, perhaps persuaded by fears that Carthaginian control of Messana would result in intervention by a major power in the affairs of

Rome's recently conquered Greek allies in southern Italy. Prospects of booty made the choice easier. Rome's decision meant war with Carthage.

The First Punic War (264–241 B.C.) was a struggle for Sicily. The Romans soon realized that they would need a navy to dislodge the Carthaginians from their seaport strongholds. With great resolve and help from their Greek allies, they soon achieved that end. There then ensued a long series of engagements for control of the waters around Sicily. Although the fledgling Roman navy suffered several defeats, the Romans persevered until

Carthage sued for peace in 241 B.C. By the treaty ending the war, Rome gained Sicily and a sizeable monetary payment to cover war expenses. With the exception of a few Greek city-states given special treatment, Sicily was organized as Rome's first tribute-paying overseas province.

But the issue between the two powers was far from settled. In the years following the peace of 241 B.C., the Carthaginians turned their attention to rebuilding their strength, seriously threatened by the loss of Sicily and the Roman challenge to their sea power. Under the leadership of Hamilcar Barca and his son, Hannibal, Carthage undertook to create an enlarged land empire in Spain as a new base for its power. Hamilcar successfully subdued the native Spanish population, recruited and trained a potent army of Spaniards, and collected a huge war chest derived from Spain's rich mines. The Romans were much too involved in other matters to pay attention to Carthage's recovery: organizing Corsica and Sardinia, treacherously seized from Carthage; extending Roman control into the Po Valley; coping with plebeian agitation for fairer distribution of public land; and curbing piracy in the Adriatic Sea. Only gradually did the Romans turn their attention to the rising power of Carthage in Spain. Their efforts to intervene there soon led to a new war, provoked in 218 B.C. by Hannibal's attack on a Spanish city that Rome claimed as an ally.

The Second Punic War (218–201 B.C.) was certainly Rome's sternest military test, due in large part to the genius of Hannibal. The initial Roman war plan anticipated sending armies to Spain and Africa to destroy the Carthaginian power bases. But Hannibal upset that plan by a boldly conceived plan of his own. His strategy centered on bringing a major military force into Italy in order to deprive Rome of the manpower provided by its Italian allies, whom Hannibal presumed would be glad to rid themselves of the Roman yoke. With characteristic daring he surprised the Romans by leading his army on a thousand-mile march from Spain across southern Gaul and the Alps into northern Italy, where he was welcomed by the Gauls, long enemies of Rome and ready to provide troops to assist Hannibal. On three different occasions between 218 and 216 B.C. the Romans challenged him with large armies, only to be crushed

each time. The last and the most disastrous of these battles, at Cannae, convinced the Romans that they could not match Hannibal in open battle. They adopted a policy of harassing his army, otherwise leaving him free to do as he pleased. Until 203 B.C.—a total of fifteen years—Hannibal maintained an army in Italy, spreading destruction up and down the peninsula; this was a remarkable feat in view of the fact that he received almost no reinforcements or supplies from Carthage or Spain. But he failed to achieve what he counted on to defeat Rome: He never persuaded a decisive number of Rome's Italian allies to desert.

While holding Hannibal at bay in Italy, Rome resolutely undertook the long struggle to crush Carthage. The Romans fought on many fronts and actually won the war outside Italy. Large armies sent to Spain slowly crushed Carthaginian power and cut off Hannibal's reinforcements. Another Roman force was dispatched to Sicily to choke off a rebellion of Greek city-states led by Syracuse in support of Carthage. Roman naval forces patrolled the western Mediterranean and the Adriatic, preventing Hannibal from getting help from Carthage or from its chief ally, the kingdom of Macedon. The Romans encouraged African peoples to attack Carthaginian territories. Rome's counteroffensive culminated in 205 B.C., when a large army under Scipio Africanus was sent to Africa. In him, Rome had found a military talent equal to that of Hannibal. Once in Africa, Scipio attacked Carthage, and Hannibal was recalled from Italy in 203 B.C. to save the city. But even he could no longer stem the tide: He met Scipio in a battle in 202 B.C. at Zama and suffered a complete defeat.

After Zama, the Carthaginians sued for peace. They were forced to surrender Spain to Rome, to destroy their navy, to accept a heavy fine to be paid over the next fifty years, and to agree never again to wage war outside Africa and within Africa only with Rome's permission. Part of Carthage's African territory was turned over to Numidia, a state Rome hoped would balance Carthaginian power in Africa. The use of such client kingdoms as a means of protecting its interests on distant frontiers soon became a regular part of Rome's imperial strategy. This settlement reduced Carthage to a minor power; victorious Rome was dominant in the western Mediterranean.

4. OVERSEAS EXPANSION: THE EASTERN MEDITERRANEAN, 200–133 B.C.

Rome's victory over Carthage was but a prelude to further successful involvement in affairs outside Italy, especially in the turbulent world of the eastern Mediterranean (see Map 8.2). Roman leaders stoutly protested that Rome's engagement there was a "just" cause undertaken to ensure Rome's safety and to protect Roman allies. However, other factors were at work to generate an expansionist, imperialistic policy. The Romans seem to have been plagued by a genuine fear of outsiders, born perhaps from an understandable ignorance about affairs in the East. As we shall see later, aristocratic Roman society was increasingly enchanted by Greek culture, causing many to feel deeply the need to protect it. The Punic Wars had demonstrated clearly that leadership in victorious wars was assurance of fame and power, as illustrated by the career of the immensely popular Scipio Africanus. Equally obvious to all Romans was the fact that successful warfare brought vast riches to Rome in the form of indemnities, tribute, and booty. Developments in the East encouraged many there to turn to "the rising cloud in the West" for help. By 200 B.C., the uneasy balance of power that had existed in the Hellenistic world since the partition of Alexander's empire in the early third century was breaking down. Ptolemaic Egypt grew increasingly weak. Aggressive leaders, such as Philip V of Macedon and Antiochus III of the Seleucid Empire, sought to capitalize on the progressively unstable situation by establishing control not only over Egypt but also over the other independent kingdoms and city-states of the East. To many in the East Rome's intervention seemed the only hope for safety against those threatening the status quo.

Rome's first involvement in the East came during the trying times of the Punic Wars. In an effort to deny the Carthaginians access to the Adriatic Sea, the Romans took steps that challenged the interests of the Illyrians, who controlled the eastern Adriatic coast. Led by an able and ambitious queen, Teuta, the Illyrians resisted and forced Rome to establish a protectorate over the coastal areas. A little later, a new threat arose when Philip V of Macedon formed an alliance with Carthage during the Second Punic War. As a counterbalance, Rome entered into alliances of friendship with Greek cities, especially the Aetolian League. These ventures increased Roman awareness of possible dangers from the East and led to more serious involvement. In 201 B.C. Pergamum, Rhodes, and several Greek city-states appealed to Rome for help against what they argued was Philip V's threat to their freedom. Although the war-weary Roman populace opposed involvement, the ruling oligarchy, led by the pro-Greek Scipio Africanus, declared war on Philip V in 200 B.C. and within three years defeated his forces. He was required to refrain from further involvement in Greek affairs. Amid considerable fanfare and with understandable praise from the Greeks, the Romans reaffirmed the autonomy of each Greek city-state, who henceforth would be Roman allies. The "liberators" of Greece then withdrew without annexing any territory or demanding any tribute.

Peace in the East was brief. In 192 B.C. Antiochus III invaded the Greek peninsula at the urging of the Aetolian League, the members of which were angry at their Roman allies for not rewarding them sufficiently for their assistance in the recent war against Philip V. Rome again sent its armies east, moved in part by the fact that Hannibal was serving as military adviser to the Seleucid army. The Roman legions drove Antiochus out of Greece and in 189 B.C. inflicted a crushing defeat on him at the battle of Magnesia in Asia Minor. He was required to keep out of Asia Minor, his fleet was destroyed, and a staggering indemnity was imposed. Rome turned over large areas of Asia Minor to Pergamum and Rhodes and sanctioned them as Roman-backed peacekeepers. Most of the Greek city-states were restored to independence, although those who had aided Antiochus were fined and forced to surrender some territory to Greek city-states who had remained loyal to Rome. Again the victors annexed no lands.

Despite what the Romans considered to be a policy to ensure peace in the East, the results were otherwise. The reduction of Macedon and the Seleucid state to secondary importance finally destroyed the balance of power in the East and opened the way for rivalry, intrigue, and strife among the petty states of the area. Even the Greeks, whom the Romans had "saved," proved treacherous and unreliable. As the chaos mounted, so did the appeals to Rome for intervention. To the ever-increasing attractiveness of imperialistic ventures was now added growing frustration on the part of the Romans. Slowly they were pushed toward a more drastic solution: direct Roman rule in the East.

Evidence of this new policy came in 171–167 B.C., when Macedonian efforts to court favor among the Greek city-states once again provoked the Romans to declare war on Macedon. Rome easily crushed the Macedonians and their allies. In the ensuing settlements, the Macedonian monarchy was abolished and the kingdom was divided into four weak states upon each of which was imposed a republican form of government. A few years later a minor disturbance in Macedon led the Romans to annex the entire territory as a tribute-paying province under a Roman governor. Persistent intrigue and disturbances among the Greek city-states resulted in increasingly stern Roman reprisals, culminating in 146 B.C. with the savage destruction of Corinth as a example to all Greeks. By that date Rome had forced pro-Roman governments on most Greek city-states. Now they charged the governor of Macedon to supervise the affairs of the Greek city-states, thus ending their freedom. Rome's allies in Asia Minor proved equally unreliable and troublesome. Such harsh measures had to be taken against them that the most important of them, Pergamum and Rhodes, were practically ruined. Finally, in 133 B.C., the last king of Pergamum willed his weakened kingdom to the Romans, who accepted it as a province. Once established in Asia, rich prizes tempted Roman imperialists: Ptolemaic Egypt and the Seleucid Empire, both too weak to offer effective resistance to the Romans.

While concentrating its attention chiefly on the East between 200 and 133 B.C., Rome continued to solidify its power in the West. The occupation of Spain and its organization into two provinces required a long and testing struggle against native resistance. The area of northern Italy between the Alps and the Apennines, called Cisalpine Gaul, was organized into a province. And the Romans finally settled scores with their ancient enemy, Carthage. Although no longer a serious threat, fear of Carthage continued to haunt Rome and prompt actions to humiliate what was now a minor state. The final step occurred in 149 B.C., when Rome declared war on Carthage on the pretext that the Carthaginians had violated the terms of the treaty ending the Second Punic War; Carthage's crime was taking up arms to protect itself against incessant harassment by the kingdom of Numidia, a North African ally of Rome. After a heroic defense Carthage was captured and destroyed in 146 B.C., and its territory was annexed as a Roman province. The destruction of Carthage was a fitting symbol of Rome's position in the Mediterranean world as the second century drew to a close. With provinces on three continents and with unchallenged military forces, the city-state on the Tiber could speak of the Mediterranean as "our sea." The fate of civilization was now in Roman hands.

SUGGESTED READING

Overview of Roman History

Karl Christ, *The Romans: An Introduction to Their History and Civilization,* trans. Christopher Holme (1984). A fine survey.

Early Italy

Jorgen C. Meyer, *Pre-Republican Rome: An Analysis of the Cultural and Chronological Relations, 1000–500 B.C.* (1983). Relying on archaeological evidence, this challenging work throws important light on the origins of Rome.

R. M. Ogilivie, *Early Rome and the Etruscans* (1976).

Michael Grant, *The Etruscans* (1980).

Mauro Cristofani, *The Etruscans: A New Investigation* (1979).

Maja Sprenger, *The Etruscans: Their History, Art, and Architecture* (1983).

Any of the above works will provide a clear picture of Etruscan society and its impact on Rome.

The Republic to 265 B.C.

H. H. Scullard, *History of the Roman World from 753 B.C. to 146 B.C.*, 3rd ed. (1961). A detailed account.

Jaques Heurgon, *The Rise of Rome to 264 B.C.*, trans. James Willis (1973). Traces Rome's development in the total setting of the western Mediterranean world.

Michael Crawford, *The Roman Republic* (1978). A challenging account of political developments with interesting interpretations.

R. Develin, *The Practice of Politics at Rome, 366–167 B.C.* (1985). A detailed study of how the early republican government worked.

E. T. Salmon, *The Making of Roman Italy* (1982). Tells how Rome forged a divided Italy into a single community.

R. M. Errington, *The Dawn of Empire: Rome's Rise to World Power* (1972).

William V. Harris, *War and Imperialism in Republican Roman, 327–70 B.C.* (1979).

These two titles deal in detail with the forces that led to Roman expansion and with its effects on Roman society.

Erich S. Gruen, *The Hellenistic World and the Coming of Rome,* 2 vols. (1984). A detailed study explaining how and why the Hellenistic world came under Roman sway; a landmark study for understanding Roman imperialism.

B. H. Warmington, *Carthage,* 2nd rev. ed. (1969). A fine treatment of the history and civilization of Rome's greatest foe.

Brian Caven, *The Punic Wars* (1980). An excellent treatment of the military history of the Punic Wars.

Biographies

Ernle Bradford, *Hannibal* (1981).

H. H. Scullard, *Scipio Africanus: Soldier and Politician* (1970).

CHAPTER 9

The Failure of the Roman Republic, 133–31 B.C.

FIGURE 9.1 A Roman Warship Warships such as the one shown in this relief, created to celebrate Octavian's victory over Antony and Cleopatra at Actium in 31 B.C., played a major role in establishing Roman dominance over the Mediterranean world during the era of the republic. Control over fleets of such ships and the soldiers they carried was also a prime factor in the rise of the military strong men—such as Sulla, Pompey, Julius Caesar, and Octavian—to positions that allowed them to end the republic. (Alinari/Art Resource)

Rome's rise to dominance in the Mediterranean world during the period 265–133 B.C. had understandably generated confidence among the Roman citizenry, especially the ruling oligarchy, that the political and social system of the republic was not only successful but also capable of meeting any situation. Developments after 133 B.C. proved that such confidence was misplaced. Between 133 and 31 B.C. a series of crises tested that system beyond its capabilities and ultimately left the traditional political system in ruins.

1. THE BURDENS OF A WORLD POWER

At the root of the crises that afflicted Rome after 133 B.C. were complex problems that were in large part a result of Rome's expansion from a small city-state to a large empire. Many of them were neglected during the era of expansion, but eventually they surfaced to demand political solutions. They need to be kept in mind if one is to understand the history of the last century of the republic.

First, Rome's conquests created a long frontier to defend and a large, diverse subject population to control. While a military force composed of Roman citizens and Italian allies had conquered this vast empire, the problem of establishing a military system to defend and maintain the empire had not been faced (see Map 8.2 for Rome's expansion during the last century of the republic).

Second, there was the problem of how the conquered subjects would be governed. In contrast with the enlightened policy originally applied to the Italian population, the Romans increasingly viewed conquered non-Italians as subjects to be exploited. Annexed territories were organized into provinces. Control over each province was entrusted to a governor invested with absolute military and civil power; little attention was given to holding these governors accountable. The residents of each province were subject to heavy tribute, the collection of which was entrusted to tax farmers (called *publicans*) who paid the Roman government what it expected from each province and then extorted all they could from the provin-

cials, often in collusion with the governors. This abusive system disrupted order among the provincials and bred discontent, resistance, and hatred.

Third, Rome's Italian allies, whose military service played a key role in Rome's conquests, were increasingly disregarded. Not only did they benefit little from the fruits of conquest, but also the prospect of citizenship implicit in Rome's earlier arrangements grew increasingly remote. As a consequence, the allies became restless and rebellious.

Fourth, Rome's economy underwent significant transformations during the third and second centuries. Rome was greatly enriched by the influx of wealth exacted from conquered peoples. Most of that wealth fell into the hands of a small segment of the population. The beneficiaries not only developed a taste for luxurious living but also sought new opportunities for investment. Although trade and manufacturing investments absorbed some of this wealth, rich aristocrats preferred investment in land and money lending. A basic transformation of the agricultural system provided ample opportunity. The traditional Italian agricultural system, based on the small, independent farm tilled by a freeholder and his family and devoted to cereal crops, was undergoing major changes. Competition from cheaper grain imported as tribute from more productive provinces eroded this system. Many small farms were ruined as a result of the devastation caused by Hannibal's wars in Italy and of the long absence of their owners in military service in far-off places. Often these citizen-soldiers borrowed to save their land, only to find themselves dispossessed for failure to repay their loans. Enterprising Romans with capital began to create large estates (called *latifundia*) by buying or seizing the land of impoverished small farmers and by using political influence to receive allotments of public land. These new agricultural units concentrated on the production of cash crops such as grapes, olives, and livestock. Increasingly the labor supply on the *latifundia* was provided by slaves, most of whom were victims of Rome's wars of conquest, or by former independent farmers forced to accept status as tenant farmer. The real victims of this transformation of agricultural life were Roman citizens and Roman allies whose loyal service as soldiers had won Rome's empire.

These fundamental economic changes caused a fifth set of problems of a social nature. Down to mid–third century B.C. the Roman social order had been relatively simple. Atop the social structure stood a relatively small circle of nobles of both patrician and plebeian origin whose authority was based on family connections, control of political life, and landed wealth. Below them was the rest of the citizen body, chiefly freeholding farmers whose economic and social status made them equals. But changing times slowly made that simple order more complex and brought increasing social tensions. As already noted, the aristocrats became richer; their wealth allowed a style of life that distanced them from the rest of the population. Although these *nobiles* were firmly entrenched at the top of society, they were increasingly challenged by a new group that came to be known as *equites.* The members of this group were wealthy entrepreneurs who grew rich as military suppliers, organizers of large-scale trading ventures, building contractors, bankers, and provincial tax collectors. Their economic interests were intimately linked to public policies with respect to war, provincial administration, public works, and taxes. Consequently, the *equites* were increasingly anxious for a share in political power and for social recognition. The continuing impoverishment of small farmers led to social distinctions within that group. Many were forced to become tenants or hired laborers, with a consequent lowering of their social status. Others in growing numbers left their farms for the cities, especially Rome, to seek livelihood as artisans, shopkeepers, and laborers; their new occupations changed their economic and social needs and concerns. Many citizens who flocked to Rome became members of what the Romans called the proletariat, a rootless and restless population endowed with rights of citizenship but victims of an unstable economic life and an uncertain social status. This volatile "mob," its members ever more dependent on the state or upon rich patrons for their livelihood, offered a tantalizing power base for ambitious political leaders willing to utilize public power to support their interests. At the bottom of the social scale was an expanding slave population; its presence sharp-

ened the concerns of economically and socially depressed freemen whose condition seemed little better than that of slaves. The stresses building up in this increasingly complex social structure had the potential for disrupting the internal order in Roman society.

Finally, Rome's entire citizen body was beginning to feel the unsettling impact of new ideological factors impinging on their lives. Large segments of aristocratic society were deeply affected by concepts and values derived from their adoption of Hellenistic culture and by the style of life their new wealth permitted. Many Romans were intrigued by the emotional, individualistic mystery religions from the East. Incessant military involvement engendered a disturbing tolerance for violence and arrogance. These currents made the Roman populace less willing to abide by traditional values and moral standards associated with the simpler, more rustic world of the early republic.

This array of problems required changes that could only be brought about by innovative political action. By 133 B.C. such decisions were in the hands of the narrow oligarchy, which had established unchallenged control over political life during the long and difficult era of expansion. This dominant group constituted a closed caste that controlled not only access to public office but also the processes by which decisions were made. Most citizens, little understanding the complicated issues of war and diplomacy and duly impressed with the success that came to Rome under the direction of the *nobiles,* willingly allowed the ruling oligarchy to decide Rome's fate. By 133 B.C. the nobles had become so accustomed to unquestioned authority that they assumed it to be their right to direct the state as they saw fit. Their conduct of public affairs between 265 and 133 B.C. suggested little awareness of the problems generated by the expansion they had so successfully managed. While this oligarchic, conservative regime seemed firmly entrenched in 133 B.C., there were ominous signs that the traditional consensus within the ranks of the *nobiles* was in danger of dissolving. Increasingly ambitious members of that group sought wealth, political and military honor, and cultural distinction that would exalt them over their aristocratic peers. Although the ruling oligarchy sought to curb such tendencies, there remained the danger that rivalries among the *nobiles* would become another disruptive force.

Thus, by 133 B.C. a dangerous situation existed. A political order shaped to allow the citizen body of a small city-state to decide its fate had fallen into the hands of a narrow, self-serving ruling caste increasingly divided within its own ranks. That government was faced with massive problems posed by the burdens of ruling a growing empire. Its inability to adjust to the changing situation produced a political upheaval that ultimately destroyed the Roman Republic.

2. ATTEMPTED REFORMS AND FACTIONAL STRUGGLES, 133–79 B.C.

The ordeal of the republic opened with a succession of political struggles that emerged from an effort to institute reforms aimed at resolving some of the most critical problems facing Rome. That effort quickly took the form of a struggle between two factions of the nobility over how the political process should work in reaching decisions about critical issues. On one side was a group known as the *optimates* (the best), representing the established ruling oligarchy, whose members believed that decision making should remain where it had always been—in the hands of the Senate and the elected magistrates drawn from the *nobiles,* a group of approximately two thousand citizens from a narrow circle of powerful families. Opposed was a faction known as the *populares* (the "people") who sought to involve a broader range of the citizen body in political decisions, utilizing for that purpose the ancient political tools of the "people"—the tribunes and the Assembly of Tribes. The *populares* were usually led by men of noble origin, often motivated by a mixture of genuine concern for Rome and ambitions to advance their careers. They sought to achieve these ends by appealing to the plebeian citizens, especially those living in Rome, and the *equites* to use their votes to shape political decisions.

The initial engagement in the struggle for reform and power occurred between 133 and 121 B.C. The champions of the *populares* were the brothers Tiberius and Gaius Gracchus. Aristo-

cratic, well educated, and ambitious, the Gracchi were deeply troubled by the threat posed to Rome's military resources by the declining numbers of citizen farmers and the increasing numbers of urban proletariat, trends that reduced the number of citizens who could afford to perform military service. Elected tribune for 133 B.C., Tiberius proposed a land law aimed at redressing this situation. The law proposed to enforce an older law limiting the amount of public land any citizen could hold. Land recovered by the application of this law would be redistributed to landless citizens. Although the law had some support in the Senate, it threatened the wealth of many *nobiles* who over many generations had gained control of most public lands. In order to pass his proposal, Tiberius resorted to political moves that were not unconstitutional but that ran counter to the way in which decisions were customarily made. He used his power as tribune to put the land law before the Assembly of Tribes; that body approved the measure without senatorial approval and despite the veto of another tribune who was rewarded for his action by being voted out of office. When Tiberius tried to apply his land law, the Senate attempted to thwart him by withholding funding. Tiberius responded by threatening to divert revenues from the provinces for this purpose, a measure that challenged the Senate's traditional control over public finances and foreign affairs. Finally, Tiberius sought reelection as tribune in order to complete his reform. Since such reelection ran contrary to the custom that limited the term of elected offices to one year, the Senate raised the charge that Tiberius was seeking to become a dictator. This inflammatory accusation led to violence and the murder of Tiberius at the hands of those calling themselves *optimates*. After Tiberius' death the application of his land law went forward, suggesting that the substance of the law was not the real issue. Instead, at the heart of the struggle was the threat to the Senate's monopoly on political power posed by Tiberius' political tactics, especially his appeal to the "people" for support.

A decade after Tiberius' death the reform issue was raised again by his brother Gaius. Elected tribune for 122 B.C., Gaius put forward a much more comprehensive program than that of Tiberius. He persuaded the Assembly of Tribes to pass new land laws, to provide cheap grain at public expense for Rome's populace, to establish overseas colonies for the resettlement of impoverished Romans, to extend political privileges to the Italian allies, and to provide to the *equites* greater control over provincial tax collection and over the juries that tried cases involving extortion in provincial administration. These measures, collectively aimed at creating broad *populares* support for Gaius, aroused bitter opposition from the *optimates* and ultimately led to violence they provoked that took the lives of Gaius and three thousand of his followers.

Although the death of Gaius Gracchus left the *populares* leaderless for more than a decade, the Gracchi had formulated a broad reform program that would provide ambitious leaders in the future with a wide range of issues upon which to build popular support. A leader capable of exploiting this situation soon appeared: Marius (ca. 155–86 B.C.). A wealthy man of nonnoble origin with small prospects of a major political role, Marius took advantage of a military crisis to gain power. The occasion was a badly managed war involving Rome with Jugurtha, a claimant to the throne of Numidia, a client kingdom of Rome in North Africa. Growing impatience with the failure of Roman armies to defeat Jugurtha and charges that this clever, unscrupulous king held his own through bribery of Roman officials generated widespread unrest in Rome. Playing upon suspicions of corruption in the Senate and proclaiming his support for *populares* reforms, Marius succeeded in winning the consulship for 107 B.C. He then persuaded the Assembly of Tribes to vote him command of the army in Numidia. In recruiting troops for his campaign, Marius took a bold and fateful step. Disregarding the traditional property qualifications for military service, he enlisted large numbers of propertyless volunteers attracted by hope of rewards from their general. The first step had been taken in the creation of private armies as a political tool.

Marius quickly justified the trust placed in him by defeating Jugurtha in 105 B.C. Then he was annually reelected as consul during the years between 104 and 101 B.C. to conduct campaigns against Germanic tribes threatening northern Italy and southern Gaul. Again Marius was successful, in no small part because of his skill in professionalizing his volunteer army. While he earned fame as a general, Marius' *populares* allies asserted pressure on the Roman government to provide land allocations for his veterans. However, during his sixth term as consul for 100 B.C. Marius was maneuvered by the Senate into using some of his soldiers to curb the increasingly violent actions of his own political allies. This action ended his leadership of the *populares* cause.

The decade of the nineties was relatively quiet, perhaps because moderate elements in the Senate made efforts to respond to critical problems. However, two issues defied its efforts and provided fuel for the next crisis. One was the festering problem of the Italian allies, long discontented over Rome's failure to recognize their contribution to military conquests and increasingly impoverished by the decline of small-farm agriculture. To relieve their situation, the allies demanded full citizenship. Although Roman leaders from Gaius Gracchus onward often proposed such a step, the Romans repeatedly refused to share the rewards of citizenship with the allies. When one more such proposal was voted down in 91 B.C., the allies joined in a great rebellion, sometimes called the Social War, which threatened Rome's very existence. Sulla (138–78 B.C.), a noble who had established a reputation while serving under Marius in the war against Jugurtha, was chosen to lead the army raised to suppress the uprising. By 89 B.C. Sulla defeated the rebels, whose cause was undermined when the Romans finally granted citizenship. For his success Sulla was elected consul for 88 B.C.

While the Social War was in progress, Rome faced another threat caused by the corruption-ridden, oppressive system of provincial administration. In 89 B.C. Mithridates VI, king of Pontus in Asia Minor, played on this discontent to launch a war of liberation in Asia Minor and Greece. Faced with the threat of loss of its empire in the East, the Senate charged Sulla with leading a campaign against Mithridates. However, a faction of *populares* leaders defied the Senate to vote the command to Marius. Sulla responded by marching his army to Rome, crushing the *populares*, and securing the command by force. His actions left little doubt where real power lay.

Sulla was able to force Mithridates to return to his old kingdom and to reestablish Roman control over the eastern provinces. But he made no decisive settlement in the East; his eyes were on Rome, where developments threatening his career were unfolding. Immediately after his departure for the East, the *populares* under Marius forced their way back into power and imposed a reign of terror on the Senate. They dominated until 83 B.C., when Sulla reappeared in Italy, greatly enriched by booty seized in the East. His battle-tested soldiers routed the *populares,* whose leader had died in 86 B.C. To seal his victory, Sulla ordered the murder of thousands of citizens from all over Italy identified with the *populares* cause and the confiscation of their property, much of which was used to reward his soldiers and his political supporters.

Once in unchallenged control, Sulla had himself appointed as dictator. Intent on restoring control of the republic to the Senate, he enacted legislation that severely limited the power of the tribunes and the Assembly of Tribes to initiate legislation. The size of the Senate was doubled, many of the new seats being granted to *equites* and upper-class Italians. Steps were taken to regularize the election procedures for the magistracies, to improve the administration of justice, and to organize provincial government more efficiently—all sources of political agitation. Confident that he had restored the ancient constitution with the Senate in control, Sulla retired from public life in 79 B.C. In fact, the Senate was in power because a powerful military leader had decreed so. The long, bitter clash between *optimates* and *populares* had resolved few of Rome's basic problems; rather, the struggle created a situation that encouraged bold, ambitious individuals to seek power by exploiting those problems. The republican form of government had suffered a mortal blow.

3. THE ERA OF MILITARY STRONG MEN, 79–31 B.C.

The Senate proved itself unable to bear the burden thrust upon it by Sulla. Its failures created successive opportunities for "strong men" to control Roman political life during the half century following Sulla. Their competition for power and the methods they employed to gain it brought the republic to an end by 31 B.C.

Between 79 and 70 B.C. the Senate was faced with several serious crises: a revolt in Italy led by a disaffected consul seeking to undo Sulla's reforms; a rebellion in Spain organized by a disillusioned Roman governor who enjoyed widespread native support; a slave uprising in Italy led by a professional gladiator named Spartacus; a mounting threat from pirates to the grain supply for Rome; and a new war with Mithridates VI of Pontus. Contrary to the principles undergirding Sulla's settlement, the Senate sought to meet these crises by granting extraordinary powers to ambitious individuals in a fashion that left the Senate little opportunity to control their actions. A protegé of Sulla, Pompey (106–48 B.C.), was given command of forces to deal with the Italian revolt and then with the insurrection in Spain (see Figure 9.2). A rich financier ambitious for a political career, Crassus (ca. 115–53 B.C.), was charged with defeating Mithridates. Both were successful, and although neither was eligible for office, they were rewarded with the consulship for 70 B.C.

During their co-consulship, Pompey and Crassus negated most of Sulla's settlement; their enactments won the applause of the remnants of the *populares* and restored the opportunity for ambitious leaders to exploit popular support as a path to power. But neither Pompey nor Crassus was satisfied. Pompey was the first to move toward greater power. By manipulation he persuaded the Senate and the people to vote him two important military commands: In 67 B.C. he was granted sweeping powers to clear the Mediterranean of pirates, a task he completed in a matter of months. Then in 66 B.C. he was selected to lead an army against Mithridates VI of Pontus, who since 74 B.C. had again challenged Rome's rule in Asia Minor. Pompey quickly defeated Mithradates. He then took it upon himself to reorganize Rome's position in the East. He annexed the combined territories of Bithynia and Pontus into a new province and created another new province in Syria. To protect these provinces, he worked out a series of agreements with small kingdoms beyond Rome's new frontier, making each a client of Rome charged with protecting the frontier in return for Roman support in maintaining each king's power

FIGURE 9.2 **Pompey and Julius Caesar** These two men, Pompey (left) and Julius Caesar (right), virtually controlled the destiny of the Roman Republic and the Mediterranean world between 79 and 44 B.C. Their busts reflect the talent of Roman sculptors in portraiture. (Pompey, Culver Pictures; Julius Caesar, Alinari/Art Resource)

over his subjects. Pompey also regulated tribute collection in the East so as to greatly increase the return to the Roman government. His efforts represented a major step in solidifying provincial administration; and it won Pompey important support from Romans whose interests were involved in the East.

Pompey's success, reminiscent of Sulla's rise to power, caused constant concern in Rome and drove other ambitious politicians to maneuver to check him. A key figure in this endeavor was Crassus, who found a skilled ally in Julius Caesar (100–44 B.C.), a man of patrician origins but with family connections that linked him with Marius and the *populares* cause (see Figure 9.2). Crassus

and Caesar promoted laws to attract popular support and spent huge sums in an attempt to secure extraordinary military commands such as those held by Pompey. The Senate resisted their maneuvers, supported in its effort by Cicero (106–43 B.C.), a "new" man who clawed his way to the consulship for 63 B.C. by utilizing his skills as an orator and a lawyer. His finest hour as consul came when he earned public acclaim for foiling an alleged conspiracy by Cataline, a frustrated power seeker and sometime agent of Crassus, to overthrow the system. While Cicero shared the ambition for power with most other political leaders of his time, he disdained one-man rule in favor of a "concord of orders" that would link the talents of the old aristocracy and the *equites* into a new ruling force capable of ending senseless political conflict.

Finally, in 62 B.C. Pompey returned from the East. Contrary to expectations, his first act was to disband his army and request that the Senate reward his veterans and legalize the settlement he had made in the East. Under the leadership of intractable conservatives, the Senate chose a course that drove Pompey, Crassus, and Caesar into a political alliance. It not only refused to meet Pompey's requests but also acted to curb a major source of Crassus' wealth by restricting the activities of provincial tax farmers and to discredit Caesar by blocking his election to the consulship. Equally frustrated, the three joined in an informal secret agreement, called the First Triumvirate, designed to ensure that each obtained what he wished. Exploiting his growing popular appeal and with the support of Pompey and Crassus, Caesar won the consulship for 59 B.C. Once in office, he forced through measures that satisfied his fellow triumvirs. His reward was a five-year command to look after Roman interests on its northern frontier in Gaul and Illyria.

During the decade after 59 B.C. Rome's political destiny hinged on the actions of the triumvirs. During the first years of the decade the triumvirate held together uneasily. It was renewed in 56 B.C. with the understanding that Pompey and Crassus would be consuls for 55 B.C. and then be granted governorships of important provinces under terms that would provide them command over armies. Caesar's command in Gaul was also extended for five years. But the arrangement was increasingly shaky. Caesar proved to be a brilliant military leader, conducting a highly publicized series of campaigns that added Gaul as a Roman province and took Roman armies into Germany and Britain. Not only did these victories enhance Caesar's reputation, but they also allowed him to create a loyal, disciplined personal army totally devoted to his cause. Crassus' long search for fame came to an end in 53 B.C. when he was killed in an unsuccessful campaign against a Roman foe in the East, the Parthians. An important link between Caesar and Pompey was broken in 54 B.C. with the death of Pompey's wife, Julia, the daughter of Caesar. Caesar's growing fame fed a familiar fear in Rome—that of a victorious general returning to

impose his will. Pompey increasingly won the favor of the Senate as its protector against such an eventuality and was voted powers that made him virtual dictator. Amid heightening tension fed by fear of Caesar and by the violent actions of his agents seeking to protect his interests, Pompey and the Senate moved to ruin Caesar. As his command in Gaul approached its legal end, Caesar sought to run in absentia for the consulship for 49 B.C. so that he could remain in public office and avoid prosecution for alleged illegal acts committed during his service in Gaul. Early in 49 B.C. the Senate decreed that he must surrender his command in Gaul, and Pompey was empowered to take necessary action to protect the state. Rather than face political ruin, Caesar chose to defy the state. He led his legions across the Rubicon River separating Gaul from Italy and plunged Rome into a civil war.

Caesar quickly demonstrated his military genius in leading his seasoned veterans against the larger forces of Pompey. In a succession of campaigns in Italy, Spain, and finally Greece, he battered Pompey's forces. The defeated Pompey finally fled to Egypt, where he was murdered. Caesar used this crime against a Roman citizen as a pretext to intervene in Egypt, where a struggle for control of the crown was in progress among members of the Ptolemaic family. Caesar supported the claims of Cleopatra against her brother-husband, Ptolemy XIV. Perhaps his decision was prompted by the fact that he had become Cleopatra's lover; but more likely he hoped that by putting the young princess on the throne, he could dominate the last independent Hellenistic kingdom and tap Egypt's fabulous wealth for Rome's benefit. From Egypt Caesar continued his triumphant march through the empire—Asia, Africa, Spain—hunting down Pompey's allies and showing his own power. Finally in 45 B.C., he returned to Rome as undisputed master of the Roman world.

Although Caesar's real power rested on his loyal army, he made an effort to legalize his authority. Despite being elected consul several times, he relied chiefly on the office of dictator as the basis for his actions. He allowed the traditional elective offices to be filled, but with men willing to bend to his will. The Senate was greatly enlarged, the new places being filled with Caesar's supporters. As a consequence, that venerable institution became little more than an advisory council to the dictator. On the basis of his dictatorial power, Caesar assumed control of crucial areas of government previously dominated by the Senate: public finances, provincial administration, command over the military forces. A grateful citizenry heaped a wide range of honors on him, creating around him the aura of superiority over other citizens. In many ways Caesar's position in Rome resembled that of a Hellenistic king; indeed, some of Caesar's contemporaries insisted that it was his intention to establish a monarchy in Rome.

In using these powers, Caesar demonstrated qualities of statesmanship to match his military genius. During his brief rule over Rome, he began shaping a reform program that addressed some of the major problems plaguing Rome: reduction of the citizens dependent on the dole by resettling them in the provinces; debt regulation; curbing violence in Rome; aid to Italian farmers; improvement in provincial administration; extension of citizenship to some provincials; reorganizing local government in Italy. It is not clear, however, whether he planned to reshape the structure of the political system to meet Rome's responsibilities as ruler of the Mediterranean world. Perhaps given more time, Caesar would have faced this issue, but that was not to be. A hard core of conservatives, including such former supporters of Caesar as Cassius and Brutus, formed a conspiracy to end what they saw as a threat to the traditional order. These guardians of "right" order struck their blow for liberty on the Ides of March (March 15), 44 B.C., stabbing Caesar to death while he was attending a Senate meeting just prior to his departure for a major campaign against the Parthians.

Caesar's murder did not lead to the restoration of the old order; rather it produced a new civil war among rivals seeking to replace Caesar. Two candidates emerged as the main contenders. One was Mark Antony (ca. 83–30 B.C.), an experienced politician who had served Caesar as a military commander. The other was eighteen-year-old Octavian, a distant relative whom Caesar had adopted as his son. Faced with efforts by the Senate to eliminate them from power, Antony and Octavian, along with another supporter of Caesar named Lepidus, joined forces in 43 B.C. to form the Second Triumvirate and to force the Senate and people to grant them jointly absolute power in the state. Within a year the triumvirs brutally murdered most of the anti-Caesar senatorial forces, including Cicero, and conducted a military campaign in Greece that destroyed the armies raised by Caesar's assassins, two of whom—Cassius and Brutus—died at the decisive battle of Philippi in 42 B.C.

After 42 B.C. Antony, Octavian, and Lepidus continued to rule Rome under the powers voted them in the legislation that established the Second Triumvirate. Actually, each was making preparations to destroy the others. Antony spent most of these years in the East, seeking to strengthen Roman control there and to mount a war against the Parthians. Although he made some progress in these endeavors, his standing in the Roman world was increasingly tainted by his involvement with Cleopatra, for whom he eventually repudiated his Roman wife—none other than Octavian's sister—and by whom he had two sons. This liaison was cleverly exploited by Octavian to portray Antony as a mad traitor and the pitiful victim of a crafty eastern harlot intent on robbing Rome of its territories to advance her own power and to reward her children.

Octavian proved more adept at building a power base. Under the arrangement agreed upon by the triumvirs, he was charged with the heavy responsibilities of providing land for the veterans from the large army that had defeated the forces of Caesar's assassins, of rooting out powerful remnants of anti-Caesar forces in the West, and of coping with the official government still operating in Rome. He worked patiently to meet these challenges, doing so in a way that gave him a solid hold over Italy and the West. Along the way, he forced Lepidus to retire from the triumvirate. Gradually, Octavian came to be looked upon as the protector of Roman interests against Antony, increasingly portrayed by Octavian's clever propaganda as an enemy of Rome. By 32 B.C. Octavian felt strong enough to refuse to rule jointly with Antony and declared war on Cleopatra. The decisive engagement between the huge armies and navies of the protagonists was fought in 31 B.C. at Actium in Greece (see Figure 9.1). Octavian's forces won an easy victory. The triumphant leader pursued Antony and Cleopatra to Egypt, where Cleopatra made one final effort to entice a Roman to support her cause. When Octavian would have none of her favors, she committed suicide, as Antony had already done. Her kingdom was annexed as a Roman province. Again the Roman world had an undisputed ruler whose sword had raised him to a position comparable to that Caesar had enjoyed in 46 B.C. Rome's future depended on what victorious Octavian would decide to do.

4. ECONOMIC AND SOCIAL TRENDS IN THE LATE REPUBLICAN PERIOD

Octavian's triumph at Actium ended a century of turmoil that from one perspective witnessed a political revolution—the replacement of the oligarchic republican system with a military dictatorship. Accompanying that violent political transformation and in part caused by it were economic and social developments that brought subtle changes in the Mediterranean world.

From an economic perspective, one of the fundamental changes of the late republican period was the emergence of Rome and Italy as the center of wealth in the Mediterranean. In large part that prosperity was due to the immense influx of wealth brutally extracted from the growing numbers of provincial subjects in the form of booty, war indemnities, and tribute. Prospects for even greater wealth remained a prime factor in continued Roman military and political expansion. Rome's predatory policy during the late republican period was economically disruptive, especially in the eastern Mediterranean area. It was not yet fully obvious to Roman decision makers that a basic consequence of this shift of wealth toward Italy was a growing economic dependency of Roman citizens on the total economy of the Mediterranean world. It remained to be seen whether Roman policy would be adjusted in directions that would replace pillage with promotion of provincial economic welfare as a prime source of Roman economic well-being.

Perhaps the realities of shifting economic trends were veiled from most Romans by continued productivity of the Italian economy in the late republican period. Agriculture remained the backbone of that economy. Despite disruptions caused by civil strife, the traditional patterns of agricultural production showed remarkable resiliency. Small farming—constantly fortified by land grants given to dispossessed farmers, landless urban residents, and discharged soldiers—still provided at least a subsistence-level livelihood to large numbers of Roman citizens. The *latifundia* system, devoted to cash crops and dependent on tenant farmers, hired labor, and slavery, continued to expand and to provide large incomes to aristocratic landowners. The expanding urban population of the late republican period stimulated industry and trade. Most industrial production in Italy was devoted to the production of items required for daily life and was organized by artisans running small-scale establishments. The products of these workshops were distributed by shopkeepers who also ran small merchandising operations. However, Rome and Italy became increasingly involved in international trading operations, especially in luxury goods and in grain, requiring capital and organization (see Figure 9.3). Although Roman aristocrats generally disdained trading activities as unworthy of their status, other Romans increasingly became involved in this lucrative activity. Many of them even settled abroad, where they increasingly expanded their participation in trade and their understanding of the interconnection between Rome's continued prosperity and the economic well-being of the entire Mediterranean world.

Outwardly Rome's social structure, rooted in an ancient class system, retained its basic forms during the late republican period. One major change was a large increase in the number of citizens as a result of the extension of citizenship to the Italian allies during the Social War (91–89 B.C.). Although the assimilation of these new citizens was not complete by 31 B.C., they were adapting to the traditional Roman class structure.

Despite the gradual erosion of its monopoly on political power during the last century of the republic, the Roman nobility retained its dominant position in society. The great noble families

FIGURE 9.3 **Aspects of Life During the Late Republic** These two scenes reflect important aspects of life in the late republic. On the left laborers unload grain brought by ship from African provinces to feed Rome's growing numbers of unemployed citizens. On the right a Roman aristocrat and his wife are instructed by a Greek slave; to be educated in Greek ways was critical to social respectability in first-century B.C. Rome. (Alinari/Art Resource)

showed remarkable ability to survive political proscription, confiscation of their wealth, and political humiliation at the hands of military dictators. During the last century of the republic the Roman nobility acquired new tastes for luxury and became more sophisticated as a result of expanding contacts with the culture of the Hellenistic world (see Figure 9.3). Many adopted freer life styles. Even aristocratic women, long completely under the domination of male heads of households, began to break the shackles of custom to become property owners, active participants in cultural and social life, and even political forces as key partners in political marriages. Although seldom involved in the mainstream of politics during the late republic, the Italian aristocracy exercised an important role in shaping local affairs throughout Italy. On the whole, the Roman nobility by 31 B.C. remained a formidable force whose support must be sought by anyone who would rule and whose ranks represented considerable talent that could be tapped to reconstruct the Roman political order.

The late republican period was marked by significant changes in the status and role of the *equites*. During a time of political turmoil and Roman expansion, the members of this nonnoble

group found countless opportunities to increase their wealth to the point where they rivaled the nobles. Although only occasionally did a member of the equestrian order find his way to the center of political power, as a group the *equites* increasingly played an unofficial role in the conduct of political life. Their engagement in banking, money lending, trade, tax collecting, contracting for public works, and procurement of military supplies made this group an unofficial arm of the government, providing crucial administrative services usually performed by a professional bureaucracy—which was lacking in republican Rome. This involvement gave the *equites* invaluable experience in and insight into foreign affairs, economic life, provincial administration, and military activity. And their expertise whetted their ambitions for a larger share in political life. Any leader who could tap the talent of the *equites* would gain formidable allies in the conduct of political life.

During the last century of the republic the plebeian order grew increasingly diverse in composition and status. Many rural plebeians survived as independent farmers but benefited little from Italy's prosperity. Even more difficult was the fate of former independent farmers forced to become rent-paying tenants or hired laborers in the service

WHERE HISTORIANS DISAGREE

Slavery in the Greco-Roman World

Most experts agree that slavery was an essential element of Greco-Roman society. As a consequence, anyone seeking to understand that society must grapple with slavery. But those who seek to respond to that challenge will soon learn an important lesson about historical investigation: The effort to describe any institution fundamental to a past society generates disagreement.

Central to the disagreement among modern historians about slavery and its role in ancient Greece and Rome is a conceptual issue. Is there such a thing as a "slave society?" That is, is there a society whose essential and unique characteristics are a consequence of the role played in that society by slavery? At this point historians—as well as economists, sociologists, political scientists, and philosophers—do not agree on an answer to this question. As a consequence, the study of slavery in antiquity proceeds from divergent perspectives.

This conceptual disagreement stems in large part from lack of consensus on many matters of fact concerning slavery in antiquity. Historians do not agree on the number of slaves, on the proportion of slaves in relation to other forms of labor, on which facets of economic life were slave-dominated, or on the source of supply of slaves. They argue about when and under what conditions the ancient slave system came into existence and ended. They debate whether slavery flourished because it was economically profitable or because there were social, moral, and psychological factors in Greco-Roman culture as a whole that made slavery necessary. They disagree on the impact of slavery on the mentality and behavior of other segments of the population and on how slaves were treated.

But why should disagreement exist? Why cannot historians working with the same body of information reach a common conclusion?

There are several reasons, which are also instructive about the nature of historical investigation. As already noted, historians often have trouble agreeing on a conceptual approach to important institutions like slavery. The surviving source material providing data about slavery in the ancient world is limited, difficult to interpret, and little concerned with issues in which modern historians are concerned. Perhaps even more significant in generating disagreement among historians is a matter raised by M. I. Finley in his book *Ancient Slavery and Modern Ideology* (1980). He argues persuasively that modern inquiries into Greco-Roman slavery have been decisively shaped by preconceived ideas—ideologies—held by the investigators. For example, the treatment of ancient slavery has been colored by convictions, often rooted in Christian moral values, concerning the moral unacceptability of the institution. Likewise, the study of ancient slavery has been distorted by what one scholar called the "religion of classicism"—the glorification of the universal values of Greco-Roman high culture to the point that whatever made it possible, even slavery, is justifiable. Still again, historians have been distracted from examining the realities of ancient slavery by dogmatic adherence to hypotheses about stages of historical development determined by economic structures, especially the Marxist concept of the slave mode of production as a necessary stage out of which emerged a feudal and then a capitalistic mode of production. In short, historians disagree because they ask different questions and expect different answers in order to support views they believe to be valid.

What then are we to conclude about what Aristotle called "property with a soul"—the slave in the ancient world? Only that there is little agreement on this important matter.

of wealthy owners of *latifundia*. Although citizens, this rural population found it increasingly difficult to participate effectively in the political process unfolding in Rome and, as a consequence, saw its social status deteriorate. The urban plebeians constituted an especially disruptive force, particularly in Rome, by now a city approaching a million residents. Its polyglot mixture of citizens, foreigners, slaves, and freedmen lived in crowded tenements without adequate police and fire protection and with minimal provisions for sanitary conditions. A considerable portion of that population earned an adequate living as artisans, shopkeepers, and laborers. But a large segment of the urban population lacked gainful employment and was dependent on the state or on rich patrons for economic survival. This city "mob" increasingly became the political tool of unscrupulous politicians. Their votes were courted in the assemblies to secure passage of legislation that would advance the personal careers of politicians, and they could be incited to acts of violence to serve political ends. In return, politicians diverted public funds to provide food and entertainment for this helpless, disruptive group. Its control and support increasingly constituted a critical social problem.

Two other components of the social structure need to be noted. First was Rome's expanding slave population, largely victims of Rome's military triumphs around the Mediterranean. Each victory resulted in hordes of war captives dumped into Italy as property of Roman citizens and assigned to labor as household servants, workers in shops and manufacturing establishments, and laborers on *latifundia*. The economic importance of slavery encouraged the development of an active slave trade. Although some slaves, especially educated captives from the Hellenistic world, were treated fairly well and often freed, the great bulk, especially rural slaves, were exploited brutally. Hardly better off were the millions of people living in the provinces who were treated without mercy by Roman armies, governors, tax collectors, and merchants. These voiceless subjects had virtually

no way to protect themselves against their Roman masters. Yet as we have noted, Rome's welfare depended increasingly on their productive skills. By 31 B.C. the hour was fast approaching when the Romans, for their own good, would have to weigh their accustomed ways of treating these subjects.

A final consequence of the long ordeal of the late republic took the form of a transformation of the collective mentality of the Roman citizenry. In various ways there was an erosion of confidence in ancient values and an opening of minds to the need for change. With good reason many groups—the peasantry, the urban proletariat, the *equites*—lost faith in the ability of the republican political order to protect their interests; often powerful individual leaders, no matter how they had come to power, served them better than did rich oligarchs spouting slogans about past glories and patriotic duty. Incessant violence generated a widespread longing for peace and order, even at the cost of some liberty. Particularly appealing to educated nobles and *equites* were the philosophical systems of the Hellenistic world, especially Epicureanism and Stoicism, both of which stressed peace of mind as the object of the good life. Hellenistic mystery religions, promising happiness in the afterlife, appealed to many at all levels of society. Expanding awareness of a world larger and more diverse than Rome not only undermined but even made ridiculous and senseless a narrow dedication to the traditions of a single city-state. Many yearned for a new vision of the good society to provide meaning to their lives in changing times.

While not as dramatic as the political upheaval that occurred between 133 and 31 B.C., these economic and social changes provide further grounds for concluding that a revolution had occurred. And they point up the fact that Roman society required more than the reconstruction of the political order if the Romans were to hold their place as rulers of the civilized world. Such was the challenge that faced Octavian at the moment when the Roman world was his to rule.

SUGGESTED READING

Political Developments

H. H. Scullard, *From the Gracchi to Nero: A History of Rome from 133 B.C. to A.D. 68,* 5th ed. (1982). A detailed history.

Ronald Syme, *The Roman Revolution* (1952).

Richard E. Smith, *The Failure of the Roman Republic* (1955).

Erich S. Gruen, *The Last Generation of the Roman Republic* (1974).

Mary Beard and Michael Crawford, *Rome in the Late Republic: Problems and Interpretations* (1985).

These four works present significant but differing interpretations of the causes of the failure of the Roman republic.

Claude Nicolet, *The World of the Citizen in Republican Rome,* trans. P. S. Falla (1980). A reconstruction of the civic life of the average citizen.

Keith Hopkins, *Death and Renewal* (1983). A study of how power and property were transferred among the members of the Roman elite.

Arthur Keaveney, *Rome and the Unification of Italy* (1987). Describes Rome's treatment of the Italians during the late republic.

A. N. Sherwin-White, *Roman Foreign Policy in the East, 168 B.C. to A.D. 1* (1984). An excellent study.

Economic and Social Developments

Henry C. Boren, *Roman Society: A Social, Economic, and Cultural History* (1977). A brief survey.

P. A. Brunt, *Social Conflicts in the Roman Republic* (1971). A good description of social tensions affecting late republican society.

K. D. White, *Roman Farming* (1970). Clarifies the problems of Roman agriculture during the republican period.

Biographies

A. H. Bernstein, *Tiberius Sempronius Gracchus. Tradition and Apostasy* (1978).

Arthur Keaveney, *Sulla: The Last Republican* (1982).

Peter Greenhalgh, *Pompey: The Roman Alexander* (1980), and *Pompey: The Republican Prince* (1981).

B. A. Marshall, *Crassus: A Political Biography* (1976).

Elizabeth Rawson, *Cicero: A Portrait,* rev. ed. (1983).

Matthias Gelzer, *Caesar: Politician and Statesman* (1968).

Arthur D. Kahn, *The Education of Julius Caesar: A Biography, A Reconstruction* (1986).

Sources

Cicero, *Selected Works,* trans. Michael Grant (1971).

War Commentaries of Caesar, trans. Rex Warner (1960). Contains two of Caesar's political works, *The Gallic Wars* and *The Civil Wars.*

CHAPTER 10
The Roman Empire, 31 B.C.–A.D. 180

FIGURE 10.1 Augustus, First Citizen of Rome This majestic statue of Octavian, or Augustus, as he came to be known soon after he seized power, was intended to idealize and exalt the man who had restored peace to the Roman world after the troubled times of the late republic. (Alinari/Art Resource)

The year 31 B.C. marked a critical point in the history of the Mediterranean world. Its destiny lay in the hands of the Romans, who during the preceding two hundred fifty years had won a series of military victories that subdued all other claimants to power. But even in the midst of victory the Romans suffered a profound internal crisis that ended with the collapse of their traditional political order. They now faced the challenge of restoring order in their own house if their dominance of the Mediterranean world was to continue in a fruitful way. During the first and second centuries A.D. the Romans met that challenge by fashioning their most notable contribution to civilization—a system of government known as the Roman Empire. This system became a powerful force promoting peace and prosperity among millions of people living in a vast territory surrounding what the Romans rightly called "our sea."

1. THE ESTABLISHMENT OF THE IMPERIAL ORDER, 31 B.C.–A.D. 14

The foundation of the Roman Empire was the work of Octavian, one of the truly great figures in all history (see Figure 10.1). His victory at Actium in 31 B.C. made him master of the Roman world by virtue of conquest. The experience of the recent past, especially the case of Julius Caesar, had demonstrated that naked power was not the answer to the ongoing crisis. With an uncanny grasp of the mentality of his times, Octavian sensed the essential issue of the moment. In the minds of the Roman citizenry any form of military dictatorship or monarchy was unacceptable because it flaunted a five-century-old tradition that held that the destiny of Rome could be determined only by the decisions of the Senate and the people acting through a set of institutions that constituted the Roman Republic. Yet the experience of the previous century had taught that the only hope for the management of the vast, problem-ridden Roman world lay in the concentration of power in the hands of a single individual. Octavian's challenge was to reconcile the collective mind-set rooted in tradition with existing reality. His solution, worked out with patience and caution during his forty-five-year rule, was masterful. He retained the outward forms of the republican constitution, but at the same time he obtained by legal means sufficient power to permit him to rule the Roman world.

For some years after 31 B.C. Octavian's legal authority was based on repeated election to the consulship. He realized, however, that a continuous succession of consulships would not serve as a permanent basis for his authority; ancient custom dictated that this highest magistracy be rotated annually among eligible citizens. In 27 B.C. he made a decisive move toward a more permanent solution. He proclaimed before the Senate "the transfer of the state to the free disposal of the Senate and the people." This surrender of all the powers he then held was interpreted as a restoration of the republic, with power again resting in the hands of the Senate, the elected magistrates, and the assemblies. Impressed by this noble gesture, fearful of the recurrence of civil war, and skillfully guided by Octavian, the Senate and the people quickly took legal action to bestow on him a wide array of powers. Included were the power of tribune for life, full consular authority without need to hold that office, *imperium* (full command) over most of the provinces, command of the armies, and the highest priestly office. To these legal powers the grateful citizenry added several honors: first senator; *augustus* ("most revered one"); *imperator* ("victorious general"); and *pater patriae* ("father of the country"). This array of legal powers and tradition-laden honors surrounded Octavian with an aura of authority so great that he began to be called *princeps,* the first citizen of Rome, trusted to do what he wished to rule the Roman world without a hint of illegal abuse of power or of violating tradition. What was essentially crucial in Octavian's position was that he did not have to share the authority legally granted him and that his power need not be renewed regularly. Not unimportant in buttressing his position as *princeps* were his immense personal fortune and his wide circle of political dependents, both created during the period of his rise to power after Julius Caesar's death.

Armed with these great powers, Augustus, as he came to be known by virtue of the title that vaguely suggested a semidivine position, turned his attention to revitalizing the citizen body—basically the population of Italy—on whose shoulders rested the responsibility for ruling the vast empire. Adhering to the ancient and widely held conviction that only a class-structured society could ensure right order, Augustus tried to redefine class divisions and to assign civic responsibilities to each group. Rigid standards of birth, wealth, and conduct were established to define senatorial ranking, resulting in a considerable reduction of those eligible for this rank in society. This elite was assigned a major role in political life. To the Senate, the traditional focus of political life for the *nobiles*, Augustus left important powers in selecting magistrates, judging cases, enacting laws, and governing selected provinces. Members of the senatorial class were expected to fill the traditional elective offices, to serve as provincial governors, and to command armies. He anticipated that the equestrian order (*equites*) would serve the state in a wide array of secondary but critical administrative positions in the army, the tax system, and the judicial system. For the plebeians, Augustus tried to provide order, economic security, and pride of citizenship, in return for which he hoped that that group would exercise its vote in support of his regime and serve as volunteers in the army. While this arrangement was sensitive to traditional class roles, it effectively defined the responsibility of citizenship in terms of service to the state at the direction of the *princeps* rather than in terms of citizen formulation of basic policy.

Beyond restructuring the social order and defining civic roles, Augustus was deeply concerned about the morale of the citizen body. This concern prompted him to take a variety of measures aimed at rebuilding a sense of community and reviving a feeling of pride in Rome, ends he hoped to achieve by playing on tradition. He made a major effort to revive ancient civic religious practices as a central part of public life. He patronized writers, such as Vergil, Horace, and Livy, and artists (see Chapter 11) willing to celebrate Rome's ancient glory and present blessings. Numerous laws were enacted in an effort to curb what Augustus believed to be vices that sapped civic virtue—luxury, sexual irregularities, divorce, childless marriages, gambling, drinking, idleness. Immense sums were spent beautifying Rome and providing better public services in the hope of eliciting pride in what was now "head of the world."

Augustus was particularly concerned with the military system. His solution was shaped by an awareness of the need for a large force to protect Rome's frontiers and by the memory of the disruptive role played by private armies during the last century of the republic. His response was the creation of a professional army directly under the control of the *princeps* consisting of twenty-five legions (about one hundred fifty thousand troops) made up chiefly of Roman citizens serving long terms. Each legion was complemented by an equal-sized auxiliary unit composed of noncitizens recruited in the provinces. Noncitizens serving in both legions and auxiliary units were granted citizenship upon completion of service. A command structure, employing carefully selected members of the senatorial and equestrian orders but always subordinate to the *princeps*, was developed. Steps were taken to provide training, discipline, systematic provisioning, regular pay, and money pensions to the soldiers. The bulk of this force was stationed in frontier provinces facing potential enemies. Only the Praetorian Guard, a select contingent of about nine thousand troops acting as a bodyguard for the *princeps*, was garrisoned in the vicinity of Rome.

During Augustus' reign the army was used both to secure control over existing provinces and to attack external foes. The most important campaigns were waged in an effort to strengthen the empire's European frontier. As a result, the Roman hold on Illyricum was made secure and the new provinces of Raetia, Pannonia, and Moesia were added along the Danube frontier (see Map 10.1). An effort to advance the German frontier from the Rhine to the Elbe ended in a crushing defeat in A.D. 9. Thereafter, Augustus gave up expansion, seeking instead to establish a fixed frontier between Romans and foreigners to be defended by the imperial army.

Well aware of the disarray produced in the provinces by Rome's predatory conduct during the republican period, Augustus made a major effort to improve provincial governance. Rome's several provinces were divided into two groups, those needing the presence of armed forces and those sufficiently secure not to need troops. Au-

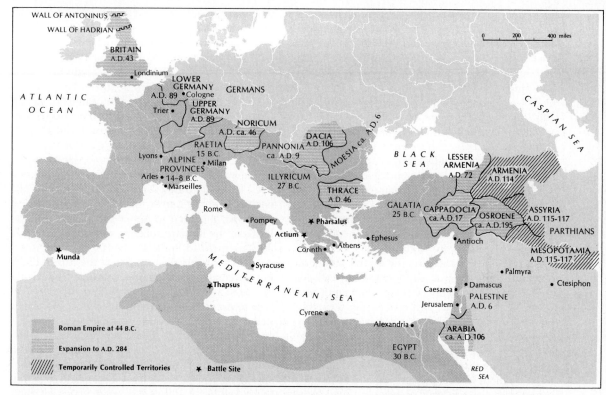

Map 10.1 **THE ROMAN EMPIRE, 44 B.C.–A.D. 284** This map shows Roman expansion during the period of the empire (44 B.C. to A.D. 284). With these additions the empire reached its greatest size. However, by the end of the second century A.D. an uneasy peace existed along the frontiers facing the Germans and the Parthians.

gustus retained control over the first group and directly supervised their administration. He was represented in each by a *legate,* usually a senator, who directed provincial administration in return for fixed pay. The *princeps* was also represented in each imperial province by a *procurator,* usually an equestrian, charged with collecting taxes and accountable to the *princeps.* This arrangement put an end to the rapacious governors and tax farmers who had for so long preyed on the helpless provincials. The provinces not needing armed forces were left under the jurisdiction of the Senate, which annually selected *proconsuls* to act as governors. However, Augustus maintained careful watch over the selection of proconsuls and over their conduct as provincial governors. This new

system almost immediately brought order and equitable treatment to the provincials.

The Augustan system of governance envisaged the sharing of governmental activities between the central government and local authorities. To achieve this end, Augustus encouraged the numerous city-states scattered across the empire to take responsibility for a wide range of matters relating to life in each city-state and its dependent countryside: police regulation, justice, public works, charity, religion. Most city-states had or were encouraged to develop a working system of government based on elected magistrates, a local senate, and assemblies—a system similar to Rome's old republican order. Local aristocracies whose interests were served by cooperating with the Roman government tended to dominate these governments. With Rome's encouragement city-states took on new vigor, and their leaders developed a strong sense of pride that made cities a vital force in promoting order across the vast Roman Empire.

The expanding range of functions associated with the office of *princeps* generated the need for permanent civil servants skilled in administration. Although Augustus and a small circle of confidants managed to handle a huge range of administrative detail, there slowly emerged around the *princeps* a corps of helpers, composed chiefly of freed slaves whose only political attachments were to the *princeps*. This embryonic bureaucracy was destined to play an ever-larger role in directing the imperial regime. In Augustus' time one of its prime accomplishments was the establishment of a sound fiscal system to support the imperial regime, especially its army. The key element of that system was a land tax and a head tax equitably imposed on noncitizens on the basis of regular census taking. Roman citizens contributed to support of the state chiefly through a form of sales tax and an inheritance tax.

Throughout his long reign Augustus was concerned with perpetuating his system. Crucial in this respect was the succession to his position as *princeps*. Fully aware that only the Senate and the people could legally bestow the powers upon which his veiled system of one-man rule depended, he saw the need to establish someone in a position where the Senate and people would have no choice except to grant that person the powers Augustus wielded. He was convinced that he should establish the principle of hereditary succession so that each future *princeps* would enjoy the prestige of descent from Julius Caesar and Augustus. Moreover, he believed that his successor should establish public visibility and gain practical political experience by actual involvement in the governance of the empire under his tutelage. Augustus' problem turned out to be finding someone who could meet these criteria. Augustus had no sons. He arranged three marriages for his only daughter, Julia, in search of an heir, but he outlived two of Julia's husbands as well as two grandsons considered as possible successors. Finally, he chose as his heir an adopted stepson, Tiberius,

who was forced to divorce a beloved wife in order to become Julia's third husband and after A.D. 4 was granted ever-greater powers by Augustus with the concurrence of the Senate. When Augustus died in A.D. 14, Tiberius was ready to assume full authority as *princeps*.

This brief summary hardly does justice to Augustus' achievement. He was not a doctrinaire idealist seeking to create a preconceived utopian order. Rather he was a patient, realistic, cautious, pragmatic, hardworking statesman. He kept certain key ideas central to his political program: the need to concentrate power in his own hands; the need to end the use of force in reaching political decisions; the need to honor the ancient political ideals of the Roman citizenry; the need to provide fair treatment to Rome's subjects; the need to set positive goals for all segments of the citizen body. But Augustus was amazingly flexible in devising means to achieve these ends. A long life gave him time to experiment and shift directions. In the end he fashioned a political order that elicited acceptance and active involvement from a crucial element in the Roman world—the Roman citizen body of Italy—and that generated confidence among millions of subjects living beyond Italy that their well-being depended on direction of their affairs by those Roman citizens led by a wise *princeps*.

2. TESTING THE AUGUSTAN ESTABLISHMENT, A.D. 14–96

During the century following Augustus' death, the Augustan system was severely tested but ultimately proved its viability. The testing took place primarily in a relatively narrow political circle involving each *princeps*, his family, his chief political agents, the senatorial class, and sometimes the army. The maneuverings, intrigues, and acts of violence of these elements, set forth in lurid details by the historians Tacitus and Suetonius (see Chapter 11), leave the impression that this era was marked by monumental misrule creating a constant state of crisis. But more constructive developments beyond this circle and outside Rome provide indisputable evidence of the success of the imperial system.

A constant source of tension within the inner circle of power stemmed from the difficulty in finding a ruler who could meet the challenge posed by the office of *princeps* as defined by Augustus. To be effective, a *princeps* needed to combine the administrative ability and the good judgment necessary in running a vast empire with the tact and the sensitivity required to ensure everyone of his respect for the authority the Augustan system entrusted to the Senate and the people. Augustus greatly limited the pool from which such candidates could come by insisting that his successors come from his family. In fact, the first four successors, called the Julio-Claudians, were related to him. But their selection bred intrigue, conspiracy, and violence and produced rulers of limited abilities whose actions provoked incessant opposition and obstructionism from the senatorial order. Augustus' handpicked successor, Tiberius (A.D. 14–37), was an able, experienced leader, but he was also cold, suspicious, distrustful, and easily provoked to brutal retaliation against those he suspected of undermining his power. Gaius (A.D. 37–41), more commonly known by his nickname Caligula, a term meaning "little boots," given to him when he was a boy strutting about military camps in small boots, was an indolent pleasure seeker whose excesses earned him an assassin's knife. Claudius (A.D. 41–54) was a timid, scholarly man who suffered a physical handicap, who was ill at ease in Roman high society, and who was constantly victimized by ill-chosen wives and advisers. Most notorious of all was Nero (A.D. 54–68), a cruel, vain degenerate eventually ousted from office, avoiding assassination by killing himself, but only after he killed his mother and two wives, disposed of numerous senators, persecuted Christians, made a fool of himself posing as an artist, and depleted the treasury to satisfy his expensive whims. It was indeed easy to conclude that none of the Julio-Claudians were worthy of respect and trust as "first citizen."

With Nero's death there occurred a development with ominous implications for the future: control of the choice of *princeps* by the army. In the span of a single year four different men were thrust into office by the army in a climate of violence reminiscent of the late republic. It was with good reason that from this point on the head of the Roman state was increasingly referred to as *imperator* (victorious general) rather than as *princeps* (first citizen). Finally, a general named Vespasian seized the office and put an end to the bloody military competition for control of the political system. Vespasian (A.D. 69–79) devoted his talent to the restoration of the fundamental features of the Augustan system. He sought to resolve the succession issue by instituting a clear hereditary principle that permitted his sons, Titus (A.D. 79–81) and Domitian (A.D. 81–96) to assume power without difficulty. These rulers, called the Flavians, were men of considerable ability who ruled constructively. However, they often acted without deferring to the Senate and thus were constantly charged with being tyrants and were obstructed in their efforts to rule effectively. The mutual disdain between senators and Flavians owed much to the fact that the Flavian family was of nonaristocratic origin. The tension between the Senate and the Flavians highlights an important cause of political turmoil during the first century. Perhaps consciously, Augustus had not precisely defined the powers belonging to the *princeps* and those belonging to the Senate and people. While the Julio-Claudian and Flavian rulers tried to honor the role of the Senate and the people in directing the state, the imprecise line between the two spheres prompted senators to charge repeatedly that rulers were usurping authority and destroying the liberties of citizens. The rulers sometimes reacted by silencing their critics; more often, they simply did what had to be done, disregarding the alleged rights of the Senate and people. Whatever the course chosen, the result was a climate of mistrust so acute that it seemed at times that civil war would again erupt to ruin the Augustan settlement.

In reality, all this strife was little more than an intriguing sideshow detracting from the substantive advances made in achieving the *Pax Romana* envisaged by Augustus. Several of the much-maligned rulers of this era—Tiberius, Claudius, Vespasian, Domitian—were able statesmen who worked patiently and effectively to resolve the problems facing the imperial regime. They maintained Rome's military capability and utilized it to defend the frontiers and to extend Rome's domain: Claudius conquered Britain and annexed

Noricum to strengthen the Danube frontier, and Domitian won territory along the upper Rhine frontier crucial to the containment of the Germanic threat (see Map 10.1). They worked hard to sustain and improve equitable administration of the provinces; especially significant was their willingness to extend citizenship to provincials. They enhanced their concerns for effective administration by promoting the development of a proficient professional bureaucracy. Vast public works were undertaken in Rome, Italy, and the provinces; and trade, industry, and agriculture were given every encouragement. For the most part, the Senate and people demonstrated little interest and less competence in dealing with these crucial matters. Despite their recurrent laments that their liberties were being usurped by rulers unworthy of such honor in terms of ancient standards, by the end of the first century A.D. most people had reached the conclusion that rule by a powerful *princeps*— or *imperator*—was the only ensurance of peace, security, and prosperity. The Augustan system had prevailed.

3. THE EMPIRE AT ITS PEAK: THE "GOOD EMPERORS," A.D. 96–180

With the end of the Flavian dynasty in A.D. 96 much of the conflict that had marked the testing of the Augustan establishment ended. During the next century, the empire enjoyed a golden age, a time of *Pax Romana*—the Roman peace. Seldom has an era produced leaders more highly praised than the five emperors who ruled from A.D. 96 to 180. Nerva (A.D. 96–98) was a respected aristocrat whose conciliatory actions calmed fears of military dictatorship. Trajan (A.D. 98–117), a native of Spain and the first emperor from the provinces, won the admiration of the entire Roman world by his respect for the Roman aristocracy, his brilliant military exploits, and his honest administration. Hadrian (A.D. 117–138) was a cultured humanitarian who spent most of his reign traveling throughout the empire promoting the cause of peace, lawful administration, and material well-being. Antoninus (A.D. 138–161), by the excellence of his character and his humane legislation, earned the title "Pius" ("devoted to duty") from a grateful

Senate. Most illustrious of all was Marcus Aurelius (A.D. 161–180), a noted Stoic philosopher who exemplified a sense of duty, a willingness to work, and a nobility of purpose in the service of the state.

The regime of the "good emperors" was one that produced little history of a conventional kind—battles, intrigues, and so forth. These emperors were sometimes engaged in warfare, chiefly in defense of Rome's sprawling, lightly defended frontiers. Trajan pursued an aggressive policy that resulted in the annexation of a crucial area north of the Danube called Dacia and of extensive territories east of the Euphrates River at the expense of Parthia. Hadrian, however, abandoned expansionism in favor of strong defense of a fixed frontier and diplomacy, a policy that led to the abandonment of much of the territory Trajan had conquered along the eastern frontier. The collective efforts of the "good emperors" by no means solved the problem of protection of the frontier, as was clear from the fact that peace-loving philosopher Marcus Aurelius had to spend most of his reign defending the northern frontier against Germans. Less spectacular were other activities of the "good emperors" related to peace and stability. They effectively removed the disturbances surrounding the succession problem by utilizing an adoptive system whereby each emperor early in his reign adopted as his son a man of ability who was then involved in imperial governance and vested with increasing legal powers to the point where he was able to take over when his "father" died. All these rulers were tactful and respectful toward the senators, who filled most of the high offices and were regularly consulted and who increasingly became staunch supporters of the imperial system. Citizenship was granted to ever-larger numbers of provincials, some of whom were elevated to senatorial rank; this policy facilitated the Romanization of the provincial population. The administrative system was steadily expanded and regularized. The rulers encouraged the development of a unified body of law for the whole empire. They championed humanitarian projects to aid the downtrodden. Every encouragement was given to city-states to determine their own course as long as that freedom did not threaten the imperial peace. The rulers worked tirelessly to establish a sound financial system to support the imperial structure. All these efforts slowly bound the diverse peoples of the empire—numbering perhaps 70 million—into a commonwealth guided from Rome.

In its mature form in the second century A.D. the imperial government was remarkably effective in shaping affairs in the empire. The way that system actually worked to act decisively in people's lives is not easy to describe. One is tempted to oversimplify the imperial government by stressing its structural features without giving sufficient attention to process. The structural aspects of the imperial government can be described in fairly simple terms. At the head of the Roman state stood a single figure, the *princeps* or *imperator,* who was vested with extensive executive, legislative, and judicial powers and with a variety of honors by the vote of the Senate and the people. Theoretically, the emperor exercised these powers by making decisions that were executed through two agencies. First was the bureaucracy, consisting of a central core of specialized departments headed by appointees of the emperor and staffed by paid "civil servants" and of agents dispatched across the empire to carry out imperial orders. Second was the army, a highly professionalized body of about three hundred fifty thousand soldiers commanded by officers appointed by the emperor and capable of enforcing imperial orders if the need arose. The emperor's authority was represented in each of the forty-five provinces into which the empire was divided by a governor (usually called a *legatus*)—with wide powers to keep order, administer justice, and protect Rome's interest—and by a *procurator* charged with collecting taxes. Provincial governors and procurators were supported by staffs of public servants. An elaborate but efficient tax system had been put in place to support this complex apparatus and to allow the imperial government to provide a wide range of public services; the burden of taxation fell most heavily on the provincials. Complementing the imperial government everywhere in the empire were active city-state governments that played a major role in directing local affairs; however, these local regimes were always open to intervention by agents of the emperor's government.

When described in terms of its structure, it is tempting to characterize the imperial government as a highly centralized, bureaucratized machine capable of imposing on a vast population a uniform policy emanating from the decisions of one man. Certainly that potential existed. However, careful study of how the imperial government impacted on the governed in specific situations presents a more subtle and complex picture.

Unquestionably the *princeps* or emperor of the second century A.D. was vested with almost unlimited authority based on legal grants and honors extended to him by agencies that at least the citizen body believed had the right to do so. The universal acceptance of the emperor as the ultimate source of authority was an important factor in giving coherence to political life because it caused everyone to turn to the emperor to get what he or she wanted. Moreover, the traditions associated with the offices upon which the emperor's authority was based dictated that the emperor "do" things; delegation of power was not an acceptable feature of Greco-Roman political thinking. The record shows clearly that second-century emperors were personally swamped with detailed administrative work: conducting military campaigns, arbitrating disputes, responding to petitions for favors, receiving embassies, and seeing to it that public property was properly exploited. Because the Roman record-keeping system was limited, all this detail had to be handled without much knowledge of specific situations. To assist in meeting this burden, emperors relied more often on their household servants than on professional civil servants; members of the imperial household became real power wielders without holding official positions or being constrained by rules defining their conduct of business. The evidence suggests that the emperors often entrusted public business to private contractors who acted according to their own lights once commissioned to perform a service for the state. Perhaps the only area where there was anything like a regularized, empire-wide administrative system was in revenue collecting, and even in this vital activity procedures were haphazard and arbitrary.

Beyond the emperor and his circle, the political process was far from systematic and uniform. It is almost unbelievable to a modern observer to realize how few public officials in the Roman system actually had the *imperium*—the power to make final decisions. Those who did—army commanders, governors, procurators—enjoyed wide latitude in making decisions. The jurisdictions given by their offices were extensive, with the result that they too were swamped with administrative details. Like the emperor, they too relied on their personal servants to assist with these details, and they too depended heavily on private contractors to get things done. All too often, things did not get done; like the famous case involving the Roman official Pontius Pilate, authorities simply "washed their hands" of problems confronting them. The army was especially active in making and carrying out decisions that impinged on the civilian population. Far from being a mechanism through which uniform decisions were imposed upon the population through uniform procedures, the Roman imperial government operated through enclaves of power in which officials vested with the authority of Rome did what they wished in the way they wished.

Probably the lives of most residents of the Roman empire were seldom touched directly by the imperial government—except in the pocketbook. For them the most important political force was the local city-state government whose far-ranging activities were encouraged by the imperial government. Each urban center with its surrounding territory was ruled by a body of local aristocrats (called *decurions*) who formed a local senate. These senates elected local magistrates, collected local taxes, assumed responsibility for keeping order and providing public facilities, held courts, and dealt with imperial officials; in short, they played a major role in governance. Although the imperial government sometimes intervened in their activities, especially in fiscal matters, the city-state regimes were allowed wide latitude to govern those in their jurisdiction as they wished.

In view of these aspects of political reality, it is obviously impossible to think of the Roman imperial regime as one headed by a wise emperor who established general policies on the basis of extensive knowledge of conditions and with the advice of informed councilors and then issued orders that were enacted by a hierarchy of public officials capable of ensuring universal conformance to the emperor's law. Instead, governance depended on the decisions and the actions of a wide array of individuals, some officials and some private parties, acting within a framework of overlapping jurisdictions where pragmatic concerns and individual judgment were more important than rules. To run a vast empire in such a manner would seem to be a formula for chaos. Yet during the second century A.D. the system worked to provide peace and order to millions. One wonders how! The explanation may seem strange to the modern conception of statecraft. Rome was governed by a narrow elite whose shared social status and common culture caused its members to think and to act politically in a common pattern. This elite viewed public life as the highest form of human activity, reflecting an attitude deeply ingrained in the Greco-Roman mentality. Whether they were public officials, senators, local decurions, army officers, or equestrian contractors, their shared social and cultural values prompted each of them to decide on a particular political situation in the same way as did all other power wielders. Thus, without the guidance of clearly formulated policies or rigid rules regulating political behavior, the ruling elite—through myriad decisions shaped by common values—quite unconsciously guided the Roman world in a common direction that especially prized peace and order. Perhaps the tone for this remarkable consensus was set by the "good emperors" whose conduct was shaped by a conviction that power entailed duty in the service of humanity—a political philosophy based on Stoic ideas. Certainly from Augustus onward successive emperors acted to sanction the social status of this elite and to replenish its ranks, especially by extending citizenship to provincials in a position to exercise power. But in the final analysis, it was the political activism of this elite bound together by shared social values and a common culture that ruled the empire in its golden days. The elements which provided the basis for this consensus emerged from the entire fabric of Roman civilization. Consequently, the political dynamism of the imperial system can never be understood fully without a grasp of the intellectual, religious, social, and cultural values shared by its ruling elite. In a real sense the future of the empire depended on the continuation of this consensus among the members of this elite.

4. ECONOMIC AND SOCIAL LIFE IN THE ROMAN EMPIRE

During the first and second centuries A.D. the general level of material life in the Roman world was higher than ever before and not to be equaled again for many centuries—although not all shared that affluence equally. Prosperity was not the consequence of any basic change in the system of production. Rather, it stemmed from the favorable environment created by peace and order, from the integration of formerly isolated areas into the total economy, from the stimulus supplied by the expanding activities of the imperial political system, and from the entrepreneurial activities of nobles and equestrians eager to expand family fortunes.

The basic element in the Roman economy was a diversified agricultural system, which occupied the energies of the great bulk of the population. Everywhere that system included a mixture of small farms cultivated by freeholders or renters and large estates tilled by sharecroppers, hired laborers, and slaves and managed by their noble owners or their stewards. In many areas these farms produced enough to support those who owned them and labored on them as well as a modest surplus to feed the population of local urban centers. However, some areas, such as Egypt and North Africa, produced large agricultural surpluses for export to the empire's great cities, especially Rome. Agricultural expansion was especially notable in Gaul and Spain, stimulated by urban growth and the presence of Roman army camps.

An important key to prosperity during the first two centuries A.D. was an expansion of trade and industry. Most of the commercial activity involved the exchange of agricultural products and simple manufactured goods on a local level. However, there was a significant movement of luxury goods, raw materials, and foodstuffs on a scale embracing the whole empire and even extending beyond to Parthia, India, China, and the Germanic world. The Mediterranean became a busy commercial roadway linking its bordering lands into an interdependent economic community. The famed Roman road system encouraged the movement of goods inland to urban centers and army camps. An array of skilled artisans pursued a variety of small-scale crafts in every major city. Many of these enterprises were financed by nobles whose slaves and freedmen produced goods and shared the returns with their masters. One of the most significant developments of this era was the remarkable expansion of industrial activity in Spain and Gaul as a result of the incorporation of these previously "backward" areas into the mainstream of Mediterranean life. A powerful stimulant to trade and industry during the period was provided by a massive building boom that occurred throughout the empire. Funded from both public and private sources, this outburst filled numerous cities, Rome above all, with forums, basilicas for the conduct of public business, temples, theaters, stadiums, palaces, baths, and private dwellings. Across the countryside were built roads, bridges, aqueducts, villas, and army camps. This vast enterprise required capital, labor, the skilled services of artisans and suppliers, and managerial skills.

Most economic life in the first and second centuries was conducted by private individuals with little interference from the imperial government, which demonstrated limited interest in economic matters except to tap the system through taxation. Yet what we would today call the public sector played an increasing role in the economy. Through its taxation system the Roman government drained off a portion of the wealth of the entire empire. That wealth was redistributed to pay salaries of officials, support the jobless in Rome, beautify the capital city, and maintain the army. As a consequence, most public expenditures tended to be concentrated in Rome and in frontier areas where the army was stationed. Such distribution of public funds tended to stimulate artificially economic activity in these areas while depriving the most productive areas of financial resources needed to sustain and expand economic activity. Moreover, the expanding role of the Roman government in utilizing the wealth of the empire made the economy increasingly sensitive to public policy decisions involving taxation, the size of the army and the bureaucracy, and the frequency of war. This development introduced an element of instability into the basic economic processes.

The basic social order prevailing in the Roman Empire was little changed from the late republican period. The distinction between citizens and non-citizens remained an important social fact, but that division was increasingly blurred by the granting of citizenship to ever-larger numbers of provincials. The citizen population was still divided into various classes recognized by law: nobles, *equites*, plebeians, and slaves. The noncitizen population of the empire was not quite so neatly categorized in legal terms, but in fact over most of the empire there prevailed a social structure similar to that in Rome. The social system provided opportunities for upward mobility, especially through the acquisition of wealth and education and through involvement in public affairs as a consequence of earning the favor of the emperor; especially fortunate in this respect were rich and powerful provincials who were accepted into the Roman nobility when they were granted citizenship.

The Roman social structure and social life were dominated by the nobles. The basis for this group is somewhat elusive to the modern mind. In essence, the nobility was self-defining; its members understood who their peers were on the basis of a variety of factors: family origin, marriage connections, wealth based on land, education, involvement in the highest levels of political life, control over a circle of clients, life style, and values. As best one can tell, the rest of society was willing to accept the superiority of those who met these standards. While small and keenly conscious of its status, the nobility was never totally exclusive. Its ranks were constantly replenished by those who could meet the standards for noble status; most often those who ascended socially were drawn from prominent equestrians and the provincial elite.

Although their wealth was based largely on landownership, Roman nobles were creatures of the city. Rome, of course, was the most attractive center, but many other cities across the entire empire had their noble circles. In this urban setting noble life centered in the family household living in a splendid dwelling, where the *pater familias* (father of the family) ruled as he wished over his wife, children, slaves, and an entourage of clients. He did not "work," as did the lower classes, but "managed" his estates, his investments in trade and industry, his loans, and often some segment of public life entrusted to him through selection

FIGURE 10.2 A Roman Lady This painting portrays a noble Roman lady of the imperial period. It suggests that Roman women were respected for their dignity, sobriety, and strength of character. Women such as this one played an important role in managing the affairs of aristocratic households and sometimes in promoting the political careers of their husbands and sons. (Courtesy of the Detroit Institute of Arts)

for an office. Always uppermost in his mind were increasing the family patrimony and enhancing its prestige. These concerns prompted a keen interest in the education, careers, and marriages of his children, especially sons; success in matters of careers and marriage depended to a considerable degree on his influence among his peers. Roman nobles participated in a constant round of social activities—banquets, festivals, races, gladiatorial contests, cultural events. A worthy noble was expected to provide the major source of funding for many of these activities. Although their legal position was surrounded by constraints that subju-

FIGURE 10.3   Scenes from a Roman Household   These two panels done in relief illustrate some of the activities associated with household life in the Roman world: storing, preparing, and cooking food. The scenes suggest that such households were the setting for a secure and comfortable life. (Alinari)

gated them to their fathers or their husbands, noble women played a prominent role in aristocratic life (see Figure 10.2). Many of them managed the family household, an operation that involved large expenditures and the management of numerous slaves (see Figure 10.3). They owned and managed property and defended their interests in courts. Not only did they take part in many social activities, but they also involved themselves in the sometimes intricate maneuvering involved in gaining and exercising political power. Not a few of them took lovers, just as their husbands did. Some evidence suggests that by the second century the traditional male-oriented mentality of the nobility increasingly viewed wives as equal partners in marriage worthy of respect and considerate treatment. Roman moralists often painted the lives of noble men and women in terms of gluttony, drunkenness, sexual excess, and idleness. However, a close reading of the evidence suggests that noble life was guided by a moral code that placed a high value on sober, ordered, restrained conduct and that sanctioned the use of great wealth to gratify private tastes but also required concern

with and involvement in public affairs in the cause of creating a civilized order. In a general way, the *equites* imitated the noble life style, often successfully in terms of wealth, sumptuous living, and education; however, members of this order were not accepted as being real nobles and thus were excluded from the summit of the social order unless the nobles chose to coopt them into the ranks of the real elite.

Rome and most other cities had a teeming lower-class population: shopkeepers, artisans, minor officials, and idle poor, as well as slaves. In Rome and Italy the bulk of these people were plebeian citizens; in provincial cities they had some status as members of the community. Strong family ties provided a bulwark in the lives of urban dwellers. Most of them devoted their time and energy to ignoble "work" through which they earned a living, an enterprise that often occupied not only heads of lower-class households but also wives and children. Some shopkeepers and artisans fared well, living in comfortable, well-furnished houses and served by slaves. But for most life was marked by poverty, misery, and contemptuous treatment at the hands of their social betters. Large numbers of poor were dependent on the state or noble patrons for the bare essentials; it has been estimated, for instance, that an average of two hundred thousand Roman residents (perhaps a fourth of the city's population) lived off the public grain dole. The Roman imperial government as well as local city-state administrations made serious efforts to provide police and fire protection, an adequate water supply, sanitary facilities, and cheap food. Nevertheless, life in the city was for many marred by poverty, violence, and insecurity.

Still, city life had its compensations, even for the lowliest. Magnificent public buildings and parks provided an impressive setting for one's life. Holidays were numerous—perhaps as many as a hundred a year by the second century A.D. Each was the occasion for splendid religious festivals centering on animal sacrifices that provided free meals, for the triumphs of victorious emperors, and for races, gladiatorial contests, and bloody combats between wild animals and between animals and human beings. Numerous and sumptuous public baths provided attractive gathering places for everyone. Social clubs (called *collegia*), usually made up of individuals sharing a common occupation, provided opportunities for banqueting and help to members in time of need. Taverns abounded as oases where one could escape from the urban desert. For the most part, the urban lower classes seemed content with their lot; there is little evidence of urban discontent.

Those who received the least benefit from the *Pax Romana* were the peasants and the slaves. Isolated from city life, the rural population seldom felt the impact of the forces that gave the Roman world its vitality. Their existence centered around the family, hard work, and simple social activities of the rural village. At best, the material return for their labor was small. Powerful trends were at work in the empire pushing many farmers into dependency on powerful absentee landlords; these dependent agricultural workers (called *coloni*) were increasingly victimized by heavy rents and by an ever-heavier share of the tax burden. To its discredit, the imperial government did little to check the exploitation of the peasantry; in fact, the aristocratic landowners who dominated the political process were quite happy to allow this drift toward peasant exploitation.

Slavery was a prominent feature of Roman imperial society. It has been estimated that in the first century A.D. perhaps one-third of Italy's population of between 7 and 8 million inhabitants were slaves. They worked as household servants, agricultural laborers, workers in urban workshops and merchant stalls, teachers, miners, and rowers; and their reward was minimal. The record is full of instances of brutal treatment by masters whose rights over slaves were complete. There is some evidence that the condition of slaves improved. Many were freed by their masters, in some cases out of gratitude for faithful service. Funerary inscriptions and literary sources suggest amicable associations between masters and slaves. Slaves were allowed to marry and maintain families. Yet in spite of such improvement, no one in the Roman world thought of ending slavery, and that institution continued to debase the lives of the victimized slaves and to poison the minds of their masters.

Even this brief description of the Roman world in the second century A.D. will elicit admiration for its peace, order, prosperity, and unity. That admiration is warranted, but it must always be tempered. The main beneficiaries of the *Pax Romana* were the members of a narrow, proud, self-satisfied, self-serving nobility who were disdainful and unconcerned about those less prominent socially. The empire had its share of poverty, injustice, oppression, and greed. Despite some of its apologists, it was far from a utopia. Some of the flaws in its structure would soon test its strengths.

SUGGESTED READING

Political Developments

Chester G. Starr, *The Roman Empire, 27 B.C.–A.D. 476* (1982).

Colin Wells, *The Roman Empire* (1984).

J.S. Wacher, *The Roman Empire* (1987).

Any of these three works will provide an excellent survey.

Fergus Millar, *The Emperor in the Roman World: 31 B.C.–A.D. 337* (1977). Although massive, this study is vital to understanding how the imperial political system worked.

Fergus Millar, *The Roman Empire and Its Neighbors*, 2nd ed. (1981). Studies the assimilation of the different provincial cultures.

J.B. Campbell, *The Emperor and the Roman Army, 31 B.C.–A.D. 235* (1984). An excellent treatment of an important aspect of the political history of the empire.

Economic and Social History

Peter Garnsey and Richard Saller, *The Roman Empire. Economy, Society and Culture* (1987). An excellent survey.

Géza Alföldy, *The Social History of Rome*, trans. David Braund and Frank Pollock (1985). Rich in details about social conditions.

Ramsay MacMullen, *Roman Social Relations, 50 B.C. to A.D. 284* (1974). Attempts to capture attitudes of major social groups.

Joan Liversidge, *Everyday Life in the Roman Empire* (1976). Excellent treatment of how the Romans lived.

Philippe Ariès and Georges Duby, eds., *A History of Private Life, Vol. I: From Pagan Rome to Byzantium*, ed. Paul Veyne, trans. Arthur Goldhammer (1987). A fully illustrated treatment of aspects of Roman history often neglected.

Judith P. Hallett, *Fathers and Daughters in Roman Society: Women and the Elite Family* (1984).

Jane F. Gardner, *Women in Roman Law and Society* (1986).

These two works, combined with those of Pomeroy and Cantarella cited in Chapter 6, will provide a good picture of the role of women in Roman society.

Keith Hopkins, *Conquerors and Slaves* (1978). A provocative study of social change in the Roman world.

Biographies

A. H. M. Jones, *Augustus* (1970).

Barbara Levick, *Tiberius the Politician* (1976).

Arnaldo Momigliano, *Claudius: The Emperor and His Achievement*, trans. W. G. Hogarth (1961).

Miriam T. Griffin, *Nero: End of a Dynasty* (1984).

Steward Perowne, *Hadrian* (1960).

Anthony Birley, *Marcus Aurelius: A Biography*, rev. ed. (1987).

Sources

Complete Works of Tacitus, ed. Moses Hadas (1942).

Suetonius, *The Twelve Caesars*, trans. Robert Graves (1957).

Two lively treatments of the history of the first century A.D.

CHAPTER 11
Roman Culture

FIGURE 11.1 **The Fruits of Peace** This relief is from a larger composition decorating the Ara Pacis (Altar of Peace) built in Rome during the first century A.D. It glorifies the benefits bestowed by Augustus. The serene goddess of fertility and her happy children are surrounded by symbols of well-being. The work reflects how art was used to promote the greatness of Augustus. (Alinari)

While the Romans were conquering and organizing a vast empire, they also produced writers, thinkers, and artists whose collective efforts made a major contribution to cultural life. Rome's prime role in the history of culture was its assimilation and dissemination of Greek culture. But in the course of adapting the basic elements of Greek culture, the Romans put their distinctive mark on thought and expression, thereby creating a Latin cultural heritage destined to influence the future decisively, especially in western Europe.

1. THE PREPARATION

Prior to the third century B.C. the Romans displayed little interest in cultural pursuits. Although Etruscan cultural models, especially in building techniques and religion, influenced early Roman society, the Romans long remained a simple people occupied chiefly with politics, war, and earning a living. However, their early experiences in these pursuits ingrained in them deep-rooted values that influenced their cultural life throughout their history.

The basic Roman outlook on life formed during the early centuries of Roman history was shaped by four major forces—family life, agriculture, warfare, and religion. The family structure was dominantly patriarchal. The authority of the male heads of households over women and children was total and absolute. Fathers impressed on other members of the tightly knit families a sense of discipline, obedience, and respect for authority and tradition. Farm life made the early Romans a practical, realistic people, content to live simply and frugally. Constant warfare in defense of hearth and city deepened the sense of duty owed to the larger community and strengthened societal discipline.

Religion had the most profound effect on early Roman life and thought. The typical Roman believed that all things in existence were animated by unseen but powerful spirits. The Romans viewed these spirits with high respect, which instilled in them a deep awe for the unseen; the Romans called such awe "piety" and lauded it as a prime virtue. In the early stages of Rome's history the chief objects of this piety were household and agricultural deities: Janus, the protective god of the doorway of each household; Vesta, the goddess of the hearth; the *lares* and *penates,* spirits guarding the productive powers of the family and its lands and flocks. As the city grew, it too developed its divine protectors. Roman civic religion centered especially on a trio of deities, perhaps derived from Etruscan models: Jupiter, the god of lightning and thunder and power; Juno, the goddess of women and family and procreation; and Minerva, the goddess of arts and sciences and wisdom. In time, other deities borrowed chiefly from the Greek pantheon, were added to this trio as major civic deities. Eventually this divine circle protecting the expanding city became the object of an elaborate mythology accounting for the behavior of each of its members. Roman mythology was borrowed in large part from the Greeks. The approach to all the gods and goddesses, whether civic or household, was highly formalized and unemotional. From very early times the Romans developed set patterns for offering sacrifices and prayers to their many deities. They also had well-defined expectations of what the gods and goddesses would return to favor families and the city. Close observance of these customary rituals became a part of responsible citizenship; any deviation threatened to earn the wrath of the deities and misfortunes for men and women. Responsibility for proper worship rested with heads of families and with priests elected to represent the city-state community before the civic gods.

Home, farm, battlefield, and altar combined to define the basic elements of the good life and to establish the values by which a Roman citizen was expected to live. Especially admired were sobriety, industry, discipline, piety, civic responsibility, and honor of the family. Less prized were originality, creativity, and individuality. As time passed, the Roman mentality tended to idealize the values of these early times and to utilize thought and expression as means of recovering the virtues they supposedly induced. This tradition was especially nurtured and prized by the Roman nobles and provided a key ingredient in the shared mentality. Thus, the traits ingrained in Roman society during its early history cast a long shadow over Roman cultural history.

2. THE HELLENISTIC TIDAL WAVE

Beginning in the third century B.C. the simple mentality of the early republic experienced a cultural revolution, brought on largely by Roman expansion. As their armies absorbed first southern Italy and Sicily and then the Hellenistic Near East, Roman aristocrats became aware of Greek culture, especially in its Hellenistic forms. They were so impressed that they were, as the first-century poet Horace put it, taken captive by those they conquered. This experience, which placed a high value on becoming culturally Hellenized, was critical in determining Rome's role in the total stream of cultural history.

One of the major consequences of this fascination with Greek culture was the introduction into Rome of a new education system. Previously, young Romans had been educated at home: males by their fathers, who taught them family customs, the principles of Roman law, civic duties, and religion; females by their mothers, who taught them the household arts. By the second century B.C. that traditional system began to be replaced by the Hellenistic pattern of education. In many aristocratic Roman households Greek slaves were employed to complement basic instruction in reading and writing Latin with instruction in the Greek language and in the Greek "classics" in literature and philosophy. Not only were young men introduced to this new education, but young women were also often involved (see Figure 9.3). Private schools emerged to provide young men with an opportunity to extend their formal education over a longer period of time. They often went to the East, especially to Athens, to finish their education. Grammar (the study of language and literature) and rhetoric (the study of effective expression and argumentation) became the touchstones of the new education. Mastery of these subjects provided the basis for a successful career in public life and for acceptance into the ranks of the *nobiles* and the *equites*.

Their fascination with Greek culture soon spurred the Romans to imitate it. Borrowing heavily from the content and forms provided by Greek models, Latin writers produced epic poems, dramas, histories, and philosophical tracts. As a result, the Latin language was enriched as a vehicle of independent literary expression. Romans were equally captivated by Greek and Hellenistic art. During the wars in the East, numerous art pieces were "liberated" to decorate Roman residences, and Eastern artists were imported to produce copies of Greek statues and paintings. The Greek style of architecture was employed for civic and private buildings so often that Rome resembled a Greek or Hellenistic city.

Even the masses in Rome felt the impact of Greek influences, but they were touched chiefly through religion. The wars of conquest left many people intellectually and emotionally lost. The formal religion of Rome offered little emotional satisfaction. The Eastern religions did. New deities and rituals taken from the Greek civic religions were added to public religion in Rome, but even these additions did not satisfy many. From Eastern slaves they learned about more exciting Hellenistic mystery religions such as the worship of Dionysus or Cybele or Isis. These emotional, personal cults increasingly challenged the traditional religion for the allegiance of the Italian population.

Some Romans fought this cultural revolution. Typical of these cultural conservatives was Cato the Elder, a second-century B.C. statesman who spent his life preaching against the Greek way. He saw the foreign culture as a threat to traditional values. But he was fighting a lost cause. Rome was destined by circumstances and choice to be heir to the magnificent patrimony of the Greeks. Many of Cato's contemporaries saw the perpetuation of Greek culture as a Roman responsibility and acted eagerly to fulfill that mission. For example, no less a person that the powerful Scipio Africanus, along with many of his descendants (including the Gracchi brothers), championed the Hellenization of Roman thought and expression.

During the first century B.C. Roman writers, artists, and thinkers began to put their own stamp on what they had borrowed from the Hellenistic world. This burst of creativity resulted in Rome's "golden age" culturally; the Augustan age marked its high point. After a brief slackening in the first century A.D., there followed a second period of considerable activity during the era of the "good emperors," often called the "silver age" of Roman culture.

3. LITERATURE

Perhaps the most impressive reflection of Rome's cultural genius is its literature. After a long apprenticeship under Greek influence during the third and second centuries B.C., a succession of writers living between about 100 B.C. and A.D. 150 produced a rich and varied body of literature. Almost without exception, these works reflect strong Greek influences in content and form. But their authors demonstrate remarkable talent in adapting Greek modes to the Latin language to produce works marked by stylistic grace and force, depth of personal conviction, a powerful grasp of social and intellectual reality, and a passion for instructing readers.

Outstanding among all Roman writers was Vergil (70–19 B.C.). Born in rural Italy, he grew to manhood during the last years of the civil wars that ruined the republic, and he personally suffered its ravages. Eventually he attracted the attention of Augustus, whose patronage permitted him to devote the last years of his life to writing. Although much of his great talent was poured out in the service of the new Augustan order, it would be erroneous to overemphasize Vergil's role as a propagandist; he wrote in support of the Augustan system out of deep conviction and enthusiasm. His *Georgics* express a strong feeling for nature and for what involvement in pastoral life can mean—especially to those corrupted by the violence and greed surrounding the last days of the republic. Vergil's masterpiece was his *Aeneid*. An epic modeled after Homer and filled with material drawn from Greek legend, this majestic work sought to show that Rome's rise to mastery of the world was divinely ordered. The plot centers on the adventures of a mythical Trojan hero, Aeneas, who after the fall of Troy was ordered by the gods to establish in Italy a new city destined to rule the world. The noble Aeneas is portrayed as an ideal Roman whose virtue is constantly tested by such challenges as the spiteful behavior of the deities, a heartrending love affair with Dido, queen of Carthage, and a horror-filled journey to the underworld. But he persists in fulfilling his mission. Never was the Roman ideal of the dedicated patriot portrayed with more intensity and dignity; and never was the theme of Rome's predestination to greatness more dramatically stated.

Two other poets, Catullus and Horace, illustrate another side of the Roman literary genius. Catullus (ca. 85–54 B.C.) was a product of high society in the late republican period. His life was lived amid a dissolute, pleasure-seeking crowd of young nobles. Among his many adventures was a love affair with a noble lady who was already married and who eventually jilted him. The experience inspired him to pour forth powerful lyric poetry portraying with great intensity the pain caused by lost love. Horace (65–8 B.C.), also a lyric poet, enjoyed the patronage of Augustus and was second in influence only to Vergil. His best work, the *Odes*, represents his personal reactions to hundreds of situations he met in his lifetime. Although he lacked the fire of Catullus, Horace spoke to a wider circle, his poems reflecting the reasoned, thoughtful reactions of an educated, humane Roman to life as a whole—a great spirit looking at the world about him with sanity, intelligence, and wit. He was and remains the ideal of a civilized person.

Lucretius (ca. 95–55 B.C.) demonstrated still another aspect of Roman poetic genius: moral seriousness. A contemporary of Catullus, he was profoundly moved by events of the civil war era. He found his personal salvation in Epicurean philosophy, which he undertook to explain in a long poem called *On the Nature of the Universe*. With almost missionary zeal Lucretius put poetry to the service of instruction. He made a noble plea to educated Romans to seek in philosophy the bases of moral regeneration and personal fulfillment. Seldom has a poet shown greater moral earnestness.

Among the lesser poets were Ovid, Martial, and Juvenal. Ovid (43 B.C.–A.D. 17) entertained Augustan high society with his *Art of Love*, a frivolous but amusing poem on the art of seduction, and his *Metamorphoses*, an entertaining, lively rendering of Greek mythological stories into Latin. Martial (ca. A.D. 38–102) and Juvenal (ca. A.D. 55–140) revealed the shortcomings of Roman society in their brilliant satires.

Cicero (106–43 B.C.) was Rome's most famous prose writer. Although an active lawyer, magistrate, and statesman, he produced a wide variety of writing, of which his speeches form a large part;

he made argumentation an art. Cicero wrote two important essays on political theory, *The Republic* and *The Laws*, defending Roman republic institutions but pleading for the establishment of a first citizen to guide the state. He also wrote several philosophical tracts that attempted to make abstract Greek thought understandable to Roman readers. His numerous *Letters* supply a brilliant picture of Roman politics and society in the first century B.C. This eloquent, learned Roman made Latin prose capable of expressing any idea.

The earliest historical writing in Latin was influenced by Hellenistic models, but the Romans again discovered their own talent. The most influential Roman historian was Livy (59 B.C.–A.D. 17), another of those inspired to creative activity under the Augustan regime. His masterpiece, the immense *History of the Roman Republic*, covers the period 753 B.C. to A.D. 9. Although a large part of the work has been lost, it is clear from what is left that Livy believed Rome had a great historical mission about which he wished to instruct his readers. Livy was not a scientific historian, interested only in the truth; his work was a conglomeration of truth and fiction put together artistically to teach a lesson. Nonetheless, the work presented with great dramatic impact the people and events that made Rome great over seven centuries and highlighted the traditional virtues that would ensure Rome's success for many centuries to come.

Less monumental but equally artistic was the work of Tacitus (ca. A.D. 55–117), who wrote about Roman history during the century after Augustus. His *Histories* and *Annals* covered large portions of the period A.D. 14–96. Although Tacitus was a man of senatorial and republic sentiments, prejudiced against the successors of Augustus, he wrote with brilliance and deep moral sense. Another of his works, *Germania*, gives important information about the Germanic barbarians, who were soon to play a part in Roman life. Suetonius (ca. A.D. 75–150) also treated the rulers from Julius Caesar to Domitian in his *Lives of the Twelve Caesars*, a racy account stressing scandal and excess.

The works of Greek writers swelled the body of excellent histories. One of the greatest was Polybius, who lived in Rome from 167 to 151 B.C. as a hostage. He became an intimate of the pro-Hellenic Scipionic circle and, greatly impressed by the Romans, produced a superb work chronicling Rome's rise to world power. Plutarch (ca. A.D. 46–120) provided a series of biographies of Greek and Roman men in his *Parallel Lives*. Several Romans produced personal memoirs that were of the nature of histories. Probably the best examples were Julius Caesar's *Commentaries on the Gallic Wars* and Marcus Aurelius' *Meditations*.

During the era when Greek ideas and art forms were first sweeping over the Roman world, attempts were made to imitate the magnificent Greek dramatic art. The most outstanding Roman dramatists were Plautus (third century B.C.) and Terence (second), both writers of comedies. But drama failed to take root among the Romans. Moreover, only occasionally did a fiction writer grace the literary scene. These gaps in the scope of Roman literary genres suggest that the creation of highly imaginative literature was foreign to the Romans, who had to be tied to reality—to history, to current moral problems, to personal experience.

4. ART

Originally inspired by Greek forms, motifs, and techniques, the artistic genius of the Romans matured slowly after about 250 B.C., reaching its full maturity during the first two centuries A.D. During that "golden age" the imperial government provided powerful impetus to artistic creativity, perhaps partly for economic and propaganda reasons, but also because a succession of emperors and the members of the ruling class in Rome enjoyed beauty and refinement. This imperial art never lost its Greek imprint, but it reflected innovations that gave Roman art a distinctive character.

Rome's most impressive artistic achievements were in architecture, where important elements were added to what was borrowed. The Romans invented concrete, which provided a cheap, durable, and adaptable building material. This material allowed architects to exploit the arch, the dome, and various forms of vaulting more effectively than had been done before and to create imaginative exteriors by the use of marble and brick facings over concrete. These technical advances permitted larger structures and innovative

Figure 11.2 A Roman Aqueduct The Pont du Gard, built across the River Gard to bring water to the Gallo-Roman city of Nîmes, is an impressive monument to Roman engineering skill. The structure rises 160 feet above the river bed and is about 900 feet in length; each of the large arches is about 80 feet across at its base. Roman architects and engineers have seldom been matched in the application of the arch to utilitarian ends. (Art Resource)

variations on the rectangular ground plans and the dominant horizontal elevation lines characteristic of the typical Greek structure.

Unlike the Greeks, the Romans did not excel in temple building; generally, they were content to imitate the Greek style, as is illustrated by the famous Maison Carrée still standing in Nîmes, France. However, they were capable of innovation. The Pantheon, built in Rome in the second century A.D., is one of the greatest round temples ever built. Its domed roof, 142 feet in diameter and supported by niche-filled concrete walls, covers a vast internal space that evokes a sense of awe. A rectangular porch, its gabled roof supported by Greek columns, leads into this inner sanctum, supplying a pleasing mixture of Greek

and Roman architectural ideas.

Much more distinctly Roman were public buildings: forums, baths, ampitheaters, aqueducts, bridges, meeting halls (basilicas), and palaces, built in abundance not only in Rome but also in provincial cities throughout the empire (see Figures 11.2 and 11.3). The Roman Forum, a huge complex of meeting halls, market facilities, and shrines, all laid out on an axial plan, reflects the Roman genius for planning and for adapting architectural forms to a variety of uses. The Colosseum, a massive sports facility begun during Vespasian's reign, accommodated fifty thousand spectators and provided special boxes for the emperors and other dignitaries. It featured an elliptical ground plan above which were elevated four

FIGURE 11.3 Roman Architecture
This photo of an arena and a theater built in Arles in southern France near the end of the first century B.C. illustrates the Roman talent for constructing impressive public buildings to serve as the focus of civic life. Arenas provided the settings for such popular activities as races, gladiatorial combats, and wild animal hunts. The close proximity of a spacious theater suited for drama, dance, song, and poetry reading suggests a wide range of interests among the citizens of a Roman provincial city. (French Government Tourist Office, New York)

levels of arch-covered passageways giving access to the seats looking down on the arena where the bloody combats so beloved by the Romans occurred. The most common Roman building was the basilica, essentially a long hall flanked by side aisles and often featuring a rounded apse at one end. The walls of the main hall extended above the roofs of the side aisles, allowing windows to be cut high in the walls. Arches and columns were skillfully used to permit access from the side aisles into the main hall and to roof the long halls; in the Basilica of Maxentius (early fourth century A.D.) a concrete roof was put over a main aisle eighty feet wide. Roman baths, which consisted of a great central court surrounded by numerous smaller rooms, demonstrated the Roman talent for organizing interior space for utilitarian purposes and for creating internal plumbing and heating systems. The Romans also built huge imperial palaces (the most famous are those of Nero and Domitian) and rural villas characterized by multistoried layouts featuring different-sized and -shaped rooms and sumptuous internal decor (see Color Plate 4). Not the least accomplishment of Roman architects was the development of living quarters suited to the needs of crowded cities: multistoried concrete structures containing standardized small apartment units suited to the needs of low-income residents.

Roman sculptors were less innovative than were architects. Greek and Hellenistic models were constantly and even slavishly imitated. The best Roman sculpture was devoted to portraiture and to relief work treating historical incidents, both art forms especially useful in serving the purposes of patrons who wished to be remembered either as individuals or as servants of the state. The artists who rendered these statues were remarkably adept at realistic portrayal, but always their work accentuated the dignity of their subjects (see Figures 8.1, 9.2, and 10.1). Roman relief carvings—featured especially on the walls of public buildings, arches and columns celebrating the deeds of emperors, and coffins honoring the dead—were remarkably effective in capturing scenes from everyday life in a way that conveyed a powerful message lauding the feats of those honored, especially in the service of the state (see Figures 9.1, 9.3, 10.3, 11.1, and 12.2). Perhaps the most remarkable example of Roman relief work is the freestanding column erected to celebrate Trajan's military triumph in Dacia. Around the column spirals a continuous scene 700 feet long that depicts in almost photographic detail the activities of about twenty-five hundred figures engaged in a military campaign. The limited survival of Roman painting (see Figure 10.2 and Color Plate 5) and mosaic work (Color Plate 6) suggests that Greek and Hellenistic influences remained strong and that these arts played an important role in decorating interiors, thus being strongly shaped by architectural plans. Painters and their patrons were especially fond of mythological subjects and portrayals of nature.

5. PHILOSOPHY, SCIENCE, AND RELIGION

Philosophical interests in the Roman world followed lines established during the Hellenistic period, focusing chiefly on applying classical Greek philosophical principles to ethical issues facing individuals and society. While many of the most significant philosophers in the Roman world were Greek speakers, educated Romans absorbed their ideas and sought to utilize those ideas to understand and to formulate answers to problems facing the Roman world. The most significant accomplishment of these Roman thinkers lay not in advancing philosophical speculation but in recasting Greek philosophy into a Roman idiom and transmitting that wisdom in the Latin language to later western European society.

Six individuals will serve to illustrate the main currents of philosophical development during the period of Roman domination; most of them were not philosophers in the strict sense but writers, statesmen, or educated citizens seeking personal and social guidance from philosophy. Cicero (106–43 B.C.), famous as a lawyer, statesman, and author, reflected a powerful tendency in philosophical thought to intermingle the viewpoints of various schools into an eclectic response to philosophical issues. But the Hellenistic schools continued to flourish. In his *On the Nature of the Universe*, the poet Lucretius (ca. 95–55 B.C.) used his talent to celebrate the Epicurean ideal of seeking pleasure and peace of mind in a materialistic universe through contemplation and withdrawal from the world. Particularly attractive to many intelligent Romans was the sober philosophy of Stoicism, which was perhaps the most influential philosophical movement of the first two centuries A.D. Three individuals were its noted advocates: Seneca (ca. 4 B.C.–A.D. 65), an essayist who served Nero; Epictetus (ca. 55–135 A.D.), a freedman who, after being exiled from Rome, spent most of his life teaching his ideas to ordinary people; and Emperor Marcus Aurelius (A.D. 121–180), whose famous *Meditations* summarized the Roman version of the Stoic world view. The Roman Stoics did not neglect the emphasis of Hellenistic Stoicism on personal peace of mind, but they gave greater attention to social responsibility and public morality. Especially influential was their expansion of the idea of an all-powerful, unchangeable law of nature governing the universe to provide a justification for a single human community governed by a system of law that conformed to the law of nature. Perhaps the thinker most important for the future was Plotinus (A.D. 204–270), an Egyptian who spent much of his career in Rome teaching a system called Neoplatonism. Derived from Plato's thought, Plotinus' system as set forth in his *Enneads* posited the superiority of the spiritual world over the material, the existence of a supreme being at the summit of spiritual reality, and the possibility of human participation in spiritual reality through a mystical experience that involved the penetration of the supreme spiritual being into the human spirit properly prepared by contemplation. Neoplatonism represented a fundamental aspect of the development of thought during the

Roman period: the merging of philosophy and religion, a trend that perhaps best met the needs of what was increasingly becoming an "age of anxiety" and that would soon provide a fertile field for Christian thinkers.

The Roman period was not marked by significant advances in science. Perhaps the most notable achievement resulted from the effort of scholars, such as Pliny the Elder (ca. A.D. 23–79), Galen (A.D. 131–201), and Ptolemy (ca. A.D. 121–151), to compile great encyclopedias intended to summarize all scientific knowledge contained in Greek and Hellenistic sources. These compilations would long remain the chief guides to understanding nature. The Romans excelled in practical science: the engineering of monumental structures; the construction of roads, bridges, aqueducts; more effective farming techniques. The technical skills developed by engineers, artisans, and farmers formed a precious heritage perhaps as important to the West as was the literary, artistic, and philosophical tradition nurtured and transmitted by Rome.

While the educated upper class of the Roman world absorbed Greek and Hellenistic philosophy and science and adjusted that material to the needs of the Roman world, the basic outlook of the great bulk of society was powerfully influenced by religion. The ancient family and civic religions continued to shape Roman thinking, and attempts were made by rulers such as Augustus to reinvigorate them. Between about 100 B.C. and A.D. 180 religious life everywhere in the empire was greatly enriched by the spread of Hellenistic mystery religions. Particularly appealing were the cults of the Great Mother goddess associated with Cybele, of the Egyptian goddess Isis, and above all of the Persian deity Mithra, which took deep roots in the Roman army. The ideas and practices associated with these religions emphasized personal identification with a deity through highly emotional rituals and life after death earned for good behavior. Such concepts tended to undermine traditional Roman religions that stressed highly formalized rituals performed by collectivities in return for material rewards. The trend already under way during the Hellenistic Age toward religious syncretism—the mingling of beliefs and practices—continued everywhere in the Ro-

man world. The ground was being prepared for the acceptance of a common religion. The advocates of that religion—Christianity—were already spreading their "good news" during the golden age of the Roman Empire.

6. LAW

One of Rome's most enduring cultural monuments was its law, vital not only as a force promoting orderly life throughout Rome's history but also as a legacy handed on to later societies to guide them in establishing effective societal relations. As early as 449 B.C. the principle was set forth in the famous Twelve Tables that citizens had rights that could be claimed and defended in courts. From thence on these rights of citizens, collectively constituting the *ius civile*, were explored, tested, and expanded in the context of changing times. During the republican period the enactments of assemblies enriched the substance of the law. Even more important, the magistrates charged with administering the law, the *praetors*, were allowed to pronounce their interpretation of the law at the beginning of their term; this practice resulted in the constant reinterpretation of the law within a framework that highlighted principles that should govern the *ius civile*. During this same period, the decisions of the judges who actually conducted cases in court constituted an ever-growing body of precedent that had the weight of law. These judges were advised by *jurisconsults*, specialists whose study of the law allowed them to assert a significant role in shaping the precedents that were applied in court as law. Roman expansion presented judicial officials with the problem of settling cases involving noncitizens. The result was the development of a law of nations (*ius gentium*), which represented a mixture of the laws of subject peoples, Roman practices, and the commonsense decisions of judges. With the institution of the Roman Empire the content of the law was further expanded by a vast outpouring of the decrees issued by the emperors attempting to ensure that the huge empire would be ruled uniformly and equitably.

As the body of the law expanded and as the society to which it was applied grew more complex, there was increasing pressure to codify the law into a single, systematic body. This concern had become central to the study of law by the second century A.D., when a series of brilliant *jurisconsults,* working under the patronage of the emperors, focused their attention on defining the principles undergirding sound law and its application. Their efforts were spurred by their realization of the importance of unified law as a tool for governing the empire and by their awareness that the distinction between citizens and noncitizens was disappearing. In addition, their thinking was decisively influenced by Stoic philosophy, which argued that there existed a law of nature (*ius naturale*) governing the universe to which human law must conform. The concept of natural law was a fruitful source of principles according to which all aspects of human law could be arranged and interrelated into a consistent, logical body. The codification of Roman law was not completed until the reign of Emperor Justinian (A.D. 527–565). But as imperial legislators, judges, and students of law moved toward that end, their efforts shaped an immense body of law that became a storehouse to which many people would turn in the future for guidance in the humane, equitable conduct of human affairs.

7. THE ROMANS AS SPREADERS OF CULTURE

When assessing the role of the Romans in cultural history, one must give them due credit for raising the level of culture in large areas previously little affected by higher civilization, especially in the western part of the empire. They were much less exclusive in their attitude toward non-Romans than were the classical Greeks, chiefly because they understood from early in their history the importance of Romanization in establishing and maintaining their domination over their culturally diverse subjects. The marks of their success as spreaders of culture are still visible. For example, the Italian, French, Portuguese, and Spanish languages are direct descendants of the Latin spread in those areas when the Romans conquered them. A modern traveler in western Europe and North Africa will repeatedly encounter the remains of Roman baths, aqueducts, temples, theaters, and roads—all evidence of the presence of the Romans as a creative force in enriching life in these areas.

The processes through which Romanization was achieved were complex. Roman soldiers, officials, merchants, and colonizers were important agents in carrying Roman culture outward across the empire. The Roman government actively promoted the creation of cities and encouraged those settling in them to imitate Roman ways. Local aristocracies were encouraged to become Romanized as a test for their eligibility for citizenship and for Roman approval of their leadership of local government. In these urban centers, schools were established to teach grammar and rhetoric and to promote the study of literature and philosophy; as a result, a common store of ideas and set of tastes spread to the far corners of the empire. The imperial government promoted extensive building activities, which led to the spread of a common style in architecture, sculpture, and painting. Scholars, religious missionaries, philosophers, artists, and teachers circulated freely throughout the empire to spread a common culture. From the third century B.C. onward, the government and the aristocracy of the city of Rome welcomed artistic and intellectual talent from all over the empire, making the capital of the empire the center of a cosmopolitan culture from which flowed influences affecting life throughout the empire. All of these factors combined to bring large numbers of people under the sway of a common culture that would decisively affect their histories for many centuries to come.

SUGGESTED READING

General Treatments

Pierre Grimal, *The Civilization of Rome,* trans. W. S. Maquinness (1963).
John Boardman et al., eds., *The Oxford History of the Classical World* (1986).
Two insightful surveys of Roman cultural life.

Religion

Margaret Lyttelton and Werner Forman, *The Romans: Their Gods and Their Beliefs* (1984).
John Ferguson, *The Religions of the Roman Empire* (1970).
Ramsay MacMullen, *Paganism in the Roman Empire* (1981).
Any of these three titles will provide rich material on religious life in the Roman world.
Stewart Perowne, *Roman Mythology,* new rev. ed. (1984). A splendidly illustrated description of Roman myths.
Alan Wardman, *Religion and Statecraft among the Romans* (1982). A fine explanation of the role of religion in political life.

Cultural Achievements

Stanley F. Bonner, *Education in Ancient Rome: From the Elder Cato to the Younger Pliny* (1977). A full treatment.
Elizabeth Rawson, *Intellectual Life in the Late Roman Republic* (1985). A landmark study dispelling stereotypes about the lack of Roman intellectual creativity.

Moses Hadas, *A History of Latin Literature* (1952). A clearly written survey.
R. M. Ogilivie, *Roman Literature and Society* (1980). Seeks to relate literature to social conditions.
F. H. Sandbach, *The Stoics* (1975). Describes the basic ideas of the Stoics.
H. F. Jolowicz and Barry Nicholas, *Historical Introduction to the Study of Roman Law,* 3rd ed. (1972). A massive survey.
Richard Brilliant, *Roman Art from the Republic to Constantine* (1974).
Bernard Andreae, *The Art of Rome,* trans. Robert E. Wolf (1978).
Cornelius Vermeule, *Roman Art: Early Republic to Late Empire* (1978).
Three well-written and -illustrated treatments of Roman art.

Sources

Kevin Guinagh and Alfred P. Darjahn, eds., *Latin Literature in Translation,* 2nd ed. (1952). A good sample of Latin literature. Better still would be to read the complete works of the major Latin authors mentioned in this chapter; their works are readily available in good translations.

RETROSPECT

Few epochs in all history witnessed greater achievement than that extending from the time when the Greeks emerged from their Dark Age about 800 B.C. to the generation that saw the Roman imperial order reach its full maturity about A.D. 180—the epoch from Homer to Marcus Aurelius. We might well ask why this epoch was so fruitful. The answer is at once simple and profound: Greco-Roman civilization made humans its central concern. Its motto was spoken by Protagoras: "Man is the measure of all things." Socrates formulated its one commandment: "Know thyself."

We cannot help being impressed at how much the Greco-Roman world discovered about humanity. At grave risk of oversimplification, we might single out a few of these discoveries as being the foundation stones of Greco-Roman civilization. First was human rationality. Second was the ordered universe that provided the setting for human activities. Third was rational humans' capacity for positive good. Fourth was the capability of people to transcend whatever they were at any instant through knowledge and good action. Last was the political nature of human beings, which gave them no alternative except to join others to realize their potential to know, to be good, and to outreach their present condition.

Yet this majestic achievement was somehow flawed, even in the minds of its creators. The Greeks and the Romans were never completely convinced that their own vision of humanity was true. They suspected that in human beings lurked an elusive element of the demonic and that beyond them existed forces they were powerless to control.

Moreover, the kind of society that emerged from the centuries-long effort to create a world fit for reasonable, good, enlightened people had some features that were disturbing. The confidence that political action could achieve perfection had given the state a dangerous dominance over its peoples at the expense of other dimensions of existence. The majestic assumptions about human rationality and capacity for good had given undue power to those who managed to acquire the symbols of rationality and good: an education, offices, wealth, and manners. These aristocrats tended to be oblivious to those who had not been enlightened or blessed with power and prestige: women, slaves, even lower-class citizens. The politicized and intellectualized flavor of classical civilization bred in those who wielded power and participated in the mainstream of cultural life a disdain for other kinds of activity—especially labor—and for other kinds of human behavior—especially that emerging from the emotional side of human nature. The rationalizing of human conduct and of nature bred an intellectual posture that saw things in terms of absolute, fixed forms and found it difficult to accept or to initiate change.

These insights might well have persuaded people living in the second-century Roman Empire of what now seems fairly evident: Classical men and women had learned much about human nature and that knowledge had liberated some of them to enliven and beautify the world, but they had not seen human nature whole. The civilization they constructed had inherent limitations arising from their restricted view of humanity. Perhaps the end product of the classical world is symbolized by a man who revealed his soul at the very end of the period—Emperor Marcus Aurelius. Marcus Aurelius was the embodiment of the best of humanity as conceived in the Classical Age: reasonable, good, serious, politically aware, sensitive to others. As ruler over a marvelous political system, he appeared to have the power to achieve whatever the good of humanity demanded. Yet in his *Meditations* he emerges as the victim of a cruel joke—a man caught up in a mechanical universe running on forever without change, a man who knew and understood but found nothing to do, a man so good that the nature of evil eluded him, a perfect citizen who was destined to the unappetizing business of fending off stupid barbarians. What was there to do but to resign oneself? One suspects that a kind of bloodless, cold, unemotional resignation in the face of what reason and goodness cannot encompass is what classical civilization finally meant. For all its accomplishments, the classical world had still not learned enough about humanity.

But whatever its limitations, classical civilization had changed the course of history. No nation, no people, no civilization of the future could escape its influence—especially not the inhabitants of Europe.

PART THREE

THE FALL OF GRECO-ROMAN CIVILIZATION, A.D. 180–500

During the second century A.D. Greco-Roman civilization had established unchallenged sway over the Mediterranean basin and extended its influence inland from the sea to three continents—Europe, Asia, and Africa. A vast community had been created; within it a bewildering variety of peoples were bound together by powerful forces. The political genius of the Romans, embodied in the imperial system of government, furnished the most potent bond of community. Almost as important were the widely shared cultural concepts that created a common basis of discourse and a common system of values. Derived primarily from the Greeks and finding expression in a remarkable literature, art, philosophy, and learning, this cultural force of unity had been adopted by the Hellenistic world and then spread through the entire Mediterranean world by the Romans. The shared political system and cultural values were powerfully reinforced by common economic ties that linked the many parts of the Mediterranean world in an interdependent material existence. The simultaneous operation of these unifying forces produced one of the most magnificent eras in all human history.

However, no human order, however strong it appears, is perfect, and no community of men and women, however confident they are of their talents, is safe from change and its tensions. As the second century A.D. drew to an end, serious stresses emerged within the basic structures of this splendid Mediterranean community. The long process leading to the formation of that community was reversed, and forces of disintegration became dominant. Within a relatively short time a vast transformation occurred in the Mediterranean basin. Greco-Roman civilization was eaten away by incurable sicknesses within its body and torn apart by the assaults of barbarians from outside. The disintegration of that civilization has always held a fascination for students of the past, prompting them to ask why it is that humanity's greatest achievement—a mature civilization—cannot be made to last. Intriguing as the question might be, the fact is that the end of classical civilization left the vast population of the Mediterranean world with no alternative but to set out again to construct new and viable patterns of life.

CHAPTER 12

The Decline of the Empire and the Rise of Christianity

FIGURE 12.1 The Ascension of Christ This ivory carving from about A.D. 400 portrays Christ's ascension into the hand of God while an angel speaks to the three Marys and soldiers cower in terror. It illustrates how Christian artists adapted classical art styles to Christian purposes; note especially the pagan sarcophagus, which certainly had no part in the scriptural account of this crucial event in Christian history. (Marburg/Art Resource)

An era of transformation of the Roman Empire began with dramatic suddenness during the century following the death of Marcus Aurelius in A.D. 180. In vivid contrast to the *Pax Romana* of the second century, the third century A.D. was characterized by almost incessant civil war that deeply disturbed the internal order of the empire and increased its vulnerability to outside attack. Amid the political crisis, basic economic and social maladjustments surfaced to add to the stress. And intellectual and spiritual confusion sapped the capabilities of society to respond to changing times. In retrospect it is clear that the old Greco-Roman pattern of civilization was dissolving and that a new order was emerging.

1. POLITICAL CRISIS, A.D. 180–284

As the second century came to a close, the peace that had prevailed throughout the Roman Empire under the "good emperors" was shattered. There followed a century of violence that led some contemporaries to believe that the Roman peace was turning to ashes and that the empire might collapse. At the heart of this political crisis were two interrelated problems: the defense of the frontier and the succession question. The resolution of each increasingly rested with the military forces.

Even during the second century the danger to the empire from its outside enemies had been ominous. During the third century that threat reached crisis proportions, especially along the northern and eastern frontiers of the empire (see Map 10.1). The increasing pressure on Roman defenses was due chiefly to developments beyond Roman control. In Parthia, a new dynasty, the Sassanian, seized power in A.D. 224. Its aggressive rulers were dedicated to the restoration not only of Persia's ancient glory but also of its ancient territory—which included most of Rome's Asiatic provinces. Along the long European frontier the Germans became ever more dangerous, chiefly because of developments within the Germanic world that caused massive movements of peoples and the formation of larger groupings of tribes into warrior-led "nations" capable of more effective military actions. During the third century these foes repeatedly intruded into Roman terri-

tory to cause widespread disruption and to focus attention ever-increasingly on the need for stronger military forces.

The ability of the Roman government to respond to the needs of defense was constantly disrupted by internal strife centering on the succession question. The death of Commodus (A.D. 180–192), the son and successor of Marcus Aurelius, was marked by a brutal struggle among segments of the army to decide on a successor to the imperial throne. The victor was Septimus Severus (A.D. 193–211), a man whose career had identified him totally with the army. His dynasty controlled the imperial office until A.D. 235 and succeeded in maintaining internal peace and frontier defenses. But the Severan dynasty followed policies that planted a time bomb. Following the advice of Septimus to favor the troops and forget the rest of the population, the Severi encouraged the soldiery to think that the state should be run to reward the army—a not illogical concept in view of the mounting dangers along the frontiers. Their appetites whetted by the prospect of such favoritism, the soldiers became vitally interested in placing on the imperial throne a leader who would serve their interests.

The intrusion of the army into the determination of succession to the imperial office led to almost constant civil war from the end of the Severan dynasty until A.D. 284. Repeatedly various army units took up arms to elevate their generals to the imperial office in expectation of special favors. Successful leaders of these uprisings—often called "barracks emperors"—barely had time to reward their troops before they were challenged by new rebels and violently removed from office. The incessant civil strife had disastrous consequences. Effective defense of the frontiers was seriously impeded. Civil administration was badly disrupted by the constant change of emperors. An immense new burden was heaped on society to meet the insatiable demands of army units for special rewards. Civil strife disrupted economic life, making it more difficult to provide for the demands of the military and at the same time maintain the level of prosperity that had prevailed during the era of the "good emperors." All of these factors suggested that the disintegration of the empire was at hand.

However, amidst this chaos subtle changes were occurring to transform the essential nature of the imperial government in ways that allowed the empire to survive the third-century crisis. In essence, the political system was becoming militarized and autocratic. The "barracks emperors" were a different breed from earlier rulers. Most were provincials whose entire careers were spent in the army. They had little experience with or sensitivity to the problems of civil administration or the needs of the civilian population. They had little understanding of the fundamental principles undergirding the Augustan principate, which called for sharing power with the aristocracies of Rome and the imperial cities. Their major policy concern was the well-being of the military establishment. The army was enlarged considerably during the third century, often by recruits from outside the empire; and it was reorganized to provide greater mobility—especially in cavalry forces—for containing the outside forces that were able to penetrate the frontier defenses. Increasingly, the chief administrative posts in the imperial government were filled from the army at the expense of the senatorial class. The emperors moved inexorably toward more thorough regimentation of civilian society and economic activity to support the army. They intruded more decisively into the affairs of local city-state governments to limit local self-determination. Rule by a *princeps*, a first citizen on the model of Augustus or Trajan or Hadrian, was being replaced with rule by a *dominus*, an absolute lord over all citizens, increasingly viewed as mere subjects. As the third century unfolded, the fruits of this change began to be evident. For instance, during the reign of Aurelian (A.D. 270–275) Roman armies were able to curb the intrusion of outsiders and to restore Roman control over frontier areas that had become virtually independent. But the path toward military autocracy threatened essential features of the traditional political order.

2. ECONOMIC, SOCIAL, AND CULTURAL STRESSES

During the third century stress and transformation were not confined to the political realm. Economic production decreased, in part due to the ravages caused by civil strife and invasions and in part due to structural limitations inherent in the traditional economic system. Most serious was a decline in agricultural production. There appears to have been a shortage of labor, probably due to a population decline in the entire Mediterranean world resulting from a serious plague. Agricultural technology did not advance to offset soil depletion and erosion. The spread of the *latifundia* was depressive, chiefly because these large estates replaced independent small farmers with dependent *coloni* and because the large-estate owners sought self-sufficiency rather than production for a market. Trade and industry also were depressed. The disturbances accompanying the civil wars impeded the movement of goods. In their search for funds to reward the army the emperors of the third century regularly debased the currency, leading to massive inflation. Increasing regimentation of the economy in the interests of supplying the enlarged army limited opportunities for new commercial and industrial ventures. New capital was scarce because the directive elements in Roman society continued to invest their wealth in land and in nonproductive military expenditures and luxurious living. The aristocratic cast of society continued to preclude any thought of generating economic growth by elevating the standard of living of lower-class members of society.

The whole structure of society was changing in the third century. The ascending military autocrats systematically eliminated the old senatorial aristocracy from their traditional places in imperial administration and military offices. In cities throughout the empire local aristocracies were crushed by the burden heaped on them to provide money and supplies for the armies and deprived of their control over local affairs by the bureaucrats representing the central authority. Artisans and merchants were increasingly forced into compulsory associations (*collegia*) through which their wages and production were controlled in the interests of the state. The peasants were steadily being driven toward hereditary tenancy and dependency on landowners, conditions that made their already depressed condition even worse.

Two elements in Roman society were advantaged by the changing order: great landowners and soldiers. The owners of large estates were able to tighten their control over agricultural production and the labor force. The imperial government, interested chiefly in securing revenue and produce from the land to support the army and the bureaucracy, gave the landowners greater freedom to exploit the peasantry and to pass on to them the burden of taxation. As their control over the *coloni* expanded, the great estateholders moved inexorably toward independence of action and the satisfaction of their self-interest (see Figure 12.2). At the same time, soldiers enjoyed ever-greater status. Men of ability from nonnoble elements of society found the army the chief avenue for social advancement; many rose to key positions in public life—even the emperorship—to challenge the old aristocracy for social dominance. Even the lowest ranks of the army enjoyed favors not open to other citizens. Because the ranks of the army were increasingly filled with recruits from the most primitive areas of the empire or from "barbarian" outsiders, people little acquainted with or committed to traditional Roman ideas and institutions now moved to leadership roles in society.

The shifting patterns of social relationships had two major effects. First, the consensus among the members of *nobiles* that had been so vital to the governance of the empire during the first and second centuries was challenged and began to dissolve. Second, these changes opened the way for the emergence of new talent with entirely different interests and perspectives. Such fundamental transformations were bound to alter the way the Roman world was controlled.

In the face of the crisis of the third century the Roman world seemed paralyzed intellectually. Culturally, the third century was one of the least productive periods of the entire classical era. Writers, artists, thinkers seemed to have lost their ability to address the problems of their time creatively and their faith in the humanistic, rationalistic values of the Greco-Roman tradition. The vaunted powers once attributed to human beings to control their own destinies at last seemed inadequate in the face of the realities of a troubled world.

In fact, the troubled society of the third century increasingly sought and found refuge in another realm—in religion. The era was alive with powerful religious currents that seriously threatened

FIGURE 12.2 Roman Aristocratic Life This scene decorating a third-century A.D. mausoleum reflects important aspects of the daily life of a typical Roman noble—returning from the hunt (top) and settling accounts with his tenants and his financial agent (bottom). (Landesmuseum, Trier)

the classical world view and undermined allegiance to the state in favor of trust in the divine. Although the ancient civic deities of Greece and Rome still had their adherents, the Eastern mystery religions, with their personal deities, emotional rituals, and promises of eternal salvation, won increasing numbers of adherents at all levels of society. There was a vast resurgence of interest in astrology and magic. Even philosophy was permeated by mystical elements. Everyone seemed in search of escape from a meaningless world through mystical contact with the divine. In this quest many Greco-Roman values, including confidence in human reason, seemed irrelevant.

3. THE BEGINNINGS OF CHRISTIANITY

Among the diverse spiritual movements contending for attention during the third century was Christianity. Although still relatively young, this religion was soon to capture universal attention and to play a decisive role in transforming the ancient world.

When it originated early in the first century A.D., Christianity seemed to hold little promise for eventual success. It began as a splinter movement within the world of Judaism, a world charged with tensions born out of repeated frustrations of the Jewish hope to recover lost national independence and the expectations that eventually God's promise of supremacy to his Chosen People would be fulfilled. Since the eighth century B.C. the ancient homeland of the Jews had been ruled by a succession of conquerors—Assyrians, Chaldeans, Persians, the Hellenistic Seleucids, and finally the Romans after 63 B.C. The Romans were willing to concede special privileges allowing the Jews to practice their religion, but they were suspicious of Jewish visions of independence. At first the Romans established a client king in Judea to keep the peace in Rome's name. The autocratic conduct of these kings, typified by the hated Herod (40–4 B.C.), goaded the Jews to constant agitation. Augustus abolished the client kingdom and imposed direct Roman rule exercised by a prefect charged with keeping order and collecting tribute. This system did not pacify the Jews, who eventually revolted in A.D. 66. The Romans reacted savagely, crushing the rebellion in A.D. 70 and destroying the Temple.

The frustration of their national aspiration had by the first century B.C. bred serious division within the Jewish community. Most Jews accepted the idea proclaimed by earlier prophets that a God-sent messiah would deliver them from their oppressors. And they all sought to abide by the Judaic law as it was interpreted by a special group of learned men called *scribes*. But they disagreed on how to act in the immediate historic setting. The Sadducees, chiefly upper-class Jews, clashed with the Pharisees, who enjoyed strong popular backing, over how to deal with the Romans and how to interpret and apply Judaic law as a means of sustaining Judaic identity and purity. Smaller groups opted for more drastic solutions. The Zealots urged taking up arms against the Romans and showed their militancy by acts of terrorism. The Essenes, whose views have become much better known since the discovery of the Dead Sea Scrolls about forty years ago, sought to break through the letter of Judaic law to a new level of spirituality and to realize their ideals by withdrawal from the Jewish community into an ascetic life marked by a sharing of wealth and prayer. Added to these groups were individual prophets, such as John the Baptist, crying out that deliverance was at hand. Of considerable importance were the Jews of the Diaspora—those dispersed by accident or choice across the entire Mediterranean world. They were strongly influenced by Greco-Roman ideas and tended to incorporate these ideas into their religious life; to most Jews of Palestine this attitude raised strong suspicions of compromise, which threatened the purity of historic Judaism.

Into this complex and highly charged scene came Jesus, born into a modest Jewish household in about 4 B.C. at almost the same moment when Augustus was taking steps to bring the Jews under direct Roman rule. When he was about thirty, Jesus began a public ministry among the Jews that lasted about three years. His message was solidly grounded in the Judaic religious tradition but had certain fresh ideas that appealed to many Jews, especially the simple, poor people. He proclaimed himself as the Son of God made man to announce the arrival of God's promised kingdom. He urged his audience to prepare for the new day now dawning by repentance and spiritual renewal based on repudiation of worldly things and on love for God and fellow men and women.

Jesus did not ask his followers to abandon their Jewish heritage but insisted that they must transcend the empty observance of the law and routine performance of the accustomed rituals by opening their hearts to God's grace. As recorded in his Sermon on the Mount, he taught that in his Father's eyes the poor, the weak, the humble, and the peacemakers had a special place; and the rich, the powerful, and the prideful stood to lose their souls. To those who repented and opened their hearts to God he promised worldly cares less than those of a child and eternal salvation. Jesus anticipated that his followers would await the final realization of the Kingdom of God as members of an organized community. He assigned a special leadership role in propagating his word to certain of his followers, whom he called his disciples. He also instituted a ritual life involving a common meal where the faithful would share consecrated bread and wine in his memory.

Jesus' preaching attracted an enthusiastic following, including many women. In his teachings Jesus gave women a place seldom accorded them in contemporary religions. But Jesus also made enemies. His attack on the empty formalism of Jewish religious practice and on the materialism of religious leaders turned "the scribes and the Pharisees" against him. To them, his message was a threat to the whole fabric of historic Judaism. The power establishment in the Jewish community, especially the Sadducees, was disturbed by his appeal to the poor and the oppressed. And many of his early followers lost much of their enthusiasm when he made it clear that his mission was not to create or rule an earthly kingdom. His command to "render unto Caesar what is Caesar's" was proof that he would not take up the sword to liberate the Jews. This was certainly a disappointment to those who had waited so long for a messiah who would recreate a powerful kingdom of the Jews in this world. This combination of hostility from his enemies and defection among his supporters led to his death in about A.D. 29. Members of the Jewish community brought charges of blasphemy against him before the Sanhedrin, the high court of the Jewish community. That body judged him guilty and received approval to crucify him from Pontius Pilate, the Roman prefect, who was afraid that Jesus' preaching would provoke civil strife among the Jews.

Jesus' death triggered a crucial development. A group of his stoutest disciples was convinced that he had arisen from the dead, proving that he was the Christ ("the anointed"), the Messiah, the Savior sacrificed in accordance with divine plan to bring about the salvation of all humanity. This belief set the little band apart from the whole world; in the words of Paul, "We preach Christ crucified, a stumbling block to Jews and folly to the Gentiles . . ." (I Cor. 1:23). A new religion had been born.

4. THE SPREAD OF CHRISTIANITY

In the first years after Jesus' death his followers carried on as a sect of Judaism. They observed the Judaic law while holding to Jesus' precepts, especially his command that they be ready for the return of Christ and for the final establishment of the Kingdom of God. The larger Jewish community continued to regard these strange people with suspicion and hostility. But the flock did grow, in part through the efforts of Jesus' disciples. Christian ideas spread to many cities, particularly in Syria and Asia Minor, where they attracted the attention of Diaspora Jews and of non-Jews (called Gentiles by the Jews) to whom the religious message of Jesus appealed. Before long many were asking to join the new community and were being received. This development posed a grave question for the foundling movement: whether or not new converts were to be held to strict observance of Judaic law and practices. There were those in the primitive Christian community who took a conservative position, but others, typified by Peter, leader of the disciples, increasingly insisted on universalizing Christianity so that it would be acceptable to Jew and Gentile alike.

A major figure in shaping the Christian mission to the Gentiles was Paul of Tarsus. Born into a Jewish family that had earned Roman citizenship, Paul was a representative of the Jews of the Diaspora—an ardent defender of orthodox Judaism but a man who was familiar with the Greco-Roman cultural life of his native city. Early in his adult life he took an active part in resisting the spread of Christianity in the Jewish community, even to the point of persecuting Christians. But then he underwent a dramatic personal conversion to Christianity. Then followed a long missionary career, beginning in about A.D. 46, which took him to Asia Minor, Greece, and eventually Rome. Central to his missionary effort was his determination to win non-Jews to Christianity. His message emphasized what he understood to be the precepts of Jesus that were applicable to all humanity—the redemption of sinners effected by the Son of God through his death, the need for moral regeneration through faith and love of God and humanity, salvation as a reward for belief in Christ and acceptance of God's grace, purity of moral life. He set down these ideas in letters written to instruct those he had converted; these epistles marked a crucial step in establishing the basic formal doctrines of Christianity. By the time of his martyrdom in Rome during the reign of Nero (perhaps in about A.D. 67), the thrust toward making Christianity a religion distinct from Judaism and directed toward a universal audience had become dominant. The separation of the Christian and Jewish communities was hastened by the Jewish revolt of A.D. 66–70, whose savage suppression by the Romans greatly discredited Judaism in the Roman world.

Once launched in the Pauline direction, Christianity steadily spread over most parts of the Roman world. During at least the first century after Jesus' death, a series of dedicated missionary preachers working under all kinds of conditions were the chief agents of expansion. They concentrated their efforts in the major cities of the empire, so that early Christianity developed chiefly as an urban religion. Often these missionary preachers began their activities in the Jewish synagogues of the cities in which they were working. Their efforts usually won a small group of adherents who formed themselves into self-sustaining "churches." The members of these cells then took up the burden of spreading the faith, working in the local communities to increase the flock.

By the end of the third century, vigorous and expanding Christian communities existed everywhere in the empire (see Map 12.1). The heaviest Christian population was in the cities of Egypt, Syria, Palestine, Asia Minor, Greece, and Italy. Christians certainly formed only a small minority of the total population by A.D. 300, but they had become a potent factor in the Roman world, one far exceeding what might have been expected in view of their inauspicious beginning and their early struggles.

The progress of Christianity was not, however, unopposed. From time to time the Roman government persecuted Christians because of their refusal to discharge any civic responsibility—including military service—that involved recognition of the Roman deities. The Christians who suffered were viewed by their fellow believers as martyrs whose heroic example strengthened the resolve of most Christians to remain steadfast. Anti-Chris-

tian feelings were felt in many elements of the Roman populace. Among the masses of people there spread a battery of vile rumors about strange beliefs and immoral, bestial practices, rumors fed by the Christian refusal to participate in public religious rites and by their private, semisecret worship services. Roman intellectuals scorned Christianity, holding up for ridicule its simplistic, illogical concepts. The leaders of the state religion and of the Jewish synagogues constantly charged the Christians with false beliefs and debased practices. Several mystery religions featuring ideas and practices similar to Christianity proved worthy rivals; especially powerful in the third century was Mithraism, which won a wide following in the army.

The Christians made difficulties for themselves as well. From the very beginning there were divisions in their ranks on what constituted right belief and proper usage. The early communities disagreed on the nature of the relationship between Christianity and Judaism. The proper moral posture for a Christian was often a subject for debate, especially because some insisted on a puritanical denial of the world and its pleasures. By the second century and increasingly in the third, Christians disagreed violently on certain fundamental doctrines, especially those relating to the nature of Jesus' relationship to God, thus generating what may be called the first heresies. These conflicts inevitably set Christian against Christian and diverted the faithful from proselytizing.

5. REASONS FOR CHRISTIANITY'S EXPANSION

Yet Christianity did expand—geographically, numerically, and substantively. Its success was due to many factors, not the least of which were favorable conditions in the Roman Empire. Despite sporadic cases of persecution, an atmosphere of religious tolerance generally prevailed. Freedom of movement allowed Christian missionaries to travel where they pleased, as is illustrated by the case of Paul. The general weakening of the traditional civic religions associated with Roman public life caused people to seek individual spiritual sat-

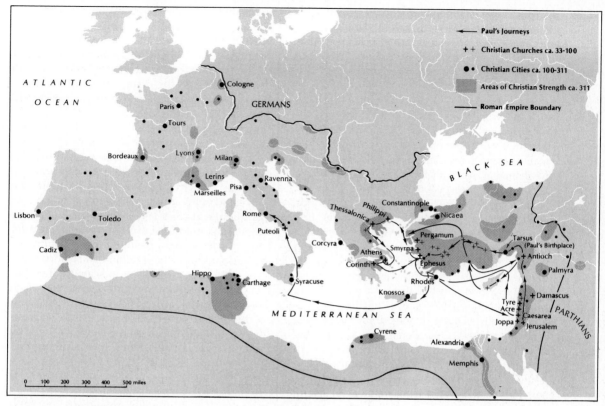

Map 12.1 **THE SPREAD OF CHRISTIANITY TO A.D. 311** This map shows how extensively Christianity had spread across the Roman Empire during the first three centuries A.D. In an important way the journeys of Paul provided a crucial beginning step in this expansion. In general, Christian life was still confined largely to cities by A.D. 311. The heavier concentration of Christians in the East is worth noting; it is perhaps understandable why the newly converted emperor, Constantine, chose to move the capital of the empire from Rome to Constantinople.

isfaction, and the chaos of the third century made the need for personal spiritual security ever more urgent. The existence of a single state uniting diverse peoples into a unified society pointed toward a single, universal religion applicable to all people regardless of origin or status. As noted earlier, powerful forces of religious syncretism had long been at work in the Hellenistic and Roman worlds, preparing for common religious life. In short, the time was ripe for Christianity. But a favorable environment cannot alone explain its expansion. Christianity proved to be a movement rich in inner resources, and it demonstrated an unusual capability to adapt to a changing world.

A fundamental source of Christian strength lay in its appeal as a religion. No matter how far in other directions we push the search for an explanation of its expansion, it is always evident that Christianity won converts primarily because its teachings answered their deepest religious needs. Such ideas as the existence of one almighty, loving, merciful God; his sacrifice of his son to redeem men and women; eternal salvation based on individual worth; damnation for sinners; and universal brotherhood supplied a powerful answer to those seeking to know about God's ways toward men and women. The humanity of Jesus, who had lived on earth not long before, gave intimacy and historical concreteness to Christianity that other religions lacked. Moreover, Christian teachings were dramatically and simply presented in a body of writing, called the New Testament, which took form during the century after the death of Jesus and which came to be accepted as the divinely inspired "good news" brought by Jesus. The Christians linked this holy book with the Jewish Bible, which they called the Old Testament, and gained a powerful weapon for presenting God's ways with respect to the world.

Another reason for Christianity's success was the organization that took shape during the first three centuries of its history. The first Christian communities consisted of a few converts lost in the non-Christian population of the cities of the Roman world. These people met together regularly to pray and sing, to share a common meal commemorating the Last Supper of Christ, and to be instructed. Leaders emerged in these cells; eventually, these leaders were given titles: *episcopus* (bishop), elder, and *diaconus* (deacon). With the passage of time problems emerged that called for firmer organization: larger numbers of Christians, persecutions, increasing wealth available to the community, disagreement over what constituted right beliefs and practice. Authority over all the affairs of the Christian community in each city began to settle on the bishop. Around this office there developed a powerful ideological justification, called the concept of *apostolic succession*. This theory argued that every bishop was a successor to the original apostles and heir to the spiritual authority that Jesus bestowed on those apostles to proclaim the faith and to forgive sinners.

In many large cities the Christian population became so numerous that one place of worship would not suffice to serve them. Additional churches were created with a priest in charge of each. However, the bishop retained final authority over these new establishments, ensuring the organizational solidarity of the Christian community on a citywide basis. This organizational evolution resulted in tightly knot, self-governing local units that reflected a basic entity in the ancient world—the city-state.

While many "churches" were being fashioned from city to city, the Christians never lost sight of their universal spiritual kinship, rooted in their belief in the one God who had given his son to ensure salvation for all his children. From this kinship resulted efforts to forge bonds of unity that would link the many churches into one Church. Jesus' disciples and the early missionaries such as Paul tried to keep in touch with as many Christian communities as possible by means of extensive travel and letter writing.

By the second century, bishops met together on a regional basis in *councils* to discuss common problems and decide on common solutions that each could apply in his own church. Certain bishops from great cities such as Jerusalem, Antioch, Alexandria, and Rome exerted considerable influence over lesser bishops in the regions surrounding these centers. These influential bishops began to be called "patriarchs" to indicate their preeminence. By the end of the third century there were Christians concerned with vesting ultimate authority over all Christians in the hands of one of these great bishops. A prime candidate was the bishop of Rome, who gained special prestige not only from the fact that Rome was the capital of the world but also from an important doctrine, the *Petrine theory*. According to this doctrine, rooted in a particular scriptural passage (Matt. 16:18–19), Jesus had granted Peter a special place as his vicar on earth; Peter had chosen Rome as the seat of that power; and those who followed him as bishops of Rome after his martyrdom were believed to have succeeded to Peter's authority as head of the total Christian community.

By A.D. 285, Peter's successors as bishops of Rome, increasingly referred to as *popes* (derived from the late Latin word *papa,* meaning "father"), were turning this claim to spiritual supremacy into active leadership in defining doctrine and prescribing discipline for Christian communities over much of the Roman Empire. And many of these communities were seeking the pope's guidance, especially in doctrinal matters. A kind of second Roman Empire was being born, subdivided into well-governed local units and headed by a spiritual "emperor."

Christianity also increased its appeal, especially to the sophisticated upper classes, by developing a systematic, reasoned statement of its

FIGURE 12.3 Honoring the Christian Dead Following an ancient Roman custom, early Christians sought to perpetuate the memory of the dead by decorating their sarcophagi with scenes from the life of the deceased. This third-century sarcophagus, clearly reflecting pagan art styles, shows the dead man (reading in the center while being prayed for) surrounded by representations of Christian history: the good shepherd, John baptizing Jesus (as a child), Jonah being washed ashore. (Alinari/Art Resource)

fundamental beliefs. This articulation of its doctrine in literary form marked a rather dramatic departure from primitive Christianity. Jesus had preached in Aramaic to an audience that was largely apart from the mainstream of Greco-Roman intellectual and literary life. The early leaders of the new religion were quite open in their rejection of pagan culture and thus established an anti-intellectual bias in the Christian community. For example, Paul could ask: "Has not God made foolish the wisdom of the world?" (I Cor. 1:20). However, this posture did not survive long. As soon as the Christians began their effort to convert Gentiles, they had to employ the Greek and Latin languages and the modes of thought and expression prevailing in the Roman Empire.

By the second century and more pronouncedly in the third, two particular forces spurred the Christians toward intellectualization of their faith: the need to answer the accusations of non-Christian intellectuals that the new religion was irrational, and the problem of resolving differences within the Christian ranks on the meaning of basic doctrines. The "apologists" answering the critics and the theologians defining the exact meaning of

the faith borrowed heavily from Greco-Roman philosophy, especially the Platonic tradition. The most influential figures in this movement wedding Christian thought and Greco-Roman culture were two scholars from Alexandria, Clement (ca. 150–216) and Origen (ca. 185–254). Their efforts increasingly persuaded Christians that classical learning had been a preparation for the true revelation and therefore useful in illuminating the meaning of God's word. The absorption of classical learning by Christianity had begun, increasing Christianity's appeal in the Roman world. The Christians were equally adept at adapting Greco-Roman art forms as a means of conveying their message (see Figures 12.1 and 12.3).

The Christians strengthened the appeal of their religion by developing ritual practices that were attractive in a world accustomed to pageantry and spectacles. Originally, Christian worship was simple. The faithful gathered in private houses to share a common meal, called the Eucharist, in commemoration of Jesus, and to pray and sing. As time passed, this ritual life became more complex, marked by the adaptation of Jewish and pagan practices to Christian uses. Special places for worship were built and adorned with art inspired by Christian beliefs. The eucharistic ceremony became more elaborate, constituting what came to be called the Mass. Ceremonies were established for such events as baptism, marriage, and burial. Special holidays—holy days to the Christians—developed to commemorate highlights in Jesus' career and the death of the early martyrs.

The Christian movement also developed a strong social consciousness. Jesus in his teachings and his life repeatedly exemplified the need for charity and kindness in dealing with others. This idea received expression in Christian practice almost from the beginning. Christians poured out their resources to help the sick, the poor, criminals, slaves, orphans, widows, and other unfortunates in society. In spite of their belief that happiness came in the hereafter, the early Christians did not close their eyes to earthly affairs.

The advance of Christianity was an amazing chapter in history. Historians have long debated whether the success of Christianity contributed to the decline of the Roman Empire. There is still no clear answer. In many ways most Christians were good Romans, as Jesus and many early Christian leaders urged them to be. They performed their civic duties as long as they were not required to deny their god. They paid their taxes and obeyed the emperor. They tried their best to help the unfortunate members of Roman society. The books they read on Christian theology contained huge portions of Greco-Roman philosophy. They worshiped in a fashion that bore a strong resemblance to non-Christian worship.

In other important ways, the early Christians were not good Romans. They served a god who would tolerate no rivals, including Roman emperors who claimed divinity. Believing that their god disapproved of the ways of non-Christians, they tended to avoid involvement in worldly affairs and to keep apart from ordinary social life. Their strong sense of sin led them to regard the world, including the Roman Empire, as a perpetual source of evil, hardly worth saving. Their belief in the omnipotence of God and in human frailty caused them to distrust human reason and to put no trust in human ability to build a paradise on earth. They thus found little that appealed to them in the basic premise of Greco-Roman civilization: the conviction that enlightened human activity could create a perfect society on earth. The Christian was a devoted, disciplined member of an organization existing independently of the Roman state. Through its evolving religious ceremonies, the Church kept before the Christians a series of symbols and arguments that made them feel their separateness and their uniqueness. Every Christian convert meant one fewer Roman citizen in the fullest sense of that word.

As the end of the third century A.D. approached, the Roman Empire had reached a critical juncture, resembling in some ways the situation the Roman world had faced at the end of the first century B.C. A long crisis had strained the imperial system and unleashed forces that pointed toward profound transformations of the political, economic, social, religious, and cultural structures of imperial society. The future of the empire depended on what kind of decisions would be made to accommodate the changing situation.

SUGGESTED READING

Decline of the Empire

Peter Brown, *The World of Late Antiquity from Marcus Aurelius to Muhammad* (1971).
Michael Grant, *The Climax of Rome: The Final Achievement of the Ancient World, A.D. 161–337* (1968).
Two provocative treatments of the late Roman Empire.

Joseph Vogt, *The Decline of Rome: The Metamorphosis of Ancient Civilization*, trans. Janet Sondheimer (1969).
Stewart Perowne, *The End of the Ancient World* (1966).
F. W. Walbank, *The Awful Revolution; The Decline of the Roman Empire in the West* (1969).

Michael Grant, *The Fall of the Roman Empire: A Reappraisal* (1976).

A. Ferrill, *The Fall of the Roman Empire: The Military Explanation* (1986).

These five works provide diverse interpretations of Rome's decline.

Rise of Christianity

Jocelyn Godwin, *Mystery Religions in the Ancient World* (1981). A good treatment of religions competing with Christianity.

E. Mary Smallwood, *The Jews under Roman Rule* (1981). A clear picture of the Jewish position in the empire.

Alan F. Segal, *Rebecca's Children: Judaism and Christianity in the Roman World* (1986). A challenging treatment of the interactions between the two religions.

W. H. C. Frend, *The Rise of Christianity* (1984).

Robin Lane Fox, *Pagans and Christians* (1987).

Two masterful, detailed accounts of the rise of Christianity.

R. A. Markus, *Christianity in the Roman World* (1974). An excellent brief account of the rise of Christianity.

Ramsay MacMullen, *Christianizing the Roman Empire, A.D. 100–400* (1984). Examines the reasons for the Christian victory.

Steven Benko, *Pagan Rome and the Early Christians* (1984). Describes how the pagans looked at the Christians.

Marta Sordi, *The Christians and the Roman Empire*, trans. Annabel Bedini (1986). Excellent treatment of relationships between the state and the Christian community down to Constantine.

Wayne A. Meeks, *The First Urban Christians: The Social World of the Apostle Paul* (1983). Excellent social history.

J. G. Davies, *Daily Life in the Early Church* (1952). Provides fascinating glimpses of the simpler aspects of early Christian society.

CHAPTER 13

The Destruction of the Roman Empire, A.D. 284–500

FIGURE **13.1** **Constantine the Great** This photo shows the surviving pieces of a huge statue, nearly forty feet in height, that Constantine had placed in a magnificent basilica he built in the Roman Forum. The massive head retains some features of earlier Roman portrait sculpture (see Figure 9.2); however, its creator was more intent in conveying Constantine's lordship than in producing a realistic portrayal of the emperor. (Art Resource)

In A.D. 284 a general named Diocletian seized the imperial throne by force. In itself this act was a repetition of what had happened repeatedly during the preceding half century; however, the accession of Diocletian marked a decisive turning point. He and his most important successor, Constantine (A.D. 306–337), undertook a reform of the empire that prolonged its vitality for another century. Then in the fifth century the empire was unable to resist the onslaught of Germanic invaders, who seized control of the western part of the empire and destroyed the unity of the Mediterranean world.

1. THE REFORMS OF DIOCLETIAN AND CONSTANTINE

Diocletian was by birth of Dalmatian peasant stock. Like so many third-century emperors, he worked his way to prominence in the military service and acquired many of the autocratic ways associated with military life. However, he did have a clear insight into the basic problems facing the Roman world and was aware of the trends unfolding during the third century to threaten imperial society. He acted decisively to carry out political reforms aimed at solving Rome's most serious problems.

Conscious of the chaos resulting from rivalry within the army for control of the succession and of the impossible burden imposed on a single ruler by the mounting problems of the empire, Diocletian sought a new arrangement to ensure orderly succession and a division of administrative responsibility. A system of shared authority was established: He and an associate each assumed the title *augustus* and to each was assigned a subordinate entitled *caesar.* When an augustus died, his caesar would succeed him as augustus and appoint another caesar. In theory the four corulers would share a single *imperium;* in practice each would be responsible for administering one of four newly established territorial units, called *prefectures,* into which the empire was divided. All would follow a common policy.

Diocletian sought to solidify and exalt the authority of the four corulers. The pronouncements of the rulers constituted the final law; no pretense was made of consulting with the Senate and the people. Various practices were adopted to lend a sacred character to the imperial office: Each ruler withdrew from public view as much as possible and adopted an elaborate court ritual designed to associate the ruler with divine powers. Each ruler began to be addressed as *dominus* (lord) rather than *princeps* (first citizen).

A significant expansion and restructuring of the bureaucracy was undertaken to ensure that the autocratic rulers were able to exercise their power. At each imperial court greater numbers of professional civil servants were organized under a chief official, called the *praetorian prefect,* whose powers were extended to embrace all civil affairs in each prefecture. The number of provinces was nearly doubled by dividing old ones, and imperial officials were installed in each to carry out the orders of the central government. An intermediary level of administration was interposed between the provinces and imperial court in each prefecture by the grouping of provinces into thirteen administrative units called *dioceses;* each had its own bureaucratic apparatus responsible to the augustus or caesar or to his praetorian prefect. This elaborate hierarchy gave the central government the means to act directly in local affairs and effectively ended the political role for the once active local city-state governments.

One of Diocletian's major concerns was the army. In part the expansion and the centralization of the bureaucracy was aimed at removing the army from involvement in civil affairs. More important was the need to increase the effectiveness of the army in the face of the external menace. Following initiatives introduced by his immediate predecessors, Diocletian sought to strengthen and regularize the permanent frontier garrisons and to develop a mobile strike force, strong in cavalry, capable of responding quickly to contain crises arising when the frontier forces were unable to cope with outside attackers. This reorganization increased the size of the army considerably—to about six hundred thousand troops—and raised monumental problems of recruitment and support.

The expansion of the bureaucracy and the army placed a massive financial burden on the imperial government. Diocletian tried to meet this challenge by restructuring the taxation system. His motives were many: dependable revenues, more equitable assessments, securing maximum income. A regular census system was instituted, which aimed at identifying units of land and human heads upon which uniform levies could be based. At the same time, the government imposed upon the key productive elements of society a requisition system aimed at extracting crucial produce in kind and services required to sustain the courts, the army, and the bureaucracy. To ensure that money, goods, and services would be available on a regular and permanent basis, Diocletian issued a series of edicts freezing large numbers of people in their occupations. As a further measure to stabilize the economy and control rampant inflation, Diocletian sought to fix prices for a wide range of commodities and services related to the operation of the bureaucracy and the army. He envisaged a regimented economy in which the state had first claim on all products and where all citizens were required to live their lives in the service of the state.

Diocletian's concept of autocracy demanded not only that citizens serve the state with their labor and wealth but also that they focus their minds on its well-being. He was convinced that religious unity was crucial in developing loyalty and devotion to the state. His reign was marked by a major effort to rally the citizenry around a worship of traditional deities, whose agent the semidivine emperor was. This policy brought him into conflict with the increasingly numerous and confident Christian community, which steadfastly refused to honor the pagan deities or to obey the state when it commanded them to do so. Such a position was intolerable to Diocletian, who responded with a series of punitive decrees in A.D. 303 and 304 that were aimed at destroying Christianity. His assault, the most serious ever faced by the Christians, took a heavy toll but failed in its prime objective. It did, however, demonstrate the degree to which religion had come to be viewed as a prime force sustaining autocracy.

When Diocletian decided to abdicate in A.D. 305, it appeared that most of his reforms had been successful in restoring order in the empire. Only one of his reforms was a signal failure—his elaborate plan for regulating the succession. Although lip service was given temporarily to its provisions, eventually there occurred a renewed outbreak of armed conflicts pitting various contenders and segments of the army against one another. The ultimate victor was Constantine, who between A.D. 306 and 324 won a series of victories that finally left him in sole control of the entire empire. Constantine was a worthy successor of Diocletian (see Figure 13.1). He vigorously pursued the main elements of Diocletian's reform program: strengthening the army; expanding and tightening bureaucratic control over imperial affairs; improving the fiscal machinery; enlarging the emperor's power; and imposing tighter control over the imperial population.

Constantine added important elements to the new order. Most significant was a new religious policy officially proclaimed in A.D. 313, when he and his co-emperor issued the Edict of Milan, granting religious freedom to all in the empire. The edict recognized the right of Christians to follow their faith. Behind the decree was an event of immense psychological impact: the conversion of Constantine himself. In A.D. 311 prior to a decisive battle in his rise to power, he had a vision that promised him victory if he would display the cross as his insignia. He did, and he won. Although Constantine was not baptized until just before his death in A.D. 337, after the Edict of Milan he gave every indication that he favored the Christian cause. He poured out money to build churches, drew clergymen into the councils of state, and extended to them a variety of special privileges. His legislation increasingly reflected Christian teachings. Although he tolerated other religions, he did little to encourage them. Every sign pointed in one direction: The empire was becoming a Christian state.

Contemporary Christians hailed Constantine's conversion as a sign of the fulfillment of God's plan; their enthusiasm laid the basis for designating him as Constantine "the Great." Many have doubted that his motives were totally religious. He certainly stood to gain politically by winning the support of the Christians. Perhaps he sensed that by committing the state to the service of Christian ends, he could create a reliable nucleus of supporters around which to build a unified empire obedient to an emperor who was God's chief servant. On the basis of the record of the preceding three centuries, it was not unrealistic to think that this aggressive religion had the potential to expand its flock to include all Romans. Constantine's behavior was not a cynical manipulation of religion. He was a man of his age, powerfully drawn to religion and especially to Christianity, not the least as a result of the influence exercised over him by his Christian mother, Helen. Whatever his motives, his action in linking the destinies of the Roman Empire and Christianity marked a turning point in history.

Hardly less momentous was his decision to build a new capital at the ancient Greek city of Byzantium, renamed Constantinople. Begun in A.D. 324 and officially dedicated in A.D. 330, this "new" Rome replicated many features of "old" Rome. Constantine's decision to undertake this expensive project was more than an autocratic whim. From the second century onward it was clear that old Rome was not the most advantageous physical center for the empire. With increasing frequency, emperors were chosen whose roots were outside Rome. The whole thrust of political development during the third century minimized the role of Rome's *nobiles* as prime factors in political life. Reflecting the obvious fact that Rome was badly located strategically in terms of frontier defenses, Diocletian's reorganization of the empire into four prefectures resulted in the emergence of new political centers: Nicomedia in Asia Minor, Milan in Italy, Sirmium in the Balkans, and Trier in the Rhineland. Prompted by such considerations, Constantine's choice for his capital was well advised. The site was nearly impregnable against attacks by land or sea. It offered more ready access to the most vulnerable frontiers—the lower Danube and the Euphrates River frontiers. The new city was close to the great centers of wealth in the East, and it was situated where Christian strength was greatest. It also offered its founder freedom from the restrictive traditions of republicanism and paganism, both deeply entrenched in old Rome.

The full impact of the founding of Constantinople was not immediately obvious. Rome remained an important city upon which Constantine continued to shower favors, including a magnificent church built in honor of St. Peter on Vatican Hill. Many could not conceive of Rome as anything except *caput mundi*—head of the world. But to some who especially cherished ancient tradition, it seemed that Constantine had turned the world around, allowing the East to surpass the West, the Greeks to prevail over the Latins. In fact, Constantine had created a bastion that in the not too distant future would serve as the center of a drastically reduced Roman Empire and as a major heir of Greco-Roman civilization (see Chapter 14).

2. AN UNEASY PEACE

Diocletian and Constantine had sought by political action to impose unity on the empire as a cure for its problems, a unity that called on all citizens to commit themselves in body and mind to the service of the state. For a time it appeared that their reforms had saved the empire. By contrast with the third century, the fourth century was one of relative order. Succession to the imperial office was usually peaceful, there was little civil strife, and the frontier defenses seemed secure. The era witnessed vigorous literary and artistic activity, much of it in the service of Christianity but some of it engendered by enthusiasm for traditional Greco-Roman culture. To many contemporaries it seemed again that the Roman political genius had saved the civilized world, as in the time of Augustus.

Yet there were ominous signs of decay in the Roman world that the reforms of Diocletian and Constantine not only failed to resolve but also deepened. Economic production continued to decline, hastened by economic regimentation and by the diversion of an ever-greater proportion of wealth to support the army and the bureaucracy. The burden of taxation, requisition in kind, and compulsory labor for the state fell chiefly on groups especially critical to economic well-being: peasants, artisans, merchants, and local urban aristocrats, all of whom took actions of some kind to avoid the burden at the expense of productivity.

The autocratic imperial government fashioned by Diocletian and Constantine revealed fatal flaws. The exalted emperors became more remote from practical affairs. The costly, ever-growing bureaucracy became intrusive, corrupt, and arbitrary to the point where it was universally detested. Considerable evidence suggests that in terms of effectiveness the army failed to respond to the immense sums spent on it. Increasingly its ranks had to be filled with German recruits, often commanded by their own chiefs, whose loyalty was suspect. The frontier garrisons were undermanned, and their troops often had to devote much of their time to supporting themselves. The actions of the military forces in laying hands on supplies were often arbitrary and brutal, generating deepening hatred between the military and the civilian population. Not a few contemporaries felt and even said that the imperial government had become a monster.

A dangerous manifestation of discontent took the form of withdrawal from public responsibilities. Citizens from all walks of life sought to evade taxation and military service. The senatorial class, once a vital element in imperial governance, turned its attention to accumulating land, creating self-sustaining estates, and living in luxury. Ensconced in their rural strongholds and often openly disdainful of "nonnoble" emperors and their lowly agents and army officers, these powerful figures defied the government's efforts to compel them to bear their share of the public burden. Usually they had their way. In ever-larger numbers peasants accepted a position as dependent tenants under these landlords as a way of escaping taxation, compulsory labor service, and military duty. In city after city across the empire members of local aristocracies fled to the countryside or took service in the imperial bureaucracy or joined the clergy in order to escape the responsibilities thrust on them by the government to deliver the money and the services due from their localities. Such evidence of disaffection pointed toward disunity rather than unity.

Equally disturbing was clear evidence that Constantine's religious policy failed to unify the state and arouse patriotic fervor. Christianity did continue its march to dominance during the fourth century, culminating when Emperor Theodosius (A.D. 379–395) made it the state religion and outlawed all others. The imperial policy of favoring Christianity alienated many Romans, especially aristocrats, who still placed trust in the ancient pagan religions. That resentment surfaced with particular vigor during the reign of Julian (A.D. 361–363), called the "Apostate" by the Christians because he repudiated Christianity and sought to replace it with a restored pagan "church." His effort failed, but it kept alive a fundamental schism in imperial society. Even the Christians were violently divided. During the reign of Constantine a bitter quarrel arose over the question of the Trinity. The Arians made God the Son subordinate to God the Father, denying the absolute divinity of Christ. The outraged Orthodox insisted that the Son was coequal with the Father and that, together with the Holy Spirit, these three "persons" formed a unity. In an attempt to settle this dispute, Constantine summoned churchmen from all over the empire to the ecumenical Council of Nicea in A.D. 325. This assemblage agreed upon the Nicene Creed, which accepted the Orthodox position and articulated a strong trinitarian position that all Christians were obliged to accept. However, the quarrel raged on throughout the century—and so did several other "heresies"—to create disarray among the Christians and to frustrate the efforts of the imperial government to impose unity. Some Christian leaders even challenged the right of the imperial government to interfere in religious affairs, claiming that the Christian community constituted a separate realm exercising an independent jurisdiction when religious issues were at stake. In short, Christianity failed to supply a vitalizing force in the service of the "new" empire; it was a movement with its own ends and strengths, not easily bent to other purposes.

Taken together these trends created divisions within imperial society and undermined the state's ability to muster its material and human resources. Their cumulative impact began to emerge at the end of the fourth century, when the empire had to face a major crisis brought on by a fundamental change in the relationships between the Romans and the Germanic peoples facing each other across the Rhine-Danube frontier.

3. THE GERMANS

In describing the decisive encounter between the Romans and the Germans during the fourth and fifth centuries, historians have traditionally referred to the Germans as "barbarians." The term is appropriate only if used to signify that the Germans differed from the Romans in terms of the basic features of the culture under which they lived. That difference is best reflected in certain fundamental Germanic institutions, each destined to play a part in shaping life in western Europe in future centuries.

The basic Germanic political institution was the *tribe,* headed by a tribal chief who was chosen primarily because of his ability as a war leader. Each tribe was composed of a number of kinship groups, or *clans.* The elders of these clans acting as a council played a decisive role in shaping tribal decisions, but all freemen capable of bearing arms were allowed to have some voice in determining collective action. Tribal government concerned itself with a limited range of affairs: war, religion, and justice. Other matters relating to group life were left largely in the hands of kinship groups; especially crucial was the responsibility of each kinship group to protect its members against injury from others. Each tribe had a body of customary law transmitted orally from one generation to another to regulate such relationships. In its substance Germanic law was primarily concerned with damages against persons. The law prescribed in monetary terms how much compensation could be demanded for various kinds of damage done to a person. That price, called *wergeld,* varied not only according to the nature of the crime but also according to the rank of the person in the kinship group. For example, any damage to a warrior commanded a higher *wergeld* than did the same offense against a woman of childbearing age; in turn, damage done to such a woman called for a higher *wergeld* than did a comparable crime against an aged person. It was the responsibility of those suffering damage or their kin group, not public authority, to initiate judicial processes to collect the *wergeld* defined by law. If the perpetrator of the damage agreed to pay the *wergeld,* then the issue was settled. If not, then the aggrieved kinship group often sought vengeance on the clan of the alleged criminal; the resultant feuds were a common feature of Germanic life. Customary law provided complex procedures for resolving disputes involving damages to persons. One such procedure, called *compurgation,* involved finding a certain number of individuals—depending on the nature of the crime and the status of the accused—who would swear under oath that the accused was innocent. Another, called *ordeal,* involved putting the accused to a test, such as holding a hot iron or being thrown into water, the results of which could be interpreted as a divine message indicating guilt or innocence.

Early Germanic economy was pastoral, but during the first centuries of the Christian era a simple agricultural economy began to develop. Although kinship groups claimed some rights over land, the basic unit of economic and social life was the household. Generally, Germanic marriages were monogamous, but some rich and powerful men had more than one wife. These households were in large part controlled by males, most of whom were presumed to be equals in early Germanic society. Although dependent on males in many ways, women enjoyed considerable status in Germanic society. Kinship ties were established through both male and female lines of clan groups. Women possessed wealth in their own right, chiefly as a consequence of gifts conveyed to them at the time of marriage. They also played an important part in the economic pursuits that supported family life.

Germanic religion was polytheistic, focusing particularly on the worship of deities embodying the forces of nature dominating the skies and the forests. An orally transmitted mythology existed to explain the nature and the powers of these deities, usually portrayed as remote, terrible forces that must be placated constantly through prayer and offerings. By about A.D. 400 the Germans had just began to develop writing. Yet they did possess a well-developed oral poetic tradition that dealt with the deities and with human heroes. Early Germanic art was devoted especially to jewelry made of precious metals and featuring animal forms and geometric patterns.

Obviously, the encounter between Romans and Germans involved the meeting of two entirely different cultures. It is important to note, however, that the Germans were not locked into a pattern of "backwardness." By the fourth century their society was changing. Small tribal groups were being unified, often by force, into *nations* ruled over by elected kings enjoying considerable powers. Within Germanic society there was also developing a unique institution—the war band (*comitatus*)—composed of warriors united by pledges made under oath to follow a military chief in return for a share of booty. These warriors became a kind of warrior aristocracy, increasingly dominant in society. The emergence of nations and of skilled war bands greatly increased the military capabilities of the Germans. As already noted, Germanic society was moving toward an agricultural economy that encouraged the development of an aristocracy of landowners at the expense of the older, more egalitarian social structure. These changing conditions made Germanic society dynamic, mobile, adaptable, and open to foreign influences.

These two different cultures had faced each other across a fixed frontier for four centuries before their decisive encounter in the fourth century. Although these confrontations had often been hostile, there were more positive aspects. The Germans often demonstrated a desire to share the fruits of Greco-Roman civilization, especially its material wealth. Although the Romans saw the Germans as "barbarians," they respected their physical prowess, their fighting skills, and their alleged moral excellence. They permitted Germans to cross the frontier as long as their movement could be controlled. Large numbers entered the empire as soldiers and farmers and became Romanized; many even rose to high places in Roman society. Roman influences sifted across the frontiers to affect Germanic society. For example, during the fourth century many Goths were converted to Christianity by Ulfilas, himself a Goth educated in Constantinople. Ulfilas provided a Gothic version of the Bible for his converts, a feat that required the creation of a written Gothic langauge. Such developments suggested that eventually the Germans might be absorbed into the mainstream of Greco-Roman civilization without causing any great disruption of its development. But that possibility depended on the ability of the Romans to control the interactions between themselves and the Germans. From the Roman perspective maintainence of the frontier defense system was the crucial factor.

4. THE GERMANIC MIGRATIONS AND THE FALL OF THE EMPIRE

At the end of the fourth century a dramatic sequence of events occurred within the Germanic world that resulted in a loss of Roman control of relations with the Germans and plunged the Roman Empire into a crisis. About A.D. 370 a horde of nomads, the Huns, suddenly swept out of central Asia across southern Russia. As they moved westward along the northern shores of the Black Sea, they encountered two settled Germanic nations, the Ostrogoths and the Visigoths. The former were quickly overpowered. The terror-stricken Visigoths begged permission to migrate as a nation across the Danube into Roman territory in the Balkans. Their request was granted. They were allowed to keep their own king and were promised land in return for military service. When the imperial government failed to provide for their needs, the Visigoths revolted and inflicted a crushing defeat on a Roman army led by Emperor Valens at the battle of Adrianople in A.D. 378. Rome now had a hostile Germanic nation within its borders. In the meanwhile, the Huns moved farther west where they created a large Hunnic nation north of the Danube and uprooted other Germanic nations (see Map 13.1 for the movements of the Germans).

For a brief time Theodosius, the last ruler of a united empire, was able to confine the Visigoths to the Balkan area by establishing them as Roman allies (*foederati*) to whom were assigned lands in return for military service. But Theodosius' death in A.D. 395 marked the end of the uneasy calm. He bequeathed his office to two sons, one assigned to rule in the West and the other in the East. Neither had much ability, and both allowed the direction of affairs to fall into the hands of ambitious generals whose power depended on Germanic troops. The result was a series of internal power struggles between the eastern and western courts that ended with loss of control over the Germanic hordes pressing on the imperial frontiers.

As the fifth century opened, the Visigoths, led by a capable king named Alaric, were skillfully playing a game of selling their services alternately to the competing emperors. Eventually they

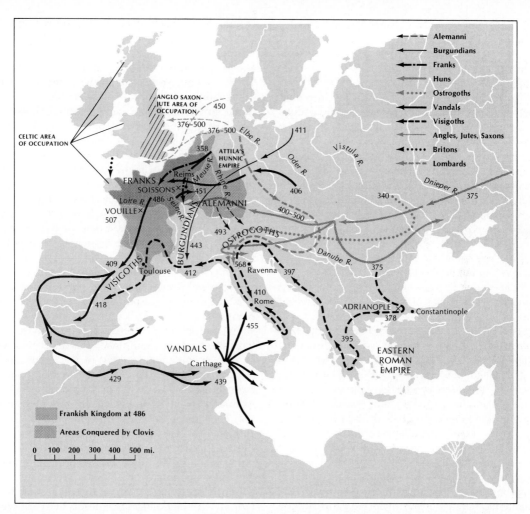

Map 13.1 **GERMANIC INVASIONS, FIFTH CENTURY** The map shows the movements of the various Germanic nations in the course of their invasions of the Roman Empire in the fifth century. Most of them ended their wandering by establishing a kingdom on Roman soil. Especially important for the future was the kingdom established by the Franks in Gaul.

turned against the West, having been promised by the emperor in Constantinople whatever lands they could conquer. Their repeated attacks on Italy necessitated the recall of troops from the Rhine and Danube frontiers and from Britain, but to no avail. In A.D. 410 they captured and sacked Rome. The frontier defenses in the West broke down, allowing other Germanic nations to pour into the heart of the empire. Their "invasions" led to the

political dismemberment of the empire in the West. In its desperation, the imperial government sought to control the Germans by assigning them areas where they could settle as allies, subject to Roman authority. In fact, wherever the Germans settled and whatever the terms, their kings and warriors soon became the real rulers. As a consequence, during the fifth century a series of independent Germanic kingdoms were founded on

Roman soil in the West to replace the unified imperial regime.

After their sack of Rome in A.D. 410 the Visigoths remained briefly in Italy and then were assigned rich lands in southern Gaul, where they established a kingdom that soon began to extend itself into Spain. Already other Germanic nations who had broken across the Rhine in A.D. 406—Vandals, Sueves, Alains—had made their destructive way across Gaul and into Spain. The Vandals, under the leadership of their one great king, Gaiseric, crossed into Africa in A.D. 429 and carved out a large kingdom that deprived Rome of access to its main grain supply. The Vandals developed sufficient sea power to allow them to pillage Rome in A.D. 455.

The Burgundians created a kingdom in southeastern Gaul in the Rhone Valley, effectively blocking the routes linking Italy to Gaul. Beginning about A.D. 425 Angles, Saxons, and Jutes came by sea to wipe out the badly weakened Roman outposts in Britain and to establish several petty kingdoms; in the process the newcomers drove the native Celtic population into Wales and across the English Channel into Britanny. Without abandoning their original homelands, Franks and Alemanni began the occupation of northern Gaul and the middle Rhine Valley. Late in the fifth century the Franks, led by a ruthless warrior king named Clovis (A.D. 481–511), seized most of Gaul as their base of power; in the process they drove the Gallic Visigoths into Spain and absorbed the Burgundian kingdom as well as much of the territory of the Alemanni. Italy, the last major territory in the West, was taken in A.D. 493 by the Ostrogoths under the leadership of King Theoderic. The confusion caused by the movements of these Germanic peoples was compounded by the presence of a powerful Hunnic kingdom established north of the Danube. Under their feared king, Attila, the Huns harassed the East and then invaded Gaul and Italy in A.D. 451–452, which were successfully defended by a coalition of Roman and Germanic troops. After Attila's death in 453, the Hunnic kingdom quickly broke up, leaving central Europe in a chaotic state.

While the boundaries of these new kingdoms remained fluid, there could be no doubt that by A.D. 500 the Germans had won the West. The fate of the empire in the East during the critical fifth century was quite different. True, German forces repeatedly ravaged imperial territory in the Balkans and sought entry into the eastern provinces. Their assaults were effectively blunted by the money, diplomacy, and military actions of the imperial government in Constantinople, which was not above bribing the Germans into diverting their attacks to the West. As a consequence, the Germans failed to penetrate the East, where the traditional imperial structures survived virtually intact.

The most dramatic result of the Germanic "invasions" was the slow dissolution of the imperial government in the West. Some of the generals serving the incompetent emperors fought valiantly to check the invasions and negotiated desperately to turn Germans against Germans. But the imperial government was simply unable to muster the resources required to contain the Germans militarily. The bulk of the Roman population showed little zeal for defending themselves; perhaps they valued the Roman imperial regime too little to spend much energy in its defense. The imperial regime in the West received little assistance from the richer East in defending the West. Although the Germans were settled under terms that gave the Roman government nominal lordship over them, in fact they took over real power. As the settlement process advanced, the Roman bureaucracy broke down, imperial income dwindled, the imperial armies melted away, and the authority of the successors of Augustus vanished. By A.D. 476 the political realities in the West were officially recognized. A German general, Odoacer, deposed the last Western emperor—ironically named Romulus Augustulus—and turned the insignia of the imperial office over to the emperor in Constantinople. In theory, this act reunited the empire under a single ruler. In reality, the emperor in the East had virtually no control over the West, where the Germans ruled by virtue of conquest. But they dominated without the benefits of the splendid political system created by the Romans. As a result, political chaos threatened.

Beyond the disruption of the imperial political system in the West, the impact of the Germanic migrations must not be overstated. The destruction of life and property was not excessive, and in most cases Germans and Romans settled side by side on peaceful terms. Except in Britain and along a thin stretch of the old empire facing the Rhine, the intruders were not sufficiently numerous to affect the ethnic composition or the language of the old Roman population. Many aspects of Roman civilization survived the shock of the Germanic intrusion to affect in a decisive way the future course of history in the West.

The main result of the Germanic migrations into the western empire was to accelerate and make irreversible certain trends in economic and cultural life that had begun before the Germans arrived. Economic decline continued through and beyond the fifth century. The new German overlords were primarily interested in agriculture; their settlement on the land hastened the trend toward a predominantly agricultural economy. City life suffered badly; most cities in the West shrank to a fraction of their old population and most of them ceased to be commercial, administrative, and cultural centers. Their decline meant the end of the urban aristocracy that had sustained Greco-Roman civilization in the West. While some Roman landlords were displaced by Germanic settlers assigned to their lands, most succeeded in retaining and even enlarging their holdings. Before the end of the fifth century, German and Roman aristocrats were intermingling to create a new ruling force in the West. Political disorder forced increasing numbers of peasants into dependency on great landowners, be they German or Roman. Most large estates became virtually self-sufficient, with the result that the West broke up into thousands of tiny self-contained economic units. Trade was substantially reduced, and manufacturing was increasingly centered in the isolated agricultural estates. All of these developments inevitably eroded the level of economic productivity.

The Germanic migrations also accelerated cultural stagnation in the West. The German rulers and some German aristocrats tried to absorb and sustain Roman intellectual and artistic life, but all they could do was imitate it; all too often their barbarism broke through the thin veneer of their adopted culture. The decline of urban life deprived traditional Roman culture of its basic environment. Educated Romans living in rural settings sought to support education, literature, and art, but their isolation and the growing irrelevance of ancient culture to a changed world made their efforts ineffectual. In fact, cultural leadership was passing into Christian hands whose cultural concerns were markedly different.

5. CHRISTIANITY IN THE LATE EMPIRE

Amidst the events of the fourth and the fifth centuries that disrupted the Roman Empire, Christianity showed great resilience and emerged from the ordeal as a decisive force in society. The fourth century was a particularly glorious period in Christian history during which it became closely identified with imperial society. Massive numbers of converts from all levels of society swelled the ranks of the Christian community to the point where Christians were the dominant religious force in the empire. Christian leaders increasingly advanced to prominent directive positions in society. The Church as a visable organization became a decisive agency in shaping life in imperial society, and its material wealth increased dramatically. The fourth-century Roman government gave powerful support to all of these developments, thereby intertwining the Church and the empire ever more closely. By about A.D. 400 the Roman Empire had truly become a Christian Roman Empire, a fact recognized by Theodosius when he designated Christianity as the state religion.

However, success brought new and serious problems. The avalanche of converts, no longer faced with the terrible possibility that baptism might spell martyrdom, diluted the spiritual fervor of pre-Constantinian Christianity. With the inadequately instructed and spiritually lax converts came an influx of pagan ideas and practices that threatened to obliterate Christian practices of worship and doctrines and that generated heresies that divided Christian from Christian. Discipline within the growing Christian ranks became more difficult. Wealth and power turned the heads of Christian leaders toward worldly pursuits. Especially threatening to the independence of the Christian community was the urge of political leaders to use the Church as a tool to advance political ends. In brief, the success of Christianity in the fourth century threatened to deprive it of its uniqueness, its zeal, its sense of mission, and its independence.

The Christian community of the fourth century proved itself to be highly resourceful in "reforming" itself to meet the challenges posed by changing times. One response was the strengthening of the powers of the clergy, especially the bishops, over individual churches and over the laity. These powers were used to define Christian behavior and modes of worship more precisely and to compel Christians to obey the evolving "law" of the Church, called *canon law*. A major beneficiary of this trend toward a stronger, more hierarchical governance system was the bishop of Rome. The fourth-century emperors showered wealth on the successors of Peter and relied on them to formulate dogma they hoped to impose on the entire empire as a means of combating heresy. The popes responded by expanding their claims to authority and by asserting that authority more vigorously, especially in matters of dogma and discipline.

During the fourth century Christianity found a new source of spiritual vision in monasticism. The monastic movement began in the late third and early fourth centuries in the deserts of Egypt. There a new breed of Christians, calling themselves "athletes of Christ," sought to follow Jesus' command to leave all worldly things behind by fleeing to the desert to seek perfection through prayer and mortification of the flesh. The first desert fathers, exemplified by Anthony, were hermits who sought perfection through individual actions. Soon these hermits began to gather into communities, or monasteries, where spiritual life was governed by rules that defined patterns of behavior and spiritual exercises for achieving perfection. Especially important in establishing modes for communal (*cenobitic*) monastic life were the rules of the Egyptian monk Pachomius and the Greek monk Basil. The spiritual heroics of the early monks electrified the Christian world. By A.D. 400, monasticism had spread over most of the Roman world. While the monastic ethos was excessive in its denial of worldly affairs and in its obsession with the danger of sexuality as a source of sin, it did remind the Christian world of the need to struggle in order to achieve spiritual ex-

cellence. It created a new type of hero to replace the martyrs of old; both men and women alike found its ideal of the Christian life irresistible. And for large numbers of ordinary men and women the holy men forged in the monastic environment became agents through whom divine favors could be gained to relieve the heavy burdens of a troubled, uncaring world.

Although most Christian leaders were quite willing to cooperate fully with the state in the promotion of a Christian empire, some resisted the claims of the state to control religion. They began to articulate concepts that limited the state's control over religion and that argued for religious liberty. Some even contended that Christian ends were more important than were secular ends and therefore must be supreme. On one occasion, for instance, the powerful bishop of Milan, Ambrose (ca. A.D. 340–397), excommunicated the Emperor Theodosius for massacring some of his subjects under circumstances that some thought exceeded the authority of worldly rulers. Ambrose justified his sentence on the grounds that the Church exercised a separate realm of jurisdiction that must take precedence over the power of the state when spiritual issues were at stake. As the concept of the independence of the Church took shape, it spurred discussion of the problem of where ultimate authority in the Christian community lay. More and more Christians agreed that the bishop of Rome, Peter's successor, was the spiritual head of the Christian world.

Perhaps the most significant success of the Christian community was its ability to generate an outburst of cultural activity that resulted in its assumption of cultural leadership in the late empire. That leadership was clearly demonstrated in the arts. Church building provided one of the chief outlets for the talents of architects, sculptors, and painters. They developed new modes of conveying the Christian message by creatively adapting the classical artistic tradition to Christian purposes (see Figures 12.1, 12.3, and 13.2). Some of the most inspired poetry of the age flowed from the pens of Christian writers seeking to express their thoughts and feelings about their faith. Christian writers such as Eusebius of Caesarea (ca. 260–340) recast the writing of history to fit the Judeo-Chris-

FIGURE 13.2   A Sixth-Century Christian Church   This magnificent church was built in Ravenna in honor of S. Apollinare. Its architectural form represents an adaptation of the Roman basilica style (see p. 146) for Christian purposes. The central hall (the nave) served as a gathering place for the faithful. An altar often stood in the semicircular apse at the far end of the nave. Aisles flanked the nave on either side, set off by columns and arches supporting the walls of the nave. These walls rose above the roof over each side aisle. At their upper levels the walls were pierced by windows that lighted the structure's interior. This style of architecture was destined to assert a powerful influence on religious architecture in later western European history. (G. E. Kidder-Smith)

tian version of historical development. Inspired chiefly by the feats of the monks, Christian writers developed a new literary genre, hagiography, devoted to the lives of the saints.

But the jewel of the period was the theological writings of a remarkable group of intellectuals known as the *church fathers*. Among the most prominent were the Greeks Athanasius, Basil, Gregory of Nyssa, and Gregory Nazianus, and the Latins Augustine, Jerome, and Ambrose. Although each was an individual intellectual in his own right, this potent group of thinkers collectively reshaped the basic thrust of intellectual life.

The fruit of their labor was a massive body of literature destined to feed intellectual life for centuries to come. Although their intellectual efforts were rooted in their deep Christian faith, they borrowed boldly and creatively from the content and the methods of the Greco-Roman literary, philosophical, and scientific tradition to build a consistent, logical, articulate statement of the Christian interpretation of the universe. In the process they not only provided reasoned and persuasive doctrinal positions but also literally redefined human values and the purpose of human existence, thereby overpowering the classical

Greco-Roman world view. Yet they did so in a way that made the Greco-Roman intellectual achievement an indispensable tool for understanding what they perceived to be ultimate Christian wisdom.

Of particular importance in establishing Christian intellectual leadership and in shaping the western intellectual tradition was Augustine (A.D. 354–430). Born in North Africa, the son of a pagan father and a Christian mother, Augustine received a good Latin education to prepare him as a teacher of rhetoric. As his education progressed, his searching mind experimented with a variety of pagan philosophical and religious systems, none of which satisfied his yearning for understanding and wisdom. Neither did the mistress he took as a young man nor the child born to that union. Eventually, he converted to Christianity and was chosen bishop of Hippo in Africa.

As a bishop, Augustine's major concern was to be an effective pastor. In that role he worked tirelessly to guide his flock toward sound belief and spiritual perfection and ended his life trying to protect his city from the Vandals. But he also turned out a prodigious body of writing on a variety of theological and moral issues. Much of his writing was prompted by his efforts to combat heresy. In his own time his writings served many as guides to a fuller understanding of the faith; for centuries to come his thought provided the basis for the major positions of the Church on most doctrinal and moral issues. Two of his many works were particularly significant. His *Confessions* recount his own spiritual pilgrimage as an educated Roman through most of the philosophical and religious systems of the ancient world to his final realization that only Christianity could satisfy his spiritual hunger. The work presents not only forceful critiques revealing the failure of Greco-Roman philosophy and religion but also a compelling argument in support of the Christian faith as the only adequate response to life's problems.

Even more influential was his *City of God*, written to answer pagan charges that the Visigothic sack of Rome in A.D. 410 was a punishment imposed on the Romans by their ancient deities who were angry at them for becoming Christians. Augustine sought to demonstrate that this "catastrophe" was only a step in the unfolding of God's plan for the universe. God, he argued, had ordained two cities, that of God and that of the world. The true city of God exists only in the other world; membership will be awarded as God wishes to those who serve the true faith without wavering. On the earth prevails the worldly city, tarnished by sin and due eventually to pass. The Roman Empire was a part of the worldly city. The coming of Christ had established an earthly embodiment of the City of God in the form of the Christian church, into whose body all must now be enfolded. Rome must pass away so that human beings can give their allegiance to the more perfect Christian community. Not despair but joy should greet the passing of Rome, since that event was a preordained step toward a more perfect world planned by God from the beginning. Almost immediately, Augustine's interpretation of the cosmos and of history as the realization in time of the divine plan replaced the various world views offered by classical philosophers.

Other Christian intellectuals helped to assure the victory of a Christian culture. One was Ambrose (ca. A.D. 340–397), bishop of Milan and a key figure in guiding Augustine to his conversion. In his writings Ambrose not only helped to shape the rationale for the independence of the Church but also persuasively articulated the basic principles of Christian morality. He drew heavily on the moral principles developed by classical thinkers, but he skillfully recast their moral values to fit within the framework of Christian doctrine. Another influential figure was Jerome (A.D. 340–419), a man of immense learning and a formidable linguist who was drawn to monastic life despite the great appeal that classical literature had for him. His voluminous letters played a significant role in guiding the spiritual life of an important circle of Roman nobles, including many women. He employed his talents to produce a Latin translation of the Old and the New Testaments. Basing his translation on both Hebrew and Greek versions of Scripture, Jerome's Bible, called the Vulgate, became the standard Latin Bible for centuries. Its existence ensured that Latin would survive as the language of the Church in the West and that its readers would retain an ability to read the literature of classical Latin antiquity. Jerome's extensive commentaries on the Bible also guided later generations in their efforts to interpret the meaning of the Bible.

Firmly in possession of its early traditions and fortified by new sources of organizational, intellectual, and spiritual vitality shaped during the fourth century, the Christian community survived the ordeal of the fifth century amazingly well. In fact, it emerged from the Germanic migrations and the collapse of the imperial government as the most potent force in society. To be sure, the fifth century produced tribulations for the Christian establishment. Churches were destroyed and Christians were killed by the Germans. Particularly disruptive was the fact that almost all of the Germanic invaders were adherents of Arian Christianity, which resulted in clashes with the orthodox Christian population and impeded the assimilation of Romans and Germans. The collapse of the Roman political system in the West deprived the Church of a major protector and a prime source of material support.

But amidst the mounting chaos the Church maintained and even strengthened its position. In many parts of the West, bishops replaced local aristocracies and bureaucrats as keepers of order, administrators of justice, and caretakers of the unfortunate. Pope Leo I (A.D. 440–461), for example, served as virtual governor of the city of Rome and as a forceful diplomat defending the city against attacks of the Vandals and the Huns. Many other bishops played a similar role in cities across the entire West. By A.D. 500 there were clear signs that the Arianism of the Germans was giving way to orthodoxy and that Germans and Romans were finding a common basis in a single faith. A key event in ensuring the victory of orthodoxy was the conversion of the pagan Frankish king Clovis to orthodoxy. Most Germanic kings, whatever their particular religious persuasion, began to lend their support to the Church and to draw on its personnel for assistance in ruling their kingdoms. As the focus of life shifted from the city to a rural setting, the Church began incorporating the neglected peasantry into the mainstream of Christian life. A sign of its concern with rural life was the emergence of a new organizational structure, the rural parish, which provided a local center from which to convert and to guide the spiritual formation of nobles and peasants increasingly bound to a rural environment. As cultural life collapsed in the declining cities, monasteries increasingly provided havens for education and the preservation of culture. By A.D. 500 the Church had become a pillar of order and stability in all aspects of life in the West. It had inherited the leadership role once held by the Roman imperial government, a role that its earliest adherents probably would never have dreamed possible nor perhaps even desirable. That leadership would have a major impact on the future.

SUGGESTED READING

Political, Economic, and Social Developments

The general history of the period covered in this chapter is treated in the works of Brown and Grant cited in Chapter 12. The following works cover more specialized aspects of the period, as indicated by their titles.

Ramsay MacMullen, *The Roman Government's Response to Crisis, A.D. 235–337* (1976).

Diana Bowder, *The Age of Constantine and Julian* (1978).

A. H. M. Jones, *Constantine and the Conversion of Europe* (1948; reprinted, 1978).

Church History

The major developments in church history are treated in the works of Frend and Fox, cited in Chapter 12. The following works treat particular aspects of religious history.

Jaroslav Pelikan, *The Christian Tradition: A History of the Development of Doctrine*, Vol. 1: *The Emergence of the Catholic Tradition (100–600)* (1971). A masterful treatment of the shaping of Christian doctrine.

Derwas J. Chitty, *The Desert a City* (1966). A colorful treatment of the origins of monasticism.

Peter Brown, *Society and the Holy in Late Antiquity* (1982). A brilliant portrayal of spiritual forces that transformed the late Roman world.

John Holland Smith, *The Death of Classical Paganism* (1976). A good account of another side of religious life in the late empire—that of the losers.

The Germans and Their Invasions

Malcolm Todd, *The Northern Barbarians, 100 B.C.–A.D. 300* (1987).

E. A. Thompson, *The Early Germans* (1965).

Either of these works will help the reader understand the nature of early Germanic society.

Hans-Joachim Diesner, *The Great Migrations. The Movements of Peoples across Europe, A.D. 300–700*, trans. C. S. V. Salt (1982). A brief account, beautifully illustrated.

Lucien Musset, *The Germanic Invasions. The Making of Europe, A.D. 400–600*, trans. Edward and Columba James (1975). A more detailed account of the Germanic migrations.

Justine D. Randers-Pehrson, *Barbarians and Romans: The Birth Struggle of Europe, A.D. 400–700* (1983). Especially good on the efforts of the Germans to establish themselves in the empire.

Biographies

Stephen Williams, *Diocletian and the Roman Recovery* (1985).

John Holland Smith, *Constantine the Great* (1971).

Robert Browning, *The Emperor Julian* (1978).

Peter Brown, *Augustine of Hippo: A Biography* (1967).

Philip Rousseau, *Pachomius: The Making of a Community in Fourth-Century Egypt* (1985).

RETROSPECT

During the three centuries prior to about A.D. 500, a complex sequence of events unfolded that brought an end to Greco-Roman civilization. The magnificent political order created by the Romans to bring peace, well-being, and concord to some 70 million people gave way to violence and chaos over large sections of the Roman Empire. Prosperity was replaced by economic stagnation and decline. The enlightened, sophisticated, aesthetically rich culture that once had supplied men and women with a sense of direction, a set of values, and occasion for pleasure lost its vitality and its appeal. Why had Greco-Roman culture not lasted? Why was Rome not eternal, as many believed it would be? Any answer to these questions is apt to convince readers that they have been witness to a great tragedy—almost Greek in character—still to be lamented.

But was the collapse of Greco-Roman civilization a tragedy? It can be argued that by the third and fourth centuries the Roman world had become a prison for the human spirit. Autocratic government, regimented economic life, militarized society, and callous social elitism may have

brought order and security, but the cost was terrible. Traditional values seemed empty forms from which flowed no inspiration capable of mitigating the burdens of civilization.

The emergence of the "barbarian" Germans as a potent force in society may, from one perspective, seem destructive; but from another, their presence infused society with an element of vitality. Here were fresh doers, learners, experimenters. The rapid advance of Christianity may have accentuated modes of thought and patterns of morality that lacked the sophistication of the concepts guiding classical civilization. Again, however, Christianity represented a fresh breeze in the Greco-Roman prison, a new vision of humanity and its destiny that provided a sense of direction and a reason for acting. The "barbarians" and the Christians held the key to the future. Both had potential to advance human destiny.

Moreover, to speak of the fall of Greco-Roman civilization is to utter only a partial truth. When the Roman Empire collapsed, it left behind monuments that would serve as guides to its heirs—a magnificent literature, a great art, model forms of government, a legal system, economic institutions and techniques, moral precepts, philosophical ideals, and scientific knowledge. In a sense, the Greco-Roman accomplishment did not disappear. Little that has happened in a large part of the world—especially the Western world—since A.D. 500 can be understood outside its Greco-Roman background. Many modern societies are children of the classical world, just as were its immediate heirs—the Christian establishment and the recently installed Germanic kingdoms. And no less important: The Roman imperial regime had survived virtually intact in the rich, creative East—that part of the world where higher civilization originated.

So history did not end with the fall of Rome! Nor did the promise of humanity perish with the end of Greco-Roman civilization!

PART FOUR

THE EARLY MIDDLE AGES, 500–1000: STRUGGLE TOWARD A NEW ORDER

The collapse of Greco-Roman civilization left the peoples living around the Mediterranean Sea with a challenge: how to replace the old order with a new civilization pattern. Despite false starts and confusion they met the challenge with remarkable creativity. Between 500 and 1000, called the early Middle Ages by modern historians, three new cultural communities were defined, each based partly on old Roman soil but each extending into "new" territory. One was the Byzantine cultural world with its center in Constantinople, its heartland in Asia Minor and the Balkans south of the Danube, and its frontier in Slavic Europe. The second was the Moslem cultural world with its heartland in the ancient Fertile Crescent, stretching from Mesopotamia to Egypt, and its frontiers eastward to India and westward across North Africa to Spain. The third new civilization was created by the Germanic nations. Gaul and Italy formed its center; its frontiers included England, Germany, Scandinavia, Spain, and the western portions of the Slavic world in central Europe.

In each of these societies there were seminal forces at work generating new institutions and new ideas. The dynamism of this age came from various sources: In all three societies powerful vestiges of Greco-Roman civilization persisted to shape essential features of each new civilization. In two of them—the Moslem and German western European worlds—new peoples, Arabs and Germans, supplied a leavening agent. But perhaps it was religion that furnished the major animating force in this period. Two new universal religions dominated the history of the period. Christianity provided that force in the Byzantine and Germanic western European cultural worlds. Islam, almost immediately establishing itself as a dominant force among the Arab founders of Moslem civilization, played a vital role in shaping the major features of the Moslem world.

Modern historians have often dismissed this age as a "dark age." Before accepting that characterization, we must try to assess the creative aspects of the period.

CHAPTER 14

Heirs to the Roman Empire: The Byzantine and Moslem Empires

FIGURE 14.1 **Moslem Mosque** This view of the interior of the magnificent mosque—built at Cordoba, Spain, in the eighth century—illustrates key features of Moslem architecture, especially the skillful use of arches and pillars to create spaces for private worship and the employment of geometric decorative designs. Many features of Moslem art represent a creative synthesis of artistic traditions borrowed from earlier cultures embraced in the Moslem world. A comparison of this mosque with a typical Christian basilica (see Figure 13.2) will suggest differences between Moslem and Christian religious practices. (Georg Gerster/Comstock)

Two of the new civilizations emerging from the Greco-Roman world—Byzantine and Moslem—had their centers in the eastern territories of the old Roman Empire. These areas, comprising the most affluent and culturally sophisticated part of the Roman Empire, provided a richer seed bed for development than did the Germanic West. As a consequence, during the early Middle Ages Byzantine and Moslem cultures were more precocious and vigorous than was that of the Germanic West. Since their very success in the early Middle Ages moved them into their own special place in history, apart from development in western Europe, we can only give them limited attention—less than they deserve.

1. BYZANTINE CIVILIZATION: ORIGIN AND HISTORY, 395–1100

Byzantine civilization, so named by modern historians after the ancient Greek city-state of Byzantium where Constantine built his capital, began as a direct continuation of the old Roman Empire. After the division of the empire following the death of Theodosius in 395, a succession of rulers in Constantinople successfully resisted Germanic attacks and maintained the basic features of late imperial society. Their claim to be the heirs to old Rome was validated in 476, when the imperial title in the West was transferred to Constantinople and the Eastern emperors were recognized as legitimate rulers over the entire Roman world, including those parts seized by Germans. But that sequence of events aimed at maintaining the fiction of Rome's survival was marked by developments in the East that by the sixth century pointed toward the shaping of a new society.

The watershed between the old and new Rome can perhaps be placed in the reign of Justinian (527–565), often called the last Roman and the first Byzantine emperor. Justinian's talents and accomplishments have been variously judged across the ages, but few would dispute the fact that he made decisions of immense importance in redirecting the course of history. He was given invaluable assistance by Empress Theodora, one of the most gifted women in history (see Figure 14.2). The daughter of a circus bear trainer, she was an actress and courtesan before Justinian took her as his wife. Intelligent, beautiful, and courageous, she was instrumental in helping her often indecisive husband make policy decisions. She was especially astute in reading the temper of the complex imperial court circle and the factious populace of Constantinople.

Justinian's claim to be called the last Roman stems from the central focus of his policy: a major effort to restore the unity of the old empire. To this end, he set out to reestablish imperial authority over the western provinces held by the Germans. Although his effort was brilliant, his success was partial. The best his armies could do was to recapture North Africa from the Vandals, Italy from the Ostrogoths, and a small strip of southeastern Spain from the Visigoths. Gaul, most of Spain, England, and the upper Danube provinces remained in German hands. More significantly, the price for these limited conquests was great, for Justinian's western policy left the eastern frontiers exposed to the Sassanian Persians, who continued their efforts to recapture the territory held by the ancient Persians. By the end of his reign, it was clear that imperial resources must be concentrated in the East if areas crucial to the survival of the empire were to be held. The Germanic West would have to be abandoned.

Justinian's reign was also significant in shaping a unique governmental system. He saw himself as the direct descendant of the Roman emperors, and he worked actively to perfect the system of absolute monarchy originated by Diocletian and Constantine. An important part of this effort led him to commission a corps of legal experts to organize into a single, consistent code the complex tradition of Roman law, which dated back at least a thousand years. That commission produced the *Corpus juris civilis,* which not only summarized the substance of Roman law as it had been defined in a long series of legislative acts and imperial edicts but also collected legal opinions that defined the principles on which the law rested. While this great monument of legal science was destined to influence considerably the development of law in the future, it served Justinian's age to legitimatize a highly centralized, absolutist government that became a distinctive feature of Byzantine civilization.

FIGURE 14.2 Justinian and Theodora These mosaic representations of Emperor Justinian and Empress Theodora were created as part of the decoration of the church of San Vitale in Ravenna (built about 574). They reflect a sense of sacred and solemn majesty that increasingly surrounded the Byzantine imperial office. Byzantine artists were highly skilled in creating mosaics to convey a message while adding color to interior spaces. (Justinian, The Granger Collection; Theodora, Scala/Art Resource)

Justinian's reign was also marked by important religious developments. Following the pattern already established by Constantine and his successors, Justinian claimed as part of his imperial authority the right to play a major role as leader of the Christian religious establishment in his empire. Particularly troublesome in his time were several violent disputes over dogmatic issues concerning the relationship between Christ's human and divine nature. The emperor sought repeatedly to settle these quarrels by imperial edicts, often

worked out after extensive discussions with prelates and theologians, which he hoped would curb violence generated by religious passion and restore religious unity. His involvement did implant the idea of a Byzantine church whose organization and doctrines were dependent on the authority of the autocratic, semisacred emperor. But his actions also alienated large numbers of his subjects.

Justinian's reign witnessed the birth of a distinctive Byzantine culture. That culture assimilated the ancient Hellenic component of classical culture with Christian ideology. Into that basic mix it incorporated cultural influences from the Near East, especially from Persia. The great symbol of this new culture was the magnificent church of Santa Sophia built by Justinian in Constantinople.

Byzantine political history from the reign of Justinian until the First Crusade (1095) was dominated by one theme: the constant struggles to fend off attacks from aggressive outsiders, especially from the east and north. These assaults reduced the Byzantine state in size and caused modifications in its internal structure that accentuated its uniqueness among its neighbors (see Map 14.1).

Hardly was Justinian dead when the first blow was struck. In 568 the Lombards, a Germanic nation, invaded Italy and seized a considerable portion of the peninsula, leaving only Venice, a corridor of land from Rome to Ravenna, and southern Italy under Byzantine control. The partition of Italy was significant for two reasons: It left Rome, the seat of the papacy, in Byzantine hands, and it provided a setting in which the Byzantine and German western European worlds would interact.

Little could be done to stop the Lombard assault because the Byzantine Empire was facing a greater menace elsewhere. Late in the sixth century the Sassanids mounted their greatest offensive in the East, seizing Syria, Palestine, and Egypt and advancing through Asia Minor to Constantinople. At the same time the Avars, an Asiatic nomadic people who established a state composed largely of Slavs north of the Danube, moved into the Balkans and toward Constantinople. In the first decades of the seventh century it appeared that the empire would perish in the Persian-Avar pincer. But a savior appeared in the person of Emperor Heraclius (610–641), who regrouped Byzantine resources and flung back the enemies in a war of liberation that permanently weakened both.

The dynasty of Heraclius soon had to face an ever-greater challenge in the form of the rampant Arabs, whose rise to power we shall trace later. Within little more than a half century in the middle of the seventh century, Moslem armies wrested Syria, Palestine, Egypt, and North Africa from Byzantine control. By the early 700s they occupied most of Asia Minor, and in 717 to 718 they placed Constantinople under siege. Again a savior appeared: Emperor Leo III, the Isaurian (717–741), who rescued the capital and eventually succeeded in liberating Asia Minor. However, the eastern provinces were permanently lost, and the Byzantine Empire was reduced to a state comprising Asia Minor and the Balkan peninsula. This was a far cry from the Mediterranean-wide empire that Justinian claimed or even the Eastern Roman Empire that he actually controlled. But it was defensible as a territorial state and would survive nearly intact for seven hundred years.

Despite Leo III's remarkable success in rescuing the Byzantine Empire from what seemed certain destruction, his successors suffered renewed trials that plagued the empire for a century after his death. In part their difficulties stemmed from internal strife brought on by their religious policy (see the next section). But outsiders again contributed to their problems. The Franks seriously undermined the Byzantine position in Italy (see Chapter 16). Even more dangerous was the emergence of a powerful Bulgar state in the Balkans. The Bulgar threat eventually produced another series of strong rulers, the Macedonian dynasty (867–1057), under whose rule Byzantine society reached its high point. The greatest Macedonian emperor, Basil II, the Bulgar Slayer (976–1025), finally destroyed the Bulgar state and extended Byzantine influence deep into the Slavic world of central Europe and Russia. Byzantine power was also increased in the East at the expense of the Moslem world, laying the groundwork for a Christian counterattack against Islam.

By the late eleventh century the Byzantine state began to decline, due in part to internal problems and in part to new assaults from the east by the Seljuk Turks and from the west by Italian cities seeking commercial advantages and Norman princes from southern Italy and Sicily seeking territorial expansion (see Chapter 21). To save the empire from these threats, the emperors appealed to the West for help, and act that was instrumental in launching the crusading movement. But this policy also meant that the fate of the long self-reliant Byzantine Empire was increasingly dependent on outsiders.

500's → Lombards, Sassinads, Avars

600's → Moslems

2. BYZANTINE CIVILIZATION: INSTITUTIONAL AND CULTURAL PATTERNS

In response to the pressures caused by incessant attacks, the Byzantine world slowly evolved institutional and cultural patterns that not only permitted its survival but also made its civilization unique and distinctive.

A major source of Byzantine strength was its government, based on the absolute authority of the emperor. That authority was defined in terms that combined traditions drawn from the Roman imperial system and from Christian concepts of governance; Constantine served as the model. To the Byzantine populace the emperor was an agent ordained by God to ensure the material and spiritual well-being of God's people. As an intermediary between God and his holy people, the emperor must be obeyed and served loyally. Without the imperial presence at the center of Byzantine life, God's favors would not be forthcoming and chaos would ensue. Although Byzantine court life was often filled with intrigues and violence, and although conspiracies and revolts deprived many emperors of their diadems and their lives, still the divinely sanctioned imperial office provided the prime directive force in Byzantine society.

The Byzantine emperors were served by a large, carefully structured bureaucracy. Each civil servant was assigned a specialized function, a rank, and a salary. Well-educated and loyal, these bureaucrats efficiently kept the fundamental activities of the state in operation. The empire was divided into a number of districts, called *themes*, where officials representing the emperor recruited troops, collected taxes, maintained order, judged cases, and enforced the emperor's edicts. The emperor's power was buttressed by a well-organized army and navy, an efficient system of taxation, and a responsive ecclesiastical establishment. Of crucial importance was the army. During the crises brought on by Persian and then Arab attacks during the seventh and eighth centuries, the government abandoned the long tradition of relying on mercenary soldiers. Instead it developed an army recruited from the free small farmers of Asia Minor and Thrace, who were granted plots of land in return for their military service. The peasant contingents were organized by themes, each under the command of a military governor. For centuries these loyal soldiers, their freedom and land carefully protected by the imperial government, stood against repeated attacks on the Byzantine state.

Agriculture formed the backbone of the Byzantine economy. Large estates, farmed by tenants, existed, but the chief strength of the agricultural system rested with small landowners. The state took a vital interest in keeping agricultural production high so that taxes could be collected from the farmers, whether large or small. The empire also enjoyed tremendous commercial activity; for many centuries Constantinople was the world's chief trading and industrial center. Through it passed a great variety of products coming from and going to places far and wide. The imperial government maintained a sound money system to support this commercial activity. Byzantine traders were supplied with many valuable products by the numerous skilled artisans who practiced their crafts in Constantinople and other imperial cities. All trade and industry were rigidly controlled by the state. Wages, prices, and profits were carefully fixed. Artisans and merchants were compelled to remain in their trades and hand them on to their sons. The imperial government itself monopolized many lucrative businesses.

The Christian religion provided another fundamental force in shaping Byzantine society. While religion touched every aspect of life, perhaps its most important function was to provide a bond linking the populace to the imperial regime, a bond that created a strong and lasting loyalty among the imperial subjects. In terms of beliefs and practices the Christians of the Byzantine Empire were like Christians everywhere. However, with passing time Byzantine Christianity underwent changes that gave rise to a separate religious establishment, now known as the Greek Orthodox church.

Following the pattern established in the fourth-century Roman Empire, the religious establishment in the Byzantine Empire remained closely allied with and subjected to the state. In contrast with the Church in the West, where the collapse of the Roman political order forced religious leaders to act independently, the Greek Orthodox church continued its development in close alliance

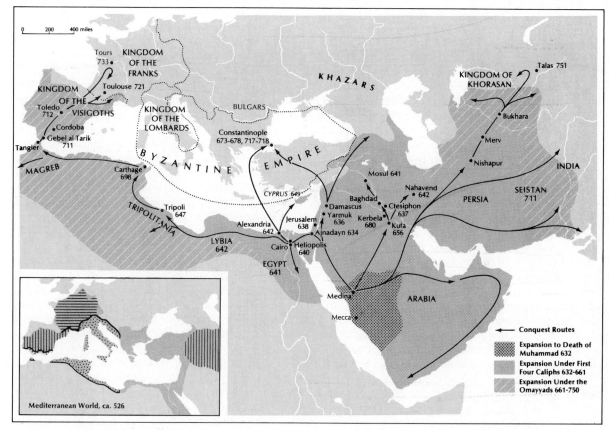

Map 14.1 THE EXPANSION OF ISLAM TO 750 This map shows the amazing success of the Arabs as conquerors during the first century after Muhammad's death in 632; the dates indicate when each major conquest was completed. It indicates clearly that the Persian Sassanian Empire and the Byzantine Empire were the major victims of Arab expansionism. By 750 large numbers of peoples in this empire had accepted Islam as their religion.

with political authorities. The emperor was accepted as the divinely ordained director of both spiritual and secular life; in fact, such a distinction had little meaning in Byzantine society. This system, called *caesaropapism* by modern historians, allowed the emperor to play a decisive role in appointing church officials, defining dogma, settling theological disputes, imposing discipline on both clergy and laity, and using the wealth and the persuasive authority of the religious establishment to serve the state. The episcopal structure of the Byzantine church, headed by the patriarch of

Constantinople, served as a powerful force in exercising imperial authority.

Byzantine religious life was given a distinctive quality by a widespread and intense interest in questions of dogma. Diverse opinions on such matters as the Trinity and the relationship between Christ's divine and human nature aroused strong feelings and fierce partisanship that produced serious political crises on many occasions, especially when the emperors tried to resolve such quarrels in the interests of unity. Greek Orthodoxy placed a strong emphasis on ritual practice as a key element of religious life, and over the centuries a rich liturgy featuring elaborate symbolism and unique musical forms evolved as a distinctive feature of Byzantine religion. On occasion both emperors and religious leaders thought this emphasis on ritual life needed to be curbed. The chief such effort led to the bitter iconoclastic struggle that raged from 725 to 843. This quarrel began when Emperor Leo III, backed by part of the clergy, attempted to remove all visual representations (icons) of the deity from churches and rites, insisting that Christians were worshiping the statues instead of God and thus were guilty of idolatry. But these iconoclasts (icon smashers) ultimately failed, and in 843 the use of icons was restored to ritual practices. Byzantine religious life gave a prominent place to mysticism—religious practices by which believers sought direct communion with God through prayer and contemplation. A powerful, active monastic establishment played an important role in encouraging this religious experience.

These unique characteristics of the emerging Byzantine religious establishment, coupled with equally unique developments shaping Christian life elsewhere, led to a growing division in the Christian world. During the fifth and sixth centuries bitter disagreements over dogma and the claims of the patriarch of Constantinople to precedence over the ancient patriarchs of Alexandria, Jerusalem, and Antioch encouraged the Christians of Egypt and Syria to separate themselves from the imperial religious establishment. The Moslem conquest of these areas reduced religious contacts with Christians in the Byzantine Empire and the West. The result was the emergence of separate Eastern churches, such as the Coptic church in Egypt and the Jacobite church in Syria. Differences also began to separate the Byzantine church from the Christians in the West. Dogmatic disagreements (particularly iconoclasm) and different ritual practices played a role in creating the rift. But especially divisive was the ever-deepening quarrel over whether the pope in Rome was superior to or coequal with the patriarch of Constantinople in terms of defining dogma and exercising disciplinary jurisdiction over the entire Christian community. Although the Byzantine emperors constantly turned to the bishops of Rome to sanction

their religious policies, they likewise supported the claims of their patriarch to exercise an authority equal to that of Rome. The slow drift toward separation between Rome and Constantinople finally culminated in 1054, when pope and patriarch excommunicated each other, creating a schism that to the present has proved irreparable.

The growing separation between Rome and Constantinople was promoted by rivalry in the missionary field. From almost the beginning of Byzantine history, Greek missionaries began to penetrate central and eastern Europe, where missionaries from the West were also active. Supported by the diplomatic, military, and material resources of the imperial government and willing to make concessions to local cultures, such as allowing rituals to be performed in native languages, Byzantine missionaries eventually converted most of the Slavs in the Balkan peninsula and Russia and attached them to the Greek Orthodox church. Not only did they give their converts a new religion, but Byzantine missionaries also spread significant aspects of Byzantine political, economic, literary, and artistic life. As a consequence, at a crucial point in the development of Slavic institutions and culture, a large part of the Slavic world was permanently oriented toward Byzantium and set apart from western Europe.

The Byzantine Empire gradually developed its own cultural life, aimed at preserving classical Greek tradition and adapting it to the Christian world view. Within a short time after Justinian's death the use of Latin virtually ceased in the Byzantine world. A vigorous education system flourished in Constantinople. The curriculum was based on a study of classical Greek literature and philosophy. At least in some aristocratic circles women were often provided a literary education in their homes. The system produced many individuals who were conversant with the literary, scientific, and philosophical masterpieces of ancient Greece and the Hellenistic world. This educated group, often associated with the imperial court, the prime patron of cultural life, also collected copies of the classics, commented on them, and wrote in imitation of them. Their efforts ensured the survival of the Greek classics and their widespread dissemination. As early as the ninth century Moslem scholars began to utilize Byzantine sources to gain access to the classical past. The cultural renaissance of fourteenth- and fifteenth-century western Europe depended almost entirely on the Byzantine world to renew knowledge of ancient Greek culture.

The all-pervasive influence of Greek models, however, tended to make Byzantine literature and thought imitative. Probably the most creative figures in Byzantine intellectual circles were the theologians, whose incessant quarrels over dogma produced a huge volume of writing in which philosophical concepts from the classical tradition were applied to Christian teachings. Byzantine historians, influenced by the models of Herodotus, Thucydides, and Polybius, also produced excellent works: Procopius (sixth century) described Justinian's wars and wrote a spicy *Secret History* describing court life; Michael Psellus (1018–1079), a high official in the imperial regime, chronicled the exploits of the Macedonian emperors; and Anna Comnenus (1083–1148), the daughter of Emperor Alexius I, described the career of her father in *Alexiad*. Byzantine poets expressed themselves most originally in hymns, some of which can still be heard in Greek Orthodox liturgy.

Byzantine art is perhaps the best mirror of the spirit of the culture. Architecture was the preeminent art. It represents a skillful fusion of Hellenistic and Near Eastern traditions. The style was formed during the fourth and fifth centuries in Egypt, Syria, and Asia Minor. It was elevated to official status by Justinian's building program in sixth-century Constantinople. The great church of Santa Sophia was based on a floor plan derived from the Greco-Roman rectangular basilica upon which was imposed a great central dome after the Persian manner. The glory of this combination lies in the internal spaciousness it permits. The dome of Santa Sophia is more than one hundred feet across and rises about one hundred eighty feet above the floor of the church. Although it rests on four great arches springing from four massive pillars that form the central square of the nave, the dome indeed seems "to hang by a golden chain from heaven," as a contemporary put it. Justinian, upon viewing the completed church, exclaimed: "I have outdone you, O Solomon."

The architectural style represented by Santa Sophia was widely imitated, and in the course of time a variation gained considerable popularity: A ground plan was based on the Greek cross with its four equal arms; each arm was crowned by a dome, as was the space where the arms cross. The famous church of St. Mark in Venice is an example of this five-domed structure. Byzantine architects also built huge and splendid palaces, most of which have unfortunately disappeared.

Byzantine architecture, for all its technical ingenuity, is incomplete without its decor. The churches and palaces were immense frames for sumptuous decoration. Santa Sophia's interior, for instance, blazed with precious metals, mosaics, paintings, jewels, and fine stone. Byzantine mosaics and frescoes centered primarily on portraying the great episodes of the Christian epic; the best surviving examples are seen in the churches built in Ravenna during the sixth century (see Figures 13.2 and 14.2). Byzantine artists made an immense contribution to the development and enrichment of Christian iconography. They were never basically concerned with portraying the world realistically; rather, they sought to use human, natural, and abstract forms to evoke spiritual understanding. Color, created by glowing combinations of stones, metals, jewels, and paints, played a crucial role in enhancing the impact of every artistic creation (see Color Plate 7).

Byzantine artists were also noted as skillful jewelers, goldsmiths, silversmiths, and manuscript illuminators. In every medium the same features predominated—the fusion of Greco-Roman and Near Eastern motifs and styles, the love of elaborate decoration and color, and the preoccupation with symbolism.

3. MOSLEM CIVILIZATION: ORIGIN AND EXPANSION

A second new civilization emerged in the eastern Mediterranean world during the early Middle Ages to rival Byzantium as an heir of the Greco-Roman world: Moslem civilization, originating among the nomadic inhabitants of the Arabian Desert. Jolted out of their traditional pattern of life by a new religion, called Islam, the Arabs exploded across a vast territory in western Asia and northern Africa and generated a new civilization whose influences still shape the lives of millions of people around the entire globe.

Although peoples from the desolate Arabian Desert had powerfully influenced the course of history in the ancient past (for example, the Akkadians, the Assyrians, and Hebrews), no one living about 600 would have guessed that the desert-dwelling Arabs were soon to have a major impact on the course of history. Although its inhabitants shared a sense of ethnic community rooted in language and common historical experiences, the Arab world was badly divided into numerous competing tribes led by warrior chieftains, called *sheiks*. The desert dwellers, called Bedouins, lived a poverty-stricken life that depended chiefly on the pasturage of animals—particularly camels—around oases. Raids on other tribes were common, so that Bedouin life was dominated by a warrior ethos. Tribal life was bound by rigid custom that governed most social relationships. Especially powerful were kinship ties, which created fierce family loyalties. Bedouin tribal life was deeply influenced by a polytheistic religious system based on the worship of deities representing the forces of nature.

For the most part the Bedouins had been little influenced by the advanced civilizations lying in a great arc around the northern end of the vast desert. However, the Arabs were not completely isolated, a significant factor in the changes that thrust the Arabs into a new historical role during the seventh century. In the long struggle between the Romans (and their Byzantine successors) and the Persians, both parties had tried to win allies among the Bedouin tribes of northern Arabia; as a result, Roman-Byzantine and Persian influences touched the lives of some Arabs in that area. The major religions of these civilizations—Christianity, Judaism, Zoroastrianism—had made modest inroads into the Arab world. Much more significant in bringing outside influences into the world of the Arabs were the overland trade routes that developed along the western side of Arabia. These caravan routes linked the rich cities of Egypt, Syria, and Asia Minor to the Indian Ocean and the Far East. During the sixth century the routes became much more important because Byzantine-Persian rivalry disrupted the trade routes running from the eastern Mediterranean area through Per-

sia to the Far East. Increased trade stimulated the growth and expanded the wealth of the Arabian cities along the caravan routes. Mecca, in particular, became a flourishing cosmopolitan center. Merchants from many places mingled with an ever-growing Arab population attracted to Mecca from the desert by the growing economic opportunities created by trade. Many Bedouin tribes came annually to Mecca to worship at a temple called the *Kaaba*, which contained a black stone that was a cult object for most Arabs. The sharp contrast between the affluent, cosmopolitan life in Mecca and the impoverished, tradition-bound Bedouin desert life began to pose questions about the value of tradition and to generate tensions that pointed toward change.

The forces of change were suddenly unleashed early in the seventh century. The catalyst was a religious prophet, Muhammad, who galvanized the Arab world into unity and jolted it out of its isolation. Muhammad was born in Mecca about 570. Orphaned in his youth, he was brought up by an uncle as a trader. Eventually, he entered the service of a rich widow whom he married, ensuring himself a respectable and leisured career. As a trader, Muhammad came into contact with foreign merchants who came through Mecca. But there is reason to suspect that the decisive aspects of his life were shaped less by these extraneous conditions than by his own introspective, brooding, ascetic spirit, which caused him to spend much of his time in prayer and meditation, often in the solitude of the desert. While the question of his own salvation may have been central to his spiritual searching, there are reasons to believe that he was troubled about the breakdown of communal values and the moral laxity evident in Mecca.

When Muhammad was about forty, he suddenly claimed that God—*Allah* in Arabic—had spoken directly to him and named him his prophet. Throughout the rest of his life these revelations continued, constituting in their entirety a full-bodied new religion. And they gave Muhammad his mission: He dedicated himself to convincing others that Allah had shown him the way to righteousness and truth.

What did Allah reveal to his prophet? The answer to this question lies in the Koran (*Qur'an* in

PLATE 1. *Gudea of Lagash* (Ruled ca. 2150 B.C.). This is one of several surviving statues of Gudea, a very active ruler of the Sumerian city of Lagash. Represented in prayer, the ruler's expression reflects the spirit of resignation which characterized the Sumerian world-view. The stylized features and the immobility surrounding the human figure was characteristic of Mesopotamian sculpture. (The Metropolitan Museum of Art, Harris Brisbane Dick Fund, 1959)

PLATE 2. **Egyptian Temple.** This photo shows the remains of a massive temple built in honor of Amon-Re at Karnak in the time of Rameses II (1299–1232 B.C.), when the Egyptian empire was at its height. The structure marked the culmination of a long tradition of temple building. The huge columns defined an inner hall which rose above side aisles also defined by columns. The columns contained numerous reliefs and hieroglyphic texts exalting Amon-Re and the feats of the pharaoh. (M. Timothy O'Keefe/Bruce Coleman)

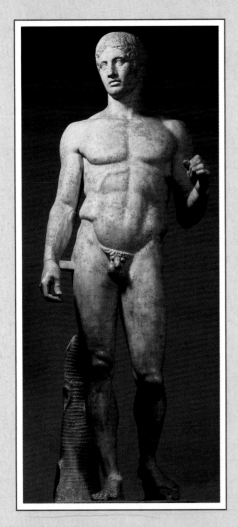 

PLATE 3 *(left and right)*. **Ideal Greek Humans.** These two statues, both Roman copies of Greek originals, reflect the search by Greek artists to represent ideal human beings. The male figure by Polyclitus (fl. ca. 450–420 B.C.) portrays a spearbearer. The female figure by Praxiteles (fl. ca. 350 B.C.) portrays Aphrodite, the goddess of love. These statues reflect the Greek genius for creating a calculated symmetry of the parts of the body without sacrificing the sense that one is observing a living human about to move. *(left,* National Museum, Naples: Scala/Art Resource; *right,* Vatican: Scala/Art Resource)

PLATE 4. A Room in a Roman Villa.
This photo shows a reconstructed room
from an aristocrat's villa near Pompey.
The decoration of such rooms occupied
much of the attention of Roman artists.
Paintings dealing with history and nature
adorned wall spaces, while elaborate
mosaics covered the floors. Examples of
such paintings are shown below. (The Metropolitan Museum of Art, Rogers Fund, 1903)

PLATE 5. *Aeneas at the Doctor.* Inspired
by Vergil's *Aeneid,* this scene from a villa
at Pompeii shows a doctor treating
Aeneas; his weeping son stands by while
Venus appears with healing herbs. (National Museum, Naples: Scala/Art Resource)

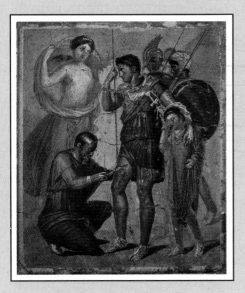

PLATE 6. *The Countryside.* This mosaic
formed part of the decoration of a magnificent villa built by Emperor Hadrian near
Tivoli. The bucolic countryside was a favorite subject of Roman artists and writers.
(Monumenti Musei e Gallerie Pontificie, Vatican)

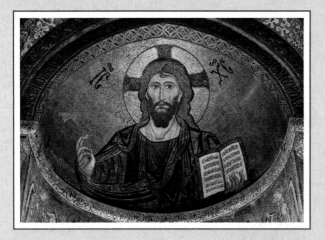

Plate 7. *Christ Ruler of the Universe.* This mosaic from the cathedral of Cefalu in Sicily portrays a theme often treated by Byzantine artists. It reflects the skill of Byzantine artists in conveying a spiritual message visually. (Scala/Art Resource)

Plate 8 *(right).* ***Christ Enthroned.*** This manuscript illumination from the Irish *Book of Kells* represents one of the major art forms of the early Middle Ages. Churches and monasteries and their patrons highly prized sacred books decorated with such illuminations. (Trinity College Library, Dublin)

Plate 9. *A Medieval Battle.* As the Latin lettering says, this scene from the Bayeux Tapestry shows the English and the French in battle. This remarkable weaving, nearly 240 feet long, portrays a series of episodes involved in William of Normandy's successful effort to conquer England in 1066. (Scala/Art Resource)

PLATE 10. Stained Glass. One of the most stunning features of a Gothic church was its stained glass windows. Although the effect such windows created is impossible to capture in a photograph, the one shown here from the cathedral at Laon in France shows how an artist could use different colored pieces of glass to tell a story, usually from sacred history. This window treats the childhood of Jesus. (Archives Photographiques, Paris: Jean Feuillie © C.N.M.H.S./S.P.A.D.E.M.)

PLATE 11. A Winter Scene. Very popular in the late Middle Ages were illustrated books of hours used for private devotions. A splendid example was one created for the duke of Berry. It contained a painting for each month of the year. The one above is for February. (Musée Condé/Chantilly: Giraudon/Art Resource)

PLATE 12. Giovanni Bellini, *Transfiguration of Christ*, Late 1480s. Giovanni Bellini (1430–1516) was one of the leading painters of the Italian Renaissance. In the *Transfiguration of Christ*, the sacred figures, Peter, James, and John crouch below Christ, who stands calmly between Moses and Elijah. In the background is a fifteenth-century town and the hills of northern Italy. The individualism of the figures, the depth and realism of the landscape, the immediacy of the scene, and the religiosity of the subject matter were characteristic of Renaissance art. (Museo di Capodimote, Naples: Scala/Art Resource)

PLATE 13. Raphael, *Portrait of a Man*, ca. 1503. While Renaissance artist's typically painted religious scenes, they also painted secular scenes—often reflecting the tastes and characters of their patrons. Raphael is considered the central painter of the High Renaissance. In portraits such as this, he conveyed the strength and individuality of important secular men without resorting to flattery or conventions. (Borghese Gallery, Rome: Scala/Art Resource)

PLATE 14. Antoine Watteau, *A Pilgrimage to Cythera*, 1717. During the Early Modern period, painting often reflected the tastes of the dominant aristocracy. This was particularly so in eighteenth-century France. This theme is one of classical mythology, but the figures are like eighteenth-century aristocrats gracefully at play in an idyllic garden of nature. The line between life and the roles they are playing blurs in this lush scene. (The Louvre, Paris)

PLATE 15. Peter Paul Rubens, *The Raising of the Cross*, 1609–1610. Baroque paintings are often extraordinarily dynamic and rich. This is particularly so in the large paintings of Rubens. In this altarpiece, the subject matter is religious, but the feeling of the painting is not one of calmness or piety. The heroic, heavily-muscled figures are caught in a moment of dramatic struggle; details are carefully rendered; even the surrounding foliage and the dog are in motion. (Antwerp Cathedral)

PLATE 16. Claude Lorraine, *The Marriage of Isaac and Rebekah (The Mill)*, 1640. This painting, with foreground figures framed by trees under a radiant sky, reveals certain characteristics of the classical style: the geometrically balanced Italian landscape, the figures in classic dress, and the general calm and discipline of the scene. Compared to the dynamic, dramatic nature of Rubens' Baroque style, the classical style is logical and restrained. Claude Lorraine (1600–1682) and Nicolas Poussin (1594–1665) helped make classicism popular in France during the seventeenth century. (Reproduced by courtesy of the Trustees, The National Gallery, London)

PLATE 17. Jan Vermeer, *The Painter's Studio*, ca. 1665. Dutch artists often painted interior scenes, depicting popular and middle-class life. In this painting a woman poses as an allegorical figure of fame. Light spreads smoothly through a window in front of her affecting everything in the studio. A map, something particularly crucial for the commercial Dutch, hangs below a geometrically precise candelabra. (Kunsthistorisches Museum, Vienna)

Arabic), the sacred book of Islam, which was compiled shortly after the Prophet's death by his associates as a record of Allah's message delivered through his prophet. The crucial teaching was that there is but one god, Allah; his followers must reject their worship of many gods for monotheism. Muhammad taught that Allah had revealed himself bit by bit down through the ages, the Jewish prophets and Jesus all being accepted as his spokesmen. However, Muhammad was the last and greatest prophet, superseding all others, and his revelation—Allah's final message—was destined to conquer the world. Muhammad insisted that almighty Allah requires complete submission to his will; the religion is thus called *Islam*, which means "submission to God." Every true adherent of Islam, called a *Moslem*, must regulate his or her life so as to abide completely to the will of Allah as revealed to the Prophet. Those who believe in Allah and submit to his law will gain a happy life after death in a sensuous heaven; nonbelievers and the disobedient will be damned to eternal suffering in hell. It is obvious that many of these fundamental teachings were closely akin to beliefs long held by Jews, Christians, Zoroastrians, and pre-Moslem Arabic pagans, a fact that has led to the charge that Muhammad was little more than a borrower of the religious ideas of others. However true this claim may be, it neglects the essential fact: The Prophet brought to the Arab world a religious vision that not only was new to the Arabs but also gave them the historic mission of spreading the true religion revealed in God's final revelation. To the Arab world this message was as radical as early Judaism or primitive Christianity was to their worlds.

To these simple articles of faith Muhammad added a list of duties required of all believers. All must pray five times daily while facing Mecca, give of their wealth to support the poor, fast during the holy month of Ramadan, and, if possible, make a pilgrimage to Mecca once in a lifetime. Muhammad also laid down strict rules regulating diet and marriage, prohibiting drinking and gambling, and demanding honesty, fair play, and respect for others. This code of conduct, strongly reminiscent of that defined for the Jews in the Old Testament, injected a strong ethical vein into the new religion. Each individual was personally responsible to Allah; there was no church, no clergy, no sacraments to assist in gaining Allah's favor.

For several years, the preaching of the new prophet netted only a few converts in Mecca. In fact, Muhammad won many more enemies than followers. By 622 these foes forced him to flee to Yathrib (later renamed Medina, which means "city of the Prophet"), north of Mecca. This flight, called the *Hegira*, marked a turning point in the history of the new religion, which the Moslems recognized by making 622 the first year of their calendar. At Mecca Muhammad—always speaking as Allah's prophet—gave increasing attention to the shaping of a religious-political community dedicated to the advance of Allah's cause by force of arms and to the enforcement of right living on the faithful. Into this community were drawn increasing numbers of Arab converts who subordinated their ancient tribal allegiances to a new, egalitarian companionship based on total submission to Allah and obedience to his prophet. The symbol of the new community was the mosque, the meeting place where the faithful gathered as equals to affirm their faith in Allah and demonstrate their unity in serving his cause. Reflecting the warrior ethos of the Arabic world, this holy community felt justified in living off the booty its warriors seized from nonbelievers, including especially the caravans of the rich Meccans. By 630 Muhammad's following was strong enough to recapture Mecca, a feat that persuaded many Arabs of the validity of Muhammad's message and led them to join his community. During his last years the Prophet used his forces to compel other Arab tribes to accept his leadership, so that when he died in 632 he was the leader of an Arab world virtually united under a religious banner.

Muhammad's success in drawing together the Arab world was impressive enough, but even more astonishing developments were to come. Almost immediately the new "nation" burst out of Arabia and began a series of military conquests that affected most of the civilized world (see Map 14.1). Between 632 and 656, the Arabs destroyed the Persian Empire; wrested the prize provinces of Syria, Palestine, Egypt, and extensive areas of North Africa from the Byzantine Empire; were probing India; and were challenging Byzantine sea power for control of the Mediterranean. After a brief interlude to settle internal problems over Moslem leadership, the advance resumed in the late seventh century. All of North Africa was conquered, and Arab forces pushed into the Indus Valley and the outer reaches of China. An offensive was mounted in Asia Minor that moved closer and closer to Constantinople. Before 700 Moslem naval forces were in virtual control of the Mediterranean. In 711 a Moslem army crossed from Africa into Europe and quickly overran the Visigothic kingdom in Spain. From there the Moslems began to raid Gaul to threaten the Frankish kingdom. But the drive was weakening: In 717 to 718 Arab forces were defeated at Constantinople by Leo III and soon after were driven out of Asia Minor. The Byzantine victory, decisive in checking the Moslem advance into Europe, was complemented in 733 when the Frankish leader Charles Martel defeated a Moslem force at the battle of Tours in Gaul.

The conquest of this vast empire within a century after the Prophet's death represents one of the great military feats in all history. Several factors played a part in this expansion. For one thing, the Arabs' opponents were weak. The Sassanid Empire was exhausted from its long struggle with the Byzantines. Religious disaffection among the Christians in the eastern Byzantine provinces caused the residents to welcome the Arabs as liberators from the religious tyranny and the fiscal exactions of the emperors at Constantinople. The conquerors interfered little with local affairs, making their overlordship easy to accept. They demonstrated great military prowess; their long training as desert warriors paid off. Their enthusiasm for their cause was also a factor. Muhammad had said, "Fight and fear not; the gates of Paradise are under the shade of the swords." Their wars were thus holy wars (*djihad* in Arabic).

4. MOSLEM CIVILIZATION: INSTITUTIONAL AND CULTURAL PATTERNS

The amazing victories of the Arabs presented the conquerors with a wide range of challenges: how to rule a huge empire inhabited by diverse peoples; how to support themselves in a different environment; how to sustain their faith in a world where other religions dominated; how to interact with different cultures. Their responses and the reactions of their subjects to their dominance produced a new, uniquely Moslem pattern of civilization of immense importance to the future history of a large part of the world.

A major problem facing the victorious Arabs was establishing a political system that would permit them to control their numerous subjects. While Muhammad had established the basis for a primitive Arab state, no one could succeed to his special place as Prophet. From his death in 632 down to 661, his close associates picked one from among them to serve as *caliph*—an Arabic term meaning deputy—to interpret and apply the law as revealed in the Koran. This office, bestowing on its holder a vast range of powers sanctioned by religion, became the key element in the Moslem political system. Whoever controlled it and used effectively the authority surrounding it could claim absolute lordship over all Moslems and all who were their subjects. But a major problem in Moslem political life centered on deciding who had a legitimate claim to the caliphate.

As long as Muhammad's personal associates were available, they could legitimately claim the office. But with their passing, a struggle developed for succession. Finally, in 661, a military leader seized control and made the office of caliph hereditary. The dynasty he founded, known as the Omayyads, held power until 750. Its legitimacy was challenged from the beginning by Muhammad's son-in-law, Ali, and his son, Hussein, who claimed authority to interpret the Prophet's word on the basis of their kinship with him. Their claims resulted in their assassinations, but their followers formed a powerful and dedicated religious-political faction, called the Shiites, which for centuries challenged the authority of successive caliphs.

The Omayyads established their center of power at Damascus. Although totally committed to Arab supremacy in the expanding empire, they realized that ruling the lands and peoples conquered by the Arab armies of Allah demanded more complex political institutions than those that characterized Muhammad's first Moslem community. Strongly influenced by Byzantine models, the Omayyads created a centralized court, a bureaucracy, and an efficient tax system. The authority of the Omayyad caliphs was exercised primarily through garrisons of Arab troops established at strategic spots across the vast empire. Bound to the caliph by ethnic and religious ties, the commanders of these garrisons controlled local affairs; often they did so by utilizing already established native political structures. These garrisons were supported by allocations from the caliph's treasury, which was supplied by taxes paid by the conquered non-Moslem population. This system meant that the Moslem world was dominated by an Arab elite whose religious convictions legitimatized for its members their right to possess and exploit what they had won by the sword. For almost a century, this system worked. Arab military supremacy gave conquered subjects little choice. Generally, the isolated, exclusivist Arab garrisons interfered little in local affairs except to collect the tribute that supported them.

But eventually the Omayyad regime was untenable. Arab strength was diluted by its dispersion over the huge empire. More important, as the number of non-Arab converts to Islam increased, resentment against Arab domination grew. Non-Arab Moslems could see no reason why their faith should not make them equal in the sight of Allah to Arab Moslems. That sentiment led to the overthrow of the Omayyads in 750—except in Spain—and the seizure of the caliphate by the Abbasid dynasty, a family of Persian origin claiming distant kinship with Muhammad. Abbasid rule meant the end of Arab domination. The capital was shifted from Damascus to Bagdad, and the political system was reshaped on the model of ancient Persia. The Abbasid caliphs reclaimed the absolute authority to interpret Allah's word for all the faithful, whatever their ethnic origin. Around their court developed a professional bureaucracy made up of educated Moslems. The caliph's authority was extended across the empire through an elaborate system of governorships over which officials representing the caliph administered justice and collected taxes. In this new political environment Arab militancy was greatly diminished.

During the eighth and ninth centuries the Abbasid caliphs enjoyed immense power, exempli-

fied by rulers like Harun al-Rashid (786–809), immortalized in the *Arabian Nights*. But by the end of the ninth century Abbasid power began to decline. Rival caliphs, challenging the legitimacy of the Abbasids to interpret Allah's will, were established in Spain, North Africa, Syria, and India and began to compete with each for a dominant position in the Moslem world. Seeking to protect themselves against these rivals, the Abbasids increasingly placed their trust in Seljuk Turkish mercenaries, nomads from Central Asia who by 1055 had made the Abbasids their puppets. By that time, Moslem political unity had vanished forever. Disunity invited attacks from outsiders, especially Byzantine and western European Christians, who had not forgotten earlier Moslem militancy.

Although the benefits were not equally shared, the Moslem world enjoyed significant economic growth. Agriculture remained the basic element of economic life. The early Arab conquerors were little interested in farming except as a source of tribute to support the military elite. As a consequence, the traditional village-farming structure of the Roman-Byzantine and the Persian worlds persisted. Later, under Abbasid rule fiscal policies were introduced that stimulated land clearance, production for urban markets, and the introduction of new crops and techniques, all of which combined to increase agricultural production. Economic growth was most marked in commerce and manufacturing. The emergence of Moslem civilization gave new impetus to urban life. Cities—new and old, large and small—became centers of life for the ruling elite and their dependents. Their needs, ranging from food to luxury items, stimulated trade and industry, which in turn filled cities with merchants and artisans. While much commerce and manufacturing filled local needs, long-distance trade routes stretching from Spain to India developed. Long-distance trade was promoted by the removal of artificial trade barriers, a sound money system, and specialized manufacturing developing in many cities (for example, the steel weapons and textiles of Damascus and the leather goods of Cordoba in Spain). The Moslem political regime allowed merchants and artisans much greater freedom than had been the case in the Byzantine and Persian empires; as a consequence, these groups exercised their entrepreneurial talents to expand wealth. On the whole, the Moslem economy was the most advanced and resourceful in the world during the early Middle Ages.

The Moslem social structure was immensely complex. Arab tradition and the teaching of the Koran emphasized the equality of all male Moslems. In fact, important social distinctions existed, initially between Arabs and non-Arabs and then between Moslems and non-Moslems. As time passed, a social elite emerged defined by office-holding, wealth, education, and living style. This elite congregated in urban centers, where its ranks were constantly replenished by those whose talents as administrators, merchants, artisans, and scholars permitted them to accumulate the wealth and acquire the social graces required for elite status. The bulk of the agricultural population and urban laborers remained outside this elite circle and were considered as inferiors. Non-Moslems, although tolerated, were also treated as inferiors, subject to special taxes and excluded from public life. The stratification of Moslem society was countered to some extent by the force of Moslem law. Already in the Koran there were rigorous prescriptions regulating the behavior of believers. This body of law constantly grew more complex to provide a common standard of conduct binding on all Moslems.

The family was a basic institution in regulating social life. But it was an institution dominated by males. Severe restrictions were placed on women, forcing them into a secluded existence and isolating them from many aspects of social and economic life. Polygamy was legally recognized and widely practiced among the affluent, putting women in a position of competing for a place in the family structure and for control over children. Husbands were able to divorce their wives easily and exercised considerable control over the destinies of children. However, Moslem law did permit women to share in inheritances and sought to protect their interests in their possessions.

The most important forces giving Moslem civilization cohesion and unity were religion and culture. The Islamic religion demonstrated an amazing power to win converts, usually without force, since Arab conquerors seldom insisted that their subjects accept the new religion. They only imposed a special tax on their non-Moslem subjects

for the privilege of retaining their old religion and excluded them from government positions. Christians and Jews were extended special privileges because they were, as Moslems put it, "people of the Book" who had received at least a portion of God's revelation. As the years passed, however, devotees of many religions—Christians, Jews, Zoroastrians, and Hindus—were converted in massive numbers, and the vast Moslem Empire became predominantly Islamic. Islam also expanded beyond the boundaries of the empire to win converts in southern Asia and sub-Sahara Africa. Important non-Moslem communities always remained in the empire, including Christian churches in Egypt, Syria, and Armenia and a significant Jewish community in Spain.

Islam itself tended to grow more complex as the centuries passed. This enrichment resulted chiefly from the efforts of a long succession of theologians, philosophers, and lawyers, all of whom reflected on the nature of their religion from different perspectives. The theologians developed a rich body of literature in the form of commentaries (called *sunnas*) on the Koran and on pronouncements attributed to Muhammad but not recorded in the Koran (called *hadiths*). The philosophers incorporated concepts derived from Greek thought into Islam in an effort to illuminate the meaning of the Koran. The lawyers constantly elaborated the body of law that governed Moslem life, seeking to make it consistent, complete, and relevant to the varied conditions of life among the faithful. The collective efforts of theologians, philosophers, and lawyers resulted in an orthodox faith much more complex than the message first proclaimed by the Prophet yet firmly rooted in the basic doctrines set forth in the Koran. The adherents of this orthodox religion, called Sunnite Moslems, constituted the vast majority in the Islamic world. But there were dissenters, the chief of which were the Shiite Moslems, who insisted that the true faith was preserved by Muhammad's blood descendants. They rejected many of the ideas about Islam proclaimed by the Sunnites and often did battle with Sunnites on many issues—a conflict that still divides the Moslem world.

The Islamic world also sustained a long tradition of seeking to deepen spirituality. The quest was carried on primarily by *sufis*, religious mystics who, through contemplation and ascetic practices, sought direct communion with the divine that would deepen their spiritual life as well as that of their followers. Despite these diverse movements, Islam as a common faith provided the prime basis of unity in the Moslem world.

Moslem expansion generated a tremendous cultural revival that brought together into a rich synthesis nearly all the world's great cultural traditions: Greco-Roman, Persian, Mesopotamian, Egyptian, Germanic, Jewish, Indian, and Arabic. Borrowing and synthesis remained a central feature of Moslem culture throughout the Middle Ages. Religion provided the matrix and the inspiration for synthesis. Since Muhammad had forbidden the translation of the Koran into any other language, all Moslems had to learn Arabic; and since the Koran contained the final truth, it was necessary to reconcile the knowledge of older cultures with Moslem religious teachings. The response to these challenges was a brilliant outburst of scholarship that rightly allowed the Moslems to claim to be the cultural heirs of the ages.

Many historians would agree that the greatest Moslem achievements were in philosophy and science. Moslem philosophers devoted their efforts chiefly to reconciling Greek philosophy with the teachings of the Koran. At the same time, they wrestled with the contradictions inherent in the Greek tradition, especially those separating Platonic and Aristotelian thought. Their efforts are closely akin to those of the scholastic philosophers of medieval western Europe (see Chapter 23). In fact, the speculations of the greatest Moslem thinkers Ibn Sina (980–1037) and the Spanish Ibn Rushd (1126–1198), known in the West as Avicenna and Averroës, exercised a direct influence on Western scholasticism.

In science the Moslem achievements were spectacular. Their efforts as collectors put at their disposal a huge body of scientific information from Greek, Indian, Persian, Mesopotamian, and Egyptian sources—more than scientists anywhere in the world had possessed until modern times. To this they added their own contributions, all of which were made widely available to a large circle of people because they were written in Arabic.

In mathematics, the Indian numerical system was adopted and the use of the zero was added to create the Arabic system of numbers almost universally used today. A Moslem, al-Khwarizmi (ca. 780–850), combined Greek and Indian concepts to create algebra. Astronomy advanced tremendously with the joining of Greek views, such as Ptolemy's, to Persian and Mesopotamian. The works of medical writers such as al Razi (865–925) and the philosopher Avicenna represent compilations from numerous sources. Moslem doctors studied diseases, dissected bodies, and experimented with drugs, adding significantly to the existing body of medical knowledge. Geographers and physicists also made significant advances.

Moslem literature demonstrated great vigor and variety. Its poetry, familiar to Western readers chiefly through the works of Omar Khayyám, is marked by brilliant imagery and highly complex technical skill in the use of the Arabic language. Perhaps the most characteristic feature of Moslem literature was the ability of writers to recast subject matter borrowed from various non-Arabic sources into masterpieces attuned to the spirit of Moslem religion and the values of Moslem society. Nothing illustrates this feature better than the *Arabian Nights;* the adventures of Sinbad the Sailor and the feats of Aladdin are stories gleaned from the literary traditions of many non-Moslem peoples, but they are given a unique coloration by the genius of Arabic authors, who retell them in a mode reflecting the spirit and the tastes of their own culture.

Like most of Islam's culture, its art reflects a creative synthesis of many traditions. Architectural talents were devoted chiefly to building mosques and palaces. The mosques, primarily places for individual prayer rather than community worship, are simple structures whose inner space is often divided by rows of graceful columns creating aisles covered by arches. As a rule, the mosques are covered by domes similar to those of Byzantine churches; above them rise graceful towers (minarets) from which the call to prayer is issued. Before each mosque is an open court containing a purification fountain and surrounded by a covered passageway. The greatest mosques, such as those at Damascus and Cordoba, are beautiful structures marked by delicacy and grace (see Figure 14.1). Surviving palaces, such as the Alcazar at Seville and the Alhambra at Granada, reflect the same architectural style but are much more elaborate.

Most Moslem buildings are rather bare on the outside but brilliantly decorated inside, especially with paintings and mosaics in splendid colors. The representation of human and animal forms was discouraged lest the faithful be tempted to compromise their monotheism by worshiping a graven image. Instead, the decorations accentuated floral designs and geometric patterns (arabesques). Exquisite artistry also manifested itself in the crafts; Moslem fabrics, tapestries, carpets, leatherwork, metalwork, weapons, and jewelry were the most prized articles in the medieval world and were key items in international trade.

The vitality of Byzantine and Moslem civilizations far excelled that which emerged in the western part of the old Roman Empire. The Germanic West lagged far behind them until at least the twelfth century. As we shall see, during the medieval centuries no aspect of western European civilization escaped the subtle influences of the Byzantine and the Moslem worlds. That immense debt was often forgotten in the West in later centuries—but not by the heirs of those who created Byzantine and Moslem civilizations.

SUGGESTED READING

Byzantine Civilization

H. W. Haussig, *A History of Byzantine Civilization*, trans. J. M. Hussey (1971).

Robert Browning, *The Byzantine Empire* (1980).

Cyril Mango, *Byzantium, the Empire of New Rome* (1980).

Each of these three works provides a full and balanced general treatment of all aspects of Byzantine civilization.

Romilly Jenkins, *Byzantium. The Imperial Centuries, A.D. 610–1071* (1966). Provides a full political history of the period in Byzantine history covered in this chapter.

J. M. Hussey, *The Orthodox Church in the Byzantine Empire* (1986). An excellent treatment.

Jaroslav Pelikan, *The Christian Tradition: A History of the Development of Doctrine*, Vol. 2: *The Spirit of Eastern Christendom* (1974). A masterful but demanding treatment of the theological issues which challenged Byzantine intellectuals.

D. Talbot Rice, *Byzantine Art*, rev. ed. (1968). A brief treatment, effectively illustrated.

Tamara Talbot Rice, *Everyday Life in Byzantium* (1967). Provides a good feel for how people lived in the Byzantine world.

Moslem Civilization

M. A. Shaban, *Islamic History: A New Interpretation*, 2 vols. (1971–1976).

Hugh Kennedy, *The Prophet and the Age of the Caliphates: The Islamic Near East from the Sixth to the Eleventh Century* (1986).

Either of these two works provides a challenging introduction to early Islamic history and civilization.

Maurice Lombard, *The Golden Age of Islam*, trans. Joan Spencer (1975). Will help the reader to understand economic and social history.

Alfred Guillaume, *Islam*, 2nd ed. rev. (1956). A clear description of the major features of Islamic religion.

Dominique Sourdel, *Medieval Islam*, trans. J. Montgomery Watt (1983). Especially good on the role of religion in shaping Moslem society.

Martin Lings, *Muhammad: His Life Based on the Earliest Sources* (1983). An excellent biography.

W. Montgomery Watt, *The Formative Period in Islamic Thought* (1973). A good introduction to early Moslem intellectual history.

David T. Rice, *Islamic Art*, rev. ed. (1975). A well-illustrated treatment.

CHAPTER 15

Heirs to the Roman Empire: The Germanic West, 500–750

FIGURE 15.1   Life in a Medieval Monastery   This scene from an illuminated manuscript reflects the essential elements of the daily routine in a Benedictine monastery: the tolling of bells to summon the monks to worship services; studying and copying manuscripts; manual labor. The combination of these activities into a disciplined routine permitted monastic communities to make a major contribution to the shaping of all aspects of medieval civilization, despite the fact that monks sought to escape the world within the confines of their monasteries. (The Pierpont Morgan Library)

The third heir to the Roman Empire, the Germanic society in the West, fared much less well than did the Byzantine and Moslem worlds during the early Middle Ages. Western Europe suffered through an age of instability and disorder. By 750 the first dim outlines of a new order were becoming evident in the form of new institutions and ideas destined to be crucial for the future of Europe.

1. POLITICAL DEVELOPMENTS

A prime factor in the history of the Germanic West between 500 and 750 was political instability stemming from two interrelated factors. First, the West was plagued by the uncertain definition of the territory belonging to each of the various kingdoms established on Roman soil during the fifth century. In 500 the boundaries of those kingdoms—Visigothic, Vandal, Ostrogothic, Burgundian, Frankish, Anglo-Saxon—were still fluid and often a matter of fierce competition. Second, all of these kingdoms lacked well-defined internal political structures capable of maintaining public order.

Between 500 and 750 there was considerable rearrangement of the fragile boundaries of the Germanic kingdoms (see Maps 13.1 and 14.1). Of prime importance was the emergence of the Franks as a major power. During the fifth century, while other Germanic groups were carving out large kingdoms in North Africa, Spain, Italy, and southern Gaul, various groups of Franks slowly penetrated northern Gaul without cutting themselves off from their homeland along the lower Rhine River. Suddenly, under their first great king, Clovis (481–511), the Franks exploded into prominence. A ruthless, able warrior, Clovis unified the Franks and unleashed their military potential. He and his immediate successors wiped out the last remnants of Roman power in northern Gaul, absorbed the Burgundian kingdom, drove the Visigoths out of southern Gaul and claimed their territory, and established dominance over Germanic peoples living immediately east of the Rhine in territories that had not been part of the Roman Empire. The Frankish cause was aided by the conversion of Clovis and his followers to orthodox Christianity, making their domination more acceptable to the population of Gaul than that of the Arian and pagan rulers they defeated.

The Byzantines and the Moslems also played a role in shaping the political map of the West. As already noted, Justinian's attempt to reconquer the West led to the destruction of the Vandal kingdom in North Africa and the Ostrogothic kingdom in Italy. However, his successors lost northern and central Italy to the last Germanic intruders into the West, the Lombards; the Byzantines retained a band of land extending across central Italy from Ravenna to Rome and southern Italy and Sicily. In 711, Moslem forces overran the Visigothic kingdom and established control over the Iberian peninsula except for small Christian enclaves in extreme northern Spain.

Meanwhile, the political map of the West was being shaped in other areas. In England, where several competing petty kingdoms had been formed by Anglo-Saxon intruders, a variety of forces were at work pointing in the direction of unification. In central Europe large numbers of Slavs moved westward and southward into lands vacated by the Germans and began to develop their own political identity. In the Scandinavian world, new political groupings were taking shape, preparing the people of the North for an important role in western European history in the future.

Thus, by 750 the political map of the West had assumed a more settled shape (see Map 14.1). The heartland of western Europe—northern Italy, Gaul, western Germany, and England—was occupied by kingdoms shaped by three Germanic peoples: the Lombards, the Franks, and the Anglo-Saxons. Facing this German-dominated world on the south were the Byzantines in southern Italy and Sicily and the Moslems controlling Spain, North Africa, and the western Mediterranean Sea. To the east and the north were the Slavs and the Scandinavians.

While the political boundaries of the West took shape, constant experimentation went on as rulers of each Germanic kingdom searched for a workable system of government to replace the Roman imperial regime. That experimentation varied from kingdom to kingdom. As a result, significant regional differences in political institutions emerged in the West during the early Middle

WHERE HISTORIANS DISAGREE

The Division of Times Past

In order to provide a framework into which random data can be arranged, historians divide past time into segments, each treated as a discrete unit that has its unique characteristics. Although necessary, attempts at *periodization* lead to basic disagreement among historians. Nowhere have such disagreements been more apparent than in the attempt to define the division between classical Greco-Roman civilization and what came after in western Europe.

The first widely accepted periodization system relating to the transition from the classical age to a new era was formulated in the early modern period. It was shaped by Renaissance humanists, Protestant religious reformers, and Enlightenment philosophers, whose various interests led them to agree that a major break occurred in the fifth century A.D. This break took the form of a "disaster" marked by the failure of the Roman political system, the triumph of Christianity, and the victory of the barbarian Germans. What followed was a "dark age." This interpretation found particularly persuasive expression in Edward Gibbon's classic, *Decline and Fall of the Roman Empire* (1776), which argued that in the fifth century a new age began with the victory of "religion and barbarism" over the rational, enlightened civilization of classical Greece and Rome.

The periodization scheme defining a decisive break in the fifth century separating the ancient world from a prolonged "dark age" dominated historical thinking well into the twentieth century. Then a new approach was developed, chiefly as a result of the work of the Belgian historian, Henri Pirenne. In his seminal work, *Mohammed and Charlemagne* (1939), he argued that in western Europe the end of the classical world came not in the fifth but in the eighth century when Moslem expansion finally interrupted the economic unity of

the Mediterranean basin. In Pirenne's words, "It is . . . strictly correct to say that without Mohammed Charlemagne would have been inconceivable." Thus, it is to the Carolingian era (ca. 750–900) that one must look for the shaping of the essential features of western European civilization, for the "first" Europe. All developments prior to 750 must be annexed to classical history.

Despite heated criticism from many quarters, the Pirenne "thesis" enjoyed wide acceptance among historians for the past half century. However, there are signs that a new periodization scheme is emerging. It is being shaped by advocates of what is sometimes called the "new social history." They are convinced that the determinant forces shaping the historical process are basic social structures that dictate the activities and thoughts of common people, the "silent," neglected actors on the human stage. Their investigations of the medieval world have led them to conclude that somewhere around 1000 there occurred changes in the basic structure of western European society so fundamental that a new age was born. These changes had not to do with politics and war and high culture but with demography, family structures, technology, social groupings, and popular religious mentalities. Compared with these changes, the Carolingian "revival" was a mere episode with little consequences. Before 1000 western Europe was a moribund society, dependent on remnants of the classical world. Only after 1000 did a unique and vibrantly creative civilization emerge in western Europe.

These brief remarks lead to two conclusions. Historians divide time past in terms of what interests them most deeply. And their periodization schemes make a difference in how historical data is organized and interpreted.

Ages, quite in contrast with the unitary political orders characteristic of the Byzantine and Moslem worlds. Out of this experimentation emerged two systems especially important for the future: that of the Franks and that of the Anglo-Saxons. We shall return to the Anglo-Saxons (see Chapter 16); here we shall concentrate on the Frankish political system to illustrate the major features of the new political order in the West.

The Franks—like most other Germans—sought to create a government based on strong monarchy. The basis of royal power was clearly staked out by Clovis. The powers he claimed were derived in part from his position as a victorious German warrior king and in part from authority he assumed as ruler over former Roman subjects. Although ancient Germanic kingship had been elective, Clovis succeeded in establishing the concept that royal power belonged to a single family whose royal blood was believed to be sacred; this principle assured hereditary succession in Clovis' dynasty, called the Merovingians, down to 751. To execute the extensive powers they claimed, Clovis and his successors created a central court of royal officials and established local units of government based on the old Roman administrative system. The kingdom was divided into local territorial units, called *counties*, where *counts* appointed by the king were charged with collecting taxes, rendering justice, maintaining order, and mustering freemen to military duty.

However, the Merovingian dynasty was unable to exercise the power its monarchs claimed in a fashion leading to uniform administration and internal order. As a consequence, royal power steadily declined to the point where the last Merovingians were justifiably dubbed "do-nothing" kings. At the heart of this failure was the inability of the Merovingians to exploit the political concepts and techniques they tried to take over from their Roman predecessors. The kings and their officials remained prisoners of the Germanic concept of king as warrior; as a consequence, rulers repeatedly resorted to force as a means of asserting their authority, often appearing as bloodthirsty tyrants rather than guardians of order and justice. Germanic custom required that warrior chiefs gain approval of their free subjects, or at least the more powerful of them, before taking political action, a

practice that put constraints on royal absolutism. The Merovingian kings had a very limited sense of public service, so that their policies tended to serve dynastic interests and to favor the selfish interests of the warrior followings whose loyal service was the chief guarantee of the survival of the dynasty. Most kings had so little managerial ability that their administrative machinery degenerated into a household officialdom serving only to meet the king's personal needs. Administrative ineptness was compounded by increasing illiteracy among all ranks of the lay population. The Merovingians were unable to sustain an effective system of taxation; increasingly they were forced to depend on their own lands and on booty they could extract by force from their subjects. Following Germanic practice they allowed each of their subjects to be judged by the law under which he or she was born, be it Frankish, Roman, Burgundian, or Visigothic; the result was chaos in the administration of justice. Especially dangerous to royal power was the persistence of the Merovingians in following the Germanic custom of treating the state as private property to be divided among their male heirs. By the early eighth century this practice had split the unified kingdom once ruled by Clovis into three distinct subkingdoms (Neustria, Austrasia, and Burgundy), each ruled by a branch of the Merovingian dynasty and each often at war with the others for control of territory. These dynastic struggles encouraged non-Frankish subject peoples to break away from Frankish control. Disorder was further promoted by feuding among powerful elements in Frankish society, including the royal family itself; following Germanic custom, entire families took up arms to avenge wrongs done to their members by other families, thereby compounding violence and disorder.

Unable to maintain a centralized government capable of exercising the powers they claimed, the Merovingian kings were gradually forced to share power with lay and ecclesiastical landowners. The emergence of the landed nobility as possessors of political power was one of the major developments of the early Middle Ages. The strength of these nobles was rooted in possession of land, family connections, control over dependents, and royal favor. Especially crucial to their advancing power were the favors extended them by the monarchs. In part those favors stemmed from Germanic custom, which demanded that warrior kings generously reward their loyal warrior followers. More significantly, they resulted from the kings' dependence on the nobles for vital political services. Lacking regular income and a professional bureaucracy, rulers were forced to rely on subjects who could and would serve the royal government at their own expense. Only the great noble families could afford such services. In return they exacted from the kings grants of land and rights to govern their possessions as they saw fit. A system of private government thus evolved with great nobles controlling affairs in their localities as they wished. This trend was accentuated by the increasing willingness of the weak in an unstable society to seek the protection of the strong. Through a process known as *commendation* individuals from all levels of society freely pledged under oath to serve others willing to offer protection and material support. Although the specific terms of these arrangements varied considerably, the result was to allow the strong to build up private followings of dependents, often called *vassals*, over whom they exercised control and upon whose services they depended to extend their power. The expanding power of the nobles was a source of incessant strife, for the demarcation between royal authority and noble privilege was imprecise, and the rules governing the relationship of one noble to another were chaotic.

These developments meant that by 750 a unique political order had begun to take shape in the West. It involved several coexisting kingdoms, each ruled by a monarch whose royal office was surrounded by religious and military sanctions that in the eyes of most made the king necessary to right order. In fact, the new monarchy was limited in terms of effectiveness by a narrow concept of public authority and by limited resources, both material and human, at its service. As a consequence, the impact of government on society as a whole was limited, especially when compared with the role played by government in contemporary Byzantine and Moslem societies. Increasingly, monarchs in the West were forced to share rulership with a powerfully established landed nobility whose members took into their own hands the control of many activities previously controlled by the Roman imperial state. It can be argued that the diminution of the power of the state was the most significant feature of the new order emerging in the Germanic West.

2. ECONOMIC AND SOCIAL PATTERNS

During the early Middle Ages economic life in the Germanic West was marked by general stagnation, which resulted in a lower level of wealth than existed in the Byzantine and Moslem worlds. As a result of a succession of plagues, incessant warfare, high infant mortality, and low life expectancy, the West was sparsely populated. Urban life continued to deteriorate, and large areas of land went uncultivated. In many ways this economic recession reflected a continuation of trends that had begun in late Roman times.

Economic life became almost totally agricultural. Possession of land provided not only the key to survival but also the measure of an individual's status in society. Agricultural production was organized in a variety of ways. In some areas, especially around the Mediterranean where Roman survivals were strongest, the *latifundia* system continued. These large estates, increasingly called *villas*, were owned by lay nobles or church officials who reserved part of the land for their own support. That land was tilled by slaves or by tenants. Such tenants were allotted a piece of land sufficient to maintain a household in return for which they performed labor on the soil reserved by the owner of the villa and rendered dues. Their status tended to become hereditary, but such status also assured them permanent use of land sufficient to support the peasant family. In a time of political chaos and population shortage the villa system offered certain advantages. It provided landowners with a permanent labor force, encouraged cooperative effort, and gave security to peasants. Thus it tended to spread across many parts of the West. In other areas, farming was organized around village communities of free landowners; in such communities each family owned and cultivated its own land but also shared common rights in forest and pasture land. Also scattered across the landscape were numerous individual farms cultivated by free peasants. Tilled land was used chiefly for cereal grains and vegetables. Yields were low, so that famine was a constant threat. The products of forests and streams and of animal herds were vital to survival. Agricultural technology was primitive, placing a premium on human labor. However, some advances were made, especially in the development of oxen-drawn ploughs capable of turning over the heavy soils of lands north of the Alps. Although the agricultural system of the Germanic West in the early Middle Ages presents a grim picture, certain developments pointed toward recovery: the disappearance of the voracious Roman taxation system; the formation of agricultural organizations (the villa and the village), which encouraged cooperation between landowners and peasants; the emergence of the family household as a key unit of production; modest technological advances; tentative population growth; and isolated efforts at land clearance.

The shift of the center of economic life to a rural setting was accompanied by the decline of urban-based commerce and industry, again continuing a trend that had begun in late Roman times. Although urban centers survived, cities served chiefly as political and religious centers rather than as centers of economic production. Near the Mediterranean in southern Gaul, Italy, Spain, and North Africa, some commercial activity did continue, and contacts with the rich East were maintained. But on the whole the West experienced a diminishing exchange of goods, a declining flow of money, and the virtual disappearance of active merchants and artisans, except as they were supported by owners of large estates to provide for local consumption. What little long-distance trade did survive was increasingly conducted by foreigners, especially Syrians and Jews. One development of the period with great significance for the future was the beginning of trading activity in the North and Baltic seas.

The social structure in the Germanic West changed in response to new conditions. The direction of change was toward a simpler system than had been characteristic of the Roman world. The distinctions between Germans and Romans gradually disappeared. Urban social groups, so vital in the Roman Empire, vanished. A new aristocracy slowly took shape, composed of resourceful, aggressive, self-made persons capable of acquiring land, seizing political power, gathering dependents around them, and defying public authority. As this new aristocracy (often referred to as the *potentes*, the powerful) took shape, the rest of the population, almost all peasants, tended to be grouped in a single lower class (often called *pauperes*, those without power). While many in this class retained legal status as free persons, increasingly the peasant population became dependents of powerful landowners, bound to the soil of a large estate and subject to various obligations in exchange for possession of a piece of land. Slavery continued to exist, especially as a means of supplying household servants, but there was a tendency to attach slaves to the land in the same fashion as other peasant workers.

Social behavior among the powerful increasingly took on Germanic values and habits at the expense of the more refined standards of conduct of the old Roman world. Increasingly illiterate and generally short-lived, aristocratic males were creatures of violence and passion, their lives centered on fighting, hunting, gaming, and sexual ventures. They loved ostentatious display, particularly in the form of personal adornments made of gold and jewels. Especially important to them were family connections, chiefly because the family circle offered security in an uncertain environment. It was not unusual for aristocrats to collect wives and concubines so as to assure themselves of many children who could be advantageously married to promote family interests. Feuds among competing noble families were a common feature of life. Although male heads of families exercised extensive powers over females, aristocratic women played a significant role in society. Dowries and gifts associated with marriage practices gave them control over considerable property. High respect was paid and special protection was extended to them because of their procreative power, the key to family survival. Their kinship ties provided a basic link in constituting extended families. The social importance of women is illustrated by the prominent role played in public life by several Merovingian queens and by the influence asserted by several gifted leaders of Merovingian monasteries for women. The life of the peasantry was marked by poverty and drudgery. The family was a vital institution to the peasants, chiefly because it was a prime unit in agricultural production.

3. THE CHURCH AND RELIGIOUS LIFE

Of decisive importance in reshaping life in the Germanic West was the Church. Although it emerged from the collapse of the Roman Empire with considerable strength, it was faced with great adversity between 500 and 750. It lost the beneficial support of the Roman government. The emerging political divisions in the West threatened unity, as did the growing isolation of the Church in the West from the Christian communities in the East. The character of religious leadership changed in ways that undermined spiritual concerns. Like all other power wielders in the West, influential ecclesiastical officials, especially bishops, paid increasing attention to gaining land and dependents. Not only did this quest detract them from pastoral duties, but also it made their offices a focus of wealth and power. These offices became the object of competition in which the worldly usually triumphed over the pious. Ecclesiastical offices were prizes that kings used to reward their followers and that self-seeking noble families sought to fill as a means of increasing their wealth and power. Discipline among the lower clergy suffered from the lack of spiritual concern among higher church officials; the result was increasing numbers of unlettered priests, ignorant of basic Christian teaching and morally lax. Powerful nobles often controlled appointments of local priests, especially those serving the increasing numbers of private churches established on local estates by nobles who viewed such churches as private property.

Although the early Middle Ages was a period of intense religious fervor among all people, religious life in general reflected inferior spiritual direction. Pagan and Christian ideas and practices mingled to produce a religious mentality that gave greater emphasis to avoiding evil spirits through magic and the intervention of the saints than to learning basic Christian doctrines and practicing Christian morality. Church writers lamented constantly about sexual promiscuity, marital irregularities, murder, rape, thievery, perjury, illicit forms of worship, and superstition; such complaints were accompanied by pleas for improvement of the clergy and more effective pastoral care.

The disruptive forces in spiritual life producing disunity, worldliness in leadership, debased religious consciousness, and moral laxness were still rampant in 750. However, some forces of renewal had begun to appear, chiefly from within the Church.

A major source of religious vitality was the Church's quest to win new converts. We have already noted that most of the Germanic invaders accepted Christianity as soon as they entered the Roman Empire. In succeeding centuries the Christian frontier continued to advance. During the fifth century missionary forces, spearheaded by St. Patrick, converted Ireland. Missionaries from the Frankish kingdom, itself Christianized late in the fifth century under Clovis, pushed the Christian frontier to the Rhine and beyond during the sixth and seventh centuries. Beginning late in the sixth century the Anglo-Saxons were converted by missionaries from Rome and Ireland. During the late seventh and the eighth centuries, English and Irish missionaries crossed to the Continent to win new converts on the northern and eastern frontiers of the Frankish kingdom. While the Christian frontier was being advanced, the work of converting the rural population of the West went forward. As new converts were won, a network of bishoprics, monasteries, rural churches, and private chapels was developed to ensure pastoral care for new Christians. The missionary establishment was often especially intent on imposing a high level of religious life, thus serving as a model of pastoral care and a source of reforming zeal.

A second positive achievement of the Church was its growing involvement in activities that were not strictly religious. It took on the burden of caring for the weak in society. It maintained the only schools and hospitals. Powerful ecclesiastical leaders played an important role in the councils of kings and royal administration, allowing them to inject Christian ideas of justice and mercy into

FIGURE 15.2 **Pope Gregory the Great** Gregory was one of the most influential figures of the formative period of medieval western European society. His varied activities as bishop of Rome put an important imprint on the office of the papacy as the leader of the Christian community in the West. Throughout the Middle Ages his successors looked back to his career as a model of Christian leadership and as a precedent for their actions. (Alinari/Art Resource)

the harsh law codes of the era. Each time the Church intervened in these matters, its prestige as a social agency and its influence over the social order increased.

A third significant development involved the Church's attack on weaknesses within its own body—corruptness and worldliness of the clergy, moral laxness, ignorance of religious precepts, and lack of discipline. Two agencies were especially important in shaping a thrust toward "reform": the papacy and the monastic establishment.

Prior to 500 the papacy had utilized the Petrine theory (see Chapter 12) to establish a strong position as guardians of true doctrine and right practice. That position was reinforced during the troubled fifth century. With the collapse of the Roman imperial government, the bishops of Rome assumed a larger role in governing the city of Rome, as was dramatically illustrated by the role played by Pope Leo I (440–461) in protecting St. Peter's city from the Huns and the Vandals. Leo I was also a fierce defender of the papal right to define orthodox doctrine, especially against the claims of the emperors and the patriarchs of Constantinople. The expanding sense of papal authority was reflected by Pope Gelasius I (492–496) in his "theory of the two swords." He argued that religious and secular power represented two separate realms of authority, each established by God to achieve different aspects of the divine plan and each independent in its own sphere. However, Gelasius maintained, whenever the two powers clashed, the spiritual sword must prevail.

However, many factors limited the ability of the popes to exert their claimed authority. The Arian Ostrogoths who ruled Italy from 493 to 554 were little inclined to respect papal authority. When Justinian reincorporated Rome into the Byzantine Empire, he treated its bishop as one of his religious agents whose authority was no greater than that of the patriarch of Constantinople. The installation of the hostile, aggressive Arian Lombards as rulers of northern Italy after 568 left the popes with no choice but to accept Byzantine protection and to acquiesce to imperial religious policy as defined by the emperor. Finally, papal influence over the Germanic West was disrupted by the control exercised by the newly established Germanic kings over the religious establishment in their realms.

The recovery of the papacy was charted by Pope Gregory I, the Great (590–604) (see Figure 15.2). A well-educated descendant of a noble Roman family, Gregory began his career in public service, ascending to the highest office in the city of Rome, but he soon abandoned the world to become a monk. He was called from monastic life to serve as a papal diplomat in Constantinople, and then he was elected bishop of Rome in 590.

Convinced that the papacy must command material resources to survive in the troubled Italian scene, Gregory spent considerable energy in the management of the patrimony of St. Peter—

that is, the property belonging to the papacy in Italy. He used the large income derived from this property chiefly to expand papal control over Rome, often with little consideration of the officials of the emperor in Constantinople who claimed legal authority to rule the Eternal City. His increasingly powerful position in Rome allowed him to play the Lombards against the Byzantines in a way that not only prevented Lombard conquest of Rome but also undermined Byzantine power in the city. This effort marked an important step in laying the groundwork for a future papal state in Italy.

But Gregory was more than a hard-headed administrator and a wily diplomat. He never forgot the pastoral responsibilities that tradition assigned to the successor of St. Peter. In this capacity he took significant steps toward reshaping the Christian message to fit the unique needs of the Germanic West and toward drawing the western Christian community to Rome for spiritual guidance. He wrote important books on theology and ecclesiastical administration that circulated widely to guide clergymen in explaining the faith and shaping the moral lives of their flocks. His powerful sermons became models for preaching as a means of improving spiritual life. He sought to provide a model of liturgical practice useful in all churches; tradition credited him with a role in developing Gregorian chant as an element of the liturgy. He wrote innumerable letters to kings and clergymen throughout the West, offering them advice on religious matters and reminding them of Rome's authority in the religious sphere. His influence was crucial in converting the Lombards and the Visigoths from Arianism to orthodoxy, thus ending a major cause of religious division in the West. He initiated the missionary effort that played a major role in converting the Anglo-Saxons of England and guided the religious organization of the new converts in a way that subordinated them to Roman authority. In short, Gregory enlarged the role of the papacy in the religious life in the West and began to direct papal efforts toward helping to resolve the particular religious problems of the Germanic West. Although Gregory's immediate successors advanced his program only slowly, the Gregorian model of papal leadership would serve for centuries as a major element in shaping religious life in the West.

A second major force in regenerating religious life in the West came from the monasteries. Monasticism had been imported from the East in the fourth century and had generated an enthusiastic response. But on the whole, early western monasticism failed to sustain its initial vitality, perhaps because it was too imitative of eastern models to address the unique conditions in the West. The West needed its own style of monastic life. Although many spiritual leaders were involved in shaping western monastic practice, two forms were especially influential.

One developed in Ireland, where the severe ascetic practices of the East took deep hold as the standard for monastic life. However, Irish monastic life became thoroughly enmeshed in Irish tribal life and became a decisive force in shaping Christian practice. This situation caused monks to be involved deeply in popular religious life. An example of this engagement was the unique system of penance developed in Irish monastic circles, involving private confession and the use of penitential books that cataloged sins and instructed confessors on the appropriate punishment for each. Irish monasticism placed a strong emphasis on learning as a dimension of piety. As a consequence, monasteries became active centers of education and of the study of sacred literature. Finally, Irish monasteries were incubators of a powerful missionary movement. During the sixth, seventh, and eighth centuries, Irish missionary monks spread over England and the Continent, bringing with them deep piety, skill in uplifting the level of religious life, and great learning.

Another powerful form of monastic life was introduced by Benedict of Nursia (ca. 480–543). Like Gregory I, he was an Italian of noble origin who abandoned the world to follow monastic life. After experimenting with the hermit life, he eventually founded a monastic community at Monte Cassino and formulated a rule to guide the lives of its members. The *Benedictine rule,* combining features from several earlier rules, emphasized that a community of dedicated individuals could serve God and each other better than could the individual hermit isolated from interactions with other humans. However, a "school for the service of God" must be made up of selected individuals willing to make a commitment to perfection. After a rigorous testing period, each new member was required to take vows to renounce all personal wealth, to remain chaste, to obey his superiors, and to remain permanently in the community he entered. The rule entrusted absolute authority over the community to an *abbot* who was responsible before God to direct each monk toward holiness; thus discipline was a key feature of a Benedictine community. A major aspect of the rule was its provision for orderly daily routine for all members of the community, consisting of specified periods of prayer, manual labor, and contemplation and reading (see Figure 15.1). This regimen ensured that the community would be self-sufficient economically and that its members would be engaged in varied activities rather than in endless ascetic practices aimed at suppressing the urges of the body and awareness of the world.

Although Benedict had no intention of devising a rule for all monasteries, his rule—given powerful endorsement by Gregory I in his popular biography of Benedict—was adopted by both male and female communities across western Europe. By 750 monastic houses, especially Benedictine and Irish houses, were asserting a powerful influence in society. Monks and nuns were the new holy people, "athletes of Christ" serving as models of piety and moral excellence for all elements of society. They were able to teach bewildered Christians the basic elements of the faith and the proper way to perform Christian worship. They were the chief preservers and transmitters of learning. They performed numerous acts of charity and goaded the rich and the powerful to emulate them. As a result of their disciplined labors in the service of God, monks carved new estates out of Europe's wilderness and made them the best-managed economic institutions in the West, from which all could learn about farm management and artisanry. They formed a bulwark against both the devil and barbarism, well worthy of emulation.

4. CULTURAL LIFE

Although the chaotic conditions prevailing in the Germanic West from 500 to 750 were hardly con-ducive to cultural activity, certain developments were significant in shaping a new culture. The chief accomplishment was the preservation of significant elements of classical and patristic literature and learning in Latin (the use of Greek virtually disappeared in the West). During the sixth century both secular society and the Church played a role in this enterprise. In Italy, Gaul, and Spain both lay aristocrats and bishops of Roman descent continued to read classical and patristic Latin authors, wrote works imitating them, and supported schools where the young could study rhetoric and grammar. Germanic courts, especially that of the Ostrogoth Theoderic, actively patronized learning and art. A luminary of Theoderic's court, Boethius (ca. 475–525), set out to translate the works of Aristotle and Plato into Latin. His famous *Consolation of Philosophy*, written while he was in prison awaiting execution for alleged treason, was a moving defense of philosophy as a guide to inner peace and happiness. Another of Theoderic's officials, Cassiodorus (ca. 490–583), left the court to found a monastery that became famous for its library of classical and patristic works.

Before the end of the sixth century, secular society ceased to play a role in sustaining cultural life; the burden fell to the Church, especially the monasteries. Irish and Benedictine monasteries established schools to teach new members to read and write, encouraged the copying of the works of classical and patristic authors, and promoted the writing of commentaries on old texts to make them understandable. Especially active in these enterprises were the Benedictine monasteries of England, where Irish and continental influences merged to generate an important outburst of literary and scholarly activity. Monastic intellectual life placed an especially strong emphasis on mastery of Scripture as the prime source of wisdom. The concerns of monks tended to be narrow, governed by a passion to know God, to understand his revealed word, and to pray well. Thus, the monks were selective in their approach to the classical tradition. And they felt no compunction about turning the classical heritage to Christian purposes, sometimes distorting classical thought almost beyond recognition.

A few figures were able to transcend mere

preservation to produce works that revealed creative talent. One was Boethius. Another was a Visigothic bishop, Isidore of Seville (ca. 560–636), whose *Etymologies* consisted of a collection of information about many subjects derived from ancient sources that encouraged the systematic organization of knowledge. Gregory the Great's writings set forth basic theological concepts in simpler terms more suited to the intellectual capabilities of his age than were the sophisticated works of the Latin fathers from whom he borrowed most of his ideas. Especially important in shaping western European intellectual life was Gregory's mode of interpreting Scripture, which sought to discover the hidden meaning behind the literal words of the Bible. A Frankish bishop, Gregory of Tours (ca. 538–594), in his *History of the Franks*, demonstrated skill at compiling historical material. The most outstanding intellectual figure of the age was the English monk Bede (673–735), whose theological, historical, and biographical writings set high standards of learning and style. His *Ecclesiastical History of the English People* is one of the best pieces of history written during the entire Middle Ages. The age was rich in saints' lives, written to celebrate the feats of holy men and women who had surrendered themselves to the service of God.

As a few struggled to preserve education and learning, the lay world sank into illiteracy. Such people were not without culture, as is evidenced by the magnificent epic entitled *Beowulf*, which is a written version in the Anglo-Saxon language of an oral tradition concerning the heroic struggles of warriors against the forces of evil. The illiteracy of the laity created a situation of immense importance for western European cultural history: The languages men and women spoke in their daily lives were different from the language of learning and literature. For centuries learning would remain the monopoly of an elite especially trained to use Latin, the language of the Church. Under such circumstances, it remained a constant challenge to prevent the world of learning from becoming remote from and irrelevant to the realities of life.

The art of the early Middle Ages reflects a mixture of old and new. Greco-Roman forms and themes persisted in architecture, sculpture, and

FIGURE 15.3 Two Thieves Awaiting the Crucifixion This sculpture from the mausoleum of a seventh-century abbot from the Frankish city of Poitiers shows two unhappy thieves bound to crosses while awaiting their end with Christ. While classical art styles persist (e.g., the representation of a building), the portrayal of the human figures indicates that new influences were penetrating artistic expression in the German-dominated world. (Marburg/Art Resource)

painting, but they were constantly modified to serve Christian ends. Many of the churches of the era followed the basilica plan characteristic of Roman structures. However, Byzantine architectural forms, shaped by Justinian's building program, asserted a strong influence on sixth-century Italy, especially in Ravenna (see Figure 13.2), and persisted there to affect building styles in other areas of the West. In sculpture and painting, classical and Byzantine influences merged to create a pictorial art emphasizing symbolical representation of religious motifs (see Figures 12.1 and 15.3). Germanic and Celtic influences asserted their effect on the pictorial arts, especially their decorative style, which used animal and geometric forms to create abstract designs. The vigor of this composite early medieval art is especially evident in designs created to illustrate handwritten manuscripts; prime examples include the Irish Book of Durrow (late seventh century), the English Lindisfarne Gospels (eighth century), and the Irish Book of Kells (early ninth century) (see Color Plate 8). Artistic expression especially emphasized the symbolic representation of religious values at the expense of realistic portrayal of humans and the world of nature.

By 750 the Germanic West had by no means emerged from the time of troubles that followed the collapse of the Roman imperial regime. Habits of violence, ignorance, poverty, and moral laxness had been ingrained into people's lives and would long affect the western European world. However, out of the experiences of the early Middle Ages had emerged innovative institutions and patterns of life: a form of limited monarchy, a new nobility, a stabilized peasantry, an involved Church, the papacy, monasticism, a store of Greco-Roman literature and learning, a new art style. Their potential had not yet been realized, but their existence pointed toward the survival of a vigorous civilization in the West that might in the future equal the level of civilized life already flourishing in the Byzantine and Moslem worlds.

SUGGESTED READING

Political, Economic, and Social History

J. M. Wallace-Haddrill, *The Barbarian West, 400–1000,* 3rd ed. rev. (1967). An excellent general survey.

Henri Pirenne, *Mohammed and Charlemagne,* trans. Bernard Maill (1939). A classic expounding the thesis that only the Islamic invasions of the eighth century brought a break with the classical world.

Edward James, *The Origins of France: From Clovis to the Capetians, 500–1000* (1982).

Katharine Scherman, *The Birth of France: Warriors, Bishops, and Long-Haired Kings* (1987).

Chris Wickham, *Early Medieval Italy: Central Power and Local Society, 400–1000* (1981).

Roger Collins, *Early Medieval Spain: Unity in Diversity, 400–1000* (1983).

These four titles provide excellent treatments of the major continental Germanic kingdoms of the early Middle Ages.

Georges Duby, *The Early Growth of the European Economy. Warriors and Peasants from the Seventh to the Twelfth Century,* trans. Howard B. Clarke (1974).

Renée Doehaerd, *The Early Middle Ages in the West: Economy and Society,* trans. W. G. Deakin (1978).

Two comprehensive treatments of economic and social history.

Richard Hodges, *Dark Age Economies. The Origins of Towns and Trade A.D. 600–1000* (1982). Uses archaeological evidence to revise current opinions about the low level of trade and urban life.

Philippe Ariès and Georges Duby, *A History of Private Life,* Vol. 1: *From Pagan Rome to Byzantium,* ed. Paul Veyne, trans. Arthur Goldhammer (1987). The appropriate chapter in this study is rich in details about social life.

Suzanne Fonay Wemple, *Women in Frankish Society: Marriage and the Cloister, 500 to 900* (1981). A balanced treatment.

Religious and Cultural History

Hubert Jedin and John Dolan, *Handbook of Church History,* Vol. 2: *The Imperial Church to the Early Middle Ages,* trans. Anselm Biggs (1980). A detailed history of all aspects of religious life.

Judith Herrin, *The Formation of Christendom* (1987). Stresses religion as a prime force in shaping the new civilizations of the early Middle Ages.

J. M. Wallace-Hadrill, *The Frankish Church* (1983). A topical approach, rich in interpretations.

Jeffrey Richards, *The Popes and the Papacy in the Early Middle Ages, 476–752* (1979). An excellent treatment.

Pierre Riché, *Education and Culture in the Barbarian West: Sixth through Eighth Century,* trans. John J. Contreni (1976). A work rich in insights into the nature of early medieval culture.

Ludwig Bieler, *Ireland: Harbinger of the Middle Ages* (1963). A brilliant treatment of Ireland's contribution to cultural life.

J. Hubert et al., *Europe of the Invasions,* trans. Stuart Gilbert and James Emmons (1969). An excellent treatment of artistic development during the early Middle Ages.

Sources

Rule of Monasteries, trans. L. J. Boyle (1949). St. Benedict's rule.

Gregory of Tours, *The History of the Franks,* trans. Lewis Thorpe.

Bede, *The History of the English Church and People,* rev. ed., trans. L. Sherley-Price (1968).

Beowulf, trans. D. Wright (1957).

All of these works illustrate various facets of intellectual activity in the early medieval West.

CHAPTER 16

The First Revival of Europe: The Carolingian Age, 750–900

FIGURE 16.1 **Dispensing Justice in the Carolingian Age** This drawing from a ninth-century manuscript shows Emperor Charlemagne and his son, Pepin, king of Italy, presiding over a court of law while a clerk is ready to record their judgment. Concern for justice was an important aspect of the Carolingian effort to provide better government. (Modena Cathedral Archives)

The slow, troubled struggle to create a new basis for society in the Germanic West suddenly quickened in the eighth century. Between about 750 and 900 a narrow but energetic segment of society, spearheaded by kings and clergy, devoted their talents to an effort to "renew" society both on the Continent and in England. Although their ambitions were by no means realized, their limited success had two important results: It made the West visible in the larger world as a coherent culture. And it gave the West an expanded awareness of its unique identity. In a sense, this renewal created the first "Europe."

1. THE RISE OF THE CAROLINGIANS

The central force promoting revival on the Continent was a new Frankish royal dynasty, the Carolingians, so named after its most famous king, Carolus, or Charles. The Carolingians originated as one of the many ambitious noble families whose power and wealth grew steadily under the Merovingians. In the middle of the seventh century, the family utilized its extensive landed possessions and its connections with the Church to gain hereditary control over the office of mayor of the palace in the subkingdom of Austrasia, where the family wealth was concentrated (see Map. 16.1). This key office allowed the family to control the weak Merovingian kings of Austrasia and to utilize royal lands to increase its wealth and its circle of dependents. As their power expanded, the Carolingians sought to extend their influence to the other Merovingian subkingdoms—Neustria and Burgundy. That effort culminated in 687, when Pepin of Herstal, the Carolingian mayor of the palace of Austrasia, defeated the Neustrian mayor and claimed the mayoralty of the entire Frankish realm.

Once established as sole mayor of the palace, Pepin of Herstal and his son and grandson, Charles Martel (714–741) and Pepin the Short (741–751), became the most powerful men in the Frankish state, far overshadowing the "do-nothing" Merovingian kings whom they served. Their efforts were aimed chiefly at checking the forces of disintegration within the kingdom and defending its frontiers. Charles Martel gained undying fame by defeating a Moslem army at the battle of Tours in 733. Their military success was due in part to their ability to take advantage of a significant military innovation that began to spread in the eighth century: the heavily armored mounted warrior. This innovation was perhaps made possible by the invention of the stirrup, which permitted a mounted warrior to keep his mount while striking or receiving blows from sword or spear. The equipping and support of a force of mounted warriors involved costs beyond the means of the impoverished royal government; increasingly it was necessary to rely on men of wealth willing to arm themselves at their own expense. Charles Martel and Pepin rewarded such service by grants of land, called *benefices*, the income from which the recipients used on the condition that they would provide military service at their own expense. Although some of these benefices were derived from royal lands, Charles Martel and Pepin made a regular practice of utilizing Church lands to provide military benefices.

Although condemned by some clergymen as pillagers of the Church, Charles Martel and Pepin courted and won ecclesiastical support vital to their growing power. Their support of missionary activity and of religious reform was particularly welcome among bishops and monks. A key figure in shaping their religious policy was Boniface, an Anglo-Saxon Benedictine monk who came to the Continent in 719 to convert the pagans living beyond the eastern frontier of the kingdom. Until his martyrdom in 755 by pagan Frisians, Boniface not only won many converts but also organized bishoprics and monasteries in newly converted territories and guided the mayors of the palace in shaping a program to reform Frankish religious life. Soon after his arrival in Francia, Boniface sought and received the blessing of the papacy for his varied activities. As a result, papal influence expanded among the Franks and the mayors of the palace gained increasing recognition as supporters of the successors of St. Peter.

Although the Carolingian mayors of the palace clearly exercised control over the Frankish kingdom, they remained legally agents of the powerless Merovingian kings. Finally, Pepin took the logical step to end this incongruous situation by

Map 16.1 **THE EMPIRE OF CHARLEMAGNE** One of Charlemagne's great achievements was his military victories, which greatly expanded the Frankish kingdom. This map shows his major conquests. The extent of his holdings indicates that he came close to dominating western Europe, an ambition that would spark the dreams of many later western European rulers. Not long after Charlemagne's death his empire would suffer savage attacks on all its frontiers and would be divided by his heirs.

transferring the crown to his own family. Concerned about the potential hostility that might arise among the Franks by a forced deposition of the ancient dynasty whose sacred blood was held in deep respect, Pepin sought to sanction his action in an unprecedented way. He sent an envoy to Rome to ask Pope Zachary whether the "right ordering of things" did not demand that he who held actual power should wear the crown. On the basis of the pope's affirmative answer, Pepin in 751 deposed the reigning Merovingian and had himself elected king by the Frankish nobles. On the occasion of his coronation, a clergyman (perhaps Boniface) gave him a special anointment never before bestowed on a Frankish king. This sequence of events indicated to many that Pepin's royal office was different from that held by his Merovingian predecessors. Although duly elected by the Franks according to Germanic tradition, papal consent to the dynastic change and anointment by the Church made Pepin an agent of God charged with caring for the material and spiritual needs of the Christian community according to God's will.

Although the bonds between the papacy and the Carolingians had been growing before 751, the papacy was especially anxious to strengthen them at that moment because of significant changes in Italy. Since Justinian's reconquest of Italy, Rome had been under the jurisdiction of the emperor in Constantinople, and the popes had relied—sometimes reluctantly—on imperial protection. During the first half of the eighth century, however, the Moslem assault on Byzantium left the emperors increasingly unable to defend their position in Italy. Moreover, the iconoclastic policy of emperors Leo III and Constantine V was condemned as heretical by Pope Gregory II and his successors. Leo III retaliated by transferring important territories from the ecclesiastical jurisdiction of the pope to that of the patriarch of Constantinople. The decline of Byzantine power in Italy encouraged its longtime rival, the Lombards, to expand their sphere of influence. Beginning early in the eighth century a succession of able Lombard kings undertook military campaigns that increasingly threatened to engulf Rome and to impose a new master on the papacy. Bereft of help from the Byzantine emperors, now both weak and heretical, the popes desperately needed a new protector.

In the face of the mounting Lombard threat, Pope Stephen II (752–757) undertook a journey to Pepin's kingdom in 754, perhaps emboldened by the fact that his predecessor had extended an important favor to the new king. After long negotiations and despite resistance by some Frankish nobles, an agreement was reached. The king agreed to protect the pope from the Lombards. In return, the pope personally reanointed Pepin as king of the Franks and bestowed on him the somewhat ambiguous title of "*patricius* of the Romans," implying Pepin's role as protector of the people of Rome, including the papacy. Pepin undertook campaigns into Italy in 754 and 756 and forced the Lombards to surrender territories in central Italy that they had recently annexed. In a grant known as the Donation of Pepin, he bestowed these lands on the papacy, despite the fact that they legally belonged to the Byzantine emperor. This grant became the basis for the papacy's claim to an independent papal state. During his negotiations with Pepin, Stephen may have persuaded the Frank of the legality of disposing lands that belonged to the emperor by confronting him with a document known as the Donation of Constantine. This document, later proved to be a forgery, claimed to date from the time of Constantine and stated that the first Christian emperor, out of gratitude for being cured of leprosy, had granted Pope Sylvester I (314–335) the rights to the western empire, especially Rome and Italy. Pepin's Donation was therefore only a confirmation of an earlier legal grant made by a universally renowned ruler whose mantle the contemporary emperor in Constantinople had inherited.

2. THE REIGN OF CHARLEMAGNE, 768–814

The foundations established by Pepin of Herstal, Charles Martel, and Pepin the Short were brilliantly exploited by Charlemagne. In the eyes of his contemporaries he possessed many qualities of greatness: imposing physical stature, prowess as a warrior, piety, generosity, intelligence, devotion to family and friends, joy for life. His actions made him a hero not only in his own time but for many future generations of Europeans.

As befitted a Frankish king, Charlemagne was above all else a successful warlord. Few years passed throughout his long reign without a military campaign; the cumulative result was a considerable expansion of his kingdom (see Map 16.1). His most severe test came from the pagan Saxons along the northeastern frontier of his kingdom; only after many campaigns extending over thirty years was he able to conquer and convert them. The northeast frontier was also advanced by the conquest of Frisia. In 774 he crushed the troublesome Lombards, assumed the title of king of the Lombards, and laid claim to all of Italy except the Byzantine territories in the south and the Papal State, over which he continued the protectorship assumed by Pepin. His armies drove down the Danube and annexed territories held by the Avars and Slavs. His attack on Moslem Spain resulted initially in a defeat at Roncesvalles, later immortalized in an epic poem called *The Song of Roland*. But persistent pressure in that direction led to the creation of the Spanish March, south of the Pyrenees. Frankish military might also curbed the separatist aspirations of the people of Aquitaine, Bavaria, and Brittany. Beyond the new frontiers established by conquest, and especially in central Europe, southern Italy, and Denmark, Charlemagne combined force and diplomacy to compel various peoples into a tributary status requiring respect for Frankish territory and Frankish interests.

A tribute to Charlemagne's skill as a military organizer, these victories yielded a rich harvest of booty, which Charlemagne dispersed liberally to sustain the services and the allegiance of the warriors who fought the many battles and to win the favor of nobles and church officials upon whose support royal power depended. But Charlemagne succeeded in surrounding his military ventures with an aura transcending mere material considerations. They were struggles against barbarians, pagans, and infidels, fought to save the Christian world and to win converts for the true religion. For his efforts he won the plaudits of popes, poets, and nobles, who hailed him as "the strong right arm of God."

Charlemagne's military successes were accompanied by a strenuous effort to improve the quality of government within his growing realm by expanding royal power. Charlemagne's concept of kingship was rooted firmly in the Germanic concept of the *bannum*, which entitled a ruler to command his subjects to serve him and to punish those who disobeyed. That Germanic basis of royal authority was elevated and enriched by ideas drawn from Christian concepts of royal authority and responsibility and of the public well-being. The Christian view of the state, rooted in Old Testament precedents and especially in Augustine's *City of God*, which was Charlemagne's favorite book, envisioned the state as a society of Christians linked together by a common faith for the purpose of realizing God's plan for humanity, including the salvation of each individual soul. To achieve that end, society must strive for right order, harmony, and justice, each defined in Christian terms. The key to achieving the good Christian society was the king. Like David, the Christian king was God's agent who, by his anointment to office, was charged with commanding his subjects to do good and with restraining them from evil. He was, in effect, God's minister in the cause of righteousness. This concept of royal power, sometimes called ministerial kingship, provided norms for defining governmental action and political behavior that were much broader than had prevailed in the Frankish state during the Merovingian period.

In applying his expanded concept of royal authority and public responsibility, Charlemagne retained the basic political structures inherited from the Merovingians. What especially marked his reign was his own vigorous action aimed at making those structures work more effectively to realize Christian right order. He was a tireless worker, traveling constantly across his realm, checking incessantly on the performance of his officials, administering justice (see Figure 16.1), and consulting frequently with those upon whom he depended to sustain political order. At the heart of his government was the royal court (called the *palatium*), made up of trusted clergy and lay nobles. Each member of the court was assigned a political function as practical needs demanded: guarding the royal treasury, judging cases, keeping records, conducting diplomatic ventures, commanding armies, providing for the material needs of the royal family. Collectively, the court circle advised the king in shaping policies. The royal court was supported chiefly by the products of extensive royal lands; additional support, never very predictable, came from war booty, tolls on trade, fines, and gifts offered the king in return for favors. The court moved constantly, chiefly to expedite military campaigns and to gain access to the produce from royal estates. Only near the end of his reign did Charlemagne establish a semipermanent residence at Aachen.

To assert his authority on the local level, Charlemagne relied on the traditional system of counties, of which there were about three hundred. In each county the king was represented by a count who administered justice, enforced order, and mustered the freemen of the county to military service. The counts were rewarded by grants of land from which they could derive income as long as they held office. The counts were served by a small group of subofficials, most concerned with administering justice. Bishops and abbots were also assigned important responsibilities in local affairs. Charlemagne tried hard to select capable men for these offices and to supervise their activities. He developed a system of sending out special agents, called *missi*, to investigate what was going on, to instruct local officials on what the king expected, and to report back to the court on local conditions. He issued a constant stream of royal orders (called *capitularies*) to inform local officials of royal intent and to direct their actions on a wide range of matters relating to public order. Almost every year, Charlemagne also called his officials and other great men of the realm to his court to an assembly where he heard their concerns and proclaimed new regulations designed to govern their actions.

The operation of this modest political apparatus, involving only a few thousand officials, depended heavily on the loyalty not only of royal officials but also of all of the king's subjects, especially the great magnates. Charlemagne was constantly concerned with expanding the bonds of loyalty. His own feats as a warrior played an important role in this respect. On several occasions he required all of his free subjects to swear an oath of fidelity, binding them to refrain from activities contrary to public order. He regularly

bestowed gifts, derived chiefly from war booty, on those whose loyalty he especially prized. Most important of all, he greatly expanded the use of commendation and benefices to bind royal officials, nobles, and churchmen to him. Those who were willing to commend themselves under oath to become his vassals were granted benefices, usually in the form of land grants or offices, to be enjoyed as long as the recipients served him faithfully. Unfaithfulness to these oaths was considered a major offense.

As is shown by his capitularies, Charlemagne's prime concern was the curbing of violence and of oppression. From his perspective as a Christian king with a God-given responsibility to sustain the Church in its mission of saving souls, religious life was a prime factor in sustaining concord and justice. As a consequence, a major part of his political program focused on religious reform. Expanding on the program begun by his predecessors, he sought vigorously to revitalize religious life. He encouraged the spread of Christianity by supporting missionary activity, even using force to compel reluctant pagans, such as the Saxons, to receive baptism. He strengthened church organization by reestablishing the authority of bishops and subordinating parish priests to them. He sought to improve the quality of the clergy by imposing higher moral and educational standards on those who assumed ecclesiastical office. Monastic establishments were encouraged to adopt the Benedictine rule as a means of upgrading discipline and spiritual life. Royal authority was used to protect ecclesiastical property and to provide material support for the religious establishment; especially important was the imposition of a tax of 10 percent of income, called the tithe, on all Christians for the support of the Church. Charlemagne made a major effort to establish uniform doctrines and ritual practices as a way of eliminating the diverse practices and bizarre beliefs that passed as Christianity. In formulating and enacting his religious program, Charlemagne relied heavily on guidance from the papacy; especially close was his relationship with Pope Hadrian I (772–795). As a result, a distinct Roman stamp was imposed on religious life in his realm. Charlemagne must be counted as a major architect of the Roman Catholic church and as a major force in enhancing the authority of the papacy in the West.

All of these achievements pointed toward the culminating event of Charlemagne's career: his coronation as emperor. The stage was set for this event when serious disturbances in Rome in 799 led to charges of misconduct against Pope Leo III (795–816), who was forced to flee to Charlemagne's court. In his role as protector of the pope and the Romans, Charlemagne went to Rome in 800 and acted directly to exonerate the pope and restore him to full authority. Then on Christmas Day in the year 800, while the king was attending Mass in St. Peter's Basilica, the pope placed a crown on his head, and the clergy and people in attendance hailed the king of the Franks as "Augustus, crowned by God, the great and peace-bringing Emperor of the Romans." For the first time since 476 a ruler from the West was emperor.

Since that momentous occasion there has been a debate about who instigated the renewal of the imperial office and what it signified. Perhaps responsibility for the event was shared by the pope, Charlemagne, and his advisers as a means of realizing different aspirations. For Leo III the bestowal of the crown certainly enhanced papal prestige. For Charlemagne the new title was a suitable recognition for his accomplishments as conqueror and protector of the Christian world. Some of Charlemagne's ecclesiastical advisers felt that such a title would enhance their ruler's authority to the point where he could play the role of a new David and a new Constantine in promoting Christian unity. Almost everyone in the West shared the opinion that the emperors in the East had failed to serve the Christian cause, especially in view of the fact that a woman, Empress Irene, held the crown at the moment. It is probably also true that the imperial title meant different things to different people. The Byzantine rulers saw it as an outrageous usurpation. The popes, at least in the long run, interpreted the event as a precedent for their right to designate the ruler of the Christian world. For many church leaders the event was a signal to intensify the effort to create the ideal Christian commonwealth.

What Charlemagne thought of his new title is likewise an enigma. He ruled as emperor for fourteen years. Some of his actions suggest that he took the title seriously. He conducted a skillful military and diplomatic campaign that finally compelled the Byzantine emperor to recognize him as emperor. He pursued with renewed vigor his religious reforms, suggesting his responsiveness to the political Augustinianism of those advisers who had encouraged him to become emperor. However, he disdained the trappings of the imperial office, and he insisted on being called king of the Franks. Contrary to all that the imperial title implied about the unity of his realm, he made plans to divide his empire in order to provide a "kingdom" for each of his three sons; such a division was avoided only because a single son, Louis, outlived him. In 813 Charlemagne personally crowned Louis as emperor without papal involvement. These actions suggest that Charlemagne viewed the imperial title as a personal honor that he had earned by his achievements and that he could dispose of as he pleased. Whatever the case, the event of 800, which translated an ancient title rich in political symbolism into a Germanic and Christian context, was of major significance in creating a western European political consciousness.

3. THE CAROLINGIAN CULTURAL RENAISSANCE

Perhaps the most lasting achievement of the Carolingian Age was a cultural renaissance that owed much to the personal interest and effort of the indefatigable Charlemagne. This revival was based on pragmatic motives. Charlemagne was convinced that political and religious renewal could be achieved only through the efforts of better-educated leaders, especially the clergy. Practical though it was, that was a radical idea in a society that had almost lost sight of the connection between learning and public order.

A major factor in generating cultural revival was Charlemagne's ability to utilize the leadership and talent produced by modest cultural revivals that had occurred earlier in several parts of the West—in Italy, Spain, Ireland, and especially England. The setting for the interaction of these leaders was what has been called the palace "school" that the king began to form in the 780s and that took on special vigor in the 790s after Aachen was established as the permanent royal residence. To this somewhat informal circle, often with Charlemagne's personal encouragement, came some of the most learned individuals from all Europe. The palace school served as a highly visible setting where individuals of varying cultural perspectives met to study, write, and reflect on intellectual issues. Because Charlemagne himself was an active and enthusiastic participant, the palace school became a visible symbol of the dedication of his regime to revitalizing cultural life; some even spoke grandly of Aachen as the "new Athens."

More significantly, the palace school became a kind of laboratory, generating ideas and techniques out of which emerged an education system crucial to the Carolingian renaissance. A key figure in shaping this education program was Alcuin (735–804), an English monk reared in the monastic cultural environment that produced Bede and Boniface. Alcuin served at the royal court from 782 to 796 and then became abbot of an important monastery at Tours, where he continued to assert leadership in cultural life until his death in 804. His concepts of education decisively shaped the thinking and the practices not only of his own generation but also of cultural leaders across the entire ninth century and even beyond.

Alcuin, and with him most Carolingian cultural figures, saw education as preparation for understanding the holy literature that contained God's message: the Bible, the writings of the church fathers, the liturgical books, saints' lives. To comprehend the message of salvation contained in the written texts, people must learn Latin. And they must acquire a body of knowledge and intellectual skills that would allow them to grasp the meaning of the holy texts. These educational objectives could best be achieved by organizing education around the old Roman system of the seven liberal arts, which consisted of two basic groupings of "disciplines": the *trivium*, embracing grammar, rhetoric, and dialectic (logic); and the *quadrivium*, comprising arithmetic, geometry, astronomy, and music.

The realization of these educational goals confronted Carolingian leaders with major challenges. They needed to provide textbooks for each of the seven arts, but especially for the *trivium*, which emphasized language study, effective writing, and logical thinking. The material for such textbooks

was to be drawn from classical Latin literature, but textbook compilers had to adapt such material to Christian purposes. Once learners had mastered the skills and knowledge embraced in the seven liberal arts, then they needed to apply their minds to the texts containing true wisdom. This objective raised the problem of the quality and the availability of books. A major effort was devoted to establishing authentic versions of Scripture, liturgical books, texts defining ecclesiastical and secular laws, writings of the Church Fathers, and even pagan Latin texts and Germanic legends. The establishment of authentic texts required linguistic skill, broad knowledge, and logical thought. Once scholars had established sound texts, then accurate copies had to be made. This need encouraged the development of workshops, called *scriptoria*, where book copying was systematically pursued; such work was particularly appropriate for Benedictine monks seeking to meet their obligation to serve God by working. Carolingian copyists, concerned with making reading easier, developed a simple but effective system of handwriting called Carolingian *minuscule*, which replaced the almost illegible Merovingian cursive writing with separately formed lowercase letters. The formation of libraries was also encouraged so that good texts would be widely available.

As the tools of education were forged, Charlemagne and his successors employed royal authority to universalize their use. Bishops and abbots were commanded to organize schools and to adopt authentic texts as a basis of teaching. This effort resulted in a significant increase in the number of schools and a heightened concern for the quality of teaching. Many bishops and abbots became active collectors of libraries and organizers of *scriptoria*. Although the palace school had declined in importance by the end of Charlemagne's reign, his successors remained active patrons of culture. However, during the ninth century cultural leadership passed to new centers, especially monastic schools, which effectively sustained the thrust of cultural revival even in the face of political decline.

Although Carolingian reform of education had only a limited impact on the massive illiteracy afflicting all levels of society, it did have significant consequences in shaping an environment more favorable to learning than had existed since late Roman imperial times. The concern with language instruction led to the development of a simplified, flexible version of Latin that became the standard means of literary expression over much of the West. The effort to establish authentic versions of a wide variety of texts created a substantial knowledge base on which a common intellectual life could be erected. That effort also reestablished contacts with the learning and literature of classical Rome and the patristic Church; almost all surviving classical Latin texts date from the Carolingian period. The capacity for clear thinking and effective writing was considerably improved. Taken together, these developments established the base from which a creative, independent western European intellectual and literary life would eventually develop.

A measure of the impact of the Carolingian renaissance can be found in the literary works produced by leading Carolingian writers and scholars. One court luminary and longtime confidant of Charlemagne, Einhard (ca. 770–840), produced an excellent biography of his master; many other writers tried their hands at biography, especially saints' lives. An Italian, Paul the Deacon (ca. 720–799), wrote a *History of the Lombards*, which reflected the capacity of Carolingian writers to produce historical works. Alcuin, Bishop Hincmar of Reims (ca. 806–882), and many others produced lively letters reflecting the major concerns of the age. Theodulf (ca. 750–821), a Spaniard, was but one among many who composed poetry. Several clerics, including Bishop Jonas of Orleans (ca. 780–843), composed books intended to guide princes, which reflect considerable sophistication in political thought. A succession of theologians prepared impressive commentaries on Scripture and compiled significant doctrinal tracts; especially notable as theologians were Hrabanus Maurus (ca. 780–856), abbot of Fulda, and John Scotus Erigena (ca. 810–877), an Irishman who lived in Francia from 850 to 875. Although most Carolingian scholarly work was derived from earlier works, it did reflect an ability to interpret tradition in terms applicable to contemporary issues.

The forces unleashed by the effort to renew Christian life and culture stimulated artistic activity. Carolingian art borrowed from diverse traditions: classical, Byzantine, Germanic, Celtic. The age produced several impressive churches; the most unique was the one built by Charlemagne at Aachen. That octagonal structure, strongly influenced by Byzantine churches in Ravenna, reflects an effort to make architecture a link between religion and the ideology of royalty. The mosaics and frescoes created to decorate churches and the miniature paintings used to illustrate manuscripts reflect skill in narrative art, especially in visually reconstructing episodes from sacred history. Carolingian artists produced fine ivory carvings, metalwork, and jewelry, much of which was employed for liturgical purposes. Underlying most Carolingian art was a powerful urge to deepen religious understanding and promote piety. In this respect, art shared the basic urge that generated and sustained the entire Carolingian renaissance.

4. THE DISINTEGRATION OF THE CAROLINGIAN EMPIRE

Charlemagne left a heavy burden for his successors. His son, Louis the Pious (814–840), continued his father's policies with some success. Although he concerned himself with good government and with defense of the empire, Louis' chief energies were aimed at realizing the universalist ideals embodied in Carolingian political ideology. This inclination led him to a close alliance with powerful churchmen, dedicated to the maintenance of unity, religious reform, and cultural renewal. His reign thus witnessed notable advances in religious reform, including the imposition of the Benedictine rule on the monastic establishment, clarification of the relationship between emperor and papacy, and an expanded role of the clergy in public life. But Louis' course, basically aimed at perfecting ministerial kingship, met resistance from powerful elements in society. The consequent tensions laid bare basic weaknesses in the Carolingian system.

The most disruptive problem in Louis' reign involved the question of succession. As we have already noted, ancient Frankish custom demanded that a ruler divide his realm among his surviving sons. The earlier Carolingians had not had to face that issue. Except for two instances which were quickly resolved, for five generations—from Pepin of Herstal's victory in 687 to Louis' accession in 814—there was only a single son to succeed to the headship of the state. But Louis did have to face the issue. His first instinct, expressed clearly in a document issued in 817, was to preserve the unity of the empire by entrusting it to his oldest son, with the younger heirs receiving minor subkingdoms subordinate to the emperor. But pressure from his younger sons and their supporters and from his second wife, Judith, intent on gaining a share of the realm for her son by Louis, gradually eroded Louis' resolve to maintain the unity of the empire. Eventually Louis agreed to provide a "kingdom" for each of his two younger sons; to the oldest, Lothair, he bequeathed the title of emperor with a vague authority over his younger brothers. Shortly after Louis' death the younger sons declared war on Emperor Lothair and in 843 forced him to sign the Treaty of Verdun. This document legalized the division of the empire into three parts: the kingdom of the West Franks (roughly modern France) to be ruled by Charles the Bald; the kingdom of the East Franks (roughly modern Germany) assigned to Louis the German; and the kingdom of Lotharingia (Lothair's realm), a narrow band lying between the West and East kingdoms and stretching from the North Sea to Italy (see Map 16.2). The Treaty of Verdun provided that the ruler of the Middle Kingdom would hold the imperial title, but his authority over the other kings was vague and ineffectual. Later in the ninth century Middle Kingdom was further divided to create three kingdoms: Italy, Burgundy, and Lotharingia. By this time succession to the imperial office became uncertain and open to competition.

The struggles surrounding the succession issue revealed another threat to imperial authority. Louis found many of his royal vassals ready to desert him and to align themselves with one or another of his sons in return for additional benefices. This situation revealed that Charlemagne's widespread use of vassalage and benefice to create bonds of loyalty to the ruler had its dangers. The granting of land to vassals began to erode the royal property, the basic source of support for government. Unless carefully controlled, the recipients of benefices used the grants of land to expand

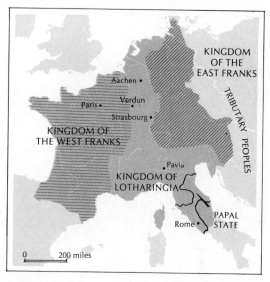

Map 16.2 PARTITION OF THE CAROLINGIAN EMPIRE, 843
This map shows the divisions of the unified Carolingian Empire arranged by the sons of Louis the Pious at the Treaty of Verdun in 843. The kingdom of Louis the German (the Kingdom of the East Franks) and the kingdom of Charles the Bald (Kingdom of the West Franks) became the bases from which Germany and France would evolve. Lothar I's kingdom was later divided into three small kingdoms, the most important of which was the Kingdom of Italy.

their independence without concern for the obligations they owed. Their growing power allowed them to demand new grants in return for service, thus creating a vicious cycle undermining royal authority and expanding the power of the landed nobility. From the end of Louis' reign onward this process accelerated at the expense of royal authority.

Still another problem began to plague the rulers: their inability to defend the Frankish realm against mounting attacks from external foes. From bases in North Africa came assaults by sea from aggressive Moslems, called Saracens, who ravaged the coasts of Italy and southern France. From the east the empire was attacked by new invaders from Asia, the Magyars or Hungarians, skilled at hit-and-run attacks by mounted warriors. Most formidable were the Vikings or Norsemen (Danes,

FIGURE 16.2   The Viking Terror   This representation of Viking ships filled with fierce warriors illustrates why they struck terror in those who witnessed the vessels approaching their undefended shores. One senses that the artist had witnessed such a scene. (Culver Pictures)

Swedes, and Norwegians). Still barbarians and pagans, the Vikings lived along the wild coasts of Scandinavia, surviving chiefly by fishing and piracy. Late in the eighth century, for reasons not entirely clear, they began to expand. Traveling by sea in small groups, they raided an immense area, touching Ireland, England, the Atlantic coast of Europe, the southern shores of the North and Baltic seas, Russia, Iceland, Greenland, and even North America (see Figure 16.2). Wherever they went, they pillaged for booty and struck terror in their victims. Gradually some of them began to settle permanently in the lands they had been raiding, especially in Ireland, northern England, Iceland, a region in northwestern France called

Normandy after them, and in the area in Russia around Kiev. Slowly their piracy gave way to trade, and they adopted the religion and culture of western Europeans. But that was too late to spare the Carolingian Empire from the destructive fury of this last wave of Germanic invaders.

The Carolingian armies, organized primarily for attack warfare, were helpless against these highly mobile marauders. The only effective way to deal with them was to organize local defenses under local leaders willing to assume that responsibility and capable of acting on their own. By assuming this burden, nobles greatly expanded their control over local political affairs. From Louis the Pious onward, kings had no choice but to reward these individuals for their military role with additional grants of land and authority, a process that further undermined royal power.

After 843 each of the Carolingian kingdoms witnessed the steady decline of royal authority. The energies of their rulers were absorbed in petty quarrels aimed at snatching territory from one another. They had no choice but to continue seeking the support of the powerful in society by granting new lands and conceding political power. As a consequence, landed nobles tightened their control over local territories, creating increasing numbers of independent principalities and forcing the peasantry into dependence. Invaders continued to pillage western Europe almost at will. The most persistent defenders of royal power were churchmen, but in the long run even ecclesiastical support worked against the interests of the Carolingians. Constantly mindful of the important role Charlemagne had attributed to the Church in creating Christian order, later Carolingian churchmen became bolder and bolder in their claims to supremacy over the state. Frankish bishops repeatedly challenged royal authority and criticized royal conduct. By the middle of the ninth century the pope was openly claiming superior authority over all Christians, including kings and emperors. Pope Nicholas I (858–867) actually tried to assert such claims by interfering in the private lives of Carolingian kings, negotiating to halt civil strife, legislating for the entire Church in the West, taking the lead in spreading Christianity, and doing battle with Byzantine emperors and churchmen over dogma and jurisdiction—all activities that Charlemagne had claimed to control as ministerial king and emperor. And even while expressing lofty sentiments about their role as protectors of Christian order, high church officials joined lay nobles in increasing their landholdings and political powers over local affairs at the expense of the royal government.

By 900 the Carolingian rulers had been reduced to impotence. The dream of Charlemagne to make western Europe a single Christian state where concord and justice prevailed had foundered. However, this failure must not hide the deeper significance of the Carolingian era. The redefinition of the nature of the state and of the role of the Christian ruler, the religious reform, the cultural renaissance, the revival of empire, the expanded role defined for the papacy, and the expansion of personal bonds as an element of public order would all affect the future shape of western European society. Much of later medieval history consisted of working out concepts about civilized life developed in Carolingian times.

5. EARLY MEDIEVAL ENGLAND

While the Carolingians were attempting to renew society on the Continent, active rulers and their followers were pursuing comparable ends in England. The Anglo-Saxon invasions of England in the fifth century had virtually wiped out Roman civilization. Latin culture, including the language, was replaced by Germanic culture and religion. The newcomers established several small kingdoms whose political institutions were almost completely Germanic. From the fifth until the eighth century these kingdoms constantly warred with one another to create a condition almost as chaotic as that prevailing on the Continent between 500 and 750.

The introduction of Christianity into this divided society provided important impetus to the development of a common culture. Late in the sixth century missionaries from Ireland and from Rome came to England and within a century had converted most of the land. For a brief period in the seventh century, Roman and Irish forces clashed over the right to dominate England. The Roman forces won, chiefly because of support offered by Anglo-Saxon kings. This victory ensured uniformity in church organization, ritual, and doctrine and put England in touch with the mainstream of continental religious life. The encounter of Irish monasticism and Roman Benedictine monasticism generated a vigorous cultural revival in England, reaching its zenith in the age of Bede in the early eighth century. As already noted, that revival produced leaders, such as Boniface and Alcuin, who helped shape the Carolingian revival and who strengthened ties between England and the Carolingian world.

Beginning in the eighth century and continuing into the ninth century, England suffered devastating blows from the Vikings. Some of these raiders occupied a large area in northern England known as the Danelaw. The Viking raids also swallowed up several of the old Anglo-Saxon kingdoms. The kingdom of Wessex became the center of resistance and eventually of counterattack against the Vikings. The reign of Alfred the Great (871–899) was the decisive moment. He not only stopped Viking expansion but also laid the groundwork for the reconquest of the Danelaw. Under his leadership the Church and cultural life were revitalized. During the tenth century, Alfred's successors rewon the Danelaw and in the process created a unified kingdom for England.

The unification of England led to a single political system, heavily influenced by ancient Anglo-Saxon institutions. A king, claiming to be supreme judge, army leader, head of the Church, and lawgiver, ruled over the kingdom. Royal authority was supported by household officials who constituted the royal court. The king supported himself and his court chiefly from the income from royal estates. However, he could levy direct taxes on his subjects; for example, several kings collected the Danegeld, a tax levied first in 991 to buy off Viking raiders. The monarch retained the authority to summon all freemen to serve in the army (called the *fyrd*). He could also depend on the military services of his noble retainers, called *thegns*, whose support was won by grants of land. He was advised on matters of public interest by the *Witan*, an assembly of great nobles and churchmen that was held to represent all freemen. However, a strong king could act without this body's approval. This complex of institutions surrounding the king made the central government of England a major factor in public life, much more effective than was that of the late Carolingian monarchs.

A crucial factor in the political order was the system of local government that had developed over a long period. The kingdom was divided into territorial units called *shires*, of which there were about forty in the tenth century. In each shire the king's interests were represented by three officials—the *earl*, the *sheriff*, and the *bishop*. The earl was the most notable in rank and prestige, but the sheriff conducted most of the royal business. A court was held in each shire twice a year, and all free individuals were expected to attend. Royal orders were proclaimed and all civil and criminal cases were adjudicated at this court. The law administered was customary law, dating from far back in Anglo-Saxon history and "remembered" by the influential members of each shire. Each shire was subdivided into *hundreds*, where courts presided over by a royal official met monthly to settle minor cases; the hundreds also provided the basis for recruiting military forces for the *fyrd*. Agricultural villages also had their own courts, usually conducted by landowners. This network of local institutions, providing a means through which royal authority could be applied at the local level, acted as a buffer against the emergence of private political power and political fragmentation so characteristic of the Continent in the tenth century.

Although by the eleventh century the Anglo-Saxon political order began to falter, the pattern of institutions created in the ninth and tenth centuries provided a heritage that would play a major role in shaping a unique English constitutional system in the future.

SUGGESTED READING

The Carolingian World

Most of the works listed in Chapter 15 provide material on Carolingian history. The following titles treat special aspects.

Louis Halphen, *Charlemagne and the Carolingian Empire*, trans. Giselle de Nie (1977). A good survey of political history.

Rosamond McKitterick, *The Frankish Kingdom under the Carolingians, 751–987* (1983). Especially helpful on the later Carolingians.

Jacques Boussard, *The Civilisation of Charlemagne*, trans. Frances Partridge (1968). A balanced treatment of Carolingian society.

Pierre Riché, *Daily Life in the World of Charlemagne*, trans. Jo Ann McNamara (1978). Rich in details on Carolingian life.

Robert Folz, *The Coronation of Charlemagne: 25 December 800*, trans. J. E. Anderson (1974). A balanced treatment of a disputed subject.

Hubert Jedin and John Dolan, eds., *Handbook of Church History*, Vol. 3: *The Church in the Age of Feudalism*, trans. Anselm Biggs (1969). A detailed treatment of religious life.

Rosamond McKitterick, *The Frankish Church and the Carolingian Reforms, 789–895* (1977). A good assessment of Carolingian religious reform.

John Marenbon, *Early Medieval Philosophy (480–1150). An Introduction* (1983). Places the Carolingian intellectual achievement in a larger historical context.

J. Hubert et al., *The Carolingian Renaissance* (1970). A magnificent treatment of Carolingian art.

Russell Chamberlain, *Charlemagne: Emperor of the Western World* (1986). An adequate biography.

The Vikings

Gwyn Jones, *A History of the Vikings*, rev. ed. (1984).

Magnus Magnusson, *Vikings* (1980).

Either of these works will help the reader understand Viking society.

P. H. Sawyer, *Kings and Vikings: Scandinavia and Europe, A.D. 700–1000* (1982). An excellent treatment of the impact of the Vikings.

Anglo-Saxon England

Peter Hunter Blair, *An Introduction to Anglo-Saxon England*, 2nd ed. (1977).

P. H. Sawyer, *From Roman Britain to Norman England* (1978).

Two concise, clearly written surveys of Anglo-Saxon history.

H. R. Loyn, *The Governance of Anglo-Saxon England, 500–1087* (1984). An excellent description of Anglo-Saxon political institutions.

Sources

Two Lives of Charlemagne, trans. Lewis Thorpe (1969). Contains the famous biography by Einhard.

H. R. Loyn and John Percival, eds., *The Reign of Charlemagne: Documents on Carolingian Government and Administration* (1975). Helpful in understanding how Carolingian government worked.

CHAPTER 17

Lordship and Dependency: Feudalism and Manorialism

FIGURE 17.1 The Bastion of Local Lordship: The Medieval Castle   Castles such as this one were built over much of western Europe during the eleventh and twelfth centuries as centers from which local potentates and their armed vassals could assert lordship over the surrounding countryside and its inhabitants. This castle, Château Gaillard, built in the late twelfth century on a cliff above the Seine River by King Richard of England to protect his Norman fiefdom from his feudal overlord, the king of France, was virtually impregnable. Outer walls (whose ruins are still visible) and a moat protected the inner fortress and its keep. Living quarters, a great meeting hall, and a chapel were built in the inner courtyard of this structure. (Copyright Stephen T. Johnson)

The inability of the Carolingian dynasty to sustain its effort to renovate society and the devastation caused by the Saracen, Magyar, and Viking assaults produced a new era of instability in western Europe during the late ninth and the tenth centuries. In some respects this period was so chaotic that historians have been tempted to describe it as a "second dark age," resembling the troubled sixth and seventh centuries. However, amidst the difficulties that marked the late Carolingian age, there occurred a basic regrouping of the population of much of the West into institutional patterns that restored stability and set the stage for vigorous growth. For the most part, the new institutional patterns were fashioned from elements that had been present in society since the end of Roman imperial order. Now, just prior to 1000, these usages, some Germanic and some Roman, were brought together to establish new human communities that proved capable of unleashing human talents in a variety of ways. The restructuring of society took a variety of forms across western Europe, thus making any attempt at generalization difficult and misleading. But everywhere certain key patterns emerged to constitute stronger foundations for society.

1. LORDSHIP AND DEPENDENCY

In broad terms a key development of the late-Carolingian period centered on the privatization of political power by powerful landholders. We have seen that a key feature of the Roman imperial order was a strong state in which extensive powers were invested in the hands of officials who exercised those powers in the interests of the public welfare. The Germanic kingdoms that replaced the Roman imperial order attempted to maintain strong central government, but the efforts of their rulers were of limited effectiveness. At the heart of the Carolingian renewal was an attempt to revitalize the state and to reestablish public order. We have traced in the preceding chapter how such rulers as Charlemagne and Louis the Pious sought to achieve this end, with the result that for about at least a century prior to 850 public authority played a prominent role in shaping affairs in the Carolingian Empire.

But the successors to the great Carolingians were unable to sustain their authority. The partition of the Carolingian Empire after 843 resulted in a diminution of royal resources in each of the Carolingian kingdoms. In their attempts to muster support, the late Carolingian kings slowly granted away their royal holdings to powerful nobles and great ecclesiastical officials; technically such grants were made in return for loyalty and service, but the recipients increasingly disregarded their obligations. The inability of the kings to defend their realms against invaders eroded their prestige and necessitated increasing reliance on local power wielders for security. Although kingdoms and kingship survived this ordeal, by the tenth century public authority had become a limited force in the lives of most people in the West.

As royal power and public authority disintegrated, a new force emerged as the dominant feature of political life. *Private lordships* replaced the state as the effective political entities. Individual landholders ruling over principalities of limited area became the only effective political force. The advancing power of landed potentates had been a characteristic of society in the West since late Roman times. By the tenth century the monopoly of power of that group became final. The political map of the West now consisted of hundreds of principalities of varying size in which power was exercised for the private benefit of the lords of these territories.

These lordships were formed in various ways. In some cases, Carolingian public officials, such as counts and dukes, simply arrogated to private use the public authority entrusted to them by the king as well as the lands and the public revenues granted to them by the king as a reward for public service. In other instances, aggressive landowners with the support of armed followers forcefully seized control of a territory and imposed their private rule on its inhabitants. Often the key to the success of such lords was their control of a military strong point, a castle (see Figure 17.1); thus, they are often referred to as *castellans*. In still other cases, enterprising nobles fashioned a lordship out of lands they received as benefices for services rendered to others under the terms of the feudal contract, which will be examined later. But whatever the means, the results were the same:

the fragmentation of kingdoms into a mosaic of private lordships where powerful individuals exercised control over those who lived within their principality. Some of these lords occasionally paid a shadowy allegiance to the impotent kings within whose kingdoms their lordships lay, but in reality each was "king" in his own principality.

As lordship developed, so did *dependency* in various forms. Since late Roman times a variety of forces had been at work encouraging or compelling individuals to place themselves in a position of dependence on other individuals under conditions that regulated their interactions on a private basis beyond the sphere of public authority. By the tenth century almost everyone who did not exercise a lordship lived in a condition of dependency in some form. The conditions of dependency varied infinitely from place to place and from person to person. However, two broad categories existed to determine the condition of most dependents.

First, some lived in a condition of noble dependency. A prime requirement for those who succeeded in creating and then sustaining independent lordships was military force. To provide this force, powerful lords gathered around themselves armed followers willing to provide military service in return for material considerations sufficient to allow them to live a life befitting a warrior. In some cases, lords supported their retainers as a part of their households, but more often military followers were given grants of land from which a living could be derived. As we shall see, the conditions governing the relationships between lords and followers came to be institutionalized in forms that defined a unique way of life for those involved. Although armed retainers were originally drawn from all levels of life, by the tenth century they along with their lords had come to claim a special status for themselves as nobles.

Second, the bulk of the population lived in a condition of servile dependency. In a world where almost everyone from the most powerful to the lowliest depended on agriculture for a livelihood, those who exercised lordship and their armed followers required a peasant labor force to till the soil from which power and wealth were derived. They gained it by asserting their jurisdiction over

the peasant population in a way that compelled peasants to perform a range of menial services related to agricultural production and that allowed the exaction of dues from the peasants which supported lordly life. The reduction of the peasantry to dependency had been evolving over many centuries, powerfully abetted by unsettled political conditions that forced peasants to seek security at whatever cost. By the tenth century the dominance of the powerful had become nearly complete, subject to almost no controls by public authority. In the process of establishing domination over their servile dependents, lords had in many cases congregated their peasants into village communities to expedite effective management of their labor and exaction of dues. As was the case with noble dependency, by the tenth century the conditions governing servile dependency had assumed institutional forms that gave stability and permanence to the system.

2. THE COMMUNITY OF THE POWERFUL: THE FEUDAL ORDER

By the tenth century relationships among the powerful were governed by a set of institutions called *feudalism*. This term is surrounded by so many ambiguities that some historians have questioned its usefulness in describing a particular sociopolitical order. However, it can still serve usefully to highlight certain practices through which members of the dominant nobility established order among themselves. Feudalism grew out of the merger, over the course of many centuries, of two practices: personal dependence and shared rights in land tenure. The first was rooted in the Germanic *comitatus* and the Roman clientage system (see pp. 103 and 172) and the second in the Germanic system of gift giving and the late Roman land tenancy system. The confusion and chaos in western Europe following the Germanic migrations encouraged the spread of these ancient institutions between 500 and 750. In search of strong protectors, many were willing to enter a *commendation* agreement, which established a personal bond linking the two individuals—often called *lord* and *vassal*—to each other in a way that was mutually useful. Likewise, those in search of a livelihood or a way to enlarge their holdings were willing to accept the use of another's land in return for some kind of service. Such grants, called *benefices*, remained the property of the grantor and thus could be made without diminishing one's basic holdings. By obtaining the use of land on a conditional basis, the recipient gained real benefit in an unsettled world where use of land was essential.

The Carolingian rulers relied heavily on these usages to expand their control over their subjects, thereby giving these practices status in public law and more precise definition. The Carolingians required the great men of the realm, including public officials, to become their vassals and rewarded them with benefices, now called *fiefs*, in return for services. Such arrangements were especially valuable in providing military service; the fief provided the means by which a vassal could arm himself at his own expense. In many cases, kings also granted their vassals *immunities*, which gave them governing powers over their fiefs and the people living on them. Vassalage and fiefs came to be interconnected to the point where personal dependence almost always involved the grant of a fief. With the breakdown of public authority and royal power after about 850, those seeking to establish private lordships utilized these practices as a means of creating a military following. They gathered around them a circle of followers who agreed to serve as vassals in return for fiefs that gave to each vassal the use of land and a labor force that provided the basis for status, wealth, and security.

Implicit in the arrangements creating the lord-vassal bond was the idea of a mutually binding contract between two free persons. The ritual that had evolved to mark the establishment of such a contract provides a convenient key to the nature of this bond (see Figure 17.2). One man knelt before another, placed his hands between the other's, and declared himself willing to become his "man." By this voluntary act, called *homage* (after the Latin word *homo*, meaning "man"), the first became a vassal and the second a lord. The lord lifted up his new "man" and kissed him, signifying that he accepted him as a vassal. The vassal then swore an oath of *fealty*, binding himself in the sight of God to be faithful to his lord. The lord then gave him some object, such as a clod of

FIGURE 17.2 The Feudal Contract: The Act of Homage This scene pictures the basic act creating the feudal contract—the act of homage by which the kneeling figures became vassals of the seated lord. (Archive of the Crown of Aragon, Barcelona/MAS)

dirt or a ring. This act was called *investiture*, symbolizing the granting of a fief—usually a piece of land but sometimes an office or a money stipend—which the vassal could use to support himself. By the acts of homage, fealty, and investiture, two individuals bound themselves together in a way that gave each rights and imposed on each obligations through which their political and social interactions were controlled. By the tenth century the lord-vassal relationship had become hereditary, ensuring that the bonds created by the contract continued for generations within the same families.

The specific rights and obligations of lords and

vassals came in time to be defined in a special legal system, called feudal law. Although feudal law varied widely across western Europe, certain rights and obligations were fairly standard.

The feudal contract generally established the lord in a position of authority over his vassal. He retained important rights in the fief he had granted to his vassal for the latter's use. The lord was obligated to protect his vassal and to provide him justice—to use his army to defend his vassal against attacks and to maintain a court where the vassal could receive a hearing for any grievances. Put briefly, the lord had the grave responsibility of running a small-scale government to serve the mutual needs of himself and his vassals.

The vassal also had important rights and obligations. He was entitled to the use of the fief and the respect of the lord. In return, he was expected to conduct himself honorably and loyally toward his lord. More specifically, a vassal owed his lord four basic obligations: First was *military service,* which required the vassal to serve at his own expense as an armed knight for a specified length of time each year, usually forty days; such service might involve guard duty at a lord's castle. Second, the vassal had to give *counsel,* usually defined by compulsory attendance at the lord's court. Third, the vassal was obligated to give *aids* in the form of money payments in certain specific situations (for ransoming the lord, the knighting of the lord's eldest son, and the marriage dowry of the lord's eldest daughter). Finally, the vassal had to extend *hospitality* to the lord and his entourage when they visited the fief that the vassal had received. In addition, the vassal was obliged to respect certain usages, called *feudal incidents,* reflecting the lord's rights in the fief. The vassal had to maintain the fief in good condition so as to sustain its value. His heir had to pay the lord an inheritance tax, called a *relief,* when he succeeded to the fief. The lord had the right of guardianship, called *wardship,* over a vassal's minor heir and of approval of the marriage of a vassal's daughter whose husband might someday become heir to the fief. Finally, the vassal was obliged to recognize that if he died without heirs, the fief reverted to the lord (the right of *escheat*).

The enforcement of the terms of the feudal contract was a major problem in a society lacking effective public authority. In fact, lords and vassals had to settle disputes surrounding rights and obligations themselves. The chief instrument was the lord's court, where the custom governing the feudal contract was applied as law. A lord could summon to his court any of his vassals accused of infidelity to be judged by the vassal's "peers"—other vassals—and, if found guilty, punished as custom dictated. To this same court every vassal could bring complaints against his lord or his fellow vassals; again, his peers decided whether he had redress. Despite this machinery, force was always the final recourse, with the result that feudal society was plagued by constant petty wars fought to force fulfillment of obligations and to gain redress for violation of rights. It would be wrong, however, to picture lords and vassals as seeking any opportunity to start a brawl. In a society that knew no other workable system for keeping order, both lords and vassals were often anxious and willing to observe the terms of the contract that served their mutual interests.

A prime result of the feudalization of western Europe's ruling class was to create circles of vassals linked together by their relationships with a common lord. In theory, the feudal order created a sociopolitical hierarchy in which each successive layer of vassals owed allegiance and service to a lord standing one step higher in the hierarchy (see Figure 17.3). At the top stood the king who was supreme lord and theoretical owner of all the land in his realm. At his pleasure he could accept as his direct vassals some of his subjects to whom he might grant large fiefs in return for service commensurate with the size of the fief. The great vassals of the king could then subdivide their holdings into smaller fiefs and grant them to other men willing to become vassals. This process, called *subinfeudation,* could continue until fiefs granted were only large enough to support a single vassal as a warrior.

In practice, the system did not work so neatly. If any lord in the hierarchy granted away too much of his land, he deprived himself of the means to compel his vassals to render him the services they owed and thus was powerless to command their obedience. As we have seen, this depletion of landed resources did happen with the late Carolingian kings; and it also happened to many others

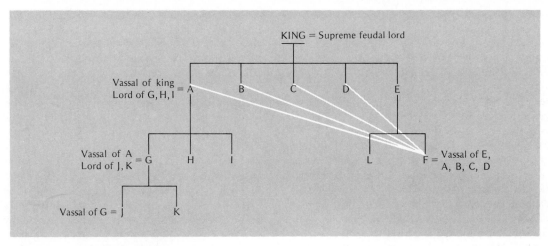

FIGURE 17.3 **The Feudal Hierarchy.**

amidst the tumult accompanying the establishment of lordships. More threatening to any neat hierarchy was the fact that subinfeudation led to the intersection of lord-vassal circles, creating conflicting loyalties and disparities in the size of landholdings. From the diagram of the theoretical feudal hierarchy, it will be apparent that an enterprising vassal (such as F) could acquire several lords; what is not obvious is where his allegiance lay if he was called upon to serve two lords at once. Moreover, such a vassal might accumulate enough fiefs from a variety of lords to possess more land than any one of them and thus be in a position to defy any of them. Attempts were made eventually to avoid such conflicting loyalties and fragmentation of authority by a system called *liege homage,* whereby a lord required not only his own direct vassals but also their vassals and subvassals to pledge prime allegiance to him. But on the whole, the feudal order led to an almost indescribable maze of contradictory allegiances and accumulations of power that made large-scale communities of lords and vassals nearly impossible. This system served best in the world of limited lordships and small principalities.

Beyond its role in shaping compact circles of lords and vassals within which order could be maintained, the feudal system served another end

vital to political and social stability: It led to the crystallization of a noble class consciously sharing a special ethos and a distinctive style of life. Although the western European nobility had roots reaching back to the Roman and Germanic worlds, the conditions that surrounded lordship and noble dependence provided a sharp focus for noble status. That group consisted of specialists in warfare and governance who felt a responsibility for protecting and ordering society.

The values of the feudal nobility were reflected with special force in two epic poems written to celebrate noble life, the *Song of Roland* and *The Cid* (see page 312). The virtues befitting noble status stemmed chiefly from what was vital to sustaining the bonds of lordship and vassalage: loyalty, bravery, faithfulness, generosity. Above all else stood prowess—the ability to excel in warfare. The life of a noble centered on a career of fighting for his lord, his lands, his family, his dependent peasants—and his God. In early youth, he began to learn his craft as an apprentice in the service of someone who already knew the art, often his father's lord. The culmination of his education was his knighting, an elaborate ceremony surrounded by religious symbolism that climaxed with his investiture with the tools of war; these were used often during his adult life. Of course, he had to sustain himself as a warrior, so the management of the lands received as a fief constituted a part of his vocation. And he had a political function stemming from his position as the vassal of another and probably as lord over still others.

The life of the nobility was generally crude and rough in the tenth century, in part because of the primitive level of economic life. The typical noble residence was a wooden fortress designed for defense rather than comfort. The living quarters were crowded, sparsely furnished, cold, without sanitary facilities, and lacking in privacy. The routine of life featured pursuits typical of male warriors: heavy eating, drinking, gambling, hunting, dancing, wenching, and warfare. Nobles were usually illiterate, "reading" by listening to tales of war sung by bards and to simple preaching of the priests. Marriage was arranged with an eye toward gaining new lands, more vassals, and stronger lords; seldom was it marred by considerations of sentiment. But the family was another matter, for a household rich in strong sons and nubile daughters was a great asset in a world of war, land acquisition, and personal relationships. The crucial importance of keeping landholdings intact and of maintaining ties with a powerful lord began to change the basic structure of the noble family. The earlier system of extended kinship ties and shared inheritance gave way to the patrilineal family in which lineage was traced from father to eldest son and inheritance was restricted to the eldest son. Nobles were religious in a simple way: They trusted God to take care of them if they were brave, faithful, and generous. Their way of expressing their faith was active, impelling them to do something visible to show their piety—build a church, give land to a monastery to assure prayers for their souls, go on a pilgrimage, or fight for God.

The feudal world was a man's world. Women were accorded inferior legal standing. They could not be lords or vassals; their social status reflected that of their fathers and husbands. Their marriage, the crucial event in determining on whom they would be dependent most of their lives, was controlled by males seeking to enhance family status in the feudal world. Unless they betook themselves to a convent, unmarried women were a liability to their families. Noble daughters married young, often to men much older. This situation, coupled with the dangers of warfare, often resulted in widowhood and the burdens of protecting the interests of minor children. Despite their general subservience, women played important roles in sustaining noble society. In a patrilineal family structure, it was the legal wife who bestowed legitimacy on the male heir who would sustain the family and its property. Women took active part in directing household servants who produced most of what was needed to sustain the noble household. On occasion, women managed fiefs when their husbands were absent. Their dowries—over which women maintained control—were often crucially important in expanding their husbands' possessions. Women were frequently called upon to witness legal transactions involving land transfers, suggesting their involvement in sustaining the family fortune and their knowledge of the substance of that fortune.

3. THE COMMUNITY OF THE SERVILE: MANORIALISM

The structures that created a nobility engaged in warfare and governance rested on an agricultural base. The feudal system provided lords and vassals with control over parcels of land of varying sizes that each noble had to exploit in order to sustain himself and his family and to fulfill the complex obligations implicit in noble status. To exploit those lands, the nobility imposed another order of dependency on the peasantry of western Europe. This system, sometimes called the *seigneurial* system, was shaped over a long period out of elements rooted in Germanic and Roman economic and social institutions. By the tenth century the essential features of the system were in place: Each noble had imposed on the peasant inhabitants of the land he controlled an organizational structure that allowed him to command their labor and to take a portion of their produce. As *seigneur*—lord—he controlled a community of humans whose function was essentially economic. Although the way agricultural production was organized varied across western Europe, the *manorial system* prevailed in the most productive areas extending from southern England across northern

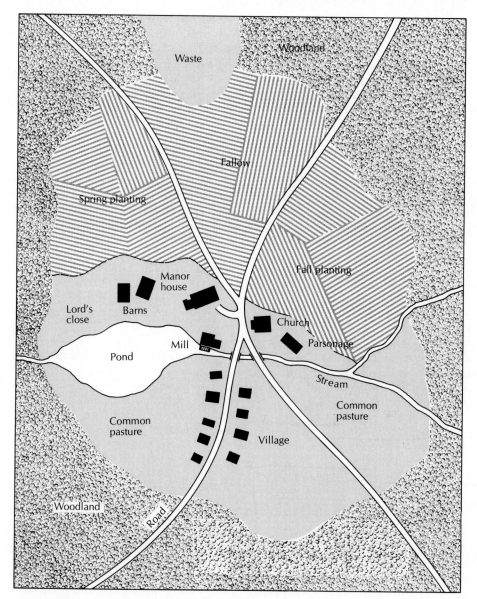

Map 17.1 **A HYPOTHETICAL MEDIEVAL MANOR** This drawing shows how a medieval manor might have been laid out. It will help identify the major components of a medieval manor as described in the text: the seigneur's manor house, the church, the village settlement, the three-field and strip system, the commons, the wood and waste land. All of these components were required to make the manor self-sufficient.

France and western Germany into northern Italy.

The manor was an economic unit organized to produce everything needed by its seigneur and his dependent peasants (see Map. 17.1). It was also a political and social unit providing for the governance of the peasants living there and defining their relationships with their seigneur and with one another. The typical manor's size was determined by the requirements of self-sufficiency. A workable manor required arable land for raising cereal crops, meadowland for animal support, woodland for fuel and building material, and a natural water supply. The seigneur usually reserved one-third to one-half of the arable land as his *demesne* from which he took all of the produce for his own support. The rest was divided into tenancies, called *mansi* or *hides,* each large enough to support a peasant household. Meadows, pastures, and woods were used in common. Under the widely used *open-field system,* the tillable land was divided into large, unfenced plots farmed by the cooperative effort of peasants. Each open field was subdivided into strips. The seigneur reserved a third to a half of these strips in each large field as his demesne; the mansus or tenancy of each peasant was made of strips in each open field.

To protect the fertility of the soil, part of the land was left idle each year. Until about 900 a *two-field system* of rotation was widely used, with half of the manor's tillable land seeded each year while the other half was left idle. Then the more efficient *three-field system* began to spread. The tillable land was divided into three open fields. Every year and in rotation, one field lay fallow, a second was planted in the fall with wheat or rye, and a third was planted in the spring with barley, oats, or legumes (such as beans or peas). Not only did the three-field system put more land under cultivation each year, but also it allowed a greater variety of crops, which improved human diet. Most peasants raised vegetables on small, well-fertilized plots surrounding their huts. In spite of the improved rotation system, yields were small and famines common. Low productivity discouraged the keeping of animals that could lighten work, such as horses and oxen, which were heavy consumers of grain and hay. However, pigs, poultry, and goats, which could live by scavenging in the woods and wastelands, were common.

Since there was little trade in the tenth century, most manufactured goods were made on the manor. Although specialized artisans such as blacksmiths and carpenters plied their trades on some manors, ordinary peasants generally made and repaired equipment, buildings, and furnishings. Women, including noble ladies, made clothing, preserved food, and concocted medicine. Only a few crucial items came to most manors from outside—metals, salt, wine.

The center of the manor was a village containing a manor house, peasant huts, a church and cemetery, granaries, a mill, a bakery, and a brewery. This village was more than a collection of buildings; it was a vital human community with a governing system and a social order. Its governor was the seigneur, who exercised the power to command, judge, and punish his dependent peasants with virtually no interference from authority beyond the manor. If he lived on the manor, the seigneur exercised his lordship in person. If he lived elsewhere, as did many nobles with numerous manors, he entrusted control of the manor to *stewards* and *bailiffs,* usually recruited from the peasantry. Although force provided a means of last recourse, seigneurial control was exercised chiefly through the manorial court. In this court the law, consisting of a body of custom defining every aspect of the relationships among those involved in manorial life, was applied to impose discipline on the peasantry and to allow individuals to gain recourse for damages done to them.

The peasant population of a typical manor included individuals whose legal status ranged from slaves to free individuals. But most were *serfs* or *villeins* who were legally bound to the soil but who held a tenancy from which they could not be dispossessed. Thus, a serf was legally unfree but possessed both a precious right in a piece of land that assured his livelihood and a place in a community that provided protection and a court of law through which rights could be protected. Serf status was passed by inheritance, as was the tenancy to which a serf was attached. Powerful forces were at work both among seigneurs and peasants to merge slaves and free individuals into serfdom.

More important to peasants than their precise legal status were the obligations they owed their seigneur. These obligations, defined by manorial custom, varied greatly over Europe, but every-where certain dues were imposed on peasants. Their chief obligation was labor service. On most manors serfs were required to spend three days a week tilling the demesne of the seigneur. In addition, they might be required to do extra days of work during the planting and the harvesting season (*boon days*) and in maintaining roads and buildings (*corvée*). Often these labor obligations extended to the serfs' wives, who were required to perform such duties as spinning, cleaning, and preparing food in the seigneur's household. Peasants were required to give to the seigneur some share of the produce of their tenancies, thus providing the seigneur with an important supplement to the produce of his own demesne. Peasants had to pay a *tithe* to the Church; often tithes found their way into the seigneur's hands. Fees, called *banalties*, were assessed for the use of the manorial mill, bakery, and brewery—facilities the seigneur alone could afford to build and over which he maintained a monopoly. The seigneur collected a death tax (*heriot*) from each peasant household when the tenancy passed from father to son and a tax (*formariage* or *merchet*) from any peasant whose daughter married outside the manor. There were, of course, fees and fines to be paid by peasants involved in litigation in the manorial court.

It is obvious that the manor provided the seigneur with many opportunities to enrich himself at the expense of the peasantry. Many exploited these opportunities to the fullest. There were limits, however. The seigneur was wholly dependent on the peasants for the one prime ingredient of the manorial economy—labor. Without peasant labor the seigneur's land would go uncultivated and his wealth and his status in the noble world would diminish. There was no other source of labor. The seigneur thus had to act with some restraint toward his laborers if he hoped to get efficient and constant work from them. Peasants were in a position to damage the interests of an overoppressive seigneur by willful neglect of crops, buildings, and animals or by calculated mischief. Killing or maiming or even irritating peasants in the interests of exacting more from them might be more costly than just treatment according to custom. The weight of custom, which tended to fix obligations over long periods, acted as a powerful brake on rapacious seigneurs.

Peasant life in the ninth and tenth centuries was brutally harsh. At best, the manorial system provided a livelihood at subsistence level. Crop failure, sickness, or warfare could erase the thin margin separating subsistence from famine and death. Too many children could overtax the meager supply of food that could be extracted from a tenancy of fixed size. The seigneur or his agents were always at hand seeking any spare wealth. The simple, one-room, scantily furnished huts offered little comfort. Neither did the monotonous diet of bread, soup, beer, cheese, and eggs, with an occasional bit of meat or fish and fruit. Yet there were compensations. The Church was ever-present, offering its solace in the face of life's hardships, including its charity at especially desperate moments, and its hopes of a better life beyond this world. Its ministrations at life's crucial moments—birth, marriage, death—helped to give dignity and significance to human existence, even in the midst of squalor and poverty. Membership in the village community provided the psychological security that stems from living among people long and intimately known. That same community provided an array of simple pleasures, often occasioned by the Church's numerous holy days—beer drinking, gaming, singing, dancing—all capable of easing the burden of a life of bare subsistence.

4. THE CHURCH IN THE WORLD OF LORDSHIP AND DEPENDENCY

The complex processes that surrounded the regrouping of society under a system of lordship and dependency had a profound effect on the Church. The reforming forces unleashed by the Carolingian ministerial kings flagged, and new kinds of problems emerged to make the late ninth and tenth centuries one of the most trying periods in the Church's history.

The Church's major difficulties emerged from its entanglement in the world of lordship and noble dependency, that is, in the feudal order. By the ninth and tenth centuries, the Church held an immense amount of landed property. Its holdings were attached to bishoprics, monasteries, and individual churches and administered by bishops, abbots, and priests. Part of its land came from gifts from the faithful, but much had been acquired in the form of fiefs granted by kings and other powerful laymen, who expected church officials so favored to render services as did any other vassals. In order to protect their holdings in a world where self-help was the key to survival, ecclesiastical officials acted like other lords. They granted church lands as fiefs in return for military and political services and thus became lords in their own rights. Like their lay counterparts, ecclesiastical lords forced the peasants on their lands into a servile condition and gave full attention to asserting their seigneurial authority. They too had to concern themselves with protecting their vassals, holding courts, and collecting dues. Such necessary preoccupations directed their efforts away from their pastoral duties. Lay leaders refused to invest any bishop or abbot with a fief unless he had the qualities of a good vassal, including military prowess and loyalty to the lord rather than to the Church as an institution. In effect, this system meant that secular leaders gained control over elections to ecclesiastical offices, often filling them with loyal kinsmen or proven vassals with little interest in spiritual matters. Secular lords treated church land received as fiefs as if it were private property, diverting the income to uses that had little to do with spiritual needs. This thoroughly secularized officialdom in control of church offices and property neglected discipline, education, charity, and moral guidance. The lower clergy was ignorant and undisciplined. The level of religious life in lay society deteriorated badly; superstition, moral laxity, and corruption of ritual practices abounded. To some contemporary pious souls, especially those who remembered the Carolingian reform effort, religious life had become a scandal worse than had ever been seen. Mammon seemingly had triumphed over God!

With due allowance for the abysmal condition into which the feudalized Church had sunk, it remains necessary to note another dimension of the Church's position in the world of lordship and dependence. Its involvement in that world drew it into contact with the basic institutions and the dynamic elements of society more intimately and

directly than ever before. Its feudalized leadership shared the mentality and felt the needs of western Europe's warrior aristocracy and peasantry. Such involvement prepared that leadership to shape a religious order responsive to reality. Even in the midst of a genuine religious crisis evidence of that response began to surface. The Church articulated a social theory positing that right order involved three orders, each with a special social responsibility: those who prayed (*oratores*), those who fought (*bellatores*), and those who labored (*laboratores*). It gave the feudal contract a religious dimension by making the oath of fealty a key element in establishing the relationship binding two men together. Its moral concepts began to shape a code of behavior known as *chivalry* befitting the warrior life (see page 251). Its leaders instituted two practices aimed at curbing violence in feudal society. One, called the Peace of God, sought to restrain acts of war against certain categories of people (the clergy, women, children); the other, called the Truce of God, tried to prohibit warfare during certain periods holy to all Christians (Sundays, major holy days, Lent). A monastic reform beginning in the tenth century, known as Cluniac monasticism (see page 296), encouraged certain practices of piety that appealed strongly to the feudal nobility. The grouping of the peasantry into organized villages provided a setting for the development of a strong parish structure through which the Christian population could be reached. Thus, despite the spiritual disarray caused by the worldliness of the feudalized Church, its immersion in the world of lordship and dependency provided new arenas where it could assert its influence over the development of European society.

The tenth-century world of lordship and dependency, of feudalism and manorialism, does not usually receive a sympathetic evaluation, especially among those who cannot conceive of a civilized order without a strong state. The violence, the oppression, the greed that surrounded the establishment of these political, social, and economic institutions seem the very antithesis of a vital society. However, despite its limitations, the system of lordship and dependency played a fundamental role in preparing a backward society for a new outburst of creativity. Feudalism and manorialism shaped small communities of people capable of concerted, disciplined action. These new groupings created a situation requiring concerted action among peoples of different social status and talents. These collectivities were especially suited to exploit Europe's chief resource, its under- utilized lands and forests. It is not coincidence that western European society began a spectacular pe- riod of growth *after* the system of lordship and dependency had become firmly established.

SUGGESTED READING

Lordship and Dependence

F. L. Ganshof, *Feudalism,* trans. Philip Grierson, 3rd ed. (1964). Stresses the legal aspects of feudalism.

Marc Bloch, *Feudal Society,* trans. L. A. Manyon (1961). A classic, approaching feudalism from a sociological perspective.

Perry Anderson, *Passages from Antiquity to Feudalism* (1978). A Marxist perspective on feudalism and its origins.

Guy Fourquin, *Lordship and Feudalism in the Middle Ages,* trans. Iris and A. L. Lytton Sells (1976). Provides insights into how power was exercised in the feudal world.

Frederic L. Cheyette, ed., *Lordship and Community in Me- dieval Europe: Selected Readings* (1968). Views by ex- perts on how the medieval system of lordship worked.

Timothy Reuter, ed. and trans., *The Medieval Nobility. Studies on the Ruling Classes of France and Germany from the Sixth to the Twelfth Century* (1978). These essays provide conflicting views on the origins and role of the medieval nobility.

Nellie Neilson, *Medieval Agrarian Economy* (1936). A clas- sic description of manorialism.

Georges Duby, *Rural Economy and Country Life in the Me- dieval West,* trans. Cynthia Postan (1968). The best work on manorial economy; provides translations of medieval sources.

Philippe Contamine, *War in the Middle Ages,* trans. Mi- chael James (1984). A good treatment of an important aspect of feudal society.

Sources

David Herlihy, ed., *The History of Feudalism* (1970). A collection of sources illustrating the nature of feudal institutions and practices.

The Song of Roland, trans. Frederick Goldin (1978).

The Poem of the Cid, trans. Lesley Bird Simpson (1957).

Aside from their literary values, these two medieval epic poems reveal a great deal about the mentality of feudal society.

RETROSPECT

In a letter written in 593 or 594, Pope Gregory I called his contemporaries' attention to the strife, suffering, destruction, and injustice seen everywhere. "See what has befallen Rome, once mistress of the world," he mourned. "What is there now, I ask, of delight in this world?"

In a way, Gregory supplied the key to the history of the early Middle Ages. Much of what had characterized Greco-Roman civilization had been lost, and society was poorer. One can easily write—as many have—the history of the early Middle Ages in terms of the destruction of classical civilization; from this perspective the era was indeed a dark age.

However, between A.D. 500 and 1000 much happened to replace what had been lost. Three new civilizations—Byzantine, Moslem, and western European—had been shaped within the confines of the classical world. Each retained precious elements of the old order. Each developed new institutions and ideas to suit its needs and situation. An inventory of what people had fashioned in these difficult centuries gives ample evidence that these "dark" years deserve a decisive place in the continuum of history. By 1000 there were still "things of delight" in the world.

The emergence of three new civilizations was not the only transformation that occurred in the early Middle Ages. In addition to the creative forces at work within each, a new dynamism had developed in the form of interactions among these civilizations. The Greco-Roman world had tended to absorb existing cultures into a unified pattern that stood counterposed to the barbarian world. By 1000 lines of interaction and points of tension existed among civilized societies rather than between the civilized and uncivilized orbits. This distinction was a forceful determinant in the course of future historical development.

The period just reviewed belonged to the East; Byzantium and Islam far surpassed western Europe in every respect. This little appreciated fact demands attention, for the accomplishments of the Byzantine and Moslem worlds in these centuries gave their peoples a proud sense of contribution to the creation of civilized life that other societies later forgot. None benefited more from the achievements of these leaders than the struggling western Europeans, whose future glory would have been different had it not been for what they absorbed from the East during the early centuries of the Middle Ages.

PART FIVE

THE HIGH MIDDLE AGES, 1000–1300: THE REVIVAL OF EUROPE

An eleventh-century chronicler named Ralph Glaber tells us that many Europeans were convinced that, in accordance with ancient prophecy, the world would come to an end at the end of the first millennium of Christian history, that is, in the year 1000. But, wrote Ralph, when that fateful year passed without the appearance of the Antichrist, "it was as if the very world had shaken itself and cast off its old age." Everywhere, he said, people rivaled each other to build better churches and were filled with new ardor for the faith. This bit of medieval legend, whatever its validity in summing up the actual state of mind of western Europeans in the late tenth century, provides a fitting introduction to this section. In actual fact, western European society did enjoy a genuine revival beginning about 1000 and continuing with unabated vigor until about 1300. This era is often referred to as the High Middle Ages. It is the period in which medieval western European society reached its full maturity.

As our account of these effervescent, creative centuries unfolds, it should become increasingly clear that the revival of western European civilization was rooted in certain basic institutions that had been forged during the preceding era: feudalism, manorialism, the Church, the precious treasure of learning stored up by Carolingian scholars. Although primitive in many ways, these institutions and ideas provided basic patterns of organization, social control, thought, and belief that permitted men and women to apply their energies and intelligences constructively. They were suddenly capable of producing new wealth. They found themselves able to construct larger political entities and to form new class relationships. Their spiritual, intellectual, and aesthetic capabilities were expanded so that a wide range of cultural achievements was possible. They found themselves able to turn outward from their beleaguered world to make a major impression on wide areas of the world heretofore little known to them. In short, the High Middle Ages was an era of creative activity that made western European civilization a factor of major significance in the world. The long centuries of painful experimentation that marked the early Middle Ages had clearly ended.

CHAPTER 18
Economic and Social Revival

FIGURE 18.1 **Medieval Farming** This miniature used to illustrate an English psalter shows peasants plowing their fields. It indicates that medieval agriculture was a cooperative effort: Peasants combined their labor, their draft animals, and their equipment to till the manor fields. The heavy moldboard plow was a major technological advance of the Middle Ages: It was especially efficient in cutting through and turning over heavy soils. Producing yields sufficient to feed both people and livestock was a major problem. (The British Museum)

Throughout the early Middle Ages a major deterrent to growth was the severely limited and constantly uncertain level of material resources available to western European society. Between 1000 and 1300 that situation was dramatically changed by a major economic expansion accompanied by significant adjustments in the social order. These changes had their source at the base of society; their agents were modest seigneurs, toiling peasants, peddler merchants, and simple artisans. The efforts of these simple people made possible the more spectacular accomplishments of the High Middle Ages in politics, religion, and culture.

1. POPULATION GROWTH

The forces that generated economic growth after 1000 were complex. However, one contributing factor is evident: The population expanded substantially between about 900 and 1350. This demographic change, reversing a trend that had prevailed since late Roman times, resulted in a doubling of the population of western Europe during that period; one generally accepted estimate suggests that the population grew from about 35 million in 900 to about 70 million in 1350. Modern demographers do not yet fully understand the causes of this growth. There is some evidence that during this period Eurasia was relatively free from killer diseases, especially bubonic plague. Perhaps the curbing of the more destructive aspects of warfare and the availability of more and better food contributed. Some have even suggested that the prospects of a better society encouraged people to have more children. Whatever the causes, the simple fact was that for three centuries a constantly expanding population put pressure on the agricultural system for greater productivity and provided a larger work force that could be turned to new enterprises.

There remain a whole series of fascinating and important problems associated with the effects of population growth on the structure of medieval society. For example, it is clear that the population growth was not uniform across western Europe, but the geographic pattern and the regional impact of growth have not been clearly established.

Neither is it clear how growth affected different age groups and social classes. What happened to life expectancy, marriage patterns, size of households, and child rearing are still poorly understood. Virtually all one can say is that population increase affected all these matters so vital to the lives of people. As historians become better able to assess the full impact of increasing population, it will be more obvious that population growth was a major dynamic force changing western European society in the High Middle Ages.

2. AGRICULTURAL EXPANSION

The most important aspect of economic growth between 1000 and 1300 was expansion of agricultural productivity. The manorial system, with its reservoir of managerial ability, disciplined labor force, and technical skills, provided the base for growth. At least five major factors were involved in expanding on that base.

First, western Europe's climate improved during this period, especially in northern Europe. Milder winters, more favorable growing seasons, better distribution of rainfall, and fewer violent storms and excessive variations in temperature all seem to have combined to create an improved setting for agricultural pursuits.

Second, as a result of an immense effort devoted to land clearance and peasant resettlement, more land was put under cultivation. Much of this land clearance involved pushing out the boundaries of existing cultivated areas, which in the early Middle Ages stood as isolated, often overpopulated islands of cultivation in vast stretches of forest. In some areas this internal expansion reclaimed lands heretofore useless: Swamps were drained in northern Italy; land was recovered from the North Sea in what is modern Netherlands. But many European cultivators, organized by enterprising landlords, moved great distances to settle on the frontiers of western Europe. The chief areas of colonization were on the German frontier east of the Elbe River, in Spanish lands being wrested from Moslem control, and in southern Italy. It appears that the cultivated acreage in western Europe nearly doubled between 1000 and 1300.

Third, technological advances greatly increased the efficiency of the labor force, especially by supplying new sources of power. The adoption of the horseshoe and the development of new harnesses, especially the shoulder collar, permitted the more efficient horse to replace the ox as a draft animal. Watermills and windmills were greatly improved, and complicated power trains were developed, which allowed the motion from these mills to be applied to such tasks as grinding grain. Traditional agricultural tools—plows, spades, hoes, harrows—were improved by more effective practices of metallurgy. Especially important was the increasing use of the wheeled, mold-board plow, which could cut through and turn over the heavy soils of northern Europe (see Figure 18.1). One suspects that these advances were due to the ingenuity and practical experience of simple peasants searching for ways to make their labor easier and more productive. Whatever the cause, the result was greater productivity and the freeing of human labor for more productive uses.

Fourth, agricultural production was increased in quantity and variety by improved methods of tillage and animal husbandry. Irrigation systems were developed in some parts of western Europe. Agricultural specialization, as in the vineyards of Burgundy and the great sheep-raising granges in England, was made possible by increasing opportunities for exchange, which we shall describe later. Greater attention was given to fertilization. The three-field system of tillage spread, which protected the fertility of the soil, promoted efficient use of labor and equipment, and permitted a greater variety of crops to be grown. Particularly significant was the increased availability of high-protein foods, such as beans, to supplement the mostly carbohydrate diet of earlier times. Better seeds were developed to take advantage of local soil and weather conditions. And improvements in animal breeds produced better animals and more animal products, such as meat and wool.

Finally, production was expanded by what we might call agricultural entrepreneurship. Planning and the adaptation of ancient customs freed labor to clear new lands, to apply new tools and techniques, and to dispose profitably of any excess production. Bold foresight resettled groups of peasants on distant lands. Innovative thinking developed new seeds, bred improved livestock

strains, and launched specialized production. Entrepreneurship, exercised in small and undramatic ways, perhaps provides the key to one of the great advances in the history of agriculture.

Modern historians have not been able to quantify very accurately the overall magnitude of the growth of agricultural production between 1000 and 1300. However, in crude terms the consequences are clear. The increased amount of land under cultivation and higher yields permitted everyone to live better and produced a surplus of food, which left more people free to devote their energies to activities other than subsistence agriculture. That critical difference made possible significant changes in all aspects of the society of the High Middle Ages.

3. REVIVAL OF TRADE AND MANUFACTURING

The expansion of agricultural production after 1000 stimulated the revival of trade and manufacturing. Trade had never entirely vanished from the western European scene, but it had declined steadily from late Roman times. By 1000 trade was insignificant in the total economic life of western Europe. Neither had manufacturing totally disappeared, but during the early Middle Ages manufacturing was restricted to the manorial setting where only a limited range of products needed for local self-sufficiency was produced. During the late tenth and early eleventh centuries, a revival began in both commerce and manufacturing; it continued until the mid–fourteenth century. During this era commerce became the catalytic force in European economy, and new forms of manufacturing emerged to provide an expanded range of products for exchange. Among the factors contributing to the commercial and industrial revival were population growth, agricultural expansion, greater political order, outside stimuli, and western European political, military, and religious expansion. But to these must be added the labors and enterprise of men and women whose activities are for the most part unknown to us.

In considerable part, the Europeans' commercial expansion was a story of their ability to break into the flourishing Byzantine and Moslem trading

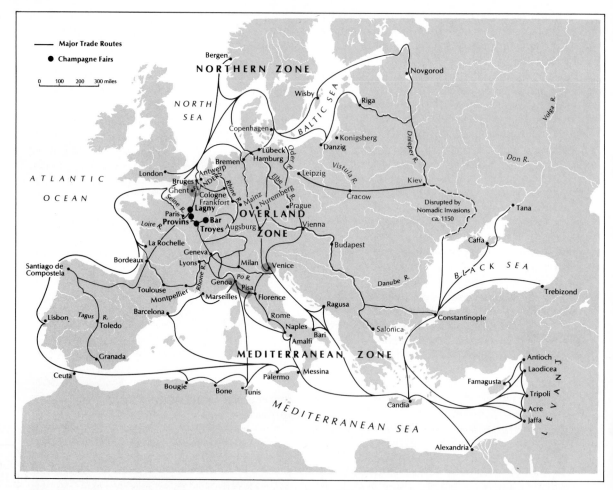

Map 18.1 **TRADE ROUTES, TWELFTH AND THIRTEENTH CENTURIES** This map shows the major trade routes developed during the twelfth and thirteenth centuries to link western Europeans with the East and to join major trading centers within western Europe. The crucial centers for international trade linking East and West were located in northern Italy, especially Venice, Genoa, and Pisa, and in Flanders, especially Bruges and Antwerp. The internal routes, focusing especially in the towns of Champagne, where great international trading fairs were held annually, spread the products of the East from the Italian and Flemish centers over much of western Europe.

complexes and to gain control of a share of them (see Map 18.1). Western Europe had always remained in touch with the Eastern trade centers, primarily through Byzantine outposts in Venice and southern Italy. In the tenth century trade activity began to quicken. The Venetians took the leading role, steadily enlarging their contacts by sea with Constantinople and bringing an ever-increasing volume of goods to the West. In the eleventh century Pisa's and Genoa's navies loosened Moslem control over the western Mediterranean, and their merchants established trade relations with the Moslems in Spain and North Africa.

The successes of the early crusading movement at the end of the eleventh century (see Chapter 21) allowed the Italian cities to establish and expand important footholds in eastern Mediterranean Moslem cities in the twelfth century. The conquest of Constantinople in 1204 during the Fourth Crusade gave the Venetians virtual control over Byzantine trade. By the thirteenth century the efforts of Italian merchants were reinforced by other traders from coastal cities in France and Spain; collectively they had become the dominant commercial force in Mediterranean trade. The lifeblood of this international trade was luxury items, especially spices and fine cloth.

Meanwhile, another window to the East was opened on the northern fringes of the continent by Viking pirates. Their raiding ventures opened a path through the Baltic Sea and along the rivers of Russia to the Black Sea and Constantinople. Traders from many areas of northern Europe eventually followed the Vikings along this route to carry a variety of goods to and from the lands bordering the North and Baltic seas and Constantinople. The focal point of this northern trading complex came to be Flanders.

No less important than international trade was the growth of trade within Europe. In part, that growth was a result of the efforts of aggressive Italian and Flemish merchants to provide Europe's aristocrats with luxury goods. Their activities created an ever-widening network of routes, especially following the river system of Europe, covering most of Europe. During the twelfth century, the chief meeting places of international traders were the fairs of Champagne in France. Here merchants from all Europe came to display their wares to other merchants, who in turn carried their purchases to local markets and prize customers (see Figure 18.2). By the thirteenth century the fairs were increasingly giving way to permanent markets established in cities.

Complementing the traffic in luxury items was an ever-growing exchange of goods between formerly self-sufficient manors and villages and the growing towns. Local trade in such items as salt, wine, and metals had always existed. From the eleventh century onward, it broadened to provide the growing towns with foodstuffs and raw materials and to carry manufactured products of the towns back to the rural settlements. In volume and number of people involved, the local town-country exchange was undoubtedly the larger component of medieval trade.

The expansion of commercial activity in western Europe promoted the growth of manufacturing. By the twelfth century the towns began to offer opportunities for skilled artisans to make a single product for sale to their fellow townspeople and rural buyers or to merchants who distributed them wherever there was a demand. Artisan manufacturing long remained a vital element of the town economy and put a vast quantity of commonplace goods into trade. Some high-quality items found an international market. By the thirteenth century some areas of Europe, particularly Flanders and northern Italy, had developed more complex manufacturing organizations where merchant entrepreneurs would "put out" raw materials into the households of hired laborers, often rural dwellers. This "putting out" system, or "cottage" industry, was especially applied to wool processing, which became international in scope: Raw wool produced in England was purchased in quantity by a Flemish entrepreneur. He organized the transportation of the wool to Flanders, where it was processed through a series of steps including washing, carding, spinning, weaving, fulling, and dyeing. Each separate operation was performed by specialized laborers, many women, who worked for hire in their own homes. The finished product was distributed by merchants contracted by the entrepreneur. A comparable system for woolen production developed in such northern Italian cities as Florence.

There is no way to tell what the revival of trade and manufacturing meant to the western European economy in quantitative terms. It is probably safe to venture that by the thirteenth century the productivity of western Europe surpassed that of the Greco-Roman world in trade and industry, and probably the contemporary Byzantine and Moslem economies as well. Agriculture was still the most important economic element, but the wealth from exchange and craftsmanship was important also. Moreover, trade and industry increasingly supplied the dynamism that encouraged continued economic growth and diversification.

FIGURE 18.2 A Medieval Fair In this scene the bishop of Paris is giving his blessing to various merchants who are waiting for the opening of the fair held annually just outside Paris near the monastery of St. Denis. Such fairs provided a major setting for the exchange of goods from far and near. The presence of a figure so important as the bishop of Paris suggests that these fairs were viewed as a vital part of life. (Bibliothèque Nationale, Paris)

4. ECONOMIC CONSEQUENCES OF INCREASED PRODUCTION

The new level of prosperity generated by the increased agricultural, commercial, and industrial productivity in western Europe manifested itself in a hundred ways: better homes, bigger churches, more elaborate dress, greater quantities and varieties of food, more art and literature, more leisure. But aside from the general increase in wealth, greater productivity had more specific results.

First, economic growth revitalized city life. Towns had never disappeared from western Europe. But between the fall of Greco-Roman civili-

zation and about 1000, they became primarily ecclesiastical, administrative, or defense centers, sparsely populated and economically dependent on agriculture. Between 1000 and 1300 ancient towns grew dramatically, and many new towns appeared. By 1300 there were cities of considerable population: Some Italian towns, such as Venice, Milan, Florence, and Genoa, had populations around 100,000; Paris may have had 80,000 people and London had 50,000. The vast majority of medieval cities probably had populations of 10,000 or less, but these modest figures did not detract from their vitality. The growing city population was constantly being fed by migration from rural areas. More significant than numbers was the fact that most urban residents earned their livelihood from trade and manufacturing, thus making the "new" urban centers quite different from the economically nonproductive towns of the early Middle Ages.

In terms of physical growth, many important towns of the era were simply enlargements of older episcopal, monastic, administrative, or military centers. Merchants and then artisans were attracted to these centers for many reasons: security, favor shown them by ruling authorities, access to rivers and roads, availability of buyers. Often they settled haphazardly outside the walls of the old center, their shops, stalls, and households creating a *suburb* (Latin, "under the city"). As commercial activity increased, the walls were extended to enclose the suburbs. Often the suburban marketplace became the center of urban life. During the High Middle Ages new towns were often established at locations favorable to commerce, and their growth resembled that of the old centers. Even some agricultural villages developed into centers of trade and manufacturing.

A second consequence of economic expansion was the growth of a money economy. Money had always circulated in western Europe, but minimally until the eleventh century. Thereafter, its use rapidly expanded to meet the needs of trade. The money economy soon spread to agriculture. The impact of the money economy was revolutionary. A whole new form of wealth emerged to challenge the monopoly held by land. Old economic relationships based on services and payment of obligations in kind were replaced by payments in money. Money could be accumulated in a way that labor services and produce could not. The liquidity of such accumulations encouraged the manipulation of money to create new economic opportunities. The possession of money allowed people to specialize their economic activities and still have the means to obtain the full range of material goods they needed. Money allowed more frequent exchanges. The exploitation of money became a new kind of economic activity.

A third major effect of economic growth was the transformation of agricultural production. The market for surplus food provided by the towns gave manorial seigneurs and peasants money incomes with which they could embellish their lives

with products from the town markets. This new potential for profit changed the emphasis on the manors from self-sufficiency to surplus production. And under this pressure the traditional system of servile dependency began to dissolve.

The dissolution proceeded in two broad directions. In many areas of western Europe, especially in the twelfth century, seigneurs began to break their demesnes into tenancies and rent them to peasants for cash. And they commuted the labor obligations of their serfs and the dues owed them in kind to money payments. Serfs could afford to buy off their obligations because the town market offered them a chance to sell produce and save a little money. But many seigneurs moved in the opposite direction, expanding their demesne and managing its cultivation themselves. A most profitable course was to concentrate on a specialized crop for sale. Seigneurs who did this often displaced peasants from their ancient tenancies and forced them to work for wages. In either case, the old manorial system dissolved over much of western Europe. In its place a variety of forms of agricultural exploitation emerged; all were dominated by the concern for profit, an end that could only be achieved by linking the countryside to the towns, their markets, and their money.

A fourth economic change involved the emergence of a new attitude toward economic activity based on profits. No longer were producers content with self-sufficiency; they worked and planned to gain more worldly goods. They began to devise strategies and techniques that would increase wealth: lending money for profit, speculating in trading ventures, manipulating land for gain, saving money. A protocapitalist economic mentality was taking shape that prized economic growth rather than stability.

Finally, western Europeans had achieved such economic growth by 1300 that they had seized economic leadership in the vast area surrounding the Mediterranean—a leadership that would eventually be extended to the whole world. No longer did Byzantium and Islam stand as advanced economic centers to a backward western Europe. As we shall see later, political factors helped the advance of the Europeans, but it is beyond question that their enterprise played a vital role in establishing their economic leadership.

5. SOCIAL CHANGE: THE BOURGEOISIE

The economic growth of western Europe during the High Middle Ages brought major changes to the simple social order of the world of lordship and dependency. Perhaps the most unexpected and significant change was the emergence of a new social group, the *bourgeoisie*. The shaping of this group represented the efforts of traders and artisans living in towns to define a place for themselves in a world lacking legal or social institutions that fitted their situation. In order to pursue their economic interests effectively, they had to seek various "liberties" or, more accurately, special privileges. Their effort slowly created for them a special collective status, distinguishing them socially from the clergy, noble warriors, and agricultural laborers.

As soon as men and women began to devote full time to commerce and manufacturing, they felt a basic need for personal freedom. Their livelihood depended on freedom to move about in a world that fixed people to fiefs and manors, to dispose of their property at will in a world where property was bound up in an intricate network of obligations, to apply their talent and labor to whatever economic opportunity arose in a world where long-sanctioned customs dictated how people spent their time and efforts. And so the merchants and artisans of the towns struggled for personal freedom and were successful in achieving it. Their methods were various: purchase; force; grants won from kings, feudal lords, and bishops. By 1300 simply living in a town meant personal freedom.

Although personal freedom was vital, it was not sufficient. Townspeople needed liberties that would allow them to determine their collective political destiny, both in terms of defining relationships among themselves and of regulating interactions with those outside their own community. To gain these added liberties, they sometimes banded together into associations to seek special privileges from those who had political authority over them and over the space their city occupied. Their efforts often resulted in a written document, called a *charter*, which defined their status and rights as a corporate body. Initially, such charters

had to be fought for or purchased at a high cost, but acquiring a charter soon grew easier as kings, feudal lords, and bishops realized the profits to be gained by having a thriving town on their domains. Charters varied greatly in content. The typical charter recognized the citizen body of the town as a *corporation* that could act legally. Usually charters granted personal freedom to the townspeople and defined what they owed to the granting authority. Finally, charters granted some degree of self-governance. In a few cases, especially in Italy, towns gained complete freedom; such towns were called *communes*. More commonly, the townspeople had only limited privileges of self-government.

In shaping political institutions the townspeople experimented considerably. In most towns there was some degree of popular participation in political life, authority being vested in an elected council. In a typical commune the council usually possessed complete power to legislate, conduct courts, levy taxes, expend money for civic purposes, and negotiate with outside powers. Its only responsibility was to the citizens of the town. Many towns chose a chief administrative official— *mayor, burgomaster, podesta*—who functioned under the supervision of the council. Judicial affairs were entrusted to specially trained judges. Towns with only limited political freedom often had to respect the authority of a royal official or a bishop or a representative of a feudal lord who exercised many powers in judicial and financial matters. Whatever the form of government, the towns quickly created an elaborate new body of law regulating civic affairs.

A grave problem facing the bourgeoisie was the regulation of economic activity among merchants and artisans, a problem for which the rest of society had no solution. The usual answer was the establishment of *guilds* within each town. The merchants of a town usually organized themselves into a single merchant guild; the artisans formed several craft guilds, one for each trade. The merchant guild existed primarily to protect the interests of merchants from outsiders and to restrain the members from taking unfair advantage of one another and their customers. Each guild enacted rules governing prices to be charged, trading practices to be observed, and the conditions under which trade could be conducted. The craft guilds similarly imposed regulations on their members concerning prices, quality of goods, conditions of labor, and quantity of production. They also controlled the conditions for entering a trade. Boys began as *apprentices* to a master, working from two to seven years under his guidance and living in his household. The apprentice then became a *journeyman* who worked for hire until he had saved sufficient money and developed adequate skill to open his own shop and become a *master*. Before he acquired that rank, he had to submit his workmanship to a rigid examination by the guild. Along with their regulative functions, merchant and craft guilds had social functions. Each usually had its own guildhall, where banquets, pageants, and religious affairs were conducted for the entertainment and edification of the members. Each guild also aided its members when sickness or death struck a family.

Like their contemporaries on the farms, city dwellers perfected a variety of technical innovations that aided their economic activities. Market facilities were created to allow the display of goods and to facilitate money-changing operations. Sound coinage systems were established, especially by the Italian towns, whose coins were used in markets all over Europe. Insurance was developed to protect merchants against losses. Bookkeeping systems were devised to keep track of exchange operations and inventories. Merchants created ways to pool their resources for mutual benefits. Partnerships, called *commenda*, were formed to finance specific ventures; under these arrangements one or more merchants provided capital to another merchant to conduct a trading enterprise in return for a specified share of the profit. Eventually permanent companies were formed in which investors made deposits and received regular dividends paid by those who actually conducted the business enterprise.

Particularly significant as a means of providing capital to promote commercial and industrial growth was the development of a credit system and of an institution specializing in credit services: the bank. Bills of exchange became available, allowing merchants to deposit money one place in exchange for a receipt that could be used to pay for goods in another place. Money lending for interest became common. At least in the early stages of commercial growth, the Church strenuously opposed usury, the lending of money for interest, as a sin because it allowed people to profit from the misfortunes of others. Gradually, resistance was modified. The Church conceded that lenders who provided funds for investment in speculative activities were entitled to compensation for the risk, and that borrowers who did not pay their debts promptly should be liable for a penalty. By the thirteenth century large-scale lending operations conducted by banks were a vital part of the economy and a source of great profit.

The urban environment allowed greater social mobility than did the worlds of nobles and peasants. Trade and industry provided diverse opportunities for merchants and artisans to increase their wealth and better their social status. The range of economic activities existing in towns allowed for a more effective use of talent than was possible for nobles and peasants. Urban political and guild life created possibilities for individuals to play a part in shaping political decisions and even to achieve major leadership roles. Women also found a wider range of economic opportunities in the towns than were available to noble and peasant women. Aside from assisting their husbands in trading and manufacturing, women could engage in economic ventures independently. Widows of important merchants often continued their former husbands' trading enterprise. Many women were members of craft guilds, especially in the textile industry. Their rights were specifically protected in guild regulations, and many apparently practiced their craft alongside men, although often at lower wages. Although urban life permitted social mobility, across the period from 1000 to 1300 bourgeoisie society tended to become stratified on the basis of wealth. An oligarchy of rich entrepreneurs, usually merchants, increasingly claimed special status and gained control of city governments and guilds. At the other end of the social spectrum from these patricians was a growing number of poor, exploited laborers who sometimes vented their discontent by rioting.

Perhaps the most tragic victims of medieval urban society were western Europe's Jews. In the early Middle Ages Jews were viewed as a unique social group and were subjected to special legal restrictions. However, they were allowed and even encouraged to engage in commercial activity, ensuring their economic well-being. As more Christians began to engage in trade and manufacturing, measures were taken to exclude Jews from these activities, driving them to rely on money lending as a means of livelihood and causing them to be scorned as usurers as well as adherents of a detested religion. By the thirteenth century Christian bankers were taking over money-lending operations, devising whatever means they could to exclude their Jewish competitors from this lucrative business. Increasingly forced out of the mainstream of urban economic life, Jews were impoverished, forced into menial occupations, compelled to live in ghettos, and often savagely persecuted by urban and ecclesiastical authorities.

The urban environment generated its own cultural needs. Commercial and industrial activities required literacy, computing skills, and rational planning. The activities of the markets and the shops raised a new range of moral problems and special kinds of spiritual longing. The circumstances of city life called for special building needs. The interaction of people from many parts of Europe and the world beyond made city dwellers aware of cultural differences and raised questions about the validity of local customs. As a result of all of these forces, cities became centers of educational, intellectual, and artistic change.

For all its success in defining a unique place for itself in medieval society, the bourgeoisie was still by 1300 not very exalted as a social class. The nobility looked down on merchants and artisans as uncultured and boorish, an attitude that often caused the bourgeoisie to spend their riches aping the habits of the nobles. The Church officially disapproved of many bourgeois activities as violations of Christian morality. The peasants were suspicious of the sharp practices of the townspeople; the "city slicker" is no recent invention of the rural mind. Still, by 1300 the bourgeoisie was solidly established in law and was in fact a dynamic factor in the social order. It is worth noting that neither the Byzantine nor the Moslem world produced a comparable "middle class," although trade, manufacturing, and city life in these societies were older and no less vigorous.

6. SOCIAL CHANGE: THE NOBILITY

In this period of rapid economic change, the nobility remained the dominant social group, its power and influence solidly rooted in feudal bonds and seigneurial control. However, changing economic conditions created new circumstances that affected the status and the life style of the nobility.

Land remained the basis of aristocratic wealth and high social status. However, the manner in which wealth was derived from land changed as the new money economy emerged, and as a consequence, nobles changed their basic modes of exploiting their lands. As noted earlier, nobles became either entrepreneurs managing their own lands or landlords collecting rents. Both courses had risks. Especially tricky was the negotiating of rents that would give them sufficient income to maintain or even improve their social status. In an age of steady inflation many aristocrats made the mistake of agreeing to long-term leases that provided them with fixed returns whose real value declined over time. As a consequence, many noble families saw their wealth and social status reduced; some even lost noble status. Some nobles turned to commercial activities to bolster their wealth, either by extracting money payments from town governments in return for privileges or by investing in commercial ventures. Whether as a commercial farmer, a landlord, or an entrepreneur involved in both agriculture and commerce, a noble of the High Middle Ages had to concern himself much more with economic matters than did his ancestors if he hoped to sustain a key ingredient of noble status: wealth.

A variety of factors were at work during the High Middle Ages to bring about a more complex stratification of the nobility than had existed earlier. The expanding economy led to wide differences in wealth within the noble class, with wealth dependent on the amount of land individuals controlled and how rationally they used its productive potential. The development of strong central governments in many parts of Europe (see Chapters 19 and 20) permitted some nobles to increase their power and prestige by close association with royal governments. Strong government, however, worked to the disadvantage of other nobles, reducing their role in warfare and the exercise of private political jurisdictions. Increasing royal power and differences of wealth also made the personal lord-vassal relationship less important in defining the condition and role of an individual noble. By 1300 the nobility consisted of a variety of groupings whose interrelationships and interactions were defined by an ever more elaborate social code defining status. There was still mobility within the noble class, but on the whole the nobility was becoming an increasingly stratified and closed social order.

In general, nobles of the eleventh, twelfth, and thirteenth centuries enjoyed an increasingly comfortable material life. Their growing wealth coupled with the reduction of violence permitted them to build dwellings that gave more attention to comfort than to physical security. Stone castles, featuring more private chambers, fireplaces vented through chimneys, and improved sanitary facilities, appeared all over Europe. For a price a typical noble could enjoy a much more varied diet, including sugar and exotic spices from the East and fine wine from southern France. A greater variety of clothing was available, especially fine woolens and imported silks. The improved material standards of living subtly refined noble life, which led to a new code of behavior for those of noble status: The code was *chivalry,* especially celebrated in the vernacular literature of the troubadours and the writers of romances (see Chapter 23).

Chivalry as a code defining ideal noble behavior was rooted in the values of the feudal warrior; it stressed loyalty, bravery, generosity, honor, and military prowess. From the eleventh century on, these values acquired new shades of meaning that—at least in ideal terms—converted the crude, brutal warrior of earlier times into the knight skilled in the practice of courtly manners. Under the code of chivalry the ideal noble was still defined as a warrior who required an elaborate training in the arts of warfare before receiving public recognition as a knight. However, chivalry restrained his behavior. He was now expected to treat knights against whom he fought according to rules of honor. He was obligated to help the Church keep the Peace of God, which meant he could not wage war against certain categories of people (the clergy, women, children), and the Truce of God, which prohibited fighting during certain periods holy to all Christians (Sundays, major holy days, Lent). In fact, the good knight sought some ideal for which to fight, such as crusading to spread the true faith or punishing evildoers who preyed on the weak. Under the chivalric code the warrior instinct tended to be channeled into carefully arranged engagements, called *tournaments,* where the martial arts were practiced under strict rules and amidst a pageantry that featured mannered behavior more than bloodshed and booty taking.

A key ingredient of chivalry was the important role given to women in the social structure. Whereas the old warrior society valued women little except as bearers of children and sources of dowries, the code of chivalry made women objects of devotion, loyalty, and sentimental attachment. A true knight was expected to develop a set of manners that would make his presence pleasing to noble women. In aristocratic circles an elaborate code of courtly love encouraged unmarried knights to demonstrate their prowess by winning the love of a noble lady—usually already married. The pursuit of the love of a lady called for patterns of behavior extending far beyond the ability to wield the tools of war, and it placed a higher value on virtues associated with women: graciousness, the capacity to give love, gentleness.

In order to respond to the new attention extended to them, noble women were expected to develop modes of behavior suited to a more refined world where males and females mixed in a courtly society. Whether the code of chivalry with its emphasis on romantic love between noble men and women improved the status of women remains a disputed question. Certainly women were treated with greater respect and gentleness than in earlier eras, and their participation in courtly social life was greatly expanded. In legal and economic practice, however, their role remained restricted. The prime object of marriage remained improving the economic and political status of the family and rearing children who would sustain the family status; marriages still served male interests and were controlled by males. Some evidence suggests that the new place defined for noble women in the chivalric code required women to be sheltered and protected as sex objects unsuited to participate in the world of work and power.

Taken together, the forces working to transform the conditions of noble life during the eleventh, twelfth, and thirteenth centuries resulted in the definition of the nobility as a leisured class of gentlemen and ladies clearly distinct from the rest of society by birth, wealth, and modes of behavior. The basic elements developed during the High Middle Ages to distinguish this dominant class survived long after the end of the Middle Ages to set the tone for genteel behavior and to define the privileges enjoyed by those claiming aristocracy.

7. SOCIAL CHANGE: THE PEASANTRY

The peasantry was also affected socially by the currents of economic change. During the twelfth and thirteenth centuries, there was large-scale freeing of serfs, especially in France, England, Flanders, Italy, and western Germany. Some peasants purchased their freedom; some gained it in return for colonizing new lands and others by leaving the manors for the city. A more important cause was the willingness of manorial seigneurs to surrender their rights to a serf's produce and services for money payments. In much of the West the serf was thus becoming a legally free tenant farmer, enjoying whatever benefits freedom brought, but also losing the paternalistic protection the manorial lord had often extended.

In a general way, the material life of the peasants improved during these centuries. Their incomes increased as a result of their greater productivity and of the inflationary trends that caused the prices they received for their produce to rise faster than the value of the obligations they owed. As they gained access to local markets, their diet was better, their health and life expectancy improved, and they were able to enjoy a wider range of products. As might be expected, significant gradations in peasant status emerged as turns of fortune allowed some peasants to acquire the use of more land than others and as some proved more skillful and intelligent than others.

Some evidence suggests that as serfdom declined the peasants gained a greater degree of self-determination than they had had when most of them were locked into the manorial structure, legally bound to the soil as a dependent population. Most peasants continued to live in small villages and had few contacts with the wider world. In some cases they banded together to gain special privileges from their political superiors, which allowed them to control some aspects of village life, much as town dwellers—the bourgeoisie—were doing. They also sometimes directly influenced the affairs of the local church. Free peasants had more opportunity to decide how they would exploit their rented lands and how they would dispose of their crops. They could leave their village to take up farming where conditions were more favorable, or they could seek their fortunes as traders or artisans in the expanding urban centers.

However, we must not push too far in assessing the improved lot of the peasantry. As a class, the peasants remained at the bottom of the social scale. Perhaps they were even further removed from the top because of the increasing complexity, refinement, and class consciousness of the nobility. Peasants became even more the object of scorn by the nobility whose members assumed that their elevated status and expanding economic needs gave them the right to exploit the peasantry economically. For the most part, peasant life remained hard, poor, and limited, and peasant conditions were still largely determined by the dominant aristocracy. As was the case with the nobility and the bourgeoisie, the basic legal and social patterns shaping peasant life became so solidly fixed during the eleventh, twelfth, and thirteenth centuries that they would persist far into the future.

Origins of the Medieval Nobility

During much of this century historians of the Middle Ages have disagreed in explaining the origins of the medieval nobility, the class which dominated political, social, economic, and cultural life.

Early in this century there was general consensus on an interpretation that was given classic expression by the French historian, Marc Bloch, in his seminal work entitled *Feudal Society*. Reflecting a view of aristocracy rooted in the Ancien Régime in France, Bloch defined "nobility" as a social class enjoying specific hereditary privileges defined by law. He argued that such a class did not emerge until the twelfth century. Prior to then there had existed a loosely defined aristocracy, the members of which enjoyed social prominence based on their personal association with royalty and on favors—chiefly land grants and offices—flowing from that connection. This social group was destroyed in the tumult following the collapse of the Carolingian empire. Amidst that chaos, "new," "self-made" men enjoying a monopoly on military power used that power to carve out a legally sanctioned position of privilege transmitted by blood. In brief, the European nobility was derived from the aggressive, ruthless feudal warriors.

Recent investigations have raised questions about this explanation. Many historians, especially those influenced by concepts of social structures formulated by social scientists, argue that noble status embraces more than inheritable legal privileges. They claim that noble status involves factors such as wealth, power over others, life style, and mental perceptions. Any effort to explain the origins of the medieval nobility that focuses on narrow legal concerns without considering these factors is faulted.

Bloch's thesis has been challenged on another ground. He argued that during the tenth and eleventh centuries there was a break in an established order which created an opportunity for "new" men to forge for themselves a unique social status. But recent historians have shown that in many cases there was biological continuity linking Carolingian noble families to noble families of the eleventh and twelfth centuries. It can be demonstrated that some warrior upstarts entered the ranks of nobility during the tenth and eleventh centuries, chiefly by marrying into old noble families. But their social ascent by attaching themselves to existing noble circles does not support the case for a "new" and different nobility in the twelfth century. The issue of origins of the nobility must involve the study of noble status in the early Middle Ages.

Further complicating our understanding of the origins of the medieval nobility is a changing view of the relationship between noble status and the warrior element in society. It was once nearly axiomatic that by the twelfth century every warrior—every knight—was *ipso facto* a noble. Historians are no longer quite so positive. There is much evidence to suggest that many knights held an inferior social status. What seems to have been more important than simply being a warrior was membership in a new kind of family structure in which the material resources of each family were transmitted from father to eldest son rather than being divided among all members of the family, as was the ancient Germanic custom. In other words, noble status in the High Middle Ages originated only with the advent of the patrimonial family structure that permitted the concentration and transmission of wealth in a narrow circle of families.

Their disagreement on the origins of the medieval nobility leaves historians at loss in explaining a key source of dynamism in the medieval world: the processes which allowed some people to establish a position of dominance over society.

SUGGESTED READING

Overview of the Period 1000–1300

Christopher Brooke, *Europe in the Central Middle Ages, 962–1154*, 2nd ed. (1987).

John H. Mundy, *Europe in the High Middle Ages, 1150–1309* (1973).

Taken together, these well-written works provide excellent coverage of the period covered in Part Five.

R. W. Southern, *The Making of the Middle Ages* (1953). A brilliant essay, concentrating on "silent" forces affecting society.

Susan Reynolds, *Kingdoms and Communities in Western Europe, 900–1300* (1984). A challenging effort to identify collectivities that shaped society in the High Middle Ages.

Economic and Social History

R. H. Bautier, *The Economic Development of Medieval Europe*, trans. Heather Karolyi (1971).

N. J. G. Pounds, *An Economic History of Medieval Europe* (1974).

Two excellent general surveys of economic history.

Georges Duby, *Rural Economy and Country Life in the Medieval West*, trans. Cynthia Postan (1968). The best description of agriculture and rural life.

Robert S. Lopez, *The Commercial Revolution of the Middle Ages, 950–1350* (1971). A persuasive defense of an interesting thesis.

Christopher Brooke, *The Structure of Medieval Society* (1971).

Charles T. Wood, *The Age of Chivalry: Manners and Morals, 1000–1450* (1970).

Two studies that seek to describe the general features of the medieval social order.

Philippe Ariès and Georges Duby, ed., *A History of Private Life*, Vol. 2: *Revelations of the Medieval World*, ed. Georges Duby (1987). Rich in details about how people lived during the High Middle Ages.

Frances and Joseph Gies, *Marriage and Family in the Middle Ages* (1987). A good introduction to a complex issue.

David Herlihy, *Medieval Households* (1985). Illuminates the nature of a basic social institution.

Maurice Keen, *Chivalry* (1984). A fine introduction.

Shalamith Shahar, *The Fourth Estate. A History of Women in the Middle Ages*, trans. Chaya Galai (1983).

Margaret Wade Labarge, *A Small Sound of the Trumpet: Women in Medieval Life* (1986).

Eileen Power, *Medieval Women* (1976).

Three of the best of many recent studies of medieval women.

Michel Mollat, *The Poor in the Middle Ages. An Essay in Social History*, trans. Arthur Goldhammer (1986). A pioneering study in a field little explored.

John M. Carter, *Sports and Pastimes of the Middle Ages* (1988). Suggests that people always find ways to have fun.

Urban Life

Henri Pirenne, *Medieval Cities: Their Origins and the Revival of Trade*, trans. Frank D. Halsey (1925).

Fritz Rörig, *The Medieval Town*, trans. D. J. Matthew (1967).

Edith Ennen, *The Medieval Town*, trans. Natalie Fryde (1979).

Howard Saalman, *Medieval Cities* (1968).

Lacking an effective synthesis of a much-studied subject, any of these four titles will provide a helpful introduction.

Joseph and Frances Gies, *Life in a Medieval City* (1969). A good reconstruction of life in a typical medieval city.

CHAPTER 19

Political Revival: The Holy Roman Empire

FIGURE 19.1 **The Holy Roman Emperor as "Agent of Christ"** This tenth-century ivory plaque shows Emperor Otto I offering a model of the cathedral church of Magdeburg to Christ who is seated in majesty. It reflects the conviction not only that the emperor controlled the Church but also that he was the intercessor between Christ and the faithful Christians on earth. (The Metropolitan Museum of Art, Gift of George Blumenthal, 1941)

While western Europe's lesser men and women were producing new wealth and rearranging their social relationships, its kings were successfully engaged in rebuilding political structures capable of controlling much larger political communities than the principalities that dominated tenth-century western Europe. By 1300 their efforts had produced a level of political order in the West that had not existed since the collapse of the Roman imperial regime. No less important, the major political entities created between 1000 and 1300 marked the origins of states that have persisted until the present. Although state building advanced over all of western Europe, we shall focus attention chiefly on political developments in Germany, Italy, England, and France.

During the High Middle Ages successful kings drew on several traditions to expand their authority: Germanic concepts of warrior kings, the Carolingian ideal of ministerial kingship, Roman law. But central to their success was their exploitation of rights bestowed on them by their position as chief lords in the feudal hierarchy, a status that provided them with extensive rights to command the loyalty, obedience, and services of their vassals. In essence, the states shaped between 1000 and 1300 were *feudal monarchies*, made possible by the exploitation of feudal practices often portrayed as the very antitheses of large states and effective central power.

1. THE FOUNDING OF THE HOLY ROMAN EMPIRE

The earliest and most impressive effort at political reconstruction during the High Middle Ages involved a political entity that later came to be known as the Holy Roman Empire. This state resulted from the combination of kingdoms established by the divisions of the Carolingian Empire. The most important was the kingdom of the East Franks defined by the Treaty of Verdun in 843 (see Map 16.2). To this German core were joined the subkingdoms formed during the ninth century by divisions of the kingdom of Lotharingia; of these, the kingdom of Italy was of special importance as a component of the Holy Roman Empire (see Map 20.1 and Map 16.2). During the late ninth and

early tenth centuries, royal power steadily declined in all of these subkingdoms. In the kingdom of the East Franks—Germany—the dukes who had served the strong Carolingian kings as royal officials usurped royal power to create virtually independent principalities, the chief of which were Saxony, Bavaria, Franconia, Swabia, and Upper and Lower Lotharingia (Lorraine in French) (see Map 20.1). These emerging territorial entities reflected pre-Carolingian tribal groupings. These ethnic ties, combined with the public powers associated with the ducal office, gave each principality an internal solidarity that hindered the complete fragmentation of Germany into petty lordships and the feudalization of relationships among the ruling nobility. An indication of the advance of ducal power came in 911, when the dukes joined hands to depose the last Carolingian king and to elect one of their own, Conrad, duke of Franconia, as king. In the Carolingian kingdoms of Italy and Burgundy-Arles, the process of political fragmentation was also proceeding rapidly; local potentates carved out principalities and imposed their lordship on the local population with little respect for royal power. To complicate the situation, in the late ninth and early tenth centuries this entire area, like most of Europe, was ravaged by the attacks of Saracens, Magyars, and Vikings.

In Germany the drift toward localism was reversed with the election of Henry I, duke of Saxony, as king in 917. His successor, Otto I, the Great (936–973), was the architect of the basic policies restoring monarchical authority. After a long struggle, he compelled the dukes to accept royal overlordship; in the course of this struggle, he managed to dislodge most of the powerful families who controlled the ducal offices, often replacing them with members of his own family. Otto earned fame as an effective warrior king by inflicting a decisive defeat on Magyar invaders at the battle of Lechfeld in 955, ending their destructive raids on Germany. Not content with this notable success, Otto encouraged military expansion, colonization, and missionary activity into the Slavic world, beginning a Germanic "drive to the East" that continued for centuries and found favor among German princes, prelates, and peasants.

Otto's success in these ventures stemmed from

his ability to strengthen the institutional base for royal power. Although he steadfastly insisted on service from the dukes as representatives of public authority, he based his power primarily on a feudal alliance with the clergy. Following a model set by the great Carolingian rulers, he made large grants of royal land to bishops and abbots on a feudal basis, creating ecclesiastical fiefs in every corner of Germany. The church officials who received royal fiefs became royal vassals, obligated to render to the king the military and political services needed to sustain royal authority. To make this policy work, Otto had to be certain of the political capabilities and the loyalty of the men who filled ecclesiastical offices and received as fiefs the lands attached to these offices. He therefore assumed the power to select those who filled clerical offices. As a consequence of this policy, called *lay investiture*, the ecclesiastical establishment became the vital element in royal administration.

Successful in uniting and defending his kingdom, Otto was drawn into Italian affairs. Certainly his urge to imitate the Carolingians was a factor in this fateful step. But political realities played a part. By mid–tenth century many Italians, including the popes, were looking for an outsider capable of doing what their feeble kings could not do: curb internal disorder and protect them from attacks by Magyars and Saracens. Otto was forced to pay heed to Italian affairs because some of his powerful subjects, especially the dukes of Bavaria, were fishing in those troubled waters in search of a power base from which to defy his royal authority. After an initial venture into Italy in 951, which resulted in his assumption of the title of "king of Italy," he returned in 961 to solidify his hold on his new kingdom. In 962 he seized Rome and was crowned emperor by Pope John XII, grateful for being freed from the oppressive clutches of greedy Roman nobles. The office created by Charlemagne was thus renewed; the imperial crown was again worn by the most powerful ruler in the West whose accomplishments had earned him this honor. A vigorous diplomatic campaign ended with recognition of the imperial title by the Byzantine emperor; Byzantine acceptance of Otto's emperorship was fortified by a marriage alliance involving Otto's son, the future Otto

II (973–983), and a remarkable Byzantine princess, Theophano. Otto I forced his authority on the Italian nobility and entrusted the exercise of royal power to powerful church officials who became his vassals. Especially significant was his policy toward the papacy. When John XII refused to accept imperial directions, Otto deposed him, dictated the election of a more pliant successor, and imposed a rule that no pope would be selected in the future without the consent of the emperor. This decision, opening an era of German domination of the papacy, punctuated the fact that the emperor was head of the Christian community, just as Constantine and Charlemagne had been.

2. OTTO'S SUCCESSORS AND THE GATHERING OPPOSITION

From Otto I's death in 973 until 1056, a succession of five emperors continued his policies with considerable success. In Germany the independence of the duchies was curbed, and their leaders were made subservient to imperial authority. The Church was skillfully manipulated to ensure its service to the emperors; in turn, the emperors acted in a variety of ways to promote its interests. To complement the administrative services performed by feudalized church officials, the emperors developed a corps of secular administrators, called *ministeriales*, recruited from the nonfree population under terms that made them totally devoted to royal service. The emperors kept a firm hold on Italy, acting there chiefly through vassal bishops. The empire was expanded on its southwestern border by the absorption of the old Carolingian subkingdom of Burgundy-Arles. Strong pressures continued to be applied in the East, so successfully that by 1056 Poland, Bohemia, and Magyar Hungary all recognized imperial overlordship. The emperors and their ecclesiastical supporters sought to surround the imperial office with a theocratic ideology that stressed the sacred role of the emperor as protector of the Christian order (see Figure 19.1). This effort reached its apogee during the reign of Otto III (983–1002), whose mother, Empress Theophano, joined forces with the leading scholar of the age, Gerbert, now reigning as Pope Sylvester II (999–1003), to promote plans for installing the emperor in Rome in a setting that would exalt not only his sacral role but also his successorship to ancient Roman emperors and perhaps his superiority over contemporary emperors reigning in Constantinople.

But the very success of the German emperors had its cost; it provoked opposition from a variety of sources. The German nobility accepted imperial authority grudgingly; all the while its members strengthened their position by extending their landholdings, consolidating their hold on the peasantry, and building their own alliances with the Church by founding monasteries over which they maintained control. The royal office was particularly vulnerable because it remained elective; despite their efforts, the tenth- and eleventh-century rulers were not able to set aside the ancient Germanic elective principle in favor of hereditary succession. In Italy the nobles resented imperial authority and foreign domination. The emerging Italian commercial cities were eager to establish their liberties at the expense of imperial control. Rulers beyond the imperial frontiers—the French kings in the West and Slavic princes in the East—were suspicious of imperial designs on their independence and their territories.

Finally and most important was the opposition generated by a powerful religious reform movement sweeping over Europe (see Chapter 22). In its ideological aspect this movement challenged the concept that secular rulers—including the emperor—were the divinely ordained leaders of Christian society. In its practical aspect the reform movement was directed against the feudalization of the Church, especially lay control over church offices and property, and against the worldly, immoral clergy produced by these practices. Support for reform came from monks, bishops, and monarchs, including even the saintly emperor Henry III (1039–1056).

Eventually, the reform movement found its leadership in Rome. Since the late ninth century, the papacy had played a modest role in directing Christian life. The papal office was controlled first by local Roman noble families and then after 962 by the Holy Roman emperors. A turning point came when Henry III installed a dedicated German reformer, Leo IX (1049–1054), as pope. Under Leo's leadership, a circle of reformers gathered at

Rome, devoting their talents to defining the goals of reform and gathering precedents to justify purifying religious life. Eventually the driving force of this group was a monk named Hildebrand, later to be Pope Gregory VII, who gave the movement a political orientation. He saw the Church as an earthly corporate body that had the responsibility to work out God's will—the salvation of humanity. To achieve that end, the Church must become a visible community with its own head, its own law, its own resources, and its own liberty. All Christians, even the greatest princes, must be directed to the proper execution of their responsibilities in the drama of salvation by the bishop of Rome, the successor of St. Peter as Christ's vicar on earth. Herein lay the radical element of the reform ideology: It denied the role of secular rulers as divinely ordained directors of Christian life. At best, princes were agents of the Church, commissioned by ecclesiastical authorities to assist in directing Christian society and subject to priestly judgment in serving their role.

During Leo's pontificate, the papacy turned its new ideology into a practical reform program that impinged directly on the existing political and ecclesiastical establishments. The concept of papal headship of the Church was widely propagated to remind lesser clergy of their obligation to look to Rome for direction. That claim was even extended to the Byzantine Empire; the result was a bitter quarrel that ended in 1054 when the pope and the patriarch of Constantinople excommunicated each other, creating a schism between the Roman and Greek churches that has persisted to the present. The popes issued a steady flow of legislation against the immorality and corruption afflicting the clergy, especially *simony* (buying and selling of church offices and services) and clerical marriage. Papal agents organized local church councils all over the West to enact reforming legislation. Popes began to build a centralized administrative machinery in Rome to enforce papal rules over all Europe. In 1059 a papal decree provided that henceforth popes would be chosen by the College of Cardinals, a body of ecclesiastical officials centered in Rome who assisted the pope in carrying out church administration. The emperor was deprived of any voice in papal elections except to approve what the cardinals decided. Seeking to strengthen its position, the papacy in 1059 formed an alliance with the Normans, a new political force emerging in southern Italy and Sicily (see Chapter 21); this pact gave the papacy a protector other than the emperor.

This aggressive policy generated resistance in many quarters. Many clergymen, long accustomed to having wives or concubines and to receiving payment for religious services, squirmed at the talk of moral reform. Bishops and abbots resented Rome's growing interference in local religious affairs that tradition had reserved to their jurisdiction. Important lords were uneasy at the prospect of losing the right to appoint church officials and to control the income from ecclesiastical property and offices. Especially vulnerable was the Holy Roman emperor, who not only relied on a subservient, feudalized Church as the chief source of his power but also claimed, by virtue of his exalted office, the God-given right to direct the destiny of Christian society. Such formidable opposition might well have blighted the reform movement had it not been for Gregory VII. A strong, willful man of great political ability and courage, he was not afraid to act to achieve what he believed was right. Once elected pope in 1073, he moved resolutely to sustain the effort to correct religious life. In 1075 he decreed that lay investiture—that is, control by lay authorities over the election and installation of ecclesiastical officials—was illegal. Henceforth, church officials would have to be chosen and installed by the Church itself. And henceforth, property pertaining to ecclesiastical offices would not be subject to lay control. This act, challenging the entire feudal order on a crucial issue, put the papacy on a collision course with most of the kings and lords of western Europe, and especially the Holy Roman emperors, in a contest known as the *investiture struggle*.

3. THE INVESTITURE STRUGGLE

As Gregory moved forward with his reform program, his most formidable foe was the young emperor, Henry IV (1056–1106). He succeeded his father Henry III, under whose rule imperial power had reached its apogee, while still a child. During his minority imperial power was severely challenged, not only by the papal reformers but also by the German nobility. But when Henry IV assumed full power in 1065, he left no doubt that he intended to follow the policies that had made his predecessors strong. Among other things, he proceeded to appoint men of his choice to episcopal office, despite Gregory VII's prohibition of lay investiture.

The break that was sure to come developed in 1075 in connection with a vacant episcopal see in Milan. Since control of this major city was vital to imperial power in Italy, Henry IV acted decisively to impose his candidate, despite the armed resistance of the city's populace. Late in 1075 Gregory sent Henry a letter ordering him to do penance for violating Church law and threatening him with excommunication and loss of his office. With the backing of most of the German bishops, Henry replied by declaring that "the false monk" Hildebrand was not even pope, since his election had been improper. Whereupon in 1076 Gregory excommunicated the emperor, suspended him from office, and invited the Germans to elect a new king. Many German nobles and bishops leaped at this opportunity to weaken the king. They commanded Henry to appear before a meeting to be held in Germany early in 1077 with the pope in attendance. If Henry could not clear himself of excommunication before this meeting, he would be deposed.

Henry IV faced a crucial issue. The specific question of lay investiture was no longer as critical as the broader implication that the pope could claim to judge the emperor unworthy of his office and bring about his deposition. Henry had to offset this claim to save his regime. His next action was tactically brilliant. He set out to intercept Gregory before the pope could reach Germany to preside over the projected meeting. In January 1077 he found Gregory at Canossa in northern Italy. In the garb of a penitent, the mighty emperor begged the pope's forgiveness. Although Gregory realized that to grant this would free a strengthened Henry to continue the imperial policy, he could not abdicate his responsibility as a priest to forgive repentant sinners. After keeping the emperor waiting in the snow for three days, Gregory absolved him (see Figure 19.2). The pope had won a moral victory by forcing the most powerful ruler in Eu-

FIGURE 19.2 A Humble Emperor: Henry IV This manuscript miniature from the early twelfth century shows Emperor Henry IV (kneeling) imploring Countess Mathilda of Tuscany and Abbot Hugh of Cluny to intercede in his behalf with Pope Gregory VII just before the fateful meeting of pope and emperor at Canossa. (Biblioteca Apostolica Vaticana, Rome)

rope to admit that he had a superior, but his action deeply disappointed his supporters in Germany and weakened the papal cause against Henry.

Henry moved at once to deal with his most dangerous immediate foes, the German nobility, some of whom persisted in their plans to depose him by electing an antiking. Henry skillfully and speedily beat down their resistance. He then turned to Italy, captured Rome, forced Gregory VII into exile, elevated a supporter to the papal throne, and had himself crowned emperor in 1084. By 1085, the year in which the disillusioned Gregory died, it appeared that Henry IV's cause had been vindicated and the tide of radical reform blunted.

But the victory was a hollow one; the papal challenge had unleashed too many enemies. Henry was unable to hold Rome against the papal allies, led by the Normans, and the papal office was returned to strong and independent hands, especially those of Urban II (1088–1099), who sustained the cause of reform and won ever-increasing support for its ideals. In Germany, the nobles kept up their resistance and slowly undermined royal power. Although Henry defended his power valiantly, by the end of his reign he was a virtual fugitive from the rebellious nobles.

Henry IV's three successors, who ruled until 1152, could not stem the assault on monarchical authority. Imperial power in Italy nearly disappeared, usurped by independent towns, nobles, and the papacy. The imperial crown became a pawn of warring noble factions, with election going to the prince who seemed least likely to exert effective power. Imperial resources were dissipated or usurped, and the administrative machinery broke down. In 1122 Emperor Henry V made peace with the Church over the specific issue of lay investiture by signing the Concordat of Worms, which provided that election to ecclesiastical offices and the formal act of installation into office be made by the Church, while the lands and secular powers associated with the office be invested by the ruler. This compromise gave the emperor an effective veto over elections by allowing him to withhold the property of the office. But it also deprived the monarch of absolute control over its major support, a loyal episcopacy selected by the ruler.

Although the specific problem of lay investiture had been resolved through compromise by the Concordat of Worms, the long struggle to arrive at that settlement had caused a fundamental change in German society (and to a lesser extent in imperial Italy) that undermined the system of royal government shaped by Otto the Great and his successors. During the years of the investiture struggle feudal practices spread rapidly through imperial society. Interminable civil wars drove the weak to seek protection by becoming vassals of the strong and allowed the strong to create independent lordships by surrounding themselves with as many vassals and fiefs as possible. The embattled emperors conceded royal lands as fiefs to princes in a desperate hope of winning support. As the process of feudalization proceeded, a hodgepodge of lordships emerged. There was no hierarchy giving the emperor a theoretical position as the ultimate feudal lord. In fact, the monarchy was left out of the emerging power structure. The real centers of power were powerful noble families who succeeded in surrounding themselves with vassals and fiefs without accepting a position of legal dependency on the emperor. By 1152 the German monarchy had lost touch with the new feudalized society that had emerged during the investiture struggle. A kingdom that had escaped feudalization in the tenth century had now acquired a feudal structure, and the monarchy had limited means of coping with it.

4. THE HOHENSTAUFENS

Despite the destructive impact of the investiture struggle, the Holy Roman Empire survived. At mid–twelfth century a new dynasty, the Hohenstaufens, took up the task of rebuilding the imperial government. The first notable Hohenstaufen was Frederick I, Barbarossa (Red Beard, 1152–1190). He resolutely set about establishing a basis for royal power that would fit the new political realities. In essence, his policy was aimed at turning feudalism to royal advantage in order to build a system of government based not on theocratic principles but on secular principles, principles that Frederick derived largely from the Roman law then enjoying a revival in western Europe.

Frederick's first task was to establish order in Germany by pacifying the powerful noble families. He made broad concessions to a few great nobles in return for their acceptance of vassalage and allowed them to curb their troublesome vassals, the lesser nobles. The chief beneficiary of this policy was the leader of the traditionally anti-Hohenstaufen Welf faction, Henry the Lion, who with royal approval became duke of both Saxony and Bavaria. But Frederick was careful to define his regalian rights clearly and to insist that his great vassals respect them. To enforce these rights, he gave special attention to increasing his royal domain, much of which was concentrated in Swabia (the Hohenstaufen homeland) and in the King-

dom of Burgundy, which became a part of the royal domain in 1156 as a result of Frederick's marriage to its heiress. A corps of nonfeudal civil servants was developed to administer this domain. He continued the old policy of turning the German Church to royal support.

From the beginning of his reign Frederick made it clear that he intended to possess the imperial title and to exercise all the powers that accrued to it. In fact, he was the first to call his realm the "Holy Roman Empire." In Italy this policy brought him into confrontation with three powerful forces: the papacy, the Italian towns, and the Norman kingdom. Initially Frederick's relations with the papacy were cordial, and Frederick was crowned emperor by the pope in 1155. However, he made it clear that he had no intention of admitting papal supremacy or of allowing the papacy to restrict what he considered to be his regalian rights over the Church. In taking this position, he aroused suspicions at the papal court that he intended to challenge the position that the papacy had defined for itself during the investiture struggle.

Even more emphatic was his position with respect to the Italian towns, from which he intended to draw material support for his system of government. By 1158 he laid down a new set of rules to govern the relationship between the emperor and the rich Italian towns. Henceforth, the emperor would reclaim the regalian rights that he argued the towns had usurped. They were to pay regular taxes, accept imperial officials as their rulers, and permit the emperor to coin money and regulate commerce. At one stroke, the freedoms the Italian cities had been fashioning during the previous century were to be severely limited.

Once Frederick had made clear his policy toward the papacy and the towns, the storm broke. For most of his reign he was forced to fight an imposing array of enemies that became known as the Guelf faction (the anti-imperial counterpart in Italy of the Welf faction in Germany). The Guelf struggle against the Hohenstaufen forces (known in Italy as the Ghibellines) was led by Pope Alexander III (1159–1181), a true heir to Gregory VII. Frederick tried to replace Alexander with a pope favorable to imperial interests but with no success. The towns of northern Italy provided the backbone of Guelf strength, especially after they joined hands in 1167 with papal blessing to form the Lombard League. In 1176 at the Battle of Legnano, this league inflicted a defeat on Frederick's army, which greatly impeded his efforts to assert his authority over the towns. The Guelfs could usually count on the support of the Norman kingdom of Sicily in resisting Hohenstaufen power.

In the long run Frederick managed to withstand this powerful coalition, chiefly by compromising some of his ambitions. In 1177 he gave up his attempt to establish a pro-imperial pope and recognized Alexander III. In 1183, at the Peace of Constance, the Italian towns came to terms, recognizing Frederick's overlordship in return for extensive specific rights that assured their actual independence. In 1186 he arranged for his son Henry to marry the heiress of the Norman kingdom of Sicily, detoothing one of his most persistent foes. Frederick's sensible compromises had not gained him full control of Italy nor subdued the papacy, but his authority in Italy was still extensive and his position as emperor intact. His long-standing policy of trying to live with a few great princes in Germany did not prove wholly successful. Eventually, he had to smash the chief Welf prince, Henry the Lion, for unfaithfulness as a vassal. Thereafter, he decided to break up the large principalities and grant the territory to many lesser nobles who would serve as royal vassals. This step relieved the immediate danger, but in the long run, by further promoting feudalization, it proved fatal to royal power.

Frederick Barbarossa's illustrious career ended in 1190 when he was drowned while leading the Third Crusade. He left behind the framework for a strong monarchy, but much needed to be done by his successors to make that system permanent. His son, Henry VI (1190–1197), began as if he would sustain his father's work, fighting a successful war to control the kingdom of Sicily, which he claimed by virtue of his marriage. But then, instead of maintaining effective control over the restless German nobility, he became enmeshed in a series of schemes to extend his power over the Mediterranean to the Holy Land, France, and Spain. As his schemes unfolded, the foes of strong central rule began to join hands. Only a premature death in 1197 saved him from paying the full price

for too great an ambition.

For the next two decades the fate of the Holy Roman Empire was determined by the most powerful of all the medieval popes, Innocent III (1198–1216). In 1198 he assumed guardianship over Henry VI's three-year-old heir, Frederick, and in that role took virtual control over the kingdom of Sicily. He sought to prevent a single Hohenstaufen from ruling Germany and Sicily, a policy that would allow him to safeguard papal power in central Italy. In Germany a faction of the nobles remained loyal to the Hohenstaufens and elected Philip of Swabia as king. Innocent immediately promoted the claims of a Welf candidate, Otto of Brunswick, the son of Henry the Lion; in 1198 Otto was also elected king. This disputed succession led to a civil war that lasted until 1212 and caused great damage in Germany. Both England and France were drawn into this struggle, England in support of the Welfs and France on the side of the Hohenstaufens. Papal diplomacy played the warring factions in Germany against each other and encouraged the northern Italian towns and the nobles of central Italy to throw off imperial control. The work of Frederick Barbarossa seemed completely ruined; the Holy Roman Empire had become a pawn of the papacy.

In 1212, with the aid of the king of France, Innocent engineered the election of his ward to the kingship of Germany and eventually to the Holy Roman emperorship. Frederick II paid for papal support by making sweeping concessions that returned control of the German church to the papacy and fortified papal independence in Italy. But he proved no docile servant of the pope. He took up the battle to build a strong Holy Roman Empire with a political skill, ruthless ambition, and personal qualities that made him one of the most intriguing figures in all medieval history. Highly educated, intelligent, cosmopolitan in tastes and outlooks, his interest in literature, science, and learning so impressed his contemporaries that he was called *stupor mundi*—wonder of the world. His enemies—and they were many—branded him irreligious, immoral, dishonest, cruel, and Antichrist; his admirers saw him as a new man driven by a secular spirit quite distinct from the religious values dominant in his era.

Frederick II took a new approach to the gov-

WHERE HISTORIANS DISAGREE

The Investiture Struggle: A Medieval Revolution?

Many historians view the investiture struggle as a revolutionary event, but they do not agree on why its impact was so important.

One school of thought sees the struggle as a revolt against a deeply imbedded system governing church property and offices. Under Roman law the Church was considered a corporate entity, capable of owning its property. But the Germans brought with them a concept that held that everything connected with a piece of land belonged to the proprietor. As a consequence, proprietors viewed churches built on their land as private property. By extension, they treated the offices and revenues associated with churches as a part of their possession to be disposed of as they saw fit. The investiture struggle was in essence an attempt to liberate church property and offices from private ownership and to vest them in the hands of the corporate Church. The consequent shifting of vast wealth and its accompanying power from secular to clerical hands was of revolutionary importance.

Another view sees the struggle as the cause of a revolution in the political system of the Holy Roman Empire. They argue that between 962–1075 the Holy Roman Empire developed into the strongest, best-organized political unit in western Europe. Its constitution was based on a mutually beneficial union between church and state. Gregory VII's program destroyed that union, thereby undermining the constitutional system of the Holy Roman Empire and allowing the secular nobles to establish independence from the emperor. The result was political chaos in Germany and Italy which kept these areas from developing strong states until the nineteenth century.

Other historians argue that the investiture struggle marked a revolution in sociopolitical ideology. For centuries, western Europeans had accepted the idea that the welfare of Christian society depended on the actions of divinely ordained secular rulers to guide society toward salvation. The royal office combined the functions of both king and priest in order to accomplish divine will. The Gregorian reforms challenged this concept of right order by insisting that priests should direct society toward its ultimate end. The true Christian community was the Church. The clergy, organized under papal control, had the ultimate authority in directing lay society, including kings, toward its God-ordained ends.

Still other scholars see the investiture struggle as a decisive turning point in defining how a Christian should act in the world. During the early Middle Ages the monastic ideal of flight from the world predominated. The investiture struggle dramatized another view: Holy people—exemplified by Gregory VII—should move out of the cloister into the wicked world to attack evil and to persuade sinful kings, nobles, clergymen, and common people to "convert" to the true Christian life. As a result of the investiture struggle the world-denying monk was replaced by the world-involved activist as the ideal Christian.

Whether these issues constitute the "stuff" of revolution is a matter of judgment. However, when a particular episode in history entails control of vast amounts of property, the constitution of a major state, the nature of right order in society, and how people act to change society, then surely major matters are at stake. One test of the argument that the investiture struggle marked a revolution might be to watch for the extent to which these fundamental issues shaped historical development after the investiture struggle.

ernance of the Holy Roman Empire. He had little interest in Germany as the base for imperial power; Italy was the focus of his political concern. After becoming ruler of Germany, he remained there only until 1220. He spent these years surrendering royal power. He was as generous to the great feudal princes as to the papacy: He made their fiefs hereditary, gave them full rights of government over the fiefs, and even turned over to them the strong position the early Hohenstaufens had established in the towns. These concessions ensured that he would receive little help from Germany in his effort to rule the Holy Roman Empire.

As he progressively disengaged himself from Germany, Frederick turned his energies toward creating in his homeland, the Kingdom of Sicily, a centralized, bureaucratic state where royal power would be absolute. Frederick spelled out the program for this regime in a code of law, called the Constitutions of Melfi, issued in 1231. This document, which was strongly influenced by concepts drawn from Roman law and by the model of the Byzantine Empire, gave the king supreme authority as lawgiver and judge, set up a bureaucracy to control local affairs, and virtually abolished all the privileges of feudal lords and towns. Frederick then attempted to impose a comparable regime on Italy. This move aroused the ancient enemies of Hohenstaufen power: the papacy and the Italian communes. Under the leadership of two extremely able and tenacious popes, Gregory IX (1227–1241) and Innocent IV (1243–1254), both uncompromising advocates of papal supremacy, the papacy and the towns battled Frederick for nearly twenty years. The emperor fought skillfully and with great flair, but he lacked the resources to establish control over Italy; papal money and the human resources of the Italian towns were too great. Papal prestige in Europe was too extensive for Frederick to form an effective antipapal alliance; in fact, most European rulers showed little interest in what appeared to be an Italian power struggle. The emperor drew almost no help from his German vassals, who were too busy enjoying the privileges he had extended them. Frederick II died in 1250 far from realizing his ambitions; in fact, his policy had irreparably damaged any realistic base for imperial authority.

Amid bickering and foreign intervention, the German nobles did not agree on a new king until 1273, when they elected Rudolph of Hapsburg, qualified chiefly by his lack of strength. In the interval 1250 to 1273, known as the Interregnum, the last vestiges of effective imperial power were destroyed. Germany had finally broken to pieces politically. Meanwhile a French prince, Charles of Anjou, accepting a papal invitation, assumed the crown of the Kingdom of Sicily in 1266. In the rest of the peninsula each city, each noble, each churchman went an independent way, respecting no higher authority and feeling no attachment to Italy. The Slavic kingdoms that had so long been under strong German influence were also free. One of the cherished dreams of medieval society—a Christian empire in which people who held one faith would enjoy one ruler and one law to guide them in the struggle for salvation—had failed.

SUGGESTED READING

The Holy Roman Empire

K. J. Leyser, *Medieval Germany and Its Neighbors, 900–1250* (1982). The best general history.

Josef Flechenstein, *Early Medieval Germany,* trans. Bernard S. Smith (1978). Especially good on background of the empire of the High Middle Ages.

Horst Fuhrman, *Germany in the High Middle Ages, c. 1050–1200,* trans. Timothy Reuter (1986). Useful on the investiture struggle.

J. K. Hyde, *Society and Politics in Medieval Italy: The Evolution of the Civil Life, 1000–1350* (1973). Effective survey of the complex history of medieval Italy.

R. Folz, *The Concept of Empire in Western Europe from the Fifth to the Fourteenth Century,* trans. Sheila Ann Ogilvie (1969). Treats the concepts undergirding the medieval ideal of universal empire.

Gerd Tellenbach, *Church, State, and Christian Society at the Time of the Investiture Contest,* trans. R. F. Bennett

(1940). A classic on the ideological issues of the investiture struggle.

Uta-Renate Blumenthal, *The Investiture Controversy: Church and Monarchy from the Ninth to the Twelfth Century* (1988). Reflects modern scholarship on a much-disputed problem.

Biography

Peter Munz, *Frederick Barbarossa: A Study in Medieval Politics* (1969).

Thomas C. Van Cleve, *The Emperor Frederick II of Hohenstaufen: Immutator Mundi* (1972).

A. J. Macdonald, *Hildebrand: A Life of Gregory VII* (1932).

CHAPTER 20

Political Revival: England and France

FIGURE 20.1 A Medieval King's Nightmares These drawings from a manuscript portray a dream of Henry I of England. He dreams that his royal power will not be sufficient to control the major elements of his subjects: the peasants, the nobles, and the clergy. Perhaps because he dreamed what he had to face, Henry I was more successful than most of his contemporaries in winning the support of his diverse subjects. (The President and Fellows of Corpus Christi College, Oxford)

W hile the German rulers struggled in vain to create an empire embracing Germany and Italy, political consolidation progressed less dramatically but more effectively in England and France. The rulers of each of these kingdoms, chiefly by exploiting their feudal rights as overlords, slowly expanded their power to the point where they exercised extensive sovereignty over all their subjects. Their lordship was made effective by their ability to create institutions of royal government capable of enforcing royal commands. Although royal power in England and France was rooted in political feudalism, the regimes the kings fashioned ultimately superseded feudalism and assumed characteristics associated with modern states.

1. ENGLAND: THE NORMAN CONQUEST

During the eleventh century, the effective system of government that had been established in England earlier (see Chapter 16) showed signs of losing its vitality. The rulers' chief local officials, the earls and sheriffs, steadily secured rights of private government. The kings began to grant royal lands to *thegns* who pledged military service in return but often failed to render it. Many free people were forced to become dependents of the powerful nobles. New Scandinavian inroads undermined royal prestige and encouraged local independence. Canute, a Dane, even took the English crown (1016–1035). He dreamed of drawing England into a vast northern maritime empire based in Scandinavia, but such aims were foiled by his early death and by ineffective successors.

After this interlude of foreign rule, the old Anglo-Saxon royal line was restored with Edward the Confessor (1042–1066) as king. His reign was characterized by a rapid deterioration of royal power to the special advantage of the great earls, of whom Godwin of Wessex was the most powerful. When Edward died without heirs, the Witan elected Godwin's son Harold as king. He was immediately faced with an invasion led by Harald Hardrada, king of Norway, who coveted the English throne. Into this mounting crisis entered William, duke of Normandy. He laid claim to the

English crown on the basis of his distant kinship with Edward and his insistence that Edward had promised him the throne. Harald and William chose almost the same moment to invade England to assert their claims, forcing a settlement on the battlefield in 1066. King Harold crushed the invading Scandinavians only to meet disaster a short time later, in October, at the Battle of Hastings, where William's Norman knights overpowered the Anglo-Saxon forces and made it possible for their leader to assume the English crown as William I (1066–1087) (see Color Plate 9).

William made it clear at his coronation that he would observe Anglo-Saxon customs and assume all rights belonging to the Anglo-Saxon kings. To gain the resources he needed to exert these rights and powers, William took a momentous step: He introduced continental feudalism into England. By virtue of his military victory William claimed large tracts of land held by his royal predecessors and by Anglo-Saxon landowners who resisted the Normans. He set aside about one-sixth of it as the royal domain and granted out most of the rest as fiefs to his Norman followers. In return they became his vassals, owing him services, chiefly military, in proportion to the size of their fiefs. Most of his direct vassals (called *tenants-in-chief* or *barons*) subinfeudated their lands and acquired their own vassals. William, however, insisted that all subvassals owed first allegiance to the king, thereby establishing a meaningful feudal hierarchy with the king at the head. Through these steps, he secured not only a valuable royal domain but also the military service of about five thousand knights, enough to ensure his mastery of England. In short, the feudal system allowed him to impose on England a new ruling elite that he as king could control.

As successor to the Anglo-Saxon kings and chief lord of the feudal hierarchy, William had the authority and resources to lay the groundwork for a strong central government. The Anglo-Saxon Witan was replaced by the feudal body called the *Curia Regis* (court of the king), at whose meetings the king's lay and ecclesiastical vassals were expected to judge cases and advise the ruler. To complement the income from his extensive domain, William continued to collect the taxes owed the king from Anglo-Saxon times, the chief one being the Danegeld, originally imposed in 991 to provide tribute payment to the Danes. He also took care to exploit the feudal dues owed him by his vassals. In 1086 William's agents compiled the Domesday Book, a survey of England's wealth fief by fief, which documented what his subjects possessed and how much they owed the king.

William was careful to retain the local units of administration he had inherited, the Anglo-Saxon shires and hundreds, and to see to it that the local officials, especially sheriffs, served royal purposes. Through this system of local government the king kept in direct touch with the English populace in matters of justice, peacekeeping, and taxation. The English system of local government prevented the fragmentation of public authority and its dispersion into private hands.

Overlooking no possible source of power and prestige, William acted to attach the Church to his new establishment. He won the support of the reformers and the blessing of the papacy by promising at the time of the conquest to undertake the reform of the badly corrupted Anglo-Saxon church. Once in control of England, he brought in a Norman, Lanfranc, as archbishop of Canterbury, who vigorously undertook the reform of religious life in England. William generously endowed the Church with property and permitted it liberty to conduct its own courts. However, he never relinquished real control over it, especially in the choice of high ecclesiastical officials.

The Norman conquest was thus a watershed in English history. A disintegrating monarchy was given new political vitality by injecting into its structure certain continental feudal practices that provided the king-lord with the resources to make himself the real master of England. Moreover, the coming of the Normans drew England into the mainstream of western European life by involving its people more directly in the vigorous economic, religious, and cultural forces that were revitalizing society on the Continent. As a consequence, many of the unique aspects of traditional Anglo-Saxon society were slowly effaced during the century following the Norman conquest. Many in England then and later lamented this development, feeling that something precious was lost. But on the whole England benefited greatly from closer contacts with continental Europe.

2. ENGLAND: GROWTH OF THE MONARCHY, 1087–1199

During the century following William I's death, his successors (known as the Norman-Angevin dynasty) were energetic, capable kings who worked hard to expand royal power: the rough, brutal William II (1087–1100); the quiet, prudent, avaricious Henry I (1100–1135); the ambitious, tempestuous Henry II (1154–1189); and the colorful, romantic knight, Richard I, the Lion-Hearted (1189–1199). Only one difficult interlude, brought about by a disputed succession, intervened to cause civil strife between 1135 and 1154. The twelfth-century kings had interests far transcending the governance of England, especially their concerns with their continental possessions, which by the reign of Henry II embraced much of France (see pp. 274–275 and Map 20.1). But we must neglect these aspects of English history in order to concentrate on the efforts of the kings to perfect strong monarchical government (see Figure 20.1).

One of the major achievements of the twelfth-century English kings, especially Henry I and Henry II, was the formation of an effective central administration. They fashioned it by combining and adapting features of the old Anglo-Saxon royal household and of the new Curia Regis in which the king's tenants-in-chief were obliged to serve as part of their feudal obligation to their royal overlord. Development moved along two complementary lines. On the one hand, the kings began to draw men from the Curia Regis who would serve for prolonged periods instead of returning to their private affairs after brief meetings of this body. On the other hand, the kings began to assign specialized functions to various members of this small council of semipermanent servants—the beginning of departments of administration. During the twelfth century, four specialized functional agencies began to take shape: the *Exchequer,* for collecting revenues due to the king from the sheriffs and for judging disputes arising out of financial obligations owed the kings; the *Treasury,* for guarding and dispensing royal money; the *Chancery,* for issuing royal orders and composing royal correspondence; and the *royal law courts.*

The kings continued to sustain and strengthen

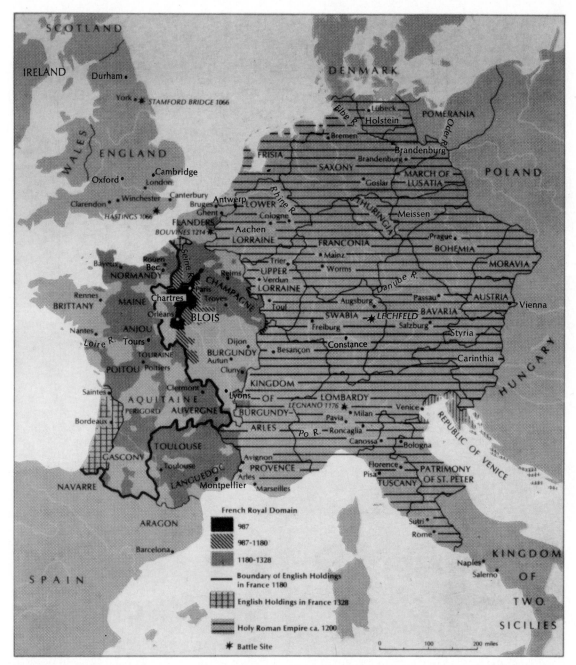

Map 20.1 **MEDIEVAL ENGLAND, FRANCE, AND THE HOLY ROMAN EMPIRE** This map shows the major political entities in western Europe about 1300. A major problem for the rulers of these states during the High Middle Ages was the establishment of control over the many principalities into which each was divided.

the traditional Anglo-Saxon system of local government. They resisted the sheriffs' ever-present tendency to usurp royal power for private advantage by using the agencies of the central government to maintain control over the sheriffs and to impose on them a broader range of activities in support of the king. Henry II was especially effective in providing clear definitions of the obligations of the sheriffs.

The kings were careful to guard the financial and military resources needed to support the growing agencies of the royal government and to restrain potential foes. The financial support of the government still depended heavily on the exploitation of the royal domain. Royal agents zealously collected every possible feudal due owed by royal vassals and all fines and fees due to the king for breaking his law or utilizing services performed by his agents. Custom duties were levied on an ever-wider scale, allowing the kings to capitalize on growing trade. The royal government also devised ways of imposing direct taxes on the income and property of its subjects. The revenues from these many sources provided the twelfth-century English kings with a sounder financial base for their power than was enjoyed by any other royal government in Europe. The king's military strength was based on the military service owed by the tenants-in-chief. To complement this feudal army, the kings maintained the ancient royal right to summon the *fyrd*, the army of all freemen in the realm. Toward the end of the twelfth century the kings began to allow those who owed them military service to make money payments, called *scutage* or shield-money, in lieu of personal service; this income was used to hire mercenary troops.

Beyond all doubt, the most important development of the twelfth century was the formation of a royal system of justice. This effort was in large part a response to the confusion surrounding the traditional system of justice. Under the old order courts were conducted by the king, his local representatives in the shires, feudal lords, seigneurs on the manors, the Church, and the towns. In each set of courts different systems of law, different procedures, and different systems of punishment were applied by judges whose legal competence varied greatly. The kings and their legal advisers sought to diminish this confusion by developing a royal system of justice common to all—a step that had the added attraction of increasing royal income derived from charges for court costs. As the system of royal justice developed, it became one of the positive benefits of strong royal government.

One of the chief measures taken to expand royal justice involved providing greater numbers of royal judges trained to apply a common system of law to cases throughout the realm. Several steps were taken to achieve this end. Henry I began the *circuit court system*, sending itinerant judges at set intervals to shires throughout England to try cases. By the time of Henry II, this system had become a regular practice; and by comparing notes, the itinerant judges were soon able to erect a common set of principles for deciding cases. A *common law* was in the making. Henry II established the first of England's great central courts, sitting permanently at Westminster to handle many cases previously heard by the Curia Regis. Eventually this body began to divide into specialized courts. The decisions of these central courts guided the activities of itinerant judges and contributed to uniformity in the legal system.

As royal judicial activity increased, the kings' agents began to challenge the jurisdiction of the baronial, manorial, ecclesiastical, and town courts. The kings expanded their authority over criminal cases by legislation that defined new crimes against the peace and ordered royal judges to punish violators. Increasing royal control over civil cases, chiefly involving property disputes, was more complicated and met strong opposition, especially from feudal and seigneural lords long accustomed to dealing with property disputes in their own courts. Insisting that no person should lose property unjustly, the kings declared that dissatisfied litigants could purchase *writs* ordering a royal inquiry into their cases. The fertile minds of the royal lawyers soon devised writs that applied to almost every conceivable kind of property dispute. In effect, purchasing a writ amounted to transferring a civil dispute from baronial or manorial courts to royal courts.

To encourage the use of royal courts, important innovations were made to ensure speedier and more efficient judicial processes: regularly scheduled court sessions, clearly fixed court fees, utilization of trained judges, uniform punishments. Most significant in this respect was the introduction of the *jury system*. For a long time English kings and their officials had been summoning groups of their subjects to tell under oath what they knew about some matter of public interest. After 1164 Henry II applied this idea to criminal cases. Sheriffs were ordered to summon in local areas within their shires a *presentment* or *grand jury,* made up of knowledgeable local residents who were required under oath to produce evidence about crimes committed in that area. On the basis of the evidence produced by these jurors, the sheriffs could proceed to bring suspected criminals to trial. By the thirteenth century, comparable groups of men known as *petit* (little) *juries* began to be used to decide on the basis of evidence presented before them the guilt or innocence of those accused of violating the law. The jury system quickly proved superior to traditional practices, which relied on trial by ordeal or by compurgation to ascertain God's will in proving guilt or innocence (see Chapter 13).

As the Norman-Angevin kings shaped a strong monarchical government, they had to concern themselves with their relationships with the Church. In general, the English kings managed the problem in a way that reinforced their authority. William I set the pattern by richly endowing the Church and supporting its reforming efforts while insisting on royal control of ecclesiastical offices and of a portion of the Church's wealth. During the reign of William II, the Church, led by Anselm, archbishop of Canterbury, challenged the monarchy's right to appoint church officials. This struggle was resolved by the Compromise of Bec in 1107, which allowed the Church to elect its own officials but gave the king the privilege of investing these officials with their lands. A more serious struggle arose in 1164 when Henry II issued the Constitutions of Clarendon, which ordered that clergymen accused of crimes be tried in royal instead of ecclesiastical courts. A one-time loyal servant of Henry II, Thomas à Becket, then archbishop of Canterbury, resisted with great vigor this attack on what he considered the Church's liberty. For his efforts he was murdered under circumstances that made it seem that the much-

FIGURE 20.2 Murder in the Cathedral: The Making of a Martyr This manuscript illustration shows agents of King Henry II murdering Archbishop Thomas à Becket in the cathedral at Canterbury. (The Walters Art Gallery, Baltimore)

provoked king was responsible. Thomas' martyrdom forced the king to concede considerable freedom to the Church in judicial matters (see Figure 20.2). On the whole, however, the English kings exercised a powerful control over the Church, and the Church gave its support to the strengthening of monarchy. Unlike the Holy Roman Empire, England was spared the disruptive impact of the investiture struggle.

3. ENGLAND: LIMITING ROYAL POWER, 1199–1307

During the twelfth century the rapid, aggressive expansion of royal authority generated surprisingly little resistance. During the thirteenth century, however, the kings met more formidable opposition. Nobles, clergy, and the rising bourgeoisie joined hands to compel the kings to recognize a principle inherent in the feudal order: that lordship—even royal lordship—was limited by the "law" of the feudal contract.

The conflict broke into the open during the reign of John (1199–1216). Politically able, although devious and rash, John brought part of his trouble on himself by making inordinate fiscal demands on his subjects. He also had the misfortune of having as his adversaries two of the most formidable personalities in medieval history, King Philip Augustus of France and Pope Innocent III. Philip captured a considerable part of the French territories under English control in a war that required John to impose a heavy burden of service and taxation on his subjects in a losing cause. John also became embroiled in a clash with Innocent III over the appointment of the archbishop of Canterbury. Again he lost and was forced to acknowledge that he was a vassal of the pope, holding England as a fief.

These rebuffs, coupled with a series of tyrannical acts by John, resulted in a great meeting of powerful nobles and clergy called in 1214 to organize a rebellion. It was led by Stephen Langton, the archbishop of Canterbury whom John had once tried to keep from office. John extricated himself from this grave danger by signing the Magna Carta in 1215. Endlessly celebrated by later generations as a charter of liberty, the Magna Carta basically affirmed the traditional privileges of nobles, clergy, and townspeople. The king promised to limit the extension of royal authority in certain areas, chiefly taxation, the administration of justice, and landholding. The charter was therefore conservative, seeking to curb unlimited expansion of royal power. Its framers had no thought of destroying effective royal government or of making all people equal. They insisted on the principle that certain of the king's subjects had rights, defined by law, custom, and contract, which the king must respect.

John's concession in no way resolved the clash between the king and the privileged over the extent and limits of royal power. It continued throughout the long reign of his weak, extravagant, foolish son, Henry III (1216–1272). Henry III caused problems for himself by spurning the advice of his own barons in favor of foreign advisers, making outlandish concessions to the papacy, and pursuing costly but futile foreign military adventures. The exasperated nobles resisted him in a variety of ways: forcing him to reissue the Magna Carta, using their influence to compel him to dismiss his foreign advisers, and forming a council of nobles to reform and supervise the operation of royal government. When these efforts failed, they resorted to a major uprising in 1264–1265 led by Simon de Montfort. The rebels won the upper hand temporarily and de Montfort summoned the nobles, the clergy, and representatives from the towns and shires to a *Parliament* that sought to establish control over the monarchy. This effort was thwarted by the inability of the rebels to agree and by the actions of Henry's son, Edward, who mustered royal arms and crushed the rebels.

The astute, capable Edward I (1272–1307) saw that few of the nobles who had opposed John and Henry III wished to end strong monarchy or destroy its institutions. In fact, during the troubled times of John and Henry III these institutions had continued to develop in complexity and effectiveness. The expansion of royal power was not the issue; the protest was against the misuse of royal authority and the abuse of ancient rights. More significantly, Edward recognized that a *community of the realm* had begun to emerge, consisting of great barons, lesser nobles, clergy, and townspeople, all of whom felt a common interest in the political affairs of England as a nation. This feeling led them to act together in confronting the royal government and to transcend on occasion the narrow confines of feudal contracts, ecclesiastical privileges, and town charters. This communal effort provided the basis for an emerging English national spirit and for new political institutions through which the community of the realm could find expression.

Edward I's reign represented an attempt to

strengthen the central government by taking these views into account. He first took steps to remove complaints that the nobles, clergy, and townspeople had raised about the administrative and judicial systems. Second, a series of fundamental laws was enacted, defining more clearly the rights and powers of the crown and how these should be exercised. In general, this legislation further limited the power of feudal lords and the Church while expanding that of the king and his courts, but Edward's political skill usually disarmed protests before they became dangerous.

Edward's chief means of avoiding opposition was the regular use of Parliament. Advisory bodies, such as the Witan and the Curia Regis, had long played a part in English political life but within a narrow framework of feudal practices. Simon de Montfort's Parliament of 1265 was a new kind of structure, joining representatives of the shires and towns to the feudal barons and clergy to create a body claiming to direct the affairs of the realm. Edward I clearly sanctioned this precedent in his Model Parliament of 1295. He commanded that each county and town select two representatives to Parliament to take counsel with the barons and ecclesiastical lords. The Parliament was soon accepted as a body with power to represent the interests of England's free population and as a place where these interests could voice their concerns about the state of the realm. Edward called Parliament primarily to serve his own purposes—especially to get extra money or to gain approval of some piece of legislation. Meetings of Parliament also served important judicial functions, so that the institution came to be viewed as the highest court in the land. Finally, Parliament provided an institutional setting where complaints against the royal government could be voiced and suggestions for change proposed; from these pleas emerged the right of Parliament to initiate legislation binding on the king and the entire realm. For at least another century Parliament's organization was vague and its powers not clearly defined. Its importance lay in Edward's recognition that the king had to listen to the demands of his subjects and his willingness to promote an institution that gave them a voice in government in a way that strengthened the emerging political community under an effective royal government.

4. FRANCE: FOUNDATIONS OF ROYAL POWER, 843–1180

The emergence of effective monarchy proceeded more slowly in France than in England and under different circumstances. Medieval France originated as the kingdom of the West Franks, a subdivision of the Carolingian Empire created by the Treaty of Verdun in 843 (see p. 221 and Map 16.2). Except for brief intervals, the Carolingian family held the crown of this kingdom until 987. During that period royal power steadily declined. The kingdom was fragmented into numerous small principalities controlled by feudal lords. These powerful figures recognized the weak kings as their feudal overlords but seldom rendered any services as vassals. The great fiefs that they had been granted became hereditary possessions virtually immune from royal control.

In 987 the French nobles and clergy finally ended the Carolingian dynasty by electing as their king one of the chief feudal lords in the kingdom, Hugh Capet, count of Paris. Hugh's descendants, called the Capetians, held the throne without interruption until 1328. The first four Capetians, who ruled from 987 to 1108, exercised almost no power outside their own royal domain, a modest but strategically well-located territory around Paris known as the Ile de France (the area shown on Map 20.1 as the royal domain in 987). Even there royal authority and resources were constantly threatened by unruly vassals. Throughout the rest of the kingdom powerful royal vassals did as they pleased in their principalities, many of which were larger and richer than the royal domain. The first Capetians did manage to establish an hereditary claim to the throne and to retain the support of the Church. And with the help of churchmen, they did maintain the important fiction inherited from the Carolingian world that the royal office was surrounded by a sacral quality and that its occupant was supreme feudal suzerain.

Between 987 and 1108 the history of France must be told in terms of the history of each of its many principalities (see Map 20.1). Most of them had been Carolingian administrative districts granted to dukes, counts, and viscounts in return for public service. These royal vassals made their fiefs hereditary and used their public authority to establish private lordships. Most of them subinfeudated their fiefs to surround themselves with supportive vassals owing feudal obligations. In many cases these secondary vassals carved out for themselves territorial enclaves, called castellanies, over which they exercised a private jurisdiction at the expense of their lords.

During the eleventh century the long process of political fragmentation slowed markedly, but not as a result of royal action. The change stemmed from the successful efforts of dukes, counts, viscounts, and castellans to establish effective lordship over their vassals. These lords, many of them royal vassals, brought order to their principalities primarily by a rigorous assertion of their rights as feudal lords. They shaped institutions that permitted them to amass sufficient military strength and fiscal resources to compel the obedience of their noble and servile dependents, to assume control over the administration of justice, and to command the support of the local ecclesiastical establishment. This local consolidation was most notable in the great royal fiefs of northern France, especially in Normandy, Flanders, Anjou, Maine, Champagne, Burgundy, and Blois. The effectiveness of such lords was exemplified by William, duke of Normandy, who was able to muster resources that permitted him to conquer England. In southern France, where feudal usages had developed more slowly, the great royal fiefs such as Aquitaine, Gascony, and Toulouse remained more fragmented; numerous petty princes paid little heed to the counts and dukes who claimed lordship over them. The kings of France played almost no role in this process of local consolidation. They were fully occupied with ruling their limited royal domain. Only rarely and seldom in any decisive way did they assert their rights over their powerful vassals whose power was increasing as a result of their expanding control over their fiefs. But neither did the kings surrender their rights.

As the twelfth century opened the position of the Capetians began to improve. Beginning with Louis VI (1108–1137), the king undertook to do what many of his vassals had already done—establish effective control over the royal domain. Louis patiently set about forcing his vassals in the royal domain to end their lawlessness, and he created an administrative machinery that allowed him to collect the dues owed the king as their overlord. His control over the royal domain provided him with sufficient resources to expand his role in the affairs of his vassals outside the Ile de France. With increasing frequency he acted as judge in disputes involving his vassals, protected weaker ones against stronger, influenced the succession to fiefs held from the king, and added small territories to his royal domain by asserting his rights under feudal law. Illustrative of his expanding strength was the decision of the dying duke of Aquitaine to entrust his daughter and heiress, Eleanor, to the protection of his overlord, the king of France. Louis VI promptly arranged for the marriage of his ward to his own son, thereby setting the stage for the annexation of Aquitaine to the royal domain.

The modest progress made by Louis VI in expanding royal influence led to a crisis in Capetian history under the reign of his successor, Louis VII (1137–1180). Thanks to the work of his father's administrators, especially the able and devoted Suger, abbot of the royal monastery of St. Denis, Louis VII maintained a firm hold on the royal domain. But beyond the royal domain, the king fared badly. He proved incapable of controlling Aquitaine, where local lords continued to act in defiance of the king's authority. Louis VII's participation as a leader in the Second Crusade not only won him no glory but also cost him a wife and her dowry. The attractive Eleanor accompanied him on that venture and was rumored to have dallied with some of the more attractive knights in the crusading army, including her uncle. This scandal was too much for the pious Louis. Moreover, Eleanor had produced no son to assure the survival of the Capetian dynasty. Perhaps Eleanor, a patroness of troubadour poets and a devotee of the ideals of courtly love, had also had enough; she is alleged to have said that she discovered she had married a monk instead of a king. In any case, Louis arranged to have the marriage dissolved; one price for this act was the surrender of his wife's dowry, the duchy of Aquitaine.

The hapless king's major difficulty, however, did not stem from his political and marital ineptitude. During his reign an unusual sequence of events unfolded to create what historians call the

Angevin "empire," which consisted of several major royal fiefs in France joined together in the hands of a single vassal of the French king. The original architects of this unusual conglomeration were the counts of Anjou, who were important royal vassals. Through an intricate process involving acquisition of fiefs, conquest, and marriage alliances, the lords of Anjou managed to establish control over a substantial territory, including Normandy, Anjou, Brittany, Maine, and the Touraine (see Map 20.1). In 1151 that territory was inherited by a certain Henry, who the next year married the recently divorced Eleanor and acquired Aquitaine as her dowry. For all of these territories, Henry was vassal of Louis VII. Then in 1154, the already well-endowed Angevin became Henry II, king of England. Obviously, his "empire" provided him with resources far exceeding those of his lord, the king of France. In fact, the very survival of the French monarchy was in question, its future put to the test by a development that could only occur in the feudal world.

5. FRANCE: THE CONSOLIDATION OF ROYAL POWER, 1180–1328

The response of the Capetians to the challenge posed by the Angevin "empire" led to the rapid expansion of royal power. The decisive turn of events came during the reign of Philip II Augustus (1180–1223), who over a long period bent every effort to destroy Angevin power in his realm. During the first two decades of his reign, he maneuvered skillfully to thwart the efforts of his vassals, Henry II and Richard I, to solidify their hold on their continental territories. With the accession of John came the opportunity to move decisively. As we have already seen, John was beset by serious challenges in England that weakened his position. His tyrannical conduct alienated many of his vassals in France, causing them to turn to his overlord for justice and protection. When John refused to appear before Philip to be judged in a case that involved John's taking as a wife a princess already betrothed to one of his vassals, Philip pronounced him an unfaithful vassal and in accordance with feudal law confiscated his fiefs. By force of arms the French king annexed Normandy, Anjou,

Maine, the Touraine, and parts of northern Aquitaine to the royal domain. Philip's control of these key territories was assured by a victory in 1214 at the Battle of Bouvines, where he crushed the forces of John and his Welf allies from the Holy Roman Empire. As master of a greatly enlarged royal domain, made up of principalities well organized by their former feudal overlords, Philip finally had the resources needed to assure his supremacy over any of his vassals.

Philip II's successors continued to follow his policy of extending the royal domain (see Map 20.1), a task made easier by the resources available from his victory over the Angevins. The kings employed a variety of means to claim territory: marriage alliances that permitted the Capetian family to inherit fiefs; confiscation of fiefs held by vassals judged unfaithful; purchase; escheat of fiefs held by vassals who died without heirs. A major addition to the royal domain, the county of Toulouse, resulted from the leadership by Philip II and Louis VIII (1223–1226) of a Church-sponsored crusade against the heretical Albigensians in southern France (see p. 301). The English sought to thwart the expansion of the royal domain and reclaim the fiefs lost to Philip II, but finally in 1259 they agreed to a treaty giving up their claims in France except for a small territory in Gascony. By 1328 a large part of France had been consolidated under direct royal rule; a kingdom of France had become a reality.

The later Capetians, especially Philip II, Louis IX (1226–1270), and Philip IV (1285–1314), worked vigorously to develop political institutions that would allow them to govern their expanding holdings effectively. They constantly enlarged the definition of their royal authority, combining concepts drawn from feudalism, Roman law, and Christian political ideology. To exercise these enlarged powers, they adapted and expanded primitive institutions inherited from the early Capetians: the Curia Regis, a court of the king's vassals; the royal household (*hôtel*), made up of officials who cared for the personal needs of the royal family; and the *provosts,* agents who managed the royal estates.

One major accomplishment of these kings was the development of a central administration located at Paris and capable of guarding the royal interests throughout the expanding domain. The Curia Regis and the royal household were gradually merged to constitute a single judicial and administrative body, which was charged with an ever-greater range of responsibilities. Originally the jurisdiction claimed by the central government was derived chiefly from the king's power as feudal lord, but by mid–thirteenth century kings were issuing ordinances to extend royal jurisdiction. The original small body of vassals and household officials serving the central government was greatly expanded by the addition of full-time, salaried administrators, many of them lawyers. During the reigns of Louis IX and Philip IV, the Curia Regis began to divide into specialized departments: the *conseil*, a small group of royal advisers; the *parlement de Paris*, concerned with administering royal justice; the *chambre des comptes*, which handled financial matters; a *chancery*, charged with producing royal orders and keeping records. Lawyers associated with the central government began efforts to establish a unified body of law, a formidable task as a result of the diverse customs that had emerged in the feudal principalities. By the reign of Philip IV the central administration of the kingdom had become a fully professionalized body of officials completely devoted to enhancing royal power and capable of asserting a collective force that guaranteed obedience to the royal will.

As the royal domain grew, the kings were faced with the monumental task of devising a system of local government. Unlike the situation in England, where kings were served by the ancient system of shires and sheriffs, local government in France had long been monopolized by feudal and manorial lords. Philip II attacked this problem by creating special officials known as *baillis* (bailiffs), whose numbers and powers were increased by his successors. Usually selected from nonnoble personnel of the royal court, these salaried officials were assigned to specific territories within the royal domain to hold courts, collect taxes, and keep order in the name of the king. Louis IX established special officers called *enquêteurs* (investigators) to check on the conduct of the bailiffs and to report misdeeds to the central government. Although the local nobility continued to perform many political functions, the bailiffs, acting in the name of the kings, steadily assumed political functions once monopolized by feudal and seigneurial lords.

The broadening range of royal activities, especially the waging of war and supporting the expanding royal administration, placed a heavy financial burden on the kings. A significant part of royal income continued to be derived from royal lands, but other sources of revenue had to be found. Aside from feudal dues, fines, and fees for royal services, the royal government had few sources of regular income. As a result, the kings often had to resort to arbitrary exactions from any source possible: towns, the Church, Jews, foreign bankers and merchants, nobles who fell out of royal favor. Especially during the reign of Philip IV, the measures used to satisfy the ravenous royal appetite for money produced complaints of royal tyranny and aroused resistance in many circles.

In the early fourteenth century, the Capetians instituted another practice that strengthened their authority. Expanding on the feudal practice of seeking counsel by calling their vassals to the Curia Regis, they began to summon representatives of the three major social groupings (*estates*)— the nobles, the clergy, and the townsmen—to advise them and approve their policies. Philip IV convoked three of these *Estates General*. In each case the assembled representatives meekly did what the king wished. But their approval added tremendous weight to royal power by making it appear that the entire nation approved of royal action. The Estates General was much more a tool of the French monarchs than was the English Parliament, chiefly because the major power groups in France, especially the nobles, failed to develop a sense of shared interest in and concern for the affairs of the entire realm.

Throughout most of the long period during which the Capetians were consolidating their hold on France, they drew invaluable aid from the Church. The kings bestowed wealth on the Church, supported reform, took its side in the investiture struggle, and respected its liberties. In return, the Church supported the royal claims to greater power and lent its wealth and talent to royal service. This fruitful relationship did not end until the reign of Philip IV, who became embroiled in a bitter struggle with Pope Boniface VIII (1294–1303) over the extent of the king's power to tax

FIGURE 20.3 A Queen at Work This manuscript illustration shows Queen Blanche of Castile, wife of King Louis VIII (1223–1226), keeping close watch over the education of her son, King Louis IX (1226–1270). Even while she was asserting her role as a mother, she was acting as regent for a kingdom that Louis IX inherited when he was an infant. Her son became a great king and a saint. (Bibliothèque Nationale, Paris ms. fr. 5716)

church property and judge the clergy. As we shall see (Chapter 25), Philip IV won a stunning victory over the mighty head of Christendom, so long successful in thwarting the Holy Roman emperors. The explanation is clear: By the early fourteenth century the king of France possessed a power base that the pope could not dissolve by simple command.

The victory of Philip IV over Boniface VIII points to a final achievement of the Capetians: their ability to endow their royal office with an image that showed kingship at its best. The prestige of the Capetians is best exemplified by Louis IX, eventually recognized as a saint by the Church. In no small part because of his actual accomplishments, Louis was hailed in his own time as a lover of justice, true Christian, gallant knight, crusader, peacemaker, promoter of morality, ideal son, husband, and father—in short, the perfect prince (see Figures 20.3 and 21.1). Most of the Capetians shared at least some of the aura of superiority so generously heaped on Louis IX, proving them as skillful in fashioning an image as in shaping effective political institutions. That image did much to enhance their real power.

Thus between 1000 and 1300 political leaders in England and France had found a solution to a problem that had persisted since the dissolution of the Roman Empire—how to create a stable political order capable of binding men and women into a large-scale community that promoted common goals. These leaders achieved that end by exploiting rights and obligations implicit in the feudal system. However, in fashioning strong monarchies, they had learned to respect the rights of privileged groups—vassals, clergy, townspeo-ple—as partners in the tasks of government. Their accomplishment laid the basis for a notable insti-tution that would play a decisive role in the future of western Europe—the nation-state.

SUGGESTED READING

England

Christopher Brooke, *From Alfred to Henry III, 871–1272* (1961). A brief, well-written survey.

Frank Barlow, *The Feudal Kingdom of England, 1042–1216,* 3rd ed. (1972).

M. T. Clanchy, *England and Its Rulers, 1066–1272: Foreign Lordship and National Identity* (1983).

Fuller accounts stressing the evolution of political insti-tutions.

Doris M. Stenton, *English Society in the Early Middle Ages (1066–1307),* 4th ed. (1965). Particularly strong in re-lating economic, social, and cultural factors to polit-ical history.

R. Allen Brown, *The Normans and the Norman Conquest,* 2nd ed. (1985). Excellent treatment of Norman ex-pansionism and its impact.

W. L. Warren, *The Governance of Norman and Angevin England, 1050–1272* (1987). A fine synthesis.

G. O. Sayles, *Medieval Foundations of England,* 2nd ed., rev. (1964). A provocative interpretation of constitu-tional development.

France

Elizabeth M. Hallam, *Capetian France, 987–1328* (1980). A balanced survey.

Jean Dunbabin, *France in the Making 843–1180* (1985). Especially good in its treatment of France's princi-palities.

John W. Baldwin, *The Government of Philip Augustus: Foundations of French Royal Power in the Middle Ages* (1986). A massive work, but useful in understanding the building of royal power.

Biographies

David C. Douglas, *William the Conqueror: The Norman Impact Upon England* (1964).

W. L. Warren, *Henry II* (1973).

Amy Kelly, *Eleanor of Aquitaine and the Four Kings* (1950).

Frank Barlow, *Thomas Becket* (1986).

John Gillingham, *Richard the Lionheart* (1978).

W. L. Warren, *King John,* rev. ed. (1978).

John Chancellor, *The Life and Times of Edward I* (1981).

Margaret W. Labarge, *Saint Louis: Louix IX, Most Christian King of France* (1968).

CHAPTER 21
The Medieval Expansion of Europe

FIGURE 21.1 Departure on a Crusade This scene depicts King Louis IX of France leaving Paris on the Seventh Crusade. It captures some of the solemnity surrounding the crusading movement. With their eyes seemingly on their distant goal in the Holy Land, Louis and his knights depart without a look backward at the group of monks blessing them. (The British Museum)

The increasing material wealth and the more effective political organization of western Europe set the stage for a decisive change in the relationship between the West and the world beyond. Between 500 and 1000 western Europeans had been almost constantly on the defensive. After 1000 that situation was reversed. During the next three centuries they employed a variety of means to expand their sphere of influence over a wide area. These efforts marked the beginning of an outward thrust by western Europeans that would continue for centuries.

1. RELIGIOUS EXPANSION

Since its beginnings Christianity had been an expansionist religion. The missionary urge remained vigorous during the High Middle Ages. As a result, the Christian world was substantially enlarged.

A major area of expansion was in Scandinavia. While the first efforts to convert the Scandinavians began in the ninth century, the crucial era in the Christianization of Denmark, Norway, Sweden, and Iceland came in the late tenth and eleventh centuries. In most cases the conversion of the kings was the decisive event. The new Christian kings received assistance in their effort to convert their people from missionaries from the south, especially from England and Germany.

Meanwhile, Christianity was carried eastward into the Slavic world. In this area the major impetus for expansion was provided by the rulers of the Holy Roman Empire and their ambitious lay and ecclesiastical vassals. Beginning in the late tenth century, the Bohemians, Poles, and Hungarians were gathered into the Roman Catholic fold. Somewhat later and again with German support, the religious frontier was advanced along the Baltic to convert the Wends, the Prussians, the Finns, the Livonians, and the Lithuanians. During this same period missionary forces from the Byzantine Empire were spreading Christianity among the eastern Slavs, especially the Russians.

During the thirteenth century missionaries from the West made efforts to win converts among the Moslems of North Africa and the Near East, and some even ventured as far afield as the Mongol Empire and China. Although these ventures produced no significant results, they opened vast new prospects for the future.

Wherever the missionary effort succeeded—Scandinavia, central Europe, Iceland, the Baltic area—the newly established Church introduced its new converts to many aspects of western European culture. As a consequence, the lives of people in these areas were decisively changed; they were "westernized" in terms of their institutions and their way of thinking.

2. COLONIZATION AND COMMERCIAL EXPANSION

The western Europeans who thrust outward with the cross were often accompanied—and sometimes led—by others driven beyond Europe's boundaries primarily by economic interests. As we have already seen, one of the great accomplishments of western Europeans during the era from 1000 to 1300 was the opening and colonization of an extensive agricultural frontier on the eastern fringes of Europe—in today's terms, a territory comprising northern Poland, most of East Germany, large areas of Czechoslovakia, and Austria. This Germanic "drive to the East" had the support of the Holy Roman emperors and of the Church, but mainly it was carried out by landowners and peasants seeking new lands to exploit. Their occupation of this frontier zone was accompanied by the implantation of western European institutions.

Likewise, between 1000 and 1300 merchants reached beyond Europe to establish the western European presence in a much larger world (see Map 18.1). Italian merchants wrested control of the Mediterranean seaways from the Byzantines and the Moslems and established trading posts in Constantinople and several Moslem seaports in Syria, Egypt, and North Africa. Northern Europeans, spearheaded by the Vikings, established settlements at Novgorod, Smolensk, and Kiev; from these emerged the Kievan principality that constituted the first effective state in Russia. Scandinavian raiders also settled Iceland and drew it into the European world. After the armies of the Fourth Crusade conquered Constantinople in

1204, western European merchants established bridgeheads around the Black Sea, which opened access to the cities of Central Asia and China. Italian traders roamed across the Asian world, reaping rich profits and reporting the potential of that vast area in travel accounts such as that composed in the late 1200s by the Venetian Marco Polo. A few bold Europeans were finding their way toward the waterways leading to India and the Indies. Simultaneously, Western seafarers were pushing southward along Africa's west coast, drawn chiefly by the fame of the gold mines of Senegal.

3. MILITARY EXPANSION IN SPAIN AND SOUTHERN ITALY

The most spectacular form of expansion during the High Middle Ages was military conquest. Europeans were impelled by a variety of motives: land hunger, quest for markets, adventure, religious zeal. Military expansionism manifested itself around the whole rim of the European heartland, but the thrust was aimed primarily at Byzantium and Islam.

One of the most important areas of expansion was the Iberian peninsula. When the Moors (as Moslems are called in Spanish history) conquered the Iberian peninsula in the eighth century, they failed to subdue small pockets of Christians in the extreme northwestern part of the peninsula. In the late eighth and early ninth centuries the Carolingians created the Spanish March from territory won from the Moors in northeastern Spain. Prior to 1000 several petty states developed in these Christian enclaves—Leon, Castile, Navarre, Aragon, and Barcelona. In these states in the early eleventh century a drive to rewin Spain was generated—a thrust that turned into a war of liberation called the *Reconquista*. The disintegration in the early eleventh century of the once powerful caliphate of Cordoba and the emergence of numerous warring Moslem principalities made the task of the Christians easier. Given this opportunity, the militant Christians turned their energies to a common assault on the Moors, usually with the strong encouragement of the Church. Large numbers of Christian knights from outside Spain,

especially from France, joined the fray. A powerful religious spirit animated these warriors, as is illustrated by two great vernacular literary works written to celebrate the feats of Christian warriors against the Moorish infidels, the *Song of Roland* and *The Cid*. The first phase of the Reconquista culminated in 1085 with the capture of the key city of Toledo. With the aid of Berber reinforcements from northwest Africa, the Moors were able to halt the Christian advance temporarily and by the mid–twelfth century even threatened to reclaim territory lost to the Christians. Shortly thereafter the Christian offensive was renewed, culminating in 1212 at the battle of Las Navas de Tolosa, where the Christian forces won a decisive victory over the combined forces of the Spanish Moors and their Berber allies. By 1300 the Christians had occupied all of the peninsula except a small region in the south called Granada (see Map 21.1).

Three major Iberian kingdoms—Castile (to which Leon was joined), Aragon, and Portugal—grew out of the territory rewon from the Moslems during the Reconquista. Each developed its own system of government, although all had certain basic similarities. Monarchy was the basic institution, and the kings steadily gained prestige as a result of their leadership of the Reconquista and Church support of their cause. Newly conquered lands gave them a chance to settle people as farmers or town dwellers under conditions that allowed the king to retain his authority. These factors initially retarded the coming of the feudal system, but eventually, feudal practices not unlike those of the French did develop. Hereditary fiefs were granted to nobles in return for services, and some vassals gained a large degree of immunity from royal control. The kings also granted extensive privileges to Spanish towns, many of which continued to be populated by Moslem and Jewish communities. The Spanish monarchs sought to develop centralized administrations, well-organized financial systems, and effective courts. Several thirteenth-century kings of Aragon and Castile legislated extensively to define royal powers and appointed local officials, comparable to the French bailiffs, to represent them. Nobles and townspeople resisted the expansion of royal power and in the long run compelled kings to accept limitations on their authority. In each king-

Map 21.1 **CHRISTIAN EXPANSION IN IBERIA**
This map shows the progress made by Spanish Christian warriors in reconquering the Iberian peninsula from the Moors during the Middle Ages. Three major kingdoms emerged from the Christian victories—Aragon, Castile (to which Leon was joined), and Portugal.

dom there developed a *Cortes,* a representative body composed of nobles, ecclesiastical leaders, and townspeople with considerable power to limit royal decisions on a variety of matters, including taxation.

As the Spanish kingdoms ruled by feudal monarchs developed, society in each took on many features common to the rest of Christian western Europe. But Spanish society retained its unique features, which were by-products of the merging of Christian and Moslem institutions and ideas during the long period of the Reconquista. As a result, Spain played a special role in the medieval West as the channel through which many Moslem influences flowed into the mainstream of western European society.

Another area of European military expansion was southern Italy and Sicily. Norman warriors from northwest France were the aggressors here. They first came to southern Italy as adventurers who, in return for land, were willing to sell their military services to local rulers competing for

power. Especially anxious for their services were Byzantine officials, seeking desperately to retain control over the area in the name of the emperor in Constantinople. Soon, however, these resourceful warriors, constantly reinforced by new migrants from Normandy, succeeded in establishing dominance over their supposed masters. By mid–eleventh century the papacy legally recognized a Norman principality in southern Italy; in return, the Normans agreed to support the papacy in its struggle with the Holy Roman emperors. These same aggressive warriors then proceeded to snatch Sicily from the Moslems. In 1130 these aggressive feats were formally recognized when the papacy sanctioned the creation of the Kingdom of Sicily, embracing southern Italy and Sicily, with a prince of Norman descent, Roger II, recognized as king. A strong monarchy was soon shaped. It incorporated a mixture of northern European feudal, Byzantine, and Moslem practices. The Kingdom of Sicily passed into Hohenstaufen hands at the end of the twelfth century and reached its apogee under Frederick II (see Chapter 19). There-after, the kingdom began to decline, chiefly be-cause it became a pawn of outside powers. But it remained in western European hands, a prize of expansion.

4. MILITARY EXPANSION: THE CRUSADES

The most dramatic expansionist effort of the west-ern Europeans involved a succession of military campaigns directed toward the eastern Mediter-ranean world over the course of nearly two cen-turies. These campaigns, called the Crusades, were viewed by contemporaries as religious wars against Islam for control of the holy places where Christianity originated. However, as they pro-gressed, their objectives became more complex.

In part, the crusading movement began be-cause developments in the Near East offered west-ern Europeans opportunities and inducements. As early as the ninth century, the vast Abbasid cali-phate began to break up into independent cali-phates bitterly contending with one another for territory and for the right to represent the true version of Islam. The rivalry was especially keen in Syria and Palestine. The aggressive Shiite Fa-timid caliphate based in Egypt sought to absorb this area at the expense of the Sunnite Abbasids. The Byzantine Empire also had ambitions in this area, which it still claimed as part of the old Ro-man Empire. In its efforts to protect its claims and to bolster its declining strength, the Abbasid dy-nasty brought a vigorous new force into the pic-ture: the Seljuk Turks. They were a people of Asiatic origin who had entered the Eastern Mos-lem world in the tenth century, became converts to Islam, and used their military prowess to ex-pand their influence. By the mid–eleventh cen-tury, the Seljuks established their dominance over Bagdad and made the Abbasid caliphs their pup-pets. They then turned their energies westward in an effort to enlarge their sphere of influence. This thrust brought them into conflict with the Fatimids and the Byzantine Empire and made the eastern Mediterranean world a confusing battle-ground. The Turkish menace became especially critical in 1070 and 1071, when the Turks seized Jerusalem from the Fatimids and inflicted a crush-ing defeat on the Byzantines at the battle of Man-zikert (see below). In the midst of this confusion, local Moslem leaders established several small principalities in Syria and Palestine; they were willing to make any arrangements that would thwart the efforts of the major rivals to establish control over this crucial territory.

The Byzantine Empire was also undergoing a crisis in the eleventh century. Under the Mace-donian dynasty (867–1057) it had enjoyed its most glorious days. But after the death of the greatest emperor of this dynasty, Basil II (976–1025), inef-fectual rulers allowed the defense system to de-teriorate by failing to protect the free peasantry that constituted its backbone from increasing ex-ploitation by the aristocracy. The Normans wrested southern Italy from imperial control and posed a growing threat to imperial control in the Balkans. The Italian city-states, especially Venice, challenged Byzantine sea power. More seriously, in 1071 at the battle of Manzikert Byzantine forces suffered a crushing blow from the Seljuk Turks, who in succeeding years conquered most of Asia Minor. This deepening crisis finally produced an effective ruler, Alexius Comnenus (1081–1118). His most pressing problem was to recover Asia Minor. But Alexius needed military help. He be-gan to appeal to the pope and the princes of west-ern Europe, arguing for help against the aggres-sive infidels who threatened Christendom. The plight of the Byzantine Empire presented western-ers with fresh opportunities and inducements to become involved in the East.

Despite the volatile and inviting situation in the East, there would have been no crusading movement without the confluence of a variety of factors in the West. Increasing material wealth provided the means for more ambitious military undertakings, and the greater political order curbed local warfare and freed the war-loving ar-istocracy for foreign ventures. Changing patterns of landholding, which confined inheritance to eld-est sons, created a large pool of young warriors seeking new opportunities to make a fortune. The military potency of feudal society was being dem-onstrated by victories on the German, Spanish, and Italian frontiers. The Italian cities were eager to advance their commercial interests in the eastern Mediterranean. The long-standing religious animosity toward Islam was sharpened by the wars in Spain and Italy. The wave of religious reform sweeping over western Europe emphasized the idea that Christians must serve God by working collectively through outward, active demonstrations of their piety. One way in which that activist vision expressed itself was through an increasing interest in pilgrimages. Thousands of people joined organized voyages to holy places all over Europe and increasingly to the Holy Land, where they were sometimes victimized by warring Moslem factions. The religious revival had an especially important impact on the chivalric ideal. Increasingly, it emphasized the responsibility of the true warrior to devote his prowess to holy war that would promote the cause of the Church and scourge its enemies, especially the hated infidels.

It was the papacy that translated the opportunities emerging in the East and the forces of militancy surging through western European society into a specific form of military action. The key figure was Pope Urban II (1088–1099), who conceived and initially proclaimed the idea of organizing an armed pilgrimage of Christian warriors who would achieve a variety of ends for the good of the true faith. This army would respond to an appeal that Alexius Comnenus made to the pope in 1095 for aid in defending the Byzantine Empire against the Moslem Seljuk Turks. In return for this help Urban hoped to gain Byzantine recognition of papal supremacy over the whole Christian world, thus ending the schism that had occurred in 1054, when the pope and the patriarch excommunicated each other. Finally, this force, aided by the Byzantines, would crush the infidels and capture the holy places in the East as a supreme act of piety in the service of God.

In 1095, after discussing his idea with important ecclesiastical and lay leaders, Urban made public his plan for a crusade in a stirring speech delivered at Clermont in France before a large audience gathered for a church council. He called on Christian knights to put aside their petty quarrels and join forces under papal leadership in an attack on the Moslems that would save Christianity in the East and liberate the Holy Land. Urban proclaimed measures to protect the property and the families of those who were willing to take

up the cross and promised that each would be rewarded in heaven for fighting this holy war.

The pope's speech at Clermont was greeted with shouts that it was God's will to do what Urban asked. That enthusiasm was soon transmitted over much of Europe by preachers of the crusading ideal. A number of feudal potentates (but no kings) began gathering separate armies in various areas. Before these armies of knights could be organized, an undisciplined horde of peasants and artisans, stirred by the appeals of enthusiastic preachers, began what has been called the Peasants' Crusade. After savagely attacking Jewish communities in several German cities, this ragtag mob moved eastward down the Danube Valley and across Hungary and Bulgaria, causing havoc as it advanced. When it finally reached Constantinople, Emperor Alexius Comnenus quickly dispatched it to Asia Minor, where it was immediately annihilated by the Turks.

By the summer of 1096 four major armies of knights began to move toward the East by different routes (see Map 21.2). Their first goal was Constantinople, where they expected to unite their forces for the attack on the Turks and the march to Jerusalem. As the armies one by one reached Constantinople during the fall and winter, protracted negotiations were necessary. The leaders of the armies from the West had no common plan of action. Although Urban II had designated a distinguished bishop to direct the crusading effort, the doughty nobles leading the various armies were unwilling to accept direction. Alexius Comnenus had expected mercenary contingents that he could simply take into his pay and order to do what he wished; the armies now converging on his capital were anything but soldiers for hire. Thus, Alexius had to negotiate an agreement with each leader. Eventually, by means that increased the distrust of the proud crusaders for the "Greeks," Alexius persuaded each of the crusading leaders to swear a personal oath of allegiance to him and to promise to release to Byzantine control conquered territories that had previously belonged to the empire. In return, he promised to provide supplies and military support.

In the spring of 1097 the crusaders began their march across Asia Minor. One decisive battle at Dorylaeum brushed aside the modest resistance

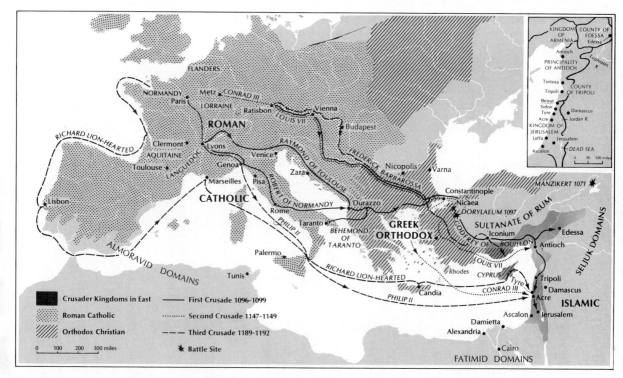

Map 21.2   THE EARLY CRUSADES   This map shows the major land and sea routes taken by various crusading armies during the First, Second, and Third crusades. The leaders of the major armies are also indicated. The distances involved in these military ventures suggest the challenges faced by the crusaders. The First Crusade established the Latin Kingdom of Jerusalem, far removed from where the armies started their trek. Most successive crusades were prompted by the need to defend that kingdom from the Moslem forces that surrounded it.

of the Turks, who were badly divided at the moment, and allowed the crusaders to pass on toward the Holy Land, paying little attention to Alexius' interest in liberating Asia Minor. Once in Syria, the armies began to split up, chiefly because their leaders were anxious to ensure their private fortunes. One group left the main body to establish control over Edessa and its surrounding territory. After the key city of Antioch had been captured in June 1098, a Norman prince, Bohemond, refused to leave it, claiming it as his by right of conquest. Not until July 1099 was Jerusalem captured by the remaining crusaders, who vented their fury by slaughtering hundreds of its inhabitants (see Figure 21.2). This great victory, a re-

markable feat considering how far the crusading armies had come and the severe tribulations they had faced for three years, made the First Crusade a success.

The crusaders disregarded both their pledge to Alexius to serve as his vassals and a papal plan to create a state subordinate to Rome. Instead, in 1100 they elected Baldwin of Flanders, a leading crusader who had established himself as count of Edessa, as king of the Latin Kingdom of Jerusalem. Baldwin retained a sizable territory around Jerusalem as the royal domain and granted out the territories of Edessa, Antioch, and Tripoli as fiefs to major crusading leaders, each of whom became his vassal. The princes acquired vassals of

FIGURE 21.2 The Capture of the Holy City, 1099 This manuscript illustration shows the crusaders making their final assault on Jerusalem in 1099 to mark the successful end of the First Crusade. Their victory ended with the slaughter of those shown defending the city. (Snark International/Art Resource)

their own, creating a typical western European feudal order. The king ruled this kingdom with the advice of his vassals, who met regularly at Jerusalem. A Latin patriarch of Jerusalem was installed, subordinating the Christian establishment to Roman authority. The native population was disturbed very little by the newcomers.

Once the Latin Kingdom of Jerusalem had been established, the defense of "Overseas" (*Outremer*, as western Europeans called their distant outpost) became a major problem. Almost immediately after the capture of Jerusalem, most of the knights from the West returned home, having fulfilled the vow they had taken to liberate the holy places. Those who stayed were few in the face of the Moslem forces whose lands they had occupied. These few took steps to protect themselves. With the aid of Italian navies they seized the chief Mediterranean seaports in Syria and Palestine; this success allowed the Latins to control the sea routes facing the Latin Kingdom, which was of decisive importance in holding their positions. They built a series of impregnable castles at strategic locations in the Holy Land. Before 1130 they established the two great crusading orders, the Knights Templar and the Knights Hospitaler; both were modeled on monastic organizations, but their members vowed to serve God by defending Christians living in and coming to the Holy Land. Later, a third such group, the Teutonic Knights, was established. Despite these measures the Christian position was always weak. That weakness repeatedly persuaded western Europeans over the next two centuries to go crusading as a way of serving God. Almost every year some western European knights at least temporarily lent their efforts to defending the Latin Kingdom. On occasion, especially at moments of crisis in the ongoing struggle, efforts were made in the West to organize more substantial forces to defend the holy places, thus permitting historians to speak of successive "crusades."

The Second Crusade (1147–1149) was prompted by the loss of Edessa in 1144 to the Turks. Papal appeals for action attracted two kings as its leaders: Conrad III, Holy Roman emperor, and Louis VII, king of France. Despite such prestigious leadership, the crusading armies were virtually destroyed by the Turks in Asia Minor. When the two rulers did arrive in the Holy Land with remnants of their forces, their misdirected military efforts aided little in the defense of the Latin Kingdom.

During the years following the Second Crusade, more effective leadership began to emerge in the Moslem world surrounding the Christian holdings. The most brilliant of these new leaders was Saladin, who joined the Moslem forces of Egypt and Syria into a powerful threat to the Latin Kingdom of Jerusalem. By 1187 he captured almost all the Christian holdings except Tyre, a few isolated castles, and the northern counties. When the news of this disaster reached the West, the pope called for a new crusade and received the promises of Henry II of England, Philip II of France, and Frederick Barbarossa of Germany to lead armies against Saladin. Frederick left first but was drowned en route. Henry II also died before he could begin his march; however, his successor, Richard the Lion-Hearted, stepped into his place. He and Philip, almost always at odds, made their way to the East by 1191. Philip was anxious to snatch away Richard's French possessions; therefore, he stayed on the scene only a minimum time. The colorful English king remained for over a year. After several inconclusive engagements with Saladin, Richard finally agreed to a truce that left Jerusalem in Moslem hands and allowed Christians to visit it. Aside from the return of a few

coastal cities to Latin control, the Third Crusade did little to improve the Christian position.

The Fourth Crusade, which in the eyes of many made a travesty of the crusading movement, was initially prompted by Pope Innocent III. However, the pope soon lost control over the forces that were raised. To ensure transportation to the East, the crusading leaders turned to the Venetians, who invested far more in ships to transport the crusaders than the disappointingly small crusading force was able to collect. To resolve this problem, the Venetians and the crusading leaders agreed to support a claimant to the Byzantine throne in return for trade concessions for Venice and money and troops for the crusaders to attack Egypt. But having ensconced the Byzantine ally in the imperial office, they found him unwilling or unable to deliver on his promises. The crusaders and the Venetians therefore decided to take Constantinople for themselves.

Their attack was successful; the city fell into Western hands in 1204 and was savagely pillaged. The crusaders immediately proclaimed a Latin Empire of Constantinople and elected a Flemish noble as emperor and a Venetian cleric as patriarch of the Greek Orthodox church, thus reuniting the Church for the moment. Somewhat reluctantly Innocent III gave his sanction to the whole arrangement. The crusading nobles immediately began to carve out rich fiefs for themselves. The Venetians, who assumed control over the chief port cities of the empire, were the real beneficiaries of the whole undertaking. The Latin Empire of Constantinople survived until 1261. Its history was mainly a story of the defense of the westerners against Greek forces whose leaders kept alive a legitimate Byzantine government in Asia Minor and fought valiantly to oust the usurpers.

After the Fourth Crusade, the crusading movement lost much of its appeal to Europeans. Innocent III organized a fifth crusade, but he died before it got underway in 1217. Its armies attacked Egypt and captured Damietta, a major Mediterranean port. The crusaders could have traded it for Jerusalem, but greed led them deeper into Egypt, where they were trapped by a Nile flood and destroyed by the Moslems.

Frederick II led the next crusade, chiefly because he wanted to secure possession of the Holy

Land, to which he had a legal right by virtue of his marriage to the heiress of the Latin Kingdom of Jerusalem. Frederick's crusade was fraught with difficulties from the very beginning. Because he refused to accept papal direction, he was in the bad graces of the papacy when he departed for the Holy Land. Once in the East, he chose to gain his ends by diplomacy rather than by the sword. In 1229 he signed a treaty with the Moslems that restored Jerusalem to the Latins and provided for a cessation of war between Christians and Moslems. This was a great victory, but the way it had been gained outraged many in the Christian West. When Frederick occupied Jerusalem, he was under a sentence of excommunication, and the city was immediately placed under papal interdict.

After this, the turmoil among the Christians in the Latin Kingdom of Jerusalem increased, making it more vulnerable; and in 1244 the Moslems again captured the Holy City. This loss prompted Louis IX of France to organize what amounted to the last major crusade (see Figure 21.1). He spent four years in the Holy Land, but his presence did little to strengthen the Christian position. In fact, his Egyptian campaign increased the danger by providing the opportunity for a strong, aggressive ruling dynasty, the Mamelukes, to establish itself in Egypt.

The increasing pressure on the Latin Kingdom of Jerusalem was relieved temporarily in the mid–thirteenth century when Christians and Moslems allied against the Mongol threat. Early in the century a great leader, Genghis Khan, had transformed the Mongol nomads of Central Asia into a potent military force that swept over Eurasia and fashioned a huge empire stretching from China to central Europe. The Mongol threat began to lessen after 1260, and the old hostilities between Moslems and Christians were renewed. In 1291 the Mamelukes took the last Christian strongholds in the Holy Land. After nearly two centuries, the Latins had finally been ousted from Syria and Palestine.

So ended the most overt and dramatic manifestation of medieval western European expansionism. However, the loss of Outremer should not detract from how significant that expansionism in all its various forms had been in changing the position of western Europe with respect to the rest of the world. Nor should it tempt us to minimize the importance of the crusading movement. Historians are not unanimous in their assessments of the consequences of the crusading movement, but they agree that at least in some respects the effects were enduring. The Crusades generated an interaction between East and West, which "educated" Europeans to new ideas, products, and styles of life. The ventures certainly extended and solidified western European commercial power. They decisively affected the histories of both the Byzantine Empire and the Moslem world, weakening the former and provoking the latter to a new aggressiveness that was to have a significant impact on Europe during the late Middle Ages and well into early modern times. Perhaps the most significant legacy of the crusading movement was the negative image of western Europeans it generated among people in the East: the greedy, faithless, crude warrior; the crafty, grasping merchant; the ambitious, worldly church official—all of whom would do anything to acquire land, wealth, and power. Such images poisoned East-West relationships for centuries.

SUGGESTED READING

Expansion in Spain, Southern Italy, and Sicily

Anwar G. Chejne, *Muslim Spain. Its History and Culture* (1974). A fine introduction to Muslim Spain.

Thomas F. Glick, *Islamic and Christian Spain in the Early Middle Ages* (1979). Treats the interaction of Islamic and Christian societies.

Angus MacKay, *Spain in the Middle Ages: From Frontier to Empire, 1000–1500* (1977). Traces the rise of the Christian kingdoms.

C. H. Haskins, *The Normans in European History* (1915). A classic.

Richard F. Cassady, *The Norman Achievements* (1986). A sound recent assessment of the role of the Normans in Europe.

The Crusades

Jonathan Riley-Smith, *What Were the Crusades?* (1977). A stimulating analysis of the nature of the crusading movement.

Carl Erdmann, *The Origin of the Idea of Crusade*, trans. Marshall W. Baldwin and Walter Goffart (1977). A fundamental work stressing ideological factors.

Jonathan Riley-Smith, *The First Crusade and the Idea of Crusading* (1986). A provocative study, challenging Erdmann's ideas.

Jonathan Riley-Smith, *The Crusades. A Short History* (1987).

Hans E. Mayer, *The Crusades*, trans. John Gillingham (1972).

Two fine short histories; perhaps the Riley-Smith work is better.

Erick Christiansen, *The Northern Crusades: The Baltic and the Catholic Frontier, 1100–1525* (1980). A full treatment of an overlooked aspect of medieval crusading.

Joshua Prawer, *The Crusaders' Kingdom: European Colonization in the Middle Ages* (1972). Portrays what happened to the Europeans in the Near Eastern environment.

Norman Daniel, *The Arabs and Medieval Europe*, 2nd ed. (1979). Treats European attitudes toward Islam.

Benjamin Z. Kedar, *Crusade and Mission: European Approaches Toward the Muslims* (1984). Examines the interactions between crusading and missionary concepts.

Michael Angold, *The Byzantine Empire, 1025–1204; A Political History* (1984). Will help the reader understand the Byzantine role in the Crusades.

Malcolm Cameron Lyons and D. E. P. Jackson, *Saladin: The Politics of the Holy War* (1982). A perceptive study of a great Moslem leader.

The works of Shaban and Kennedy cited in Chapter 14 are useful in portraying conditions in the Moslem world during the crusades.

Sources

James A. Brundage, ed., *The Crusades: A Documentary Survey* (1972).

Louise and Jonathan Riley-Smith, eds. and trans., *The Crusades: Idea and Reality, 1095–1274* (1981).

Two collections of materials throwing light on how contemporaries experienced the crusading movement.

CHAPTER 22

The Revival and Triumph of the Church

FIGURE 22.1 **The Last Judgment** This magnificent scene carved above the main portal of the west façade of the Gothic cathedral at Chartres illustrates a fundamental idea of medieval Christian teaching: the Last Judgment—when Christ will make a final determination of the eternal lot of all people. Christ is surrounded by symbols of his glory and by life-size representations of individuals who played a role in the unfolding of the Christian drama. The scene conveys a powerful message to the faithful who might stray into sin: The time is at hand to enter the church and partake of grace-giving sacraments so that one will be ready to receive Christ's approval at the final hour. (Scala/Art Resource)

Between 1000 and 1300 powerful religious movements surged through western European society to bring about changes that some refer to as a "reformation." The reform movement of the High Middle Ages was complex, involving diverse approaches to the structuring of Christian society and to the attainment of Christian perfection. It tested to the limits a variety of traditional assumptions about religion and society. It called forth a major intellectual effort seeking to discover in the rich Christian tradition guides that would help shape a fuller religious life. Its impact was felt at all levels of society. In its totality the reform movement represented the major force binding all Europeans into a unified civilization. Thus, in a real sense, the medieval reformation constitutes the central "event" in the history of the High Middle Ages.

1. ORIGINS OF THE REFORM MOVEMENT

As we have seen (see Chapter 17), religious life in western Europe reached a low ebb in the tenth century, chiefly as a result of the feudalization of the Church's property and its leadership. Even in the midst of that difficult time the signs of religious renewal began to appear. Its first manifestations came in the monastic world, which for centuries had served as a focal point for those intent on the quest for spiritual perfection. Especially important was the monastery of Cluny, founded in Burgundy in 910 by a pious lay prince (see p. 296). The new monastery was dedicated to strict observance of the Benedictine rule, to freeing the community from lay control, and to elevating the intensity with which God was worshiped. A succession of dedicated abbots worked diligently to spread the Cluniac model, so that by the early eleventh century Cluniac establishments existed all over Europe as centers of spiritual guidance. Monastic reform was not confined to the Cluniac movement. During the tenth century monastic reforms were initiated in Lotharingia, Italy, and England, each stressing various patterns of renewal: denial of the corrupt material world in favor of poverty; a search for moral perfection; a quest for a better understanding of the Christian heritage.

Many bishops sought ways to improve the moral condition of the lower clergy under their jurisdiction and to intensify the teaching of their flocks. Pious rulers, and especially their queens, began to patronize reform activities. Some feudal potentates gave generous support to reformed monastic houses, especially Cluniac establishments, attracted chiefly by the willingness of the monks to pray for their souls after death. Even the peasantry felt the pull of reform, chiefly by outcries against abuses and corruption.

At its beginnings in the late tenth and early eleventh centuries, the quest for spiritual renewal was diffuse, disorganized, lacking in specific direction, and even contradictory. Although elements of spontaneity continued to surround the reforming effort until well into the thirteenth century, from the early eleventh century onward certain major trends dominated the medieval "reformation." One of them, spearheaded by the Roman popes with the support of some secular rulers and the intellectual establishment, sought to establish the "liberty" of the Church, to perfect its organization, and to impose on the faithful a uniform discipline and doctrine. A second, focused chiefly in the monastic world but also drawing strength from intellectuals, constantly probed for deeper spirituality, for moral improvement, and for more meaningful ways of worshiping God. A third involved a vibrant upsurge of popular piety, seeking ways by which the poor and the meek might share the promises of Jesus. Although these major components of the reform movement constantly intersected and reinforced each other, an examination of each of them separately will provide the most effective means of comprehending the magnitude of religious ferment during the High Middle Ages.

2. PAPAL REFORM: ORGANIZATION AND UNIFORMITY

The medieval reformation was well under way before the papacy began to play a significant role in its progress. An ancient tradition, reinforced during the Carolingian Age, attributed to the bishops of Rome headship over the Christian community by virtue of Jesus' commission to Peter, the first bishop of Rome. But during the tenth and early eleventh centuries the papacy had become bogged down in corruption and was dominated first by Roman nobles and then the Holy Roman emperors. As a consequence, it earned little respect from the Christian community of western Europe. In fact, that community was fragmented into many churches, most of which were led by a feudalized clergy dominated by secular lords and concerned chiefly with issues of power and wealth.

The situation began to change in the middle of the eleventh century when a circle of radical reformers, led by Hildebrand, later Pope Gregory VII (1073–1085), established control over the papacy. These reformers were men of deep moral convictions and well schooled in the traditions of the Church. They were convinced that the moral degeneration afflicting the contemporary religious world could only be cured by the reassertion of the authority of the Church. As we have seen (see Chapter 19), the Gregorian reformers envisaged the Church as a visible earthly community charged with guiding the members of that community to salvation. They believed with a passion that the community needed its own head, its own laws, its own resources, and its own liberty. On the basis of the ancient Petrine theory, they claimed for the bishop of Rome the divinely sanctioned authority to head the Christian community as God's earthly vicar. Borrowing from patristic thought and the pronouncements of earlier popes, they argued that God entrusted to his vicar two kinds of divinely ordained power, spiritual and temporal. The pope held the spiritual sword but granted the temporal sword to lay princes to be used to repress evil forces that impeded the faithful from gaining God's favors on earth and from earning eternal salvation. He retained full authority to direct the use of the temporal sword by any prince and to withdraw it if spiritual needs so dictated.

As pope, Gregory VII acted to convert this ideology into a reform program that addressed what he perceived to be the evils of his day. He launched an effort to free the Church from lay control by prohibiting lay investiture of clergymen with their offices and lands, thereby opening a prolonged political struggle with the princes of western Europe, especially the Holy Roman emperors. He initiated a legislative program aimed at using papal authority to eliminate moral abuses among the clergy, especially the selling of church offices and services (simony) and clerical marriage. To ensure that these efforts at reform were observed, he charted a program aimed at centralizing ecclesiastical authority in papal hands. Even before his pontificate, the papal reformers had instituted the College of Cardinals as the body empowered to elect the pope, thereby putting the papal office beyond lay control. Gregory took important steps to make that body the nucleus of a papal administrative machine. Papal *decretals* (legislative enactments) were issued with increasing frequency, laying down regulations for church governance and clerical conduct. Papal legates were sent across Europe to enforce this legislation. The papacy encouraged regional church councils to enact measures aimed at correcting abuses wherever they existed in the Christian world. Provisions were made to expedite the appeal of difficult cases to Rome for settlement. Special attention was given to regularizing and increasing papal income so as to ensure independence of action.

Gregory VII did not live to see his program succeed, but it remained a blueprint for his successors. The consolidation of papal power met resistance from many quarters, particularly from bishops and princes, who rightly sensed that their ancient freedoms were threatened. But Gregory's successors pursued his policy of centralization with skill and persistence. Their efforts were abetted by the willingness of the popes to retreat from Gregory's radical position on the supremacy of ecclesiastical over secular power. This compromise led to extensive mutual support between Church and state in establishing a more effective ecclesiastical organization; many kings found such an organization useful in supporting their own efforts to curb stubborn nobles and towns. By the thirteenth century such popes as Innocent III (1198–1216), Honorius III (1216–1227), Gregory IX (1227–1241), and Innocent IV (1243–1254) presided over an immense organization capable of directing religious life all over western Europe in minute detail.

These thirteenth-century papal monarchs controlled an elaborate Church bureaucracy located in Rome and called collectively the papal *curia*. This body was divided into specialized departments dealing with finances, correspondence and records, judicial cases, doctrine, and the discipline of sinners. It was staffed by trained clerical specialists who made careers of papal administration. The College of Cardinals, made up of churchmen especially selected by the pope, sat with the pope in special meetings (called *consistories*) to formulate major policies; its members often served as heads of the specialized departments that handled routine administrative matters. From the curia flowed a steady stream of legislation touching on every conceivable aspect of religious life. The papal court system handled an ever-increasing volume of cases appealed to Rome from throughout Europe. The Roman curia extended its authority beyond Rome through a system of papal agents, called *legates*, sent from Rome to supervise the enactment of papal orders. Some legates resided for extended periods in specific areas, while others were commissioned to deal with a specific problem. The legatine system, coupled with the curia's extensive correspondence and judicial appeals to Rome, kept the popes well informed about local affairs throughout Europe. A huge and constantly increasing income—derived from papal property, gifts, fees for judicial services, payments for dispensations from papal regulations, and assessments levied on the lower clergy and the laity—sustained this huge organization.

Papal authority was extended downward through the age-old hierarchy of archbishops, bishops, and priests. By 1300 the exact functions of each level were carefully defined, and papal control over the election and supervision of archbishops and bishops was extensive. Each archbishop was entrusted with the supervision of several bishops in his *province*, and each bishop was empowered to direct the activities of the priests and the laity residing in his *diocese*. These officials headed a small-scale model of the papal curia, called a *cathedral chapter*, staffed by *canons* who had a voice in episcopal elections, advised their superior, and carried out provincial and diocesan administration. The administration included conducting judicial proceedings, collecting and dispensing revenues, managing episcopal property,

and supervising parish priests who were charged with ministering the sacraments and preaching to the Christian populace. One of the major accomplishments of the era was the establishment of a firm structure of local parishes across western Europe. For the most part, these territorial units, often coinciding with manors and agricultural villages or with specific quarters in urban centers, were freed from lay control over the appointment of priests and parish income and placed under episcopal direction. They provided a key element through which Christian teaching and practices could be extended to all people.

Although by 1300 some were beginning to think otherwise, the inspiration behind this effort at centralization was not merely a quest for power. Papal leaders and many of their episcopal subordinates genuinely believed that only through effective organization could the Christian flock be guided toward right behavior and right belief. As a consequence, a major aspect of the papal reform movement was an attempt to define and standardize church law and doctrine vital to the proper care of souls.

By the eleventh century the Church possessed an immense body of law derived from many sources: scriptural precedents, the writings of the early Church Fathers, the acts of a long succession of church councils, and the pronouncements of many popes and bishops (some of which were forged) on issues dealing with religious practices and discipline. Many of the provisions of this body of law were confused and contradictory, and some no longer applied to contemporary realities. Moreover, the issues posed by the reform movement demanded new legal solutions. These problems produced a new breed of specialists: trained lawyers working to create a consistent, organized body of law that would sustain the effort to create an independent religious community with its own rules. A decisive figure in the effort to create a "code" of law for the Church was Gratian. In 1140 he published his *Decretum*, which represented an effort to apply the rules of logic to the vast body of past precedents in a way that would remove contradictions and produce a consistent set of laws. Gratian's work immediately became the guide for Church administration and discipline. Among many other things, his code defined the powers of each rank of the clergy, the jurisdiction of ecclesiastical courts, crimes against the Church and their punishments, the proper use of Church income and property, and the manner of conducting religious ceremonies. Throughout the work ran one predominant idea—the supremacy of the papacy in the governance of the Church. Subsequent codifications that incorporated new legislation and extensive commentaries aimed at relating canon law to the real world greatly enriched the Church's law. By 1300 a powerful instrument for directing Christian society had been forged.

A comparable movement occurred in the field of doctrine. By 1000 the Church had accumulated a rich body of teachings defining right belief, but this material was disorganized and often contradictory. To cope with this problem, another kind of specialist, the trained theologian, emerged. Perhaps the decisive figure in developing systematic theology was a French schoolmaster, Peter Abelard (1079–1142). Calling attention to the conflicting teachings of Scripture, the Church Fathers, and tradition on certain doctrine questions, he urged that scholars apply human reason to resolve these differences. Most theologians adopted his approach, which came to be called Scholasticism. During the thirteenth century, a series of great theologians, the chief of whom was Thomas Aquinas, worked to systematize the Church's teachings and eliminated most of the earlier confusion. In the process, they tried to weave all human knowledge into a unified body consistent with revealed truth, giving the Church a single truth to teach to all.

Although the essence of Christian doctrine was stated in succinct form in the Nicene Creed, originally promulgated in 325, at the heart of the theological system of the twelfth and thirteenth centuries stood the doctrine of grace and the sacramental system. According to the theologians, God had created human beings in order that they might enjoy eternal salvation, human life being but a test of worthiness. Since humans were corrupted by original sin—the stain imposed on all by the disobedience of Adam and Eve—men and women needed God's grace to save them. That grace was bestowed through the sacraments instituted by Christ as an essential part of his mission of redemption (see Figure 22.2).

By the twelfth century the number of sacraments was set at seven; each drew its efficacy by virtue of the fact that it was administered by the Church, without whose services no Christian could expect to be saved. *Baptism,* usually administered at infancy, removed the stain of Original Sin and initiated its recipients into the Christian community; without it no Christian could be saved. *Confirmation,* usually received during the difficult years of adolescence, infused into Christians the Holy Ghost, strengthening their faith and fortifying them against the devil at a particularly critical moment. *Extreme unction,* administered to those in danger of death, strengthened them at the moment they must face the judgment of the Almighty and removed from their souls the stain of minor (or venial) sins. *Marriage* sanctified the wedded state and family life. *Holy orders,* or ordination, conferred on select Christians the priestly powers that permitted them to act as valid successors of Christ and the apostles in teaching the faith and administering the grace-giving sacraments, especially the Eucharist and penance. The *Eucharist* was the sacrament by which Christ himself was present to the faithful. Its exact nature was not defined until the Fourth Lateran Council in 1215, held under the direction of Innocent III, pronounced the doctrine of *transubstantiation:* When a priest consecrated bread and wine at Mass, their substance changed miraculously into the body and blood of Christ, although their external accidents (color, shape, taste, etc.) remained the same. Partaking of this sacrament—receiving Communion—infused the grace of Christ's substance into the soul. No punishment was more terrible than excommunication—being cut off from receiving the Eucharist. The last sacrament was *penance,* whereby Christians who confessed their sins to a priest and resolved not to repeat them received God's forgiveness, provided that they made some sacrifice or did some good work assigned by the priest. Since the stain of sin barred one from heaven, Christians constantly needed to resort to the confessional to ensure that their souls, freed from Original Sin by baptism, were constantly repurified by the removal of all stains caused by the sins they committed in the course of their lives. The Fourth Lateran Council decreed that the faithful must confess at least once a year.

FIGURE 22.2 The Sacraments These scenes from a fourteenth-century manuscript illustrate three of the seven sacraments—baptism, the Eucharist, and marriage. According to the Church's teaching, only through participation in the sacraments could a Christian gain salvation. (Bibliothèque Nationale, Paris, ms. n. s. fr. 4509)

Embroidered on the sacramental system was a rich array of Church-sanctioned practices and beliefs to facilitate the winning of God's favors. By the thirteenth century Christian life was surrounded by an array of prayers and ritual ceremonies that invoked God's help in every conceivable situation. Sacred objects, especially relics, available to almost every Christian possessed powers to draw God and the devout faithful together. An army of saints filled heaven to plead the cause of humanity with God and to assist in frustrating the hordes of devils that schemed under Satan's command to corrupt men and women. These adjuncts to the sacramental system were enlarged and enriched during the High Middle Ages, a process that added a powerful emotional dimension to the rather awesome concepts of the sacramental system.

The major fruits of papal reform—the centralized administrative system, the wide-ranging body of canon law, and the theological system making the Church essential to the salvation of all—permitted Church leaders to extend their influence far beyond the religious sphere. Nothing illustrates this influence better than the role played by Innocent III in European affairs. We need only recall how he manipulated affairs to make his ward, Frederick II, Holy Roman emperor. He took an active role in the complex political interactions involving the numerous Italian city-states. After a long quarrel he compelled Philip II of France to take back a wife he had repudiated. He forced or persuaded John of England and several other rulers to accept the status of vassal of the pope. Innocent was active in promoting the crusading movement. He was instrumental in organizing a crusade against the heretical Albigensians of southern France, thereby helping the French kings to expand their royal domain. Innocent's story was replicated in the careers of most thirteenth-century popes and, on a smaller scale, in those of countless bishops. In short, papal monarchs and their episcopal agents used religious weapons to gain political ends and political and economic pressures to advance ecclesiastical interests. They often summed up their authority by speaking of their God-given right to exercise "the fullness of power" over all Christians. By that they meant that they had the right to make the final decisions affecting any aspect of Christian society. While they conceded that lay leaders had the authority to direct worldly affairs, they claimed the ultimate authority to judge how well these authorities used their power to achieve Christian ends.

3. MONASTIC REFORM: SPIRITUAL SEEKING

While the quest for greater order in the organization of the Church and its law and theology was advanced by popes, bishops, canon lawyers, and theologians, others sought for deeper spiritual understanding. Although those promoting reform on the papal model were always concerned with spirituality, it was in the monastic world that the urge to deepen spiritual life was felt most strongly. Those interested in expanding spiritual horizons faced a religious mentality of limited dimension in the year 1000. Most believed in a God perceived as a stern judge whose wrath might fall on helpless, sin-tainted humans at any time and in any form (see Figure 22.1). Human life was surrounded by constant danger from the devil and his demons, present everywhere and armed with almost irresistible powers to entice men and women ever deeper into sin, for which God's anger would only be greater. The best humans could hope for was to do something that would be pleasing to God or that would persuade the legions of angels and saints who served the judgmental deity to intercede in their behalf. As a consequence, religious life was highly externalized. Men and women sought to propitiate God by offerings of their material goods, acts of charity, prayers, and veneration of relics of the saints. They searched for acts of penitence to win forgiveness for their sins—fasting, abstinence from fleshly pleasures, pilgrimages. Nothing brought greater comfort

than miracles whereby God or his agents overturned the natural order to cure sickness, turn sure defeat in war into victory, save the harvests, or confound the devil at the crucial moment when he was about to trap someone into sin.

The dominant monastic force during the tenth and eleventh centuries was the Cluniac movement. The Cluniacs reinforced the ancient ideal that God could be served best by a retreat to a cloistered stronghold. The movement sought to restore the primitive purity of the Benedictine rule as a means of ensuring that an elite would serve God well. The founder of Cluny, a pious French noble, freed it from lay control, and its first abbots sought successfully to extend its influence by founding dependent houses that took directions from the abbot of the mother house. In a spiritual sense, the Cluniac movement emphasized an elaborate daily round of prayer and celebration of sacred rites as the main duty of the monks. The Cluniac liturgy was a splendid model of externalized religion that the contemporary world found so attractive. Many feudal aristocrats established close ties with Cluniac communities, chiefly to gain assurance that the monastic congregations they supported would include them in their prayers for the dead. As sponsors of the Peace and the Truce of God, the Cluniac order made a notable contribution to curbing feudal warfare and promoting the concept of holy warfare as an act pleasing to God. And as promoters of the cult of saints and pilgrimages, the Cluniac monks provided an important outlet for the widespread urge for penitential actions pleasing to God.

By the end of the eleventh century the Cluniac movement began to lose its appeal. In part, this decreased interest was a consequence of the excessive wealth and the spiritual complacency of the Cluniac order. More important, spiritual seekers increasingly found the externalized forms of piety promoted by Cluny unduly limited and not attuned to changing concepts of the nature of God, of human capabilities, and of the needs of Christian society, especially as highlighted by the Gregorian reform. These views tempered God's harsh judgmental qualities with a new emphasis on his love for humanity (see Figure 22.3). They invited a search for the human capacity to absorb God's love internally and to progress toward perfection through human powers. They encouraged activities born of human love that promoted the welfare of earthly society.

The expanding confidence in the human capacity for personal perfection led to a revival of hermit life based on the model provided by the desert fathers of the fourth and fifth centuries. Many of the hermits of the eleventh and twelfth centuries pursued their search for perfection individually. However, the hermit ideal did produce the Carthusian order, established in France in the late eleventh century. Selecting the most unattractive sites for monastic houses and imposing a severe regimen of poverty, fasting, and prayer, the Carthusian order encouraged its members to strive for a spiritual condition that would open the human heart to divine love. The order impressed upon an admiring world a model of denial of self and of the world as a means of preparing to meet God.

The monastic movement that during the twelfth century played the most important role in shaping a new spiritual vision and in projecting it into the world was the Cistercian order. Founded in 1098 by a Benedictine who felt that the ancient rule was not being properly observed by the then-dominant Cluniacs, the Cistercian movement stressed the need for separation from the world and for an austere life of prayer and labor. Cistercian houses were usually established on remote, uncultivated sites; like other agricultural colonizers of the era, the Cistercian monks employed their labor and technical ingenuity to create thriving agricultural establishments. Cistercian houses, both male and female, soon sprang up all over Europe, held together by a unique provision in the Cistercian rule stating that policy and regulations for all houses would be decided by regular meetings of their heads.

Especially influential in shaping the Cistercian spiritual message was Bernard of Clairvaux, who viewed monastic life as a preparation for action in the cause of God. That preparation was aimed at the inner spiritual development of each individual monk rather than the elaborate, communally organized round of external religious acts that characterized Cluniac practice and that dominated the religious mentality of most contemporary Christians. Monks needed to practice physical depri-

Figure 22.3   A Loving, Caring God   This sculpture from Chartres Cathedral shows God creating Adam. This Creator is not the awful judge of the last day (see Figure 22.1). Rather, this scene reflects the new understanding of God that had such a powerful effect on the spirituality of the twelfth and thirteenth centuries. (Archives Photographiques, Paris)

vation, work, and prayer as a part of their spiritual training. Equally important was contemplation and devotion. Bernard's prescription for individual spiritual development focused attention on a loving God reaching out to unleash the potential of the human soul to participate in divinity. The human spirit could best reach back toward that God by contemplating the human, suffering Jesus and by seeking to share the feelings of Mary, Mother of God, of Jesus' disciples, and of those he taught as all of them lived in the presence of God made human for the salvation of other humans. Bernard was fully confident that the love and understanding flowing from such an approach to God would prepare human beings to go forth to fight sin and spiritual poverty without fear of corruption. In his own life he exemplified this new kind of spiritual activism. During his long career in the Cistercian order (1113–1153), he was involved in nearly every important event in Europe as a spiritual activist. He was the chief instigator of the Second Crusade, proclaiming that involvement was a manifestation of love for God and of service in the divine cause. He served the papacy doggedly in rooting out corruption in the clergy (he even censured papal conduct on occasion). He was a relentless foe of unorthodox and heretical thinking. He hounded Europe's kings constantly to improve their lives and their governments. He had no peer as a popular preacher and as a promoter of the use in the entire Church of the devotional practices that were at the heart of Cistercian spirituality. He and other Cistercians served as industrious soldiers of Christ whose chief armament was their sense of godliness derived from their inner spiritual life. Their target was the souls of men and women who possessed but did not properly use the power to make themselves better Christians.

Other developments in the monastic world of the twelfth century contributed to the deepening of religious life and the expansion of monastic influence on society. The number of monastic houses for women—nunneries—increased dramatically, usually governed by a version of the Benedictine or the Cistercian rule. These centers enlarged the visibility of women as models of piety and offered many of them opportunities for education and service. An order called the Augusti-

nian Canons was organized as a means of improving the moral quality of the clerics who served in cathedral chapters. Its rule bound the canons to poverty, prayer, and moral excellence while permitting them to continue their responsibilities as pastors and episcopal administrators. Perhaps the most unusual application of the monastic model was the establishment of the crusading orders—the Templars, the Hospitalers, and the Teutonic Knights. Following a model defined by Bernard of Clairvaux, those who entered these orders took a monastic vow stressing obedience, poverty, and service to God as warriors defending the Christians in the Holy Land. Their service earned these orders not only high respect but also immense wealth, which led to their involvement in landholding, commerce, and money lending.

The expansion of monastic involvement in the world and the monastic search for new spiritual horizons reached a culmination in the early thirteenth century with the establishment of the mendicant (begging) orders, the Dominicans and the Franciscans. These orders were a response to several problems that increasingly challenged the Church's traditional pastoral activities: the growth of urban life, with its unique institutions and tensions; the emergence of more sophisticated law and theology; the growing criticisms of the wealth and power of the ecclesiastical establishment; and doctrinal heresy. The mendicant movement sought to prepare pastors who could go forth into the world to address these problems without being burdened by material concerns or by the stigma of wealth—widely believed to be a barrier to spiritual perfection. To achieve this end, the mendicant orders insisted on absolute poverty after the model of Jesus and his disciples; neither the individual monk nor the corporate order was to possess wealth. Material support was to be derived from charity extended by those being served; begging for such charity was a key element of the vocation of the mendicants. Although the mendicants were mindful of the necessity of developing inner spiritual life, the range of problems they sought to address as pastors called for the development of intellectual skills. As a consequence, their preparation for active monastic life stressed education devoted to mastering the intricacies of canon law and theology and to developing skills needed for effective expression of the Church's teachings.

The Dominican order drew its name from its founder, a Spanish canon named Dominic (1170–1221). He was inspired to found a new order as a result of a tour through southern France, where the Albigensian heresy was rampant despite the efforts of the local bishops and Cistercian monks to curb it. Dominic became convinced that orthodoxy would prevail only if preachers learned in theology and free from all suspicion of wealth mingled intimately with the heretics to teach them the true faith. In 1215 Pope Innocent III authorized him to organize a new order dedicated to the destruction of heresy by preaching. The rule provided that Dominic's followers would commit themselves to complete poverty and to preaching; their collective activities would be directed by a master general and his subordinate priors who commanded the provinces into which the order was divided. The rule placed heavy stress on the education of each monk in theology and law. The Black Friars, or Friars Preachers, as the order came to be called, quickly established themselves as a major force across Europe, active in preaching and in controlling the formulation and teaching of theology in the universities. Their involvement in university education allowed them to play a major role in shaping the religious leadership of the entire Church during the thirteenth century.

The inspiration for the Franciscan order was supplied by one of the most appealing figures in all religious history, Francis of Assisi (1182–1226) (see Figure 22.4). The son of a wealthy Italian merchant, Francis, while still a young man who had previously enjoyed the pleasures of life, underwent a fundamental spiritual conversion that convinced him that he must imitate Christ in a most literal sense. As he put it, he married "Lady Poverty" and turned his energy to preaching and performing charitable works. He was especially charismatic as a preacher, exuding joy and a sympathy for all God's creatures, especially unfortunate, suffering human beings. To his followers, he was "God's own troubadour," filled with happiness and love. Almost immediately both men and women began to follow him. They surrendered their wealth, worked or begged for a livelihood, and preached a simple message of love for

FIGURE 22.4   Francis of Assisi: "God's Own Troubadour"   St. Francis of Assisi, portrayed here in a painting done by Cimabue ca. 1280, was perhaps the most powerful spiritual force in the thirteenth century. His ideas on poverty and love deeply affected many of those searching for religious values in his age. (Alinari/Art Resource)

God and humanity. In 1210 Francis asked Innocent III for permission to organize a formal religious order that would practice absolute poverty and dedicate its efforts to preaching and good works. Innocent hesitated, feeling that Francis' demands on his followers were too severe and perhaps concerned that the simple message of love and repentance would breed a crop of dissenters with little regard for the machinery that the organized Church supplied for saving souls. Finally, however, he consented. Between then and 1226, when Francis died, the order grew rapidly, spreading to nearly every part of western Europe and even beyond. As the order expanded, its governing rule was modified to provide a more structured organization and a discipline more formal than the founder's simple command that his followers imitate Jesus. The rule of absolute poverty was modified to allow the order to acquire wealth and to place greater emphasis on formal education as preparation for a preaching career. To many devoted Franciscans these compromises represented a denial of the Franciscan ideal; as a result of these concerns, the order was plagued by bitter internal conflicts. The Friars Minor, or Grey Friars, also met strong opposition from local clergy, who resented their exaltation of poverty and their effective skills as preachers and confessors. Despite these obstacles, the Franciscans asserted a powerful influence on religious life at all levels of society. Together, the Franciscans and the Dominicans became pillars of strength for the thirteenth-century Church in terms of propagating its teachings, containing voices of dissent, and expanding spiritual consciousness.

4. POPULAR REFORM: ENTHUSIASM, DISSENT, HERESY

The highly visible efforts of reformers to impose order on religious life and to expand spiritual visions were accompanied by considerable religious ferment among people of modest social status. Reform of this kind manifested itself in the activities of diverse peoples: simple priests, maverick monks, peasants, merchants, artisans, women, even children. What motivated their efforts at religious renewal are difficult to discern. Perhaps they were stimulated by a deeper understanding of the Christian message brought to them by the priests and monks produced by the papal and monastic reform movements. Perhaps they were introduced to new religious ideas by the slowly expanding number of literate laypersons, especially in towns, who were able to explore sacred literature and articulate their own interpretation of its meaning. The social and economic changes affecting society at all levels created new pressures that provoked a rethinking of traditional religious values. In reviewing the evidence, one suspects that many simple, uneducated, illiterate people were able to extract from their limited knowledge of God's ways and of Jesus' message fresh religious insights that made their lives more mean-

ingful. Whatever the source, there can be no question that the period 1000 to 1300 witnessed significant religious stirrings throughout the population.

One manifestation of popular religious ferment was the enthusiastic response of simple people to externalized cult practices aimed at seeking God's favor and doing penance for sins. Such people eagerly participated in the cult of relics and the veneration of saints. Simple people participated in pilgrimages to holy places, whether the holy place be a shrine located a few miles away or the scene of Jesus' earthly life in distant Palestine. The infamous Peasants' Crusade reflects the fervor aroused in the popular mind by the crusading movement; even more bizarre was the Children's Crusade of 1212 during which several thousand children were organized for an expedition to the Holy Land and proceeded as far as Marseilles in southern France before less pious merchants sold them into slavery.

Another fairly frequent manifestation of popular religious enthusiasm was the response given to charismatic preachers, who some credit with laying the groundwork for a Christian evangelical movement. Building their message around Jesus' poverty, humility, and love, these preachers often established bands of followers who shared their wealth, engaged in works of charity, cared for the sick, and worshiped in unique ways that emphasized emotion and intimate companionship. Some of these leaders spiced their exhortations to live like Jesus and his apostles with passionate attacks on the moral flabbiness of the clergy and the wealth of the contemporary Church, thus making anticlericalism a regular part of popular religious reform. On occasions, this anticlericalism led to overt action against the established clergy. For instance, in 1145 an Italian monk, Arnold of Brescia, so aroused the populace of Rome against the wealth and secular power of the papacy that the pope was forced to flee and only succeeded in recapturing control of the city by calling upon Frederick Barbarossa to use force to capture and execute Arnold.

On occasion such popular reform efforts extended beyond what the Church and secular authorities would tolerate as dissent and became heresy. Such was the fate of the Waldensian movement. This group was inspired by Peter Waldo, a rich merchant from Lyons in France. In 1173 he gave away his wealth and took up a life of poverty in imitation of Christ—much as Francis of Assisi would do later. Soon after he began his preaching, Peter went in person to Rome to seek papal permission to establish a monastic order based on poverty. The pope denied him permission to continue his work. Disregarding this prohibition, the group continued, gradually becoming more radical. Practicing poverty and a strict moral life reflecting many Cistercian ideas about sobriety, temperance, and simplicity, Waldensian leaders went among the common people, especially in urban centers, preaching and praying in the vernacular language. They condemned the clergy, arguing that all Christians could serve a priestly function, and denied the need of the sacraments in gaining salvation. They developed their own ministers and their own ritual practices. Eventually they were accused of heresy, and the Church undertook to suppress the movement. Some Waldensian groups, especially in France, returned to orthodoxy, but in northern Italy the movement withstood persecution and has survived to the present.

Far more radical were the Cathari (from a Latin word meaning the "pure"), also called Albigensians (from Albi, the southern French city where the movement was especially strong). Their fundamental belief was rooted in a radical dualism, a concept that originated in the Near East as early as the fourth century, probably from the mixing of Christian and Zoroastrian ideas. The movement spread slowly westward, finally reaching northern Italy and southern France in the tenth century. By 1200 its influence was felt throughout Europe, with its major center of strength in southern France, a land that was politically fragmented and culturally unique

The Cathari believed that two powers, good and evil, coexist and constantly compete in the universe. Only things spiritual, including the human soul, were good. Everything material was evil, including the flesh within which the soul is entrapped and the earth itself. This position caused the Cathari to deny the humanity of Jesus and the validity of what he had instituted in this world as instruments of salvation, including the earthly Church, the ordained priesthood, and the sacraments, all of which partook in some way in the evil material world. True Cathari—the "perfect," as they called themselves—sought to liberate their souls by escaping the material world. They refused to marry, holding that human procreation was the greatest of all evils. They ate no meat, milk, or eggs, all the products of sexual union. They owned no property and refused to shed blood. Allowances were made in the Cathari communities for those incapable of the rigorous life imposed on the "perfect." Second-grade Cathari, called "believers," were permitted to indulge in things material more freely, although "believers" hoped someday to join the ranks of the "perfect" who alone would be saved. The Cathari developed their own clergy, their own religious services, and their own rules of conduct. Their fervor and discipline produced communities that were remarkably resourceful in asserting political and economic dominance over the areas where they lived. But above all else, the Cathari impressed those around them with their austerity and moral earnestness.

Needless to say, the unique beliefs and the material success of the Cathari aroused the ire of those outside their exclusive communities and brought charges of heresy against them. As a consequence, the Church moved to suppress the movement. Local bishops attempted to convert them by persuasion; that failing, they then hailed them before Church courts to try and punish them under the provisions of canon law that provided death sentences for heresy. As we have noted, first the Cistercians and then the Dominicans tried to persuade the Cathari to return to orthodoxy. However, these measures failed, in part because of the dedication of the Cathari and in part because the movement had support from many local nobles. Pope Innocent III finally took a more drastic step: He organized a force of French knights, most vassals of kings Philip II and Philip III of France, to mount a "crusade" against the heretics. This ferocious Albigensian Crusade (1209–1229) destroyed the main centers of Cathari power and exterminated many members of the movement. To hunt down those that remained, the papacy utilized a special court, the Inquisition, and empowered it to employ special legal techniques, including secret witnesses and torture, to identify suspected heretics and to bring them to trial that resulted either in their return to orthodoxy or their death. These drastic measures provided a final solution for Catharism.

5. THE CONSEQUENCES OF THE MEDIEVAL REFORMATION

During the thirteenth century there were increasing signs that the reform movement was losing its vitality. Most of the forces that generated reforming ideas and practices during the eleventh, twelfth, and early thirteenth centuries had been successfully encapsulated into the formal structures of the Church as official parts of its organization, its doctrine, its law, its ritual, its moral code, and its spirituality. In a sense, what we identified as papal reform had absorbed and legitimized most other kinds of reform. There remains but one question: What were the consequences of all the energy spent trying to elevate the level of religious life? Historians have differed widely in their answers to this question, chiefly because they cannot agree on a standard by which the quality of religious life can be judged. But perhaps most would accept certain outcomes of the medieval reformation.

First, the medieval reformation certainly strengthened the organization of the Church. In contrast to its position in 1000, the Church by 1300 had the power and the resources to impose on its vast membership one body of belief, one code of conduct, and one set of religious practices. Seldom in history has an institution been in a position to direct society so decisively. But that position was not gained by accident; it required sustained creative effort.

Second, the reformation redefined the relationship between church and state. Whereas in 1000 the Church was dominated by secular powers whose authority was surrounded by a sacral aura, by 1300 the Church had defined for itself an area of liberty into which no other authority could intrude. Acting within this sphere, the Church was able to play a vital role in influencing societal development according to religious norms. The existence of separate realms for church and state would powerfully affect Europe's future.

Third, the challenges posed by the effort to renew religious life unleashed intellectual and artistic talents in ways that stretched the mental capabilities and the artistic sensibilities of western Europeans far beyond the boundaries of the mentality existing in the year 1000. In short, religious renewal sparked a multifaceted cultural renaissance that might not otherwise have happened except for the troublesome issues raised by the intense search for God and for more effective ways of serving his will.

Fourth, the medieval reformation broadened the range of spiritual possibilities far beyond what had been available to Christians in the early Middle Ages. The probing for the meaning of religious life that occurred between 1000 and 1300 in the monastic world and among simple people produced spiritual concepts that greatly enriched Christian life. Perhaps the most notable discovery was the spiritual frontier that existed within the individual Christian.

Finally, it can be argued that the medieval reformation caused as many religious problems as it solved. As its most notable monument, the medieval reformation created a powerful, rich, highly structured institution, deeply involved in the affairs of the world. In its theology and its law, that Church had defined a highly formal system of religion that claimed to hold the keys to salvation. It remained to be seen whether society would continue to accept that monolithic system in its entirety. Would kings and princes allow the Church to direct many aspects of worldly society according to its own rules? Would men and women find the answers to their spiritual needs in the strictly defined system of belief and worship prescribed by the Church? Was there any flexibility within this highly centralized, legalistic, formal religious structure to allow adjustment to changing times and ideas? In short, did the far-reaching consequences of one powerful religious reformation create conditions that would soon demand another?

SUGGESTED READING

General Surveys of Church History

Bernard Hamilton, *Religion in the Medieval West* (1986). A valuable guide to the basic tenets and practices of the Christian faith.

Jeffrey Burton Russell, *A History of Medieval Christianity: Prophecy and Order* (1968). A good brief treatment.

Hubert Jedin and John Dolan, eds., *Handbook of Church History*, Vol. 4: *From the High Middle Ages to the Eve of the Reformation*, trans. Anselm Biggs (1970). A detailed history of religious life.

R. W. Southern, *Western Society and the Church in the Middle Ages* (1970). Stresses relationships between the Church and the world.

Reform: Papal, Monastic, Popular

Walter Ullmann, *A Short History of the Papacy in the Middle Ages* (1972). A compact, provocative summary of papal history.

Charles M. Radding, *The Origins of Medieval Jurisprudence. Pavia and Bologna, 850–1150* (1987). Treats the origins of medieval canon law.

Jaroslav Pelikan, *The Christian Tradition. A History of the Development of Doctrine*, Vol. 3: *The Growth of Medieval Theology (600–1300)* (1978). A challenging treatment of the search for a uniform body of doctrine.

Bernard Hamilton, *The Medieval Inquisition* (1981). A clear study.

Christopher Brooke, *The Monastic World, 1000–1300* (1974).

C. H. Lawrence, *Medieval Monasticism: Forms of Religious Life in Western Europe in the Middle Ages* (1984). Two good descriptions of various forms of medieval monasticism.

R. I. Moore, *The Origins of European Dissent* (1977). Traces the development of dissent, with a stress on social factors.

Walter L. Wakefield, *Heresy, Crusade and Inquisition in Southern France, 1100–1250* (1979). Excellent on the Cathari.

Rosalind and Christopher Brooke, *Popular Religion in the Middle Ages: Western Europe, 1000–1300* (1984). A fine introduction.

Biographies

Helene Tillmann, *Pope Innocent III*, trans. Walter Sax (1980).

Watkin Williams, *Saint Bernard of Clairvaux* (1953).

Adolf Holl, *The Last Christian*, trans. Peter Heinegg (1980). Treats Francis of Assisi.

Etienne Gilson, *Héloise and Abelard*, trans. L. K. Shook (1951).

Pierre Mandonnet, *St. Dominic and His Work*, trans. Mary Benedicta Larkin (1945).

CHAPTER 23

Intellectual and Artistic Achievements

FIGURE 23.1 Gothic Sculpture
These Gothic figures from the south portal of the cathedral at Chartres, France, illustrate the warmth and realism of Gothic sculpture. (Jean Roubier)

The crowning achievement of western Europeans during the High Middle Ages was their original and creative work in thought, literature, and art. The foundations for this cultural outburst had been painfully shaped during a long apprenticeship culminating in the Carolingian revival; the immediate stimulus was provided by the powerful political, economic, and social changes occurring after 1000. The achievements played an important role in giving western European civilization its unique character and in establishing western European preeminence in a world setting.

The cultural achievement of the High Middle Ages can best be understood by a topical approach concentrating on certain areas of cultural activity that dominated thought and expression. However, it is important to note that the cultural development occurring during the period from 1000 to 1300 had a chronological dimension. In broad terms, cultural change occurred in two phases. The first, extending from about 1000 to 1170, was marked by vigorous exploration and experimentation that immensely expanded the cultural horizons and skills of thinkers, writers, and artists. As one American scholar put it, that era witnessed a "renaissance." As the twelfth century neared its end, the cultural climate began to change. The buoyant, questing spirit gave way to a concern for organizing and summarizing the diverse accomplishments of the earlier period. This age of synthesis, extending across the thirteenth century, produced the most mature expressions of medieval culture, but its accomplishments lacked the freshness and spontaneity characteristic of the earlier "renaissance."

1. THE WORLD OF LEARNING: EDUCATION

The cultural life of the High Middle Ages was divided into two distinctive spheres. In one, Latin was the vehicle of expression. In the West, Latin was the language in which the prime sources of the Christian faith were enshrined: Scripture, the writings of the Church Fathers, the liturgy, the canon law. And it was the language employed to explain the meaning of the faith. Those who used that language, chiefly members of the clergy, be-

came the "learned" in society, a group accorded high respect because its members had access to the written sources that opened the way to salvation. In the other cultural sphere, the languages of the people, the vernacular tongues, prevailed, first as spoken vehicles of communication and then as written languages devoted chiefly to expressing the interests, tastes, and values of the nobility. Although these two cultural spheres intersected and interacted, each made its own unique contributions to the cultural life of the High Middle Ages.

In the world of the "learned" education was of crucial importance. During the early Middle Ages Latin increasingly became a foreign language that had to be learned by those seeking access to religious truth. This crucial need required schools designed primarily to sustain Latin learning. What was taught in those schools and how it was taught became a prime factor in shaping the mentality of the learned world.

As we have already noted (see Chapters 15 and 16), prior to 1000 educational activity was largely confined to monastic schools, although by 1000 a few modest cathedral schools still survived from Carolingian times, and in Italy some municipal schools continued. A curriculum based on the study of the seven liberal arts had been fixed, and basic textbooks defining the content of these disciplines had been established, chiefly during the Carolingian period. The monastic schools touched a narrow segment of the population and cultivated a limited range of intellectual interests.

During the eleventh and twelfth centuries the educational system underwent a significant expansion and a fundamental change in character. Part of the stimulus came from intellectual ferment within the monastic world (see Chapter 22). More decisive, however, was a shift in the social value of education. Education became the avenue by which increasing numbers prepared themselves for career opportunities opened up by the demand in the Church, royal governments, and towns for literate people capable of handling the complexities of administration and commercial exchange. Cathedral and municipal schools were better prepared to meet this challenge than monastic schools and enjoyed a remarkable growth in number and size. Especially in the cathedral schools there was a marked intensification and expansion of the study of the seven liberal arts, particularly the *trivium*—grammar, rhetoric, and dialectic (logic). In the municipal schools in Italy, the study of law took on new vigor. Many of the most prominent cathedral schools of the early twelfth century, such as those at Paris, Chartres, Laon, and Reims, owed their fame to individual masters who specialized in one of the liberal arts and was thus able to enrich its content and its methodology. In fact, being a master became a career in itself, marking the appearance of the professional intellectual as a key force in the world of learning. The content of grammar, rhetoric, and dialectic derived chiefly from classical Latin models, so that the cathedral schools became centers of more intensive and critical study of the classics. The other four liberal arts (the *quadrivium*)—arithmetic, geometry, astronomy, music—were less important in training literate, articulate people to serve new social roles. Still, their content was constantly expanded, chiefly as a result of the renaissance of classical studies.

Toward the end of the twelfth century the monastic, cathedral, and municipal schools no longer met the needs of the world of learning. Because they were often dependent on a single master teaching a specialized discipline, they lacked continuity and curricular breadth. Also, their masters had opened up intellectual vistas and generated specialized scholarly interests that abbots, bishops, and town councils had little practical interest in fostering. Moreover, during the last half of the twelfth century western Europe was flooded with a huge body of new knowledge coming from the Greek and Moslem worlds. Primarily philosophical and scientific in content, this new knowledge challenged existing religious beliefs and demanded levels of learning well beyond that needed to prepare people for careers. The response was a new institution, the university, consisting of a community of teachers and learners engaged in a collective effort to expand, organize, and transmit knowledge and intellectual skills.

The earliest universities, those at Bologna and Paris, came into existence about 1200; not long after others emerged in various urban centers across Europe. Following a pattern already used by urban dwellers and by merchants and crafts-

men seeking to establish a place for themselves in society, the founders of universities organized themselves into self-governing corporations, or guilds (the general Latin term for "guild" was *universitas*). At Bologna the students, for the most part law students, formed a *universitas* because they felt they needed protection from the townspeople and their masters. At Paris the teachers of the arts in the city's episcopal school broke away from the bishop's control and founded a self-governing body, the faculty of the arts, to control the educational process. A crucial step in establishing a university was gaining legal recognition from a public authority—king, bishop, town council—allowing the corporation to exercise certain privileges. The privileges claimed were wide-ranging, but one was vital: the right to grant a degree certifying that a learner had completed a specified program of training defined by a faculty. Once a guild of teachers and students had established its legal status, it developed its own internal structure and operating rules. This process was often lengthy and beset by fierce struggles within the *universitas*.

The core curriculum of the typical university was based on training in the seven liberal arts conducted by a faculty of masters of arts, each a specialist in one of the arts. Completion of the arts program, usually requiring four years, resulted in a bachelor of arts degree, which qualified its literate recipients for a variety of careers. Those wishing to teach the arts either in a university or some other kind of school pursued their studies in one of the arts for another year or two and earned a master's degree. Those who aspired to a teaching career beyond instructing students in the liberal arts or who hoped to serve in high places as authorities on technical disciplines could pursue a doctorate in theology, law, or medicine. This degree required additional years of study, research, and public professing. At Paris, for example, the theology doctorate took at least thirteen years of study. Although the ultimate objective of university study was earning a degree, many students spent time at universities without earning degrees; just being at a university earned them preferment in advancing their careers and some degree of social respectability.

The basic teaching method at universities focused on acquainting students with authoritative texts in the various disciplines. Usually these texts were works by ancient authors; but as the High Middle Ages progressed, the works of "modern" authorities were added (such as Peter Lombard and Gratian). Since books had to be handwritten, they were scarce and expensive. In the face of this problem, the master read the text (thus the origin of the lecture method, derived from the Latin word for reading, *lectio*), and the students took notes. As the master read the text, he commented on the issues it raised, often citing the opinions of other authorities on each issue and employing logical argumentation to reconcile differences. The purpose of this enterprise was to convey fundamental truths and to train students in the art of defending them through argumentation (*disputatio*)—an art that required acquiring a body of knowledge, developing a capacity for logical thinking, and perfecting skills in oral argumentation. Proof of worthiness for a degree was established by a student's performance in a public examination. Such a test required the student to expound on a text, develop and defend a thesis with respect to it, and respond to challenges to the thesis posed by the examining masters. This method produced minds that held a high respect for established authorities, were adept at textual analysis, were skilled in reconciling contradictory positions by logic, and were inclined to settle differences by argumentation.

The early universities were communities of people rather than physical entities. Most classes were held in rented halls. Students took lodgings in private homes. In time, however, universities did take on a physical presence. Patrons began to endow establishments, called *colleges*, for housing and feeding students. The first such institution was the Sorbonne at Paris, named after its patron, Robert de Sorbon, a rich courtier. Chapels, manuscript-copying services, and libraries were built to serve those engaged in learning. Thus, a university quarter began to emerge in some medieval cities, usually a welcome adornment to urban life.

University students were almost exclusively male and came from a mixed social background; predominantly they were the offspring of people of modest means—petty nobles, merchants, artisans, even affluent peasants—who saw education as a means of economic and social advancement. They ranged in age from fourteen or fifteen to thirty or thirty-five. Since universities were few, students gathered at each from afar, thus constituting a population of strangers in most university towns. Many were supported by their parents or by patrons—usually inadequately, if we can believe the constant pleas for funds voiced in surviving student letters. These letters, however, seldom talk of student expenditures in taverns and on other frivolous pursuits that are recorded in other surviving documents. Students engaged in endless clashes with townspeople, who viewed them as foreigners, idlers, and wastrels but also as targets for exploitation. Since students were legally considered members of the clergy and of a privileged corporation, it was difficult for town governments to exercise legal control over them. Town-gown rivalry, often surrounded by bitter recriminations and even violence, became a regular part of urban life in every university center.

2. THE WORLD OF LEARNING: THE MEDIEVAL "SCIENCES"

The evolution of the medieval educational system promoted the structuring of intellectual activity into what medieval scholars would have called "sciences," by which they meant bodies of interrelated knowledge capable of describing and explaining meaningful segments of the universe. In a sense, each of the seven liberal arts constituted a science in the medieval scheme of things, and medieval scholars and teachers greatly enriched each of them, but especially grammar and dialectic. However, the chief monuments of medieval intellectual activity came in more exalted "sciences": theology (which embraced what we would call philosophy), or the study of God; law, or the study of human society; and nature, or the study of the material order. Aside from the challenging intellectual issues innate in each of these areas, various pressing problems in a changing society forced learned men to explore each and to struggle to bring order to what was known.

The queen of medieval "sciences" was theology. Although it had always engaged Christian thinkers, theology made a quantum leap forward during the High Middle Ages. That advance was due in part to the urgent need felt within the Church to unify and systematize its basic teachings as an aspect of its effort to reform Christian society. But also stimulating theological activity were the expanded competence in thinking techniques and the critical issues raised by new knowledge.

During the early Middle Ages theological inquiry sought primarily to understand and to explain the meaning of certain authoritative texts that contained the divine truth—above all else, Scripture. The approach was primarily literary, seeking by careful reading and meditation to discover the levels of meaning contained in the word of God. In the eleventh century, a subtle change in approach to texts began to occur, providing the key to the emergence of the "science" of theology. Prompted by their growing awareness of the contradictions in Scripture and in the way past authorities had interpreted the revealed truth, scholars began to explore the extent to which human reason could be useful in grasping religious truth. In this pursuit they turned to the methodology of dialectic or logic, using the rules of formal thinking to test and to demonstrate the validity of religious propositions.

Some of the early proponents of this new approach were naïve and were viewed with suspicion because of their unorthodox conclusions. A key figure in turning the tide was Anselm (1033–1109), abbot of the monastery of Bec in Normandy and later archbishop of Canterbury. A man of learning and of unquestioned orthodoxy, Anselm proclaimed as his central intellectual tenet that faith should seek understanding, by which he meant that one steeped in revealed truth should strive to understand that faith in human terms. To demonstrate his point, he undertook to develop a logical proof of the existence of God, one that could stand on its own without dependence on revelation. His famous proof, which has intrigued many generations of thinkers, legitimized human reason as a valid tool in the search to understand what revelation meant.

The study of dialectic and its application to various problems became a passion in the schools of the early twelfth century. A leader was Abelard (1079–1142), a key figure in creating the science of theology. Son of a minor Breton noble family, Abelard studied with several leading masters in various cathedral schools in France and then became a successful master himself. His promising career was disrupted by a love affair with one of his pupils, Heloise, which led to secret marriage, a child, the emasculation of Abelard by Heloise's outraged kinsfolk, and the separation of the lovers. These "calamities," as Abelard put it, condemned the victim to a life of wandering from monastery to monastery and school to school— perhaps always haunted by his memory of true love but also driven by an urge to know and to understand more fully. Abelard's career was filled with controversy, stemming partly from his prideful, combative personality and partly from the force of his ideas, which posed a revolutionary challenge to traditional theological inquiry.

Superbly skilled as a logician, Abelard made a major contribution to systematizing the use of dialectic as a tool of theological inquiry. In a bold book entitled *Sic et Non (Yes and No)*, he set down a series of cases in which authorities disagreed on fundamental doctrinal questions. His approach implied that only the use of reason could resolve these contradictions. Abelard also developed new insights into how human beings came to know. He maintained that the truth consists of concepts formed in the mind from the study of created things, such concepts being the nearest approximation to the perfect knowledge that is God. A philosopher's task is to organize in a logical fashion all that is known so as to create a mental image of God's universe. Abelard's dialectical approach to theology aroused strong opposition, led by the formidable Bernard of Clairvaux. But the resistance was to no avail, and the new theology became predominant. It was given special impetus by Peter Lombard (1100–1160), who used the dialectical methodology as the basis for his *Sentences*. In it Peter employed logic to resolve contradictory positions contained in Scripture and the writings of the Church Fathers on a large number of topics relating to basic Christian doctrine. The result was a unified body of theology, systematically organized. The *Sentences* quickly became the basic text for teaching theology, and its dialectical methodology became standard.

The value of the dialectical approach became

even more evident during the late twelfth and thirteenth centuries, when scholars in the West came into possession of a vast body of new knowledge derived from Greek philosophy and scientific knowledge along with the Moslem commentaries on that material. During the early Middle Ages western Europeans had lost contact with almost all of Greek philosophy and science. However, from as early as the ninth century Moslem scholars became deeply interested in this material, had translated most of material into Arabic, and had commented on it extensively (see page 197). Beginning in about 1150 this huge body of knowledge again became available in the West, primarily as a result of the labors of scholars working chiefly in Spain and Sicily to translate Arabic texts into Latin. The new material included most of Aristotle's writings, and he quickly became the leading authority on logical methods and on philosophical and scientific learning—the Philosopher, as Western thinkers soon called him. The new learning posed a serious challenge: Not only did it provide scholars with heretofore unfamiliar knowledge about a wide range of matters, especially about the natural world, but it also confronted them with logically demonstrated systems of truth that directly contradicted many basic Christian teachings.

The major concerns of thirteenth-century theologians, collectively called the Scholastics, centered on mastering the new knowledge, organizing it into a rational system, and reconciling it with Christian doctrine in a way that met the tests of logic. Their assault on these problems was motivated not only by the intellectual challenges innate in these issues but also by their urge to serve the Church in its quest for doctrinal clarity and uniformity. These concerns, explored most intensely in the universities, evoked a variety of responses, often accompanied by bitter intellectual warfare that belies the notion that the Middle Ages was a time of uniformity and conformity in the realm of ideas.

One especially controversial approach to these fundamental issues was formulated by a group of scholars called the Averroists, after a famous Moslem thinker who had commented extensively on Aristotle's works. The adherents of this school wholeheartedly accepted Aristotelian rationalism,

arguing that reason was capable of defining an order of truth that had its own validity irrespective of the tenets of the faith. At the opposite pole was a school of thought that found Aristotelianism to be of little value in leading to the truth. This school reasserted the Platonic-Augustinian tradition that had long prevailed as the prime approach to theological wisdom. The most notable figure in this group was Bonaventura (1221–1274), a Franciscan teacher in Paris who later became head of the Franciscan order. Bonaventura argued that reason could not discover the ultimate truth, which must come to the intellect intuitively through an illumination from divine sources beyond the power of human reason. Although Bonaventura did not deny the value of a rational consideration of natural phenomena, he held that no fundamental truth would result; in fact, he was convinced that rationalism would ultimately end in doctrinal error.

But the most representative response to the major issues posed by the new knowledge was formulated by a succession of scholars who tried to reconcile revelation and reason. By far the most influential advocate of this approach was Thomas Aquinas (1225–1274), an Italian Dominican whose active career was divided between teaching at the university in Paris and serving at the papal court. During his career as teacher and scholar he produced a huge body of theological writing. His chief works, the *Summa contra Gentiles* and the unfinished *Summa Theologiae*, represent medieval theological and philosophical thought at its most advanced level. In all of his works Thomas begins with the assumption that God created the universe in such a way that all its parts fit together and have a single purpose. Every human being has the duty to know God and his works, and each has the ability to achieve that end as a result of human reason. There are two paths to this single, unified order of truth: revelation and reason. The task of the mind is to seek the truth by applying itself to those things that are the proper subjects for reason while accepting on faith those things that can be learned only by revelation. Thomas accepted on faith such doctrines as the Creation, the Trinity, and the Incarnation but applied reason to such problems as the existence of God, immortality, the operation of the natural world, the nature of government, and ethics. He was certain that reason directed to the proper ends and guided by sound methodology would provide the intelligence with an order of truth that fitted into the order of truth contained in revelation. If there is a conflict between revelation and reason, it results from faulty reasoning.

Following the rules of logic formulated by Aristotle and relying heavily on him for knowledge of subjects proper to human reason, Thomas measured the whole realm of human knowledge item after item with a view toward reconciling that knowledge with the revealed truth. His method consisted of a rigorously applied series of steps: formulating a proposition stating some aspect of the truth, setting forth all possible contrary positions, demonstrating the logical fallacies in these contrary positions, and finally showing the logical validity of the true position. Each single truth in Thomas' system is part of an interlocking structure of thought that relates all things to a perfect truth. The final result of his work—his *summae,* or summations—is a synthesis of all knowledge into one vast structure glorifying God and demonstrating the perfection of his creation in terms comprehensible to the human mind. The Thomistic synthesis perhaps best represents the overall spirit of medieval thought: the quest to integrate existing knowledge into a single structure; new knowledge was seldom a concern of theologians or philosophers.

Another "science" that developed during the High Middle Ages involved the systematic study of law. Although several universities had faculties of law, the major center of legal studies was at the University of Bologna. By the eleventh century strong pressures were felt in society, especially in the Church and the royal courts, to develop unified, consistent bodies of law as an instrument promoting order in society. However, legal systems existing at that time were surrounded with confusion and contradictions. Like the theologians, students of law began to employ dialectic as a tool to resolve this problem. We have already noted the work of Gratian, who in his *Decretum* (1140) created a model compendium of canon law, based on the collection and rational reconciliation of a wide range of precedents. Gratian's work became the basic text used in teaching canon law.

A long succession of twelfth- and thirteenth-century canon lawyers continued the work of compilation and commentary; by the thirteenth century their labors had produced a highly sophisticated, consistent body of law essential to the governance of the Church.

The development of canon law was greatly stimulated by a revived interest in the study of Roman law. Except for a few places where written law had remained in use during the early Middle Ages, such as southern France and northern Italy, Roman law had long been neglected in the West. But then in the eleventh century its study was taken up with great vigor, mainly because the chief embodiment of Roman law, the Code of Justinian, provided an ideal model of law organized on a rational basis. Civil lawyers spent their energies writing commentaries (called *glosses*) on the code to try to elucidate its meaning and relate its principles to existing society. Aside from producing an immense body of legal literature, their work decisively influenced the kind of law administered in the rising monarchies and shaped the concepts defining royal power. The legal concepts set forth by the students of Roman law prompted efforts to codify the confused bodies of customary law existing over much of western Europe. An example was the important treatise on English common law compiled by Henry Bracton in the thirteenth century.

Although a precise "science" of society did not emerge in the High Middle Ages, theologians and lawyers had much to say about the nature of human society and of the political order. Discussions on these matters were spurred by a variety of influences: explorations by religious reformers of the ancient Christian concepts of the nature of the state and society; the conflict between church and state; the need to justify the claims of the new monarchies; the revival of Roman law; the recovery of classical Greek and Roman works on political theory (especially Aristotle). Gradually the serious study of political theory led to a new view of the nature of society and the political order. Traditional political thought, derived chiefly from Augustine, viewed the state as an instrument for suppressing the sinful nature of human beings; by filling this negative role, rulers prepared the ground for the spiritual perfection of human beings through the efforts of ecclesiastical leaders. Increasingly during the twelfth and thirteenth centuries the state came to be defined as an integral part of the natural order asserting a unique and necessary positive force for the full realization of human potential.

Thomas Aquinas played an important role in articulating this new view of the state. Strongly influenced by Aristotle, he argued that the state is a part of the natural order, existing to permit human beings to live in an ordered community where each could realize his or her innate potential for good. The proper form of government was a result of rational reflection on human needs. In Thomas' view, the ideal state was one in which various classes performed specific functions under the guidance of a just ruler in the interests of providing for the needs of all. Such a system ensured justice, which was the ultimate objective of government. Upon the ruler of the good state fell the heavy responsibility of discovering and applying the principles of natural law required to regulate human society in accord with the divine order. In discovering a positive role for the state as an instrument shaped by rational human actions for promoting human welfare, the political theorists of the High Middle Ages established the foundations for future study of the state and its functioning in a context which took into account existing realities.

In the "science" of the natural world the achievements of medieval thinkers seem pale by the standards of later ages. The most advanced area of scientific study was medicine, which constituted a separate field of study in some universities, especially at Salerno in Sicily. The study of medicine focused primarily on mastering medical knowledge derived from the Hellenistic and the Moslem worlds. However, the High Middle Ages did witness one development of major significance for the study of the natural world. During the early Middle Ages thinkers had adhered to a view of nature rooted in Neoplatonism. This view considered the natural world an inferior order of reality, representing an illusory reflection of nonmaterial perfect forms. As this Neoplatonic concept was translated into a Christian idiom, nature came to be viewed as part of the universe corrupted by the Fall. Given powerful impetus by a monastic

ideal that spurned material things, early medieval thought was biased against serious concern with nature. That changed during the High Middle Ages. The Scholastic effort to unite all knowledge into a single truth and the vastly increased knowledge of nature resulting from the rediscovery of Greek and Moslem scientific works generated an effort to study the natural world as a prime manifestation of God's created cosmos. That study led to the conclusion that the material world was good by virtue of being part of God's creation, that there was order in nature because it was part of God's perfect order, and that the natural world was intelligible to human reason. In short, nature had to be understood if theological and philosophical knowledge was to be complete. This fundamental shift in attitude constituted a prime achievement of the medieval search for truth. The discovery—perhaps rediscovery is a better term—of nature provided the starting point for great advances in knowledge *about* nature.

Even in the High Middle Ages the first tentative steps were taken to learn more about the natural world than was contained in the ancient authorities, especially Aristotle and Scripture. An important group of scholars, most of them Franciscans, centered at Oxford in the thirteenth century pointed the way. Robert Grosseteste (1168–1253) and his pupil Roger Bacon (ca. 1214–1294) were its most distinguished members. These men insisted that the truth about the natural world could be gained only through observation and experimentation. Bacon argued that most Scholastics put too much trust in ancient authorities, and he engaged in experimentation, especially in optics. The efforts of Bacon and his fellow scholars were helped by an increasing body of knowledge and technical expertise being accumulated by artisans, medical practitioners, mechanics, and farmers engaged in the routine affairs of life. The ground was being prepared for a later explosion of scientific knowledge.

3. BEYOND THE LEARNED WORLD: VERNACULAR LITERATURE

Complementing the writings of theologians, lawyers, and scientists was another rich and varied body of literature created during the High Middle Ages. It aimed primarily at instructing and entertaining a broader audience than the learned world.

Much of this second kind of literature was written in Latin to serve the increasing numbers of Latin readers and speakers produced by the schools. This literature was strongly influenced in style and language by classical Latin authors whose works provided the models upon which the study of grammar and rhetoric was based. However, Latin authors in the High Middle Ages demonstrated considerable skill in using those models in innovative ways. The Latin vocabulary was constantly enriched by the infusion of new words and meanings, and classical literary forms were modified to permit Latin authors to treat matters that concerned them in creative ways. Perhaps the best Latin writing of the High Middle Ages took the form of lyric poetry on religious themes, often composed to serve the religious liturgy, especially as hymns. Much of this poetry used a new verse technique based on rhyme and accent rather than on long and short vowels, the classical technique. The new style lent itself to nonreligious poetry, exemplified by the many student songs, collectively called Goliardic poetry, celebrating drinking, sensual love, gambling, and other worldly themes. Between 1000 and 1300 there was also a great outpouring of prose literature devoted to history, biography, saints' lives, devotional literature, letters, and political polemics.

But it is vernacular literature, written in the tongues that Europeans spoke in their daily lives, that represents the most creative literary accomplishment of the High Middle Ages. By 1000 the language map of western Europe had become a tower of Babel. That map had emerged slowly during the early Middle Ages out of three basic root languages: classical Latin, which evolved into Romance tongues, such as French, Provençal, Italian, Spanish, and Catalan; Old German, out of which came German, English, and the Scandinavian tongues; and Celtic, which evolved into Irish and Welsh. Each of these basic vernacular languages was further divided into local dialects, and many of them were enriched by extensive borrowings from each other. How these various tongues came to be instruments of written expression is badly understood, but the fact that writers did develop the capability of using these languages to create unique literary works marked a major landmark in western European cultural development.

Most vernacular literature was written for an aristocratic audience and reflects the values of that class. One of the earliest forms was the epic, a song setting down in writing the deeds of great warriors that had been preserved in oral tradition. The great Anglo-Saxon epic *Beowulf*, composed about 800, recounts the deeds of a warrior living in a pre-Christian Germanic society. So also do the Scandinavian sagas, the *Poetic Edda* and the *Prose Edda* of Snorri Sturlson, not put in written form until the twelfth and thirteenth centuries but reflecting a much earlier pagan society dominated by violence. The chief Germanic epic, the *Nibelungenlied*, composed about 1200, reflects a tradition dating back to the time of the Germanic invasions. The chief *chanson de geste* ("song of deeds") produced in French was the *Song of Roland*, written about 1100 to retell the story of Charlemagne's expedition of 778 against the Moors in Spain, which ended in the defeat of the Frankish forces at Roncesvalles. However, the unknown author adorned his account of this historical event and its hero, Roland, with the ideals and customs characteristic of eleventh-century feudal society; particular emphasis is given to Roland's prowess as a warrior, his loyalty to his lord, and his willingness to give his life to defend his faith. The same themes dominate the Spanish epic, *The Cid*, which glorifies the deeds of a famous knight involved in the Reconquista of Spain from the infidel Moors.

The epic genre was rivaled by a new vernacular literary form, the lyric, which during the twelfth century enjoyed a tremendous vogue in the courtly circles of the chivalric nobility. This poetry developed first in Provence, in southern France, and soon spread over most of Europe. Its creators, called *troubadours*, were chiefly young men whose lack of great fiefs and firm family ties rooted in proper marriages placed them on the fringes of noble society. Through their poetry they sought to expound their sensual love for a noble lady, usually already married, in a fashion that would earn them honor in her eyes and thus status in the society to which she belonged. The troubadours (called *trouvères* in northern France and *minnesängers* in Germany) formulated a new set of values for noble society. Their poetry argued that the emotions associated with love—longing, suffering, anticipation of a lover's favor—had the power to ennoble just as much as did prowess in battle or loyalty to a male feudal lord. The search for self-understanding and the emotional probing associated with the quest for love refined the inner spirit and evoked patterns of behavior that combined to create the gentleman as the epitome of noble existence. The lyric writers thus played a crucial role in transforming values and behavior patterns upon which the concept of male excellence was based. They also were instrumental in attributing to women a vital role in shaping nobility, a role based on their sexuality and their power to give pleasure. The impetus for this new morality derived primarily from qualities innate in human nature and had little to do with moral values rooted in religion, an interpretation that raised grave suspicions in the minds of church leaders about troubadour poetry.

Toward the end of the twelfth century, the epic and the lyric traditions merged to produce a third type of vernacular literature, the *romance*. Romances were stories combining the love theme with adventure, written chiefly to entertain court society; the immensely popular romances enjoyed the special patronage of high-placed noble women, such as Eleanor of Aquitaine. The adventure element in these stories was drawn from sources with vague roots in history, especially materials relating to King Arthur and his court. The authors of the romances used this "historical" material with complete freedom. The treatment of love in these stories reflected continued probing of themes contained in troubadour poetry. The most gifted romance writers fashioned works with enduring appeal. Among them was Chrétien de Troyes, a late-twelfth-century French author who skillfully exploited the Arthurian material to create an intriguing picture of the ideal knight struggling to achieve chivalric excellence through pursuit of love and adventure and of the noble lady serving as a prime agent in shaping the consummate knight. Another writer, the thirteenth-century German Gottfried von Strasbourg, in *Tristan and Isolde*, masterfully reveals the meaning of love in

the lives of two who were its prisoners. *Parzival*, written by his countryman Wolfram von Eschenbach, is an appealing picture of a man pursuing an unobtainable ideal, symbolized by the Holy Grail. The mature concepts of chivalry found their fullest expression in the romances. The themes and actions treated in them had a powerful impact on the behavior of the nobility for centuries and continued to intrigue writers and audiences down to the present, influencing poetry, operas, and even modern musicals.

While the epics, lyrics, and romances were being written, sung, and read by nobles, other forms of literature evolved to appeal to the tastes and interests of nonnobles. Especially notable were dramas and *fabliaux*. Medieval drama began as part of church liturgy; dramatized parts of services eventually moved outside the church into the marketplace. By the thirteenth century the guilds had taken over the responsibility for producing these dramas on religious festivals. Each guild would take responsibility for presenting one scene from a connected series of scenes that constituted the entire play. Several types of dramatic production developed: mystery plays, enacting scenes from the Bible; miracle plays, treating the highlights of saints' lives; morality plays, personifying human virtues and vices. The presentation of these serious, sacred dramas was punctuated by earthy language and comical portrayals of the key characters. The *fabliaux* were short tales recited in public squares to entertain the crowds. Whatever the subject—it could be almost anything—the *fabliaux* were always close to city life, representing everyday events in the lives of ordinary people. They were filled with vulgar humor and satire aimed especially at priests, betrayed husbands, and scheming women effective in getting what they wanted from young men. The most famous collection of *fabliaux* was the *Romance of Reynard the Fox*, made up of stories in which animals symbolize people and human characteristics.

Of the many writers during the High Middle Ages one genius, Dante Alighieri (1265–1321), towers above all others. He was to literature what Thomas Aquinas was to theology. Dante was a product of the vibrant urban life of Florence. In his youth he fell in love with a girl named Beatrice, who later married someone else and died young.

Beatrice became for Dante the ideal woman as defined by the code of courtly love. Dante was a learned man who wrote on a variety of subjects. He was also active in Florentine political life, ultimately suffering expulsion from the city because of his identification with a faction that lost control of the city government. While suffering in what he called "an undeserving exile," he wrote in his native Tuscan dialect his masterpiece, *The Divine Comedy.* Outwardly, it tells of Dante's journey through hell, purgatory, and heaven. Tired, discouraged, and confused at the outset, the pilgrim slowly begins to comprehend the harmony, order, and purpose in the universe; his spirit is progressively uplifted and his soul cured of its discontents. Guided through hell and purgatory by the Latin poet Vergil and through heaven by his beloved Beatrice, he is permitted to see all things from the depths of hell to God himself. Within this framework Dante weaves with dazzling poetic skills a rich tapestry reflecting medieval thought. He is a philosopher, presenting with consummate skill the medieval idea that all things in the universe are ordered by God in a cohesive, intelligible scheme. He is a mystic, yearning to the depths of his soul to catch a glimpse of God so that his longing may be satisfied. He is a love poet; Beatrice, his guide in heaven, is a symbol of human love, a purifying and uplifting emotion. He is a scientist, incorporating into his poem many medieval ideas about the structure of the physical universe. He is an admirer of Greek and Roman writers and thinkers, although he has to condemn them to hell as non-Christians. He is a keen political observer, full of fierce partisanship. On his

long journey from the gates of hell to its very pit, where Lucifer chews up three great traitors, Brutus, Cassius, and Judas, Dante discusses with Vergil nearly every kind of sin, showing a deep understanding of human nature and its weaknesses. The ascent from hell through purgatory to the seat of God in heaven offers him equal chance to discourse on every aspect of virtue. Few artists have grasped human life and human aspirations more fully or written of them with greater artistry.

4. THE VISUAL ARTS

During the High Middle Ages the visual arts provided the cultural media common to all, rich and poor, literate and illiterate, learned and ignorant. This era marked a decisive epoch in art history. Two major styles, Romanesque and Gothic, were perfected between 1000 and 1300. Both styles were preeminently religious in inspiration, created primarily to provide suitable places of worship, and the Church was the prime agency promoting artistic endeavor.

The Romanesque and Gothic styles were the fruits of a long artistic evolution. The starting point of medieval church architecture was the Roman basilica, the rectangular meeting hall. The early Christians placed their altars in the semicircular *apse* at the rear and conducted the mass there. The *nave* provided space for the faithful participating in the sacred rites. Side aisles often flanked the nave. The upper walls of the nave rose above the side aisles and were pierced with windows allowing light into the nave. A lateral

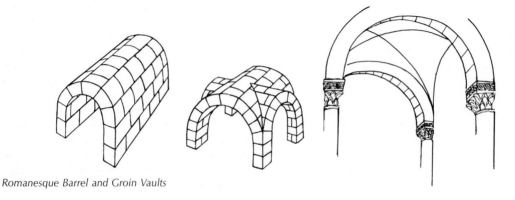

Romanesque Barrel and Groin Vaults

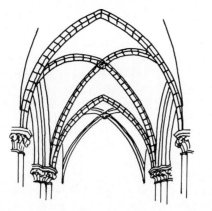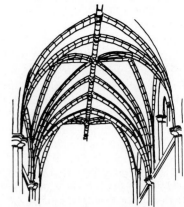

Gothic Ribbed Vault

aisle, called the *transept*, sometimes crossed the nave just in front of the apse, so that the early church took the form of a cross. Over the centuries, this basic ground plan of church architecture and the art that decorated it were considerably modified by influences from the Byzantine, Germanic, and Celtic worlds and by new creative forces emerging from daily life. During the High Middle Ages artists finally succeeded in blending these many tributaries into distinctive new styles.

Romanesque architecture first appeared in the late Carolingian period and flourished through most of the twelfth century. Its main features are admirably illustrated by several churches still standing: Notre Dame la Grande in Poitiers, the cathedral of Saint-Sernin in Toulouse, the cathedral church of Worms, the Abbey Church of Maria Laach in Germany, and the church of Sant' Ambrogio in Milan. The Romanesque style was characterized both by technical innovations and by a new spirit. The monastic world, especially the Cluniac reformers, played a dominant role in developing and spreading this style. The Cluniac emphasis on elaborate rituals and their concern for providing the proper setting for the veneration of relics and for gatherings of pilgrims dictated churches large enough to house a number of chapels and accommodate great crowds. Architects also wanted to find a replacement for the traditional wooden roofs, which were so often destroyed by fire. The solution was a capacious church built entirely of stone.

So that liturgical needs were met, the basic ground plan of the traditional basilican structure was modified. The nave was extended beyond the transept to create a *choir*, a space where the main altar was located and where the clergy and monks could gather for worship. The side aisles were also extended around the choir, creating a passageway or ambulatory that encircled the nave and the choir. A series of chapels were constructed off the side aisles and the choir ambulatory, providing spaces for many simultaneous religious services and special shrines for relics. To replace the wooden roof, architects developed techniques that allowed them to throw a barrel vault made of stone over the full length of the nave and choir and the side aisles. These heavy roofs were supported by massive stone walls. Where openings were needed through these walls—such as passages between the nave and the side aisles—round arches set on heavy pillars were used to support the structure above the opening. Groin vaults, again supported by arches and pillars, were evolved to cover the square or rectangular area where the axis of the nave and the choir was crossed by the transept. However, the barrel vault system of creating a stone roof was satisfactory only for relatively small structures. As the Romanesque style evolved, architects developed a method of building stone roofs over larger naves and choirs. They begin to break up the long barrel vault with rib arches crossing the nave and choir and resting on pillars on opposite sides of the nave and the choir. This technique created a series of bays or "squares" marked off by pillars at each of the four corners. Each bay could then be covered with cross vaults. The space between the rib and the cross vaults could be filled in with relatively light stone pieces, reducing the roof weight and concentrating its downward thrust on the pillars at the corners of each bay (see illustration, p. 314). Despite these innovations, the stone vaulting covering the structure remained massive and exerted tremendous downward and outward thrust. For this reason Romanesque churches required heavy walls and massive internal columns; the few windows had to be kept small. Thus the typical Romanesque structure had an atmosphere of muted darkness and mystery that was not dispelled by the decorative paintings on piers, arches, and walls and the candles that supplied artificial light. Yet this atmosphere was also due to the religious mentality of an age that viewed the church as God's citadel standing against a world filled with evil forces, a sacred fortress where men and women could commune with the God who protected them from the howling demons and the frightening forces of nature that raged outside this holy refuge (see Figure 23.2).

By the mid–twelfth century the European world was changing rapidly, and the new environment produced a new architectural style, the Gothic. It appeared first in Ile de France, the domain of the Capetians; the earliest full-scale Gothic church was the Abbey Church of St. Denis near Paris, built in 1137–1144 by Abbot Suger, the adviser to kings Louis VI and Louis VII. From here the Gothic style spread over much of Europe.

The Gothic style evolved out of a desire for height and light in churches, a desire derived largely from new intellectual and spiritual concepts that fostered a more rational view of God and saw his chief attributes in terms of reason, light, and proportion. The Gothic church was an attempt to leave behind the mystery-shrouded, awesome world of the Romanesque and move into the light and purity of paradise—the paradise Dante pictured in poetry. Among the Gothic structures that achieve this effect magnificently are the cathedrals at Paris (Notre Dame), Chartres, Reims, Amiens, Strasbourg, and Bourges in France; at Lincoln, York, and Salisbury in England; and at Cologne in Germany.

Technically, this transformation was made possible by the pointed arch, which carried thrust downward, and the ribbed vault, used to concentrate the thrust at a few points. Architects were able to combine them to fashion tremendously tall skeletons of stone whose weight flowed to earth through a series of slender pillars. The outward thrust, greatly reduced by the pointed arches and concentrated by the rib vaults, could be offset by thickened columns at the outside of the building or by flying buttresses, pillars set away from the main structure and joined to it by bracing arches high above the ground (see illustration, p. 315). Thin walls, supporting nothing but their own weight, could be filled in between pillars. More important, light could be let into the structure by great arched windows cut through the thin walls. These windows, often interlaced with delicate decorative stonework, pierced the lofty clerestory and the side aisles, and majestic round windows were placed high above ground level at the ends of the nave, the choir, and the transept. The windows were often filled with many-hued stained-glass figures or scenes that suffused the interior with a breathtaking display of colored light (see Figure 23.3 and Color Plate 10).

Nearly every other visual art was put to work to decorate medieval churches. The exterior of a Romanesque church was generally plain except for the west façade, where the great arches built to provide doorways leading to a nave and side aisles provided a setting for sculpture. As illustrated by churches at Arles and Vézelay, these spaces were filled with massive, highly symbolic sculpture done in high relief; they portrayed human figures, animals, and abstract decorative patterns. A favorite subject was the Last Judgment, in which a stern Christ was portrayed relegating men and women to heaven or hell (see Figures 22.1 and 23.2). Within a Romanesque church there was more sculpture, chiefly decorative carving adorning the massive piers. The wall spaces were decorated with frescoes portraying scriptural scenes, particularly those that stressed the suffering of Christ and his judgment on humanity. Romanesque sculpture and painting is somber, with human beings small, powerless, and dependent, surrounded with symbols of the terrors that beset spiritual life; it grips the emotions rather than the mind.

Gothic architecture brought about changes in the other arts. The exteriors of Gothic churches

FIGURE 23.2 Romanesque Art These photos of the church of Sainte Madelaine at Vézelay in France illustrate some of the main features of Romanesque art. The nave (top right) features round ribbed arches, heavy columns, and thick walls pierced by small windows. Above the main portal (upper left) is a sculptured complex showing Christ instructing his disciples; comparable scenes over entrances were usual in Romanesque churches. The many capitals atop the pillars (lower left) of the nave and the porch leading to the main entrance provided space for carved scenes illustrating biblical themes. Romanesque sculpture was less concerned with realism than with reminding viewers of a religious truth and with moving their emotions. (Nave, Marburg; portal, Scala/Art Resource; sculpture, Marburg/Art Resource)

provided innumerable places for decorative sculpture, giving stone carvers an opportunity to experiment with a fantastic array of decorative motifs. Statues, sometimes executed in the round as well as in relief, became more realistic and humanistic, expressing more the human qualities than the mystical powers of Jesus, the Virgin, the apostles, and the saints (see Figures 22.3, 23.1, and 23.3).

The interior of Gothic churches offered less space for painting and sculpture than did Romanesque churches; decoration was concentrated chiefly on columns and arches. Not images but light fills the Gothic church. The painted walls of the Romanesque church were replaced with stained-glass windows. Their creators drew their themes chiefly from scriptural sources, but in their renditions they reflected in amazing detail the daily activities of medieval people. The stained glass at Chartres and in the beautiful Sainte-Chapelle built by Louis IX in Paris enthrall the viewer.

A variety of minor arts were employed to adorn these structures and to serve in carrying out religious services. Skilled metalwork was used for door handles and hinges, candleholders, chalices and pitchers, reliquaries, and railings to divide the space within the church. Woodwork provided pulpits and highly adorned seats for the celebrants of sacred services. Intricate needlework was employed to create splendid vestments for the clergy and tapestries to cover wall spaces. Skilled copyists and miniature painters fashioned beautiful liturgical books: bibles, missals, psalters, hymnals. Ivory carvings were used to fashion covers for these books. In all these forms, artists demonstrated highly developed skills and imagination to create works that fitted the grand style dictated by architecture and that reinforced the atmosphere of sanctity proper to holy places. Attendance at religious services constantly exposed the entire population to a dazzling display of the visual arts.

Another art associated with religious activity, music, also developed significantly during the High Middle Ages. Church music consisted primarily of melodies with verses taken from Scripture (especially the psalms) or composed for liturgical events (such great hymns as *Dies Irae* and *Stabat Mater* came from the Middle Ages). *Gregorian chant* (its alleged inventor was Pope Gregory

I) or *plain song* developed as early as the sixth century. At first, the singing was in unison, but over the centuries variations worked on plain song developed into contrapuntal music. By the thirteenth century, complex and moving contrapuntal compositions, rendered by many voices and various instruments, filled the churches with sounds almost as heavenly as the light that poured through the stained-glass windows.

The great cathedrals commanded the best artistic talent and the bulk of the wealth that medieval society had to devote to art. However, there were other lines of artistic pursuit. Living quarters for bishops and the cathedral clergy and for monastic communities were constructed in both the Romanesque and Gothic styles. Many feudal castles, massive rather than elegant or comfortable, were built in the Romanesque style. In the towns, especially from the thirteenth century onward, beautiful town halls and guildhalls were constructed, putting Gothic principles to new uses. These buildings were decorated with paintings and carvings and furnished with skillfully wrought furniture and utensils for daily living. These structures were impressive signs that the Church never completely absorbed artistic energies.

5. THE UNDERLYING SPIRIT OF MEDIEVAL CULTURE

Certainly it is not easy to find a common denominator for Thomas Aquinas, Dante, the architects and sculptors who built the churches at Poitiers, Amiens, and Chartres, the troubadours, the romance writers, and the authors of *fabliaux*. However, the more one experiences medieval culture, the more one senses an underlying, unifying spirit.

Medieval thought, literature, and art are permeated by a quest for truth and light beyond the world of human existence. This reaching out of the mind and the imagination sprang from the almost universal belief that God controlled the universe and that it was the duty of mortals to know and worship him. The artist and the writer stood in awe of God and humbly used their talents to serve him. Medieval culture viewed as a whole,

FIGURE 23.3 The Gothic Style The splendid church of Notre Dame at Amiens in France exemplifies the Gothic style. Its lofty nave (top left) is vaulted with pointed arches whose ribs carry weight down to the columns flanking the nave. Note the high arches that lead to aisles on either side of the nave. Above these arches is the clerestory, pierced by huge windows lighting the nave; the expanse can be seen in the apse at the far end of the building. The aerial view of the structure (bottom left) shows the flying buttresses used to offset the outward thrust of the roof on its supporting stone skeleton. Also evident is the transept crossing the nave. The façades of the main structure and the transept were decorated with numerous sculptures. Greeting those who entered the south transept was the "Golden Virgin" (top right), a wonderful example of the warmth and realism of Gothic sculpture. (Aerial view, Hunting Aerofilms; nave and sculpture, Archives Photographiques, Paris)

therefore, has an atmosphere of otherworldliness and of surrender to a power beyond human understanding.

Yet intertwined with this aspiration toward and submission to the divine is a warm, sympathetic feeling for humankind. Medieval people believed that a human being was God's finest creation. Artists and writers were never disdainful of human powers and potentialities. They took joy in presenting humanity as it was and wrestled constantly with the problem of understanding human nature more fully.

The medieval genius shines most brilliantly in attempts to synthesize these two outlooks. Thinkers, writers, and artists seldom felt that otherworldliness and secularism, spirituality and humanism were contradictory terms. They respected their own powers enough to believe that they could reach out toward God—by building higher cathedrals or by putting together greater *summae* of knowledge or by flights of poetic fancy. Yet they were filled with a faith great enough to believe that their human quest would lead them to a power infinitely greater than themselves and that ultimate illumination would allow them to realize their full potential as God's creatures.

SUGGESTED READING

General Surveys

John W. Baldwin, *The Scholastic Culture of the Middle Ages, 1000–1300* (1971). A perceptive brief survey.

C. H. Haskins, *The Renaissance of the Twelfth Century* (1927). A classic treatment.

Philippe Wolff, *The Cultural Awakening*, trans. Anne Carter (1968). A good assessment of the revival of cultural life.

Robert L. Benson and Giles Constable, eds., *Renaissance and Renewal in the Twelfth Century* (1982). An informative collection of essays on various phases of medieval cultural revival.

The Learned World

Alan B. Cobban, *The Medieval Universities: Their Development and Organization* (1975). A good description of medieval universities.

Michael Haren, *Medieval Thought: The Western Intellectual Tradition from Antiquity to the Thirteenth Century* (1985). Especially good in showing continuity between the ancient and medieval worlds.

John Marenbon, *Later Medieval Philosophy (1150–1350): An Introduction* (1987). A clear treatment; should be used along with Marenbon's volume on an earlier period, cited in Chapter 14.

Etienne Gilson, *History of Christian Philosophy in the Middle Ages* (1955). A classic treatment providing a positive assessment of medieval thought.

Richard E. McKeon, ed., *Selections from Medieval Philosophers*, 2 vols. (1929–1930). Selections from medieval philosophers.

Harold J. Berman, *Law and Revolution: The Formation of the Western Legal Tradition* (1983). A seminal study rich in insight.

A. C. Crombie, *Medieval and Early Modern Science*, 2nd ed., 2 vols. (1959). A good survey.

Walter Ullmann, *A History of Political Thought: The Middle Ages* (1965). A provocative survey.

Ewart Lewis, ed., *Medieval Political Ideas*, 2 vols. (1954). A collection of medieval writings on political theory.

Literature and Art

W. T. Jackson, *The Literature of the Middle Ages* (1960). A useful survey. More valuable is reading medieval literary works; the works mentioned in this chapter are easily available in excellent translations.

Georges Duby, *History of Medieval Art, 980–1440* (1986). A topical approach with splendid illustrations.

Henri Focillon, *The Art of the West in the Middle Ages*, 2nd ed., 2 vols., trans. Donald King (1969). A masterful detailed treatment.

Georges Duby, *The Age of the Cathedrals: Art and Society, 980–1240*, trans. Eleanor Levieux and Barbara Thompson (1981). A challenging attempt to interrelate art and social developments.

Jean Gimpel, *The Cathedral Builders*, trans. Teresa Waugh (1984). Describes the techniques of medieval builders.

Henry Adams, *Mont-St.-Michel and Chartres* (1913). A classic work contrasting the spirit of Romanesque and Gothic art.

Erwin Panofsky, *Gothic Architecture and Scholasticism* (1951). A stimulating effort to interrelate the intellectual and artistic worlds.

RETROSPECT

The era from 1000 to 1300 was of decisive importance in shaping the essential features of western European civilization. It was a time of remarkable expansion changing every aspect of the primitive society that had been so painfully and tenuously pieced together in the first five centuries after the collapse of the Roman order. After 1000 there occurred at every level of society and in every phase of life sustained, creative activity that increased wealth, secured order, shaped a more complex social order, expanded mental horizons, deepened understanding of the human condition, and enlarged the capabilities for expression. Many of the creations of the High Middle Ages remained essential features of western European society almost until the present. Included were the youthful national states, towns, the centralized Church, the universities, the basic social classes (nobility, bourgeoisie, peasantry), the vernacular languages, Romanesque and Gothic art, legal systems, and commercial and agricultural technologies. Any attempt to understand later European history must take these medieval creations into account.

But the era had another, equally important dimension. While gathering strength internally, western European society began to impinge on the world beyond its boundaries. During the High Middle Ages the first decisive steps were taken toward the establishment of European preeminence in the world. Anyone who would understand the contemporary world situation would be well served by attempting to identify the forces that by 1300 had given western Europeans the capabilities to influence the destinies of non-Europeans.

In reflecting on developments during the High Middle Ages, one is struck by the fact that as western European society matured, its institutional and ideological fabric was interlaced with dichotomies and contradictions. Examples leap immediately to mind: strong monarchy opposed to the privileged Church, nobility, towns; universal empire in competition with national states; Church versus state; urban society contrasted with rural society; universal Latin culture opposed to localized vernacular cultures; faith pitted against reason; the spirit against the flesh; guild protectionism versus capitalistic enterprise. One is almost forced to conclude that as a consequence of its historical development during the High Middle Ages, western European civilization became, in a unique way, an order compounded of contradictory thrusts. It was like a Gothic cathedral in which height competed with thrust, light with dark.

Can we say perhaps that this juxtaposition of opposites that emerged in the period between 1000 and 1300 constitutes the essence of postmedieval western European civilization? Dare we suggest that these medieval contradictions have supplied the Western world with its dynamism? Might we suspect that the history of the West after 1300 may be a story of the resolution of these contradictions? These issues are worth watching.

PART SIX
THE LATE MIDDLE AGES, 1300–1500

Historians have used various and contradictory phrases to label the late Middle Ages, that is, the period from 1300 to 1500: "the age of the Renaissance," "an age of transition," "the dawn of a new era," "the autumn of the Middle Ages," "the waning of the Middle Ages," "the age of adversity." All of these labels suggest that change was the keynote of the era; but they also suggest that historians do not agree on the direction of that change. Some emphasize new forces emerging; others stress the dissolution of old ways.

We shall take our clue for our treatment from those who lived during the period. Reading the literature and viewing the art of the era, one is struck by the bitterness, frustration, morbidity, and doubt gripping people's minds. They seemed to have sensed that something was amiss, and they reacted by losing confidence and hope. Their state of mind suggests that they saw their age as a time of decline and disintegration. Following that lead, our treatment will seek to show that the equilibrium established in the thirteenth century began to break down, resulting in widespread tensions and the deterioration of old patterns of civilization. But in taking that approach, we need to be mindful that those tensions also generated powerful new forces, capable of transforming society; we shall return to them in later discussions. However, men and women living during the period from 1300 to 1500 could not sense their promise as well as we can, gifted as we are with hindsight. To those people their times were disturbing, marked by the passing of the known and the familiar.

CHAPTER 24
Political, Economic, and Social Tensions

FIGURE 24.1 **Medieval Siege Warfare** This scene portrays the siege of an English castle in southern France by French forces during the Hundred Years' War. It illustrates very accurately the main weapons used in warfare. Engagements of this type drained large amounts of resources from both the English and the French royal governments. Providing the needs of the armies in these encounters often resulted in the pillaging of the countryside, which disrupted agricultural production and commercial exchange and caused untold misery to many. (The British Museum)

olitically, the fourteenth and fifteenth centuries were filled with disorder and strife. All of the major political entities that had been shaped during the High Middle Ages suffered dislocation in some form. Their inadequacies bred civil strife, class struggles, internal wars, and internal misgovernment throughout western Europe. In part, these political troubles rose from structural limitations and weaknesses in the institutions of these states. In part, they were a consequence of a new range of problems that the existing regimes had not previously faced. The most serious of these new problems were economic and social difficulties arising from the limitations and inadequacies of the traditional agricultural, commercial, and industrial systems.

1. THE DECLINE OF THE HOLY ROMAN EMPIRE

We have previously traced the efforts of a succession of rulers between 950 and 1250 to join Germany, Italy, and the western fringes of the Slavic world into a Holy Roman Empire and the powerful opposition, led by the papacy, these efforts generated (see Chapter 19). The death of the last great medieval emperor, Frederick II, in 1250 marked a decisive turning point: Not only did the empire as an institution disintegrate in the late Middle Ages; so did the political ideal that had given it a rationale—that a Christian commonwealth uniting the faithful under a single Christian prince could be created and sustained.

Frederick II's death opened a long period of decline in the authority of the emperor in Germany. After a strife-torn period without a ruler (called the Interregnum, 1250–1273), the German nobility elected a succession of rulers from three different families—the houses of Hapsburg, Luxembourg, and Bavaria—only to repudiate each family in turn when its ruling representative threatened to become too powerful. While demonstrating their unwillingness to accept a ruler with any effective power, the nobles, clergy, and townspeople successfully extended their independence from the central government. The resistance to effective monarchy was given legal definition by Emperor Charles IV (1347–1378), who in 1356

issued a decree called the Golden Bull. It provided that the German ruler would be chosen by seven princes designated as *electors:* the archbishops of Cologne, Trier, and Mainz, and the princes of Saxony, Brandenburg, the Palatinate, and Bohemia. Each elector was granted almost complete independence within his own territory.

After 1356 the Holy Roman Empire progressed rapidly toward decentralization. Other princes and cities demanded and gained the same kind of independence enjoyed by the electors, making the empire little more than a confederation of hundreds of independent political entities. The emperor could call together the princes, church leaders, and representatives of the towns in meetings called *diets,* but he lacked any means of enforcing decisions; he had no national army, no tax system, and no court system. Within their small principalities, many princes created stable, well-organized political systems—Germany was not a lawless, ungoverned land by any means. But Germany did lack unity, a condition that would cost it dearly in the future.

In Italy, the trend toward decentralization after 1250 was even more pronounced. The elected emperor was in theory the ruler of Italy, and from time to time some Italians did seek to have him exert his authority. After the early fourteenth century, the emperors seldom even tried to exercise any influence over their Italian realms, and a welter of independent states emerged. Among them, a few stand forth as most important.

In southern Italy the old Norman-Hohenstaufen state was divided after 1282 into the Kingdom of Naples, ruled by a French prince, and the Kingdom of Sicily, ruled by a member of the royal family of Aragon. Their rivalry and misrule brought steady decline to this once rich area. Finally, in 1435 the two kingdoms were united under Aragonese rule. However, by that time the area was so disturbed that it was destined to remain poor for centuries. The Papal States dominated central Italy. Papal overlordship was bitterly resisted by the local nobles, and it was badly compromised by the absence of the papacy from Rome during much of the fourteenth century (see Chapter 25). However, during the fifteenth century a succession of able, ruthless popes restored their authority, making the Papal States a major force in Italian political life.

Northern Italy was divided into many small city-states, most of which were constantly agitated by political conflicts. By the beginning of the thirteenth century concessions forced from their political overlord, the Holy Roman emperor, assured their political independence. After the death of Frederick II, they battled one another for land, trading advantages, power, and security. Some of the more powerful of the city-states, especially Milan, Venice, and Florence, were able to impose their rule on other small cities to create territorial entities that tended to dominate political life in northern Italy.

Internally, the political system of most of the city-states tended to move from an order with considerable citizen participation toward a system dominated by a single individual (the *signore*, "lord") or by an oligarchy of the rich. The pressure of intercity warfare and of class strife within each city-state encouraged the trend. Milan was taken over by a despot early in the fourteenth century when the Visconti family established its power. Visconti domination, which made Milan rich and greatly expanded its territory, lasted until 1447, when the Sforza family replaced them. Florence resisted despotism longer; in fact, through most of the period Florence retained the façade of a republican form of government that allowed its citizens considerable power to decide public issues. Under this system the city was constantly agitated by political strife. Gradually there emerged a behind-the-scenes power that used patronage, bribery, and personal influence to control rivalry and shape political decisions. After about 1430 that role was played by members of a rich banking family, the Medici. Although they held no exalted titles, the Medici in effect ran Florence as if they were despots. Venice always remained subject to an oligarchy of rich merchants whose methods did not differ greatly from those of the despots. The turbulent, strife-filled times in Italy promoted a new style of politics, later described brilliantly in Machiavelli's *The Prince*. The new order tended to place heavy emphasis on the absolute sovereignty of the state, its right to create its own moral sanctions, its superiority over its subjects. Many historians see these developments as prototypes for the absolute sovereignty claimed

by modern states.

Despite the vitality of the Italian Renaissance states, the fragmentation of the peninsula doomed Italy to weakness in the face of larger, better-organized states, such as Spain and France and even the larger German principalities. In 1494 Charles VIII of France was called into Italy by the Sforza ruler of Milan in order to gain advantage for his city; the French invasion opened a long era when the many states of Italy became pawns in European power politics.

2. THE FAILURE OF FEUDAL MONARCHY IN FRANCE, ENGLAND, AND SPAIN

After 1300 England, France, and the Iberian kingdoms encountered troubles nearly as serious as those of the Holy Roman Empire. As the fourteenth century progressed, the well-organized feudal monarchies developed during the twelfth and thirteenth centuries (see Chapter 20) began to show signs of instability and inadequacy. The heightening of tension in each kingdom led to civil wars that pitted the crown against the nobles and noble factions against each other. Under constant stress, the essential features of feudal monarchy and the concepts that animated the political order of the High Middle Ages broke down.

The histories of France and England from 1300 to 1500 were linked together by the Hundred Years' War (1337–1453). This struggle was an extension of a conflict that began in the twelfth century over possessions on the continent held by English kings as fiefs from the French kings. The first phase of the struggle, highlighted by Philip II's victory over John, was settled by the Treaty of Paris (1259), which recognized the French king's control over the northern part of the old Angevin Empire but left the English king holding as a fief important territories in Aquitaine (see Map 24.1). However, the rivalry continued, especially as a result of pressures exerted on English holdings by the strong French kings, Louis IX and Philip IV. English and French interests also clashed in the county of Flanders, where the English sought to resist French domination to protect their interests in the Flemish woolen industry, which depended on English raw wool. French support of the efforts of the Scots to win their independence also troubled the English, especially after the Scots virtually assured that end with their victory at the battle of Bannockburn in 1314.

These festering issues came to a head during the reign of Edward III of England (1327–1377). In 1328 the last member of the direct Capetian line died. Although Edward III had the best hereditary claim to the French throne, the Estates General selected as king Philip of Valois, representing a collateral line of the Capetian family. Philip VI acted aggressively to assert his authority in Flanders, provoking a revolt there. The pro-English Flemish rebels urged Edward to claim the French throne so that he could become their king. In the meantime, Philip began to harass the English territory in Aquitaine and to press his claim to lordship over his vassal, the king of England. When Edward resisted Philip's demands, the French king confiscated Aquitaine in 1337 on the grounds that Edward had refused to honor his obligations as a vassal. Edward III then asserted his claim to the French throne, provoking a major war.

The first phase of the Hundred Years' War, lasting until 1360, was nearly fatal to France. Having established control of the English Channel, the English put armies in France, which in two great battles at Crécy (1346) and Poitiers (1356) cut to pieces the flower of the French nobility. At Poitiers, King John of France was captured and taken to England. An internal crisis ensued in France, marked by an effort of the Estates General to take control of the government, by a peasant rebellion, called the *Jacquerie*, in 1358, and by the ravaging of a large part of France by bands of unpaid soldiers. Eventually John bought his release by agreeing to the Treaty of Brétigny (1360) in which he agreed to pay a huge ransom and to give Edward III full title to Guienne as well as a small territory in northern France, including the key port of Calais. Edward renounced his claim to the French throne.

The Treaty of Brétigny did not end the ancient rivalries. The next phase of the war, extending from 1364 to 1415, saw sporadic but indecisive fighting. Effective military action was impeded by serious internal problems in both of the rival kingdoms. France enjoyed a brief recovery under Charles V (1364–1380), who rebuilt French military strength and increased royal income to the point where he seriously threatened England's hold on Guienne (see Figure 24.1). However, these gains were undone during the reign of his pitiful successor, Charles VI (1380–1422). A minor when he became king, Charles VI was victimized by greedy relatives acting as regents. The most powerful was an uncle, Philip, duke of Burgundy, who was determined to control the weak monarch in order to enlarge his already substantial principality. Philip was thwarted, however, when Charles, on reaching his majority, fell under the spell of his brother, Louis, duke of Orléans. Moreover, Charles began to suffer spells of insanity, each of which required a reinstitution of the regency. Burgundians and Armagnacs (partisans of the duke of Orléans) competed bitterly for control of the regency and the kingdom. Powerful nobles joined the struggle in an effort to serve private interests. This selfish, violent rivalry plunged France into civil chaos from which much of the population suffered badly.

England was hardly less troubled during these years. Edward III ruled until 1377 amid deepening trouble. To wage the increasingly costly war against France, he needed money, and the easiest way to get it was to call Parliament. Frequent meetings resulted in the rapid development of parliamentary organization: The *House of Lords*, comprising the great feudal barons and high church officials, separated from the *House of Commons*, made up of townspeople and of the lesser gentry representing the counties. Aside from its extensive control over taxation, Parliament began to gain a voice in spending money, controlling royal officials, and initiating legislation through petitions presented to the king. The advancing power of Parliament became particularly notable in the reign of Richard II (1377–1399). His reign was troubled by economic and social problems that led to a Peasants' Revolt in 1381 and by deep dissatisfaction among the nobles with the king's autocratic ways. Eventually, Parliament deposed Richard II and chose in his place Henry IV (1399–1413), whose sole right to rule was based on Parliament's approval. Obviously, that institution had assumed a crucial role in political life. However, Parliament proved neither capable of directing the kingdom nor willing to trust the king to do so. It became a forum for factional agitation aimed at dominating the king in order to gain greater privileges.

Henry V (1413–1422) hastened both England and France on their troubled ways by reopening the Hundred Years' War. In 1415 he invaded France and crushed a French army at Agincourt. With the support of the Burgundian faction, he established control over most of France north of the Loire River. In 1420 he forced the humiliating Treaty of Troyes on Charles VI. By its terms, Henry married Charles' daughter; Henry or his heir by that marriage would rule France after Charles' death; in the meantime Henry would serve as regent. The legitimate heir to the throne, the dauphin Charles, was disinherited. France seemed on the verge of destruction.

But the English were not to enjoy their triumph long. After both Henry V and Charles VI died in 1422, leaving the infant Henry VI as king of both nations, the French made a spectacular recovery. The rallying point was the dauphin Charles, who controlled considerable territory south of the Loire and had the support of many royal officials, military captains, and nobles. Timid by nature, Charles did not capitalize on these resources until he was moved to action by a strange turn of events. In 1429 a simple peasant girl, Joan of Arc, came to him claiming God had revealed to her that Charles must free France of the English and assume the crown that rightly belonged to him. Her message bestirred the dispirited Charles and pumped new confidence into the French soldiers loyal to him. Dressed like a man, Joan herself was with the army that in 1429 defeated an English army besieging the key city of Orléans; this was the first French victory for many years. On the strength of it, Joan persuaded Charles to be crowned king, a venture that turned into a triumph.

From 1429 to 1453, the French won victory after victory, until the English held only Calais. But Joan did not live to see these triumphs. In 1430 she was captured by the Burgundians and turned over to the English. She was tried by the Church for heresy and burned at the stake in Rouen in 1431. Despite her tragic end, Joan's dream of a reborn France soon came to pass. Under Charles VII, royal power made a remarkable recovery in France. Well served by excellent ministers, Charles was able to build a well-trained army paid for by the king, thus ending his dependence on a feudal army and on troublemaking mercenaries. In 1439 the Estates General granted the king power to impose a direct tax, called the *taille*, on his subjects. Although many powerful nobles in France continued to act in their own interest, political life more and more focused on the royal government with its increasing ability to establish order and curb the irresponsible behavior of the princes. The old feudal basis for royal power was rapidly eroding. In its place was a growing consciousness of the king as the head of a nation of subjects held together by common interests that the state should serve. When Charles VII died in 1461, his son, Louis XI (1461–1483), inherited a solid base from which to rule. His accession marked the beginning of a new era.

England was in a less happy state during much of the fifteenth century, chiefly because of a deepening factionalism among a few privileged families seeking control of the government as a means of enhancing their power. Surrounding themselves with private armies, these factions pushed England toward civil war. The struggle began to take shape during the reign of Henry VI (1422–1461). Because he became king in infancy, there was a

Map 24.1 **THE HUNDRED YEARS' WAR** In the Hundred Years' War the English fought to regain their once extensive possessions in France (see Map 20.1), and the French sought to add these territories to the royal domain. The map shows the ebb and flow of that prolonged struggle. When the war began in 1337, England held only a modest territory in southwest France. At the height of their fortunes in the first half of the fifteenth century, they controlled most of northern France. But not for long. When the war ended in 1453, the French had driven them off the Continent except for the city of Calais.

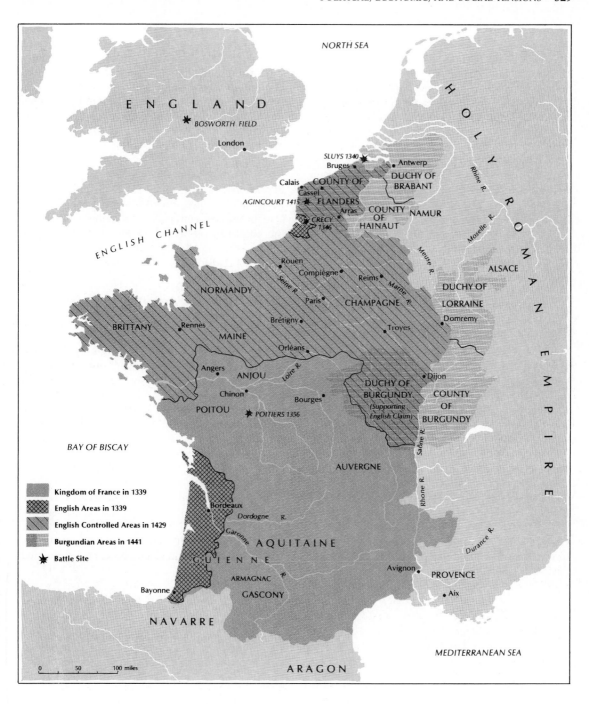

NORTH SEA

ENGLAND

BOSWORTH FIELD

London

SLUYS 1340
Bruges
Antwerp
Calais
COUNTY OF
DUCHY OF
BRABANT
Cassel
AGINCOURT 1415
FLANDERS
Arras
COUNTY OF
HAINAUT
NAMUR
CRÉCY
1346

ENGLISH CHANNEL

Rouen
Compiègne
Reims
ALSACE

NORMANDY
Seine R.
Paris
CHAMPAGNE
Marne R.
DUCHY OF
LORRAINE
Domremy

BRITTANY
Rennes
MAINE
Brétigny
Troyes

Angers
Orléans
ANJOU
Loire R.
Chinon
Bourges
Dijon
DUCHY OF
BURGUNDY
(Supporting
English Claim)
COUNTY
OF
BURGUNDY

POITOU
POITIERS 1356

BAY OF BISCAY

AUVERGNE

Rhine R.
Moselle R.
Meuse R.
Saône R.
Rhône R.

HOLY ROMAN EMPIRE

Kingdom of France in 1339

English Areas in 1339

English Controlled Areas in 1429

Burgundian Areas in 1441

Battle Site

Bordeaux
Dordogne R.
Garonne R.
AQUITAINE
GUIENNE
ARMAGNAC
Bayonne
GASCONY
Avignon
PROVENCE
Aix
Durance R.

NAVARRE

0   50   100 miles

MEDITERRANEAN SEA

ARAGON

long regency. Moreover, his family, the Lancastrians, elevated to the throne by parliamentary act in 1399, did not have as strong a hereditary claim to the throne as did another family, the Yorkists. Followings of nobles formed around the Lancastrians and the Yorkists, leading to a bitter civil war, the War of the Roses, so called because the opposing forces adopted the white and the red rose as their symbols. While this struggle for the crown raged, the regular processes of orderly government were disrupted. Tyranny, intrigue, murder, confiscation of property, and pursuit of private ends were the order of the day. Finally, in 1485, Henry Tudor, a Lancastrian, defeated his Yorkist rival, King Richard III, in a pitched battle at Bosworth Field and assumed the throne as Henry VII.

Although Henry's claim to the crown was extremely tenuous, the nation, weary of civil disorder, was willing to follow anyone who promised to restore peace and security. The desire for order was strong among the lesser nobles, the *gentry* made up chiefly of rural landowners, the prosperous peasant yeomen, and the well-to-do bourgeoisie. Taken together these elements constituted a substantial force willing to support effective royal government. The old noble factions were badly discredited as a result of their brutal, self-seeking conduct during the War of the Roses. As a result, the new king had considerable freedom to act as he pleased. Henry used the opportunity to end the feudal state and create a strong central government that united the English people into a nation.

The three major Iberian kingdoms—Aragon, Castile, and Portugal—also had their difficulties during the late Middle Ages. By 1300 the holy war against the Moslems had ceased to be the significant factor in Spanish affairs, for the Moslems had been confined to the narrow territory of Granada (see Map 21.1). The Christian kingdoms then turned on one another, competing bitterly for territory. At the same time almost constant civil strife raged within each kingdom, replicating the struggles in England and France. Castile was plagued by a long series of disputed successions that undermined royal authority. Aragon's internal order was compromised by the aggressive overseas policy pursued by its kings, especially in Italy, a pol-

icy seldom favored by the nobility, and by conflict between the landed and the commercial interests. These senseless quarrels finally began to abate in 1469 when the heiress of Castile, Isabella, married Ferdinand, the heir of Aragon. In 1479, when this couple had succeeded to both thrones, they quickly took steps to end the strife, unify their lands into a single state, and to impose stronger royal control over their subjects.

Portuguese kings did not meet such violent resistance as did the other Iberian kings, and their heroic struggle to prevent Castile from absorbing Portugal won them broad internal support. They also promoted commercial ventures throughout the fifteenth century, backing Portuguese merchants who expanded southward along the African coast and found lucrative markets.

3. EASTERN EUROPE AND THE MEDITERRANEAN WORLD

While the western European states were undergoing internal crises and engaging each other in rivalries that sapped their strength, highly significant political changes were unfolding along Europe's eastern and southeastern frontiers. These developments drastically altered the relationships that had been established between the West and these eastern areas in the High Middle Ages (these changes can be followed on Map 24.2).

The Byzantine Empire never fully recovered from the attacks of the Seljuk Turks in the late eleventh century and the capture of Constantinople by western Europeans in 1204 during the Fourth Crusade. After the Europeans were finally ousted in 1261 and Greek emperors again assumed

---

Map 24.2 CENTRAL EUROPE AND WESTERN ASIA, ca. 1500 This map shows the major political entities in central Europe and western Asia about 1500. Especially threatening to Poland, Lithuania, and Hungary—and to western Europe in general—were two rapidly expanding powers: the Ottoman Empire and the Grand Principality of Moscow (the future Russia).

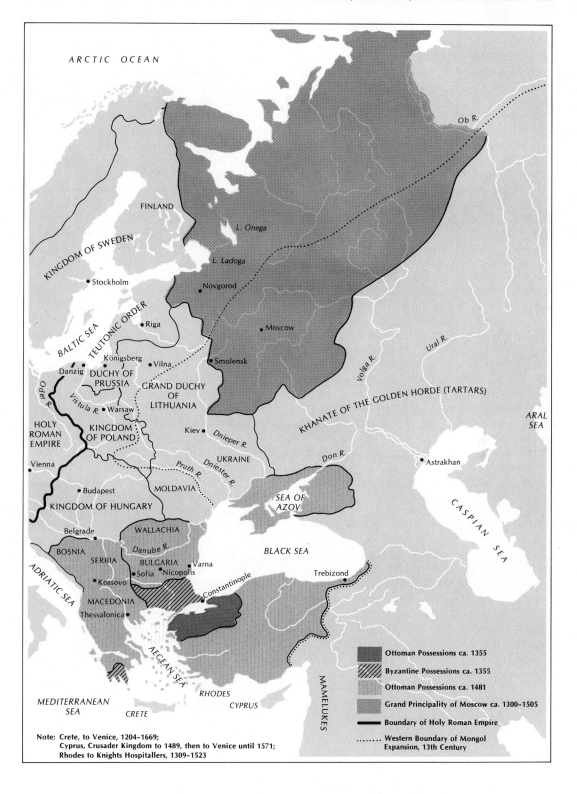

ARCTIC OCEAN

Ob R.

FINLAND

L. Onega

L. Ladoga

KINGDOM OF SWEDEN

• Stockholm

• Novgorod

TEUTONIC ORDER

• Riga

BALTIC SEA

• Moscow

Königsberg

• Vilna

Ural R.

Danzig

DUCHY OF PRUSSIA

• Smolensk

Oder R.

Vistula R.

GRAND DUCHY OF LITHUANIA

Volga R.

KHANATE OF THE GOLDEN HORDE (TARTARS)

ARAL SEA

• Warsaw

HOLY ROMAN EMPIRE

KINGDOM OF POLAND

• Kiev

Dnieper R.

Vienna

UKRAINE

Don R.

• Astrakhan

Pruth R.

Dniester R.

• Budapest

MOLDAVIA

CASPIAN SEA

KINGDOM OF HUNGARY

SEA OF AZOV

Belgrade

WALLACHIA

BOSNIA

Danube R.

BLACK SEA

SERBIA

BULGARIA

• Varna

• Sofia

• Nicopolis

• Kossovo

Constantinople

• Trebizond

ADRIATIC SEA

MACEDONIA

Thessalonica •

AEGEAN SEA

MAMELUKES

MEDITERRANEAN SEA

RHODES

CRETE

CYPRUS

Ottoman Possessions ca. 1355

Byzantine Possessions ca. 1355

Ottoman Possessions ca. 1481

Grand Principality of Moscow ca. 1300–1505

Boundary of Holy Roman Empire

Western Boundary of Mongol Expansion, 13th Century

Note: Crete, to Venice, 1204–1669;
Cyprus, Crusader Kingdom to 1489, then to Venice until 1571;
Rhodes to Knights Hospitallers, 1309–1523

power, a fatal illness afflicted the empire. Civil strife slowly sapped the strength of its government. The Italian city-states, led by Venice, deprived the empire of much of its trade, and bit by bit its territory was pared away, especially by the Ottoman Turks. The emperors of the fourteenth and fifteenth centuries appealed desperately to the West for help but received little. Finally, in 1453 Constantinople was captured by the Ottomans, who made the city their capital under the name Istanbul. The fall of Constantinople ended forever the power that had so long shielded Europe.

The Ottoman victory in 1453 marked the reappearance of a Moslem threat to the West, a danger that western Europeans had not faced for centuries. The Ottoman Turks were originally Asiatic nomads who were uprooted and pushed westward by the Mongols. They settled in Asia Minor in the thirteenth century, accepted Islam, and adopted many of the ways of Moslem society. Under their first great ruler, Osman (or Othman, whence the term *Ottoman*) (1290–1326), the new state began to expand in Asia Minor and then into the Balkans, largely at the expense of the Byzantine Empire. Early in the fifteenth century, Ottoman power was nearly destroyed by Tamerlane, a Mongol warrior who sought to reconstruct the empire of Genghis Khan (see Chapter 21). Tamerlane's empire collapsed soon after his death in 1405, allowing the Ottomans to recover their power and continue their expansion. They completed the conquest of the Byzantine Empire by 1453. Early in the sixteenth century, they conquered Syria, Palestine, and Egypt. As the Middle Ages ended, their vast empire loomed as a major threat to the West.

As the Ottoman Turks extended their territorial sway, they fashioned political institutions that gave their empire strength and stability. The Ottomans constituted an elite claiming supremacy over their subjects, many of them Christians, by right of conquest. They retained a strong sense of community based on their ethnic identity and their religion. The Ottoman state was headed by the *sultan,* whose extensive power over all aspects of life was based on his claim to be the successor of Muhammad, empowered to interpret the Moslem law that all followers of Allah were required to obey. A well-organized bureaucracy developed,

modeled on both Byzantine and Abbasid models. Local units of government were developed across the empire to carry out the sultan's policies, collect taxes, and administer justice. In practice, the Ottoman regime allowed local communities broad authority to regulate their own affairs as long as they did not disrupt internal peace or challenge the sultan's supreme power. Aside from taxes, the Ottomans extracted human resources from their subject population to sustain their regime. Young boys, often of Christian or Jewish origins, were claimed as slaves, converted to Islam, and rigorously trained for specialized duties in the civil service or the army. The military corps created from these slaves, called the Janissaries, developed into a highly professional, dedicated force that played a key role in Ottoman expansion and in maintaining Ottoman domination over the large empire. Young girls were also enslaved to serve in Ottoman harems, including that of the sultan.

Central and eastern Europe began to assume a modern shape in the wake of the decline of the Holy Roman and Byzantine empires. The south coast of the Baltic Sea was dominated by Germans, an expansion spearheaded by the crusading order of the Teutonic Knights who brought traders, missionaries, and agricultural colonists in their wake. Their presence filled the Slavs of central Europe with an abiding distrust and fear of the Germans. The Germanic threat resulted in a union of the ruling houses of Poland and Lithuania under the Lithuanian prince Jagiello, who married a Polish princess and governed both states as King Ladislas II (1386–1434). The house of Jagiello exerted strong military pressure on the Baltic Germans and the Russian states to the east during much of the fifteenth century, but it never succeeded in creating an effective government for its huge kingdom. To the south, Hungary continued to develop, but its energies were increasingly absorbed in defending itself against the Ottoman Turks and holding back ambitious German nobles bent on taking the Hungarian throne. Until the Ottomans seized control of the Balkans at the end of the fourteenth century, a flourishing Serbian kingdom dominated that area; after its destruction, the Hungarians stood as western Europe's outpost against the Turks. Farther east a vigorous Russian state was emerging. We shall return to the story of its development later (see Chapter 34). Suffice it to say here that by 1500 Russia was beginning to play an important role in determining the fate of eastern Europe.

4. ECONOMIC AND SOCIAL TENSIONS

The political difficulties of the late Middle Ages were brought on partly by basic economic and social problems troubling most of Europe. By 1300 the long period of economic growth that western Europe had enjoyed since about 1000 (see Chapter 18) was ending; for the next century and a half its economy suffered contraction and depression, and social disequilibrium grew. Although the nature and impact of economic and social dislocation varied from region to region, certain broad patterns affected western Europe generally.

The economic growth of the period from 1000 to 1300 had been powerfully stimulated by sustained population growth. The depression that afflicted western Europe after 1300 was in important ways a by-product of a dramatic population decline. Modern demographers have produced considerable evidence to suggest that by 1300 much of western Europe had reached the point where the population level was straining the food supply. Also, the early decades of the fourteenth century were marked by a succession of famines, due in part to unfavorable climatic conditions and in part to increasing dependence on poorer agricultural lands. Perhaps the combination of a population pushing the limits of productive capacity and an increasingly unfavorable pattern of weather might have been sufficient to cause a population downturn. To these conditions, however, was added a demographic catastrophe.

That disaster took the form of a devastating pestilence: the Black Death, an epidemic of bubonic plague that first spread over Europe with deadly effect between 1347 and 1350 and then returned periodically during most of the fourteenth century and far beyond into the seventeenth century. The scourge was brought to Europe from the East by rats infested with fleas whose bites transmitted the bacilli to the human bloodstream. Once the disease was loosed in

FIGURE 24.2 **The Plague** This painting captures the terror inflicted on the population of a city by the Black Death. Even while shrouding the dead for burial, people were suddenly struck down, as is the man shown falling to the ground. Neither the prayers of the clergy nor the pleas of the saints, represented in this scene by St. Sebastian, could help. (The Walters Art Gallery, Baltimore)

western Europe, it caused an immense loss of life. The best estimates suggest that a third of Europe's population was wiped out between 1347 and 1350. Periodic recurrence of the plague continued the downward spiral of the population, so that by the early fifteenth century western Europe had barely half as many people as it had had in 1300. Such a drastic demographic change had massive effects on the level of production, the demand for goods, the labor supply, prices, social relationships, and mass psychology (see Figure 24.2).

While population decline was a prime force in curbing economic growth in the late Middle Ages, it was only one factor. The economy also suffered from structural limitations rooted in the traditional system of production and from disruptive forces outside the economic system. Especially damaging to economic life during the fourteenth and fifteenth centuries was the reduction of commercial exchange. The population decline drastically reduced demand and limited the productive processes that supplied goods for exchange. Vast disturbances in eastern and central Asia ended opportunities to penetrate new areas of commercial opportunity. The rise of the Ottoman Empire seriously disturbed the favored position that Italian merchants had long enjoyed in the eastern Mediterranean. The independent cities that had been the source of commercial growth earlier became increasingly restrictive, chiefly in an effort to protect local merchants and to monopolize regional trade. Sustained cooperation among commercial cities for mutual benefit proved nearly impossible. The most successful effort of this kind was the Hanseatic League, which linked about seventy cities in northern Germany, Scandinavia, and the Low Countries. But ultimately the League declined, chiefly because its members refused to sacrifice local interests.

Industrial production experienced a comparable constriction. Labor shortages increased labor costs to the point where many kinds of industrial production were unprofitable. To redress this situation, some manufacturers—particularly in the wool industry—began to move their operations into rural areas where labor was cheaper. And they joined landowners to pressure governments to pass legislation, such as the English Statute of Laborers (1351), attempting to freeze wages. The guild system, which had once promoted industrial production, grew increasingly restrictive. Seeking to protect their monopoly over the production of goods in each city, the guilds passed rules limiting the volume of production, setting prices, excluding the products of outsiders, barring technical changes, and limiting entrance into each craft. Although some industrial operations, such as wool production, continued to flourish, the general effect of such measures was to depress industrial production.

Agricultural production was likewise depressed and dislocated. Widespread and persistent warfare ravaged many lands. Colonizing opportunities had nearly disappeared. Famine and plague decimated the rural labor force and sharply reduced the urban demand for food products, especially cereal grains. Large areas of marginal land were taken out of production, dislocating many agricultural workers. Many landowners were sorely pressed to make ends meet. Their solution usually involved abandoning the traditional manorial system. Some rented their domains to enterprising peasants eager to gain access to more land. Others enclosed their manors in order to concentrate on specialized crops and livestock raising; these operations increasingly depended on hired labor. Both solutions resulted in the dislocation of serfs traditionally attached to the land.

Economic dislocation and contraction led to widespread social tension and disturbance in the late Middle Ages. As we noted earlier, even before 1300 Europe's aristocracy was becoming stratified, chiefly on the basis of wealth. That stratification continued and became even more pronounced during the late Middle Ages. These were tenuous times for the highest nobility, not only because changing economic conditions strained their fortunes but also because the unsettled political situation demanded their involvement in violent factionalism and civil war if they were to retain their position of prestige and power. Some did not survive the murderous conflicts. However, the powerful aristocratic families that did survive held their fortunes and increased their privileges, so that their social position became more distinct than ever. Increasingly, these powerful nobles owed their status to their close connections with the monarchs. The high aristocracy pursued an ever more splendid and exclusive life style; it was based on an exaggerated practice of behavior patterns dictated by the code of chivalry.

Although many lesser nobles were also sorely tested by the agricultural depression, they solidified their position as a country gentry asserting a powerful influence over local life. Their key to success was the careful management of production on their landholdings and the exploitation of the local labor supply. They often strengthened their local position by allying themselves with great nobles and by seeking favors from royal governments. While duly impressed by the life style of the great nobles, the lesser nobles were not able and did not try to imitate it. They began to develop a simpler life style attuned to the activities of the small country estate and the local town. By 1500 this gentry had become a powerful force interested primarily in order and stability and support for their economic interests; they became a source of support for the increasingly strong kings. Thus, by 1500 a powerfully entrenched aristocracy continued to dominate society. However, its inner structure as a class was being altered, and its power base was shifting from the relationships defined by feudal connections to those defined by birth, by wealth, and by royal favor.

The peasant world underwent significant changes during the late Middle Ages. The developments in agricultural production noted above gave added impetus to the decline of serfdom, so that by 1500 servile dependence—a key component of the agricultural system before 1300—had virtually disappeared in western Europe. While this development improved the legal status of most peasants, it deprived many of the economic security that had characterized serf status in earlier times. Population decline and the dismantling of manors seriously disrupted community groupings that had been a vital part of peasant life. Economically, peasants were thrown more and more on their own as renters or hired laborers, often with disastrous results in a period of economic instability. Hard-pressed landlords preyed on peasant misfortunes to force on them added financial obligations, higher rents, and lower wages. Royal taxes fell heavily on the peasants, and the wars they thus paid for often ravaged their farms. With reduced opportunities in the troubled cities and a vanishing frontier, many peasants were trapped in a position of poverty and oppression. They expressed their discontent by frequent and violent rebellions, most of which were brutally crushed by kings, nobles, and clergy (see Figure 24.3). Despite the generally grim picture surrounding peasant life in the late Middle Ages, there were peasants who succeeded in increasing their landholdings either by purchase or by renting and who found ways of expanding their productivity and wealth in a volatile age. This element of the peas-

FIGURE 24.3 Peasant Violence Pressed by a variety of miseries, peasants often resorted to violence in the late Middle Ages, as illustrated in this drawing showing peasants attacking a knight with axes and daggers. (Bibliothèque Nationale, Paris, ms. fr. 87)

ant class would eventually make important contributions to the agricultural recovery of western Europe (see Color Plate 11).

Equally disadvantaged and discontented were certain elements of the urban population. The depression in manufacturing and exchange reduced many small-scale artisans and shopkeepers to the status of laborers for hire or to the ranks of the unemployed. They were also increasingly deprived of a significant voice in urban government, such as they had enjoyed during the twelfth and thirteenth centuries. Dominated by rich entrepreneurs, city governments and the guilds sought to regulate more stringently the economic activities and the wages of urban laborers. This element of the bourgeoisie demonstrated their discontent by frequent rioting and rebellion, usually with little more success than the peasants had.

The social group making the greatest advance in the fourteenth and fifteenth centuries was an elite segment of the bourgeoisie engaged in capitalistic ventures. Their success is exemplified by the Medici and the Bardi in Italy, the Fuggers in southern Germany, Jacques Coeur of France, and some of the entrepreneurs associated with the Hanseatic League. Members of this group amassed huge fortunes in such fields as banking, money lending, and the wool industry. Seeking to use that wealth to create more, these entrepreneurs increasingly determined the course of economic development. They seized political control of most city governments and found favor with kings. Culturally they were able to patronize the learning and art of the Renaissance movement advancing in much of Europe and to set standards of fashion. In a sense, this group now represented the bourgeoisie; others who had formerly been counted in this class—simple artisans and small shopkeepers—were becoming a group apart, a laboring class. The new bourgeoisie was destined to play a major role in the future of the West.

By approximately 1450 the worst of the economic and social stresses of the late Middle Ages was over, and there were signs of recovery everywhere. Aside from the return of political order accompanying the restoration of royal authority, the population had begun to grow again. The agricultural system became increasingly stable, chiefly on the basis of a rental system that bound landlord and peasant together on a money basis and a more rational management of land and labor in relation to the realities of the market. Innovative techniques were being devised for accumulating capital and organizing large-scale manufacturing production and commercial enterprises. New technological advances were being made and were being applied more widely—water mills in the textile industry, better mining techniques, printing, improved shipbuilding, the compass, the astrolabe, gunpowder. New frontiers were opening by way of the seas that washed Europe's western shores. All these forces pointed toward new growth in western Europe. It was obvious, however, that this growth would be achieved in ways different from those that prevailed in medieval Europe.

SUGGESTED READING

Overview of the Period 1300–1500

Robert Fossier, ed., *The Cambridge Illustrated History of the Middle Ages*, Vol. 3: *1250–1520*, trans. Sarah Hanbury Tenison (1986).

Daniel Waley, *Later Medieval Europe: From Saint Louis to Luther*, 2nd ed. (1985).

George Holmes, *Europe: Hierarchy and Revolt, 1320–1450* (1975).

Any of these three works will provide an excellent overview of the major developments during the period.

Western Europe

Bernard Guenée, *States and Rulers in Later Medieval Europe*, trans. Juliet Vale (1985). A comparative study of political developments.

F. R. H. DuBoulay, *Germany in the Later Middle Ages* (1983). A clear treatment of Germany's complex history.

Brian Pullan, *A History of Early Renaissance Italy. From the Mid–Thirteenth to the Mid–Fifteenth Century* (1973). Helpful in showing general political and economic trends in Italy.

George Holmes, *The Later Middle Ages, 1272–1485* (1962).

Trevor Rowley, *The High Middle Ages, 1200–1550* (1986).

Either of these works will provide a clear picture of developments in late medieval England.

John Gillingham, *The War of the Roses: Peace and Conflict in Fifteenth-Century England* (1981). Stresses the political and military aspect of England's internal strife.

P. S. Lewis, *Later Medieval France: The Polity* (1968). One of the few works in English on late medieval France.

Christopher Allmond, *The Hundred Years' War. England and France at War c. 1300–c.1450* (1988). A well-done treatment stressing the effects of the war.

Eastern Europe

Donald M. Nicol, *The Last Centuries of Byzantium, 1261–1453* (1972). A clearly presented account.

Halil Inalick, *The Ottoman Empire: The Classical Age, 1300–1600*, trans. Norman Itzkowitz and Colin Imber (1973). The best treatment of a subject not always given an objective evaluation.

David Morgan, *The Mongols* (1986).

G. Vernadsky, *The Origins of Russia* (1959). A brilliant treatment.

Economic and Social History

C. M. Cipolla, *Before the Industrial Revolution: European Society and Economy, 1000–1700* (1976). Effectively places late medieval economic and social history in a larger context.

Harry A. Miskimin, *The Economy of Early Renaissance Europe, 1300–1460* (1969). A detailed study; more general treatments can be found in the works of Bautier and Pounds, cited in Chapter 18.

Specialized aspects of late medieval economic and social history are treated in the following works.

Johannes Schildhauer, *The Hansa: History and Culture*, trans. Katherine Vanovitch (1985).

Robert S. Gottfried, *The Black Death: Natural and Human Disaster in Medieval Europe* (1983).

Graham Twigg, *The Black Death: A Biological Reappraisal* (1984).

Michel Mollat and Philippe Wolff, *The Popular Revolutions of the Late Middle Ages*, trans. A. L. Lytton-Sells (1973).

CHAPTER 25

The Decline of the Church

FIGURE 25.1 Pope Boniface VIII This fresco from the Church of St. John Lateran in Rome shows Pope Boniface VIII proclaiming the great jubilee held in Rome in 1300. The artist, perhaps Giotto, catches something of the autocratic spirit of the proud pontiff whose efforts to assert papal authority led to deep trouble for the Church. (Alinari/Art Resource)

The tensions that beset western European political, social, and economic institutions in the fourteenth and fifteenth centuries afflicted the Church even more severely. After 1300 this powerful institution, which had earlier decisively influenced all aspects of human activity, encountered increasing difficulties in asserting its traditional leadership role. Its teachings, its system of government, and its leaders were subjected to merciless criticism and open defiance. And the Church failed to discover effective ways to respond to these mounting criticisms.

1. A CRISIS IN CHURCH GOVERNANCE

One of the major results of the reform movement of the High Middle Ages had been the creation of a highly centralized, hierarchical system of church governance capable of imposing a uniform pattern of belief and discipline on the Christian community of western Europe. During the late Middle Ages that structure faltered in a variety of ways.

The most dramatic challenge to that system focused on its very center: the papacy. The authority of the papal office, brought to its apogee by the talented popes of the thirteenth century, was vigorously contested during the pontificate of Boniface VIII (1294–1303). This vain, ambitious "prince of the new Pharisees" (see Figure 25.1), as Dante called him, met stern resistance from the kings of England and France. His failure to respond effectively to that test dramatized the vulnerability of the papacy and led to increasing attacks on the papal office.

Boniface's first setback came when he attempted to stop Edward I of England and Philip IV of France from imposing new taxes on the Church in their realms to help finance their wars with each other. In a pronouncement intended to be binding on all Christians (called a papal bull) entitled *Clericis laicos*, Boniface forcefully maintained that only with papal consent could taxes be laid upon the Church. Edward and Philip responded by cutting off revenues from their kingdoms to Rome, forcing Boniface to retreat from his position.

Before long Boniface and Philip again clashed, this time over the question of whether the king or the Church had jurisdiction in legal cases involving the clergy. Against the strong-minded pope stated his case unequivocally. In a bull entitled *Unam sanctam* he not only stated the Church's right to judge its clergy but also insisted that the French king and all other Christians must subject themselves to the pope to be saved. Philip countered with a masterful propaganda campaign, highlighted by blatant distortion of the papal position, which successfully discredited the pope in the eyes of the French public. He capped that campaign by sending his agents to Italy to capture Boniface. They were successful, and the pope escaped what might have been an even more painful defeat by dying. St. Peter's vicar had suffered a humiliating defeat.

Philip IV capitalized on his victory by using his influence over the College of Cardinals to ensure the election of a French bishop as pope. Aware that he would be unwelcome in the turbulent Papal States, the new pope in 1309 took up residence at Avignon, a city located on the east bank of the Rhone River, just outside French territory. Until 1377 this city remained the residence of the papacy. During these years of what the Italian writer Petrarch called the "Babylonian Captivity"—referring to the episode in Jewish history when God's chosen people were held captive in Babylon by the sinful Chaldeans, now equated with the French monarchy—the popes were accused, unfairly, of being pawns of the French kings. The English, who were locked in the Hundred Years' War with the French, used the situation to reduce papal control over English ecclesiastical affairs. The German emperors and princes were equally defiant. Many Christians were troubled by the fact that the pope's claim to power was based on succession to St. Peter as bishop of Rome, not Avignon. These critics were not impressed by the plea of the papacy that Rome was not safe; neither had it been for Peter nor for many earlier popes. The Babylonian Captivity caused scholars and writers to raise major questions regarding church government and to arrive at answers that challenged papal supremacy.

The Avignon papacy was extremely active in pursuing policies intended to strengthen papal control over the entire ecclesiastical organization of the Church. Several of the Avignon popes were highly skilled administrators whose efforts brought the long-standing trend toward centralization of Church organization to a culmination. Their most pressing concerns were financial. Cut off from the traditional revenues derived from their control of the Papal States in Italy, these popes worked hard to exploit old sources of revenue from across all Europe and to develop new forms of income. They vastly expanded their control over appointments to major ecclesiastical offices, "reserving" for themselves the right to fill these offices with those willing to pay the price. Payment usually took the form of conceding to the papacy all or part of the income associated with the office for a specific period of time. The popes earned a lucrative income by granting dispensations from the regulations of canon law for a broad spectrum of matters ranging from the dissolution of marriages to the relaxation of obligations associated with holding religious offices. Another expanding source of income was the sale of indulgences, a practice that allowed sinners to do penance by making payments in money. They steadily increased the number of cases that had to be adjudicated in papal courts and derived a huge income from this activity. They enlarged the papal bureaucracy beyond anything previously known. In terms of revenues, subordinates, and business transactions, the Avignon popes were actually more powerful than even their illustrious thirteenth-century predecessors.

However, this emphasis on organizational affairs did their prestige more harm than good. Abuses of the worst kind began to plague the papal government. The growing horde of papal bureaucrats engaged in every type of corruption, such as selling offices and accepting bribes to assure the desired outcome of judicial cases tried in papal courts. Many buyers of Church offices were interested only in income and never went near the office; absenteeism thus became a major problem. It was common for one individual to purchase several offices; this pluralism again contributed to neglect of the responsibilities associated with religious office. Bishops and abbots in all parts of Europe resented growing papal interference in local Church affairs and tried to escape papal control, often by turning to their kings, who gladly

protected them—for a price. Papal taxation aroused bitterness and resistance everywhere. Edward III of England reflected the dislike of the money-grabbing popes when he said: "The successor of the Apostles was ordered to lead the Lord's sheep to the pasture, not to fleece them." Perhaps the king's criticism was less than candid. One reason why the popes were able to increase papal income was that they shared their take with the royal governments of western Europe, which were not too disturbed by additional burdens on their subjects as long as they profited. The officials of the papal curia spent much of this wealth on luxurious living; a symbol of their luxury was the splendid papal palace built in Avignon. The ecclesiastical life style of the city, which Petrarch called "the sewer of the world," aroused the bitter anger of many in Europe whose lot was poverty and suffering in the wake of the Black Death and widespread economic depression. The Avignon popes seemed powerless to curb these excesses, and thus suffered the blame.

The Babylonian Captivity finally ended in 1377 with the return of the pope to Rome. However, this move led to the election by a part of the College of Cardinals of a second pope, who continued to live at Avignon. Thus began the Great Schism, forty years in which the Church was headed by two popes directing two administrations, two tax systems, two sets of Church courts. Everyone was at a loss to know who was the right pope. Corruption and fiscal exactions increased. Rival popes played politics furiously, each seeking to gain enough allies to oust the other. Many Europeans—and especially princes—thought in terms of obeying the pope who offered the most advantageous concessions in terms of controlling Church wealth within each kingdom or principality. Few took seriously the claim of either pope to be spiritual leader of Europe; popes who competed with one another and encouraged the division of Christendom seemed little better than greedy politicians.

As a result of the schism, many leaders—bishops, canon lawyers, theologians, and even princes—began to search for ways of ending what seemed a scandalous situation. Their search eventually focused on an institution that had played a major role in the early history of the Church: a general council. The chief advocates of the conciliar theory argued that an ecumenical assembly of bishops possessed an authority superior even to that of the pope and thus provided a legitimate means of healing the schism and reforming the clergy. Despite the threat of conciliarism to the concept of papal supremacy, its advocates carried the day. Between 1409 and 1449 four councils were held, each a stormy affair marked by interminable negotiations. The Council of Pisa (1409) addressed the issue of the schism but ended with the installation of a third pope to further complicate that problem. The Council of Constance (1414–1418) finally succeeded in restoring a single pope.

In the subsequent two councils, the popes devoted singular attention to controlling proceedings and thus disarming this dangerous threat to papal authority. Their task was not too difficult, since the council membership was often divided by quarrels among ecclesiastical leaders representing different nations. A major tactic used by the popes to curb the claims of the conciliarists to exercise final authority over the Church was to make concessions to monarchs in return for their support of papal power. For example, the pope accepted the Pragmatic Sanction of Bourges, issued in 1438 by Charles VII of France with the backing of the French clergy; this agreement gave the French monarch extensive rights over ecclesiastical income and the clergy. Comparable agreements worked out with other rulers seriously limited papal power and hastened a trend toward the creation of "national" churches.

Probably the greatest failure of the councils was their inability to institute meaningful reform. Despite numerous attempts to enact legislation aimed at curing many of the Church's ills, the members of the councils were never able to agree on a practical reform program. When the last council disbanded in 1449, most people had lost confidence in this means of revitalizing the Church. The greatest influence of the conciliar movement was indirect: It opened the Church's traditional organization to question and caused many to conclude that the pope's claim to the "fullness of power" was not divinely ordained.

The popes of the last half of the fifteenth century concentrated on strengthening their control over the Papal States in Italy and competing in the many power struggles raging in Italy in this period. On the whole, they were successful. But the methods they employed led many to view the pope as nothing more than a secular prince, scheming, bribing, and brawling to get what he desired for himself, his family, and his friends and enjoying a luxurious existence. A few led scandalous lives and several became patrons of Renaissance artists and writers who were openly advocating ideas and values that challenged Christianity. The popes ceased to enjoy the respect and veneration of most Christians. No one would deny that the popes were powerful in terms of wealth and political resources. What they had lost was the moral authority that had been their chief source of influence in the thirteenth century, and without that authority, the papacy was in no position to exercise effective authority over the faithful.

The disarray in church governance resulting from the problems besetting the papacy and the decay of papal prestige was compounded by a steady deterioration of the effectiveness of the entire body of the clergy in the performance of their pastoral and administrative responsibilities.

Especially pronounced was the decline of monasticism. Between 1300 and 1500 not a single new order of any importance was established in western Europe, and many of the older monastic institutions became increasingly corrupt and ineffectual in providing spiritual leadership. Monasteries were no longer a refuge for the spiritually dedicated or a stage from which the zealous could launch their efforts to purify religious life.

The Franciscans and the Dominicans were the most powerful and active orders during the late Middle Ages. Except for a few purists, most mendicants forgot their ideals of poverty and pastoral service and turned to the pursuit of wealth and power. Most of the other orders fell into the same pattern. Monks and nuns were lax in observing monastic rules governing discipline and defining moral norms. Little attention was paid to the quality of recruits entering monasteries; many were aristocratic ladies who could not find husbands, younger sons without land, and commoners who sought to escape the hardships of life. Absentee abbots thought only of garnering the income from monastic property. Of course, not all monks were

FIGURE 25.2   Misconduct of Monks   Some of the most savage criticism of the late medieval church was aimed at the monastic establishments. These scenes reflect some of the causes of that criticism. Left, a monk and his mistress are held in stocks for passersby to jeer at. Right, a monk drinks excessively. (The British Library)

morally lax or without religious fervor. However, the culprits, as usual, caught the public eye and the innocent shared their bad reputation. One needs to read only a little of the literature of the fourteenth and fifteenth centuries, such as some of the stories in Boccaccio's *Decameron* or Chaucer's *Canterbury Tales*, to realize that monasticism was held in low repute. Monastic life had come to signify laziness, greed, immorality, and hypocrisy (see Figure 25.2).

The secular clergy, charged with the Church's everyday ministry to the Christian populace, was equally plagued by corruption and moral laxness. The tone was set by the powerful officials of the papal curia, especially the cardinals, whose vast entourages, immense wealth, and talent for political machinations indeed made them "princes of the Church." Many bishops purchased their offices, paying prices that left them little choice but to wring money out of their subjects, and heavy papal taxes tempted them and the lesser clergy to undertake shady financial practices. Some held several offices at once, making it impossible for them to perform the duties of any. Absenteeism was common; many bishops and priests preferred life at Avignon or at a royal court to life in their episcopal sees or parishes. Absentee clergy often turned their religious duties over to poorly trained, poorly paid clerks who were incapable of guiding religious activities. Services, instruction,

confessions, preaching, and counseling were slighted, leaving people with religious problems lost and unhappy.

Given these conditions, it was not difficult for many people in the fourteenth and fifteenth centuries to judge the Church as an institution harshly. In their minds it was too rich, too power-hungry, too bloated with self-serving officials. It had become an institution chiefly concerned with sustaining its power and wealth at the expense of a vast Christian community that was already troubled by a variety of economic, social, and political dislocations.

2. CHALLENGES TO TRADITIONAL RELIGION

Especially damaging to the Church's traditional leadership role was its inability to accommodate or control the frequent and extremely heterodox religious movements welling up in the tension-filled society of western Europe during the late Middle Ages. Chiefly as a result of the intense effort to impose uniformity on religion during the High Middle Ages, after 1300 Roman Catholic belief and religious practices fell into a rather unbending, formal pattern that became ever more mechanical; most ecclesiastical leaders were content to equate piety with going through the motions of attending services, receiving the sacraments, and obeying the clergy.

Dissatisfaction with this situation was demonstrated in many ways. One of the most important was an increase in the number of mystics, that is, persons who believed they could experience and know God directly through intuitive powers. Mysticism was present throughout the Middle Ages; St. Bernard and St. Francis of Assisi were mystics. But the fourteenth and fifteenth centuries produced an especially large number of people who sought ways to catch their personal vision of God. Many of the most influential were simple men and women who never wore clerical garb, like Joan of Arc. None was more prominent than Catherine of Siena (1347–1380). On the basis of visions of Christ she claimed to have experienced, as well as through her efforts to help the poor, the sick, the criminals, and the downtrodden, she earned a reputation as a saint. Although she, as well as many like her, was never seriously at odds with the Church, Catherine practiced a kind of Christianity unfamiliar to contemporary officials of the cult.

The activities of the mystics led to the development of communal movements that operated almost independently of the Church. A prime example was the Brethren of the Common Life (and its female counterpart, the Sisters of the Common Life), founded by a lay preacher named Gerard Groote (1340–1384), who was one of the many spiritual heirs of the great German mystic Meister Eckhart (1260–1327). This loosely knit movement was a product of a new kind of piety, called the *devotio moderna*, which stressed prayer, love, and direct communion with God. Devotees of the new piety joined together as brothers and sisters in communities where they shared their worldly goods, joined in common worship, confessed their sins to each other, devoted themselves to works of charity, sought to educate members of the community, and even produced their own devotional literature. One of the best examples of their literature, still read today as a spiritual guide, is Thomas à Kempis' *Imitation of Christ*. The many communities of brethren seldom strayed into heresy, but their piety, their puritanical life, and their mysticism set them apart. Not surprisingly, the brethren were often attacked for spreading dangerous ideas; perhaps there was some substance to this charge in view of the fact that such important later reformers as Erasmus and Martin Luther were educated in their schools. Akin to the brethren were the Beguines, associations of laywomen who led a common life, committed themselves to chastity and good works, and supported themselves by working or begging. Similar communities of men, called Beghards, were also established. More radical were the Brethren of the Free Spirit, who among other things denied the existence of sin on the basis of their belief that God existed in all things, an idea that resulted in their condemnation.

The fourteenth and fifteenth centuries produced a hardier crowd of radicals—usually condemned as heretics—who voiced ideas that provoked many to violent actions against the Church. Some were intellectual figures, such as Marsiglio of Padua, whose devastating book, *The Defender of the Peace*, appeared in 1324. Its thesis was that the Church was obligated to fulfill certain spiritual duties but was not entitled to any secular powers. Marsiglio advocated that it be deprived of its wealth and made a branch of government, subservient to the ruler. He argued that the Church as a community of all Christians should be ruled by a council representing all elements in Christian society, not by a clerical hierarchy headed by the pope. He denied that the papal office had divine sanction; the pope was simply an ecclesiastical administrator whose powers were defined by the Christian community and who could be limited any way that community wished.

Somewhat later, John Wycliffe (1320–1384) delivered even heavier attacks on the Church. This Oxford scholar and teacher entered the ranks of rebellion late in life, apparently moved by a growing tide of anticlericalism and antipapalism emerging in an England troubled by the Hundred Years' War and internal stresses. In his first attacks on the Church he argued that the Church had abused its right to hold property and that all church property should be confiscated by the state. Later he advocated the destruction of the whole clerical hierarchy on the ground that salvation depended not on the clergy but on the power of God; every person was his or her own priest. Here, of course, he was striking at a key idea on which the medieval Church based its institutional position: the idea that salvation depended on the ministry of a clergy set apart from and above the laity by the sacrament of ordination. Wycliffe also attacked many of the religious practices of the Church—elaborate rituals, prayers to saints, veneration of relics, pilgrimages, and the like. He even questioned the validity of the sacraments as necessary to salvation. He argued that Scripture alone must be the authority for Christian doctrine and translated the Bible into English so that all could read it.

Although Wycliffe was soon condemned as a heretic and forced to leave Oxford, his teachings attracted many followers, known as the Lollards, and for many years Lollard preachers and writers agitated for their master's ideas in England. In time, however, they came to challenge all authority, and the English kings of the fifteenth century joined the clergy in destroying the movement.

Wycliffe's ideas had their most significant effect not in England but in Bohemia (modern Czechoslovakia). The leading disciple there was John Huss (ca. 1373–1415), a priest who taught at the University of Prague. When his preaching of Wycliffe's precepts raised a protest from the clergy and ruling faction, most of whom were German and were passionately hated by the native population, Huss became a national hero of the Bohemians. Like Wycliffe, he too was excommunicated. Eventually, Huss sought and received permission to appear before the Council of Constance to defend his teaching. The Holy Roman emperor promised him safe conduct for his appearance. Once in Constance, however, Huss was imprisoned, tried, and executed as a heretic in 1415. A rebellion broke out immediately in Bohemia and raged until 1436. Crusade after crusade was preached by the papacy against the Hussites; several German armies, led by an emperor who was anxious to reclaim Bohemia, were soundly thrashed by the aroused Bohemians. Eventually peace was restored when certain religious concessions were granted to the Hussites. However, a faction of the followers of Huss and Wycliffe, called Taborites, was not satisfied by these concessions and became practically a church apart in the last years of the Middle Ages.

Manifestations of religious ferment and frustration took many other forms during the four-teenth and fifteenth centuries. Any number of fiery preachers proclaimed the end of the world and the coming of God's wrathful final judgment. Wildly emotional cults, such as the Flagellants, who whipped one another to atone for the world's sins, preyed on people's religious sensibilities, especially in times of great crisis such as the Black Death. Brutal massacres of the Jews in the name of Christian righteousness marred the histories of many cities. A fear of witches flourished on an unprecedented scale, accompanied by numerous trials of those suspected of witchcraft. Increasingly people sought assurances of salvation by purchasing indulgences, which they believed would ensure that the punishment due for sins would be removed. Never were relics more appealing and more brazenly manipulated, as illustrated by Chaucer's pardoner with his bag full of "pigs' bones." Literature, art, and sermons were preoccupied with death in particularly horrible forms. All of these unusual forms of religious expression reflected a psychology of fear and uncertainty, sometimes reaching the proportions of mass hysteria.

Clearly, religious ferment in Europe was powerful and widespread. Neither the gentle mystics nor the fiery-tongued rebels, neither the adherents of the occult nor the victims of hysteria were at home in the Roman Catholic church. People were striking out in all directions, questioning ritual, organization, and dogma. But the institution that claimed to care for the souls of the disturbed and the dissatisfied either ignored the quest for religious satisfaction or ruthlessly crushed the discontent. The Church was failing its central mission: to meet the basic religious needs of its vast flock. More importantly, it seemed unable to discover ways of restoring its power to cure souls.

3. THE FAILURE OF INTELLECTUAL LEADERSHIP

The Church suffered another serious blow as a consequence of fundamental shifts in the intellectual development of the late Middle Ages. This transformation was not dramatic, but it undermined the Church's control over a supportive intellectual establishment and generated new criticism of the world view upon which the Church's authority was founded. Outwardly, the life of learning continued down familiar paths. The universities remained the focal points of scholarship and teaching in the liberal arts, theology, law, medicine, and science and provided the major attraction to most intellectuals. The Scholastic method, although increasingly pedantic and trivial in its approach and its accomplishments, reigned supreme. But the emphasis in intellectual endeavor underwent a subtle change. The majestic Scholastic synthesis of the thirteenth century, exemplified by the works of Thomas Aquinas, failed to hold its sway over theological and philosophical deliberations. It left so many questions unanswered that many thinkers not only despaired of the dream of reconciling revelation and reason into one consistent, complete order of truth but also began to attack the basic proposition that faith and reason were compatible. Synthesis gave way to analysis. As we have seen, even while the Thomistic synthesis was being hammered out, some people refused to accept it; the resistance intensified after 1300.

Shortly after Thomas Aquinas' death in 1274, the attack on his position quickened and took forms that raised fundamental philosophical questions. The Franciscan scholar John Duns Scotus (ca. 1266–1308) argued with great force that God's freedom and power were so exalted that all attempts to describe his attributes rationally imposed untenable limits on divine power. In effect, Duns Scotus was saying that theology was not a proper matter for rational speculation. This trend of thought was expanded by William of Ockham (ca. 1300–1349), an English Franciscan who taught at Oxford and served in the court of Emperor Louis IV of Bavaria until the Black Death claimed his life. A powerful logician, Ockham assailed the basic rational supports of Thomistic theology. In his mind knowledge of such things as the existence of God and the immortality of the soul came only by intuition and mystical experience. Theology and philosophy thus became separate "sciences," incapable of reconciliation. In defining the realm of reason, Ockham argued that only by sense perception of individual objects could humans know; in this respect he was a philosophical *nominalist*, repudiating the long tradition that

ideas constituted the ultimate reality (philosophical *realism*). Duns Scotus and William of Ockham gained powerful disciples who followed up the assault on Thomism. The crescendo of attacks shattered the thirteenth-century confidence in one all-embracing truth and with it a powerful prop of the Church.

The disarray among the Scholastics encouraged thinkers to take new intellectual paths. Since reason was distinct from faith, political theorists like Marsiglio of Padua constructed new concepts of the governance of church and state that were especially destructive to theologically based justifications of the Church's power over the social order. The attack on rational theology nourished mysticism and opened the way for the radical theological concepts of Wycliffe and Huss. Many intellectuals, disillusioned by the barren exercises of late medieval Scholasticism, found intellectual sustenance in classical literature and philosophy, drawing from these sources a secular, humanistic world view and value system. Most important for the future was the growing interest in science. Following Ockham's argument that rational inquiry must confine itself to tangible objects, scholars, especially at the universities of Paris and Oxford, produced a considerable body of scientific knowledge and provided significant corrections to Greco-Arabic scientific generalizations. Their efforts laid the groundwork for the revolutionary scientific discoveries of Copernicus, Galileo, and others in the sixteenth and seventeenth centuries. As intellectual life became more pluralistic and more oriented to worldly, secular concerns, the potential for criticism of the Church increased, and the Church's ability to control intellectual activity for its benefit decreased.

4. THE THREAT OF NEW FORCES

While the Church decayed from within and was unable to cope effectively with religious and intellectual movements diverging from traditional patterns, it had to contend with powerful forces outside the sphere of religion that challenged its leadership and depleted its following. Many of these forces portended a new era in western European history; they will receive fuller treatment later. Here, it is important that they be noted as threats to the Church's dominance.

The aggressive national states beginning to take shape in the fifteenth century represented one such force. Although still Catholic, ambitious rulers sought to limit and dominate the religious establishment in their realms. In England kings and Parliament joined in enacting laws to prevent the papacy from taxing church property and controlling ecclesiastical appointments. In France, the royal government worked steadily, often with the help of the French clergy, to establish a "Gallic" church, independent of the papacy and subservient to the crown. In Spain late in the fifteenth century the monarchs even undertook to reform the Church independently of the papacy. These cases were all clear indications that as 1500 approached, "national" churches were becoming a reality at the expense of the universal Church.

Equally threatening to the Church's position was the capitalistic ethos emerging in economic life, especially among urban patricians but also among members of the rural gentry and affluent peasants. Challenging the Church's ancient distrust of wealth and materialism, this new ethos viewed wealth and its acquisition as a positive force in society. Its adherents would have liked to see the Church's wealth put to new uses. Most of them paid little heed to religious arguments condemning the charging of interest, price manipu-

lation, and profit seeking. Implicit in the capitalist ethos was a mentality oriented toward competition, worldliness, individualism, pragmatism, and a work ethic—all values that did not fit easily into the Church's concept of how the drama of salvation should be played.

Finally, a new breed of thinkers, writers, and artists, sometimes collectively called *humanists*, was emerging to criticize many teachings and practices supported by the Church. The new humanism, developing first and most vigorously in Italy and then spreading to other parts of western Europe, found its intellectual sustenance and its aesthetic values in classical rather than medieval models. It posed a major challenge to the world view long promoted by the Church in the name of Christian truth.

The irresolvable internal difficulties and challenging outside forces that combined to undermine the authority of the Church in the late Middle Ages provided the surest indication that an epoch was ending. Admittedly the stresses and strains affecting political, economic, and social institutions all pointed toward the transformation of basic structures characteristic of medieval western European civilization. However, for centuries the religious establishment—the Church—had been the main force giving that civilization its unique features. The faltering of the Church truly heralded the end of an epoch in western European history.

SUGGESTED READING

Decline of the Church

Francis Oakley, *The Western Church in the Later Middle Ages* (1979).

Steven Ozment, *The Age of Reform (1250–1530). An Intellectual and Religious History of Late Medieval and Reformation Europe* (1980).

Two excellent treatments of all aspects of religious history.

Yves Renouard, *The Avignon Papacy, 1305–1403*, trans. Denis Bethell (1970). A concise survey; good on the impact of this chapter in papal history.

Walter Ullmann, *The Origins of the Great Schism: A Study in Fourteenth Century Ecclesiastical History* (1948). A careful analysis of the factors that produced the Great Schism.

Daniel MacCarron, *The Great Schism: Antipopes Who Split the Church* (1982). Biographical sketches of the popes involved in the schism.

Brian Tierney, *Foundations of the Conciliar Theory; The Contributions of the Medieval Canonists from Gratian to the Great Schism* (1955). Stresses the legal basis for conciliar ideas.

Antony Black, *Council and Commune: The Conciliar Movement and the Fifteenth-Century Heritage* (1979). Discusses the political ideas of the conciliarists in the context of history and theology.

New Religious Movements

Rufus M. Jones, *The Flowering of Mysticism; The Friends of God in the Fourteenth Century* (1939).

James M. Clark, *The Great German Mystics: Eckhart, Tauler, and Suso* (1949).

Anne Bancroft, *The Luminous Vision: Six Medieval Mystics and Their Teachings* (1982).

Any of these three titles will help the reader to understand the nature and influence of late medieval mysticism.

Albert Hyma, *The Christian Renaissance: A History of the "Devotio Moderna,"* 2nd ed. (1965). A full treatment of a movement that deeply affected late medieval religious life.

Richard Kieckhefer, *Unquiet Souls: Fourteenth-Century Saints and Their Religious Milieu* (1984). Rich in insights into the nature and causes of religious "unquiet" in the fourteenth century.

Norman Cohn, *The Pursuit of the Millennium: Revolutionary Millenarians and Mystical Anarchists of the Middle Ages,* rev. ed. (1970). A brilliant description of aberrant religious movements in the later Middle Ages.

Malcolm Lambert, *Medieval Heresy: Popular Movements from Bogomil to Huss* (1977). An excellent synthesis.

Cultural History

Georges Duby, *Foundations of a New Humanism, 1280–1440,* trans. Peter Price (1966). A remarkable synthesis linking many aspects of late medieval cultural history.

Gordon Leff, *The Dissolution of the Medieval Outlook: An Essay on Intellectual and Spiritual Change in the Fourteenth Century* (1976). A perceptive but challenging interpretation of late medieval intellectual development.

RETROSPECT

By 1500 there were many signs that western European society was again on the threshold of a remarkable era of expansion, comparable in many ways to the great leap forward that occurred between 1000 and 1300. Yet it is understandable that most people living in 1500 were dimly, if at all, aware of the promise before them. Like men and women in most ages, they were better instructed by the immediate past and the present than by the unrealized future. Our treatment of the late Middle Ages has made it clear that both past and present were troubled, filled with tensions rooted in limitations inherent in the basic structure of medieval western European civilization. Given the magnitude of those troubles, it is not surprising that people's thoughts were filled with pessimism and anguish and that their reactions to life were marked by excess and violence.

In retrospect, the causes of the adversities of the late Middle Ages seem clear. The major institutions, thought patterns, and value systems shaped prior to 1300 as essential features of civilization had unstable features that began to emerge after 1300. The medieval ideal of a Christian commonwealth was flawed by fundamental disagreement about the leadership of that commonwealth and by deep-seated localism. Feudal monarchies were beset by conflicts between royal authority and private privilege. The universal Church, with its central leadership and uniform doctrine, law, and liturgy, could not contain the ferment that was seeking new ways of understanding and living Christian life. Localistic, monopolistic, self-sufficient economic structures con-tended with international, profit-seeking, individualistic enterprises. Faith and reason, Latin and vernacular cultures, religious and secular values vied for people's minds. The precarious balance among such conflicting elements, which had been shaped during the High Middle Ages, began to fall apart in the late Middle Ages. Thus the turmoil of that age.

Some aspects of the history of the late Middle Ages remind one of the events of the third and fourth centuries that resulted in the collapse of classical Greco-Roman civilization. But the situation was fundamentally different; a catastrophic collapse of an established civilization was not at hand. It was not the exhaustion of a total civilization that caused the troubles of the fourteenth and fifteenth centuries. Rather, those troubles stemmed from the clash of contradictory elements folded into the medieval synthesis. Once the collective decision was made to opt for one way or the other between the alternatives posited by the medieval synthesis, new energies were released. By 1500, choices began to be made in favor of strong central government, national states, rationalism, religious diversity, a pluralistic culture, and a capitalistic economy as the essential components of European life. All these were medieval in origin, just as were their opposites. Postmedieval Europe was thus shaped by choices made from the rich, varied institutional and ideological creations of medieval people. "Modern" Europe originated in the Middle Ages. Its history is unexplainable and unintelligible without a knowledge of medieval history.

PART SEVEN

The Beginning of Early Modern Times: Fifteenth and Sixteenth Centuries

In the previous section, we observed the various tensions and weakening institutions that marked the decline of the medieval world during the fourteenth and fifteenth centuries; now we shall see how the institutions we have come to call early modern grew out of the decaying medieval system.

The earliest changes occurred in the urban societies of northern Italy. There, during the fourteenth and fifteenth centuries, the culture of the Renaissance was born. Strongly rooted in classical Greek and Roman civilizations, this self-conscious culture developed thought, values, and institutions that would characterize early modern times. During the later fifteenth and the sixteenth centuries, the Renaissance spread north of the Alps, where scholars, writers, and artists adapted it to their own needs and concerns.

In place of the declining feudal monarchies and empires, powerful monarchs created the national or territorial state, which became the dominant political institution of the early modern era. The first of these national states to emerge were Spain, France, and England. From then until now, the history of the Western world has revolved around them and the other national states that were patterned after them.

The overseas expansion of Europe reflected the political vitality of the age. National states supported voyages of discovery and the establishment of empires around the globe. This expansion took advantage of and stimulated new economic development. Europe's medieval economy, characterized by subsistence agriculture, monopolistic guilds, and localism, slowly gave way to capitalistic practices and institutions. The old landed aristocracy that had dominated the medieval economy now found itself challenged and threatened by new intruders into its class and by a new middle class of aggressive merchants and entrepreneurs.

The decline of the Western Christian Church in the last two centuries of the Middle Ages culminated in the Reformation. During the first half of the sixteenth century, the Western Church itself split, and much of northern Europe became Protestant. This split, in turn, hastened reform within the Roman Catholic church. In this deeply religious age, however, such a momentous disintegration of religious unity created turmoil and violence. For almost a hundred years religious and political conflict became intertwined in the bloody Wars of Religion.

Since these five great movements—the Renaissance, the rise of national states, the expansion of Europe, the rise of commercial capitalism, and the Reformation (Protestant and Roman Catholic) occurred primarily during the fifteenth and sixteenth centuries, it may be useful to conceive of the fifteenth as a century of transition and the sixteenth as the first century of the early modern era.

CHAPTER 26
The Renaissance: Italy

FIGURE 26.1 Leonardo da Vinci, "The Virgin of the Rocks," ca. 1485 With Leonardo da Vinci (1452–1519), Renaissance painting, with its emphasis on humanism, reached its peak. In this painting, the Virgin is a beautiful woman, and the Christ child is a playful, cuddly little boy. The rock formation is authentic, and the plants are identifiable specimens. (Archives Photographiques, Paris)

While most of European society during the fourteenth century was still medieval, Italian society was already changing, developing some of the characteristics that would become common during the early modern period. Most important, Italian society produced a new culture with roots in both medieval Christian civilization and classical Greek and Roman civilizations. This culture, called the Renaissance, would continue to grow in Italy during the fifteenth century and then spread throughout Europe. The Renaissance became a basis upon which thought, literature, and art during the early modern period rested.

1. ITALIAN ORIGINS

Although historians have debated the causes for the rise of the Renaissance in Italy, they usually point to a few factors that distinguish Italy, and particularly northern Italy where the Renaissance was centered, from the rest of Europe.

Above all, northern Italy was unusually urbanized—there were more and larger cities than in most other areas of Europe. The first and most important Renaissance city was Florence, but other cities such as Venice, Pisa, and Milan became centers of the Italian Renaissance. By the fourteenth century these cities had gained economic prosperity from long-distance trade, commerce, industry, and banking.

These cities marshalled their economic strength to expand and gain power over surrounding lands once controlled by the landed aristocracy. They also took advantage of the exhausting struggles between the Holy Roman emperor and the papacy, two powers that might have been strong enough to hinder the growing political independence of the cities. Political life within the cities became dynamic, often chaotic, but most of the time controlled by the new commercial elite.

The society of these large, commercial cities became more fluid as position began to be determined more by wealth than by blood. Medieval aristocratic strictures were weakened. The elite of the cities, continually infused with new members of the wealthy bourgeoisie and outside talent attracted to the vibrant cities, participated in commercial and industrial exploits—activities usually rejected as inappropriate to the aristocracy elsewhere in Europe. This elite included a large number of relatively young people, more aggressive and individualistic than traditional groups elsewhere.

This urban elite needed to be literate and well educated in practical matters. Schools arose to serve them and taught a curriculum appropriate for their practical interests. The elite also had great wealth to spend, and they turned to culture in general and art in particular. They may have wanted art as an investment, as a means for promoting their own political and social ambitions, or as a matter of civic pride. In any case they became patrons of the arts. Now art was being produced not only for clerical and traditional aristocratic patrons but also for rich, middle-class, and urbanized aristocratic patrons who had different outlooks.

As the demand for art grew, so did the prestige of the artist. In medieval society artists were little more than low-paid artisans. In Renaissance society they became well-paid professionals and part of a respected intellectual elite that included writers and philosophers.

Finally, the physical and human environment of the Italian cities included advantages not present elsewhere in Europe. The remains and traditions of Greco-Roman civilization were still evident in Italy and its cities. Moreover, these cities, thanks to their proximity to the East and their commercial and political ties to Byzantine lands, often came into contact with the sophisticated Byzantine culture.

Thus the thriving Italian urban society—with its commercial wealth, its political independence, its social fluidity, its schools, its artists, its intellectual elite, and its cultural environment—was the fertile ground in which the Renaissance first grew.

2. GENERAL NATURE

The term *renaissance* means "rebirth." One of the central characteristics of the Renaissance was the self-conscious revival of classical civilization and the sense of creating something different from medieval civilization. Renaissance scholars rejoiced in discovering, mastering, and making available the cultural products of Greece and Rome. At the same time they criticized medieval Scholasticism and medieval culture in general. They envisioned themselves as being part of a new civilization based on a revival of classical civilization intertwined with the purest elements of Christian civilization.

The emphasis on reviving classical civilization reflected greater concern with secular life. The medieval focus on theology—concern with the spiritual world and formal religious doctrines—changed toward a focus on human beings, their nature and their actions. Medieval Christian theologians distrusted the flesh as an enemy of the spirit and human wisdom as unable to perceive divine truth by rational processes unless guided by Christian inspiration. Renaissance scholars and artists glorified the human form as beautiful and the human intellect as capable of discovering all truth worth knowing. They viewed human beings as three-dimensional, part of an immediate, concrete, recognizable physical environment.

However, care must be taken in characterizing Renaissance culture as secular. The Renaissance was not antireligious; there was no fundamental questioning of Christian beliefs in this still-religious age. Much of the secularism of the Renaissance was in a Christian and even a pious context. Part of the concern with reviving secular classical civilization stemmed from a desire to better understand early Christianity and Christian principles. Moreover, the secularism of the Italian Renaissance was not a sharp, sudden break with the immediate past. Secular interests had never completely died out, even at the peak of the Church's prestige in the Middle Ages. The twelfth century had already witnessed a revival of interest in classical civilization. It would be better to say that during the Italian Renaissance there was a significant intensification of the secular spirit in thought, literature, and art, all still within a fundamentally Christian environment.

Individualism was another important facet of the Renaissance spirit. In this respect, the difference between the medieval and the Renaissance spirit was primarily one of degree. Christianity did much to elevate the dignity of the individual soul and the individual personality. But the medieval clergy feared pride as a sin. They taught that the individual ego must be carefully held in check. Medieval monasticism attempted to suppress the individual ego and submerge it in the group. In practice, then, medieval Christianity tended to be collectivist. Church artists and writers usually did not sign their names to their work, which was supposed to contribute only to the greater glory of God. Renaissance individualism was prideful, even lusty. People of accomplishment were self-consciously confident, even boastful. They wanted the glory that their work would bring them. People such as Boccaccio (1313–1375), Alberti (1404–1472), Machiavelli (1469–1527), and Cellini (1500–1571) were proud of their identity and uniqueness.

Many of these great scholars and artists displayed another element of the Renaissance ideal—versatility. The educated person of the Middle Ages was usually a specialist—a theologian or church artist or administrator. But the most renowned Renaissance schoolteachers taught many subjects in addition to the traditional formal ones—dancing, fencing, poetry, and vernacular languages to mention a few. Many of the Renaissance schools broadened the old theology-oriented seven liberal arts and made much greater use of pagan classical literature and philosophy in the curriculum. One of the most popular books in Europe in the sixteenth century was Castiglione's *Book of the Courtier*. The ideal courtier, said Castiglione, is not only a gentleman and a scholar but also a man of action—a soldier and an athlete. Probably the best illustration of versatility in any age is Leonardo da Vinci (1452–1519). This revered Renaissance figure, one of the most celebrated painters of all time, was also an able sculptor, architect, mathematician, philosopher, inventor, botanist, anatomist, geologist, and engineer.

Finally, the Renaissance was urban and socially limited. While many products of the Renaissance were public and even unavoidable in Italian cities, only an elite participated in or directly supported the Renaissance. It scarcely touched most people in the cities and was unheard of in the countryside. Moreover, the Renaissance was of different significance for women than men, even among the elite. On the one hand, women often participated with men in the new urban schools and played a growing role within the household. Indeed, marriage patterns often resulted in widowed women retaining the family's wealth while not remarrying, giving them considerable economic freedom. On the other hand, women during the Renaissance were losing some of the status and public position they held during the Middle Ages. More than before, they were relegated to domestic life, where they played a supportive, decorous, and sexually inferior role to their husbands. This changing status was particularly evident within the rising middle class, but even noble women lost power and the independence they had enjoyed when medieval courtly manners and love held sway. Women were generally excluded from active, public participation in the culture and society of the Renaissance.

3. HUMANISM

During the fourteenth century, Italy witnessed the rise of humanism. Historians have debated the exact meaning of Italian humanism. Narrowly defined, it means classical scholarship—the study of original Latin or Greek manuscripts. Broadly defined, it means the recovery of classical manuscripts, educational reform to include greater emphasis on classical scholarship, rejection of medieval Scholasticism and professionalism, and optimistic emphasis on human beings—on their capabilities as powerful, rational Christian and secular beings on this earth. Understood in this broad sense, humanism encompasses in its literature, its educational reforms, and its philosophy the main characteristics of the Italian Renaissance.

Literature

The characteristics of Renaissance humanism are richly illustrated by the Italian literature of the fourteenth century. The best of that literature was produced by the Tuscan Triumvirate—so called because it consisted of three men who lived in Florence in the old Etruscan province of Tuscany. The first was Dante Alighieri (1265–1321). In an earlier section (see Chapter 23) we discussed Dante as the greatest of the late medieval writers.

His masterpiece, the *Divine Comedy*, is so full of medieval Christian lore and theology that it has been called a *Summa Theologiae* in poetry. Nevertheless, there is so much of the humanistic spirit in the *Divine Comedy* and in Dante's other writings that he belongs also to the Renaissance. In the ''Inferno'' of the *Divine Comedy*, Dante paints vivid, sensuous word pictures that seem to characterize this world rather than the next. The blazing fires and sulfurous fumes of hell, the cries of lament and curses of the damned come alive in our imagination. Furthermore, the author venerates such pagan classical writers as Vergil and Cicero to a much greater degree than had the medievalists (although a number of medieval writers had tried to make Vergil a Christian).

Dante's other major writings are even more humanistic. His love lyrics, written in his native Tuscan vernacular and addressed to Beatrice, are among the most beautiful in any language. In fact, Dante's writings greatly enriched the Florentine dialect and raised it eventually to the status of the national language of Italy.

Dante was also versatile; he was a man of public affairs as well as of letters. An active participant in the turbulent politics of Renaissance Italy, he was exiled from his native Florence when his faction lost. Dante even went so far as to fill hell in the *Divine Comedy* with his political enemies.

Petrarch (1304–1374), the second of the Tuscan Triumvirate, is often considered the father of Italian humanism. In his writing and his life he rejected medieval Scholasticism and culture as inferior to classical culture. He argued for the recovery of classical manuscripts, the mastering of Latin, and educational reform. He is best known for his superbly crafted letters to great figures of the past, such as Cicero, Vergil, Livy, and St. Augustine, and for his love sonnets in the Tuscan vernacular to Laura, a married woman whom he saw at mass and loved from afar.

Boccaccio (1313–1375) did for Italian prose what Dante and Petrarch did for Italian poetry. In his *Decameron*, a collection of one hundred tales or novelettes, Boccaccio exhibits little Christian restraint. He relates bawdy romances with skill and grace, condoning and even glorifying the seamy side of human nature.

Classical Manuscripts

The passionate quest for Latin and Greek literary manuscripts sometimes conflicted with the creation of original Italian literature by siphoning off the interest and energy of the writers. This conflict is illustrated by Petrarch, who rather early in life ceased writing what he called his "worthless" lyrics in order to discover lost classical manuscripts and to copy their style. He did succeed in bringing to light many priceless classical literary gems, but his epic *Africa* (relating the exploits of Scipio Africanus), written in Latin after the style of Vergil's *Aeneid*, lacks spontaneity and is all but forgotten.

Petrarch interested Boccaccio in the recovery of Greek and Latin manuscripts, and the search soon spread. Popes, princes, rich merchants, and bankers subsidized the humanists. In the fifteenth century, Italy was busy with professional humanists hunting, copying, translating, and editing ancient manuscripts.

Educational Reform

Working with classical manuscripts was related to a broader educational reform encompassed in the humanist movement. Humanists such as Petrarch argued that medieval schooling was too narrow, that the goal of education should be to produce more rounded, eloquent, virtuous individuals who were able to pursue the good life. Classical literature became a larger part of an educational curriculum that increasingly stressed practical learning. Educational reformers such as Pietro Paolo Vergerio (1349–1420) and Vittorino da Feltre (1378–1446) modified the Scholastic tradition and infused the curriculum with physical exercises, music, philosophy, Latin, and Greek as well as classical literature.

Philosophy

The study of classical masterpieces led to a variety of philosophical inquiries. This phase of humanism had many facets, including a new stress on the rational capabilities of humans, the development of a critical attitude, and a change in the concept of politics.

In 1396 Manuel Chrysoloras, a Byzantine scholar from Constantinople, was invited to Florence. He and other Greek scholars stimulated the study of Greek manuscripts during the fifteenth century. This study led to a revival of interest in Platonism and the establishment of the Platonic Academy in Florence under Marsilio Ficino (1433–1499) and Pico della Mirandola (1463–1494). They believed that, properly understood, Platonic philosophy and Christianity were compatible. They argued that human beings had great freedom and abilities, above all an ability to use will and reason to strive for the good life.

Another element of the humanistic view of life was the development of an analytic attitude. When Lorenzo Valla (1407–1457) proved by linguistics that the Donation of Constantine was a forgery, the scholarly and secular-minded pope raised no objections, although this was one of the documents upon which the papacy had based its claims to temporal power in the West. In fact, Pope Nicholas V made Valla his secretary. By making this discovery, Valla established himself as the father of modern critical historical scholarship.

The Florentine Niccolò Machiavelli (1469–1527), in his celebrated *The Prince*, suggested that Christian morals have little to do with the actual practice of politics. To acquire and maintain political power, the prince (or ruler or governing officials) must be willing to use both amoral and ruthless means. Since politicians, like all human beings, are self-seeking animals, the prince should assume that all rival princes and even his own lieutenants are conspiring for his power. Therefore, the prince should be willing to set his own chief subjects against each other and maneuver them into impotence. A wise prince deceives and treacherously attacks his foreign rivals at the most favorable moment before they can do the same. While Machiavelli was trying to remedy the deplorable reality of a divided Italy overrun and pillaged by more powerful foreign enemies, he also reflected the reality of secular attitudes and politics in fifteenth- and sixteenth-century Italy. His was a political theory that separated politics from ethics, stressing how people behaved rather than how they ought to behave. Few books have had more influence on, or been more descriptive of, modern political thought and practice.

4. FINE ARTS

Several characteristics of the Italian Renaissance are vividly illustrated in the Italian fine arts of the fourteenth, fifteenth, and sixteenth centuries.

Painting

Medieval painting in Europe had been closely allied with the Church. Painters deliberately penalized human flesh in order that the spirit might shine forth unimpeded. The figures, nearly always saints, were stiff, haggard, flat, and elongated. The physical world too was blanked out with solid gold backgrounds. The styles were stereotyped.

In the early fourteenth century Giotto, a contemporary of Dante, began to break this medieval mold of artistic custom by humanizing his figures and painting functional landscape backgrounds. Although his magnificent frescoes in the church of St. Francis at Assisi depicting the life of St. Francis were still rather flat, with diffused lighting, this did not make them less decorative—an artistic principle known to ancient Egyptian artists. True, Giotto's subject matter was almost entirely religious, but his treatment of it was such that the humanistic spirit made definite advances at the expense of the medieval. In the early fifteenth century Masaccio greatly developed the trend begun by Giotto a century earlier. He increased the illusion of depth by introducing atmospheric perspective and by further developing linear perspective. He also introduced the principle of the known light source, which thereafter replaced diffused light in painting. His nude human forms were further rounded and humanized (see Figure 26.2). His landscape backgrounds were realistic and detailed. With Masaccio and later painters such as Bellini (see Color Plate 12) and Botticelli (see Figure 26.3), the transition from medieval to Renaissance painting was completed and the stage set for such towering geniuses of the

---

FIGURE 26.2 **Masaccio, "Expulsion of Adam and Eve"** Masaccio, early in the fifteenth century, developed still further the trend toward humanism and naturalism begun a century earlier by Giotto. His "Expulsion of Adam and Eve from the Garden of Eden" depicts a religious subject in a human, realistic, and detailed manner. The nude figures are rounded and individualized. (Alinari/Scala Art Resource)

FIGURE 26.3 Botticelli, "Adoration of the Magi," ca. 1477   The theme of this painting is religious, with the Christ child in the center. However, the human figures are depicted with individualism, and the models (Lorenzo de Medici kneeling next to the Christ child; the artist, Botticelli standing proudly to the far left) are secular and contemporary. (Uffizi/Art Resource)

Italian High Renaissance as Leonardo da Vinci, Michelangelo, Raphael, and Titian.

It would be difficult to find a more representative figure of the Italian Renaissance than Leonardo da Vinci (1452–1519). All the colorful facets of the Renaissance spirit are richly illustrated by the career and work of this versatile genius. Leonardo was an illegitimate child, as were a number of the famous figures of the Renaissance. He was

born near Florence and began his career there, but some of his most productive years were spent in the employ of the duke of Milan. He finally followed King Francis I to France, where he died. Like most Renaissance artists, Leonardo dealt primarily with religious subject matter; but, also like the others, his treatment of it was more secular and human. In his *Virgin of the Rocks* (see Figure 26.1), for instance, Leonardo creates with exquisite grace and beauty the Virgin Mary and the Christ child. The Virgin, however, is the loveliest of women, and the Christ child is a plump and playful baby boy. The characters are human, not divine. The background is a strange rock formation, naturalistic enough to reveal a keen interest in this material earth and yet arrestingly abnormal. The plant forms in the background are actually identifiable. Leonardo's *Last Supper* depicts the reactions of the twelve disciples to Christ's words, "One of you shall betray Me." This celebrated fresco, exhibiting the artist's complete mastery of technique and draftsmanship, is essentially a study in human psychology—a subject in which Leonardo showed a special interest. The famous *Mona Lisa* is not religious in subject matter; it is the portrait of a real woman. The mysterious half smile—the mouth smiles but the eyes do not—so captivates the viewer that one is likely to overlook other features of the picture, including the hands, which are said to be the most sensitive ever painted.

Michelangelo (1475–1564) is second only to Leonardo da Vinci as a versatile Italian High Renaissance genius. Since Michelangelo was primarily a sculptor, his painting is sometimes called "painted sculpture." Although a Florentine, much of his life was spent in Rome, where he labored in the service of the popes. His greatest painting was the ceiling fresco in the Vatican Sistine Chapel. The hundreds of individual figures, representing nine scenes from the book of Genesis, marvelously blend together into one harmonious whole. Later Michelangelo painted the *Last Judgment* as an altarpiece for the same chapel. The Christ in this picture is more like a pagan giant than the Jesus of medieval Christianity.

Some critics believe Raphael (1483–1520) to be the greatest painter of all time; others say that he merely synthesized the original work of others. The output during his brief life was enormous. His favorite subjects were religious, but his Madonnas were feminine, gracious women and his Christ child pudgy and mischievous. His best-known paintings, the *Sistine Madonna* and the *Madonna of the Chair*, both in oil, well illustrate this secular treatment of a sacred theme. Many of his vivid portraits are of lay princes and tycoons (see Color Plate 13). His monumental fresco *The School of Athens* reveals the veneration felt for the glory of Greece during the Renaissance.

The fourth of the great painters of the Italian High Renaissance was Titian (1477–1576). A citizen of Venice, the most powerful commercial city of the fifteenth and early sixteenth centuries, Titian reflected the humanistic spirit of the Renaissance to an even greater degree than his three renowned contemporaries. Although a considerable portion of his painting was of religious subjects, his focus was nearly always the pomp and pageantry of the Church rather than its teachings. But a large part of his subject matter was more secular. The wealth and brilliance of Venice, overflowing with cargoes of luxurious fabrics, tapestries, and gems from the East, provided a challenging array of sensuous and colorful material for the artist to depict. And in the use of color, particularly vivid yellows, reds, and blues, Titian had no peer. He painted the hair of his women a reddish-gold hue that has come to be called titian. His portraits of some of the great lay personages of the sixteenth century, such as Francis I of France, Emperor Charles V, and Philip II of Spain, are masterful character studies. With Titian, the break with medieval painting begun by Giotto and Masaccio and widened by Leonardo, Michelangelo, Raphael, and many other great Italian painters was completed.

Sculpture

In sculpture, the artist without peer in any age is Michelangelo. It is true that he had Roman copies of the sculpture of Hellenic Greek masters such as Praxiteles and Scopas to guide and inspire him. But the gifted Florentine was no mere copier. The Greek masterpieces, for all their beauty and grace, were idealized types—half human, half divine. Michelangelo and his lesser-known immediate predecessors and contemporaries added a typically Renaissance characteristic to sculpture: individuality. The statues of the Italian Renaissance are not only human beings but also human individuals. Even Michelangelo's *Pietà*, which represents the mother of Jesus holding the dead body of her son as she looks down piteously, is a study in human emotions. The helplessness and hopelessness of the huge, all-engulfing mother displays the human resignation at the finality of death—not the Christian hope of resurrection and eternal life. His *Moses* portrays the fierce and rugged strength of man, not God. Moses' beard, as crude as icicles beneath a water tank in the month of January, displays the sculptor's ability to distort deliberately for effect. The three-dimensional medium of marble enabled Michelangelo to exploit to the full his favorite subject, the masculine nude. Numerous statues of David are used to convey not only the virile muscular power but also the agile grace of the male animal. His *Dying Slave* (see Figure 26.4) is a sublime portrayal of both the human form and the human spirit struggling to free themselves from bondage. Some critics think that the great sculptor's finest genius is displayed in the companion statues of two members of the Medici family—Lorenzo, the contemplative type, and Giuliano, the man of action. In these two pieces the master craftsman and artist exhibits every technique of sculpture. The work of Michelangelo is probably our best example of the Renaissance glorification of the human being.

The subject of Renaissance sculpture cannot be dismissed without brief mention of the work of Benvenuto Cellini. His work in gold and silver was of an exquisite delicacy that has never been equaled. His most famous larger work is the bronze statue of Perseus holding up the Gorgon's head. In this amazing conglomeration of unrealities, Cellini showed complete disregard of all accepted traditions and standards, yet with happy results. Such bold and original pioneering was typical of the self-confident, secular nature of the Renaissance mind.

Architecture

Renaissance architecture, like Renaissance sculpture, drew heavily from Greek and Roman sources (see Figure 26.5). From Greece by way of Rome came columns (now merely decorative) and horizontal lines; from Rome came the dome, the arches, and the massiveness that characterized Renaissance buildings. All of these features (except massiveness) represented a revolt against the Gothic architecture of the later Middle Ages, although the Gothic style had never gained much of a foothold in Italy.

FIGURE 26.4 Michelangelo, "The Dying Slave"
The genius of Michelangelo, master sculptor of the Renaissance, is exemplified in this work, "The Dying Slave," now in the Louvre, which glorifies both the human form and the human spirit. (Courtesy Michigan State University)

The two greatest monuments of Italian Renaissance architecture are the dome of the cathedral in Florence and St. Peter's Basilica in Rome. The Florentine cathedral is essentially Tuscan Gothic. Its ornate rectangular façade and bell tower reflect Byzantine and Islamic influences. But its most distinguishing feature is its gigantic octagonal dome, designed and constructed by Brunelleschi in the

FIGURE 26.5 Circle of Piero Della Francesca: An Ideal Town   This mid-fifteenth-century townscape painting expresses ideals of Italian Renaissance architecture: geometry, logic, individuality with order, lightness, and spaciousness. (Anderson/Art Reference Bureau)

early fifteenth century. This symbol of the grandeur of ancient Rome served as a model for such later great domes as St. Peter's in Rome, St. Paul's in London, and the Capitol building in Washington, D.C.

But the most grandiose achievement of Renaissance architecture is St. Peter's. This magnificent structure was to the Renaissance era what the Pyramids, the Parthenon, the Colosseum, and the Gothic cathedrals were to their respective epochs. It was built by the popes during the sixteenth and early seventeenth centuries at a cost that shook all western Europe religiously and politically. Its numerous architects drew primarily on classical Greek and Roman sources for their inspiration. Even seventeenth-century baroque features eventually entered into its design. Raphael served for a time as chief architect, and Michelangelo designed the dome. One has to step inside St. Peter's to appreciate the breathtaking grandeur of this awesome structure. Its lofty proportions and gigantic pillars, its brilliant paintings and sculptures, its gold, marble, and mosaic decorations all glorify the material things of this world as well as the spiritual aspects of this world and the next.

Music

Music was another field of art in which many original contributions were made during the Renaissance period, particularly the sixteenth century.

Although most of these developments occurred in northern Europe, especially the Netherlands, Italy was a scene of some importance. Instrumental music became popular, and great improvements were made in the instruments. The harpsichord and the violin family of instruments came into existence. Musical techniques such as major and minor modes, counterpoint (the blending of two contrasting melodies), and polyphony (the interweaving of several melodic lines) rapidly developed. The most illustrious musician of the sixteenth century was Palestrina, chief musician to the pope and probably the greatest master of polyphonic music of all time. Although most of the music of the Renaissance still centered about the Church, it was now more sensuous and versatile. Moreover, new secular forms appeared. The madrigal, popular throughout Europe in the late sixteenth century, was a musical rendition of stanzas of secular lyrical poetry. Renaissance musicians laid the foundations for modern classical music in all its major forms—concerto, symphony, sonata, oratorio, and opera.

5. DECLINE

During the sixteenth century, the Italian Renaissance lost some of its vigor and originality. Certainly this loss did not occur overnight. For decades, and even into the seventeenth century, Italy was recognized as a center of the fine arts and cultural sophistication. Italian art, heavily patronized by the Church, retained much of its momentum. However, the center of Renaissance activity was shifting from Italy to northern Europe, paralleling the shift of commerce from the Mediterranean to the Atlantic. When Venice, Florence, and Milan were the most prosperous commercial and banking centers in Europe, they were the most vigorous seats of Renaissance culture. With the shifting of the trade routes to the West, their cultural vigor declined.

Other sixteenth-century developments probably played roles in the decline of the Italian Renaissance. The invasions of Italy by the French, Spanish, and German armies and the general military and political instability of the sixteenth century seem to have contributed to the decline. The flowering of culture and relative political stability in other parts of Europe may have made Italy a less important or attractive cultural center. In any case, cultural momentum shifted northward as the Renaissance spread outside of Italy.

SUGGESTED READING

General

G. A. Brucker, *Renaissance Florence,* rev. ed. (1983). A useful book on Renaissance Florence.

J. Burckhardt, *The Civilization of the Renaissance in Italy* (1867, 1983). A classic that has influenced all subsequent studies of the subject.

J. R. Hale, *Renaissance Europe: The Individual and Society, 1480–1520* (1978). Strong on individualism.

L. Martines, *Power and Imagination: City-States in Renaissance Italy* (1980). A highly respected recent study.

J. H. Plumb, *The Italian Renaissance* (1965). A good, well-written survey.

Humanism

F. Chabod, *Machiavelli and the Renaissance* (1960). A solid analysis by a leading authority.

Paul O. Kristeller, *Renaissance Thought: The Classic, Scholastic, and Humanistic Strains* (1961). A highly respected study of Renaissance thought.

W. H. Woodward, *Vittorino da Feltre and Other Humanist Educators* (1964). A good study of Italian humanist education.

The Fine Arts

James Beck, *Italian Painting of the Renaissance* (1981). A good recent study.

Bernard Berenson, *The Italian Painters of the Renaissance* (1968). A classic.

Sources

B. Castiglione, *The Book of the Courtier* (1976). Contemporary textbook for gentlemanly behavior.

B. Cellini, *Autobiography* (1956). The artist's own account of an adventuresome life.

N. Machiavelli, *The Prince* (1961). A classic of political theory.

P. Taylor, *The Notebooks of Leonardo Da Vinci: A New Selection.* Well illustrated.

CHAPTER 27
The Renaissance: The North

FIGURE 27.1 Dürer, "The Four Horsemen of the Apocalypse," ca. 1497–1498 In this woodcut the great German artist Albrecht Dürer exhibits a skill in his engraving and woodcutting that matched the painting genius of his Italian contemporaries, Leonardo and Michelangelo. His painting of this apocalyptical scene reveals the piety, the mysticism, and the concern with death that were important elements of the northern Renaissance. (The Art Museum, Princeton University)

The northern Renaissance occurred later than the Italian Renaissance and was in large measure imported from Italy. Although northern scholars such as Chaucer visited Italy as early as the fourteenth century, it wasn't until the late fifteenth century, when journeys by scholars, students, and merchants to Italy were commonplace, that the Renaissance flowered in the North. The northern Renaissance also had its own roots and characteristics. It was located more in the courts and universities than in large commercial cities. Northern humanism was more intertwined with Christian pietism than in Italy. In a broad sense, the northern Renaissance sought to humanize Christianity, to reconcile the sacred and the secular.

1. NORTHERN HUMANISM

The trend toward humanism as a basic attitude toward life began in earnest in northern Europe in the late fifteenth century. One of the central figures of northern humanism was Johann Reuchlin (1455–1522), a German scholar. After a sojourn in Italy during which he became imbued with the ideas of the Italian humanists, Reuchlin undertook to introduce the new classical learning into Germany. Specifically, he sought to broaden and enrich the university curriculum by establishing the study of the "un-Christian" Hebrew and Greek languages and literature. The Church and university interests vested in the medieval order of things attempted to thwart him, invoking the Inquisition to try him on grounds of heresy. Reuchlin fought back courageously and enlisted a large and enthusiastic following. Eventually the pope condemned him to silence. However, the victory really lay with Reuchlin and his humanist supporters. During the first few decades of the sixteenth century the new humanistic curriculum became established in all the major universities of Germany.

Meanwhile, in England a group of Oxford professors was accomplishing with less opposition what Reuchlin had fought for in Germany. John Colet (1467–1519) was the most prominent member of this group. He, too, visited Renaissance Italy. In true northern humanistic fashion he gave a critical and rational slant to his preaching and teaching of the Scriptures at Oxford. Probably the greatest of Colet's contributions to the new learning was the founding of St. Paul's grammar school in London, with a largely classical curriculum. To guarantee its humanistic orientation, he chose as trustees a guild of London merchants. St. Paul's soon became a model for many other such schools throughout England.

The most famous of the early-sixteenth-century English humanists was Sir Thomas More (1478–1535), Lord Chancellor of the Realm. More's *Utopia*, like Plato's *Republic*, blueprinted an earthly, not a heavenly, paradise. In picturing his ideal commonwealth, More indicted the social, religious, and political events of his own time. Utopia was a society in which private property and profits were unknown. Much attention was given to public health and education. The economy was planned and cooperative. War was outlawed except in self-defense. Religious freedom was granted to all but atheists. Although More eventually was to accept death by beheading rather than to recognize Henry VIII as head of the English church in place of the pope, his ideal society was ethical and secular. Humans through their own wisdom would create their own perfect world here on earth.

Towering above all the other northern humanists was Desiderius Erasmus (1466–1536). Erasmus was born in Rotterdam in the Netherlands, the illegitimate son of a priest. Reared as an orphan, he was educated in a school run by the Brethren of the Common Life, a pietistic order of laymen that taught the Greek and Latin classics and emphasized simple inner piety rather than ritual and formal creed. (Martin Luther, the great contemporary and adversary of Erasmus, also attended a school of the Brethren of the Common Life.) At the age of twenty-one Erasmus entered an Augustinian monastery (again like Luther) and was eventually ordained. Instead of serving as a priest, however, he studied his beloved classics—a pursuit he was to continue at the Sorbonne and for the rest of his life.

Erasmus' vast erudition combined with his great personal charm made him a much sought-after man. His first book was *Adages*, a collection of wise sayings of the Greeks and Romans with his own comments. It was an immediate success, and other books soon followed. His greatest work was the *Praise of Folly*, in which he ridiculed with subtle humor and delightful satire the ignorance, superstition, credulity, and current practices of his day, particularly those connected with the Church. The folly that he praised was a very human lightheartedness, a sense of humor. Wherever Erasmus went—France, England, Italy, Switzerland, Germany, the Netherlands—he was received with admiration and awe. No other individual so advanced the cause of northern humanism by popularizing the study of the Greek and Latin classics.

In addition to popularizing the new humanistic learning north of the Alps, Erasmus is significant in history for at least two other reasons—his influence on religious and social reform, and his efforts to humanize and intellectualize Christianity. He was at his best when laughing to scorn the abuses and superstitious practices of the Roman Catholic church. The taking of money from the poor and ignorant masses by wealthy and corrupt clergy, veneration of relics, and unquestioning belief in the miraculous were in the eyes of Erasmus beneath the contempt of enlightened men and women. But he was clever enough to sheathe his barbs with humor, thus making them more subtle and effective. Erasmus, however, was no Protestant. When Martin Luther first began his attacks on the Roman Catholic church, Erasmus thought that he was merely seeking to correct glaring abuses and hailed him as a fellow spirit. But when Erasmus discovered that the German reformer was primarily interested in doctrinal reform and that the Protestants were as dogmatic as the Roman Catholics, Erasmus would have nothing more to do with him. Nevertheless, Erasmus' incessant attacks on the abuses in organized Christianity undoubtedly encouraged both Protestant and Roman Catholic reformers.

Erasmus made great efforts to humanize Christianity. Although he never did specifically say so, the implication running through his writings is that Jesus was also a human being—a person to emulate. Erasmus would bypass formal creed, dogma, ritual, organization, and seek the "historical" Christ. Erasmus attempted to steer Christianity into a practice of following the example of a humanized Christ, stressing love, piety, civic virtue, and the best of classical values.

2. LITERATURE

During the late fifteenth and early sixteenth centuries Renaissance literature in the North was closely connected to the spirit of northern humanism with its stress on combining classical scholarship and Christian concerns. Scholars and educators such as Ulrich von Hutten (1488–1523) in Germany, Jacques Lefèvre d'Etaples (1454–1536) in France, Francisco Jiménez de Cisneros (1436–1517) in Spain, and William Grocyn (ca. 1446–1519) in England helped establish traditions of literary humanism in their countries. During the middle of the sixteenth century Renaissance literature in the North became more distinctly secular. The most important literary developments in the decades from the mid–sixteenth to the early seventeenth centuries were in England, France, and Spain.

The reign of Elizabeth I (1558–1603) was a period of great energy and optimism in England, and this was reflected in its literary outpourings. England became "a nest of singing birds" such as the world had never seen nor heard. Edmund Spenser's *Faerie Queen* (1590) glorified the versatile individual of the Italian humanists, particularly the ideal set forth by Castiglione in his *Book of the Courtier*. Christopher Marlowe (1564–1593) in his brief life wrote human-centered plays of such caliber that some critics think he would have achieved the stature of Shakespeare had he lived. His *Tamburlaine the Great* and *Edward II* treat the worldly drama of royal ambition. The central figure in *The Jew of Malta*, a forerunner of Shylock, is a product of the revived commercial capitalism. *Doctor Faustus* dramatizes the theme, later immortalized by Goethe, of the intellectual who in true Renaissance fashion sold his soul to the devil in return for earthly knowledge and pleasure.

Mightiest of all the writers of the English Renaissance was, of course, William Shakespeare (1564–1616). So little is known of Shakespeare's life that some still wonder whether he actually wrote all the poems and plays we attribute to him.

Although his lyrical poetry was beautiful, his most important work was in drama. Here he was heavily indebted to his contemporary, Christopher Marlowe, as well as to the ancient Greek and Roman dramatists. Marlowe developed the blank verse form, which Shakespeare perfected. In plays such as *Hamlet, Macbeth, Othello, King Lear, The Merchant of Venice, As You Like It, Henry IV, Romeo and Juliet,* and *Julius Caesar,* Shakespeare displayed a mastery of every known technique of the dramatic art.

More important for the student of history, he exemplified and dramatized the secular spirit of the Renaissance. The individual is Shakespeare's subject matter. Rugged, distinctive human personalities are the heroes and villains of his plays. No human emotion, aspiration, or psychological conflict escapes his eye. On the whole, Shakespeare, unlike the Greek dramatists, makes each person the master of his or her own fate. Admiration for Greece and Rome, a keen interest in newfound lands, the first stirrings of modern natural science, the commercial revolution and social problems arising from the emergence of the capitalistic middle class, the rise of national monarchy and a national patriotic spirit—all enter into the fabric of the plays.

The two chief figures in French Renaissance literature were François Rabelais (1494–1553) and Michel de Montaigne (1533–1592). Rabelais was a renegade priest, a bored physician, and a loving student of the classics. Although he stumbled quite by accident and late in life upon his gift for writing, he turned out to be one of the great creative geniuses in the history of literature. His masterpieces are *Pantagruel* and *Gargantua.* They are fantasies about two completely unrestrained giants who wallow and revel unashamedly in sensual pleasures. These works are an open assault on Christian moral standards and restraints. The wit is coarse and lewd and sympathetic toward the frailties of human nature. Rabelais' rich imagery, his marvelous gift of expression, and his graceful artistry combine to make him one of the founders of modern French prose.

Montaigne was a prodigy born of a wealthy family. Like Rabelais, he was an ardent lover of the classics. The result of his life of study and reflection was his *Essays.* Montaigne was a skeptic.

To arrive at reliable truth, he believed, one must rid oneself of all religious prejudice. He was a moral and spiritual relativist, rejecting all absolutes. Unlike his successors of the eighteenth-century Enlightenment, he distrusted the authority of human reason. Unable to replace the authority of Christian dogma with any other firm conviction, Montaigne was nearly always negative in his conclusions. But he immensely enjoyed this game of intellectual hide-and-seek. In fact, Montaigne believed that the chief purpose of life is pleasure—not the "eat, drink, and be merry" pleasure of Rabelais, but urbane, sophisticated, restrained, intellectual pleasure. The influence of Montaigne has been enormous—obviously on essayists from Bacon to Emerson and later, but also on the development of modern rationalism in general.

Standing out above all others in Spanish Renaissance literature are Miguel de Cervantes (1547–1616) and Lope de Vega (1562–1635). Cervantes was a contemporary of Shakespeare, the two dying within a few days of each other in 1616. Cervantes' early life, like Shakespeare's, is obscure. In time he became a soldier of fortune, fought heroically and was wounded in the great naval battle of Lepanto with the Turks, suffered a five-year imprisonment in Algeria, and finally served as a quartermaster for Spain's Invincible Armada. In poverty-stricken later life he settled down to write his famous novel *Don Quixote.* This masterpiece of Spanish literature relates with urbane grace and humor the adventures of a confused knight, who filled his noble head too full of the lore of chivalry, and of his groom, Sancho Panza. Sancho, a squat plebeian on a donkey, and Don Quixote, an emaciated knight on a tall, lean horse, go about Spain from one delightfully charming adventure to another. Cervantes' most immediate purpose was to satirize what was left of medieval chivalry. At a deeper level he probes the balance between the idealism of Don Quixote and the realism of Sancho Panza, revealing that there is some of each in all of us. Finally, since all types and classes of people throughout Spain are lucidly portrayed, *Don Quixote* is a valuable historical source for descriptions of life in sixteenth-century Spain.

Lope de Vega wrote a fabulous number of works in practically every known genre. His plays

FIGURE 27.2 The Gutenberg Bible
An illuminated page from the Gutenberg Bible, after a facsimile. This forty-two-line Bible, printed by Johannes Gutenberg in about 1456, is the earliest known book printed by movable type in the Western world. The craftsmanship exhibited by this illustration is remarkable. Gutenberg's invention launched a revolution in communications. (Rare Book Division, New York Public Library, Astor, Lennox and Tilden Foundations)

alone exceed in number those of any other writer, whether we accept the writer's own claim to at least eighteen hundred or recognize only the five-hundred-odd plays that can be accounted for today. The secular person, pictured in every conceivable dramatic situation, is the hero of the great Spanish playwright.

Thus the writers of the northern Renaissance had much in common. Their chief interests were contemporary human beings and the exciting, rapidly expanding material world around them. Their chief inspiration was the classical literature of Greece and Rome. They were on the whole nationalistic and wrote in the new national vernaculars.

3. PRINTING WITH MOVABLE TYPE

The spread of humanism and literature in general was stimulated by the invention of printing on paper with movable type. In ancient and medieval times manuscripts were written and copied in longhand on parchment or papyrus, a slow and costly process that greatly retarded the dissemination of knowledge. In the fourteenth century printing from carved wooden blocks came to western Europe from China by way of the Moslem world and Spain. This process too was tedious, costly, and limited. Also from China came paper, made of various fibers, silk, cotton, or flax. Paper was a great improvement over parchment or pa-

Figure 27.3 Matthias Grunewald, "The Crucifixion," ca. 1510–1515 This northern Renaissance painting from the "Isenheim Altarpiece" by the German artist Grunewald combines a deeply pious subject matter reminiscent of late Gothic traditions with Renaissance perspective and individualism. (Musée Unterlinden, Colmar)

pyrus for purposes of mass production. [Even the art of printing by movable type itself was a Chinese (Korean) invention, although this is not believed to have influenced its invention in the Western world.]

Johannes Gutenberg set up the first practical printing press using movable type in Europe at Mainz in western Germany. The Gutenberg forty-two-line Bible printed in about 1456 is the earliest known book to be printed by the new process (see Figure 27.2). The invention was an immediate success and spread quickly to all the other countries of western Europe. It is estimated that by the end of the fifteenth century more than twenty-five thousand separate editions and nearly 10 million individual books had been printed. Printing was now much cheaper, much quicker, and much more accurate. Its effects spread beyond greater access to religious and secular literature. The printing press encouraged a growth of literacy and made the spread of political and commercial documents easier.

4. ART, ARCHITECTURE, AND MUSIC

Northern Renaissance art was influenced by Italian art and shared many of its characteristics, but it had stronger roots in the Christian, pietistic culture of the late Middle Ages. Generally the subject matter of paintings was less secular than that of Italian Renaissance paintings. Northern artists tried to bring the concrete details of Christian life into immediate focus and with great emotional impact (see Figure 27.3).

The most noteworthy fifteenth- and sixteenth-century painters in the North were the Flemings (Belgians) and the Germans. The Van Eyck brothers, Hubert and Jan, lived in Ghent in the Flemish Netherlands in the fifteenth century. Like Masaccio, their Italian contemporary, they brought to near completion the transition from medieval to Renaissance painting (see Figure 27.4). Their greatest joint work is *Adoration of the Mystic Lamb*. Not the least of their contributions to painting was

FIGURE 27.4 Jan Van Eyck, "The Virgin and Chancellor Rolin" The Van Eyck brothers, Hubert and Jan, of Ghent in the Netherlands, were fifteenth-century contemporaries of Masaccio. This painting illustrates the clear, naturalistic perspective, the precision of line and detail, and the religious theme that were characteristic of northern Renaissance painting. (Scala/Art Resource)

the development of oil as a medium. It was from them that Leonardo da Vinci learned to work in this medium, which he perfected in such masterworks as the *Mona Lisa* and the *Virgin of the Rocks*.

In sixteenth-century Germany, Albert Dürer of Nuremberg and Hans Holbein the Younger of Augsburg were the leading painters. Dürer was primarily a master craftsman of delicate and graceful line. Probably for this reason, his woodcuts and engravings are better than his paintings, and in these media he is without peer in any age (see Figure 27.1). Holbein was a skillful sketcher and woodcutter, but he made his greatest contributions in the field of portrait painting. He painted several portraits of Erasmus and illustrated Erasmus' *Praise of Folly* with pen-and-ink drawings. Many of his most productive years were spent in England in the employ of Henry VIII. Among his greatest portraits are those of Henry VIII (see Figure 28.1), Edward VI, Mary Tudor, and Sir Thomas More.

Renaissance architecture was less prominent in the North. The largest Renaissance structure outside Italy is the vast Escorial near Madrid, which Philip II of Spain built as a royal palace and mausoleum. Its rugged massiveness, rectangular shape, and horizontal lines typify the Renaissance style. Some of the best examples of northern Renaissance architecture are the Renaissance wing of the Louvre in Paris, which is the world's largest and probably greatest art gallery, and some of the largest chateaux along France's Loire River. This architecture was essentially derivative; the French Renaissance chateaux were really fortresses being played with.

The music capital of the Western world during the Renaissance period was the Netherlands. It was from the Flemings that the Italian Renaissance musicians, including Palestrina, derived much of their knowledge and inspiration (see p. 360).

5. SIGNIFICANCE OF THE RENAISSANCE IN HISTORY

In retrospect, then, it is apparent that the Renaissance was part of a transition from the Middle Ages to the early modern period. In some measure it was a rebirth of the classical civilizations of Greece and Rome, but it was not merely that. There was much in the Renaissance that was fresh and original, and there was a self-consciousness among Renaissance scholars, writers, and artists that they were part of something new. In some ways the Renaissance represented a new emphasis on secularism and a rejection of the scholastic Christian culture of the Middle Ages, particularly in Italy. Yet in other ways it remained fundamentally a Christian civilization and an era that, in our terms, was quite religious. Indeed, the depth of religious sentiment during the Renaissance, particularly in the North, is revealed by the Reformation.

The intellectual and cultural themes established during the Renaissance would continue to grow throughout the early modern period. As we shall see, their effects would be felt in the politics, the commerce, and the society of Europeans during the sixteenth, seventeenth, and eighteenth centuries.

SUGGESTED READING

General

J. Huizinga, *The Waning of the Middle Ages* (1954). A superb interpretation important for an understanding of the early northern Renaissance. (See also items at the end of Chapter 26.)

Northern Humanism

E. H. Harbison, *The Christian Scholar in the Age of the Reformation* (1956). By a leading scholar in the field.
J. Huizinga, *Erasmus and the Age of the Reformation* (1957). Probably the best single volume on Erasmus.
R. Marius, *Thomas More: A Biography* (1984). A recent study.
M. M. Philips, *Erasmus and the Northern Renaissance* (1965). A good general study.

England, France, and Germany

Fritz Caspari, *Humanism and the Social Order in Tudor England* (1968). Focuses on connections between humanism and sixteenth-century English society.

L. Febvre, *Life in Renaissance France* (1977). A highly respected account.
Werner L. Gundersheimer, ed., *French Humanism 1470–1600* (1969). A solid collection of essays.
J. H. Overfield, *Humanism and Scholasticism in Late Medieval Germany* (1984). Focuses on universities.
Lewis Spitz, *The Religious Renaissance of the German Humanists* (1963). Broad and well written.

Art and Printing

Elizabeth Eisenstein, *The Printing Press as an Agent of Change* (1978). A superb, exhaustive interpretive study.
W. Stechow, *Northern Renaissance Art: 1400–1600* (1966). A useful survey.

CHAPTER 28
The Rise of National States

FIGURE 28.1 Hans Holbein the Younger, "Portrait of Henry VIII," 1540
Henry VIII and his father, Henry VII, were two of the most forceful of the new monarchs that arose in Europe between 1450 and 1550. These monarchs increased the power of the central government as well as their own personal power. (Alinari/Art Resource)

In the fifteenth and sixteenth centuries, monarchs in western Europe succeeded in creating powerful national states. These monarchs, often referred to by historians as the "new monarchs," aggressively built their dynastic power in three main ways. First, they undermined their competitors, above all the feudal barons. Monarchs turned to members of the lesser nobility and the middle class for backing. Second, they developed new methods of financial and administrative support. National taxes gave monarchs new, independent sources of income, and expanding governmental bureaucracies staffed by officials who owed allegiance to the monarchs extended royal authority throughout the land. Third, they brought the Church more under their command. In some cases they gained the right to appoint church officers within their lands; in other cases they actually established new official churches.

The new monarchs used other methods as well and took advantage of developments occurring at that time. Applying principles of dynastic succession, they married to expand and unify their lands. They increased their income by promoting and tapping into reviving commerce, which brought with it a moneyed economy and a prosperous middle class. With their greater financial resources, new monarchs established standing professional armies that could use the new military tactics and technology that were lessening the importance of the independent mounted armored knight. They suppressed internal violence and made law enforcement more the responsibility of their own agents. To legalize their growing power, the monarchs utilized the principles of Roman law, which considered kings to be sovereigns in whose hands the welfare of all the people was placed.

The most important of these new monarchs arose in Spain, France, and England. Although other factors retarded unification in Italy and Germany until the nineteenth century, Spain, France, and England were already well on their way to becoming powerful national states in the late fifteenth century.

---

[1]Isabella ruled Castile from 1474 to 1504, and Ferdinand ruled Aragon from 1479 to 1516.

1. SPAIN

Spain became the most powerful and influential of the new states at the opening of the early modern era. The energy and enthusiasm that Spain displayed at this time may be attributed in part, at least, to her long and finally successful struggle against the Moors. By the middle of the thirteenth century the Moors had been driven out of the entire Iberian peninsula except for the southernmost province of Granada. Furthermore, the numerous medieval feudal holdings in what is now Spain had been consolidated into four large kingdoms—Castile, Aragon, Granada, and Navarre (south of the Pyrenees). The marriage of Ferdinand of Aragon and Isabella of Castile in 1469 united to some extent the two largest kingdoms. During their reign (1474–1516)[1] Granada and Navarre were conquered and ties between their lands were strengthened. Thus, within a forty-seven-year span from 1469 to 1516 the Spanish national state was created.

Ferdinand and Isabella strove for political and religious unity. In order to suppress further the jealous nobility, they allied themselves with *hidalgos*—members of the lesser nobility—and the middle class, leaning heavily on them for financial and administrative assistance. In return, the joint sovereigns did everything in their power to advance their fortunes. Vigorous enforcement of law and order, stabilization of the currency, building of roads and bridges, tariff protection of home industries—all served to advance the economic prosperity of Spain in general and the middle class in particular. This commercial expansion was greatly enhanced in 1492 with the discovery of the New World in the name of Spain. The ensuing profits and loot further strengthened the hands of the Spanish sovereigns by freeing them from dependence on the Cortes (the representative bodies dominated by the nobility) for funds.

In religious affairs, also, Ferdinand and Isabella gained power over the Church and unified their country. They acquired the right to appoint bishops, reformed the Church, and gained access to some of its wealth. By the end of their reign, the Church in Spain was in effect at the command of the Spanish state. Against the two non-Christian groups in their realm, the Jews and the Moslems, the "Catholic Sovereigns" waged a campaign of conversion or expulsion. The Jews had long been the object of hatred and persecution in Christian Europe. In part this hatred derived from religious differences, but there was also an economic factor. Church laws against usury had given the Jews a monopoly on money lending, a precarious but often profitable activity. The envy and hatred of the Christians led to periodic outbreaks of violence. In the late fourteenth century, an outbreak of unusual severity forced many Spanish Jews to seek safety in outward conversion. But these Marranos, as the pseudoconverts were called, were the object of increasing suspicion. Finally, Ferdinand and Isabella, despite some reluctance, introduced the Inquisition into Spain. At the mercy of this court, the Marranos were terrorized by imprisonment, torture, and loss of life and property. In 1492 the remaining Jews were ordered to leave the country. The exiles thus banished (estimated to be in the neighborhood of one hundred fifty thousand) took much of their wealth and all their economic energy and skills with them.[2]

Shortly afterward the Moslems suffered a similar fate. Upon surrendering their last stronghold in Granada, in 1492, they had been promised religious freedom in return for submission to the political authority of the Spanish crown. However, again the "Catholic Sovereigns" yielded to the increasing pressure of religious intolerance, and in 1502 the Moslems were ordered to accept Christianity or leave Spain. Although thousands did leave, even more thousands remained and went through the farce of outward conversion. But these "converts," called Moriscos, only delayed their fate. In the two succeeding reigns they too were persecuted and expelled.

Spain, then, was unified religiously under the crown, but at an economic and intellectual cost. Nevertheless, territorially consolidated and politically unified by Ferdinand and Isabella, enriched by the wealth of the New World, and inspired by the crusading zeal of a purified and triumphant religion, Spain was to be the most powerful and influential of the new national states during the first century of the early modern era (see Figure 28.2 and Map 28.1).

2. FRANCE

The reign of Louis XI (1461–1483), known as the "Spider King," may be said to mark the beginning of France as a modern national state. Louis came to the throne of France eight years after the end of the Hundred Years' War with England. His predecessor, Charles VII, had used the war emergency to obtain powers over taxation (*taille*) and a standing army for the crown. During the last phase of the war a great upsurge of French national spirit, aided by the exploits of Joan of Arc, made possible, at long last, the expulsion of the English invaders. Louis XI put these inherited advantages to clever use. First of all, he set out to crush the power of the feudal nobility who had taken advantage of the royal distress during the Hundred Years' War to assert their virtual independence of the crown. By craft and by direct military force he broke up the league that the insubordinate nobility formed against him and reduced the individual nobles to submission. In order to achieve this goal, Louis utilized the rising middle class. In return for its support he placed many members of this class in his councils and in key administrative posts, enabling some to enter the nobility. He also did what he could to foster commerce and industry. Roads, harbors, and waterways were improved. Shipbuilding, commerce, and industry were encouraged by royal subsidies and protective regulation.

Louis XI virtually completed the territorial consolidation of the French national state. He brought province after province under direct royal control, until by the end of his reign France had acquired all of its modern territory except the northwesternmost peninsula of Brittany (which was acquired by Louis' son) and a few territories along the fluid northeastern frontier. This expansive movement brought Louis XI into conflict with Charles the Bold of Burgundy. Charles the Bold (perhaps "the Rash" would have been a more accurate title) had inherited rich and strategically

---

[2]The Jews had earlier been expelled from England, France, and the German states.

FIGURE 28.2 Ferdinand and Isabella   A coin of Ferdinand and Isabella, sovereigns of Spain. Spain was the most powerful of the new national monarchies and her coins enjoyed wide circulation in Europe and predominance in the Spanish and English empires in North and South America during the sixteenth, seventeenth, and eighteenth centuries. The Spanish piece-of-eight was commonly called the "dollar," and in 1787 the dollar was adopted by the United States as its standard unit of value. (American Numismatic Society)

located territories that included the Netherlands, the duchy of Burgundy, and the free county of Burgundy. These he hoped to consolidate into a great national state—the old Middle Kingdom of Charlemagne's grandson Lothair—between France and Germany. Had he succeeded in doing so, the course of history might have been changed significantly. However, Charles the Bold and his successor, Mary of Burgundy, were no match for the "Spider King" of France. Charles was killed battling the Swiss, and Mary was unable to prevent Louis XI from seizing the duchy of Burgundy, Picardy, and part of Flanders. (The abortive Burgundian "Middle Kingdom" has been a battleground between France and Germany throughout much of the modern period.) Thus consolidated and enlarged, France was to play a dominant role in European affairs in the centuries that followed.

Louis XI's schemes, however, did not include the betterment of the condition of the lower classes. Having paid for his ambitious programs with heavy taxes but having received little in return, the lower classes remained disaffected and discontented.

3. ENGLAND

Early modern times, so far as English history is concerned, may be said to have begun with the reign of Henry VII (1485–1509), the first of the Tudor dynasty. The political unity of the English national state had been brought about as early as 1066 by William the Conqueror (aided to a considerable degree by geography). However, the feudal system, with its decentralization of administration and society, the Hundred Years' War with France (1337–1453), and the Wars of the Roses (1455–1484) between the rival houses of Lancaster and York, had by the last quarter of the fifteenth century brought England to a state of turmoil bordering on anarchy. Henry Tudor acquired the English throne by victory on the battlefield over the Yorkish King Richard III, who was slain. Himself a member of the Lancastrian family, Henry ended the bloody dynastic feud by marrying Elizabeth of York.

The most pressing task confronting the strong-willed new monarch was the suppression of the turbulent nobility. The great feudal barons had

Habsburg Dominions

Ottoman Empire

Boundary of the Holy Roman Empire

NORWAY

Bergen •   Oslo •   • Stockholm

SCOTLAND   SWEDEN

• Edinburgh   NORTH
                     SEA   DENMARK   Copenhagen •   BALTIC SEA

IRELAND   • Danzig

• Dublin   • York   ENGLAND   Hamburg •   Vistula R.

                                                              BRANDENBURG   Warsa

ATLANTIC OCEAN   London •   DUTCH Munster   • Berlin

                        • Canterbury   NETH.   Cologne   Wittenberg •   SILESIA
                                         Antwerp •   • Breslau
                                         Brussels   Schmalkalden •   SAXONY   BOHEMIA   Craco
                        BELG.   Prague •
                   Rouen •   NETH.   LUX.   • Trier   • Worms   MORAVIA
St. Malo •   • Metz   Ratisbon •
                   Paris •   PALATINATE   Strasbourg •   Augsburg •   Vienna •
              Orléans •   • Strasbourg   Munich •   AUSTRIA   • Buc
                                        FR.   • Basel   BAVARIA
         Bourges •   FRANCE   COMTÉ   SWISS   TYROL   HU
Angoulême •   CONFEDERATION   Trent •
         Bordeaux •   BURGUNDY   • Geneva   Venice •   VENETIAN   Mohacs •
                                        SAVOY   Milan •   REPUBLIC
Santiago •   DAUPHINE   • Genoa   Parma •   BOSNIA
                   Bayonne •   Avignon •   • Florence   DALMATIA
Oporto •   Valladolid • Burgos   PYRENEES   Marseilles •   PAPAL
                   NAVARRE   STATES   MONTENEGRO
PORTUGAL   SPAIN   ARAGON   CATALONIA   Corsica   Elba
              (Castile)   • Barcelona   (to Genoa)   (to Florence)
         Escorial • • Madrid   Rome •
Lisbon •   Toledo •   NAPLES
                   • Valencia   Sardinia   (Aragon)
                        Balearic I.   (to Aragon)   Naples •

              • Seville   MEDITERRANEAN SEA   Palermo •   Io
Cadiz •   • Granada   Sicily   (V
         GRANADA   Algiers •   • Tunis   (to Aragon)
Melilla (Spain) •   Malta (Knights of St. Joh

SULTANATE   SULTANATE OF ALGIERS   SULTANATE OF
OF FEZ   TUNIS

          B A R B A R Y   S T A T E S

0   100   200   300 miles

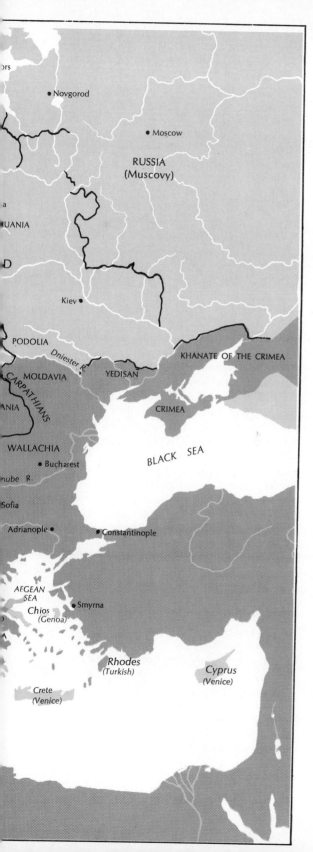

taken advantage of the decades of civil war and of the long rule of a weak king prior to the war to defy royal authority. They retained their own private armies and overawed the local courts. At once and with great vigor Henry VII proceeded to enforce the laws against livery and maintenance,[3] thereby destroying the illegal feudal armies. Since the regular local courts were too weak to proceed against the nobility, Henry set up his own Court of Star Chamber, which, backed by the royal army, was able to overawe the most powerful barons and bring them to justice and to submission to the crown.

In these undertakings Henry VII had the support of the lesser gentry and the middle and lower classes, all of whom yearned for peace and order. The middle class, particularly, desired stability for the sake of its growing business activities, and it was with this class that the Tudors allied themselves. Henry selected many of his counselors and administrators from the ranks of the bourgeoisie. He made favorable commercial treaties with the Netherlands, Denmark, and even with Venice, the jealous queen of the rich eastern Mediterranean trade. Navigation acts were passed to protect English shippers. Henry's frugality and careful collection and handling of revenues not only were good business but also freed the king of dependence upon Parliament for funds.

Henry VII died in 1509, but he passed along to

---

[3]So called from the practice of the peasantry's wearing the lord's badge or livery, signifying membership in his private army, in return for the lord's promise to maintain (support) them in courts of justice.

Map 28.1 EUROPE, 1526 This map indicates how widespread the Hapsburg dominions were under Charles V. In addition, Charles V exercised some indirect control over most of the territory within the Holy Roman Empire as its selected emperor. As the Spanish monarch, his lands included Spanish holdings in the New World. The map also shows France nearly surrounded by its Hapsburg rivals and the Isamic Ottoman Empire as a threat to Christian Europe.

his glamorous son, Henry VIII, a united and orderly national state and a well-filled treasury. And under his granddaughter, Elizabeth, England rose to a position of first-rate importance in European affairs.

4. ITALY, GERMANY, AND THE HOLY ROMAN EMPIRE

Italian- and German-speaking people have played a vital role in modern European history, particularly in making important contributions to the arts and sciences. However, they did not achieve political unity at the opening of the early modern period, and that disunity created political problems that persisted into the nineteenth and twentieth centuries.

At the opening of the early modern period the Italian peninsula was divided into five major independent states: the Kingdom of Naples, the Papal States, Florence (Tuscany), Venice, and Milan. The Kingdom of Naples, the poorest of the Italian states, occupied the southern third of the peninsula and at times the large island of Sicily (see Map 28.2). During the fifteenth and sixteenth centuries it was a bone of contention over which France and Spain repeatedly fought. The Papal States occupied the central portion of the peninsula. These states were ruled by the pope not only as a supreme pontiff but also as political head. Florence and Venice, republics in name, were dominated by rich banking and commercial families. Milan, another thriving center of commerce, was ruled by an autocratic duke.

The main reason for Italian disunity in the early modern era was the long tradition of independence among the city-states. There the spirit of local rather than national pride and loyalty prevailed. Instead of forging common bonds, the major Italian city-states such as Florence, Venice, and Milan competed with each other for control over the smaller ones, such as Ferrara, Modena, and Mantua. Possibilities of unification under the papacy or the Holy Roman emperor were undermined by a long history of struggles between these two powers. For awhile, the Treaty of Lodi (1454–1455), which allied Florence, Milan, and Naples, and alliances between Venice and the Papal States

created a balance of power and some stability on the Italian peninsula. But this stability broke down in 1494. In the following decades Italy was repeatedly invaded by France and the Holy Roman Empire. The political division of the Italians in an age of powerful national states continued to be a standing invitation to aggression against them.

During the fifteenth century German-speaking peoples remained split up into more than three hundred virtually independent units. The only political bond between them was the impotent government of the Holy Roman Empire. This ramshackle institution—a survival of the organization set up by Charlemagne in 800 and revived by Otto the Great in 962—purported to be a restoration of the old Roman Empire, but it never was. In the Middle Ages, when the Spanish, French, and English sovereigns were consolidating their territories and their authority, the German emperors were frittering away their time and energy trying to bring Italy under their control. While they were away from Germany on these quixotic ventures, the local feudal barons conspired against them, consolidated their own power, and built up hereditary states of their own within the empire. Meanwhile, territory after territory slipped from under the emperor's control, until by the opening of the early modern period, the Holy Roman Empire included for all practical purposes only the German-speaking states (plus Czech-speaking Bohemia).

Eventually seven of the emperor's most prominent subjects gained the right to elect him. This elective feature not only diminished the prestige of the emperor but also forced candidates to bribe the electors and bargain and promise away any chance of strengthening the imperial office. Since the emperor had no sure income, he had no military force with which to enforce his will. Even to defend the empire, he was forced to call upon his subject princes to furnish troops. The lawmaking and taxing powers lay in the hands of the Diet, which was composed of three houses: the house of electors, the house of lesser princes, and the house of representatives of the free imperial cities. The Diet had no regular time or place of meeting and was seldom able to reach agreement on any important question. In the late fifteenth century an imperial court was set up to settle disputes between member states. However, lacking any

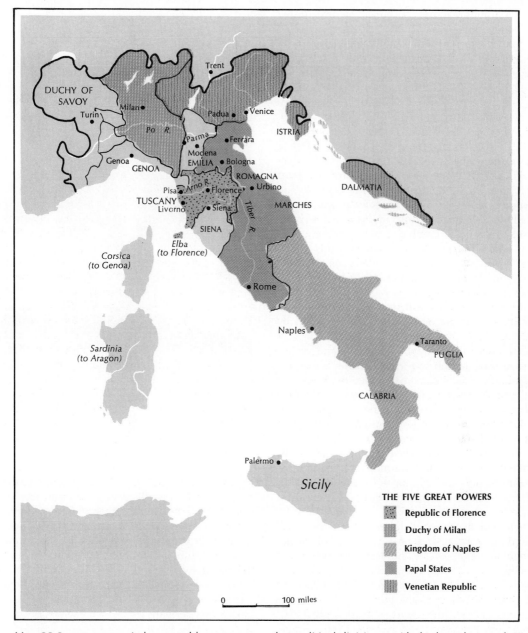

Map 28.2 ITALY, 1454 Italy as unable to overcome her political divisions, with the large but weak King-dom of Naples controlled by outside powers, the center controlled by popes opposed to national unification, and the rich urbanized North divided among cometing states.

The map labels, from the legend and across the map:

THE FIVE GREAT POWERS
- Republic of Florence
- Duchy of Milan
- Kingdom of Naples
- Papal States
- Venetian Republic

DUCHY OF SAVOY — Turin — Milan — Trent — Padua — Venice — ISTRIA — Po R. — Parma — Ferrara — Modena — EMILIA — Bologna — ROMAGNA — Urbino — DALMATIA — Genoa — GENOA — Pisa — Arno R. — Florence — TUSCANY — Livorno — Siena — MARCHES — Tiber R. — SIENA — Elba (to Florence) — Corsica (to Genoa) — Rome — Sardinia (to Aragon) — Naples — Taranto — PUGLIA — CALABRIA — Palermo — Sicily

0   100 miles

means of enforcing its decisions, this instrument too proved ineffective.

The one factor that gave any semblance of vitality to the Holy Roman Empire was the Hapsburg family. A Hapsburg was first elected emperor in 1273. After 1438, with only one brief exception, no one but a Hapsburg was elected until the empire finally died at the hands of Napoleon in 1806. By marriage and diplomacy, the Hapsburgs expanded their original Austrian lands until they possessed at the opening of the early modern period one of the largest and richest dynastic estates in Europe. Although, therefore, the Holy Roman emperor as emperor was virtually powerless, as head of the house of Hapsburg he was one of the most influential of monarchs. Nevertheless, all efforts of the Hapsburgs to strengthen the central government of the empire foundered on the rocks of German particularism—the local interests of the jealous princes.

During most of the first half of the sixteenth century the house of Hapsburg was headed by Emperor Charles V (see Figure 28.3). Charles V inherited from his parents and four grandparents a vast array of territories and claims. From his grandfather Maximilian he inherited the Hapsburg provinces generally spoken of as Austria, to which were added in Charles' lifetime Hungary, Bohemia, Moravia, and Silesia. As a Hapsburg, he also inherited a good claim to the imperial crown of the Holy Roman Empire. From his grandmother Mary he inherited the Burgundian lands: the free county of Burgundy (Franche Comté), the Netherlands, Luxembourg, Flanders, Artois, and claims to the duchy of Burgundy and Picardy, which had been seized by Louis XI. From his grandfather Ferdinand he received Aragon, the Kingdom of Naples, and numerous islands in the Mediterranean. From his grandmother Isabella he received Castile and a claim to the entire Western Hemisphere based on the papal Line of Demarcation (1493) and the Treaty of Tordesillas (1494). And from Ferdinand and Isabella jointly, he inherited Granada and Spanish Navarre.

The very size of Charles V's far-flung holdings spelled perpetual trouble. (See Map 28.1.) The language problem alone was appalling. To this were added differences in local customs, tastes, and eventually religion. Moreover, Charles V was sure

FIGURE 28.3 This 16th century engraving by Sichem shows Emperor Charles V with symbols of the Holy Roman Empire, sword and crossed Globe. (The Bettmann Archive)

to become involved in all the major international conflicts of Europe. Born and reared in the Netherlands, Charles was accepted in Spain only after a serious opposition and open revolt. His efforts to strengthen the government of the Holy Roman Empire and to raise money and troops there were frustrated by the local German princes. Finally, the Lutheran revolt further split the empire and shattered completely the personal power of Charles in Germany.

5. INTERNATIONAL RIVALRIES, 1516–1559

The rise of national states failed to bring peace to Europe. The national monarchs, supported by the bourgeoisie, had justified their own aggrandizement on the grounds that it was necessary to end the interminable feudal wars, and they had in fact established a large measure of internal law and order. However, the little feudal wars were followed by big national and dynastic wars. Although these monarchs established modern diplomatic institutions (earlier developed by Italians in the fifteenth century), such as permanent ambassadors, they also utilized larger armies and new military technology in their wars.

Throughout the sixteenth century international strife revolved around the house of Hapsburg. Charles V found himself almost continually at war with Francis I of France. Each feared the other's power. Francis I had continued the process initiated by his predecessors of increasing the power of the French monarchy, above all by securing new revenues through the sale of governmental offices, by swelling the state bureaucracy, and by gaining the right to appoint France's bishops and abbots. Francis vigorously contested Charles' election as Holy Roman Emperor. They fought over conflicting territorial claims in Italy, the Burgundian lands, and along the French-Spanish border. Charles won nearly all the battles, but he was never able to make his victories permanent.

The relations between Charles of Hapsburg and England were limited to a personal family quarrel. When Henry VIII sought an annulment of his marriage to Catherine of Aragon, the aunt of Charles V, Charles used his influence with the pope to block the proceedings, thus touching off a chain of events that ended with Henry taking over the Church in England and separating it from the Roman Catholic church. It was under Charles' son, Philip II, that conflict between Spain and England was brought to a climax.

Among Charles V's more concrete achievements were his marriage to Isabella of Portugal, which brought about a brief union of Spain and Portugal under Philip II, and his repulse of the Ottoman Turks. The Ottoman Turks had migrated to Asia Minor from Central Asia in the thirteenth century, converted to Islam, and by the beginning of the sixteenth century had built an empire that extended from Egypt to the Danube. Under Suleiman the Magnificent (1520–1566), their ablest ruler, they crushed the Hungarians at Mohacs (1526), swept across Hungary, and in 1529 laid seige to Vienna, the capital city of Hapsburg Austria. At the same time they conquered all of North Africa as far west as Morocco, and their fleets dominated the Mediterranean. It was feared that all Western Christendom might fall to the Moslems. At this point, Charles V rallied the forces of the empire and the Hapsburg provinces and drove the Turks back into Hungary. His captains also administered some defeats to the Moslem Barbary pirates in the western Mediterranean.

In 1555 Charles V began to divide his holdings between his son, Philip II, and his brother, Ferdinand. To Philip he gave the Burgundian provinces and Spain, with its appanages in Italy, the Mediterranean, and the New World. To Ferdinand he gave the Austrian provinces and successfully promoted Ferdinand's candidacy to the crown of the Holy Roman Empire. Henceforth there were two branches of the Hapsburg dynasty—Austrian and Spanish—both of which would long continue to play important roles in European and world history.

In 1559 the Treaty of Cateau-Cambrésis ended the dynastic wars between the Hapsburgs and the French Valois kings. Spain gained dominance in Italy, the center of power in Europe shifted to Spain, and a new era of revolts and wars entwining religion and politics unfolded.

6. THE POLITICAL MAP OF EUROPE IN 1559

At the beginning of the early modern period, then, powerful monarchs established national states in Spain, France, and England. These national states rose to dominate Europe. Germany and Italy were divided into many small states. The German states and Slavic Czech-speaking Bohemia were in the Holy Roman Empire. The Netherlands, owned by the Hapsburgs, was a part of the empire. Switzerland, nominally in the empire, was in reality an independent confederation of semiautonomous cantons. Elsewhere in Europe, Scotland was still independent, and England's control over Ireland was only tenuous. Denmark owned Norway and was in temporary union with Sweden. Poland, including Lithuania, occupied a large stretch of territory east of Germany, but its anemic government made Poland impotent at home and abroad. Russia, under Ivan III, had just freed itself from Mongol overlordship and as yet counted for little in European or world affairs. The Balkan peninsula and most of Hungary were part of the Ottoman Empire.

Spain, France, and England represented the political wave that most of Europe would eventually follow. But their new internal strength brought not a more peaceful international order but war on a larger, more violent scale.

SUGGESTED READING

General—The Fifteenth and Sixteenth Centuries

Margaret Aston, *The Fifteenth Century: The Prospect of Europe* (1968). A general survey with emphasis on social history.

De Lamar Jensen, *Renaissance Europe: Age of Recovery and Reconciliation* (1981). A good recent treatment.

Eugene F. Rice, Jr., *The Foundations of Early Modern Europe, 1460–1559* (1970). The best general survey of the period, with an excellent bibliography.

The New National Monarchies

J. H. Elliott, *Imperial Spain, 1469–1716* (1964). An excellent account of Spanish history during this period.

G. R. Elton, *The Tudor Revolution in Government* (1959). An important analysis of English political history during the fifteenth and sixteenth centuries.

J. Lockyer, *Henry VII* (1972). A recent biography with accompanying documents.

R. J. Knect, *Francis I* (1982). An authoritative study.

J. J. Scarisbrick, *Henry VIII* (1968). A fine biography.

J. H. Shennan, *The Origins of the Modern European State* (1974). An excellent brief analysis.

A. J. Slavin, ed., *The "New Monarchies" and Representative Assemblies: Medieval Constitutionalism or Modern Absolutism?* (1964). A sampling and comparison of scholarship on the political history of the period, particularly the rise of the "new monarchs."

The Hapsburgs

K. Brandi, *The Emperor Charles V: The Growth and Destiny of a Man and of a World Empire* (1939). A classic biography.

H. B. Koenigsberger, *The Hapsburgs and Europe: 1516–1660* (1971). A solid account of Hapsburg rule.

CHAPTER 29

European Expansion, Commercial Capitalism, and Social Change

FIGURE 29.1 **Columbus Discovers the New World** This illustration is from a letter of Columbus to the treasurer of the king of Spain, published in Basel a year after his first voyage. Here the Spaniards are offering the Indians gifts as they approach the West Indian island. The Indians are portrayed as naked and perhaps even childlike, emphasizing the European perception of them as lesser, uncivilized beings. Pictures such as this excited the wonder and greed of many Europeans during the Age of Discovery. (NYPL Picture Collection)

The rise of national states was closely associated with the expansion of Europe and new economic development. Monarchs who created national states supported voyages of discovery and the overseas conquests that resulted. They took advantage of the wealth that poured in to finance their growing governments and their wars. They also allied themselves with the rising middle class against the feudal aristocracy. The strength of this middle class lay in its commercial wealth and its use of capitalistic methods to gain that wealth. Together, this European expansion and economic development represented a new level of power and wealth that would make Europe dominant over large parts of the globe.

1. THE AGE OF DISCOVERY

In the late fifteenth and early sixteenth centuries European mariners made a series of daring voyages in which they discovered not only the New World but also new and much better routes to the East (see Map 29.1). These voyages were made possible by a number of recent developments. Important improvements in the technology of shipping and navigation were being made. New armaments and military tactics gave Europeans advantages over those resisting them. Commercial and organizational skills increased the chances of success for these risky voyages. The governments of the national states along the Atlantic coast promoted these voyages and provided needed financial support. Their principal motive was a desire to bypass the Venetians, the Moslems, and the land barriers that separated them from the riches of the East. But there was also a powerful outward impetus in the spirit of inquiry and adventure kindled by the Renaissance interest in the secular world, and in the Christian missionary zeal that had always been a spur to expansion.

The first to begin these voyages in the fifteenth century were the Portuguese. During the first half of the fifteenth century, Prince Henry the Navigator (1394–1460) established a school of navigation and base of operations on the southwestern tip of Portugal from which he sent expeditions down the west coast of Africa. In addition to curiosity, his motives were mercenary and religious:

He wanted to capture the gold trade in western Africa and hoped to find the legendary Christian kingdom of Prester John. A broader goal of this Portuguese effort was to find a new route around Africa to India. Pushing steadily down the coast of West Africa, the Portuguese developed a lucrative trade in gold, ivory, sugar, and slaves. In 1488 Portuguese explorers rounded the Cape of Good Hope. In 1498 Vasco da Gama, in what was probably the greatest voyage in the history of navigation, reached India, the object of the quest. Vasco da Gama was out of sight of land ninety-three days—three times as long as Columbus on his voyage to the New World. That the Portuguese knew what they were up to is proved by the fact that Vasco da Gama's return cargo sold for sixty times the cost of the expedition. These glad tidings sent a host of Portuguese adventurers hurrying to the East Indies, where they carved out a huge commercial and political empire. One of these adventurers, Cabral, swinging too far westward, touched the eastern bulge of South America, thus laying the basis for Portugal's claim to Brazil. With their discovery of this all-water route to the East, the Portuguese broke the Arab and Venetian monopoly over the spice trade. From that point on, the center of commercial activity shifted westward toward the Atlantic seaboard.

Meanwhile, Spain was sending its mariners westward, for by the late fifteenth century most educated people in western Europe assumed that the earth was round, although they greatly underestimated its size. Many navigators therefore believed that the East Indies could be reached by sailing west. The first European to attempt it was Christopher Columbus. (Nothing had come of the tenth-century voyages to Greenland and northern America of the roving Norsemen, Eric the Red and Leif Ericson.) Columbus was born in Genoa but moved to Portugal. When, however, Portugal failed to support his proposed westward voyage, he turned to Queen Isabella of Castile, who gave him the necessary backing. His three ships touched a West Indian island on October 12, 1492. Thinking that the West Indies were islands off the east coast of Asia, Columbus made three further voyages in the hope of bypassing these barriers and sailing on to his real goal, the East Indies. Instead, he was turned back by the South and

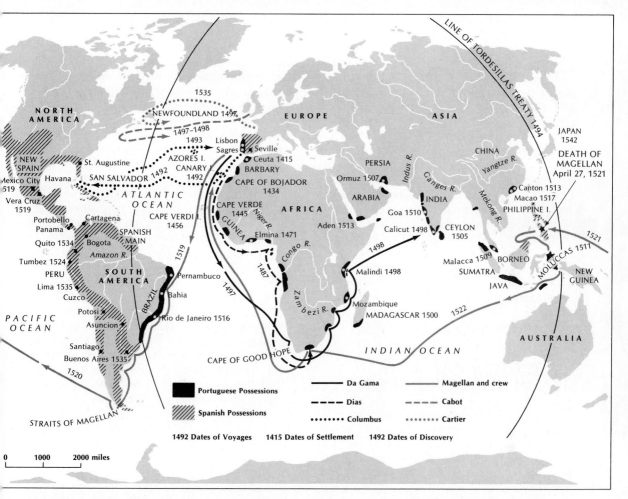

Map 29.1 **EXPLORATION AND CONQUEST, FIFTEENTH AND SIXTEENTH CENTURIES** This map shows the routes taken by some of the early explorers. It indicates some of the distinctions between the Portuguese and Spanish empires—the Portuguese concentrated in Africa and the East and focused primarily on sea power and trading posts; the Spanish concentrated in the New World and focused primarily on conquest and colonization. Early English and French efforts were more limited and farther north.

Central American mainlands and died disappointed, not having realized the magnitude of his discovery.

But others soon realized it, and in the first half of the sixteenth century, Spanish expeditions to the New World multiplied. In 1493 the pope drew a line of demarcation dividing the non-Christian world between Spain and Portugal. This line was somewhat altered in favor of Portugal the following year by the Treaty of Tordesillas. Since all of North and South America except the eastern part of Brazil and most of Greenland fell to Spain, the Spanish sailors continued to move westward. Ponce de Leon, de Soto, and Coronado explored the southern part of what is now the United States. Balboa crossed the Isthmus of Panama and looked out upon the Pacific Ocean. In 1519 Magellan set out around the world by way of the Straits of Magellan. Although he himself was killed in the Philippines, one of his ships in 1522 completed the circuit. Also in 1519 Cortez began the conquest of the Aztec Empire in Mexico. In 1531–1532 Pizarro conquered the Inca Indians in Peru.

The other two national states, England and France, were relatively inactive in discovery and exploration during the fifteenth and early sixteenth centuries. The English crown did, however, sponsor voyages to northern North America by the Italian mariner John Cabot in 1497–1498. These voyages became the basis for England's claims to North America, where England later built a great empire. The French government sponsored Jacques Cartier, who in 1535 sailed up the St. Lawrence to what is now Montreal and claimed Canada for France. Nonetheless, it was not until the seventeenth century that Spain and Portugal were replaced as the world's leading imperial powers.

2. THE FOUNDING OF THE SPANISH NEW WORLD EMPIRE

Although much of the Western Hemisphere at the beginning of the sixteenth century was sparsely inhabited by native or "Indian" tribes, the Spaniards encountered two highly organized societies: those of the Aztecs in Mexico and the Incas in Peru.

The first inhabitants of the Western Hemisphere are generally believed to have immigrated from Asia across the Bering Strait, perhaps as long as forty thousand years ago. They organized into hundreds of tribes throughout the North, Central, and South America.

The first of these tribes to build a highly organized society were the Mayas. They are believed to have come into what is now Guatemala and the Yucatán peninsula of southeast Mexico from the northwest about 1000 B.C. Their civilization reached its height between A.D. 400 and 600. It was a city-state civilization resembling that of ancient Greece approximately a thousand years earlier. Their writing, most of which has been lost, was a combination of pictures and ideographs.

Their best art was brightly colored pottery, gems, gold and silverware, and sculpture. Probably their most remarkable creations were a system of mathematics based on the decimal (actually vigesimal) system and a calendar based on astronomy, both of which were in advance of those used in contemporary Europe. Their massively walled stone cities were connected by elaborately paved roads. These cities, however, were continually at war with one another, and in the twelfth century the less culturally developed but better-organized Toltecs conquered the Mayan city-states much as Philip of Macedon conquered the Greeks.

In the fourteenth century the warlike Aztecs came down from the north and founded a city on an island in Lake Tezcoco—the present Mexico City. From this base they conquered and organized a military empire or confederacy comprising most of what is now southern Mexico. The Aztecs were the Romans of the New World, and like the Romans they acquired most of their culture from the earlier civilization (Mayas). Theirs was the gift of military and political organization. They developed an elaborate, though stern, system of justice. Their religion was important and highly organized. Several thousand priests, both regular and secular, tended the impressive temple and supervised education and morals. The numerous gods, taken mostly from the Mayas, were headed by the terrible war god, who demanded human sacrifice, usually prisoners of war. And yet the rank-and-file Aztecs were gentle lovers of poetry and art. Flourishing commerce, agriculture, and mining added to the wealth obtained by conquest.

An even more colorful civilization was that of the Incas on the Andean Plateau of South America. In the eleventh century the Inca Indians began to extend their sway over their neighbors until their empire covered an area fifteen hundred miles long and three hundred miles wide—including present-day Ecuador, Peru, and parts of Bolivia and Chile. An elaborate system of roads and communications tied this vast and lofty empire together. Incan society was a combination of benevolent despotism and socialism. The all-powerful Inca ruler was treated as a god. However, he had a body of advisers and administrators, chosen from the upper classes. All land and all production were owned and directed by the state. The regi-

FIGURE 29.2   The Aztec Perception of the Spanish   Although there are many Spanish records of their arrival and explorations in the New World, this Aztec manucript (ca. 1519–1522) is one of the few surviving Indian versions of the coming of the Europeans. This illustration shows Cortez arriving in Mexico. Note the depiction of some of the crucial elements of Cortez's conquest: the sword, the horse, the flag, and the cross. (Biblioteca Apostolica Vaticana, Rome)

mented lower classes did all the work under close supervision and shared from the common stores. A high degree of specialization was practiced. Agriculture was well advanced, and huge terracing and irrigation projects had been developed to overcome the difficulties of the Andean terrain. Religious worship, particularly of the sun god, was an important feature of national life. Outstanding were Incan pottery, architecture, textiles, and gold and silver ornamental objects.

The native American civilizations were no match for the marauding Europeans. Spanish military men, particularly those of the lesser nobility

(*hidalgos*), were part of a centuries-old tradition of crusading for Church, crown, and profit. Cortez, with a band of some six hundred soldiers and eighteen horses, overcame the Aztecs by a combination of treachery, tactics, weapons, and determination. He took advantage of divisions and hostilities between the Aztecs and the subject tribes as well as the Aztec belief that the Spaniards were ancient gods whose return had long been expected. Once inside the capital city, the Spaniards were too strong to be expelled. They slaughtered and looted the poorly armed Aztecs without mercy (see Figure 29.2).

Even more spectacular was the conquest of the Incas. Like Cortez, Pizarro used disunity within the Incan Empire as well as trickery and brutality to defeat the Incas. At one point, Pizarro enticed the Incan emperor into a conference. At a given signal Pizarro's small but well-armed band of Spanish soldiers fell upon the splendidly dressed but primitively armed Incan troops and slew them by the thousands. Pizarro promised to free the Incan chieftain in return for a ransom of gold objects sufficient to fill a room seventeen by twenty-two feet to a height of nine feet, plus a larger amount of silver. This ransom was collected and paid, but Pizarro, who never really intended to free the emperor, had him put to death anyway.

Spanish administrators soon replaced these conquerors, and throughout the sixteenth century Spaniards flocked to the New World. By 1607, when the first permanent English colony was founded in North America, a quarter of a million Spaniards had settled in the vast Spanish Empire stretching from what is now Arizona to Cape Horn. A number of distinguished missions and cathedrals had been erected, and several thriving universities had been founded. The native civilizations had been almost wholly destroyed and replaced by the Christian civilization of Spain.

3. CAPITALISM AND THE COMMERCIAL REVOLUTION

The discovery of the New World and of all-water routes to the Far East fueled an expansion of European commerce that was already underway. A crucial aspect of this expansion was the development of capitalistic methods. The use of capitalistic methods and the scale of commercial growth was so great that the term *commercial revolution* is used to describe it.

The term *capitalism*, stripped to its barest essentials, means a system whereby private individuals put money to work to make more money. Individuals, competing in a market to maximize their profits, determine what to produce, how to produce it, and what price to charge. It involves, among other things, private property, the profit motive, a substantial amount of free enterprise, the hiring of labor for wages, and the lending of money for interest.

Elements of capitalism had been in existence for centuries, but to a lesser degree and in much more limited form than during the sixteenth century. During most of the Middle Ages agriculture operated at only a subsistence level and was carried out under feudal restrictions. Commerce was a trickle of luxuries for the rich and necessities such as iron, implements, and salt. Guilds hampered commercial and industrial enterprises. The Church supported the concept of the "fair price" rather than competitive pricing and frowned on the lending of money for interest (usury).

During the eleventh century, commercial activities began to revive, and by the thirteenth century a pronounced recovery was underway. The Crusades contributed significantly to this revival. The huge movement of men and supplies from western Europe to the Holy Land enriched the merchants and shippers of Venice and other Italian cities. Some of them set up permanent trading posts in the Near East and introduced the luxuries of the materially more advanced Moslem and Byzantine worlds to western Europe. The Fourth Crusade, which the Venetians diverted to the looting of Constantinople, was particularly fruitful. The Venetians seized not only a great hoard of gold and silver in the stricken Eastern imperial capital but also a large part of the territory of the Byzantine Empire itself. This wealth flowed into the stream of western European commerce.

Foremost among the centers of this newly revived commerce and capitalism were the city-states of northern Italy, such as Venice, Genoa, Florence, and Milan. Venice was the queen of the Mediterranean in the thirteenth, fourteenth, and fifteenth centuries. After crushing the sea power of her chief rival, Genoa, in the fourteenth century, Venice enjoyed a virtual monopoly over the lucrative trade with the East. At the peak of its prosperity, Venice's merchant marine numbered some thirty thousand sailors. Milan was the starting point of the overland traffic across the Alps to northern Europe. In the late fourteenth century Milan gained control of the port city of Genoa. Florence manufactured large quantities of fine woolen textiles on a capitalistic basis, and in the fourteenth and fifteenth centuries it was the banking capital of the Western world. The Medici family alone possessed at one time some two hundred branch banks scattered throughout western and central Europe.

In northern Europe, the Hanseatic League, composed of some eighty German Baltic and North Sea cities, enjoyed a brisk trade in such commodities as fish, furs, grain, and timber. In southern Germany and the Rhine Valley, numerous trading centers such as Augsburg, Nuremberg, and Cologne sprang up along the overland route between Italy and northern Europe. Finally, the Netherlands, Paris, and London shared in this early period of revived commercialism.

As the main trade routes shifted from the Mediterranean to the Atlantic during the fifteenth and sixteenth centuries, new commercial centers to the west began to flourish. Contrary to what one might have expected, Spain, surfeited with gold and silver from Mexico and Peru, never developed a thriving commercial capitalism. And although Lisbon became the first great terminus of goods pouring in from the East, the Portuguese, like the Spanish, were so preoccupied with their vast overseas empire that they neglected the marketing opportunities in Europe itself.

These lucrative opportunities were first seized by the Dutch. Enterprising Dutch merchants purchased the goods in Lisbon, shipped them to the Netherlands, and sold them at a nice profit throughout northern and western Europe (see Figure 29.3). In the sixteenth century Antwerp, with its excellent harbor and location, was the leading commercial center in Europe. In the seventeenth century, following the sack of Antwerp in 1585 by Spanish troops, Amsterdam and London led the commercial world. The Dutch even took advantage of their newly won independence from Spain and of Portugal's temporary conquest by Spain in 1580 to seize the best part of Portugal's Eastern Empire, the area of present-day Indonesia.

Another phase of the commercial revolution was the advent of more bounteous supplies of commodities. Spices, coffee, tea, sugar, dyes, tropical fruits, fine textiles, tapestries, and precious stones, long known but in scarce supply and too expensive for all but the very rich, now came into Europe in ever-increasing volume. From the New World came potatoes, corn, tobacco, and

FIGURE 29.3 Jan Gossaert, 'Portrait of a Merchant,'' ca. 1530 This portrayal of a banker by the Flemish painter Gossaert reflects the spirit of commercial capitalism. This serious, self-assured banker works with pen in hand and business letters in the background. His clothes and rings reveal controlled wealth. (National Gallery of Art, Washington, D.C.; Alisa Mellon Bruce Fund)

chocolate (all of which were previously unknown to Europe), new dyes and medicines, gold and silver.

A different kind of new product—black slaves—also helped to swell the rising stream of commerce. This modern traffic in human beings was first begun in the later fifteenth century by the men of Portugal's Prince Henry the Navigator. It was later taken over by the Spaniards to supply labor for their empire in the New World. Native Indian populations were decimated by disease and the harsh conditions imposed by the Spaniards. Those that survived proved to be poor·slave laborers. The Spaniards turned to tropical Africa to supply slaves for their mines and plantations. Thousands of blacks were bought from local chieftains and crowded into the holds of ships. Many of them died during the crossings, but the survivors were sold like cattle for a high price in the New World markets. So heavy was this immensely profitable traffic that the racial and social complex of the New World society was drastically altered.

New types of business organizations were developed to accommodate the expanding volume of commerce. *Chartered companies* were organized to bypass the medieval guilds, which were unable or unwilling to meet the new demands. The most efficient type of chartered company proved to be the joint stock company. The members of a joint stock company pooled their resources, hired or elected their management, and shared in the profits in proportion to the amount of stock owned. In this way permanence was achieved, since the stock of any individual member could be bought or sold while the company remained intact.

Two of the earliest joint stock companies were the British East India Company, founded in 1600, and the Dutch East India Company, founded two years later. The British company was given not only a trading monopoly over British India but political control of the area as well. The Dutch company was given a monopoly over all Dutch trade east of the Cape of Good Hope. Annual profits of 300 percent were not uncommon for these giant companies. The annual profits of the Dutch East India Company never fell below 12 percent over a period of two hundred years.

Banking expanded in proportion to commerce. In the sixteenth century the Fugger family of Augsburg occupied the place in the financial world that the Medicis of Florence had held in the fifteenth. Jacob (the Rich) Fugger loaned Charles V the money with which he bribed his way to the emperorship of the Holy Roman Empire. In the seventeenth century the Bank of Amsterdam and the Bank of England were founded on a seminational basis. Both of these banks were really private joint stock companies, but in return for certain monopolies, such as the handling of government funds and the issuance of currency, they were obliged to accept a degree of government regulation. Banks of this size were able to mobilize sums of money and credit sufficient not only to launch and control large-scale commercial ventures but to influence government as well.

The commercialization of agriculture was of especially great significance. In some areas, particularly England, it sped up the process of combining smaller plots of land oriented toward subsistence farming into larger plots of land specializing in certain crops or herding for export. The commons—land available for the use of poor tenants—was taken away by large commercial landlords. Increasingly, small farmers were turned into wage laborers, either on the lands of commercial farmers or in the cities. The ranks of the landless poor swelled, while the productive commercial farmers gained wealth.

Industrial activity expanded in this period, particularly mining, shipbuilding, printing, armaments, and textiles, but guilds and governmental restrictions hindered the spread of capitalistic methods in these industries. The greatest expansion of capitalistic practices came with the growth of the domestic, or "putting out" system. Merchants or entrepreneurs would purchase the raw materials and distribute them to artisans, who would do the piecework in their cottages. Then the entrepreneur would collect the finished products, pay the cottagers for their work, and market the goods at a profit. While this system had certain advantages, it limited the volume of production. Until the coming of the machine and the factory system in the late eighteenth and early nineteenth centuries, therefore, large-scale capitalism was to remain commercial rather than industrial.

Part of this commercial revolution was fueled by the extraordinary rise in prices during the sixteenth century. This price inflation was probably related to the dramatic influx of gold and silver from the New World into Europe. However, historians now point to other causes for the price inflation that were perhaps more important, including the increase of population, the growing sense of confidence, and the increased purchasing of goods by governments; all combined to push demand for goods beyond available supplies. Traders, merchants, and commercial farmers were in a particularly good position to benefit from the rising prices for commodities, which encouraged them to invest in commercial activities.

4. MERCANTILISM

Governments attempted to exercise some control over economic developments. From the beginning of the Age of Discovery in the late fifteenth century until the end of the eighteenth century, all the governments of western Europe except the Dutch Netherlands pursued a policy that has come to be called *mercantilism*. Mercantilism was, in essence, economic nationalism. While the monarchs of the new national states were consolidating their political power, they were also attempting to unify and centralize their national economies. Efforts were made to standardize national currencies and weights and measurements. Internal commerce was encouraged by improving communications and reducing or removing internal tariff barriers. These efforts, however, were only partially successful. More attention was paid to the aggrandizement of each nation's economy at the expense of its neighbors. The basic assumption of mercantilist theory was that gold and silver are the true measure of national prosperity and power. Gold and silver, the mercantilists believed, in addition to being convenient mediums of exchange, could purchase anything—consumer goods, armies, navies, and administrative personnel. Spain's good luck in Mexico and Peru and its sixteenth-century brilliance and influence undoubtedly strengthened this view.

Spain alone was fortunate enough to come upon the gold and silver directly. All the other states had to devise more roundabout means of acquiring the precious metals. The favorite device was to seek a favorable balance of trade. The importation of expensive manufactured goods was discouraged by high tariffs, whereas the exportation of manufactures was encouraged, if need be, by subsidies. The reverse was true of inexpensive raw materials. The national aim was to buy low and sell high. Colonies were sought as sources of raw materials and markets for manufactured goods. But the colonies were not to be permitted to compete with the manufacturers and shippers of the mother country. Navies were advocated for the protection of the colonies. Sometimes the mercantilists closely regulated a nation's manufactures with a view to maintaining a reputation abroad for high quality. This phase of mercantilism reached its highest development in France in the seventeenth century under Louis XIV's economic minister, Colbert. It was not until the latter part of the eighteenth century that the British economist Adam Smith and the French Physiocrats began to undermine faith in the validity of mercantilist principles and to prepare the way for an era of *laissez faire*, or free trade.

5. POLITICAL AND SOCIAL CONSEQUENCES

One immediate political consequence of the rise of commercial capitalism in western Europe was the strengthening of royal absolutism. The monarchs made use of the merchants and bankers in order to increase their own power at the expense of the rival nobility. More money was now available for the royal treasury and the royal army. The middle classes, of course, shared the benefits of their alliance with the royal monarchs. Many members of the bourgeoisie were appointed to key positions in the royal administrations. With their increased wealth came increased social and political influence. The strongholds of their influence were the towns and cities whose growth paralleled the expansion of commerce. Western European society was becoming more urban—yet another change from the medieval pattern.

As the power of the national monarchs and the middle class grew, the position of the old nobility weakened. Their wealth and power were based on land, and now money was of growing importance. The inflation of prices further hurt the old nobility in relation to the moneyed bourgeoisie. Not overnight, but slowly and with occasional setbacks over the decades and centuries, the old nobility of western Europe was being displaced in political and social influence.

Yet in some ways the nobility was not being replaced but was rather being infused with new, though suspect, blood. The successful, wealthy middle class generally dreamed of joining the privileged nobility rather than replacing it as a social class. They did just that by purchasing aristocratic titles, acquiring large estates, and marrying into the nobility. Moreover, various opportunities were grasped by bolder but less established members of the nobility. Many nobles of minor importance in Spain were able to become wealthy and powerful in Spanish lands overseas. In England and the Netherlands many members of the aristocracy openly engaged in business operations, thereby adjusting successfully to changing economic conditions.

The ascendance of the middle class and changes within the nobility did not bring an immediate improvement in the condition of the lower classes. Indeed, the *nouveaux riches* often proved to be harsher taskmasters than the older aristocracy, who had stronger ties to medieval traditions of social responsibility. The urban wage earners were especially hard-hit by the inflation. Sixteenth-century cities, while increasing in size and number, witnessed an even greater growth of poverty, begging, vagrancy, and crime. In France and England some peasants who had converted their feudal dues to money payments profited, but most of the peasants in western Europe and all of those in central and eastern Europe suffered from the inflation. Landlords and those wealthier peasants who adapted well to the commercialization of agriculture profited, but they usually left in their wake large numbers of peasants worse off than before. Distressed landlords were likely to pass their hardships along to the peasantry. The number of landless poor grew. Peasant revolts became common throughout Europe in the sixteenth century. However, the rise of the middle class and the weakening of feudal class lines produced a more fluid social structure and made possible future political change. Money is more easily acquired by the commoner than is blue blood or title.

Finally, commercial capitalism probably diminished women's economic status. Most women still worked in traditional occupations—remaining in the countryside, assisting in their husbands' trades, or engaging in typical women's jobs such as domestic service, midwifery, and nursing. In the newer commercial, industrial, or professional occupations stimulated by commercial capitalism, women usually were either excluded or relegated to the lower-status and lower-paid jobs such as carding and spinning wool. As work became increasingly defined as labor for paid wages, the domestic tasks performed by women lost their status as work. Ultimately some women would gain options for greater independence from spreading commercial capitalism, but they had much to overcome.

6. EUROPEAN DOMINATION OF THE GLOBE

Thus we see Europe's agricultural, collectivist, "fair price" economy was being transformed into a much more dynamic, urban, competitive, profit-motivated economy. The rise of commerce and capitalism not only changed the nature of European society but also provided much of the explosive force that enabled tiny Europe to dominate most of the rest of the world.

During Europe's Age of Discovery much of the Western Hemisphere, southern Asia, and the coastal areas of Africa were quickly brought under European domination. This amazing expansion continued until by the end of the nineteenth century practically the entire world was dominated by Europe and European civilization. Spanish, Portuguese, English, French, and Dutch colonists, followed later by the nationals of all the other European countries, flocked to the New World, taking their Western Christian culture with them. The brilliant Aztec and Incan civilizations of Mexico and Peru were destroyed. The tribes of American Indians were exterminated, absorbed, or confined to reservations. The Moslem, Hindu, Buddhist, and Confucian civilizations of Asia and Africa were not so quickly or extensively destroyed, but they were clearly affected. The details of European expansion (and eventual contraction) constitute a considerable portion of the history of Western civilization since the sixteenth century.

SUGGESTED READING

The Age of Discovery

C. M. Cipolla, *Guns, Sails, and Empires: Technological Innovation and the Early Phases of European Expansion, 1400–1700* (1965). Stresses connections between technology and successful expansion.

D. P. Mannix and M. Cowley, *Black Cargoes: A History of the Atlantic Slave Trade* (1968). An excellent detailed account.

J. H. Parry, *The Age of Reconnaissance* (1963). A good survey of the causes and consequences of the early voyages.

Overseas Empires

Charles R. Boxer, *The Portuguese Seaborne Empire* (1970). An excellent study of the Portuguese Empire.

Charles Gibson, *Spain in America* (1966). A good study of the Spanish Empire in the New World.

B. Keen and M. Wasserman, *A Short History of Latin America* (1984). A useful recent text.

Commercial Capitalism and Social Change

F. Braudel, *Civilization and Capitalism, 15th–18th Century,* trans. S. Reynolds, Vol. 2: *The Wheels of Commerce* (1982). Highly acclaimed and sophisticated.

R. Bridenthal, C. Koonz, and S. Stuard, eds., *Becoming Visible: Women in European History, Second Edition* (1987). Contains good material on this period.

C. M. Cipolla, *Before the Industrial Revolution: European Society and Economy* (1980). Particularly good on demographic and economic change.

Ralph Davis, *The Rise of the Atlantic Economies* (1973). Contains a good survey of sixteenth-century economic history.

Richard Ehrenberg, *Capital and Finance in the Age of the Renaissance* (1963). A good study of sixteenth-century capitalism and the Fugger bank.

CHAPTER 30

The Reformation

FIGURE 30.1 Cranach the Younger, "Protestant Reformers," 1543 This painting shows some of the crucial figures of the Protestant Reformation. In the center stands Elector John Frederick of Saxony, whose family protected Luther and other Protestant reformers. Luther is to the far left, his associate Philip Melanchthon is to the far right, and between Melanchthon and Frederick is Huldreich Zwingli, a leading reformer in Zurich. (Toledo Museum of Art, Toledo, Ohio; gift of Edward Drummond Libbey)

Sixteenth-century Europeans were intensely interested in religion. Although Renaissance culture, political developments, and commercial expansion were of great concern, the church was still at the very center of their lives. The Reformation probably touched more people than any other development of the sixteenth century.

The Protestant Reformation, initiated in the second decade of the sixteenth century by Martin Luther, swept through much of northern Europe. Reform within the Roman Catholic church, often called the Catholic Reformation, followed and included both internal reforms initiated independently of the Protestant Reformation and reforms undertaken to counter Protestantism. In the end, the Reformation split western Europe into hostile religious camps, destroying the medieval unity of the Western Christian Church.

1. BACKGROUND

In the late Middle Ages, discontent with the Church grew. Large numbers of people felt spiritually dissatisfied with what the Church offered. Greatly concerned with their own salvation and with leading a more pious life, people looked outside the formal institutions of the Church for guidance and examples. The growth of lay religious organizations such as the Brethren of the Common Life, the popularity of traveling preachers, the continuing search for mystical experiences, and the graphic pious art all testified to widespread and deep spiritual needs that were not being met through the Church. The Church seemed to have departed too far from the spirit and practices of the apostles and early fathers.

People voiced other complaints about the Church, particularly about many abuses that arose during the fourteenth and fifteenth centuries when the Church was torn by the Babylonian Captivity, the Great Schism, and the struggles between popes and councils (see pp. 339–342). The lack of education and the worldliness of the clergy, the sale of Church offices and services (simony), the favoring of relatives for lucrative Church offices (nepotism), and the holding by one man of more offices than he could adequately serve (plu-

ralism)—all were subjects of loud and growing complaint. Many of the higher clergy, even the popes, became preoccupied with their own secular concerns and Renaissance culture. Those who recognized a need to remedy these problems were unable to do enough until it was too late. Eventually the Church hierarchy took steps to remedy abuses, but not until much of Western Christendom had already left the Roman Catholic fold.

In addition to these spiritual dissatisfactions and complaints about abuses within the Church, other developments made certain areas of Europe fertile for the growth of reform movements. In Germany the Holy Roman Empire lacked the political unity that had helped national monarchs in Spain, England, and France gain control over their national clergy and access to the accumulated wealth of the Church. Local governments grew jealous of the immunities from civil laws and taxation enjoyed by the clergy. People resented the drain of wealth to the clergy and the institutions of the Church outside their territories, especially to Italy. These localities supported lay preachers, who gave numerous popular sermons throughout the year. In some of these same areas, particularly in university towns, Christian humanism took hold. Thanks to the printing press, criticisms of the Church by Erasmus, Ulrich von Hutten, and other humanists became widespread.

For the most part, this growing dissatisfaction with the Church was not revolutionary and did not yet challenge the fundamental doctrines of the Church. There was no widespread sense that the Church was about to be torn apart or that the only alternative was to make a complete break from the Church. On the other hand, the depth of the problems facing the Church is indicated by the radical reform movements occurring prior to the sixteenth century. As early as the fourteenth century reformers such as John Wycliffe in England and John Huss in Bohemia had voiced their protests against the Church. These protests turned into threatening movements of heretical dissent and social revolt, and authorities put them down only with great difficulty. When movements of dissent and revolt against the Church arose in the sixteenth century, they proved to be too powerful and well supported to be suppressed.

FIGURE 30.2   Cranach the Elder, "Martin Luther," 1521   Martin Luther often referred to himself as "a peasant, the son of a peasant." His father, though of peasant stock, was an ambitious miner who moved into the ranks of the bourgeoisie. A complex character, Luther had the brilliant mind and personal force of one of the great leaders and movers of history. (Culver Pictures)

2. LUTHERANISM

The Protestant Reformation was composed of four major distinct but related movements—Lutheranism, Calvinism, Anglicanism, and Anabaptism. From these four main stems have sprung the hundreds of Protestant denominations that exist today. The Lutheran revolt was first in point of time.

Martin Luther (1483–1546) was the son of an ambitious miner of central Germany (see Figure 30.2). At a boarding school run by the pietistic Brethren of the Common Life he, like his contemporary Erasmus, was introduced to a type of Christianity that emphasized simple piety rather than dogma and ritual. Later at Erfurt University he received a traditional liberal arts education. He was an excellent student. However, upon the completion of his undergraduate course and just as he was ready to begin study of the law, he suddenly renounced the world and entered an Augustinian monastery. This decision was no passing whim. As a child, Luther had been much concerned over the fate of his soul, and throughout his university days, his religious yearning had increased.

But the young friar found no satisfaction in the monastic life of the sixteenth-century Church. He scourged himself, donned beggar's garb, and went out among his former fellow students with sunken cheeks and gleaming, feverish eyes. It was not until, on the advice of a perceptive supervisor of his monastic order, he began to read the writings of St. Augustine and St. Paul that Brother Martin found the answer to his lifelong quest. On reading in Paul's Letter to the Romans (1:17) "the just shall live by faith," he concluded that here was the true means of salvation—not good works, sacraments, and rituals, but simple faith in Christ. Over a period of years he developed a theology based on the fundamental concept that righteousness is a gift of grace from God attained by faith in Christ's righteousness—justification by faith alone.

In the meantime Luther had become a member of the faculty of the newly founded University of Wittenberg in Saxony. For several years he taught philosophy and theology, quite unaware that his belief in salvation by faith alone was in fundamental conflict with the dogma of his church. Students flocked from afar to listen to him.

One day a friar named John Tetzel came into the vicinity of Wittenberg selling indulgences. According to the doctrine of indulgences, which had grown up in the late Middle Ages, Christ and the saints, by their good works while on earth, had accumulated in heaven a treasury of excess merit that the pope could apply to the credit of penitent sinners, thereby shortening for them or their loved ones their stay in purgatory. By the opening of the sixteenth century the dispensing of this vague, extrasacramental means of grace had become hardly more than a money-making venture. Huge sums, taken from all over Europe, were brought to Rome for the construction of St. Peter's or for other costly papal projects.

On October 31, 1517, Martin Luther posted on the church door in Wittenberg his Ninety-Five Theses, or propositions, concerning the doctrine of indulgences, which he proposed to be debated publicly. It did not occur to him that this event would mark the beginning of an upheaval to subside only after nearly half of Western Christendom had broken away from the Roman Catholic church. He was astonished and at first dismayed to find himself suddenly the national hero of all the various disgruntled elements throughout Germany. When, however, two years later in a public debate at Leipzig Luther finally realized that his position was hopelessly at odds with that of the Church, he lost no time in making the break clean. He published a series of pamphlets in which he violently denounced the pope and his organization and called on the German princes to seize the property of the Church and make themselves the heads of the Christian Church in Germany.

A papal bull of excommunication (which Luther publicly burned) soon followed. A few months later Emperor Charles V called the troublesome monk to appear before the Diet of the Holy Roman Empire at Worms (1521). There Luther boldly refused to recant and was outlawed by the highest civil authority in Germany. Although Luther remained under this death sentence with a price on his head for the rest of his life, he was protected by his prince, the elector of Saxony, and by German public opinion.

By this time all Germany was in religious and social turmoil. Nearly everyone with a grievance of any kind was looking to Luther for leadership. Religious zealots, such as the Anabaptists, began preaching individualistic and more radical doctrines in his name, and he found it necessary to repudiate them. Taking a somewhat more conservative stand, he decided that only those features of the Roman Catholic church that were opposed to the Scriptures ought to be rejected. In the early stages of the conflict Erasmus and many other humanists thought they saw in Luther a kindred spirit, but this alliance was short-lived. Erasmus soon found Luther to be as dogmatic and

uncompromising in matters of doctrine as the Roman Catholic theologians, if not more so.

Luther also found it necessary to break with a group of rebellious peasants in south Germany. The condition of the peasants was bad and growing worse. The landed aristocracy, themselves losing ground to the rising middle classes, were depriving their peasants of long-established manorial rights such as free use of meadows and woodlands. In 1524 widespread disturbances broke out in southwestern Germany. The next year the peasants published a list of demands, including an end to serfdom, elimination of certain taxes, confiscation of Church property, and reform of the clergy. When these were refused, the peasants rebelled in the name of Luther, whom they believed to be against all oppressive authority. Luther was sympathetic with some of their demands, particularly the confiscation of Church property and reform of the clergy, but otherwise he proved to be socially and politically too conservative. He rejected their attack on authority as too broad and pleaded with them to refrain from violence. When the rebellious peasants did not follow Luther's advice and continued their violent uprisings in Luther's name, he repudiated them and called on the civil authorities to suppress the revolt by force. The armed authorities did so with a vengeance.

Luther's new religion, as he eventually formulated it, made the Scriptures the sole authoritative source of Christian dogma. That all might have access to the Bible, he translated it into German.[1] He conceived of the Church as the whole body of believers in Christ, not the Roman Catholic church or any other specific organization. He abolished the hierarchy of pope, cardinals, and bishops, and he reduced the importance of the clergy in general, proclaiming the priesthood of all believers. The ritual of worship was made much simpler. Of the seven sacraments of the Roman Catholic church, Luther kept only the two he found mentioned as sacraments in the Bible: baptism and the Eucharist. He rejected the Roman

---

[1]Luther's translation was in such excellent German that it had great influence on the standardization of the modern literary German language.

Catholic doctrine known as transubstantiation.[2] Luther interpreted the scriptural passages that refer to the Holy Eucharist, or Lord's Supper, to mean that during the administration of the sacrament Christ's body somehow enters into the bread and the wine, but the bread and wine remain—consubstantiation. He denied the Roman Catholic belief that a sacrifice is involved. He abolished monasteries and the celibacy of the clergy. Luther himself married a former nun. In general, he sharply distinguished religious matters from political and social matters, leaving the believer spiritually free and the secular rulers in charge of ·political and social matters.

The Emperor Charles V was greatly distressed by this religious revolution, which further divided his scattered and chaotic empire. Many German princes saw in Lutheranism a chance to increase their own political and financial independence from Charles V and the Italian papacy. Although determined to suppress the Protestants, Charles V was too busy with his wars against the French and the Turks to make much headway. Years of indecisive fighting between the Roman Catholics under Charles V and the Protestants ended in 1555 with the compromise Peace of Augsburg. Each of the more than three hundred German princes was left free to choose between Lutheranism and Roman Catholicism; his subjects were to abide by his choice. Luther himself died in 1546, just before the fighting began. By this time, Lutheranism had triumphed in the northern half of Germany and soon had spread, under the leadership of Scandinavian monarchs, to Denmark, Norway, Sweden, and most of the Baltic provinces (now Latvia, Estonia, and Finland), which were then under Swedish control. In addition, Lutheranism heavily influenced all later Protestant movements, the most important of which was Calvinism.

3. CALVINISM

John Calvin shares with Luther the position of first

importance in the founding of Protestant Christianity. Born in France in 1509, John Calvin was twenty-six years younger than Luther. He was the son of a lawyer who was secretary to the bishop of Noyon in Picardy. Young Calvin had a radiant personality that made for warm friendships. Long association with aristocratic friends probably accounts for his elegant manners. His father sent him first to the University of Paris for a thorough grounding in the humanities and theology and then to the best law schools in France. Upon finishing his legal training, he entered a humanistic literary career. Suddenly, at the age of twenty-four, after reading Luther's writings and having an intensely personal religious experience, Calvin converted to Protestant Christianity.

The zealous young reformer soon aroused the ire of Roman Catholic authorities in France and of the French government and was forced to flee for his life. Calvin then spent the next two years in hiding writing the first edition of *The Institutes of the Christian Religion*. Published in Basel, Switzerland, when Calvin was only twenty-six, this theological treatise was to become the most influential writing in the history of Protestantism. Its precise and forceful logic reveals the fine legal training and powerful intellect of the author. Its lucid and facile style influenced the formulation of modern literary French. It immediately made Calvin an important name in literary and theological circles.

Probably Calvin's most significant contribution to Christian theology is his sublime concept of the majesty of God. To the author of the *Institutes*, the Divine Creator is so majestic and awe inspiring, and human beings so insignificant by comparison, that salvation by election, or *predestination*, as it is more often called, seems to follow logically. According to Calvin, God in the beginning planned the whole universe to the end of time. For unfathomable reasons of his own, God selected those human beings who would be saved and those who would be damned. He planted in the minds of the elect a saving faith in Christ and an insatiable desire to live the Christian life and to bring about the Kingdom of God on earth. In no other way could one acquire this faith and this desire. Calvin based this doctrine on the Scriptures (particularly the writings of St. Paul), which he considered to be the sole authoritative source for Christian the-

---

[2]*The New Catholic Dictionary* defines transubstantiation as "the marvellous and singular changing of the entire substance of the bread into the entire substance of the Body of Christ and of the entire substance of the wine into His Blood."

ology. St. Augustine, the most influential of the early Church Fathers, and Luther also believed in salvation by election, but neither they nor anyone else had ever spelled out the doctrine so precisely.

Shortly after the publication of the *Institutes*, Calvin went to Geneva. That city, like most of the rest of Switzerland, was in the throes of religious and political revolt brought on partly by the influence of Luther and the native Swiss reformer, Ulrich Zwingli (1484–1531). At first accepted by Protestant leaders, then rejected, Calvin finally returned in 1540 to try to make Geneva a model city of God on earth. Calvin, by sheer force of personality and intellect, soon rose to a position of great power in the city. He brought the town council, which was remarkably democratic and representative for the sixteenth century, under the dominance of a consistory composed of Protestant pastors and laity. Under Calvin's leadership the town council and the consistory set up a strict system of blue laws. Churchgoing was compulsory. Dancing, cardplaying, theatergoing, drinking, gambling, and swearing—all were forbidden. Enforcement was vigorous and penalties severe, even for the sixteenth century. The most famous penalty was the burning of Michael Servetus, an eccentric amateur scientist and theologian whom the Roman Catholic church had already condemned to death for heresy.[3] Servetus escaped his Catholic persecutors and came to Geneva. When Servetus arrived, he was seized, tried, convicted, and burned at the stake.

Calvinist ritual was even simpler than that of the Lutherans. The worship service consisted of preaching, praying, and psalm singing. Like Luther, Calvin retained only two of the seven sacraments—baptism and the Holy Eucharist, or Lord's Supper. But to Calvin, Christ was present only in spirit in the bread and wine and only for the elect. Calvin patterned his system of church government after that of the very earliest church as described in the Bible (Acts of the Apostles). The local churches were governed by laymen called *elders* who were elected by the congrega-

tions. A measure of unity in faith and practices was maintained by means of a hierarchy of representative assemblies.

During the second half of the sixteenth century it was Calvinism rather than Lutheranism that became the most dynamic force in Protestantism. Protestant Christians came from many countries to sit at the feet of Calvin and to study at the University of Geneva, which he founded. John Knox, who came from Scotland to study under Calvin, called the Genevan theocracy "the most perfect school of life that was ever on earth since the days of the apostles." Calvinists combined vigorous evangelical appeals with a systematic theology and a well-organized church. The Calvinist ethic of "the calling" to one's station on earth, no matter what it was, dignified striving and hard work.

Calvinism became dominant in most of Switzerland (Swiss Reformed), the Dutch Netherlands (Dutch Reformed), Scotland (Presbyterian), and the German Palatinate. It also had a strong minority following in England (the Puritans) and a smaller but vigorous following in France (the Huguenots), Bohemia, Hungary, and Poland. The Calvinists played an important part in the founding of the United States, particularly the Puritans in New England, the Dutch Reformed in New York, and the Scotch-Irish Presbyterians along the frontiers of all the original states. Such well-known denominations in present-day America as the Congregationalists, the Presbyterians, and the Baptists are Calvinist in origin.

4. ANGLICANISM

Foundations for the Reformation in England had been developing for many years before it was actually initiated by the actions of King Henry VIII (1509–1547). Lollardy, a movement of religious and social dissent stretching back over a hundred years, persisted as an underground movement into the sixteenth century. Humanism and anticlerical sentiments were gaining in strength. In 1525, William Tyndale (1494–1536), influenced by Luther, started printing an English translation of the Bible. However, the occasion of the beginning of the Reformation in England was the desire of

---

[3]The most serious of Servetus' heretical views were his denial of the Trinity, which cast doubt on the divinity of Christ, and his rejection of childhood baptism.

Henry VIII for a new wife and a male heir. Catherine of Aragon, to whom he had been married for eighteen years, had given him only a daughter, Mary. When it became apparent that Catherine would have no more children, Henry decided to ask the pope to annul the marriage. The pope, however, was in no position to grant the annulment. Catherine was the aunt of the Emperor Charles V, whose troops were at that very moment in control of the city of Rome. When Henry finally realized the pope was not going to accommodate him, he took matters into his own hands. At his bidding a subservient Parliament passed the Act of Supremacy (1534), making the king of England, not the pope, head of the Church in England. Later the monasteries, strongholds of papal influence, were dissolved and their holdings confiscated by the crown. Meanwhile, Thomas Cranmer, whom Henry made archbishop of Canterbury, had arranged the annulment, and Henry had married Anne Boleyn. (He was to marry six times in all.) Henry was, of course, excommunicated by the pope.

But Henry VIII was no Protestant. In the days before the annulment controversy the pope had given him the title "Defender of the Faith" for his anti-Lutheran writings. Now he had Parliament pass the Six Articles reaffirming the Catholic position on all controversial doctrinal points except that of papal supremacy. Protestants, on the one hand, and Roman Catholics who refused to acknowledge the headship of Henry VIII in place of the pope were persecuted with equal severity.

It was during the reign of Henry VIII's young son, Edward VI (1547–1553), that the Anglican church first became Protestant. Archbishop Cranmer drew up a *Book of Common Prayer* and Forty-two Articles of Faith that were definitely Calvinist in flavor. Edward VI was succeeded by his elder sister, Mary (1553–1558), who was the daughter of Catherine of Aragon and a devout Roman Catholic. Mary's ambition was to restore her kingdom to the Roman Catholic fold. Her first step was to marry her cousin, Philip II of Spain, the most powerful champion of resurgent Roman Catholicism in all Europe. Next she asked and received papal forgiveness for her wayward people. Finally, "Bloody Mary" burned at the stake some three hundred Protestants, including Archbishop Cranmer. But Mary's marriage to a man soon to be king of Spain, England's most dangerous rival, and her persecutions were extremely unpopular in England; in the long run her policies hurt rather than helped the Roman Catholic cause there.

Elizabeth I (1558–1603), the Protestant daughter of Anne Boleyn, followed Mary on the English throne. This high-spirited, cynical, and politically minded queen found theology tiresome. Her chief interest was to find a satisfactory compromise that would unify her people. During the course of her long reign the Anglican church became definitely, but conservatively, Protestant. Cranmer's *Book of Common Prayer* was readopted with slight alterations. The Forty-two Articles were changed to the Thirty-nine. Some of the more controversial doctrinal points that seemed to prevent the various Protestant sects from uniting were reworded. Although celibacy of the clergy was abandoned, the episcopal system (government of the church by bishops) was retained. A rather elaborate ritual was adopted. Two of the sacraments, baptism and the Eucharist, were retained.

Although the great majority of the English people appeared to have accepted Elizabeth's compromise settlement, two groups remained dissatisfied. An extreme Calvinist element sought to "purify" the Anglican church of all remaining traces of Roman Catholicism. These Puritans were to increase in strength until under Oliver Cromwell's leadership in the next century they gained temporary control of the country. The Roman Catholic minority, on the other hand, lost steadily in numbers. The support that some Roman Catholics gave to Philip II's attempt to conquer England and to the effort of Mary, Queen of Scots (a Roman Catholic), to overthrow Elizabeth (see Chapter 31) tainted all of them with the suspicion of treason and played into Elizabeth's hands. By the end of her reign, England was one of the Protestant countries of Europe.

5. THE ANABAPTISTS

Some reformers believed that Luther, Calvin, and the Anglican leaders had not gone far enough. They would break more sharply with all the existing institutions of the early sixteenth century—

political, economic, and social as well as religious. Hence the term *radical* is often applied to them. Since these "radicals" were highly individualistic in their approach to religion, it is difficult to generalize about the many sects with their widely differing views and points of emphasis.

Generally, these sects tended to emphasize the evilness of the world, the mystical communion with God, the Second Coming of Christ, and the righteousness of the poor in their struggle against the rich. In some cases, religious reform became a means of social reform—a revolt of the poor against the rich.

These sects commonly rejected the doctrine of infant baptism. The true Christian, they believed, was one who was "born again" and baptized as an adult according to Scripture. Those who had been baptized as infants must be rebaptized. Anabaptism means *re*baptism. The Anabaptists believed that the true church of Christ on earth is a gathered church composed only of born-again Christians. The Anabaptists attempted to live lives of uncompromising holiness as dictated by the Bible or by the Holy Spirit speaking directly to each individual. These sects refused to recognize or participate in civil government, take oaths of allegiance, recognize titles, or serve in armed forces. Some practiced a shared economy. Most of them were poor. They were feared and persecuted by Roman Catholics, Lutherans, Calvinists, Anglicans, and secular leaders alike.

A few of the early Anabaptist leaders were violent activists, such as Thomas Müntzer, who inflamed the peasant rebels of southwest Germany, and John of Leyden, who set up a violent dictatorship in Münster in northwest Germany. This bizarre "heavenly Jerusalem" held out for more than a year against besieging Lutheran and Roman Catholic armies. The leaders were then tortured to death and their bodies hung in iron baskets from a church tower as a warning to radical dissenters. But the great majority of the Anabaptist leaders were pious and gentle—in fact, pacifists. Conrad Grebel, the first prominent Anabaptist leader, was a humanist from an upper-class family of Zurich, Switzerland. Probably the most successful and influential of all the Anabaptist leaders was the convert Menno Simons, a gentle former Roman Catholic priest from the Dutch

Netherlands. His followers, the Mennonites, spread throughout much of western Europe and later the United States. Also in the Anabaptist tradition was the Society of Friends, commonly known as Quakers. Founded by George Fox in England in the mid–seventeenth century, this pietistic and pacifistic sect has spread to many parts of the world.

6. CATHOLIC REFORM

The rise of Protestantism touched off an aggressive Catholic reform movement during the 1530s and 1540s, but even before this movement some efforts to revitalize Roman Catholicism had already taken place. In Spain, around the turn of the sixteenth century, Cardinal Ximenes had forestalled a possible protest movement by enforcing strict discipline on the clergy and waging bitter warfare against heresy. During the first few decades of the sixteenth century several religious orders such as the Theatines, the Capuchins, the Barnabites, and the Ursulines were founded and dedicated themselves to clerical reform and education within the Catholic church. Even before the revolt of Luther and Calvin, Catholic leaders from several countries pushed for the calling of a general council to authoritatively enact badly needed reforms. However, the secular interests of the Renaissance popes and the popes' fears that an assertive reform council might again challenge the absolute authority of the papacy prevented a coordinated European-wide reform. The last council to meet before the Reformation, the Fifth Lateran Council (1513–1517), bowed to the pope's control and enacted no major reforms.

After the 1520s and 1530s, with area after area becoming Protestant, countermeasures of a rather drastic nature became imperative. There were two schools of thought concerning the proper course of action. One, led by the liberal Cardinal Contarini of Venice, advocated compromise and conciliation. Contarini eventually went so far as to meet with Melanchthon, a close friend of Luther and an important figure in the Lutheran revolt, in earnest quest of an acceptable compromise. They were unsuccessful; the two religions appeared to be incompatible. The other school of thought was led by the conservative Cardinal Caraffa of Naples. Caraffa believed that many corrupt practices in the Church needed to be reformed but that no compromise whatever should be made in the dogma. He believed that the Protestants were heretics and could reunite with the Roman Catholic church only by recanting and submitting to the pope. This is the school of thought that triumphed, and Caraffa became Pope Paul IV. The upshot of this line of thinking was the calling of a Church council at Trent, an imperial city in northern Italy.

The Council of Trent

The Council of Trent, which was in session off and on for eighteen years from 1545 to 1563, was probably the most important council in the history of the Roman Catholic church. The popes skillfully controlled its membership and voting procedure. The ultimate decisions of the council were in two categories: dogmatic and reformatory. In matters of faith or dogma, all the traditional doctrines of the Church were reaffirmed and redefined, especially controversial ones such as the sacraments, transubstantiation, auricular confession, celibacy of the clergy, monasticism, purgatory, invocation of the saints, veneration of relics, and indulgences. The dogmatic canons and decrees of the council concluded: "Anathema to [accursed be] all heretics! Anathema! Anathema! Anathema!" The council also took stern measures to stop corrupt practices. Simony, nepotism, pluralism, and immorality and ignorance among the clergy were condemned. Schools for the education of the clergy were advocated. Bishops were admonished to exercise closer supervision and discipline over the lower clergy. To implement its canons and decrees, the council endorsed the Inquisition, which had recently been set up in Rome to combat heresy, and inaugurated the Index of Forbidden Books to prevent the reading of heretical literature except by authorized persons. Both instruments were placed under papal control and supervision.

Thus the Roman Catholic church at last spoke out, selected its weapons, and girded itself for more effective battle against the Protestants. At its service was the militant new Society of Jesus.

FIGURE 30.3 Ignatius Loyola (1491–1556) Ignatius Loyola, by founding the Society of Jesus (the Jesuits), played a key role in the Catholic Reformation. Although not as scholarly as Luther or Calvin, he was a superb organizer and leader. (Culver Pictures)

The Society of Jesus

The founder of the Society of Jesus, Ignatius Loyola (1491–1556), was a member of the Spanish lesser nobility, and until early middle life he was an obscure soldier (see Figure 30.3). In a battle with the French his leg was crushed by a cannonball. During the months of agony and convalescence Loyola read lives of the Christian saints and underwent a deep spiritual conversion. He determined to devote his tremendous energies and latent talents to the service of the Roman Catholic church—to become a soldier of Christ, the Virgin Mary, and the pope. He set off for the University of Paris to begin his education. Loyola was, how-

WHERE HISTORIANS DISAGREE

The Meaning of the Reformation

Most historians agree that the Reformation was of major significance, but when they address the more difficult questions of its exact causes and nature, agreement ends.

Before the twentieth century, historians often confused their own religious preferences with historical analysis, becoming more interested in assigning blame or praise. Protestant scholars focused on the corruption of the Roman Catholic church, the heroic piety of Protestant figures, and the positive force of the Protestant Reformation in the modern world. Catholic scholars contended just the opposite, arguing that there was no crying need for doctrinal reform, that Protestant leaders were self-centered and ignorant theologians, and that the Protestant Reformation was to blame for the flood of secularization in the West.

Most twentieth-century historians look at the Reformation in more complex terms. Many favor sophisticated religious and cultural interpretations of the Reformation. These historians argue that the Reformation grew out of deep and widespread spiritual longing and dissatisfaction with the practices of the Catholic church. They emphasize that whatever other qualities Protestant leaders may have had, they were deeply religious people whose reforming doctrines and practices appealed to the spiritual and cultural needs of many. These historians also stress the spiritual concerns revealed in Catholic reform. To these historians, the sixteenth century was an age of religious reform.

Other historians think of the Protestant Reformation in primarily political terms. They stress that the time was ripe for the Reformation not only because of religious tensions but also because secular authorities favored it. They emphasize that vast numbers of people became Protestant or remained Catholic (or reconverted) because their political leaders demanded it. They view the various religious movements of the sixteenth century as associated with nationalism. They believe it to be significant that the Protestant Reformation began in Germany, where there was no strong central government and where Luther strongly and openly appealed to German nationalism against Rome. By contrast, the strong rulers of France and Spain were able to extract such concessions from the pope as to create what amounted to a Gallican church and Spanish Catholic church, while successfully withstanding the Protestant challenge. The various Calvinistic churches were generally set up along national lines, such as the Swiss, Dutch, German, and Scottish Reformed churches. And of course the Anglican church was a national church.

Still other historians interpret the Reformation from an economic perspective. They point out the hunger for the rich lands held by the Roman church, the resentment over the tax exemption of these lands and over the draining away of money to Rome, and the opposition of the commercial class to the Church's ban on usury. Related to these points is the "Weber thesis." Max Weber and other scholars have argued that the hard work and asceticism which Calvinism stressed fit well with the emerging spirit of capitalism, which emphasized hard work, savings, and reinvestment. Thus Calvinism appealed particularly to commercial centers in Holland, England, Switzerland, and New England. From this perspective, then, Protestantism helped solve various economic problems of the era.

The long history and depth of these controversies over the meaning of the Reformation reveal how difficult evaluation of major religious change can be for the historian.

ever, not a scholar nor theologian but a man of action. He soon began to attract a band of followers, with whom he organized the Society of Jesus.

The Jesuit order, as the Society of Jesus was commonly known, was founded along military lines. Absolute and unquestioning obedience was the first requirement. Loyola admonished his followers, ". . . if she [the Church] shall have defined anything to be black which to our eyes appears to be white, we ought in like manner to pronounce it to be black." Applicants for membership were carefully selected and trained. For the spiritual guidance and inspiration of the members of the Society, Loyola wrote the *Spiritual Exercises*. The *Exercises* guide the member through a solid month of concentrated meditation, a week each on the horrors of sin, the life of Christ to Palm Sunday, his suffering and crucifixion, and his resurrection and ascension. This remarkable work has proved to be a powerful tool for training and rededication. Jesuits served as priests, teachers, medics, diplomats, or in almost any other capacity suitable to their talents and training—but always with the interests of the Catholic church in mind. After years of service a few of the most outstanding were admitted to the highest circle of officers who, under a general elected for life and residing in Rome, governed the order.

Loyola's high standards, far from deterring applicants, served as a challenge and an attraction. The Society of Jesus grew rapidly. As priests, the Jesuits were nearly always the best trained, the most popular, and the most influential. As teachers, they were usually more highly educated, devoted, and attractive than their competitors. They have always been keenly aware of the power of education, especially for the very young. "Give me the child, and I care not who has the man." The Jesuits soon gained control of education in most Roman Catholic countries.

These dedicated soldiers of Christ also made the best missionaries. In North and South America the dauntless Jesuits went among the Indians and converted most of them to Roman Catholic Christianity. In the Far East, Francis Xavier, second only to Loyola himself in Jesuit history, converted tens of thousands.

Not the least important of Jesuit activities was that of gaining the confidence of kings, princes, and other political personages, and thereby influencing state policy. This militantly zealous order was a powerful stimulant to the wavering cause of Roman Catholicism. In Italy, Spain, Portugal, and Ireland, where Protestantism had only a weak foothold, the Jesuits helped stamp it out altogether. In France and Belgium they helped to turn the tide against the Protestants. In southern Germany, Poland, and the Austrian Hapsburg lands, all of which seemed to be on the verge of going Protestant, the Jesuits reversed the trend and helped make those lands strongholds of Roman Catholicism.

7. WOMEN AND THE REFORMATION

As with the Renaissance, scholars question whether the Reformation benefited women socially or in any aspect of public life. Although Luther may have encouraged greater sharing within the household—the ideal of the companionate marriage—and acceptance of sexuality within the marriage, it is difficult to argue that his reforming ideas greatly improved the condition of women. In his eyes, women were expected to be satisfied as pious wives, mothers, and household managers, remaining clearly under the authority of their husbands. Despite some advocacy of mutual cooperation within the marriage, Calvin also rejected female independence and placed the husband at the head of the household.

The Protestant abolition of monasteries included women's religious orders, thereby eliminating one of the few occupational outlets available to sixteenth-century women. Protestantism offered no comparable alternatives for the thousands of women who left the often socially prestigious Catholic convents. Only well into the seventeenth century and in certain Protestant sects such as the Quakers did women start to play a public role as preachers.

Catholic reform resulted in few if any significant changes for women. Only the growth of pious Catholic women's organizations, such as the Ursulines, who were devoted to teaching girls, gave women some opportunity to play a more active role within the Church.

If the direct effect of the Reformation on women is uncertain, it is clear that women during that era suffered from an explosion of witch-hunts and prosecutions for infanticide. Beliefs in witchcraft dated back for centuries, but it was not until the sixteenth century that large numbers of women were actually prosecuted and put to death on charges of witchcraft. Protestants and Catholics alike charged women, usually older, lower-class women living in rural villages, with the heretical crime of making a pact with the devil and causing harm to their enemies. Tens of thousands of women were tried for witchcraft and perhaps a third of them were put to death.

Concurrent with these witchcraft hunts of the Reformation era came a flood of prosecutions for infanticide. While authorities prosecuted far fewer women for infanticide than witchcraft, those prosecuted were more likely to be found guilty and executed. Usually the objects of these prosecutions were poor unmarried younger women living in cities.

How much the Reformation itself had to do with this wave of lethal prosecutions of women is unknown. Perhaps more important were the growing efforts by the state to regulate behavior, the environment of fear during this period, and the general suspicion of women out of the norm in this male-dominated society. In any case, during the sixteenth and seventeenth centuries both Catholic and Protestant authorities, whether religious or secular, found sufficient theological and civil justifications to carry out these prosecutions that cost so many women their lives.

8. SUMMARY

Protestantism grew out of a widespread desire for greater spiritual satisfaction and correction of abuses within the Western Christian Church. Political and economic factors soon came into play to broaden the appeal and strength of the Protestant Reformation. Towns, princes, and kings saw the advantages of acquiring control over religious institutions and the tremendous wealth controlled by these institutions. This wealth and control served to strengthen their own political power. Since religious affiliation was viewed as integral to political and social order, conversion of political leaders eventually meant conversion of most of their people.

Initially Lutheranism was the dominant Protestant denomination, but in the second half of the century Calvinism became the most dynamic. By the end of the third quarter of the sixteenth century, Protestantism had triumphed in the northern half of the Germanies, in Scandinavia, in most of the Baltic provinces, in most of Switzerland, in the Dutch Netherlands, Scotland, and England. In addition, it had gained a strong minority following in France, Poland, Bohemia, and Hungary.

No matter how much the various Protestant denominations disagreed among themselves, they shared beliefs that put them at odds with the Roman Catholic church. They believed in justification by faith alone. They believed that the Roman Catholic church had departed so far from the spirit and practices of the apostles and early Fathers that it could no longer be considered God's appointed custodian of the Christian religion. Scripture alone, not the decisions and traditions of the Roman Catholic church, was their sole authoritative source for Christian dogma. They emphasized the direct relationship between human beings and God. They thought of the church as a priesthood of all believers. They rejected papal supremacy, the divine sanction of the Roman church, the celibacy and indelible character of the priesthood, monasticism, and such other characteristic Roman Catholic doctrines as purgatory, transubstantiation, invocation of saints, and veneration of relics.

The Roman Catholic church was not impotent in the face of these challenges. It had already initiated some internal reform efforts of its own prior to the outbreak of Protestantism, and those reform efforts grew throughout the sixteenth century. It also initiated a broad-based counter-Reformation to strengthen its hold in areas that remained Roman Catholic and to try to regain areas lost to Protestants. Despite some successes, however, it was never able to reconquer or reconvert the territories in which Protestants had gained a clear majority. The Reformation definitively split Western Christendom into hostile religious camps, and this religious hostility would spill over into decades of bloody wars and revolts.

SUGGESTED READING

General

G. R. Elton, *Reformation Europe 1517–1559* (1966). Particularly good for its treatment of the political context.

H. J. Grimm, *The Reformation Era* (1973). Sound and readable.

De Lamar Jensen, *Reformation Europe, Age of Reform and Revolution* (1981). A very good work.

R. L. de Molen, *Leaders of the Reformation* (1984). Portraits of key figures.

L. W. Spitz, *The Protestant Reformation* (1985). A solid, recent survey.

Lutheranism

J. Atkinson, *Martin Luther and the Birth of Protestantism* (1968). Good introduction.

E. Erikson, *Young Man Luther: A Study in Psychoanalysis and History* (1962). A highly important and influential interpretation.

H. G. Haile, *Luther: An Experiment in Biography* (1980). A modern treatment.

Calvinism

J. T. McNeil, *The History and Character of Calvinism* (1967). By a leading authority.

W. E. Monter, *Calvin's Geneva* (1967). Fine study of the Reformation in Geneva.

F. Wendel, *Calvin: The Origins and Development of His Thought* (1963). A good introduction to Calvin and Calvinism.

Anglicanism

A. G. Dickens, *The English Reformation* (1974). Best survey.

The Anabaptists

G. H. Williams, *The Radical Reformers* (1962). Excellent survey.

J. J. Scarisbrick, *The Reformation and the English People* (1985). A short survey.

Catholic Reform

A. G. Dickens, *The Counter Reformation* (1969). A brief well-written introduction.

René Fülop-Miller, *Jesuits: A History of the Society of Jesus* (1963). A thorough study with a psychological perspective.

H. Jedin, *A History of the Council of Trent*, 3 vols. (1957–1961). The standard, definitive work on the subject.

Women and the Reformation

M. J. Boxer and J. H. Quataert, eds., *Connecting Spheres: Women in the Western World, 1500 to the Present* (1987). Includes useful material on the period.

R. Bridenthal, C. Koonz, and S. Stuard, eds., *Becoming Visible: Women in European History, Second Edition* (1987). Includes a good chapter on this period.

CHAPTER 31
Politics and the Wars of Religion

FIGURE 31.1. François Dubois, "St. Bartholomew's Day Massacre"   This painting of the St. Bartholomew's Day Massacre in 1572, by François Dubois, a contemporary Protestant painter, shows soldiers indiscriminately killing Huguenots in Paris. (Musée Cantonal des Beaux-Arts, Lausanne)

The Peace of Augsburg in 1555 brought an end to war between Catholics and Lutherans in Germany, and the Treaty of Cateau-Cambrésis in 1559 ended the Hapsburg-Valois wars. But these halts to long conflicts did not bring an end to the bloodshed. On the contrary, the period between 1560 and 1648 witnessed an outbreak of revolts, massacres, civil wars, and international wars that was unprecedented. While people in several areas suffered, the most intense and extended fighting occurred within the boundaries of the Holy Roman Empire. By the end of the Thirty Years' War in 1648, probably a third of the German population had died from the war.

Certainly religious differences were involved in these conflicts and accounted for the ferocity of the struggles (see Map 31.1). But politics and greed were also intertwined, with leaders vying for political gain and mercenaries thirsty for loot. Both crossed religious lines to make war for their own purposes.

1. THE CRUSADE OF CATHOLIC SPAIN

Emperor Charles V had bequeathed the greater part of his vast empire to his son Philip II (1556–1598) (see Figure 31.2). In addition to Spain, Philip's inheritance included the Netherlands, Franche-Comté, Milan, the Kingdom of Naples, Sardinia, and the Spanish Empire overseas. In 1580 Philip conquered Portugal in the name of his Portuguese mother and became master (at least in name) of Portugal's huge Eastern empire.

Philip II, unlike his father, was a native Spaniard. He utilized the gold and silver flowing in a steady stream from the New World and the lucrative commerce of the East Indies and of the busy Netherlands in the interests of Spain. Ignoring the Cortes and the local rights of Aragon and tending personally to the myriad details of government, the meticulous and stubborn Philip brought Spain under his sway to an extent that Ferdinand and Isabella and Charles V had never been able to do. With the best army in Europe and the will to use it, there is little wonder that the king of Spain was the most feared man in Western Christendom.

The Roman Catholic church was of great im-

FIGURE 31.2. Philip II Philip II of Spain was the most feared monarch in the Western world during the second half of the sixteenth century. A meticulous and stubborn ruler, he struggled to extend his own power and the dominance of the Roman Catholic church over Protestantism. (Alinari/Scala/Art Resource)

portance to Philip II. He conceived it to be his chief mission in life to use the great wealth and power of Spain to restore the dominion of the Roman church over all of Western Christendom. In the Netherlands, in England, and in France, Philip II threw the might of Spain on the side of the Roman Catholics in their counteroffensive against the Protestants.

Revolt in the Netherlands

Philip II, unlike his father, Charles V, was considered by the Netherlanders to be an unsympathetic foreigner who taxed their prosperous commerce and industry for the benefit of Spain. The abso-

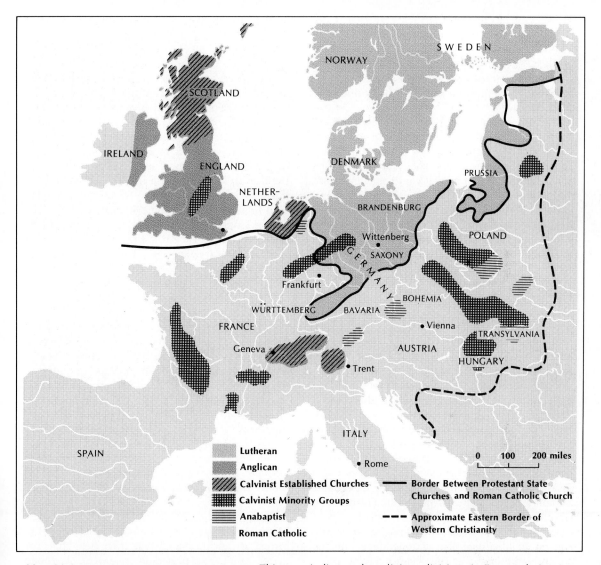

Map 31.1 **RELIGIOUS MAP OF EUROPE, CA. 1560** This map indicates the religious divisions in Europe during the Reformation. In the turmoil between 1560 and 1648, most of those areas that had already turned Lutheran or had established Calvinist churches would remain Protestant. Those areas in which Protestant groups were in the minority would be subject to pressures and change.

lutist monarch and his Spanish administrators also overrode the traditional political privileges of the nobles and the cities in the Netherlands. Nonetheless, religion was the foremost cause of dissension. By mid–sixteenth century, nearly half the people in the Netherlands had become Protestant. Most were Calvinists, but a considerable number were Anabaptists. Philip II, who would tolerate no heresy in his empire, took stern measures to stamp out Protestantism. The Inquisition was used to enforce the laws against heresy. In 1566, bands of outraged Protestants began to deface Roman Catholic churches. Philip thereupon dispatched Spanish troops under the duke of Alva to reduce the Netherlands to submission. A six-year reign of terror followed, in which thousands were put to death.

Far from being cowed, however, the Netherlanders resisted fiercely. They found a brilliant leader in William of Orange, or William the Silent, as he came to be known. They took to the sea, playing havoc with Spanish commerce and communications. When, in 1580, Philip conquered and annexed Portugal, the hardy Dutch "Sea Beggars" seized the richest parts of the Portuguese Empire in the East Indies. The Spanish infantry quickly overran the ten southern (Belgian) provinces, but against the seven northern (Dutch) provinces, made up largely of islands and peninsulas and skillfully defended by the Dutch fleet, Spain's armies could make little headway. Most of the Protestants soon fled north from the Spanish-occupied southern provinces. Likewise, most of the Roman Catholics fled south from the Protestant-dominated north. In 1579 the ten Roman Catholic southern provinces (now Belgium), fearful of the growing power of the Protestant northern provinces (which also spoke a different language), submitted to the Spanish yoke. The seven northern provinces, however, banded together in the Union of Utrecht and continued the struggle for independence. When in 1584 William the Silent was assassinated by a hireling of Philip II, other able leaders arose to take his place. Finally in 1609, eleven years after Philip's own death, Spain agreed to a twelve-year truce, and in 1648 Spain recognized the complete independence of the Dutch Netherlands, as the seven northern provinces are commonly called. In the seventeenth century the little Dutch republic led the world in commerce, in banking, and in painting and was second to none in science and philosophy.

Thus Philip II's crusade in the Netherlands was only partly successful. He saved the southern provinces for Spain for another century, and for the Roman Catholic church, but the Dutch provinces, the richest in his empire, were lost both to Spain and to the Church.

Struggles with England

Most grandiose of all Philip II's crusading efforts was his attempt to restore wayward England to the Roman Catholic fold. His first move was to marry England's Roman Catholic queen, Mary Tudor. They wed in 1554, two years before his own rule over the Spanish Empire. However, Mary's marriage to the king of a feared and hated rival power and her persecution of English Protestants only increased her own unpopularity and that of the Roman Catholic cause in England. Moreover, the marriage failed to produce an heir. When Mary died in 1558, Philip sought to continue his influence in England by trying to marry her successor, Elizabeth. But Elizabeth, a Protestant and a high-spirited English patriot, refused.

Elizabeth proved to be one of England's ablest monarchs (see Figure 31.3). In style and policy, she was a *politique*—a ruler who avoided strong religious stands and emphasized moderation, pragmatism, tolerance, or avoidance in religious matters. For her, like other *politiques* such as William of Orange, religious concerns were subordinated to the need for political unity. She guided the Anglican church to a moderate Protestant position.

Spain's military successes led Elizabeth to support Spain's opponents. In the 1570s and 1580s she signed an alliance with France and aided the Dutch Protestant rebels. She also encouraged English sea dogs to plunder Spain's treasure ships sailing from its New World colonies—indeed, to plunder the colonies themselves. When in 1587 Spanish plots against Elizabeth clearly implicated Mary, Queen of Scots (a Catholic), Elizabeth was forced to execute her. It was then clear that England would not peacefully rejoin the Catholic fold.

Philip II tried to conquer England by direct military action. In 1588 his "Invincible" Armada sailed forth—130 ships, many of them great galleons. Aboard was a formidable Spanish army. The Armada was to go first to the Netherlands and pick up additional soldiers. In the English Channel it met the somewhat larger English fleet, composed mostly of smaller but swifter and more heavily armed ships. The Spaniards fought well

FIGURE 31.3. Marcus Gheeraert, "Queen Elizabeth I" Marcus Gheeraert's portrait of Queen Elizabeth I shows this monarch at the height of her power (a picture of her victory over the Spanish Armada in the background, the crown to her right, her right hand on the globe) and wealth (her jewel-laden attire). (Cooper-Bridgeman Library)

until finally their formation was broken by English fire ships sent into their midst. Once scattered, the Spanish ships were no match for the English fleet. Storms played a major role in the loss of Spanish ships. Only about half the ships ever reached Spain. It was at this point that England began to wrest control of the seas from Spain. Not only had Philip II failed to exterminate Protestantism in England, but the Roman Catholic cause there was now tainted with treason, and Protestantism was stronger than ever.

Confronting the Ottoman Turks

In the sixteenth century, the Ottoman Empire under Suleiman had grown in power to its greatest extent. Victories over Christian troops in Hungary had threatened central Europe. Ottoman fleets dominated large parts of the Mediterranean. The Hapsburgs had traditionally led in the struggle against the Ottomans and Islam in general, and Philip II took up the challenge with vigor. Under the urging of the pope, Venice, Genoa, and Spain amassed a fleet of more than two hundred vessels under the command of Philip's illegitimate half brother, Don Juan. In 1571 this fleet caught and annihilated the somewhat larger Turkish fleet off Lepanto on the coast of Greece. This was one of the few clear-cut successes of Philip's career. Lepanto greatly diminished the Turkish menace to Christendom by sea and marked the beginning of a long, slow period of decline for the Ottoman Empire.

2. THE RELIGIOUS WARS IN FRANCE

In France and Germany during the late sixteenth and first half of the seventeenth centuries, struggles between Protestants and Catholics combined with conflicts between different political factions to break out into bitter wars, usually called the Wars of Religion.

In France Calvinism had made slow but steady progress during the reigns of Francis I (1515–1547) and Henry II (1547–1559) in spite of vigorous persecution by those Roman Catholic monarchs. By 1559 the Huguenots, as the French Calvinists were called, numbered possibly a twelfth of the total population. However, since their ranks included many of the prosperous bourgeoisie and some of the greatest noble families of France, their influence was far greater than their numbers would indicate. Enmity between the Huguenots and the Roman Catholics, which had smoldered under the strong rule of Francis I and of Henry II, broke into open and consuming flame under Henry II's three ineffective sons, who ruled in succession from 1559 to 1589. All three were dominated by their powerful and ambitious mother, Catherine de Médicis. This situation invited political as well as religious faction and intrigue, and in the civil wars that followed politics and religion were intertwined.

The leadership of the Roman Catholic faction was assumed by the powerful Guise family; that of the Protestants by the influential Bourbon family, who were related to the royal line. The first eight years of fighting were ended in 1570 by an uneasy truce. However, Catherine de Médicis became fearful of the growing influence of the Huguenots. She turned for support to the Catholic

Guises, and under their influence she agreed to a plan to massacre the Huguenots. At a given signal at midnight, August 24, 1572 (St. Bartholomew's Day), the Roman Catholics in Paris fell to slaughtering the Protestants. The massacre soon spread to the provinces and went on for a number of weeks. Thousands of Huguenots were slain.

The ablest of the Huguenot leaders, young Henry (Bourbon) of Navarre, escaped and rallied the remaining Protestant forces for the war that was now renewed in earnest. The wealth and energy of the numerous bourgeois and noble members of the Huguenot faction, plus the brilliance of their dashing young leader, offset the superior numbers of the Roman Catholics. Eventually Henry III, the third son of Catherine de Médicis to rule France, organized a moderate Roman Catholic faction to stand between the uncompromising Guise faction and the Protestants. The struggle now became a three-cornered "War of the Three Henrys" (Henry, duke of Guise, Henry of Navarre, and Henry III, king of France). Philip II of Spain threw his support to Henry, duke of Guise. Henry III, now regarding Henry, duke of Guise, as the greater menace to his own royal authority, had him assassinated in 1588. The next year an agent of the Guises assassinated Henry III. This left Protestant Henry of Navarre, by right of succession, King Henry IV of France. However, it was only when he abjured Protestantism four years later and went through the formality of becoming a Roman Catholic that the great majority of his subjects, who were Roman Catholics, allowed him to enter Paris and be legally crowned. "Paris is worth a Mass," he is alleged to have remarked. Five years later (1598) he issued his famous Edict of Nantes (see p. 420), which, by granting tolerance to the Protestant minority, ended religious strife in France for nearly a century.[1] By these acts, Henry revealed himself as a *politique*, favoring national unity over religious concerns. He enjoyed some of the same success and popularity as other *politiques*, such as Elizabeth I in England and William of Orange in the Netherlands.

---

[1] The Huguenots rose up in a brief rebellion (1627–1629) against Cardinal Richelieu when he removed their military and political privileges (see p. 421).

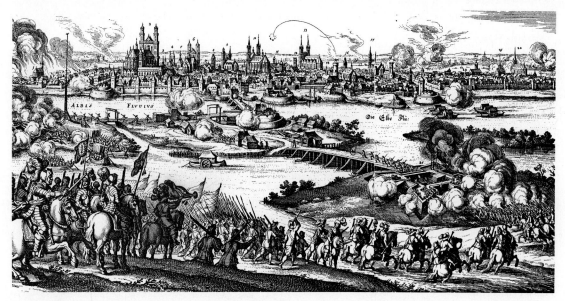

FIGURE 31.4. The Thirty Years' War This print shows Magdeburg, where in 1631 one of the battles of the Thirty Years' War was fought. The last and the bloodiest of the religious wars that accompanied the Reformation, the Thirty Years' War devastated much of Germany and exhausted its participants. (NYPL Picture Collection)

3. THE THIRTY YEARS' WAR IN GERMANY

The Peace of Augsburg (1555), which had brought to a close the first armed conflict in Germany between the Roman Catholics and the Lutherans, proved to be only an uneasy truce. Since the signing of the treaty, which recognized only Roman Catholics and Lutherans, the Calvinists had made strong headway in several states of the Holy Roman Empire and demanded equal recognition. Furthermore, lands of the Roman Catholic church were constantly being secularized in Protestant areas in violation of the treaty. On the other hand, the Roman Catholics, being more aggressive as a result of the clarification of their position by the Council of Trent and the activities of the militant Jesuits, talked of exterminating Protestantism in the Holy Roman Empire and recovering all their lost lands and souls. The Protestants in alarm formed a defensive league. The Roman Catholics countered by forming a league of their own.

The increasing tension finally erupted into the Thirty Years' War (1618–1648) (see Figure 31.4). In this war the religious issue was complicated and often confused by political and dynastic issues. The individual princes of the empire were struggling to maintain or even increase their independence from the emperor. The Hapsburg dynasty, both Austrian and Spanish, threatened to become so powerful that the apprehensive Bourbons of France entered the war against them. The upshot was that eventually the Roman Catholics, the Holy Roman emperor, and the Hapsburg dynasty (the emperor was an Austrian Hapsburg) formed one faction against which were arrayed the Protestants, most of the individual princes of the empire, and the Bourbons.

The long-brewing Thirty Years' War began in 1618 when a group of Bohemian nobles, mostly Calvinists and fearful of losing both their religious and their political rights, declared their Hapsburg ruler deposed and chose the Calvinist elector of the Palatinate as their king. The Hapsburg Holy

Ottoman Empire
Austrian Hapsburgs
Spanish Monarchy
Swedish Dominions
Brandenburg-Prussia
Boundary of the Holy Roman Empire

0   100   200   300 miles

SHETLAND I.

ORKNEY I.

NORWAY

• Bergen

SWEDEN

Stockholm •

KINGDOM OF
DENMARK AND NORWAY

SCOTLAND

• Edinburgh

NORTH SEA

DENMARK

Copenhagen •

BALTIC SEA

IRELAND

Dublin •

ENGLAND
(COMMONWEALTH
1649–1660
UNITED KINGDOM
1707)

SCHLESWIG

HOLSTEIN

SWEDISH
POMERANIA

BRANDENBURG-PRUSSIA

• Danzi

UNITED
PROVINCES

Hamburg •

Bremen •

POMERELIA

Vistula

ATLANTIC OCEAN

London •

Amsterdam •
Ryswick •

HANOVER

BRANDENBURG

Berlin •

GREAT
POLAND

ENGLISH CHANNEL

SPANISH
NETH.

• Brussels

Leipzig •

SAXONY

SILESIA

L
PO

C

Paris • Verdun •

MINOR
GERMAN STATES

BOHEMIA

Toul •

FRANCHE
COMTÉ

LORRAINE

ALSACE

BAVARIA

MORAVIA

FRANCE

Augsburg •

AUSTRIA

Vienna •

Kingdom of Hungary

SWISS
CANTONS

SAVOY

PIEDMONT

REP. OF VENICE

Bue

HUNGAR

Milan •

Venice •

SLAVONIA

Marseilles •

Parma •

BOSNIA

TUSCANY

Zara •

ADRIATIC SEA

MONTENEGRO

SE

PORTUGAL
(TO SPAIN
1580–1640)

PYRENEES

CATALONIA

CORSICA
(Genoa)

PAPAL
STATES

Lisbon •

Madrid •

ARAGON

Rome •

Bari •

CASTILE

SPAIN

BALEARIC I.

MINORCA

SARDINIA

Naples •

KINGDOM OF NAPLES

IONIAN
(Venice

MAJORCA

GIBRALTAR

Tangier
(Portugal)

Ceuta (Spain)

Algiers •

MEDITERRANEAN

Palermo •

SICILY

Oran (Spain) •

Tunis •

FEZ AND MOROCCO

BARBARY STATES

ALGERIA

TUNISIA

SEA

MALTA (Spain)

Roman emperor, aided by the Roman Catholic League and by Hapsburg and Roman Catholic Spain, took the field and easily crushed both Bohemia and the Palatinate. Hundreds of Calvinist Bohemian nobles were executed and their property confiscated. Protestantism was outlawed in Bohemia. The Calvinist Palatinate was annexed to Roman Catholic Bavaria. This quick and crushing victory by Roman Catholic and imperial forces frightened not only the Protestant princes of northern Germany, but also the Protestant neighboring states.

In 1625 Lutheran King Christian IV of Denmark, who held numerous bishoprics in Germany that had been illegally secularized, entered the war against the Roman Catholic and imperial forces. Christian IV was aided by English subsidies and numerous German Protestant princes. At this critical juncture a brilliant soldier of fortune, Albrecht von Wallenstein, offered his services to the emperor. This military genius raised a volunteer army of fifty thousand adventurers of various nationalities. Wallenstein's army, together with the regular imperial and Roman Catholic forces, defeated Christian IV and drove him out of Germany. The Danish king was deprived of nearly all his German holdings. Upon the conclusion of this phase of the war in 1629, the victorious emperor issued the Edict of Restitution, restoring to the Roman Catholic church all the lands illegally secularized since the Peace of Augsburg—more than a hundred tracts, large and small.

The whole Protestant world was now genuinely alarmed at the resurgent power of the Roman Catholics. The German princes were faced with the loss of their powers to the Holy Roman emperor. The French Bourbons were concerned

Map 31.2 EUROPE, 1648 This map of Europe after the Treaty of Westphalia in 1648 shows that what would eventually become unified into Germany during the nineteenth century was still greatly divided within a Holy Roman Empire that was weaker than ever. With the rapid decline of Spain, most political conflict in the century after 1648 would be between France, England, Austria-Hungary, and Brandenburg-Prussia.

about the rapidly growing strength of the Hapsburgs. At this juncture another Protestant champion stepped forward—Gustavus Adolphus of Sweden. This Lutheran "Lion of the North" was a military leader of great ability. Furthermore, he was well backed by French gold. Gustavus Adolphus led his army victoriously through the Germanies, gaining allies among the Protestant princes as he went. The Hapsburg emperor hastily recalled the ambitious Wallenstein, whom he had dismissed upon the conclusion of the Danish phase of the war. Two of the ablest military commanders of early modern times now faced each other. In the battle of Lützen (1632) Wallenstein was defeated, but Gustavus Adolphus had been killed and the victory was far from decisive. Fortunately for the Protestants, Wallenstein was dismissed and two years later was assassinated. Since Sweden had failed to turn the tide of the war, the Bourbon king of France in 1635 threw the full weight of his military might directly into the fray. For thirteen more years the war dragged on until all participants were exhausted. The Treaty of Westphalia in 1648 finally brought the struggle to a close (see Map. 31.2).

In general, thanks largely to the intervention of France, the Roman Catholics, the Holy Roman emperor, and the Hapsburgs suffered a setback. Not only were the Roman Catholics thwarted in their efforts to exterminate Protestantism in Germany, but the Calvinists now gained equal status with the Lutherans and Roman Catholics in the Holy Roman Empire. The Edict of Restitution was nullified. The Holy Roman Empire practically fell apart. According to the terms of the Treaty of Westphalia, each of the more than three hundred individual princes could now make his own treaties. Three of the most important princes, the rulers of Brandenburg, Bavaria, and Saxony, made sizable additions to their territories. Sweden gained strategic territories along the German Baltic and North Sea coasts. France gained the important bishoprics and fortress cities of Metz, Toul, and Verdun, and the province of Alsace except for the free city of Strasbourg. These former imperial territories gave both Sweden and France a vote in the Diet of the Holy Roman Empire and a say in German affairs. The complete independence of Switzerland and the Dutch Netherlands was officially recognized. The Austrian Hapsburgs retained their hereditary possessions but lost prestige as emperors of a disintegrating Holy Roman Empire. Also, their relative position declined as that of France rose. The Spanish Hapsburgs fared worse. After eleven more years of fighting with France they yielded a strip of the Spanish Netherlands and another strip along the Spanish border to France. Spain's days of greatness were finished.

The immediate effect of the Thirty Years' War on Germany was disastrous. For three decades hostile German and foreign armies had tramped back and forth across Germany, killing, raping, and looting the defenseless inhabitants. In the wake of Wallenstein's army of fifty thousand, for instance, swarmed one hundred fifty thousand camp followers bent on plunder. To the usual horrors of war was added religious fanaticism. Some 30 to 40 percent of Germany's inhabitants lost their lives from this war. Many years would be required for Germany to recover from these wounds.

The Thirty Years' War was the last and the bloodiest of the religious wars that accompanied the Reformation. Although there would still be much religious strife and controversy, the religious map of Europe henceforth would change very little. After 1648 political rather than religious affairs would occupy center stage in the Western world.

SUGGESTED READING

General

T. Aston, ed., *Crisis in Europe 1560–1660: Essays from Past and Present* (1965). An important interpretation of the whole period as one of general crisis.

R. Dunn, *The Age of Religious Wars, 1559–1689* (1979). A good, brief survey.

T. Rabb, *The Struggle for Stability in Early Modern Europe* (1975). Analyzes the "crisis" interpretation.

The Crusade of Catholic Spain

W. T. MacCaffrey, *Queen Elizabeth and the Making of Policy, 1572–1588* (1982). A good recent analysis.

G. Mattingly, *The Armada* (1959). Brilliantly shows the impact of the Armada's failure on all of Europe.

Geoffrey Parker, *Spain and the Netherlands, 1559–1659* (1979). A clear introduction.

P. Pierson, *Philip II of Spain* (1975). A well-written biography.

Religious Wars in France

J. H. M. Salmon, *The French Wars of Religion: How Important Were Religious Factors?* (1967). A collection of provoking interpretations.

J. H. M. Salmon, *Society in Crisis: France in the Sixteenth Century* (1975). Focuses on French institutions.

The Thirty Years' War

Georges Pagès, *The Thirty Years' War: 1618–1648* (1971). A clear history of the conflict.

T. K. Rabb, ed., *The Thirty Years' War* (1981). A collection of differing interpretations of the war and its significance.

RETROSPECT

During the fourteenth and fifteenth centuries, various tensions and a weakening of social institutions marked the transformation of the medieval world. During the fifteenth and sixteenth centuries, the institutions and developments that would characterize early modern times grew out of the changing medieval system. The five most important developments of the fifteenth and sixteenth centuries were the Renaissance, the rise of national states, the expansion of Europe, the rise of a capitalistic economy, and the Reformation.

The first challenge to the medieval system came in the cities of northern Italy during the fourteenth and fifteenth centuries. There the ideas, values, and culture of the Renaissance arose. Scholars, writers, and artists began looking back to classical Greece and Rome for models instead of accepting medieval scholastic authority. Cultural leaders focused more on individual human beings living in a concrete, material, Christian world rather than on medieval theology.

Western Europeans of the social and cultural elite were becoming more self-centered, proud, versatile, and materialist. These Renaissance qualities produced new, vibrant literature and art, making northern Italy the cultural center of the West.

During the fifteenth and sixteenth centuries the Renaissance spread from Italy to northern Europe, particularly to the courts of princes and kings and to university towns. There the Renaissance took on a more piously religious character as northern humanists tried to reconcile Christian and classical cultures.

In place of the declining feudal monarchies and empires arose the national or territorial state, which became the dominant political institution of the early modern era. The rise of the national states ended the independence of numerous feudal lords by bringing them under the authority of national monarchs. Talented monarchs such as Ferdinand and Isabella in Spain, Louis XI in France, and Henry VII in England increased their own power and established foundations for the continued growth of national monarchical power. Those areas that did not unify into national states, such as in Germany and Italy, suffered from political weakness.

National monarchs encouraged Europeans to expand into the non-Western world. Voyages of discovery soon led to commercial trade, spreading Christianity, and political control. During the fifteenth and early sixteenth centuries, Portugal and Spain led in this expansion of Europe. England, France, and the Netherlands soon followed. By the end of the sixteenth century, large parts of the rest of the world, particularly in the Western Hemisphere, southern Asia, and coastal Africa, had come under European economic and political domination.

The expansion of Europe was also stimulated by new economic developments. Europe's medieval economy, characterized by subsistence agriculture, monopolistic guilds, and localism, slowly gave way to capitalistic practices and institutions. Increasing population and rising prices spurred commerce and created social turmoil, with poorer peasants suffering the most. The old landed aristocracy was now threatened by newcomers into the class and by a new middle class of aggressive entrepreneurs, merchants, bankers, and lawyers. It is true that the bourgeoisie sought most of all to enter the ranks of the nobility, and did so whenever possible, and that the nobility held the upper hand politically and socially for two or three more

centuries. But by 1600 class lines had become more fluid.

The fifteenth and sixteenth centuries were marked by a deepening concern for religious matters. During the 1500s the Western Christian Church, which had monopolized religious life and strongly influenced the intellectual, political, and economic life of Europe during the Middle Ages, was split asunder by the Reformation. Great religious leaders such as Martin Luther and John Calvin broke from the Roman church and laid the foundations for the various Protestant churches. Much of northern Europe became Protestant. This advance of Protestantism stimulated reform efforts already underway within the Roman Catholic church. Catholic doctrine was forcefully affirmed at the Council of Trent, and new religious orders such as the Jesuits reinvigorated the Church.

The religious struggles of the Reformation combined with political forces to give rise to the Wars of Religion. From the middle of the sixteenth to the middle of the seventeenth centuries, much of Europe was struck by war and political turmoil that was connected to religious issues. The most devastating of these wars was the Thirty Years' War, which broke out in Germany in 1618 and was not concluded until 1648 with the Peace of Westphalia. By this time, the developments initiated during the fifteenth and sixteenth centuries were achieving a new maturity. Europe was already entering into the Age of Royal Absolutism.

PART EIGHT

THE AGE OF ROYAL ABSOLUTISM, SEVENTEENTH AND EIGHTEENTH CENTURIES

As we have seen, the fifteenth and sixteenth centuries were a period of change and upheaval. The Renaissance, the Reformation and the Wars of Religion, the rise of the new monarchs, the commercial revolution, and the expansion of Europe marked the period as substantially different from the preceding Middle Ages and as the beginnings of early modern times. The seventeenth and eighteenth centuries constituted a period when the society, culture, and institutions of early modern Europe matured. The mid-seventeenth century to the last decades of the eighteenth century was a period of relative stability. Historians have often referred to this period of European history as *"l'ancien régime,"* the Old Regime before the French Revolution of 1789.

The dominating development of this period was the growing power of central governments, particularly in the form of royal absolutism. The government of France under Louis XIV epitomized this royal absolutism. An important contrasting trend to royal absolutism was constitutionalism, where the king lost the struggle for greater power. The most striking examples of constitutionalism were in England and the Netherlands.

In most other ways the society and culture of the seventeenth and eighteenth centuries evolved only slowly, reflecting the growing power of central governments and their reigning monarchs. Aristocrats remained socially dominant but with some exceptions, such as in England and the Netherlands, were domesticated by royal monarchs or integrated into the service of the crown's central government. Life for most people still took place in the countryside and in traditional villages, which were only starting to evolve as the tentacles of central governments and economic change reached them. Here it was only in the second half of the eighteenth century that the agricultural revolution and the spread of cottage industry quickened economic and social change. Most religious affiliations remained as determined during the course of the Reformation and Wars of Religion, with established churches usually working hand in hand with monarchs and aristocrats. The most important cultural trends—the baroque and the classical styles—reflected royal grandeur and aristocratic tastes.

Intellectually, however, two developments occurred that would eventually undermine this traditional order of early modern Europe and provide a foundation for the modern society of the nineteenth and twentieth centuries: the Scientific Revolution and the Enlightenment. Yet even these intellectual developments took place only among a small elite and within the political and social context of the seventeenth and eighteenth centuries.

This period, then, is best organized around its most dominating and striking development—the rise and maturation of royal absolutism. The first two chapters examine royal absolutism and the challenges to royal absolutism in western Europe. The third chapter traces the rise of royal absolutism in eastern Europe. The next chapter turns to the competition among states for power, colonies, and empire—in many ways another element of the growing power of central governments. Focus then broadens to economic, social, cultural, religious, and intellectual developments of the period, most of which in some ways reflect the rise of and struggle with royal absolutism in the seventeenth and eighteenth centuries.

CHAPTER 32

The Dominance of France:
The Age of Louis XIV

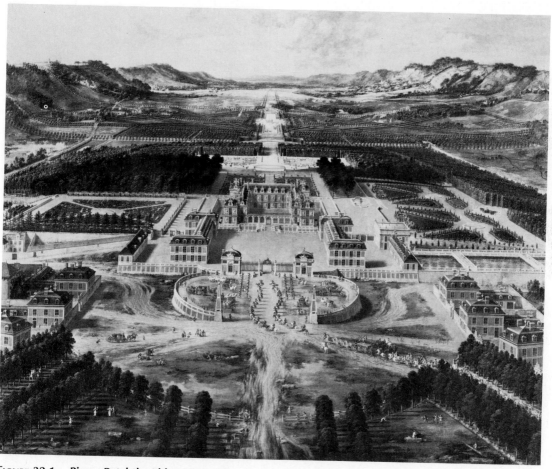

FIGURE 32.1.   Pierre Patel the Elder, "Versailles," 1668   This painting shows Louis XIV's palace and grounds at Versailles in 1668. The scale and order of Versailles reflected the grandeur of the French monarchy at its height. Other European monarchs modeled their palaces after Versailles in an attempt to increase their own prestige. (Lauros-Giraudon/Art Resource)

France was the dominant nation in Europe throughout most of the seventeenth and eighteenth centuries. Under Louis XIV royal absolutism not only reached its peak in France but also served as a model that other monarchs sought to emulate. The well-lighted stage across which the "Sun King" strode was set for him by three able predecessors—Henry IV, Richelieu, and Mazarin.

1. THE RISE OF FRANCE UNDER HENRY IV, RICHELIEU, AND MAZARIN

When Henry IV became king of France in 1589, his country was torn from several decades of bitter religious war. Respect for law and order had broken down. The feudal nobility had in many cases reasserted its own authority. The finances of the central government were in chaos. Roads and bridges were in disrepair. French prestige abroad was at a low ebb; even the city of Paris was garrisoned by the Spanish troops of Philip II.

Henry of Navarre, the first of the Bourbon dynasty to rule France, set out to change all this. The new king, in his prime at the age of thirty-six, was debonair and witty, courageous, generous, and optimistic. His slogan, "A chicken in the pot of every peasant for Sunday dinner," was more than an idle phrase; it is little wonder that *Henri Quatre* became the most popular monarch in French history. The romantic Henry had in the duke of Sully an able, methodical administrator to serve and steady him. The most urgent task was to restore the authority of the central government. This Henry set out to do by vigorously suppressing brigandage and enforcing the law. The lesser nobility was brought to heel directly and quickly. The powerful nobility was dealt with more gingerly, but by the end of Henry's reign real headway had been made toward reducing the nobles to obedience to the central government.

Henry and Sully launched a comprehensive program of economic reconstruction. Agriculture and commerce benefited from the increased security of life and property, from the repair of roads, bridges, and harbors, and from the freeing of internal and external commerce of many obstructions and tariff barriers. Marshes were drained for farming. Better breeding methods were introduced. The peasants' livestock and implements were protected against seizure for debt or taxes. New industries producing glass, porcelain, lace, tapestries, and fine leather and textiles were subsidized and protected by the state. Silk culture, which brought vast wealth to France, was introduced. The building of France's overseas empire began in 1608 when Champlain founded Quebec, the first French colony in the New World.

When Henry IV came to the throne, only about a fourth of the heavy taxes, from which the clergy and the nobility were largely exempted, ever reached the national treasury. The rest went into the pockets of corrupt officials and tax farmers, that is, the collectors who bid a fixed sum for the privilege of collecting the taxes and were permitted to keep anything over and above the contracted amount. Sully was unable to change this vicious system, but by means of careful bookkeeping, efficient administration of expenditures, and elimination of corruption, he was able to show a surplus for the first time in many years.

Another major achievement of Henry's reign was the granting of religious toleration to the Huguenot minority. A *politique,* Henry abjured Protestantism in order to gain acceptance as king of an overwhelmingly Roman Catholic nation. The Edict of Nantes, which Henry IV issued in 1598, granted the Huguenots not only complete freedom of conscience and limited public worship but also civil and political equality. Moreover, they were given military control of some two hundred fortified cities and towns as a guarantee against future oppression.

Having laid the foundations for royal supremacy, economic health, and religious toleration, Henry IV in the last years of his reign devoted an increasing amount of attention to foreign affairs. His goal was to make France first secure and then supreme in Europe by weakening the power of the Spanish and Austrian Hapsburgs. In 1610 he readied his armies for a campaign, but just as he was preparing to join them he was assassinated by a fanatic.

After fourteen years of retrogression under Henry IV's Italian wife, Marie de Médicis, and their young and inept son Louis XIII (1610–1643), Cardinal Richelieu gained active control over the

FIGURE 32.2.   Champaigne, "Cardinal Richelieu"
The imperious and ruthless Richelieu played a major role in making the royal power supreme in France and France the supreme power in Europe. Here he poses in church robes befitting his office as a cardinal. (Scala/Art Resource)

lieu crushed them both. With the royal army at his disposal, he boldly destroyed the castles of the nobles who remained defiant, disbanded their private armies, and hanged a number of the most recalcitrant. The special military and political privileges that the Huguenots enjoyed under the Edict of Nantes were considered by Richelieu to be intolerable, giving them the status of a state within a state. After a bloody two-year struggle, he stripped the Huguenots of these privileges, although he left their religious and civil liberties intact.

In order to bypass local political influence, which in some provinces was still strong, the dynamic minister divided France into some thirty administrative districts called *généralités*, each of which was placed under the control of an *intendant*,[1] who was an agent of the crown. So absolute was the power of the *intendants* over local affairs, even of the most minute nature, that they came to be called the "thirty tyrants of France." They were chosen from the ranks of the bourgeoisie and were shifted around frequently lest they become too sympathetic with the people over whom they ruled. The royal will was thus extended to every part of France.

Although Richelieu was a cardinal in the Roman Catholic church, he did not hesitate to plunge France into the Thirty Years' War in Germany on the side of the Protestants. His purpose, of course, was to weaken the Hapsburgs, chief rivals of the French Bourbons for European supremacy. When Richelieu died in 1642, he had gone far toward bringing to fruition Henry IV's policies of royal supremacy in France and French supremacy in Europe. Richelieu, however, did not share Henry IV's concern for the common people. Their lot became harder under the imperious and ruthless cardinal, at whose death they rejoiced.

Richelieu was succeeded by his protégé, Cardinal Mazarin. Louis XIII's death in 1643, one year after that of his great minister, left the throne to Louis XIV (1643–1715), a child of five. Mazarin played the same role in the early reign of Louis XIV that Richelieu had played during most of the

government of France (see Figure 32.2). Although technically a mere servant of the fickle Louis XIII, the masterful cardinal made himself so indispensable that for eighteen years (1624–1642) he held firm control over French affairs. Handsome, arrogant, and calculating, Richelieu was a true Machiavellian. His twofold policy, from which he never veered, was similar to that of Henry IV—to make the royal power supreme in France and France supreme in Europe.

Believing the high nobility and the Huguenots to be the chief threats to royal absolutism, Riche-

---

[1]The *intendants* existed before Richelieu's time, but he greatly increased their power and functions.

reign of Louis XIII. From the death of Richelieu in 1642 until his own death in 1661, Mazarin vigorously pursued the policies of his predecessor. The Thirty Years' War was brought to a successful conclusion. All who challenged the crown's absolute authority were crushed.

The most noteworthy events during his administration were a series of uprisings between 1648 and 1652, known as the *Fronde*. The Fronde was a revolt of the disgruntled nobility and townspeople against the ever-increasing authority of the central government. At times it looked as if the rebels might succeed, but the rebellious factions could not unify. In the end only Mazarin and the monarchy represented order in the face of apparent chaos, and the rebels were defeated. The failure of the Fronde marked the last overt resistance to royal absolutism in France until the French Revolution in 1789. When Cardinal Mazarin died in 1661, he passed along to young Louis XIV a royal power that was at last absolute and a national state that was easily the first power of Europe.

2. LOUIS XIV AND HIS GOVERNMENT

Louis XIV was twenty-three years old when, in 1661, he stepped forth as the principal actor on the world's gaudiest stage. Young Louis was well fitted for the part. He had a sound body and a regal bearing. His lack of intellectual brilliance and of deep learning were more than offset by a large store of common sense, a sharp memory, a sense of responsibility, and a capacity for hard, tedious work. From his Spanish mother, from Mazarin, and from his tutors he had gained the conviction that he was God's appointed deputy for France. In Bishop Bossuet he had the most famous of all theorists and exponents of royal absolutism. Bossuet in numerous writings argued that absolute monarchy is the normal, the most efficient, and the divinely ordained form of government. He contended that, furthermore, the royal monarch, the image of God and directly inspired by God, is above human reproach and accountable to God alone. These ideas as acted out by Louis gained and held the ascendancy throughout the continent

of Europe during the late seventeenth and most of the eighteenth centuries.

Absolute though he might consider himself [the words *"L état, c'est moi"* ("I am the state") are often attributed to him], Louis could not possibly perform all the functions of government personally. Actually, the great bulk of the decisions and details of government were handled by a series of councils and bureaus and were administered locally by the *intendants*. Distrusting nobles, Louis appointed members of the middle class to the important offices of his government. The functions of the chief councils, such as those of state, finances, dispatches, and the privy council, appear on paper to have been overlapping and ill defined. As supervised by the industrious Louis XIV, however, the administrative machinery worked smoothly and efficiently. In fact, it was the envy of his fellow monarchs and probably constituted his most constructive achievement. There was no semblance of popular participation in government. The role of the people was to serve and obey; in return, they enjoyed reflected glory and received such benefits as the monarch might be willing and able to bestow on them. The Estates General was not called once during the seventy-two years of Louis XIV's reign or the fifty-nine-year rule of his successor.

3. THE KING AND HIS COURT: VERSAILLES

In line with Louis XIV's concept of divine right absolutism, he believed that he should have a palace worthy of God's chief deputy on earth. Hating tumultuous Paris, congested and crowded with vulgar tradespeople, he selected Versailles, eleven miles southwest of the city, to be the new seat of government. There as many as thirty-five thousand workmen toiled for thirty years, turning the marshes and sandy wastes into the world's most splendid court. The cost was so staggering that Louis destroyed the records. The greatest artists in the land were employed in the creation of the palace and the grounds. The most costly marbles, glass, tapestries, paintings, and inlaid woods were used in profusion in the ornate baroque style

FIGURE 32.3. **Charles Lebrun, "Chancellor Seguier"** Chancellor Seguier, a patron of the seventeenth-century French artist Lebrun, is shown here as an ambitious courtier to Louis XIV. In formal robes, this member of France's new nobility *(noblesse de robe)* is attended by pages as if he were a monarch. (The Louvre, Paris)

of the period. Hundreds of acres of gardens, parks, walks, canals, and artificial lakes were laid out with mathematical precision. Playing fountains and marble statues formalized the landscape.

Around his court Louis XIV gathered the great nobles of France (see Figure 32.3). Henry IV, Richelieu, and Mazarin had broken their power; Louis XIV turned them into court butterflies. The inevitable jostling for the king's attention, which was the one source of preferment, and the conflicting claims of so much titled rank necessitated

the drawing up of an elaborate code of etiquette. The king was dressed and undressed, bathed, and fed by the highest noblemen in the land—all in strict ritual. The household personnel consisted of ten thousand soldiers in brilliant uniforms and four thousand civilians. Nor was the pageant of Versailles mere glitter alone. Louis XIV subsidized or gathered around himself the leading French artists and literary figures.

But there was a reverse side to the coin. Versailles was a showplace, not a comfortable home for the king. It was cold, drafty, and inconvenient. The balls, parades, hunts, and social ritual were not sufficient to absorb the energy of the vivacious and ambitious nobility of France. The court seethed with gossip, scandal, and intrigue. Nor did the hard-toiling, heavily taxed French masses, who were supposed to enjoy the reflected glory of the monarch, always appreciate such extravagant glamour. Indeed, there were increasing expressions of discontent.

4. COLBERT AND THE FRENCH ECONOMY

Louis XIV was fortunate to have at his command during the first half of his reign a prodigious financial manager. Jean Baptiste Colbert (1619–1683) was an inordinately ambitious social climber who realized that, because of his bourgeois origin, his only means of advancement was through indispensable service to the king. An engine of efficiency, he toiled endlessly, supervising the countless details of the French economy.

Colbert's first and probably his most difficult task was to balance the national budget, which had become badly unbalanced under Richelieu and Mazarin. The careful accounting of receipts and expenditures that Sully had inaugurated three-quarters of a century earlier was resumed. Some of the debts that the government had contracted at exorbitant rates of interest were canceled; on others the rates were reduced. Dishonest tax collectors were dismissed and punished.

With Colbert, mercantilism reached its peak. French industries were protected by prohibitive tariffs, while exports and new industries were subsidized. Raw materials, however, were strictly husbanded. Imperial and commercial activities in India and North America were vigorously promoted. To protect this growing empire and the commerce that it generated, a large navy was built. But Colbert did not stop with these traditional mercantilist practices. In order to gain a world-wide reputation for the uniformly high quality of French products, all manufacturing was subjected to the most minute regulation and supervision. So many threads of such and such quality and color must go into every inch of this textile

and that lace. A veritable army of inspectors enforced the regulations. This extreme policy of mercantilism, the economic adjunct to royal absolutism, has come to be called Colbertism. It achieved its immediate end so far as quality and reputation were concerned, but it stifled initiative and retarded future industrial development. That Colbert was able to balance the budget and achieve general economic prosperity in the face of Louis XIV's lavish expenditures, including the building of Versailles, was a remarkable feat. It is well, however, that Colbert died in 1683, for Louis' wars of aggression eventually wrecked most of the great minister's work. Much of Europe copied Colbert's policies and techniques during the latter part of the seventeenth and most of the eighteenth centuries.

5. ABSOLUTISM AND RELIGION

It was virtually inevitable that Louis XIV's concepts of divine right monarchy would have religious repercussions. First, they ran counter to the claims of the pope. All his life Louis considered himself to be devoutly loyal to the Roman Catholic faith, as were the majority of his subjects. But when it came to matters of church administration Louis was not willing to have his royal authority limited, even by Rome. Numerous conflicts between king and pope led to the calling of a great council of the French clergy in 1682. This council, under the domination of Bishop Bossuet, faithful servant of Louis XIV and famed exponent of the theory of royal absolutism, drew up a statement of Gallican Liberties, special privileges or freedoms of the French church from Roman domination. The Gallican Liberties brought the French church to a position close to that of the English church under Henry VIII. They might even have led to eventual separation from Rome had not Louis XIV in later life fallen increasingly under the influence of the Jesuits and the pious Madame de Maintenon, who were able to rekindle his loyalty to the pope.

Louis' absolutism also ran afoul of the Jansenists, so called because they were followers of a Belgian bishop, Cornelis Jansen. This group represented a Puritan movement within the Roman Catholic church. The Jansenists had no intention of breaking away from the Church, to which they considered themselves entirely loyal. It was their wish to return to the teachings and practices of the Church in the days of St. Augustine. They emphasized predestination, inner piety, and the ascetic life. A number of intellectuals and people of means were attracted to their ranks, including the dramatist Racine and the mathematician and philosopher Blaise Pascal. At Port Royal near Versailles a group of prominent Jansenists practiced a communal life and established an excellent school that attracted much favorable attention. Eventually the Jesuits persuaded the pope to declare Jansenism heretical and aroused Louis XIV against the Jansenists. He outlawed the sect and destroyed its buildings.

The chief religious victims of Louis XIV's absolutism were the Huguenots. Although the Huguenots numbered not more than a tenth of the total population in France, many of them were industrious, prosperous, and educated members of the middle class. The Huguenots were subjected to a variety of persecutions. Regular army troops were quartered in Huguenot homes and instructed to cause havoc. Whole Huguenot communities would abjure their faith at the approach of the troops. Finally, in 1685 the Edict of Nantes was revoked and the Protestant religion outlawed. Although Huguenots were forbidden to emigrate, many—probably a quarter million—succeeded in doing so, taking much of their wealth and all their economic knowledge and skills with them. Not only were these industrious citizens lost to France, but they strengthened some of France's rivals and enemies, such as England, the Dutch Netherlands, and Brandenburg, which welcomed them. Forbidden to enter the underpopulated French colonies, many Huguenots helped to people the English colonies in America.

6. LOUIS XIV'S WARS OF AGGRESSION

The Sun King was not content to rule the world's most powerful nation. Louis' immediate and expressed goal was to extend his rule to France's natural frontiers. Since the French boundaries were already delimited by mountains and sea on every side but the northeast, it was in that direction that Louis looked for expansion. He claimed that only the Rhine River would provide France with an adequate natural strategic boundary on that side. An advance to the Rhine would involve France in war with most of Europe. Between the French frontier and the Rhine lay the Spanish Netherlands, much of the Dutch Netherlands, imperial territory belonging to the Austrian Hapsburgs, and many German states. England, too, would be threatened, and the balance of power upset. But Louis felt himself equal to the task of defeating these powers.

Louis' war minister, Louvois, organized France's huge military establishment on a scientific and businesslike basis, replete with supply depots and hospitals. He introduced strict discipline, uniforms, and marching drill. Vauban was one of the great designers of fortifications and of siege operations. It was a common saying that a city defended by Vauban was safe and that a city besieged by Vauban was doomed. Condé was an able and dashing military leader, and Turenne a masterly planner of campaigns and battles.

During the last four decades of his seventy-two-year reign Louis XIV fought four wars of aggression. In 1667 he unceremoniously sent French armies in to conquer the Spanish (Belgian) Netherlands. Spanish power had declined rapidly since the sixteenth century, and Louis' armies captured one fortress city after another. The Dutch, however, took alarm and formed an alliance with England and Sweden to check the French menace. This array of powerful nations along with Spain caused Louis to accept a peace that granted him only a slice of the Spanish Netherlands.

The frustrated Grand Monarch determined to punish the upstart prosperous Dutch. He sent huge French armies into the Netherlands. The cause of the Dutch seemed hopeless, and in desperation they opened their dikes. Large portions of their land were flooded, but the French were held at bay. Meanwhile, the power of France frightened Spain, the Holy Roman emperor, Brandenburg, and several small German states into joining the Dutch in alliance. Louis XIV won many victories over the allies, but when the English Parliament forced Charles II to break his agreement with the French king and join the alliance against him, Louis XIV decided to make peace. Again hapless Spain was the loser, giving up to France the long-coveted Franche-Comté (free county of Burgundy) and another strip of the Spanish Netherlands.

At the end of the Dutch War (1678) Louis XIV stood at the peak of his power (see Map 32.1). He had defeated all the greatest military powers on the western European continent and had gained valuable territories. But the tide was about to turn. Turenne was killed near the end of the Dutch War, and the aged Condé retired at the end of the war. No comparable generals were found to replace them. Colbert's hard-won surplus and balanced budget were now things of the past, and France's economy was suffering. All Europe had become alarmed by the French aggression.

No sooner had the Dutch War ended than Louis began trumping up claims to various territories in Alsace and Lorraine and sending in his armed forces to occupy them. The result was another defensive alliance against Louis composed of the Dutch Netherlands, Spain, Sweden, the Holy Roman emperor, and a number of small German states. The heart of the alliance was William of Orange, stadholder of Holland, and when the redoubtable Dutchman became King William III of England after the Glorious Revolution of 1688, England, too, was brought into alliance against Louis. The alliance was called the League of Augsburg. After nine years of fruitless struggle, Louis accepted a peace giving him only the city of Strasbourg.

But the Sun King was not about to give up. He persuaded the last monarch of the Hapsburg line in Spain just before he died in 1700 to choose one of Louis' grandsons as king. The prospect of Spain and the Spanish Empire joined to the already inordinately powerful French monarchy frightened the other powers of western Europe into once more forming an alliance against France. The ensuing War of the Spanish Succession lasted eleven years (1702–1713). The allies administered to the French and Spanish armies a series of severe defeats. In 1713 Louis XIV, beaten and exhausted, was forced to accept the Treaty of Utrecht. The settlement was complicated, but France had been somewhat humbled. It was beginning to lose ground overseas to Great Britain and in Europe had been halted short of the Rhine. But France was still the most powerful single nation in Europe.

Louis XIV lived only two years after the signing of the Treaty of Utrecht. He had long outlived his popularity. As the body of the grandest of all the absolute monarchs was drawn through the streets of Paris, some of his abused people cursed in the taverns as the coffin passed.

7. THE DECLINE OF FRENCH ABSOLUTISM

The French monarchy never again achieved the power it wielded under Louis XIV. Certainly France remained a first-rank power, with a large army, a centralized bureaucracy, and a growing economy. But between 1715 and 1789 the monarchy slowly declined.

Louis XIV was succeeded in 1715 by his five-year-old great-grandson, Louis XV. Louis XV was never interested in the day-to-day affairs of government like Louis XIV. Most historians consider him a mediocre king, concerned with his own pleasures and willing to leave governmental administration to his ministers, most of whom were of questionable quality. Until 1720 the duke of Orléans ruled as regent. He diminished the prestige of the monarchy by backing the financial schemes of John Law, which resulted in a scandal known as the Mississippi Bubble. The duke of Orléans also opened the door to the crown's greatest competitor—the aristocracy—by strengthening the *parlements*—courts dominated by aristocrats that declared laws or acts of the monarch valid or invalid.

From 1726 to 1743 Cardinal Fleury served as chief minister. The most effective of Louis XV's ministers, Fleury brought relative stability to political affairs and a needed period of peace. But neither he, nor the less effective advisers of Louis XV that followed, nor the monarchy of the indecisive Louis XVI that succeeded in 1774 were able to solve fundamental problems weakening the monarchy.

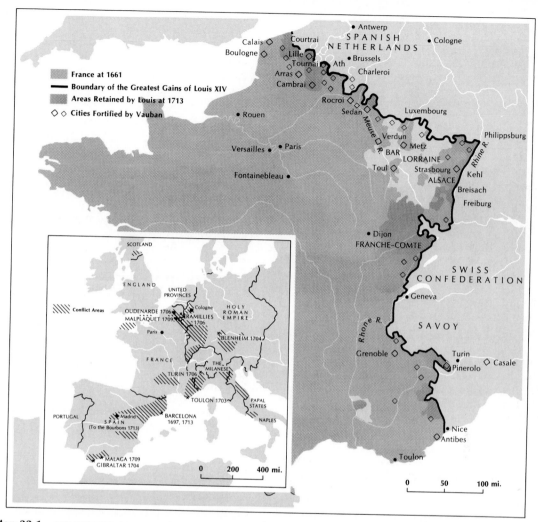

Map 32.1 **THE GROWTH OF FRANCE UNDER LOUIS XIV** These maps indicate the extensiveness of the wars waged by Louis XIV during his reign and the areas in which he made the most significant gains—along the eastern border of France.

Expensive wars and unreformed taxation policies left the treasury depleted after Louis XIV's death. The clergy and nobility retained most of their immunities from taxation despite efforts of several ministers to break those privileges. The debt grew, and the monarchy was weakened by its inability to reform its finances to lessen the burden of that debt.

Underlying these political and financial problems was a resurgence of the aristocracy. In the decades between 1715 and 1789 the monarchy was faced by an increasingly assertive aristocracy, anxious to recapture some of its old political power. Ambitious aristocrats thwarted the kings' efforts to reform taxes. They set themselves up as centers of aristocratic opposition to the monarchy, above all through their control of the *parlements* (law courts).

Thus by the middle decades of the eighteenth century, the French monarchy had clearly declined from its heights under Louis XIV. When problems came to a head in the 1780s, the king was unable to handle them and the monarchy was toppled by a great revolution.

SUGGESTED READING

General

P. Anderson, *Lineages of the Absolutist State* (1974). A good Marxist analysis.

G. N. Clark, *The Seventeenth Century* (1961). Good brief survey, emphasizing cultural aspects.

R. N. Hatton, *Europe in the Age of Louis XIV* (1979). A well-illustrated survey.

Rise of France Under Henry IV, Richelieu, and Mazarin

L. A. Moote, *The Revolt of the Judges: The Parlement of Paris and the Fronde 1643–1652* (1971). A detailed analysis of the Fronde.

V. L. Tapié, *France in the Age of Louis XIII and Richelieu* (1974). A good survey.

Louis XIV and His Court

W. F. Church, ed., *Louis XIV in Historical Thought* (1978). Conflicting interpretations of Louis XIV.

P. Goubert, *Louis XIV and Twenty Million Frenchmen* (1970). A respected study of French society and politics.

H. Rowen, *The King's State: Proprietary Dynasticism in Early Modern France* (1980). Analyzes the theory of Louis XIV's rule.

A. Trout, *Jean-Baptiste Colbert* (1978). Analyzes his economic policies.

J. B. Wolf, *Louis XIV* (1968). An excellent biography.

The Decline of French Absolutism

A. Cobban, *A History of Modern France, Vol. 1* (1966). A clear, well-written interpretation.

Sources

L. R. Saint-Simon, *The Memoirs of the Duc de Saint-Simon.* A disgruntled courtier's detailed eyewitness account of Versaille under Louis XIV.

Marie de Sévigné, *Letters from Madame la Marquise de Sévigné,* ed. and trans. Violet Hammersley (1956). Well-written eyewitness account of life at Versailles.

CHAPTER 33

The Challenge to Absolutism: England and the Dutch Netherlands

FIGURE 33.1. **The English Cabinet** This scene shows Robert Walpole, who served as prime minister of England from 1721 to 1742, presiding over a session of the cabinet. Walpole and the other cabinet members shown here all were members of Parliament and belonged to the majority party in that body. In sessions such as this they decided upon the major policies to be followed by the government; their control of Parliament allowed them to enact their decisions. Thus, the cabinet became the effective executive power in Great Britain, a position that it still holds today. The emergence of the cabinet system was one of the major outcomes of the bitter political struggle in seventeenth-century England. (The Bettmann Archive)

While royal absolutism was being perfected in France and elsewhere on the Continent, England and the Dutch Netherlands moved toward a form of government that placed limitations on the authority of the executive and on the power of the state. This constitutional system gave to a representative body the authority to define the law. It also sought to create a balance between the power of the state and the rights and liberties of citizens of the state. The constitutional changes made in England and the Dutch Netherlands during the seventeenth century strongly influenced later struggles against absolutism in many parts of the world.

1. EARLY STUART ABSOLUTISM

The absolutism shaped by the Tudors (see Chapter 28) was subjected to serious challenges during the seventeenth century. "Good Queen Bess" died in 1603 without a direct heir. She was succeeded by a distant cousin, James Stuart (1603–1625), king of Scotland. He was an avowed absolutist, but he was woefully ignorant of the delicate working of the Tudor political system and not suited by temperament for the hard work nor gifted with the political adroitness needed to keep that system working. His political ineptitude led to a progressive breakdown of the Tudor system and to a polarization of political forces.

But not all of the troubles of James I's reign were the making of a king known in his own days as "the wisest fool in Christendom." New problems were facing England that threatened the general satisfaction that most people had felt toward Tudor governance. Major economic changes were in process, creating new opportunities in agriculture, manufacturing, trade, and the professions. Enterprising groups seeking to take advantage of these opportunities were eager to assert greater control over royal policy in order to promote their economic interests. These same changes were adversely affecting other groups, especially rural tenants and laborers, thereby fostering popular discontent. A major realignment of power was taking shape in Europe, marked by the ascendancy of France. This development encouraged the English rulers to seek closer ties with their traditional enemy, Spain, a course that many still basking in the glories of the victory over the Armada viewed as unpatriotic.

The very structure of the Tudor political system lacked key elements conducive to effective absolutism. Too much depended on the personal qualities of the monarch and a narrow circle of royal advisers. There was not a well-developed bureaucracy nor a well-organized military force. The central government had limited control over local government, dominated by a local gentry, the members of which were jealous of their offices and protective of their local interests. The traditional system of common law served to limit arbitrary acts by the royal government. Most serious of all were the limited financial resources of the crown. It could not manage on the traditional sources of revenue—income from royal lands, customs duties, and feudal dues. Additional income could only be derived from taxes, which Parliament had long since established the right to approve. If absolutism was to continue, significant political reforms aimed at increasing the power of the monarch were required. Such changes posed a threat to powerfully entrenched interests in England.

Another increasingly acute source of tension involved religious issues. Many were not satisfied with the Anglican settlement carried out during Elizabeth's reign (see Chapter 31). The major dissenters were the Puritans, who wanted reforms that would make the established religion more "Protestant": simpler ritual, more emphasis on Scripture, less episcopal control over local churches. There also remained many Roman Catholics who hoped to undo the Reformation; their presence was a cause of constant concern for all Protestants.

During James I's reign these issues found their focus in Parliament, especially in the House of Commons, a body theoretically representing the entire English populace but actually dominated by the country gentry, merchants, and lawyers. The king was forced to summon Parliament because of the constant and increasing need for money. Although Parliament usually provided some financial aid, its members constantly raised issues that challenged royal policy. They criticized James I's royal advisers for corruption, favoritism, and incompetence. They questioned his unwavering support of Anglicanism and his lenient policy toward the Catholics. They condemned the alliance he made with Spain early in his reign and his failure to support the Protestant forces when the Thirty Years' War began in 1618. James responded by repeatedly dismissing Parliament. He then tried to utilize other means of raising money, but these efforts were challenged in the courts as contrary to custom and thus illegal. The king answered by dismissing judges, leading to more parliamentary criticism. Throughout this long series of clashes, Parliament proved itself to be an undisciplined, intemperate body. But its confrontations with the king heightened the fear that the royal government was bent on extending its prerogatives to the point where the constitution and the law would be subverted, opening the way to tyranny.

Under James' successor, Charles I (1625–1649), the conflict deepened into civil war. Charles was no less stubborn than James in his insistence on royal absolutism and in his refusal to bend before the claims of Parliament and the courts. The king's major problem continued to be a need for funds, a need made more desperate by a blundering foreign policy that resulted in costly military ventures in France and Spain that produced no victories. Charles was forced to request taxes from Parliament, which responded by challenging royal policy on a variety of issues. Increasingly, the leaders of Parliament began to make specific their definition of what they meant by royal violation of the constitution and the law. Their views found expression in the Petition of Rights submitted to the king in 1628. This bold document demanded that the king desist from various illegal acts: imposing martial law in peacetime, levying taxes without Parliament's approval, imprisoning citizens without trial, and quartering soldiers with private citizens. Desperate for money, Charles accepted the Petition of Rights, thereby admitting that he had acted illegally. But when Parliament in its next session in 1629 insisted that the king respect the petition's provisions on taxation, Charles dismissed Parliament, over the bitter protests of its leaders.

For the next eleven years Charles ruled without Parliament. To do so he was forced to rely on a variety of means of raising funds that pushed royal authority to the limits of legality. Ultimately, it was Charles' religious policy that forced him once again to confront his enemies on their ground—in Parliament. With Charles' support, his chief religious adviser, William Laud, archbishop of Canterbury, initiated a vigorous "reform" aimed at giving greater emphasis in the Church of England to elaborate rituals, episcopal authority over local churches, and the doctrine of free will. To the Puritans Laud's reforms were detestable, the very opposite of the most fundamental precepts of Protestantism. Many of them fled to the New World in search of a setting where they would have the freedom to institute real Protestantism. Laud's policies also alarmed many Anglicans, who sensed that England was on a course that would lead it back to Roman Catholicism. But it was the absolute refusal of the Scotch Presbyterians to accept the "beauty of holiness," as Charles called Laud's reforms, that precipitated a crisis. In 1639 they revolted, posing a military crisis that forced Charles to summon Parliament into session in 1640 in order to raise money to resist the Scotch threat to the kingdom.

The first Parliament of 1640, called the Short Parliament, was dismissed after three weeks because it again challenged royal authority. But the Scots continued to press and Charles was forced to capitulate. He summoned the Long Parliament, so called because it was to sit for twenty years. With an amazing show of unity Parliament proceeded to legislate the end of Stuart absolutism. It forced Charles to sacrifice his chief ministers, including Laud. It abolished the hated extraordinary courts, including the Star Chamber and the Court of High Commission, which had long been tools used by the crown to avoid the common law. An act was passed requiring a meeting of Parliament every three years and curbing the power of the king to dismiss Parliament. Severe limitations were placed on the king's power to tax without parliamentary approval. To all of this Charles acceded, chiefly because he needed money to fight the Scots.

Up to this point Parliament had succeeded brilliantly in legislating what amounted to a bloodless revolution that established limited monarchy. But the parliamentary forces then began to falter over the question of how to use Parliament's power. In general, its leadership was forced in directions that caused alarm in many quarters and drove many back toward support of the king. Charles helped to cause this split by giving every sign that he would resist being a limited monarch. Suspicion of his motives caused parliamentary leaders to remove from his hands control of the administration and the army and to impose taxes that seemed as burdensome as those imposed by Charles earlier. Religious opinion in Parliament moved in the direction of ending Anglicanism "root and branch" in favor of some form of Presbyterianism. This mounting extremism caused many influential leaders to believe that Parliament was setting a course that would upset the established order. The division in the parliamentary ranks emboldened Charles to try to restore his control; he went so far in early 1642 as to attempt to arrest the leaders of Parliament. This action was a call to arms, pitting against each other elements of a ruling class that had lost its community of interest, an interest that had long focused on the monarch.

2. ENGLISH CIVIL WAR, COMMONWEALTH, AND PROTECTORATE (1642–1660)

The opening of armed strife divided England along lines that defy easy definition. The opposing forces did not represent clear-cut economic interests or social classes. A considerable following, soon known as the Cavaliers, rallied around Charles, who represented himself as the champion of the established order against the political and religious radicals in Parliament. The backbone of the Cavalier forces came from the great noble families and their clientele among the country gentry living in the more economically backward areas of northern and western England. Although the opposition, called the Roundheads, had its noble supporters, it drew its main strength from lawyers, the gentry of the south and the east, and the commercial interests; many from these elements were Puritans. This core was soon reinforced by radical elements from the poor and op-

pressed, especially those living in London. In the intricate matter of choosing sides, there figured complex personal factors—family ties, friendships, personal loyalties—much after the fashion of the American Civil War.

The first phase of the civil war lasted through 1646. While neither side was prepared militarily, for a time the Cavaliers seemed to have the upper hand. But the Roundheads had forces working in their favor: support of the navy, domination of the richest part of England, control over the regular administrative system and Parliament, power to vote taxation. In 1643 the Roundhead cause was bolstered by an alliance with the Scots. But ultimately the outcome of the struggle was determined by the success of the Roundheads in creating an effective army. The chief architect of the victorious army was a simple farmer with strong Puritan convictions, Oliver Cromwell. He organized a cavalry regiment of disciplined, deeply religious recruits who proved more than a match for the Cavalier forces they faced. His system was soon applied to the entire Roundhead force to create the New Model Army, made up of selected troops paid and equipped in a businesslike fashion. It quickly proved itself superior to the Cavalier army, so that by 1646 the Cavalier army was crushed and Charles was forced to surrender.

However, with victory in their grasp, the Roundheads were unable to work out an acceptable settlement. After the defeat of the Cavaliers the Roundheads were led by moderates who wished to establish a limited monarchy and a Presbyterian religious order. Charles remained unwilling to accept such a settlement and raised fears of a renewal of the civil war by fleeing his captors and allying himself with the Scots. More ominous was the increasing prominence of Roundhead leaders who demanded a more radical religious reform favoring the independence of local churches and freedom of conscience. These religious Independents were joined by the Levellers, political radicals who advocated the end of monarchy, democratic elections, and the redistribution of wealth. The strength of these religious and political radicals became centered in the New Model Army, where discontent was fed by the fact that pay was considerably in arrears. Fearful that the radicals would seize complete control, the moderate Roundheads ordered the army demobilized. And they turned back to the king, who suddenly expressed considerable enthusiasm for parliamentary control over the monarchy and for Presbyterianism. The Independents, led by Cromwell, would not be denied. They destroyed the hope of Charles and his Scotch army in a single battle in 1648 and, along with it, the cause of the Cavaliers and the moderate Roundheads. Backed by the New Model Army, Cromwell acted decisively to ensure the position of the Independents. He purged the Long Parliament of all members not dedicated to his cause and gave to the so-called Rump Parliament chief authority in the land. It immediately legislated out of existence the Anglican church, the House of Lords, and the monarchy. And at Cromwell's urging it decreed the execution of the king in 1649 on the grounds that he was "a tyrant, traitor, and murderer."

For eleven years after Charles I's death Cromwell's forces sought to rule England without a king. Always in a minority and dependent on the army, their desperate experimentation failed to establish a stable order. England steadily retreated from revolution.

The first experiment sought to create a republican form of government called the Commonwealth. A one-house Parliament was made the supreme authority, with a state council of forty-one members charged with conducting the daily affairs of government. The political and religious extremists in the army were curbed, and considerable toleration was extended to all Protestants. Severe measures were taken to subdue the rebellious Irish and the Scots. An aggressive foreign policy, aimed at promoting English commercial and colonial interests, was undertaken. Navigation acts were passed to ensure that trade within England's emerging empire would be monopolized by England. War was waged on the Dutch, England's chief commercial rival. None of these policies, however, helped to popularize the Commonwealth. The Cromwellians could not shed their image as regicides and Puritan extremists (see Figure 33.2). Resistance to the Commonwealth grew steadily.

Cromwell ultimately blamed the failure of the

O liver seeking God while the K. is murthered by his order.

FIGURE 33.2. A Satire on Cromwell The deep religious fervor of the Puritans and the taint of regicide that lingered throughout the Commonwealth and the Protectorate are satirized here as Oliver Cromwell is shown at prayer while Charles I is being executed. (NYPL Picture Collection)

Commonwealth on what he considered the self-seeking leaders of the Rump Parliament. Finally, in 1653, he dissolved the Rump by force and tried to replace it with a handpicked body (called the Barebones Parliament, in honor of Praise-God Barebones, the first name on its roll). This body failed to distinguish itself in any way, and it too was dissolved. Finally, the very instrument that had stood against tyranny—Parliament—was gone. The tide of revolution had peaked with Cromwell and his army in control.

In pursuit of what he called a "healing and settling" course for England, Cromwell tried one more experiment, called the Protectorate. A written constitution was drawn up entrusting power to a lord protector (Cromwell), who was advised by a Council of State and guided by a one-house Parliament elected by property holders. From the beginning the lord protector and Parliament clashed on most issues, largely because the elected Parliament represented political and religious positions that ran contrary to the convictions of those who alone could sustain Cromwell in power, the "godly" men of the New Model Army. Despite the constant turmoil the Protectorate achieved some successes. The specter of radical political change was dispelled by the suppression of the Levellers. The central administration was honestly administered. Traditional patterns of local government were restored. A variety of Protestant groups enjoyed considerable independence and freedom of religious choice. Cromwell pursued a firm foreign policy that pacified Ireland and Scotland, extended English overseas colonies, and promoted commercial interests. But never could Cromwell escape the fact that the army, not civilian consent, kept him in power.

As the Protectorate floundered, opinion began to run in favor of the restoration of monarchy. In 1657 Parliament asked Cromwell to become king, an honor he declined, but he did agree to remain lord protector for life. Thus, when he died in 1658, the wheel had come nearly full circle: A man who had led his soldiers to the abolition of monarchy was himself king without title.

At Cromwell's death, his son, Richard, became lord protector. This weak figure was soon swept aside by forces favoring the restoration of monarchy. By 1660 elements in the New Model Army joined with people of property and commerce to end the Protectorate. The Long Parliament voted to dissolve itself. A new Parliament was elected and soon invited Charles Stuart, the son of Charles I, to return from exile and assume the crown in 1660.

3. THE ENGLISH RESTORATION (1660–1688)

The Restoration of the Stuarts by no means resolved the basic problems that had divided England since 1603, particularly those involving the relationship between king and Parliament and the religious establishment. Between 1660 and 1688 these problems continued to disturb society. However, the struggles of the Restoration era were more moderate than had been the case in the preceding two decades.

The reign of Charles II (1660–1685) began in a climate of forgiving compromise. The king and Parliament joined in repealing all the acts of the Commonwealth and the Protectorate. Only a few Cromwellians were punished for their part in killing Charles I. Confiscated property was returned to property owners. The king was assured of a sizable income on a regular basis, but he was deprived of many ancient feudal rights that had allowed his predecessors to exact taxes without approval of Parliament. Not only was control of taxation reserved to Parliament, but the Triennial Act was passed to ensure that it would meet every three years whether or not the king so wished. However, this settlement did not get to the basic political issue: where ultimate authority rested.

Even less satisfactory was the religious settlement embodied in a series of parliamentary acts passed in 1661 and 1662 and known as the Clarendon Code after Charles II's chief adviser, the earl of Clarendon. These acts not only reestablished the Anglican church but also threatened to destroy the Independents and Presbyterians. The Act of Uniformity required all clergy to abide by the Book of Common Prayer. The Corporation Act ruled that all members of city governments worship in the Anglican church. The Conventicle Act made religious meetings other than Anglican illegal, and the Five Mile Act forbade all preachers who were not Anglican to come within five miles of any city. In brief, the Clarendon Code promised to nonconformists (that is, non-Anglicans) little better than criminal status.

These troublesome issues soon began to surface, to divide opinion and generate conflict. They were intensified by a series of disasters that befell England during the early years of Charles' reign.

He involved England in a war with the Dutch that led to a humiliating defeat. In 1665 a plague struck England, to be followed the next year by a fire that destroyed most of London. Many god-fearing English felt that these misfortunes were divine retribution for the immorality of the royal court, where the model of profligacy was set by the king himself.

Parliament again became the center of dissatisfaction. It reacted to public wrath by forcing Clarendon out of office in 1667 and by becoming stingier in approving taxes needed to fund an unsuccessful war and Charles' personal extravagances. Charles paid little heed to the growing opposition, choosing instead to pursue two policies he personally favored: an alliance with France and religious tolerance in England that would permit Roman Catholics to worship freely. In 1670 he signed a treaty with Louis XIV agreeing, in return for a subsidy, to join France in a war on the Dutch and to promote the Catholic cause in England. In 1672 Charles issued a Declaration of Indulgence, which set aside laws restricting the practice of Roman Catholicism. An outraged Parliament forced the king to withdraw the Declaration of Indulgence and passed the Test Act (1673), which excluded Catholics from all public offices. And when Charles joined France in another unsuccessful war against the Dutch in 1672–1674, Parliament forced him to seek peace by refusing financial support.

Although the tensions continued, especially those involving religious issues, Charles showed considerable ingenuity in neutralizing Parliament during the last years of his reign. An improving economy resulted in growing tax returns, minimizing Parliament's power to control the crown by controlling taxation. Louis XIV's subsidies helped ease the financial burden on the king. More significantly, Charles skillfully built a political following—an embryonic "party"—devoted to strong monarchy and Anglicanism. Its members, scornfully dubbed "Tories" (a term used to designate Irish bandits) by the opposition, could often control Parliament in support of the king. An opposing "party," committed to parliamentary supremacy and religious tolerance for all Protestants, was also formed; its members were called "Whigs" (after a term used to designate Scottish

horse thieves and murderers). Charles' successes led many to feel that absolutism was returning to England. But one obstacle kept Charles from totally controlling English political life: a rising fear that the king was determined to restore Catholicism.

James II (1685–1688) inherited a strong position from his brother, based in large part on the Tory majority in Parliament, a sound financial position, and general satisfaction with legitimate succession. But he soon dissipated this strength by his open avowal of Catholicism and attempts to improve the position of Catholics in England, which neither Tories nor Whigs would tolerate. When in 1688 a son was born to James and his Catholic wife and baptized in the Catholic faith, ensuring that the Stuart dynasty would be perpetuated by a Catholic successor, Tory and Whig leaders invited James' Protestant daughter, Mary, and her husband, William of Orange, the stadholder of several provinces in the Dutch Netherlands, to assume England's throne. When William invaded England in late 1688, the great majority of the people rallied to his side; James II fled to France. For a second time, the unhappy Stuarts had been forced off England's throne, but this time the revolution was bloodless.

4. ENGLAND'S GLORIOUS REVOLUTION AND ITS CONSEQUENCES

The flight of James II, unlike the execution of Charles I, did not lead to radical political experimentation. Instead, what the English call a Glorious Revolution was carried through in the form of several fundamental legal enactments that pacified England and established the basis for its future political system.

Immediately after the triumph of William and Mary, Parliament declared the throne vacant by reason of James' abdication. It then voted to grant the crown to William and Mary. A Bill of Rights was passed in 1689. This fundamental charter asserted Parliament's authority to depose a king and choose a new one. It assured to the members of Parliament the right of free speech, immunity from prosecution for statements made in debate, and freedom from royal intervention in elections. It forbade a variety of acts that had long been the basis for royal absolutism: taxing without consent of Parliament, dispensing with laws, maintaining a standing army in peacetime, requiring excessive bail, depriving citizens of the right to trial in the regular courts, interfering with jurors, and denying people the right to petition the king. The Bill of Rights implied that government was based on a contract between ruler and ruled, a concept of government increasingly attractive among "enlightened" leaders in western Europe. This theory of government was set forth with special force by John Locke in his *Two Treatises on Civil Government*, published in 1690. Locke argued that a government was the product of a contract entered into by rational people in order to establish an authority capable of protecting rights that belonged to all humans by the laws of nature: the right of life, liberty, and property. Any government that violated these natural rights broke the contract that brought it into existence; in this event its subjects had a right to correct or even overthrow it. For settlement of the long-standing religious issue a Toleration Act was passed, allowing religious freedom to Puritans and Independents but not to non-Protestants. Finally, the Act of Settlement was passed in 1701 to ensure that none but Protestants could inherit the throne.

The initial settlement marking the Glorious Revolution certainly addressed in a positive way fundamental issues that had troubled England for nearly a century. However, there remained problems still to be resolved. The accession of William and Mary resulted in a basic reorientation of England's foreign policy, which called on the nation to commit its resources to a long, burdensome series of wars in many parts of the globe to prevent France from establishing world dominance. We have already seen (Chapter 32) the decisive role that England played in foiling Louis XIV's ambitions. Closer to home Ireland was brought under English control. Early in his reign William led an army into this unhappy land, where discontent had long festered and which now became a center of Stuart intrigue—funded by the French—aimed at recovering the English throne. Having established control by force, William instituted a policy of suppression, reducing Ireland to colonial status, a policy that provided splendid opportunity for English landlords to uproot Irish Catholic landowners and take possession of their property. Scotland enjoyed an easier fate in the face of increasing English power. Early in his reign William began negotiations with the Scots that finally bore fruit after his death. In 1707 Parliament passed the Act of Union, which joined the two kingdoms into a single nation henceforth known as the United Kingdom of Great Britain. The settlement gave the Scots a liberal number of seats in Parliament and guaranteed their Presbyterian religious establishment.

The burdens of global war placed stresses on the political system and led to important changes. As we have already seen, Parliament was actively engaged in defining the settlement after the Glorious Revolution. Its role in political life intensified thereafter, chiefly because its approval was needed for taxes. Annual government expenditures increased threefold between the reign of Charles II and the reign of William and Mary. To meet these expenditures, the monarchs had to call Parliament nearly every year. Frequent sessions of Parliament required that the royal government pay special attention to the election process in search of sufficient votes from qualified voters—chiefly property owners—to secure a majority in Parliament willing to support royal policy. Because Parliament was increasingly important, party strife between Whigs and Tories became a decisive feature of political life. Party leaders played an ever-larger role in counseling the rulers and overseeing public affairs. This ever-increasing identification of Parliament with the management of the nation's affairs probably did more than the noble principles of the Bill of Rights to make secure parliamentary control of public life.

The progress toward parliamentary supremacy following the Glorious Revolution left unresolved one major constitutional issue—that of the exact nature of the executive power responsible for the conduct of the routine affairs of state. For centuries, English kings had relied on powerful ministers to assist them in conducting government affairs and in shaping policy. Until 1688, these ministers had usually been chosen by the king and were responsible to him. After the supremacy of

Parliament was established in 1688–1689, this system began to change with the emergence of the *cabinet system*. Royal ministers were increasingly chosen on the basis of their ability to influence Parliament, especially the House of Commons. Since Commons tended to divide into parties that controlled large blocs of votes, it proved wisest for the rulers to seek out party leaders from that body for appointment as ministers responsible for exercising executive functions.

With the accession of Anne (1702–1714), this trend developed rapidly. Neither she nor the first Hanoverians, George I (1714–1727) and George II (1727–1760), were especially qualified for or interested in the rigorous tasks of administration. As a consequence, the direction of the government and the formulation of policy fell into the hands of royal ministers able to secure from Parliament approval to carry on the affairs of state in the name of the monarch. This *cabinet* of ministers slowly learned to accept mutual responsibility for the total operation of the government, which required that they all be members of the same party and that they use their collective influence in Parliament to ensure approval of their program. If they failed to command a majority in that body, then they had to surrender their positions as ministers in favor of a new cabinet that did have a parliamentary majority. One member of the cabinet, the *prime minister*, came to be recognized as the leader and spokesperson of the whole group; a major qualification for this designation was leadership of the majority party in Commons.

Although Queen Anne relied heavily on John Churchill, duke of Marlborough, to conduct her government, the first real prime minister and architect of the cabinet system was Robert Walpole (see Figure 33.1). A longtime member of Commons, he became George I's chief minister in 1721, primarily because of his leadership of the dominant Whig party in Commons. From then until 1742 he virtually ran England by surrounding himself with fellow ministers who could control votes in Parliament. Not until he lost control of Commons over a foreign policy issue was he forced to relinquish his position as prime minister. However, the king had little choice but to appoint another prime minister and cabinet that could command a majority in Parliament. Henceforth to the present the executive functions of government in Great Britain would be carried out in the name of the monarch by a circle of party leaders who could command a majority in the House of Commons but who were likewise required to render account to that body for their conduct of public affairs.

The Glorious Revolution and the settlement that followed it marked a turning point in Great Britain's history. Two great decisions had been reached. First, royal absolutism had been repudiated in favor of a limited monarchy in which ultimate authority was entrusted to an elected Parliament. Second, religious uniformity had given way to religious toleration for all Protestants. The resolution of these issues restored Great Britain's internal stability and provided a basis for its rapid advance to the status of world power. However, the "revolution" had its limitations: Even as it unfolded, steps were taken to limit eligibility for Parliament to men of wealth, chiefly landowners. Until the nineteenth century these "gentlemen" dominated Great Britain in a fashion that served their collective interests.

5. THE DUTCH NETHERLANDS

Absolutism was also successfully challenged during the seventeenth century by the Dutch. Their success led to the creation of a new nation in which prevailed a political and social environment that allowed the Dutch to forge for themselves a leadership role in European commerce, banking, and intellectual and artistic life. That new nation emerged from the Dutch refusal to accept the absolutist system that Philip II of Spain attempted to force on them (see Chapter 31). Although Philip II was able to impose Spanish rule over the ten southern provinces of the Netherlands (now Belgium; see Map 33.1), the seven northern provinces resisted and by 1609 had established effective independence as the United Provinces of the Netherlands; independence was officially recognized by the Treaty of Westphalia (1648).

The new state adopted a republican form of government. Each province, ruled by an elected executive (called the stadholder) and a provincial representative assembly, retained extensive control over local affairs. Although most of the stad-

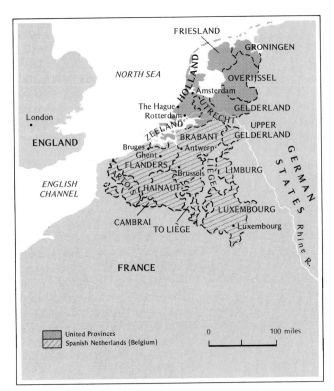

Map 33.1 **THE UNITED PROVINCES, 1609**
This map illustrates how small a territory the Dutch Republic occupied in its golden age—no larger than a corner of England. Yet through the cities of this small area flowed much of the commerce of the seventeenth and eighteenth centuries. With that commerce came a flow of money that made such cities as Amsterdam the financial centers of the world.

holders came from the landed aristocracy, especially from the House of Orange, a powerful family that had played a crucial role in the struggle for independence, the provincial governments were dominated by commercial and financial leaders who resisted the establishment of strong central government. The only truly national political institution was the States General, made up of delegates from each province who acted only on instructions from the provincial governments. It enjoyed limited powers and asserted very little direction over national affairs. The citizens of the Dutch Netherlands enjoyed considerable freedom to pursue their personal and collective interests. Particularly noteworthy was religious freedom. The Reformed church, strongly Calvinist in doctrine and practice, was established by law, but other religious groups, including Roman Catholics and Jews, were tolerated, a fact that attracted religious refugees from other European nations.

The Dutch Netherlands, a nation of only about one million, made its chief mark on the seventeenth-century world in commerce and finance. That success was based on the seafaring skills of its people and the entrepreneurship of its vigorous bourgeoisie. Those talents, developed over many centuries, allowed the Dutch to become world leaders in commerce. Experienced Dutch sailors plundered Spanish commerce and overseas colonies to reap a rich reward. When Spain temporarily annexed Portugal in 1580, the Dutch seized most of Portugal's lucrative holdings in the East Indies. The Dutch East India Company, set up in 1602 to develop trade with the East Indies, returned huge profits to its stockholders during the entire seventeenth century. The Dutch established a flourishing colony in North America. Dutch traders also took advantage of their favorable geographical position at the mouth of the Rhine and its tributaries and of their excellent harbors along the northern European trade routes to gain a near-monopoly of the carrying trade of Europe. A large

FIGURE 33.3. **Rembrandt, "Syndics of the Cloth Guild"** In the Dutch Netherlands of the seventeenth century, commerce was king. Under the leadership of such men as shown here, the tiny Dutch Netherlands attained a first-rank position in the world of science, philosophy, and trade. Rembrandt, one of the greatest portrait painters of all time, was probably also the greatest of the baroque painters. (Fotocommissie Rijks-museum Amsterdam)

proportion of Europe's ships were built in Dutch shipyards.

The extensive trading activities of the Dutch led to a huge flow of wealth into the hands of Dutch merchants. This capital allowed them to become Europe's leading money lenders, serving princes, merchants, and landowners willing to pay for the use of Dutch capital. The financial activities of the Dutch were institutionalized in the Bank of Amsterdam, set up in 1609. It became a model for national banks later established elsewhere in western Europe. Its location in Amsterdam reflected the fact that that city had become the world's chief commercial and financial center.

The wealth and the freedom of Dutch society generated a vigorous cultural outburst. Some of the chief intellectuals in Europe found refuge in the United Provinces, including the philosophers René Descartes from France, John Locke from England, and Baruch Spinoza, a Jewish refugee from Portugal. Among the notable Dutch intellectuals was Hugo Grotius, whose *On the Law of War and Peace* was the first great treatise on international law and has remained a classic on the subject ever since. Freedom of the press enabled the United Provinces to become the leading European center of book publishing. This was the golden age of Dutch painters. While baroque painters in other countries were glorifying royalty and nobility, Jan Vermeer, Franz Hals, and above all, Rembrandt van Rijn were celebrating the spirit of Dutch society by dignifying—sometimes glamorizing—the middle and lower classes (see Figure 33.3). Dutch scientists played an important role in advancing the Scientific Revolution, including the invention of the telescope and the microscope. All of these activities gave the Dutch an important role in western European literary, intellectual, and artistic life.

As the seventeenth century drew to a close, the Dutch preeminence in commerce and banking began to decline, especially in the face of England's sea power and France's land might. But that decline could not efface the notable contributions of the Dutch to seventeenth-century western European civilization, a contribution due at least in part to the freedom enjoyed by Dutch citizens to assert their talents as they chose.

SUGGESTED READING

General Treatments

J. P. Kenyon, *Stuart England* (1978).
Barry Coward, *The Stuart Age. A History of England 1603–1714* (1980).
Either of these works will provide a fine overview of Stuart England.
Derek Hirst, *Authority and Conflict: England, 1603–1658* (1986).
J. R. Jones, *Country and Court, England, 1658–1714* (1978).
These two volumes, parts of a new general history of England, give a balanced treatment of the period.
Christopher Hill, *A Century of Revolution, 1603–1714*, 2nd ed. (1982). A provocative study from a Marxist perspective.
C. G. A. Clay, *Economic Expansion and Social Change, England, 1500–1700*, 2 vols. (1984). An excellent synthesis, rich in details.

From Civil War to the Glorious Revolution

Robert Ashton, *Reformation and Revolution, 1558–1660* (1985). Helps to establish the background for England's revolutionary age.
Lawrence Stone, *The Causes of the English Revolution, 1529–1642* (1972). Analyzes various interpretations of the causes of the English revolution.
G. E. Aylmer, *Rebellion or Revolution? England, 1640–1660* (1986). A balanced treatment of the civil war and the era of Cromwell.
C. V. Wedgwood, *The King's Peace, 1637–1641* (1955); *The King's War, 1641–1647* (1959); and *A Coffin for King Charles* (1964). Brilliant treatments of the crucial years of the English civil war.
Christopher Hill, *The World Turned Upside Down: Radical Ideas During the English Revolution* (1972). An important work on radicalism.

Patrick Morrah, *Restoration England* (1979). A good social history.
John Miller, *The Glorious Revolution* (1983). A brief, thoughtful description and assessment of the Glorious Revolution.
P. Laslett, *The World We Have Lost*, 2nd ed. (1971). A brilliant evocation of the English society of about 1700.

The Dutch Netherlands

Pieter Geyl, *The Netherlands in the Seventeenth Century*, rev. ed., 2 vols. (1961–1964). An excellent detailed treatment.
Charles Wilson, *The Dutch Republic and the Civilisation of the Seventeenth Century* (1968).
K. H. D. Haley, *The Dutch in the Seventeenth Century* (1972).
Two brief treatments that will help the reader to understand Dutch society in its most glorious age.
C. R. Boxer, *The Dutch Seaborne Empire, 1600–1800* (1965). A good description of the source of much of Dutch wealth.
Simon Schama, *The Embarrassment of Riches. An Interpretation of Dutch Culture in the Golden Age* (1987). A brilliant portrayal of social life.

Biographies

Pauline Gregg, *King Charles I* (1981).
Antonia Fraser, *Cromwell. The Lord Protector* (1973).
Antonia Fraser, *Royal Charles: Charles II and the Restoration* (1979).
S. Baxter, *William III and the Defense of European Liberty, 1650–1702* (1966).

CHAPTER 34

Eastern Europe and the Rise of Prussia and Russia

FIGURE 34.1. Frederick II Before His Troops During the seventeenth and eighteenth centuries, the rulers of Brandenburg-Prussia used their armies to build up the state, making it one of the major powers of eastern and central Europe. Here, Frederick II of Prussia is shown in a characteristic military pose, exemplifying the strong alliance of the monarchy and army. (The Mansell Collection)

At the beginning of the seventeenth century eastern Europe exhibited certain characteristics that set it in sharp contrast to western Europe. Economically, the states east of the Elbe River were less commercially developed than those in western Europe. Estate agriculture (large landed estates owned by lords and worked by their serfs) remained the rule. Socially, the landed aristocracy dominated these areas to a greater extent than in western Europe. Indeed, this aristocracy had generally succeeded in reversing medieval trends toward greater freedom for the peasantry and the growth of towns. During the fifteenth, sixteenth, and seventeenth centuries serfdom was reimposed with greater severity than ever, and the landed aristocracy won in its struggle with competing urban centers. Politically, many areas lacked the strong central government found in the western European states. In political struggles the nobility had sometimes gained the upper hand over monarchs. Nowhere was this pattern more marked than in Poland, where there was a corresponding decline in the strength of the state to the point that Poland was literally divided and annexed by outside powers during the eighteenth century. Yet the seventeenth and eighteenth centuries would witness some important changes in eastern Europe, particularly in political affairs.

The most significant political developments in central and eastern Europe during the seventeenth and eighteenth centuries were the rise of Prussia and Russia. At the opening of the seventeenth century, the two chief powers in central and eastern Europe were the Ottoman and Hapsburg empires. Although the Moslem Ottoman Turks had been restrained by Hapsburg military power in the sixteenth century on both land and sea, they were about to renew their effort to conquer Christian Europe. The Austrian Hapsburgs, in addition to disputing the control of southeastern Europe with the Turks, dominated the Holy Roman Empire, which included all the German states. In northeastern Europe, Sweden, Prussia, Poland, and Russia competed for hegemony. Among all these powers, Prussia and Russia had hitherto been the least conspicuous in world affairs. During the seventeenth and eighteenth centuries, Prussia and Russia would become major powers and assume active roles in international politics.

1. THE EARLY HOHENZOLLERNS

The history of Prussia is in large measure the history of the Hohenzollern family. This aggressive and prolific dynasty was first heard of in the tenth century. At that time the Hohenzollerns were obscure counts ruling over the castle of Zollern and a tiny bit of surrounding territory in southwest Germany just north of the Swiss border. In the twelfth century they became burgraves of Nuremberg, an important commercial city in Bavaria. Early in the fifteenth century the Holy Roman emperor, looking for an able ruler for the mark of Brandenburg, a military province near the exposed northeastern border of the empire, chose the head of the house of Hohenzollern. Although its ruler was one of the seven electors of the Holy Roman emperor, Brandenburg was a bleak and thinly populated little province. Yet around this nucleus the Hohenzollerns built the important state of Prussia and, later, the German Empire (see Map 34.1).

From the time the Hohenzollerns became margraves of Brandenburg (1415) until they were finally overthrown at the end of World War I in 1918, they followed a threefold policy: militarism and territorial aggrandizement, paternal despotism, and centralized bureaucracy. The first to take major steps toward making Brandenburg an important power was Frederick William (1640–1688), the Great Elector. One of the ablest of all the Hohenzollerns, he acquired several new territories at the end of the Thirty Years' War. He centralized and administered the governments of his scattered territories with energy and skill. He won in his struggles with the Estates, the representative assemblies of the realm, gaining the crucial power to collect taxes and eliminating the Estates as a functioning institution. He established and strengthened his standing army. He managed an important compromise with the landed aristocracy, allowing them complete control over their serfs but committing them to his government as members of his bureaucracy and his military officer corps. He protected the native industries, improved communications, and aided agriculture. In a most intolerant age he followed a policy of religious toleration. When Louis XIV revoked the Edict of Nantes in 1685, Frederick William wel-

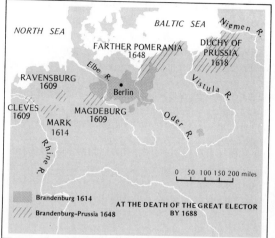

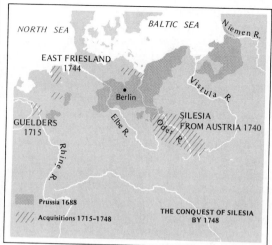

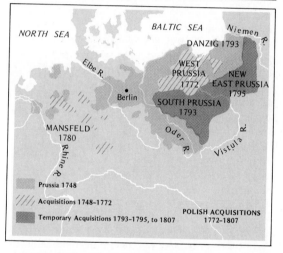

Map 34.1 **THE GROWTH OF PRUSSIA, 1614–1807**
These maps show the growth of Brandenburg-Prussia during the seventeenth and eighteenth centuries. The maps reveal the lack of connections between many of Brandenburg-Prussia's lands; one of Prussia's long-term goals in the eighteenth and nineteenth centuries was to connect those territories it already controlled as well as to expand its holdings.

comed thousands of industrious Huguenots to Brandenburg. At the death of the Great Elector in 1688, Brandenburg was on the road to becoming a great power.

The next Hohenzollern, Frederick I (1688–1713), acquired the title of king for the dynasty. The Hapsburg Holy Roman emperor in 1701 granted Frederick the title in return for aid against Louis XIV in the War of the Spanish Succession. Frederick I chose Prussia rather than Brandenburg for the name of his kingdom, since Prussia was outside the Holy Roman Empire and a free sov-

ereign state. Hence Brandenburg became Prussia.

From 1713 to 1740 Prussia was ruled by a vigorous militaristic autocrat, Frederick William I (since he was the first Frederick William to be king). Unquestioned absolutism, machinelike centralized bureaucratic administration, and, above all, militarism were his obsessions. He built the Prussian army into the most efficient and one of the largest fighting forces in Europe. And yet Frederick William was so efficient and miserly that he was also able to pass along to his talented son, Frederick II, a well-filled treasury.

2. COMPETITION WITH THE AUSTRIAN HAPSBURGS AND THE EMERGENCE OF PRUSSIA AS A GREAT POWER

In the same year that Frederick II became king of Prussia (1740), the beautiful and gracious young Maria Theresa became archduchess of the Austrian Hapsburg dominions. These dominions included, in addition to the Austrian lands, the Kingdom of Hungary and the triune crown of Bohemia, Moravia, and Silesia. After the Thirty Years' War, the Austrian Hapsburgs initiated a long policy of centralizing their power in those lands they directly controlled (rather than the Holy Roman Empire) and expanding to the east. This policy was effectively carried out during the second half of the seventeenth century and the eighteenth century. The monarchy improved its administration, established a powerful standing army, gained at least a fragile allegiance of the nobility, and acquired territories at the expense of the Ottoman Empire and Poland. Maria Theresa's father, Emperor Charles VI, had spent much time in his last years attempting to safeguard his daughter's accession to the Hapsburg throne. He succeeded in obtaining the signatures of virtually every European sovereign, including the king of Prussia, for a document called the Pragmatic Sanction, which guaranteed the integrity of Maria Theresa's crown and territories. Two months after Charles VI died, however, Frederick II, without a declaration of war, marched his troops into and seized Silesia, one of the richest of the Hapsburg provinces. This Machiavellian act of the young Prussian king plunged most of the major European states into a series of wars for the mastery of central Europe.

The War of the Austrian Succession lasted for eight years (1740–1748). Maria Theresa successfully repelled the Bavarians, Saxons, French, and Spaniards, but she was unable to dislodge Frederick II from Silesia. Frederick, on his part, cynically deserted his allies as soon as he had achieved his own purposes. The Treaty of Aix-la-Chapelle in 1748 brought the hostilities to an end. Frederick retained Silesia, and Maria Theresa's husband, Francis of Lorraine, was recognized as Holy Roman emperor. The only real gainer from the war was Frederick II. Silesia, a fertile province inhabited by more than a million German-speaking people, nearly doubled the population and resources of Prussia.

The Hapsburgs, however, had no intention of being thus despoiled of one of their fairest provinces by the upstart Hohenzollerns. Proud rulers over territories many times the size and population of Prussia and for centuries emperors of the Holy Roman Empire, they viewed the Hohenzollerns with condescension. Maria Theresa's able diplomat, Count Kaunitz, was soon at work lining up allies. Saxony, Sweden, Russia, and even France were won over. Spain, now ruled by the Bourbons, later followed France into the alliance. This time, however, Great Britain took the side of Prussia. Great Britain did this in order to oppose its archenemy France, with whom it was already at war in India and North America, and to safeguard Hanover. This double shifting of alliances came to be called the Diplomatic Revolution.

Frederick was not one to wait for his enemies to strike first. As soon as he became aware of their designs, he opened hostilities by overrunning Saxony. Thus began the Seven Years' War (1756–1763). Frederick, with his slender resources, soon found himself at bay; the four greatest military powers on the continent of Europe were closing in on him from all directions. After tenaciously holding his enemies off for six years, defeat appeared to be near. Then in 1762 the Russian Tsarina Elizabeth, one of his bitterest enemies, died and was succeeded by the ineffective Peter III, who was an ardent admirer of Frederick II and who put Russia's forces at the disposal of Prussia. Although Peter III was soon murdered by a group of his own officers and court nobility and Russia withdrew from the war, the remaining allies had no further stomach for the fight. The Peace of Hubertusburg in 1763 left things as they were at the beginning of the war, Prussia retaining the controversial Silesia. In the same year the Treaty of Paris brought to a close the colonial struggle between Great Britain and France in India and North America, leaving Great Britain master of both.

Having so narrowly escaped destruction, Frederick the Great spent the remaining twenty-three years of his life reconstructing his war-ravaged territories. He encouraged agriculture, subsidized and protected industry, and invited immigrants into his well-governed territories. At no time, though, did he neglect his war machine. In 1772 he joined Austria and Russia in the first partition of Poland. Frederick took West Prussia, thus joining East Prussia with the main body of the Prussian state. When Frederick II died in 1786, Prussia had been raised to the status of a great power, sharing equally with Austria the leadership of central Europe. During his reign Prussia's size and population had more than doubled, and its military exploits pointed to a spectacular future.

3. RUSSIA BEFORE PETER THE GREAT

While Prussia was becoming a great power in central Europe, Russia was rising to prominence to the east. The first shaping of some of the Slavic tribes of eastern Europe into what eventually became the Russian national state was begun by Viking invaders in the ninth century. These intrepid seafarers moved out from their Scandinavian homes in all directions—across the Atlantic, into the Mediterranean, and up the rivers of what are now England, France, Germany, and Russia (the word *Russia* is apparently derived from the Swedish word for rower). Their most important commercial and political center in eastern Europe was Kiev, which became Russia's first capital. Eventually the Norse invaders adopted the Slavic culture of their subjects.

In the tenth century Christianity was brought to Russia by missionaries from Constantinople. Through the influence of the Greek Orthodox church, whose headquarters were in Constantinople, Russia became a somewhat Byzantine civilization, differing from the Greco-Roman and Roman Catholic culture common to the countries of central and western Europe.

A second crucial influence on Russian civilization was the Mongol conquest of the thirteenth century. Around the turn of the thirteenth century the Mongol conqueror Genghis Khan (1162–1227) had established a vast empire in eastern Asia. Shortly after his death the Golden Horde, as the

Mongol warriors were called, swept westward into Christian Europe. The thirteenth-century Europeans were no match for the Mongols. Russia was easily overrun, and in 1241 a combined German and Polish army was defeated at Liegnitz in the heart of central Europe. All Christian Europe appeared to be at the mercy of the invaders. At that moment, however, the great khan died in eastern Asia, and the Mongol commander withdrew his forces to Russia and hastened back to seize his share of the spoils. The Golden Horde never resumed its triumphal surge westward, but for two and a half centuries it inundated Russia and there was considerable mixing of cultures.

During the Mongol occupation the grand dukes of Muscovy managed to ingratiate themselves with their Mongol masters and build up their own influence and power. The first of the grand dukes of Muscovy under whom Russia took on the shape of a modern national state was Ivan III (1462–1505). In 1480 Ivan III defeated the rapidly declining Mongols and limited their power in Russia to the southeastern area. Ivan greatly extended his sway both to the north and to the west by military conquest. After his marriage to Sophia Palaeologus, heiress to the now-defunct Byzantine (Eastern Roman) Empire, Ivan declared himself successor to the Eastern Roman Caesars—hence the title Tsar. When he died, the foundations of a Russian national state had been laid (see Map 34.2).

Ivan IV (1533–1584), "the Terrible," added both to the authority of the Russian tsars and to the territories over which they ruled. He destroyed the remaining power of the Mongols in southeastern Russia and annexed most of their territory. The Ottoman Turks, however, seized the strategic Mongol territory north of the Black Sea. Although Ivan IV established trade relations with England by way of the White Sea and the Arctic Ocean, his efforts to gain a foothold on the Baltic were frustrated by Sweden and Poland. It was during Ivan IV's reign that Russia's conquest of Siberia was begun. Half a century later the Russian flag was planted on the shores of the Pacific.

The twenty-nine years following the death of Ivan IV are known as the Time of Troubles (1584–1613). Weak rulers and disputed successions resulted in such anarchy that the Poles were able to

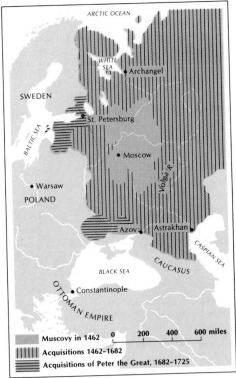

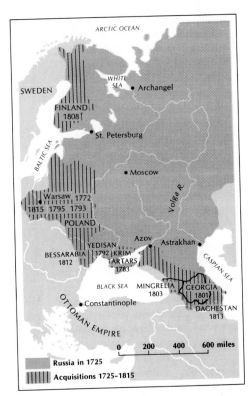

Map 34.2 **THE GROWTH OF RUSSIA IN THE WEST** These maps show the steady expansion of Russia to the west and south, acquiring access on the Baltic Sea and Black Sea under Peter the Great and extending its territories further in the course of the eighteenth century.

capture Moscow and hold it briefly. To end the political chaos, a group of leading nobles in 1613 chose Michael Romanov as tsar.

The early decades of the Romanov dynasty, which was to rule Russia until the Revolution of 1917, were not easy. There were great popular discontent and numerous uprisings between the late 1640s and the early 1670s as the lower classes rebelled against the nobles and the central government, who were making serfdom even more onerous and life for townspeople more difficult. The discontent reached a climax with the revolts led by Stenka Razin in the late 1660s and early 1670s. Razin was finally caught and executed, soon ending that series of threats. During this

same period problems within the Russian Orthodox church broke out as many, known as the Old Believers, rejected liturgical changes initiated by the patriarch of Moscow. The effect of this controversy was to drive the Church into greater dependence on the secular government. Nevertheless by the final decades of the seventeenth century the Romanov tsars had managed to overcome these problems, improve the central administration, and extend their authority. They gradually established commercial and cultural contacts with the West. Increasing numbers of traders, artisans, and adventurers from central and western Europe, particularly Germany, came to Russia to seek their fortunes. Thus the stage was set for Russia to become more fully involved in European affairs. This involvement became especially important during the reign of Peter the Great.

4. RUSSIA UNDER PETER THE GREAT, 1689–1725

Peter I (1689–1725) was an unusually large, vigorous, and ambitious individual (see Figure 34.2). At the age of seventeen he seized the reins of government from his elder sister. For the next thirty-six years he devoted his boundless energy to the twofold policy of strengthening his own authority and his military forces and of gaining access to the west on the Baltic and Black seas.

Peter concluded that one of the best ways to increase his own political and military power was to copy Western practices. He traveled in western Europe and learned much about Western customs and techniques, which he proceeded to introduce into Russia. After crushing a revolt of his bodyguard with a ruthlessness that cowed all potential troublemakers, he adopted the bureaucratic system of western European monarchs in both central and local government to make his authority more absolute. Western technicians were brought to Russia in large numbers and new industries were subsidized and protected by mercantilist policies. Western, particularly French, social customs were introduced to the upper and middle classes of Russian society. Women were brought out of seclusion, and the long beards and flowing Oriental robes of the men were banned. These reforms hardly touched the peasant masses, who were increasingly tied down in a system of serfdom bordering on slavery—a process that had been going on in Russia throughout the sixteenth and seventeenth centuries. When the patriarch of the Russian Orthodox church opposed the tsar's authority and some of his Westernizing policies, Peter abolished the patriarchate. He placed at the head of the church a Holy Synod composed of a committee of bishops and presided over by a lay procurator-general, all appointed by the tsar. Henceforth, the Orthodox church was a powerful instrument of the Russian government. But Peter the Great's chief concern was always his military

FIGURE 34.2. Peter the Great Peter the Great was a physical giant. This portrait gives us a hint of the vigor and forcefulness that he put to use in Westernizing and modernizing Russia, making the nation a military power to be reckoned with. (Culver Pictures)

establishment. He built a navy and patterned his conscript army after that of Prussia. By the end of his reign, Russia had one of the major fighting forces of Europe.

When Peter became tsar, Russia had no warm-water access to the West. Sweden held the coveted shores of the Baltic Sea, and the Ottoman Turks occupied the territory north of the Black Sea. Peter's efforts to dislodge the Ottoman Turks were not very successful, but after an extended, costly war with Sweden, in which Peter lost early battles to his adversary Charles XII, Peter's efforts were rewarded. By the Treaty of Nystad in 1721, Russia received the Swedish Baltic provinces of Livonia, Estonia, Ingria, and Karelia. On the Neva River near the Baltic, Peter built a new modern capital, St. Petersburg, facing the West. At his death in 1725, Russia was a great and growing power ready to play a major role in European affairs.

5. RUSSIA UNDER CATHERINE THE GREAT, 1762–1796

Peter the Great was followed by a succession of weak or mediocre rulers. After an interval of thirty-seven years, Catherine the Great (1762–1796) ascended the Russian throne. Catherine was an obscure princess from one of the little German states. She had been married for political reasons to young Peter III, grandson of Peter the Great, while he was still heir to the Russian crown. After he became tsar, Peter III quickly alienated all classes of his subjects. Less than a year after her husband became tsar, Catherine conspired with a group of aristocratic army officers, who murdered Peter and declared Catherine tsarina of Russia.

The Machiavellian tsarina prided herself on being an enlightened despot, as was fashionable in the late eighteenth century, but few of those enlightened ideas were translated into political or social deeds. Some apparent reforming efforts ended when Russian serfs rose in one of the greatest insurrections in history. In 1773, under the able leadership of a Don Cossack, Pugachev, hundreds of thousands of serfs marched against their masters. The rebellion was put down with difficulty. The cruel repression left Russian serfs almost as slaves to the privileged nobility.

The chief significance of Catherine the Great in political history lies in her aggressive foreign policy (see Figure 34.3). Peter the Great had reached the Baltic by despoiling the Swedes. Catherine reached the Black Sea, the Balkan peninsula, and the heart of Europe by defeating the Turks and destroying Poland. In two major wars between 1768 and 1792 Catherine defeated the Turks and seized all of their territory north of the Black Sea as far west as the Balkan peninsula. Russia also gained a vague protectorate over the Christians in the Ottoman Empire, which provided a standing opportunity to meddle in the internal affairs of the Turks. But Catherine fell short of her real goal, Constantinople. By 1772 Russia, Prussia, and Austria had already seized strips of Poland. In 1793 Russia and Prussia enlarged their holdings, and in 1795 the three powers divided among themselves the remainder of the once huge Poland. Catherine's share, which was about two-thirds of the total, brought Russia's western boundary deep into central Europe. The second and third partitions of Poland and concern over the French Revolution, which began in 1789, absorbed Catherine's energies during the last years of her life. When she finally died in 1796, Russia was a nation ominous in size and power and a major factor in European and world affairs.

6. THE DISAPPEARANCE OF POLAND AND THE DECLINE OF SWEDEN AND THE OTTOMAN EMPIRE

Poland, at the opening of the eighteenth century, was the third largest country in Europe, exceeded in size only by Russia and Sweden. In the sixteenth and seventeenth centuries it had appeared that Poland would become a major power. Taking advantage of Russia's Time of Troubles (1584–1613), the Poles had captured Moscow. In the latter part of the century they had saved Vienna from the Turks.

Actually, however, the Polish nation was far from strong. Sprawling over a large area between Russia and the German states, it enjoyed no natural boundaries either to the east or the west. The eastern half of its territory was inhabited by Russian-speaking people. The northern provinces were peopled largely by Latvians, Lithuanians, and Germans. There were also many Germans in the west. Religious cleavages followed the language lines.

Moreover, there was no strong middle class to vitalize Poland's economy. In the late Middle Ages a sizable overland commerce between the Black and Baltic seas had flowed across Poland. But with the shifting of commercial routes and centers to the west in the early sixteenth century, Poland's commerce had withered. Furthermore, the Polish nobility, jealous of its own power and fearful of

FIGURE 34.3. Catherine the Great Catherine the Great's territorial ambitions are satirized in this cartoon, which shows her leaping toward her coveted goal, Constantinople, as the pope and other European leaders look on in dismay. (NYPL Picture Collection)

an alliance between the bourgeoisie and the king, deliberately penalized commerce with severe restrictions. The great mass of the people were serfs, tilling the soil of the powerful nobility.

In the face of so many divisive forces, only a strong central government could have made Poland a stable national state. But here lay Poland's greatest weakness. The kingship was elective, and the great nobles who held the elective power saw to it that no strong king ever came to the throne.

During the eighteenth century the kings were all foreigners or puppets of foreign powers. The legislative Diet was completely monopolized by the nobility. So that each noble's rights were safeguarded, unanimity was required for the passage of every measure. Thus any noble could veto any proposed law (*liberum veto*). In addition, any noble could disband ("explode") the Diet and cancel all its acts. This system guaranteed virtual political anarchy. National spirit was weak. The all-pow-

Map 34.3 EASTERN EUROPE, SIXTEENTH–EIGHTEENTH CENTURIES Between the sixteenth and eighteenth centuries, political power in central and eastern Europe shifted fundamentally. The first map shows the Holy Roman Empire, Poland, and the Ottoman Empire in the sixteenth and early seventeenth centuries. The second map shows that by the eighteenth century, these powers had all but been replaced by Prussia, the Russian Empire, and the Austrian Empire.

erful nobles were far more concerned for their own private interests than for the well-being of the nation.

It would have been surprising had such a power vacuum as eighteenth-century Poland not invited the aggression of its ambitious neighbors. In 1772 Catherine the Great and Frederick the Great bargained to take slices of Polish territory. The somewhat less greedy Maria Theresa of Austria, fearful of being outdistanced by Russia and Prussia, joined them. This aggression at long last stirred the Poles to action. Sweeping reforms were passed, improving the condition of the peasants and the bourgeoisie and giving the king and the Diet power to act effectively. But it was too late. Russia and Prussia were determined to prevent the emergence of a vigorous Polish nation. In 1793 they marched in and seized additional slices of territory. The Poles, under the leadership of Thaddeus Kosciusko, now flew to arms, although the arms were often only agricultural implements. They were no match for the professional armies of Russia, Prussia, and Austria, who in 1795 divided the remainder of Poland among themselves.

Poland was not the only victim in eastern Europe of the powerful Russian, Prussian, and Austrian armies. Sweden and the Ottoman Empire declined, both relatively and actually. Sweden had become the dominant military power in northern and eastern Europe under Gustavus Adolphus in the early seventeenth century. At the opening of the eighteenth century Sweden was second only to Russia in size among the nations of Europe, holding large areas east and south of the Baltic in addition to the homeland. However, its population and resources were too small to hold for long such far-flung territories, which were coveted by ambitious and growing Prussia and Russia. Charles XII made a spectacular effort to hold them, but in the end he lost all his trans-Baltic territories except Finland, and he dissipated Sweden's strength in so doing. Sweden has never been a major power since.

The Ottoman Turks, after reaching the gates of Vienna early in the sixteenth century and again late in the seventeenth century, weakened rapidly. The Treaty of Karlowitz in 1699 limited their power in Europe to the Balkan peninsula and a strip of territory north of the Black Sea. Their two serious defeats at the hands of Catherine the Great marked the beginning of the breakup of the Ottoman Empire.

By the end of the eighteenth century, the three dominant powers in central and eastern Europe were the relativeiy static Austrian Hapsburg Empire and the two rapidly rising states—Prussia and Russia (see Map 34.3). Each of these states had developed strong central governments with standing armies, large bureaucracies, and organized systems of taxation under the monarch's control.

SUGGESTED READING

General

D. McKay and H. Scott, *The Rise of the Great Powers, 1648–1815* (1983). A good recent survey.

I. Woloch, *Eighteenth-Century Europe: Tradition and Progress 1715–1789* (1982). A recent, thorough introduction.

Rise of Prussia

F. L. Carsten, *The Origins of Prussia* (1954). A solid, brief account of the reign of the great elector, Frederick William.

G. Craig, *The Politics of the Prussian Army, 1640–1945* (1964). A highly respected analysis of the influences of the Prussian Army.

H. Holborn, *A History of Modern Germany 1648–1840* (1966). Best on the subject.

H. C. Johnson, *Frederick the Great and His Officials* (1975). Focuses on Prussian administration.

The Austrian Hapsburgs

R. J. Evans, *The Making of the Hapsburg Empire, 1550–1770* (1979). A solid, recent account.

Rise of Russia

P. Dukes, *The Making of Russian Absolutism: 1613–1801* (1982). A solid survey.

I. de Madariaga, *Russia in the Age of Catherine the Great* (1981). Highly regarded recent study.

B. H. Sumner, *Peter the Great and the Emergence of Russia* (1962). A brief introduction.

A. Yanov, *Origins of Autocracy: Ivan the Terrible in Russian History* (1981). Excellent recent analysis.

Disappearance of Poland and Decline of Sweden and Ottoman Empire

P. Coles, *The Ottoman Impact on Europe, 1350–1699* (1968). A well-written study.

O. Halecki, *A History of Poland* (1961). Sound coverage of the partitions.

R. N. Hatton, *Charles XII of Sweden* (1968). An excellent, thorough biography.

CHAPTER 35

Overseas Colonization and Competition for Empire

FIGURE 35.1. The Taking of Quebec, 1759 This eighteenth-century engraving shows British forces capturing Quebec from the French in 1759. This victory was a major turning point in the eighteenth-century competition for world empire. (Library of Congress)

During the age of royal absolutism, the European nations intensified their competition for overseas possessions and commerce. They were spurred on in large part by the riches that flowed to Europe from these possessions but also by a conviction that overseas possessions enhanced the power of nations. Whereas Spain and Portugal had led the way beyond the Atlantic frontier during the sixteenth century, England, France, and the Netherlands threw themselves vigorously into colonizing and commercial expansion in various quarters of the globe during the seventeenth and eighteenth centuries. The newcomers indeed outstripped their older rivals and established themselves as the leading European colonial powers. As large as the world beyond western Europe was, the competition for it led to struggles among the leading European powers; the outcome of these struggles decisively affected the power relationships among the competing nations. And while the Europeans colonized, traded, and competed around the globe, European civilization spread with them, impacting with varying results on the native populations encountered by the Europeans. The seventeenth and eighteenth centuries marked a decisive turning point in the establishment of western European domination over much of the world. No less significantly, European expansion laid the basis for a global economy.

1. THE NEW WORLD: THE ENGLISH, THE FRENCH, AND THE DUTCH

One of the areas attracting the English, French, and Dutch was the New World, where all three nations established thriving colonies during the seventeenth century and eventually became embroiled in bitter rivalry for dominance. The northern European nations had their appetites whetted by the fabulous profits reaped from the New World by the Spanish and the Portuguese during the sixteenth century. These two powers retained their vast empires in Central and South America during the seventeenth and eighteenth centuries and continued to earn a rich reward from their enterprises. During the seventeenth century the hauls of gold and silver declined, and the Spanish

and Portuguese turned their energies toward creating large plantations worked by oppressed natives and imported African slaves to produce products marketable in western Europe. Their presence in South and Central America forced the attention of the English, French, and Dutch toward North America and the Caribbean area.

The English were the most successful colonizers in North America. Although some settlers were prompted by political and religious reasons, most were lured by the prospects of available land. Colonizing ventures were organized by joint stock companies chartered by the government to plant settlements in the New World or by individual leaders granted huge tracts of land for the purpose of colonization. Between 1607, when the first colony was planted at Jamestown, Virginia (see Figure 35.2), and 1733, when a colony was founded in Georgia, England established control of the Atlantic seaboard from Maine to the Spanish colony in Florida. In the thirteen colonies a stable order soon emerged that showed considerable potential for agricultural and commercial growth. This growth was promoted by a steady flow of emigrants, not only from England but also from other northern European nations. By the beginning of the eighteenth century the English settlers were beginning to push westward out of the coastal colonies in search of new lands to occupy. English explorers and traders penetrated into the Hudson Bay area in Canada and claimed for England a huge territory, where soon a profitable trade in fur developed. Flourishing English colonies were established in the West Indies, the chief ones being Barbados, Jamaica, and Bermuda. In this area the English concentrated on developing highly profitable sugar plantations, utilizing African slaves as a labor supply.

France also undertook to colonize in the New World, although not as successfully as England. Its first American colony was established by Samuel de Champlain at Quebec on the St. Lawrence River in 1608. Champlain later explored and claimed for France the entire St. Lawrence Valley from the Atlantic to the Great Lakes. Toward the end of the seventeenth century during the reign of Louis XIV the French extended their holdings in North America by claiming a huge territory called Louisiana, stretching down the Mississippi

FIGURE 35.2. The New World Frontier   This representation of the first settlement at Jamestown, Virginia, suggests something of the drastic changes that affected those who left European society—symbolized by the great ship standing at anchor—to face the wilds of the New World. (Culver Pictures)

Basin from the Great Lakes to the Gulf of Mexico. The French also established prosperous colonies in the West Indies, especially on Martinique and Guadeloupe, where sugar production was the major economic activity.

Except for the West Indies, settlers were slow to come to France's vast, rich lands in the New World, in part because of governmental policy. France closed its empire to non-Catholics, thus excluding an element so important in populating England's colonies—the religiously dissatisfied. By adopting a policy of land allocation that favored the aristocracy, the French government made it difficult for commoners to obtain land overseas. The opportunities for profits offered by the fur trade discouraged agricultural settlement. When England seized France's American empire in 1763, perhaps no more than eighty thousand settlers lived in New France, compared with the 1.5 million inhabitants of the English colonies. But that sparse population left its marks, especially in the form of Roman Catholicism, the French language, and the imitation of French social practices by

settlers in the St. Lawrence Valley and southern Louisiana—marks that persist to the present to give a distinctive character to society in these areas.

The Dutch also became involved in the colonizing of North America. In 1621 the Dutch West India Company was chartered to undertake colonizing and commerce in the New World. In 1624 a Dutch colony was planted on Manhattan Island, a location made especially attractive because of its potential as a center from which trade could be controlled. Soon other Dutch communities were established in the valleys of the Hudson, Connecticut, and Delaware rivers. However, the Dutch did not push their colonizing effort very seriously. Their interest was chiefly in trading activities, leading them to concentrate their energies on the more profitable East Indies. Their American colonies became a bone of contention in the Anglo-Dutch struggles that preceded the Glorious Revolution in England. In 1664 the English seized New Netherland, ending Dutch colonization in North America.

2. EUROPEAN PENETRATION OF THE FAR EAST AND AFRICA

During the sixteenth century, Portugal had established supremacy in the Far East. In the seventeenth century, however, the Dutch, English, and French aggressively entered into the area (see Map 35.1). The Dutch were the first. In 1602 all the competing Dutch companies interested in Far Eastern trade were joined into a single Dutch East India Company, to which the Dutch government gave almost complete freedom of action. The company soon drove the Portuguese out of the Spice Islands, which became the center of the Dutch trading empire. In 1641 Malacca on the Malay peninsula was seized, giving the Dutch control of the seas around the East Indies. Ceylon and the Celebes were also captured. The English tried to seize a share of this rich area, but they were driven out by the Dutch as early as 1623. To safeguard the sea route to the Indies, the Dutch established a colony at the Cape of Good Hope in South Africa. Its growth was slow, but the Dutch influence was eventually strong enough to influence the history of South Africa to the present. To watch its interests in the Indies, the Dutch East India Company established a governor-general in Java, who in turn set up several other fortified governmental centers in the island empire.

For years after, the Dutch continued to profit from their holdings in the Indies. They demonstrated remarkable skill in utilizing the native agricultural economy to produce commodities such as spices that were in great demand in western Europe. Consequently, their presence disturbed very little the existing patterns of life in the area. The Dutch also made attempts to penetrate China and Japan but enjoyed only limited success, chiefly because neither the Chinese nor the Japanese welcomed them. Both were too strong to permit entrance by force.

The English, although shut out of the East Indies by the Dutch, made rapid progress toward replacing the Portuguese in India. The English East India Company was chartered in 1600 and given a monopoly of English trade in the East. This company concentrated chiefly on India, slowly forcing the Portuguese to let English traders into that rich land. The company founded its own "factories" (trading posts) at key locations—Surat, Madras, Bombay, and Calcutta (see Figure 35.3). For a long time the East India Company was content to exploit the trading opportunities available in these cities; the merchants interfered little with Indian affairs and had little influence on Indian society.

Rather belatedly, the French entered the competition in the Far East. Colbert organized a French East India Company (1664), which soon established a French outpost at Pondicherry in India. From this center the French company built up a prosperous trade that returned large profits.

During the seventeenth and eighteenth centuries, western Europeans made significant crossroads into sub-Saharan Africa. Again the Portuguese had been the early leaders, but they were eventually joined by others. It was the establishment of the plantation system in the New World that sparked a new interest of Europeans in Africa. The plantations needed labor; African slaves could provide that commodity. Portuguese, Dutch, English, French, and North American traders and adventurers, acting with the support of their governments, established a series of trading posts along the West African coast stretching from modern Senegal to Angola chiefly for the purpose of purchasing slaves to be transported to the New World.

3. THE IMPACT OF EUROPEAN EXPANSION: THE NATIVE AMERICANS

The increasing presence of European colonists and traders around the world during the seventeenth and eighteenth centuries had a significant impact on the native populations of the areas to which Europeans went. In many ways these encounters between Europeans and natives set a pattern that was destined to impose a bitter heritage on the modern world.

Of all the non-Europeans who felt the impact of the white man, the native Americans—the American Indians—were perhaps most immediately and drastically affected. Their patterns of life, ranging from the highly sophisticated civilizations of the Incas in Peru and the Aztecs and Mayas in

Mexico and Central America to the simple pastoral and hunting cultures of the North American Indians, were irreparably disrupted by the onslaught of the intruders.

We have already described the destructive impact of the Spanish and Portuguese *conquistadors* on the Aztecs, Mayas, and Incas. During the seventeenth and eighteenth centuries, the dislocation continued. Spanish and Portuguese colonial policies cast the Indians into the role of laborers on the expanding plantation system and in the reviving mining enterprises from which the Europeans drew huge profits. To add to the disruption of native social and economic life, the new masters imported large numbers of black slaves from Africa. Although the foreign Europeans were few in number, they dominated political, economic, and social life with little respect for the established practices of native life.

Despite their indifference to established native American culture, the Europeans in Latin America were never numerous enough to exterminate the native Americans or their cultures. Inexorably, their blood and their culture intermingled with those of the native Americans. As a result, significant elements of native American culture survived, especially in family structure, agricultural techniques, art motifs, and even religion. Although the ancient Indian civilizations of Central and South America were forever disrupted, enough Indian culture survived to give Latin American society a special hybrid character that has survived to this day.

The Indians of North America suffered a dif-

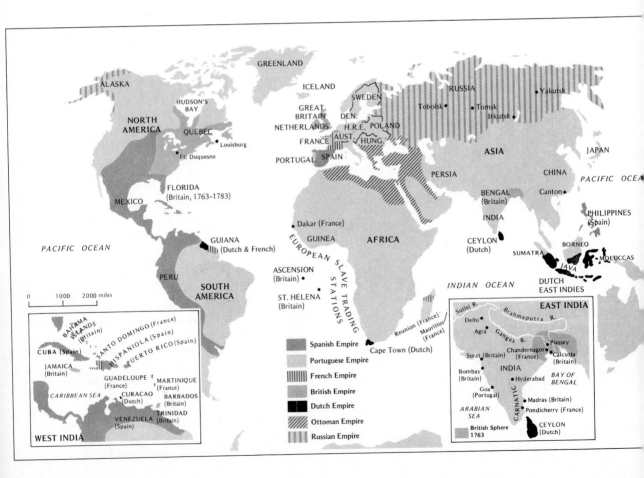

ferent, and perhaps a crueler, fate. In general, the interactions between French settlers and the Indians were not particularly disruptive to Indian society, chiefly because the French were few in number, usually more concerned with trade than land occupation, and interested in the Indians as potential converts to Christianity. The English settlers pursued a more ruthless course. From the beginning they were chiefly interested in occupying and exploiting the land, an intent that demanded the displacement of the natives. Although English-Indian relationships were occasionally marked by friendliness and mutual assistance, the burgeoning seaboard population began to assert inexorable pressure on the Indians. As a consequence, the Indians began to disappear from "new" America; their demise was often accompanied by conniving and brutality on the part of the settlers, who began to perceive themselves as *the* "Americans." In the effort to protect their land, the Indians fought back savagely. Their resistance nourished a feeling among the colonists that the native Americans were inferior savages whose extermination would best serve everyone's interest. The British government struggled from afar to establish an Indian policy aimed at respecting Indian rights to their lands and dealing with them honorably in resolving conflicts. But the westward-bound, land-hungry newcomers paid little heed and proceeded with the grim business of displacing or exterminating the Indians in the vast Indian stronghold lying between the Appalachians and the Mississippi. The resultant dislocations completely undermined the foundations of native American culture and condemned the Indians to a long-standing inferior status in America.

Map 35.1 OVERSEAS POSSESSIONS, 1763 This map shows the extent to which the major European powers had established control over the world by the middle of the eighteenth century. It especially points up the success of England in the quest for overseas possessions. The rich trade flowing to and from Europe to the overseas possessions had become a vital factor in the economies of these nations. Increasing its overseas possessions and trade was of vital importance to every Euorpean state.

4. THE IMPACT OF EUROPEAN EXPANSION: THE FAR EAST

In contrast with the impact of Europeans on the New World, their impact was minimal on the peoples of the Far East. Few Europeans went to that part of the world as colonists. Those few who did isolated themselves in trading depots located in seaboard cities in India and the East Indies, where their contacts with the natives were slight. The limited impact of the Europeans on the world of the Far East resulted also from the fact that the newcomers encountered ancient cultures and solidly established societies.

When the Europeans first began the penetration of India, that ancient land was politically unified for one of the rare moments in its history. Unity had been imposed by Moslem foreigners, the Moguls, a branch of the Mongol horde of Tamerlane. Mogul rule brought prosperity to India's upper classes and a brilliant chapter in India's already rich cultural history. As the seventeenth century progressed, Mogul power began to decline. Political power increasingly fell into the hands of native local princes, a development that proceeded rapidly during the eighteenth century. Because this situation aided the English and the French in establishing their commercial interests in India, the intruders encouraged political localism. Thus, their presence had a significant impact on the political structure of India.

However, Indian society retained its cohesion and its unique identity despite the presence of the foreigners, be they Moslem Asiatics or Christian Europeans. Its primary social institutions—the family, the village, and the caste system—remained intact, fundamentally untouched by the outsiders. Undergirding these ancient social institutions were powerful religious beliefs and practices, embodied above all in Hinduism, which emphasized the acceptance of the existing order as a part of the divine order. Hindu Brahmins, or priests, played a crucial role in sustaining the traditional order. Indian social institutions, religion, and culture combined to incline Indians to accept their situation in the present world because each individual's lot represented a necessary step in the progression toward ultimate fulfillment in another

FIGURE 35.3. A Refuge in a Foreign World. This drawing shows a European factory, or trading settlement, built in seventeenth-century India. Within the confines of such structures were warehouse, places of residence, market facilities, and even a church. The structure illustrates how the Europeans isolated themselves from the native population in the Far East. (The Bettmann Archive)

world. Progress, competition for wealth, and the search for new things did not hold the same attraction for Indians as they did for Europeans. Indians were not impressed by European civilization. They were convinced that they had reflected as deeply on human problems as the foreigners and had arrived at superior answers. Indians could point to a remarkable art and literature as proof of the vitality of their way of life. Little the Europeans could offer to India seemed able to improve on Indian institutions and values. The outsiders found that a few hundred soldiers and a few cannon could not shake the Indians'

confidence in their village and family life, their caste system, their religion, and their culture. Moreover, the continued existence of the basic pattern of Indian civilization in no way impeded the Europeans from reaping huge profits from their commercial enterprise in India. Only slowly and almost imperceptibly did the European way of life make any significant impression on India. And as time passed, Europeans developed a deep respect for some aspects of Indian civilization.

The Dutch presence in the East Indian world likewise had little effect on native society. In fact, the Dutch found it in their interests to sustain the existing order because it lent itself easily to commercial arrangements favorable to the outsiders.

The other major cultural centers in the Far East—China and Japan—were also little affected by the intrusion of Europeans during the period from 1500 to 1800. Again, this was a consequence of the vitality of native civilizations. In China the Manchu dynasty established a strong political regime during the seventeenth century that brought internal peace, prosperity, and a revitalization of Chinese social, religious, and cultural life along traditional patterns. Chinese civilization came to be greatly admired in Europe in the eighteenth century. However, the Manchus carefully controlled the activities of Western traders—called "Ocean Devils" by the Chinese—with the consequence that European influences were barely felt in China. Japan also enjoyed internal stability under the rule of the Tokugawa shoguns, who in the early seventeenth century established firm control over Japan's ancient feudal system and encouraged close adherence to ancient social, cultural, and religious customs and values. The new rulers soon adopted a policy of excluding all Europeans from access to Japan, a policy of isolationism that continued until the nineteenth century and that ensured that European influences would be minimized.

5. THE IMPACT OF EUROPEAN EXPANSION: SUB-SAHARAN AFRICA

European expansion into sub-Saharan Africa during the seventeenth and eighteenth centuries had a decisive effect on the societies existing in that vast territory. The centuries prior to 1500 had witnessed the formation of several prosperous states across a wide belt of territory south of the Sahara from the Atlantic to the Indian oceans and then far southward along that inviting sea. These states—Ghana, Mali, Songhay, the kingdoms of Hausaland, and the Swahili city-states on the east coast of Africa—were strongly influenced by Moslem religion, culture, and technology from North Africa. However, in all of them the imprint of much older native African cultures was also strongly felt, producing an amazingly cosmopoli-

tan culture, especially in the cities that dominated these states. The remarkable affluence of these states depended on a vigorous trans-Saharan and Indian Ocean trade that carried gold, ivory, slaves, and many other products northward to the Moslem world and Europe and eastward to India. In fact, many of these states were brought into existence by enterprising native chieftains who organized extensive realms so as to control more effectively the trading ventures that brought such great riches. Because their existence depended so heavily on trade and because the techniques their rulers borrowed to assert their power had little impact on the great bulk of the native population, these African states tended to be unstable. Nonetheless, their creation and their active intercourse with outside cultures marked an important stage in the development of sub-Saharan Africa and its involvement with the larger world. Farther to the south, beyond the sphere of Moslem influence, the native population continued its agricultural existence according to ancient customs, as yet little touched by developments to the north.

These developments in pre-1500 sub-Saharan Africa created a situation that made Africa particularly susceptible to the onslaught of the western Europeans, chiefly because the destiny of so many African states was tied directly to trade with the outside world. Coming by sea to the coastal areas of sub-Saharan Africa, the Europeans almost instantly caused a redirection of trade routes from the traditional trans-Saharan routes toward the coastal regions that gave access to western Europe and the expanding European empires in the New World and the Far East. The newcomers made little effort to settle in sub-Saharan Africa, partly because the Africans resisted their settlement but more importantly because they could get what they wanted by doing little more than establishing a few trading posts in the coastal cities of Africa. What they wanted were the valuable raw materials of Africa, especially gold, and then before long the Africans themselves—as slaves to perform the arduous labor of creating a rich agricultural establishment in the New World. Throughout the seventeenth and eighteenth centuries massive numbers of black Africans—perhaps as many as 9 or 10 million—were uprooted from their native soil, often as a result of the efforts of their black compatriots, sold into the hands of English, French, Dutch, Portuguese, Spanish, and American slave traders, and distributed under inhuman conditions far and wide to toil as chattels in the service of white landowners intent on exploiting the vast agricultural potential of the New World.

As the Europeans opened slave stations along the coasts of sub-Saharan Africa, significant new political alignments occurred in Africa. African kingdoms along or with access to the Gold Coast flourished as a result of their domination of trade flowing from inland into the hands of European traders. Among the most prominent of these kingdoms were Oyo, Benin, Asante, Kongo, and Ngola. Often the ruling elements of these kingdoms became prime agents in supplying slaves to the Europeans, leading them to intervene among inland tribes to find slaves to sell. Native chiefs living inland likewise became caught up in the slave trade. Armed with deadly weapons from Europe, the native tribes began to wage war on one another as a means of procuring slaves. The Europeans asserted subtle influences on the coastal states in order to enhance their own trading interests, thus promoting a slow deterioration of the capability of the Africans to control their own destiny. As the demand for slaves increased and the prices commanded by the African slave suppliers rose, European traders moved farther and farther south along the west coast of Africa to turn the attention of more and more native Africans toward serving European trading interests, especially slavery, with the same disruptive consequences. European influences, especially Portuguese, on the east coast of Africa were equally disruptive of the brilliant Swahili civilization flourishing there. Only deep in the central part of Africa did the native population remain relatively free of the impact of European intrusion.

On the whole, the development of sub-Saharan Africa was seriously impeded by the encounter of its peoples with the western Europeans during the seventeenth and eighteenth centuries. Africa's human resources were depleted, her natural resources plundered, and her political and social structures disoriented. The Europeans gave little in return, especially when compared with what the Moslems of North Africa had contributed to the enrichment of sub-Saharan Africa prior to

1500. Despite the traumatic consequences of European expansion in this era, the Africans retained many elements of their native tradition, which would later reassert itself as a significant aspect of the liberation of Africa from European domination. And those who were uprooted from Africa in this period took much with them to add important elements to the civilization that was forming in the New World, where they were laboring as slaves.

6. THE STRUGGLE FOR OVERSEAS EMPIRE

In spite of the vast lands to occupy in the New World and rich trading opportunities to exploit in the highly civilized East and in sub-Saharan Africa, the aggressive European nations could not keep out of one another's way in their overseas expansion. As a consequence, the rivalry of European nations became global. The outcome of these struggles began to determine the destinies of peoples only remotely involved in the competition of the European states.

The competition for empire was rooted in two interrelated factors: the essential importance of overseas trade to the expanding economies of the major European nations and the policy of mercantilism practiced by most European powers.

The growing importance of overseas commerce to national economies was abundantly clear. New products from abroad—among others, spices, sugar, tobacco, cotton, silk, tea—were in high demand. So also were some manufactured goods from the Far East, especially cotton textiles and chinaware. Colonists needed the products of European manufacturers. The opportunities to transport these goods stimulated shipbuilding. The need to distribute products from abroad created new opportunities for merchants. The funding of overseas trading and colonizing ventures stimulated the development of banking and credit. The profits garnered from overseas trading activities not only improved the standard of living of those who earned the profits but also became a prime source of capital for investment in agriculture, manufacturing, and commerce. Even governments relied on the gains from overseas trade to provide taxes and loans. In short, Europe's economy had become the focal point for a global system. Control of that economy was vital to the well-being of European nations, even to the point of fighting others for a share of the lucrative overseas trade.

The realities of seventeenth- and eighteenth-century economic life found expression in the widely accepted economic policy of mercantilism, which accentuated the importance of competition for overseas trade and colonies. Mercantilist policy was based on the conviction that the economic well-being of a nation depended on directing the total national economy in a way that would produce a favorable balance of bullion coming into the economy. Among other things, this policy saw colonies as a source of cheap food and raw materials and an outlet for manufactured goods that would return a profit to the mother country. Such a view made the accession and the careful management of the colonies crucial to each nation that aspired to be powerful. Especially important was the need to monopolize trade with a nation's colonies, which placed a premium on developing naval power. Likewise, mercantilism dictated that every effort be made to restrict the colonizing ventures of rival nations and to deprive them of their colonial possessions whenever possible. Thus, every conflict among the major European nations in the seventeenth and eighteenth centuries was extended to their colonies, and every major peace settlement included a redistribution of overseas possessions (see Chapters 32 and 34 for the European aspects of these wars).

The competition for the fruits of overseas empires began in the sixteenth century with the English and Dutch assaults on Spanish and Portuguese trading activities and overseas holdings. By the middle of the seventeenth century competition began to intensify and to become more general. More than any other country, England allied governmental economic policy with private commercial interests, with a view toward promoting national well-being. This approach cast England into a particularly aggressive role in the competition for empire and trade. As early as 1651 England passed its first Navigation Act, providing that all goods coming to and from England and its overseas possessions must be carried in English ships.

This policy posed a challenge to Dutch commercial power, which was especially successful in providing shipping services to other nations. It also encouraged the growth of the English merchant fleet and the navy, badly neglected during the early Stuart period. On three different occasions between 1651 and 1688, England engaged the Dutch in warfare. As a result, Dutch commercial ascendancy began to be undermined while England's commercial power grew; the Dutch also lost their North American colonies.

Toward the end of the seventeenth century the English and the Dutch began to see that France was the chief threat to both. The result was an Anglo-Dutch alliance made by William of Orange when he became king of England in 1689. By that time the Netherlands was no longer the major sea power in Europe. The Dutch were increasingly content to keep their already established holdings in the East Indies, to continue their declining but still profitable carrying trade, and to reap a great profit as the chief bankers and money lenders of Europe.

From 1689 until 1763 England and France fought each other regularly in Europe, and each engagement had its repercussions abroad (see Map 35.1). Several times during the War of the League of Augsburg (1688–1697), the English and the French forces engaged in North America, where the war was called King William's War. Neither in Europe nor in America was the action decisive, and no changes were made in the holdings of either combatant. England had more success during the War of the Spanish Succession (1702–1713). In North America, where the struggle was called Queen Anne's War, England captured Acadia (Nova Scotia) and received recognition of its claims to Newfoundland and Hudson Bay. From France's ally, Spain, England received Gibraltar and Minorca, assuring entrance into the Mediterranean. Spain also granted to England the right to supply Spain's colonies with slaves (the *asiento*) and the privilege of sending one ship a year to the Spanish colonies in America. These concessions ended Spain's long effort to close its empire to outsiders and gave England the advantage over other nations in exploiting trading opportunities provided by the Spanish overseas holdings.

From 1713 to 1740 England and France remained at peace. During this calm neither nation was idle in overseas matters. France, realizing the weakness of its position, was especially active in North America. France tried to protect its holdings from English sea power by building a strong fort at Louisburg at the mouth of the St. Lawrence. France also began constructing and garrisoning a series of forts in its territories west of the Appalachians designed to keep the English colonists pinned to the Atlantic seaboard. England concentrated its efforts on widening the commercial breach it had made in Spain's empire in 1713. A new European war in 1740, the War of the Austrian Succession, led to a sharp conflict between England and France in America (King George's War) and in India. At the end of the war in 1748 each power restored its spoils to the other, England giving up Louisburg and France restoring Madras.

An eight-year truce ensued in Europe, each side preparing desperately for the struggle that everyone knew would soon reopen. In North America, France went back to the policy of building a barrier against the westward expansion of the English colonies. The inevitable clash came in 1755, when the British unsuccessfully tried to stop the French from occupying Fort Duquesne, at the present site of Pittsburgh. The issue was clearly joined; one power must destroy the other in America.

In India a no less dramatic struggle was shaping. France had entered the scene later than England but had made steady progress up to 1740. Between 1740 and 1756 the French and British manipulated the internal chaos in India resulting from the decline of Mogul authority to wring for themselves concessions from India's various princes or political factions. Competition became so vicious that soon an undeclared war was on in India. Thus, at the opening of the Seven Years' War (French and Indian War in America) in 1756, France and England were pitted against each other on three continents. In that war England, led by William Pitt, threw its chief efforts into the naval and colonial war and won a smashing victory. In North America the French held their own until 1757. After that the superior British forces, supported by the navy, overpowered the French outposts one by one. The decisive blow came in 1759, when the British captured Quebec, opening all Canada to the British (see Figure 35.1). British naval units captured the chief French holdings in the West Indies. In India, Robert Clive, a resourceful agent of the East India Company, gave the British a decisive victory at the battle of Plassey in 1757. Clive added large territories to England's sphere of influence by conquering several native Indian states.

The Seven Years' War ended in 1763 with the Treaty of Paris. France surrendered Canada and all Louisiana east of the Mississippi (except New Orleans) to England. Spain, which had been an ally of France, ceded Florida to England. By a special treaty France compensated Spain for this loss by giving Spain the rest of Louisiana (west of the Mississippi). All French possessions in the West Indies except Guadeloupe and Martinique also fell to England. France's empire in India likewise went to Britain. The French were permitted to enjoy trading privileges in India and to keep Pondicherry, but Britain controlled the chief centers of trade, ending any hope of a French recovery of power there. The Treaty of Paris closed an era in European expansion. Although the Dutch and the Spanish still had extensive holdings abroad, Great Britain had fought its way to supremacy in colonial and commercial affairs. The English could now turn to the exploitation of that empire.

Since Columbus' voyage the Europeans had wrought an important change around the world. Energetic colonizers had planted European civilization on the soil of the New World. Enterprising merchants had begun to tap the wealth of a considerable part of the Far East and of sub-Saharan Africa, creating for the first time a global economy in which the level of prosperity in European nations was directly related to their access to the labor and products of peoples all over the earth. European patterns of civilization had begun to alter the lives of peoples who had developed their own cultures long before the Europeans came. For good or bad, the Europeanization of the world had begun. And European history never again ceased to have a world-wide scope.

SUGGESTED READING

European Expansion

J. H. Parry, *Trade and Dominion: The European Oversea Empires in the Eighteenth Century* (1971).

Holden Furber, *Rival Empires of Trade in the Orient, 1600–1800* (1976).

Either of these studies will provide an excellent account of the building of commercial empires.

The Impact of European Expansion

Bernard Bailyn, *The Peopling of British North America: An Introduction* (1986).

W. J. Eccles, *France in America* (1972).

These two works will help the reader understand the occupation of North America by Europeans.

Wilcomb E. Washburn, *The Indian in America* (1975). A good survey.

Karen Ordahl Kupperman, *Settling with the Indians: The Meeting of English and Indian Cultures in America, 1580–1640* (1980).

James Axtell, *The Invasion Within: The Contest of Cultures in Colonial North America* (1985).

Two excellent studies of the impact of European civilization on native American life.

James Lockhart and Stuart B. Schwartz, *Early Latin America: A History of Colonial Spanish America and Brazil* (1983). A good survey.

Stanley Wolpert, *A New History of India*, 2nd ed. (1982). The appropriate parts of this work will provide a good introduction to Indian society at the time of the European intrusion.

Roland Oliver and Anthony Atmore, *The African Middle Ages, 1400–1800* (1981). A clear treatment of a complex subject.

James A. Rawley, *The Transatlantic Slave Trade. A History* (1981). A balanced account.

Imperial Rivalry

W. L. Dorn, *Competition for Empire, 1740–1763*, rev. ed. (1963). A classic work.

CHAPTER 36

Society, Faith, and Culture in the Seventeenth and Eighteenth Centuries

FIGURE 36.1. **Gainsborough, "Miss Catherine Tatton"** Although the middle class was growing during the early modern era, the culture of the period was still dominated by the aristocracy. This portrait of an aristocratic lady by Thomas Gainsborough (1727–1788) reflects the luxury and tastes of the eighteenth-century aristocracy, which commissioned many such paintins. (Scala/Art Resource)

For most people the structure of society, the way of life, and the relevant social institutions changed only slowly throughout most of the seventeenth and early eighteenth centuries. More rapid change occurred thereafter, but it was usually concentrated in certain areas and classes. Despite the continued rise of the bourgeoisie and considerable political change, the aristocracy remained socially dominant and governments headed by kings generally continued to centralize their power. Religious faith remained of great importance to most people, but after the middle of the seventeenth century new religious movements such as pietism were no longer the revolutionary force they had been during the previous century. The literature and arts of the period reflected the spirit of royal absolutism and the values of the aristocracy, with their exaltation of kings, princes, and nobility and also their concern for order and form. The classical style prevailed in literature and music and shared dominance with the baroque in painting and architecture.

1. SOCIETY

Population Growth and Social Structure

One of the greatest sources for change in Western society has been population growth. As we have seen (see pp. 388–390), European population grew substantially during the sixteenth century, putting pressures on economic life, adding to social turmoil, and creating changes in the quality of life for different classes of people. This population growth leveled out during the first two decades of the seventeenth century. On the whole, Europe's population was able only to maintain itself or grow slightly during the seventeenth century. In some areas population declined markedly. The typical enemies of population growth were poverty, disease, famine, and war. Most people lived close to the subsistence level. Any disturbance—a poor harvest, a natural catastrophe, a war—quickly used up their meager reserves of food and opened the door to hunger, declining health, disease, and famine. The Thirty Years' War was particularly devastating, leading to a decline in German population of some 40 percent during the

first half of the seventeenth century. The relatively late age of marriage—in the late twenties for men, the mid-twenties for women—also helped keep down the number of births in a society in which life expectancy was short and only about half of the babies born would reach maturity.

During the eighteenth century, particularly after the 1730s, European population grew sharply—from approximately 110 million in 1700 to 190 million in 1800. Although the causes are unclear, it seems that an increasing birth rate and declining death rate were achieved by earlier marriages, better and more regular nutrition, fewer plagues, and less devastating wars. Agricultural and commercial prosperity, along with continuing improvements in transportation facilities, diminished the periodic famines in many areas. Historians credit in particular the introduction of the potato from the New World and its widespread cultivation in eighteenth-century Europe with crucially increasing supplies of nutritious food. Certainly medical practices were not one of the causes for population growth. With the exception of developing small pox inoculation, which was little used outside of England until the nineteenth century, eighteenth-century doctors, hospitals, and medicines probably caused more deaths than they prevented.

Seventeenth- and eighteenth-century people viewed their society as divided—into different occupational groups and classes—and hierarchically ordered—the different groups and classes ranked from high to low status by birth, office, wealth, or education. Mobility between these ranked orders of society was viewed as the exception. People considered the social order to be relatively rigid and correct. In fact, however, mobility and change occurred. Wealth, education, and new opportunities for governmental service opened avenues for middle-class merchants, bankers, and professionals to move into the ranks of the aristocracy. Nevertheless, social mobility was never the option for many, as it would become during the nineteenth and twentieth centuries.

Rural Life

Seventeenth- and eighteenth-century Europeans lived predominantly in rural settings. In western

FIGURE 36.2. Louis Le Nain, "The Cart," 1641 In contrast to most seventeenth-century artists, Le Nain shows the life of the French peasantry. This farmyard scene (notice the mixture of ages), so typical of the countryside, contrasts sharply with life for the aristocracy. (The Louvre, Paris)

Europe approximately 80 percent still lived in the countryside; in the less urbanized eastern Europe the percentage was even higher. In rural areas life was centered on the traditional village (see Figure 36.2). There life was communally oriented: villagers knew each other, strangers stood out, and almost all effective authority was local. Community pressures limited what we today would consider the rights of dissent or privacy.

This pattern of life was slowly being altered. The traditional village was experiencing intrusion from the outside, change in its age-old pattern of life, and loss of people to the growing cities. The political isolation of the village was being broken by the increased presence of officials from the growing central governments, by the growing absence of the local nobility (who were attracted to the courts and capital cities), and by the decline of communal political institutions. Above all, economic life was being changed by the agricultural revolution and by the spread of cottage industry—both facilitated by improving means of transportation.

The Agricultural Revolution At the beginning of the seventeenth century, crops and animals

were raised in western Europe much as they had been since the Middle Ages. Most fields were open and divided into various strips of land. Crops were rotated and land allowed to lie fallow (unplanted) one out of every two or three years to keep the soil fertile. Large strips of land were set aside as "commons"—open areas where villagers grazed their animals and gathered food and hay. Decisions about crops, animals, and land use were usually determined by tradition and the practices of the community.

During the seventeenth and eighteenth centuries, changes in agricultural production initiated in Holland spread to England and then to other areas of western Europe. These changes were so important that they have been called an agricultural revolution. New crops such as potatoes, turnips, and clover were introduced. New methods of rotating crops, such as from grains to tubers (potatoes and turnips) to hay (grasses for animal fodder), were developed. Fertilization of the soil was increased by using manure from larger animal herds. These changes enabled farmers to eliminate fallow land. In addition, Dutch innovators developed methods of draining wetlands so that new crops and methods could be introduced easily.

They also experimented with breeding to create new strains of productive cattle.

In the early eighteenth century, the new crops and methods spread to England. Charles "Turnip" Townsend experimented with crop rotation and the use of turnips and clover. His contemporary and compatriot, Jethro Tull, advocated the use of a seed drill, which made planting more efficient and productive. Another Englishman, Robert Bakewell, improved the existing types of sheep and cattle by selective breeding.

These changes were sometimes connected to the enclosure of open fields and commons, particularly in England. The consolidation and enclosure of scattered strips and farms allowed larger landowners the freedom to apply new agricultural methods. Enclosures had been used in Great Britain since the sixteenth century, but the profits that could be made in commercial agriculture employing new crops and methods stimulated numerous landlords to seek enclosures during the eighteenth century. After 1750 Parliament authorized a wave of enclosures that transformed the British countryside. While these enclosures hastened the agricultural revolution, they left large numbers of rural poor unable to survive as small farmers. Many of them were forced into the ranks of rural or urban workers.

Cottage Industry   During the seventeenth and eighteenth centuries, "cottage industry," or the "putting-out system," expanded greatly in rural areas. According to this system, a merchant-capitalist provided raw materials (usually for textile production such as wool or linen) and sometimes equipment (such as a handloom or spinning wheel) to peasants. Peasants, working in their cottages, turned these raw materials into finished products—spinning and weaving wool into cloth (see Figure 36.3). The merchant periodically returned, paid for the peasants' labor by the piece, and distributed the finished products to distant markets. The pay was low, lower than that offered in cities, but it was enough to help large numbers of peasants and rural workers to survive. The growth of cottage industry during the eighteenth century, particularly in Great Britain and parts of France and Germany, helps explain how so many people could remain in rural areas.

Urban Life

Cities grew during the seventeenth and eighteenth centuries, but unevenly. Until the middle of the eighteenth century, most of the growth was in the capital and port cities, particularly in northern and western Europe. These cities swelled with the growth of central governments and commerce. After the 1750s new cities arose and small cities grew, reflecting the general population growth and new concentrations of agricultural and industrial activity—particularly in Great Britain.

This urban growth meant greater prosperity for some, but the urban masses were not the beneficiaries. Most continued to live precariously at little more than a subsistence level. Any improvement in the standard of living was enjoyed almost exclusively by the middle and aristocratic classes, particularly those taking advantage of opportunities in commerce and industry and in the expanding governmental bureaucracies. A growing class of urban professionals attended institutions of higher education. In an expanding number of colleges they joined young aristocrats sent by families who felt that more education and culture was appropriate to members of the aristocracy. The middle classes continued to use their wealth to enter the aristocracy through the purchase of titles and offices, the acquisition of large estates, and judicious marriages.

The Family

The family, so central to social life and the socialization of future generations, is usually one of our most conservative institutions, evolving only gradually over time. This pattern of subtle, slow change held true for most of the seventeenth and eighteenth centuries.

The family functioned as both a social and an economic unit. In this household economy (or family economy), everyone who could worked for the good of the household. Husband, wife, children, servants, and apprentices were part of this unit of production and consumption. Even those who earned wages elsewhere usually sent part of their earnings back to the family. Children were often sent away to other households when they could earn more outside their own family.

Child rearing and attitudes toward children

FIGURE 36.3. Cottage Industry Most cottage industry was in textiles. Here the various members of a rural household in Ireland work together, beating and combing flax into linen, which will be spun and woven. (The Mansell Collection)

were strikingly different from those of today. Children were generally not at the center of family life nor of primary concern. Infanticide was not unknown, abandonment was a common practice, and what we would consider neglect was more often the rule than the exception. Much of this behavior may be explained by the high rate of infant mortality, the generally precarious state of the household economy, and simple poverty. Parents usually had to view their children not only as family members, but as assets or liabilities in the survival of the family. With life so precarious for their children, great emotional involvement with them was risky.

It was once thought that most people lived in extended families—more than one married couple and their children in the same household; how-

ever, most historians now agree that as a rule people lived in a nuclear family household consisting of one couple and their children. Nevertheless, the typical family household during the sixteenth, seventeenth, and most of the eighteenth centuries was a much more populated, public place than the household of a modern nineteenth- and twentieth-century nuclear family. At various times a variety of relatives lived in or moved through the household, as did domestics and laborers. The household was far more open to members of the community and pressures from the community at large. The father, older children, other relatives, and community adults in general participated with the mother in raising and socializing young children.

Marriages continued to be entered into for primarily economic and social reasons. The land, the wealth, the skills, and the position one held were the most important considerations in contemplating marriage; sentiment, particularly being in love, played a secondary role. Children were the expected product of a successful marriage. Typically, a married woman gave birth to more than five children, though odds were that many of those would fail to reach adulthood or even get beyond the first few years of childhood.

Significant change came during the second half of the eighteenth century. Sentiment was becoming more important as a motivation for marriage; economic and social considerations, while still important, were not quite as dominant as before. Premarital sex and sex outside of marriage were on the increase, as evidenced by the growing number of births registered within a few months of marriage and by rising rates of illegitimacy. People were marrying at an earlier age and moving around more. Child rearing and homemaking were being turned into a woman's profession in middle-class households. Along with the rising likelihood that most babies born would survive came a changing perception of children as more special, precious, and loved—not miniature adults to be used, as they were more often perceived in the sixteenth and seventeenth centuries. Indeed, what was happening during the second half of the eighteenth century was a slow transformation to the modern family, which would come into bloom with the spread of industry and the dominance of the middle class during the nineteenth century.

Women

Women, while continuing to play a subordinate role to men, were central to the economic well-being of the family among the lower classes. Their work started when they were children, helping with the lighter tasks of farming or cottage industry. In her early teens, a girl often left home to work as a servant, trying to gain the skills and money for her future marriage and the establishment of a new household. As a married woman, her tasks as a child bearer and child rearer were important but secondary to her other economic and social functions. In addition to the standard household chores, women were expected to work

as much as possible. Women participated in the collecting and threshing of grain, took primary responsibility for gardening, raised the poultry, supervised and processed dairy production, and shared in the manufacture of household items and products for commerce (particularly spinning) as the putting-out system spread. When women worked in wage-earning occupations, it was generally at less pay and in lower-status positions than men. The line between acceptable "women's work" and "men's work" widened as the emphasis on women's domestic responsibilities grew. Outside a household, women were particularly vulnerable. They lacked many legal rights and were denied most alternatives for independent employment.

Middle- and upper-class women had fewer opportunities for participation in economic life. Respectable careers open to unmarried middle-class women were limited to those of governess or lady-in-waiting. Once married, the middle-class woman was at the center of the family, but for any real economic independence she had to wait for the death of her husband. More than lower-class women, middle-class women were increasingly seen as responsible for upholding standards and supervising the help within the home. Aristocratic women were similarly limited in the economic roles they played, but they could turn to influential social and cultural roles (see Chapter 38).

2. FAITH: THE GROWTH OF PIETISM

After the end of the Wars of Religion in the mid-seventeenth century, a relative status quo existed between Catholicism and Protestantism. While hostility still existed between believers of different Christians faiths, it no longer broke out into the violence and revolution characteristic of the Reformation era. Religious life remained centered in the local parish. In his church, the priest or pastor conducted services and supervised various charitable and educational activities. Although most people retained allegiance to established Catholic or Protestant churches, some new religious movements did arise during the seventeenth and eighteenth centuries. The most important were a number of pietistic sects, which stressed the importance of active faith in leading a religious life.

In Germany Philipp Spener (1635–1705) and Count Zinzendorf (1700–1760) became leaders of pietist movements of considerable dimensions. Spener, a Lutheran pastor, recoiled from the formal officiousness that his church had fallen into after the heated religious strife of the sixteenth and early seventeenth centuries. He minimized dogma and external forms in favor of inner piety and holy living. His largely Lutheran following included some of the leading intellects of Germany. Count Zinzendorf, a well-to-do Saxon noble man, undertook to restore the Bohemian Brethren, the persecuted and scattered followers of the early-fifteenth-century reformer John Huss. He called his group the Moravian Brethren. The Moravians, too, shunned intricate dogma and formal ritual. They set up model communities based on brotherly love, frugal living, hard work, and inner piety.

In Lutheran Sweden, Emanuel Swedenborg (1688–1772), a distinguished scientist, inventor, and public servant, founded a movement somewhat like the Moravian Brethren, based on his visions, which he took to be direct revelations of God. Swedenborg wrote several learned theological works stressing inner and outward piety and individual communion with God.

England, however, was the seat of the most widespread and influential pietistic movements of the seventeenth and eighteenth centuries. The first was the Society of Friends, or the Quakers, as they were generally called, founded by George Fox (1624–1691). Fox, a man of great energy and stubborn independence, detested formalism in religion as well as in society and government. He believed that true Christianity is an individual matter—a matter of plain, pious living and of private communion with God under the guidance of divine "inner light." Opposed to war, to rank, and to intolerance, the Quakers refused military service, the use of titles, and the taking of oaths. In these respects the Quakers were different from most of the other pietists. They were considered dangerous to the established order and were severely persecuted.

A more moderate and popular pietist movement was Methodism. The prime mover in Methodism was John Wesley (1703–1791). John Wesley and his brother, Charles, became converted to a more fervent, evangelical type of Christianity. When the Anglican churches closed their doors to John Wesley, he preached emotional sermons to huge throngs in the streets and fields. George Whitefield, the most eloquent of all the early Methodists, electrified tens of thousands in England and America and converted many to pietistic Christianity. The real founder of Methodism in the American colonies was Francis Asbury (1745–1816), who duplicated in many respects the work of John Wesley in England. In both England and America the Methodists grew rapidly in numbers, mostly among the middle and lower classes.

The various pietist groups were definitely not political revolutionaries. They were intensely interested in social reform—in education, health and sanitation, temperance, penal reform, and abolition of the slave trade. But they hoped to achieve these reforms by private charity rather than political action. They tended to accommodate themselves to political status quo in the belief that spiritual and social conditions could be improved within that framework of government.

3. CULTURE

The cultural styles of the seventeenth and eighteenth centuries reflected the dominance of royal and aristocratic tastes—particularly in the baroque, classical, and rococo styles. The main exceptions came in the Dutch Netherlands and eighteenth-century England, where paintings and literature often reflected the tastes of the ascending middle class.

Literature

The reign of Louis XIV (1643–1715) was the golden age of French literature. The elegance, the sense of order, and the formalism of the court of the Grand Monarch were all reflected in the literature of the period, sometimes called the Augustan or the classical period of French literature. It was in the field of the drama that the French writers attained their greatest success. Corneille wrote elegant tragedies in the style of and often on the same subjects as the ancient Greek tragedies. The struggles of human beings against themselves and against the universe furnish the dramatic conflicts. Corneille's craftsmanship and style are handsomely polished, though often exalted and exaggerated.

Even more exquisitely polished were the perfectly rhymed and metered couplets of Racine's tragedies: *Andromaque* relates the tragic story of Hector's wife after the death of her husband at the hands of Achilles and the ensuing fall of Troy. *Phèdre* is about the wife of the legendary Greek king Theseus who falls in love with her stepson. This story had also been the subject of plays by Euripides, Sophocles, and Seneca.

One of the greatest of all the French dramatists was Molière. In his charming and profound comedies—such as *Tartuffe, Le Misanthrope,* and *Les Femmes Savantes (The Learned Ladies)*—Molière devastatingly portrays and satirizes the false, the stupid, and the pompous: egotists, pedants, social climbers, false priests, quack physicians. The tragic conflicts and the personality types of Corneille, Racine, and Molière are universal and eternal.

Other major French writers of the age of Louis XIV were Blaise Pascal, the scientist and mathematician who also wrote the marvelously styled *Provincial Letters* against the Jesuits and the deeply reflective *Pensées (Thoughts);* Madame de Sévigné, who wrote almost two thousand letters to her daughter, each a work of art; and duke de Saint-Simon, who spent the latter part of his life writing forty volumes of *Mémoires.* Madame de Sévigné and the duke of Saint-Simon, both of whom were eyewitnesses of the court of Louis XIV, constitute two of the most important sources we have for the history and the life of that period.

The common denominator among all these writers is their emphasis on and mastery of elegant and graceful form. In this emphasis they reflect the spirit of royal absolutism at its height. However, the form is valued not merely for its own sake but as an artistic clothing for subtle and critical thought. French literature in the late seventeenth century overshadowed that of all other countries of Europe, much as did French military

and political influence. The lucid and graceful French language became the fashionable language of most of the royal courts and courtiers on the European continent.

French literature in the eighteenth century continued for the most part in the classical vein. Voltaire wrote dramas and poems carefully tailored to the dictates of classical formalism. His prose works exalted logic and the ideals of Greece and Rome. Only Rousseau among the major eighteenth-century French writers departed from the classical spirit to anticipate the romanticism of a later era.

Next to France, England produced the most important literature in the seventeenth and early eighteenth centuries, and like the French, the English authors generally wrote in the classical vein. The giant of English letters in the mid–seventeenth century was John Milton (1608–1674). This learned Puritan was steeped in the literature of ancient Greece and Rome. His exquisite lyrics *L'Allegro* and *Il Penseroso* and incomparable elegy *Lycidas* are thickly strewn with references to classical mythology. The conscientious Milton contributed much of his great talent and energy to public affairs. During the Puritan Revolution he went blind while working as pamphleteer for the Puritan cause and as secretary for Oliver Cromwell. The chief literary product of this period of his life is *Areopagitica,* probably the noblest defense of freedom of the press ever penned. Milton's masterpiece is *Paradise Lost,* written in his blindness and after the restoration of the Stuart kings had ruined his public career. *Paradise Lost* is a poem of epic proportions based on the Genesis account of the rebellion of Satan against God and the temptation and fall of human beings. This majestic theme is treated in stately blank verse of formal elegance. Even in this deeply religious work, Holy Writ is interwoven with classical pagan myth.

The two greatest poets to succeed Milton were John Dryden in the late seventeenth century and Alexander Pope in the early eighteenth century. Both were satirists, both displayed a massive knowledge of Greek and Roman lore, and both wrote chiefly in the formal rhymed couplets typical of the classical period. In the precision of their form, as in the sharpness of their satire, their appeal was to reason rather than to emotion.

The eighteenth century in English literature was an age of great prose. Following the upheavals of the seventeenth century, the Puritan and Glorious revolutions, it was a time of political and religious bitterness and bickering. In pungent and incisive prose Jonathan Swift, in his *Gulliver's Travels* and political essays, and Richard Sheridan, in his numerous dramas, pilloried the fops, pedants, bigots, and frauds of the day, much as Molière had done a century earlier across the channel. It was in the eighteenth century that the English novel was born. More than other literary forms, it was aimed at and reflected the tastes of England's rising middle class. Samuel Richardson, in *Clarissa Harlowe*, and Henry Fielding, in *Tom Jones*, used this medium to analyze human personality, emotions, and psychology, just as Corneille and Racine had used the poetic drama in France for the same purpose.

In the eighteenth century several writers—Robert Burns in Great Britain, Rousseau in France, Schiller and Goethe in Germany—anticipated romanticism (see Chapter 45). But the prevailing spirit in eighteenth- as in seventeenth-century literature was classical. Precision, formalism, and ofttimes elegance marked the style. Ancient Greece and Rome furnished the models. The appeal was generally to reason. The royal monarchs and their courts had little to fear from this literature. They could derive comfort from its formal order and laugh with the rest of the world at its satire, which was aimed at humankind in general rather than at ruling regimes.

Painting and Architecture

If the literature of the seventeenth and eighteenth centuries did not offend the absolutist kings and their aristocratic courtiers, the visual arts of the period usually glorified them (see Color Plate 14). The dominant style of painting and architecture during the seventeenth century was the baroque, which used elaborate swirling forms and colors to achieve dramatic, emotional effects. The baroque style was originally associated with the Roman Catholic Reformation and reflected the resurgence of a revitalized Roman Catholic church led by the militant Jesuits. Later its massive and ornamental elegance reflected the wealth and power of the absolutist monarchs and their courts, then at the peak of their affluence.

The most popular of the baroque painters of the early seventeenth century was the Fleming Peter Paul Rubens (1577–1640). After studying the work of the Italian High Renaissance masters, Rubens returned to Antwerp and painted more than two thousand pictures, many of them huge canvases. He operated what amounted to a painting factory, employing dozens of artists who painted in the details designed and sketched by the master. Rubens, a devout Roman Catholic, first painted religious subjects (see Color Plate 15). His later subjects were pagan mythology, court life, and especialiy voluptuous nude women—all painted in the most brilliant and sensuous colors (see Figure 36.4).

Spain boasted two of the greatest seventeenth-century painters: El Greco and Velásquez. El Greco, whose real name was Domenikos Theotokopoulos, was a native of the Greek island of Crete (hence "The Greek"). After studying the Italian Renaissance masters, he settled down in Toledo and developed a style of his own. By deliberate distortion and exaggeration he achieved sensational effect. *View of Toledo, St. Jerome in His Study,* and *Christ at Gethsemane* illustrate his genius. El Greco's favorite subject was the reinvigorated Church of the Roman Catholic Reformation. Considered to be a madman by his contemporaries, he is now regarded as the forerunner of several schools of nineteenth- and twentieth-century painting. Velásquez was a painter of great versatility. Although much of his earlier work was of a religious nature, he also painted genre subjects (depicting the life of the common people) and, later, portraits. He is considered one of the greatest of portrait painters. As official court painter, he exalted and glorified the Spanish royalty and ruling classes at a time when they had really passed their peak in world affairs.

During the second half of the seventeenth and then the eighteenth century, classicism, with its greater emphasis on control and restraint, gained favor. Good examples of classicism are in the works of the French artists Nicolas Poussin and Claude Lorrain (see Color Plate 16). Poussin spent most of his life in Italy studying the Renaissance masters. Although his biblical and mythological

FIGURE 36.4. Peter Paul Rubens, "Henry IV Receiving the Portrait of Marie de Médicis," 1621–1625 Rubens was commissioned by Marie de Médicis, widow of King Henry IV of France, to paint this allegorical scene showing Henri IV considering a proposed marriage to Marie de Médicis. The swirling lines, dramatic perspective, rich color, and opulence are typically baroque. (The Louvre, Paris)

scenes are more vibrant and pulsating than the Italian Renaissance paintings that inspired them, they are much more serene, subtle, and controlled than the works of Rubens and El Greco.

In eighteenth-century Great Britain, Reynolds, Gainsborough, Romney, and Lawrence vied with each other for commissions to paint the portraits of royalty and aristocracy. The results were plumes, jewels, buckles, silks, brocades, and laces in dripping profusion (see Figure 36.1).

In the Dutch Netherlands painting did not reflect royal and aristocratic tastes. Here in the busy ports and marketplaces commerce was king, and the great Dutch painters of the seventeenth century, notably Frans Hals, Jan Vermeer, and Rembrandt van Rijn, portrayed the bourgeoisie and

the common people (see Color Plate 17). Rembrandt is universally recognized as one of the greatest artistic geniuses of all time. As a portrayer of character he has never been surpassed. His mastery of light and shade (*chiaroscuro*) made it seem as if the very souls of his subjects were illumined. *Syndics of the Cloth Guild, Night Watch,* and *Anatomy Lesson of Dr. Tulp* (see p. 439) are among his most powerful portrait studies. These three paintings also vividly depict the commercial prosperity, the festive urban life, and the growing interest in natural science, respectively, in seventeenth-century Dutch Netherlands.

Baroque architecture, like baroque painting, was an elaboration and ornamentation of the Renaissance and a product of the Roman Catholic

FIGURE 36.5. **The Baroque Style** This photo is of the interior of the basilica St. Andrea della Valle, which was built in the latter part of the seventeenth century. It well illustrates the elaborate, gaudy splendor of the baroque style, the hallmark of the age of royal absolutism and affluence. In this case the royal monarch was the pope, ruler of a Church reinvigorated by the Roman Catholic Reformation. (Alinari/Scala/Art Resource)

Reformation (see Figure 36.5). In the late sixteenth, the seventeenth, and the eighteenth centuries Jesuit churches sprang up all over the Roman Catholic world. The most important and one of the best examples of the baroque style is the Jesuit parent church, Il Gesù, in Rome. Also, like the painting, baroque architecture was later used to represent the gaudy splendor of the seventeenth- and eighteenth-century absolute monarchs and their courts.

Towering over all other monuments of baroque architecture, much as St. Peter's towered over all

other Renaissance structures, was the Versailles Palace of Louis XIV (see Figure 32.1). The exterior of Versailles is designed in long, horizontal, classic lines. The interior is lavishly decorated with richly colored marbles, mosaics, inlaid woods, gilt, silver, silk, velvet, and brocade. The salons and halls are lighted with ceiling-to-floor windows and mirrors and crystal chandeliers holding thousands of candles. The palace faces hundreds of acres of groves, walks, pools, terraces, fountains, statues, flower beds, and clipped shrubs—all laid out in formal geometric patterns. So dazzling was this symbol of royal absolutism that many European monarchs attempted to copy it. The most successful attempt was Maria Theresa's Schönbrunn Palace in Vienna.

In England Sir Christopher Wren was the greatest architect of the baroque period. The great fire that destroyed most of the heart of London in 1666 provided Wren with an opportunity to build numerous baroque structures. His masterpiece is St. Paul's Cathedral, with its lofty dome and columns.

In the eighteenth century, architecture tended to become less massive, relying heavily on multiple curves and lacy shell-like ornamentation. This style is usually referred to as rococo. One of the best examples of the rococo style is Frederick the Great's Sans Souci Palace at Potsdam. The rococo style, like the baroque, represented an age of royal and aristocratic affluence.

Music

The classical spirit pervaded the music of the seventeenth and eighteenth centuries as it did the literature and the visual arts; and like the literature and the visual arts, the music was an outgrowth of Renaissance developments.[1] The piano and the violin family of instruments, whose forebears appeared in the sixteenth century, developed rapidly in the seventeenth. In the late seventeenth and early eighteenth centuries, three Italian families, the Amati, the Guarneri, and the Stradivari, fashioned the finest violins ever made. The seventeenth century was also marked by the rise of the opera. Alessandro Scarlatti in Italy, Lully in France, and Purcell in England popularized this grandiose combination of music and drama. The eighteenth was the great century of classical music—the age of Bach, Handel, Haydn, and Mozart.

Johann Sebastian Bach (1685–1750) was a member of a German family long distinguished in music. Noted in his own lifetime chiefly as an organist, he composed a vast array of great music for

FIGURE 36.6. Mozart Mozart, shown here as a boy, gained fame as an infant prodigy. Mozart died when he was thirty-five, but this prolific genius composed over six hundred works. (Mozart Museum, Salzburg)

organ, harpsichord, and clavichord (forerunner of the piano), orchestra, and chorus, much of which has been lost. Most of Bach's compositions were religiously inspired, and he holds the same position in Protestant music that the sixteenth-century Palestrina does in music of the Roman Catholic church. Bach was not widely appreciated in his own day. It was not until Felix Mendelssohn in the nineteenth century "discovered" him that he became widely known.

George Frederick Handel (1685–1759) was born in central Germany in the same year as Bach and not many miles distant. He studied Italian opera in Germany and Italy and wrote forty-six operas himself. He became court musician of the elector of Hanover. Later he made his home in England, as did the elector, who became King George I of

---

[1]Some music historians designate the music of the seventeenth and early eighteenth centuries, including that of Bach and Handel, as baroque, which was a forerunner of the classical.

England. Handel wrote an enormous quantity of music, both instrumental and vocal. All of it is marked by dignity, formal elegance, and melodious harmony—fitting for and appreciated in an age of royal splendor. His best-known work is the majestic oratorio *The Messiah*, heard every Christmas season.

Franz Joseph Haydn (1732–1809), unlike Handel, was primarily interested in instrumental music; he was the chief originator of the symphony. During his long career in Vienna, which he helped to make the music capital of the world, he wrote more than a hundred symphonies in addition to scores of compositions of other forms of music, particularly chamber music. It was in his hands that orchestral music really came into its own. All his work is in the formal, classical style. He became a friend and an important source of inspi-

ration for the younger Mozart.

Wolfgang Amadeus Mozart (1756–1791) is regarded by many students as the greatest musical genius of all time. Born in Salzburg, he spent most of his adult life in Vienna. Mozart began composing at the age of five (possibly four), and gave public concerts on the harpsichord at the age of six (see Figure 36.6). At twelve he wrote an opera. Before his untimely death at the age of thirty-five, he wrote more than six hundred compositions in all the known musical forms. Symphonies, chamber music, and piano sonatas and concertos were his favorite forms. His best-known operas are *The Marriage of Figaro*, *Don Giovanni*, and *The Magic Flute*. In the masterful hands of Mozart the classical style reached the peak of its perfection. Never was music so clear, melodic, elegant, and graceful.

SUGGESTED READING

General

F. Braudel, *The Structures of Everyday Life: The Limits of the Possible* (1982). A massive, highly respected social history.

H. Kamen, *European Society, 1500–1700* (1985). A solid survey.

G. Rudé, *Europe in the Eighteenth Century* (1972). Emphasizes social history.

Society

P. Ariés, *Centuries of Childhood: A Social History of Family Life* (1962). A path-breaking work.

J. Blum, *The End of the Old Order in Rural Europe* (1978). Excellent comparative study.

M. W. Flinn, *The European Demographic System, 1500–1820* (1981). A recent survey.

P. Laslett, *The World We Have Lost* (1965). A classic study of English society during the period.

E. Shorter, *The Making of the Modern Family* (1975). Interpretive, controversial, and well written.

L. Stone, *The Family, Sex and Marriage in England, 1500–1800* (1977). A sophisticated interpretation.

L. Tilly and J. Scott, *Women, Work and Family* (1978). A highly respected work.

J. de Vries, *European Urbanization, 1500–1800* (1984). Broad recent survey.

Faith

A. Armstrong, *The Church of England, the Methodists, and Society 1700–1850* (1973). A broad survey.

G. R. Cragg, *The Church and the Age of Reason* (1961). A solid survey.

Culture

A. Adam, *Grandeur and Illusion: French Literature and Society 1600–1715* (1972). A thorough survey of French literature and its relation to seventeenth-century society.

P. Burke, *Popular Culture in Early Modern Europe* (1978). Focuses on ordinary people.

C. Palisca, *Baroque Music* (1968). Excellent survey.

C. Rosen, *The Classical Style: Haydn, Mozart, Beethoven* (1972). Excellent study.

V. L. Tapié, *The Age of Grandeur: Baroque Art and Architecture* (1960). A solid survey of art history.

I. Watt, *The Rise of the Novel: Studies of Defoe, Richardson, and Fielding* (1957). A good introduction.

CHAPTER 37

The Scientific Revolution

FIGURE 37.1. Isaac Newton Isaac Newton (1642–1727) became the leading figure of the Scientific Revolution, employing the new methods of science and drawing together discoveries in astronomy and physics to create a systematic explanation of the physical laws of the universe. This portrait suggests his youthful vigor and keenness. He was still in his twenties when he developed some of his greatest theories. (The Bettmann Archive)

Until the seventeenth century even the most learned scholars of Europe agreed with the standard medieval understanding of the physical nature of the earth and the universe. This medieval understanding was based on the views of the fourth-century B.C. Greek, Aristotle, as modified by Ptolemy and medieval Christian scholars. According to this Christian medieval understanding the earth was stationary and at the center of the universe. Around it moved the planets, the sun, the stars, and the heavens in an ascending series of spheres. This universe was finite and and focused on the earthly center of God's concern. "Scientific" investigation generally took the form of making deductions from accepted, authoritative medieval assumptions about the physical universe. The questions asked were usually the more philosophical or theological ones of ultimate causes for an event—guesses on why something occurred.

During the seventeenth century a relatively small number of scholars undermined this medieval understanding of nature and replaced it with a modern scientific view. According to this new scientific view, the earth was a moving body and no longer at the center of the universe. Rather it, along with the planets, moved around the sun in an infinite universe of other similar bodies. Scientific investigations generally took the form of observing, measuring, experimenting, and coming to reasoned conclusions through the use of sophisticated mathematics. Medieval assumptions about the physical universe were viewed with a skeptical eye. The questions asked were usually the more concrete, pragmatic ones of how an event occurred rather than the ultimate reasons for why such an event occurred. The new scientific synthesis was one of a mechanistic universe of forces acting according to mathematically expressible laws and open to human reason and investigation.

Until the eighteenth century the impact of this modern scientific view, known as the Scientific Revolution, was limited. Nevertheless, it was an intellectual revolution of great significance, for with it Western civilization was making a turn from its medieval assumptions and embarking in a direction unique among the cultures of the world. Science would grow to become one of the main factors distinguishing the West and accounting for its power and dynamism.

1. CAUSES AND SPREAD

There were several causes for the development and spread of the Scientific Revolution, some of which extend back to the late Middle Ages and Renaissance. Medieval universities had been growing for some time and included the study of philosophy and other subjects that would be central to the Scientific Revolution, including astronomy, physics, and mathematics. Certainly the emphasis and the greatest prestige was accorded to theology and nonscientific study in these medieval universities, but nevertheless there were places on the faculty for many of the central figures of the Scientific Revolution, such as Galileo and Newton.

The Renaissance involved a search for classical writings. The discovery of Greek authorities who contradicted Aristotle and the growth of Neoplatonism as an alternative to Aristotelian thought in Renaissance Italy encouraged scholars to question medieval scientific assumptions. The Renaissance stimulated interest in analyzing and describing physical reality, a key concern of the Scientific Revolution. The Renaissance was also an age of commercial and geographic expansion in the West, which created a demand for new instruments and precise measurements, particularly for navigation in the open seas. This demand encouraged scientific research, especially in astronomy and mathematics. In turn, the better instruments developed during the Renaissance helped scholars make accurate measurements, something crucial for the new science. During this same period, the printing press was invented, which facilitated the dissemination of the new science, even if initially to only a select few.

The Reformation played a mixed role in the Scientific Revolution. Generally, both Catholics and Protestants criticized the scientific discoveries that so threatened the medieval-Christian view of the universe. During the sixteenth century there was perhaps more room within the Catholic church for scientific research than among Protestants, but by the middle of the seventeenth century this was clearly not the case. By then the Counter-Reformation Catholic church had turned into an enemy of much of the new science, while Protestants began to accept it. This was particularly so in England, where the Puritans encouraged the new science and where science took hold most firmly.

During the seventeenth century, governments gave support to science, in part hoping that scientific inquiry would yield discoveries that would increase the power and prosperity of the state. With governmental support scientific academies were established and played a significant role in the advancement of science. The earliest and most important of these were the Royal Society in England, chartered in 1662 by Charles II, and the Académie des Sciences in France, founded by Colbert four years later. These organizations and others patterned after them furnished laboratories, granted subsidies, brought scientists together to exchange ideas, published their findings, and encouraged scientific achievement generally. They also helped make scientists a more socially acceptable group and contributed to the creation of a new set of values supportive of the new science.

Finally, religious and psychological factors played an important, if difficult to evaluate, role in the development and spread of the Scientific Revolution. Many of the new scientists had strong, though not always traditional, religious motives for their work, particularly a desire to gain insight into the perfection of God's universe.

2. ASTRONOMY AND PHYSICS: FROM COPERNICUS TO NEWTON

The first branches of modern natural science to attract systematic attention were astronomy and physics. Discoveries in these fields would dramatically alter the perception of nature and the earth's place in the universe.

Nicolaus Copernicus

The first steps were taken in the sixteenth century by Nicolaus Copernicus (1473–1543), a Polish cler-

gyman interested in astronomy, astrology, mathematics, and church law. Like so many other northern European scholars in the fifteenth century, he crossed the Alps to study in an Italian university. There he was influenced by the rediscovery of Greek scholarship, particularly Platonic and Pythagorean thought, that differed from the accepted, mathematically complex Aristotelian-Ptolemaic tradition. This rediscovered Greek thought emphasized the importance of a hidden, simpler, mathematically harmonious reality underlying appearances. With a religious, mystical passion, Copernicus sought a simpler mathematical formulation for how the universe operated. This search convinced him that the earth was not the center of the universe but, rather, that the sun was the center. Moreover, the earth was not stationary but moved in perfect divine circles around the sun, as did other bodies in the universe. This change from an earth-centered (geocentric) to a sun-centered (heliocentric) universe has come to be known as the Copernican revolution (see Figures 37.2 and 37.3).

Copernicus worked on his heliocentric model of the universal for almost twenty-five years, but fearing the ridicule of the laity and the ire of the clergy, he did not have it published until 1543, the year of his death. Few knew of his views and even fewer accepted them. Nevertheless, their significance and their threat to the Christian conception of the universe would be recognized and condemned by Catholic and Protestant authorities. They denounced the Copernican system as illogical, unbiblical, and unsettling to the Christian faith. Nevertheless, his views would stimulate other scholars investigating the physical nature of the universe.

Tycho Brahe

After Copernicus, the most important astronomer of the sixteenth century was a Danish aristocrat, Tycho Brahe (1546–1601). He persuaded the king of Denmark to support him, and he built the most advanced astronomy laboratory in Europe. There he gathered unusually accurate, detailed information about the planets and stars (even though the telescope had not yet been invented). Partic-

FIGURE 37.2. The Medieval View of the Universe
This woodcut (1559) shows the traditional Ptolemaic conception of the universe. At the center is the earth, surrounded by ascending spheres of air, fire, the sun, the planets, the stars ("firmament"), the crystalline ring, and the "primum mobile." (The British Museum)

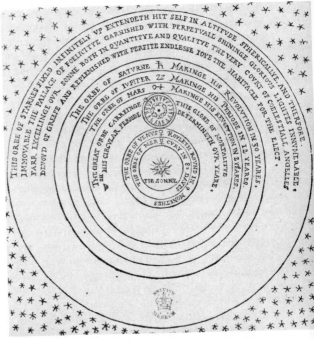

FIGURE 37.3. The Copernican conception of the universe (woodcut, 1576). At the center is the sun, surrounded by the circling planets (one of which is the earth), all bounded by an infinity of stars and the heavens. One of the central developments of the Scientific Revolution was the replacement of the Ptolemaic geocentric by the Copernican heliocentric conception of the universe. (The British Museum)

ularly important were his discoveries of a new star in 1572 and a comet in 1577, both of which undermined the Aristotelian assumptions about a sky of fixed, unalterable stars moving in crystalline spheres. He did not share Copernicus' belief in a heliocentric universe nor did he grasp the sophisticated mathematics of the day. He believed that the earth remained the stationary center of the universe, as argued by Aristotle and Ptolemy, but he concluded that the other planets revolved around the sun, which itself moved around the earth and moon. However, the astronomical observations he gathered would be used by other scholars who became convinced that the earth moved around the sun.

Johann Kepler

Tycho Brahe's assistant, Johann Kepler (1571–1630) built upon Brahe's observations while returning to the Copernican heliocentric theory. A German Lutheran from an aristocratic family, Kepler believed there was an underlying mathematical harmony of mystical significance to the physical universe. He sought such a mathematical harmony that would fit with Brahe's observations. His most important findings were the three laws of planetary motion, proposed between 1609 and 1619: first, that the planets moved in ellipses around the sun; second, that their velocity varied according to the distance from the sun; and third, that there was a physical relationship between the moving planets that could be expressed mathematically. He thus further undermined the Aristotelian universe accepted by medieval thought and provided support for the Copernican revolution. Moreover, he extended the Copernican revolution in ways that would be fully realized by Galileo and Newton.

Galileo Galilei

The Italian astronomer, physicist, and mathematician Galileo Galilei (1564–1642) believed, like Copernicus and Kepler, that there was a hidden harmony to nature. He felt that this harmony could be discovered through experimentation and mathematics. He investigated motion through controlled experiments and demonstrated that motion could be described mathematically. He showed that bodies once set in motion will tend to stay in motion and described mathematically the speed of falling bodies. He thus undermined Aristotelian physics and established rules for experimental physics.

Galileo then moved to astronomy, using a telescope he built in 1609. The telescope revealed to Galileo that the moon had a rough surface not unlike the earth's, that Jupiter had moons, and that the sun had spots. He confirmed the Copernican hypothesis and provided support for the view that other heavenly bodies were like the earth and imperfect. By implication, this finding meant that the natural universe was ordered and uniform, without the hierarchical distinctions of the accepted medieval view.

Galileo aggressively published and defended his views against detractors, most notably in *Dialogue on the Two Chief Systems of the World,* published in Italian in 1632. This text brought him into conflict with conservative forces in the Catholic church, which condemned his theories at an Inquisition in 1633, forcing him to recant.

Isaac Newton

The uphill trail blazed by Copernicus, Brahe, Kepler, and Galileo was continued on to a lofty peak by Isaac Newton (1642–1727). As a student at Cambridge University, he distinguished himself enough in mathematics to be chosen to stay on as professor after his graduation. Starting in his early twenties, Newton came forth with some of the most important discoveries in the history of science—or indeed of the human intellect. He developed calculus and investigated the nature of light. He formulated and described mathematically three laws of motion: inertia, acceleration, and action/reaction. He is probably best known for the laws of universal attraction, or gravitation. The concept matured and was refined in Newton's mind over a period of years. As it finally appeared in 1687 in his *Principia (The Mathematical Principles of Natural Knowledge),* the law is stated with marvelous simplicity and precision: "Every particle of matter in the universe attracts every other particle with a force varying inversely as the square of the distance between them and directly proportional to the product of their masses." This law, so simply expressed, applied equally to the movement of a planet and a berry falling from a bush. The secret of the physical universe appeared to have been solved—a universe of perfect stability and precision.

What Newton had done was to synthesize the new findings in astronomy and physics into a systematic explanation of physical laws that were true for earth as well as for the heavens. This Newtonian universe was uniform, mathematically describable, held together by explainable forces, atomic in nature. The universe was essentially matter in motion.

Newton, like most other figures of the Scientific Revolution, was profoundly religious; he believed in God and a God-centered universe, as well as alchemy. By the later years of the seventeenth century and the beginning of the eighteenth century, the new science was becoming more acceptable than it had been for Newton's predecessors, as is illustrated by his career. He became a member of Parliament and served for many years as director of the Royal Mint. He was knighted by Queen Anne. His acceptance, as contrasted with the ridicule and persecution suffered by Copernicus and Galileo, indicates the progress that had been made by the scientific attitude between the sixteenth and the eighteenth centuries.

3. SCIENTIFIC METHODOLOGY

The scientists who made discoveries in astronomy and physics succeeded in undermining the medieval view of the universe as stable, fixed, and finite, with the earth at its center. They replaced it with a view of the universe as moving and infinite, with the earth merely one of millions of bodies, all subject to the laws of nature. In the process they were also developing and using new methods for discovery, for ascertaining how things worked, and for determining the truth. Indeed, at the heart of the Scientific Revolution was the new methodology of science. According to this new methodology, earlier methods for ascertaining the truth, which primarily involved referring to traditional authorities such as Aristotle, Ptolemy, and the Church and making deductions from their propositions, were unacceptable. The new methodology emphasized systematic skepticism, experimentation, and reasoning based on observed facts and mathematical laws. The two most important philosophers of this new scientific methodology were Francis Bacon and René Descartes.

Francis Bacon

Francis Bacon (1561–1626) was a politician and once was lord chancellor of England under James I. He had a passionate interest in the new science. He rejected reliance on ancient authorities and advocated that scientists should engage in the collection of data without holding preconceived notions. From that information, scientific conclusions could be reached through inductive reasoning—drawing general conclusions on the basis of many particular concrete observations. He thus became a proponent of the empirical method, which was already being used by some of the new scientists. In addition, he argued that true, scientific knowledge would be useful knowledge, as opposed to medieval Scholasticism, which Bacon attacked as too abstract. He had faith that scientific discoveries would be applied to commerce and industry and generally improve the human condition by giving human beings greater power over their environment. He thus became an outstanding propagandist for the new science as well as a

FIGURE 37.4. Title Page of Bacon's *Novum Organum* This title page from Francis Bacon's *Novum Organum (New Instrument)*, published in 1620, shows a ship of discovery sailing out into the unknown. Below is the quotation, "Many shall venture forth and science shall be increased." (The Bettmann Archive)

proponent of the empirical method (see Figure 37.4). He did not, however, have a good understanding of mathematics and the role it could play in the new science. Descartes did.

René Descartes

René Descartes (1596–1650) was born in France and received training in Scholastic philosophy and mathematics. He spent his most productive years as a mathematician, physicist, and metaphysical philosopher in Holland. In 1619 Descartes perceived connections between geometry and algebra that led him to discover analytic geometry, an important tool for scientists. He expressed his philosophy and scientific methodology in his *Discourse on Method* (1637), a landmark in the rise of the scientific spirit. It was an eloquent defense of the value of abstract reasoning. He would question all authority no matter how venerable—be it Aristotle or the Bible. He tried to remove systematically all assumptions about knowledge to the point where he was left with one experiential fact—that he was thinking. "I think, therefore I am," he believed to be a safe starting point. From this starting point he followed a rigorous process of deductive reasoning to come to a variety of conclusions, including the existence of God and the reality of the physical world. He argued that the universe could be divided into two kinds of reality: mind, or subjective thinking and experiencing; and body, or objective physical substance. According to this philosophy, known as "Cartesian dualism," the objective physical universe could be understood in terms of extension and motion. "Give me extension and motion," said Descartes, "and I will create the universe." Only the mind was exempt from mechanical laws.

Descartes, like Bacon, rejected Scholastic philosophy as not useful (although there were similarities in his deductive method and the reasoning used in Scholastic thought). He emphasized the power of the rigorous, reasoning individual mind to discover truths about nature and turn them to human needs. Unlike Bacon, he emphasized mathematical reasoning, not empirical investigation. By challenging all established authority, by accepting as truth only what could be known by reason, and by assuming a purely mechanical, physical universe, Descartes was in dispute with medieval thought and established an influential philosophy and methodology for the new science.

4. OTHER DISCIPLINES

The individuals who made the great discoveries of the Scientific Revolution all used, to varying degrees, the new scientific methodologies promoted by Bacon and Descartes during the first half of the seventeenth century. Clearly astronomy and

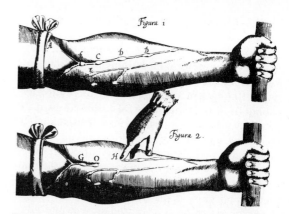

FIGURE 37.5. Modern Anatomy This illustration from an anatomy book published in 1639 by William Harvey shows the circulation of blood. Harvey's empirical, descriptive approach was typical of the new science. (Art Resource)

physics led the way, but important discoveries were made in other sciences as well.

In the sixteenth century Vesalius, a Fleming living in Italy, wrote the first comprehensive textbook on the structure of the human body to be based on careful observation. Because he dissected many human bodies in order to make his observations, he ran into serious opposition from clerical authorities. In disgust he gave up his scientific studies and became the personal physician of Emperor Charles V. In the seventeenth century William Harvey, an Englishman who also studied in Italy, discovered the major principles of the circulatory system, thus making it possible for surgeons to operate on the human body with somewhat less fatal consequences than had previously been the case (see Figure 37.5). Vesalius and Harvey are regarded as the founders of the science of anatomy.

In the seventeenth century, an Irish nobleman, Robert Boyle, laid the foundations for modern chemistry by attacking many assumptions inherited from the ancients and by beginning the systematic search for the basic physical elements. He relied on the experimental method and argued that all matter was composed of atoms. He discovered a law of gases that still bears his name.

The language in which science is expressed is mathematics. In the early seventeenth century a Scotsman, Sir John Napier, invented logarithms, by which the process of multiplying and dividing huge numbers is greatly simplified. Shortly afterward the system was applied to the slide rule. About the same time, René Descartes adopted the symbols now used in algebra and devised analytic geometry, a method of combining and interchanging algebra and geometry. In the latter part of the seventeenth century Newton and the German Wilhelm Leibnitz, working independently, invented calculus, upon which many of the most intricate processes of advanced science and engineering are dependent.

During the seventeenth century some of the basic scientific instruments were invented. Both the telescope and the microscope were products of the Dutch Netherlands. However, it was Galileo who first used the telescope in systematic astronomical observations. Leeuwenhoek, a Dutchman, was the chief pioneer in the use of the microscope. He discovered bacteria two hundred years before Pasteur learned how to combat them; he also observed the cellular structure of plant and animal tissue, the structure of the blood, and its circulation through the capillary system. Another Dutchman, Huygens, invented the pendulum clock, making possible for the first time in history the precise measurement of small intervals of time.

The methods and discoveries of the Scientific Revolution spread to disciplines outside of what are usually considered the sciences. A good example is political theory, with the seminal thought of Thomas Hobbes (1588–1679) and John Locke (1632–1704).

Hobbes gained contact with the new sciences from several quarters. As a young man he served as a secretary to Francis Bacon. While traveling on the continent, he came into contact with René Descartes and Galileo. He studied the writings of William Harvey. Hobbes acquired an expertise in both geometry and optics. Toward the middle of his life Hobbes became involved in the political events of his times and turned his attention to political theory. Dismayed by the civil strife raging during the civil war in England, Hobbes developed a political theory justifying absolutism in the name of law and order. In his *Leviathan* (1651), Hobbes started from a very few principles about human nature and rigorously deduced explanations for the founding and proper functioning of the state. He argued that human beings are most concerned with the preservation of their own lives, the avoidance of pain and the pursuit of pleasure, and the striving for power to protect themselves and get what they want. In the hypothetical state of nature, people are in a continual competitive struggle with each other. Self-interest and reason eventually lead people to exit the state of nature by way of a social contract between themselves. This social contract creates and grants massive powers to a sovereign, who uses those powers as necessary to keep the peace. Hobbes, like other seventeenth-century scientists, assumed a mechanistic, materialistic universe. His reasoning was much like Descartes'—rigorous, mathematical, and deductive. In the end, Hobbes concluded that absolutism was in accordance with natural law, though his method of reasoning pleased neither kings nor aristocrats.

John Locke was also heavily influenced by the new seventeenth-century science. He acquired a medical education at college, read the works of leading scientific thinkers such as Francis Bacon and Isaac Newton, and was a friend of Robert Boyle. Like Hobbes, Locke was involved in some of the political events of his times. Locke also started with human beings in a state of nature, made some basic assumptions about the human condition, and traced the exit from the state of nature by way of a social contract. Yet Locke came to some significantly different conclusions. Assuming that human beings were not quite so self-centered and that things were not so bad in the state of nature, Locke argued that the sovereign had far fewer powers than Hobbes had claimed and that individuals retained the right to revolt under certain circumstances. Applying reasoning similar to that of seventeenth-century scientists, Locke concluded that British constitutionalism was in accordance with natural law.

Thus both Hobbes and Locke extended the Scientific Revolution to new fields. While their conclusions differed, they set a new standard for political theory, becoming two of the most influential political theorists of modern times.

By the end of the seventeenth century, the Aristotelian-medieval world view had been broken and replaced by the Copernican-Newtonian world view. The methodology of modern science was established. Scientists had created the foundations for the modern sciences of astronomy, physics, mathematics, chemistry, and anatomy, and study in other disciplines was underway. Although the new scientists' work had gained considerable acceptance, their ideas were still known to only a few. During the Enlightenment of the eighteenth century, the ideas of the Scientific Revolution spread widely and were applied in new ways.

SUGGESTED READING

General

J. Ben-David, *The Scientist's Role in Society* (1971). A sophisticated social interpretation.

A. R. Hall, *The Scientific Revolution 1500–1800: The Formation of the Modern Scientific Attitude* (1966). A good analysis.

M. Jacob, *The Cultural Meaning of the Scientific Revolution* (1987). A strong interpretation.

A. G. R. Smith, *Science and Society in the Sixteenth and Seventeenth Centuries* (1972).

Astronomy and Physics

Ludovico Geymonat, *Galileo Galilei* (1965). A solid biography.

T. S. Kuhn, *The Copernican Revolution* (1957). An excellent analysis.

F. Manuel, *A Portrait of Isaac Newton* (1968). Uses a psychoanalytic perspective.

R. S. Westfall, *Never at Rest: A Biography of Isaac Newton* (1981). An excellent new biography.

Scientific Methodology

T. S. Kuhn, *The Structure of Scientific Revolutions* (1962). An important, influential interpretation of the Scientific Revolution.

Other Disciplines

P. Laslett, *Locke's Two Treatises of Government* (1970). Includes an introductory analysis with the texts.

C. B. MacPherson, *The Political Theory of Possessive Individualism: Hobbes to Locke* (1962). A controversial, Marxist interpretation.

Sources

M. B. Hall, ed., *Nature and Nature's Laws: Documents of the Scientific Revolution* (1970). A good collection.

CHAPTER 38
The Enlightenment

FIGURE 38.1. "Madame Geoffrin's Salon," 1755 Meetings in aristocratic Parisian salons such as this were typical of the Enlightenment. Here thinkers, artists, musicians, writers, and aristocrats exchanged views and helped spread the philosophy of the Enlightenment. (Giraudon/Art Resource)

As a period of intellectual history, the eighteenth century is usually referred to as the Enlightenment, or the Age of Reason. The Enlightenment was initiated toward the end of the seventeenth century by a number of intellectuals who attempted to popularize the ideas of the Scientific Revolution. During the eighteenth century this popularization continued, and new attempts were made to apply the methods of natural sciences to human behavior and social institutions. Western thinkers were speculating on the broader meaning of science—its ethical, political, social, and economic implications. They subjected almost everything to the critical standard of reason. In doing so, Enlightenment thinkers rejected the assumptions of their medieval and Renaissance predecessors who looked to the Christian or classical past for guidance. Enlightenment thinkers argued for reform and change. They felt that people were ready to shrug off the shackles of tradition and custom and participate in the progress of civilization; to these optimistic intellectuals, people were ready to become enlightened.

The Enlightenment was limited in some respects. During the eighteenth century the Enlightenment was centered in western Europe. Moreover, Enlightenment thought spread primarily to only the elite of the urban aristocracy and middle classes. Nevertheless, the ideas and attitudes developed during the Enlightenment would come to dominate most parts of Western civilization over the next two centuries.

1. ENLIGHTENMENT CONCEPTS

Although Enlightenment thinkers differed widely among themselves, they shared a belief in certain broad concepts that together make up the philosophy of the Enlightenment. The three most important concepts were reason, nature, and change and progress.

Enlightenment thinkers argued that all assumptions should be subjected to critical and empirical reasoning. Traditional institutions or customs should not be accepted because they have been long-lasting but rather should be examined critically and held up to the standard of reason. True knowledge is gained empirically. All we know and all we can ever know is what we perceive through our senses and interpret with our reason. There are no such things as innate ideas or revealed truth.

Enlightenment thinkers believed that nature is ordered, functions reasonably, and constitutes a standard for judgment. Nature is governed by a few simple and unchangeable laws. Those who think they can change one of these laws—who think they can, by praying, for instance, bring down the rain on parched crops and perchance a neighbor's unroofed house—are dupes of their own egotism. Nature does not act capriciously. Proper empirical analysis will show that nature functions in line with the laws of reason. Nature is good and beautiful in its simplicity. Human beings have corrupted it with their complex political, social, and religious restrictions. A move to nature is a move toward wholesome vigor and freedom.

Most Enlightenment thinkers felt that change and progress work hand in hand as human beings work to perfect themselves and their society. Change should not be viewed with distrust as a deterioration from a previously superior, more perfect state of things. Change, when dictated by reason and when in line with nature, liberates individuals and should be pursued. Such change contributes to individual and social progress on earth. Human beings are naturally rational and good, but the proponents of mystic religions have distorted human thinking and prevented proper progress by preaching false doctrines of original sin and divine moral laws. Rid people's minds of these religious hindrances and they can and will build for themselves a more perfect society.

The concepts of reason, nature, and change and progress worked together in the minds of Enlightenment thinkers and generally formed a structure for their more specific ideas. Enlightenment thinkers used reason and nature to criticize institutions and customs of the past, which still dominated their eighteenth-century society. Reason and nature further guided these thinkers as they determined what changes should take place. They felt that as individuals and societies made appropriate changes, human life would become more informed by reason and more compatible with nature. They believed human beings were on the verge of enlightenment—of great progress—if people would simply open their eyes and become mature, reasoning adults. This progress would take the form of people leading increasingly happier, freer, more moral lives.

2. THE *PHILOSOPHES*

Enlightenment ideas were put forth by a variety of intellectuals who in France came to be known as the *philosophes*. *Philosophes* is French for philosophers, and in a sense these thinkers were rightly considered philosophers, for the questions they dealt with were philosophical: How do we discover truth? How should life be lived? What is the nature of God? But on the whole the term has a meaning different from the usual meaning of "philosopher." The *philosophes* were intellectuals, often not formally trained or associated with a university. They were usually more literary than scientific. They generally extended, applied, popularized, or propagandized ideas of others rather than originating those ideas themselves. The *philosophes* were more likely to write plays, satires, histories, novels, encyclopedia entries, and short pamphlets or simply participate in verbal exchanges at select gatherings than to write formal philosophical books.

It was the *philosophes* who developed the philosophy of the Enlightenment and spread it to much of the educated elite in western Europe (and the American colonies). Although the sources for their philosophy can be traced to the Scientific Revolution in general, the *philosophes* were most influenced by their understanding of Newton, Locke, and English institutions.

The *philosophes* saw Isaac Newton as the great synthesizer of the Scientific Revolution who rightly described the universe as ordered, mechanical, material, and only originally set into motion by God, who since then has remained relatively inactive. Newton's synthesis showed to the *philosophes* that reason and nature were compatible: Nature functioned logically and discernably, and what was natural was also reasonable. Newton exemplified the value of reasoning based on concrete experience. The *philosophes* felt that his empirical methodology was the correct path to discovering truth.

John Locke (1632–1704) agreed with Newton but went further. This English thinker would not exempt even the mind from the mechanical laws of the material universe. In his *Essay Concerning Human Understanding* (1690), Locke pictured the human brain at birth as a blank sheet of paper on which nothing would ever be written except by sense perception and reason. What human beings become depends on their experiences—on the information received through the senses. Schools and social institutions could therefore play a great role in molding the individual from childhood to adulthood. Human beings were thus by nature far more malleable than had been assumed. This empirical psychology of Locke rejected the notion that human beings were born with innate ideas or that revelation was a reliable source of truth. Locke also enunciated liberal and reformist political ideas in his *Second Treatise of Civil Government* (1690), which influenced the *philosophes*. On the whole Locke's empiricism, psychology, and politics were appealing to the *philosophes*.

England, not coincidentally the country of Newton and Locke, became an admired model for many of the *philosophes*. They tended to idealize it, but England did seem to allow greater individual freedom, tolerate religious differences, and evidence greater political reform than other countries, especially France. England seemed to have gone furthest in freeing itself from traditional institutions and accepting the new science of the seventeenth century. Moreover, England's approach seemed to work, for England was experiencing relative political stability and prosperity. The *philosophes* wanted to see in their own countries much of what England already seemed to have.

Many *philosophes* reflected the influence of Newton, Locke, and English institutions, but perhaps the most representative in his views was Voltaire (1694–1778) (see Figure 38.2). Of all the leading figures of the Enlightenment, he was the most influential. Voltaire, the son of a Paris lawyer, became the idol of the French intelligentsia while still in his early twenties. His versatile mind was sparkling; his wit was mordant. An outspoken critic, he soon ran afoul of both church and state authorities. First he was imprisoned in the Bastille; later he was exiled to England. There he

FIGURE 38.2 Frederick the Great with Voltaire
Voltaire, seated, talks with Frederick the Great.
This picture reveals the image of the great Enlightenment thinker at work with books, papers, and pen and with the international stature sufficient to gain the ear of enlightened despots such as Frederick. Yet Frederick's enlightenment may have been more form than substance. Bibliothèque Nationale, Paris)

encountered the ideas of Newton and Locke and came to admire English parliamentary government and tolerance. In *Letters on the English* (1733), *Elements of the Philosophy of Newton* (1738), and other writings, he popularized the ideas of Newton and Locke, extolled the virtues of English society, and indirectly criticized French society. Slipping back into France, he was hidden for a time and protected by a wealthy woman who became his mistress. Voltaire's facile mind and pen were never idle. He wrote poetry, drama, history, essays, letters, and scientific treatises—ninety volumes in all. The special targets of his cynical wit were the Catholic church and Christian institutions. Few people in history have dominated their age intellectually as did Voltaire.

The work that best summarizes the philosophy of the Enlightenment is the *Encyclopedia*. The *En-*

cyclopedia was a collaborative effort by many of the *philosophes* under the editorship of Denis Diderot (1713–1774) and jean le Rond D'Alembert (1717–1783). This gigantic work undertook to explore the whole world of knowledge from the perspective of the *philosophes*. Its articles on subjects ranging from music to machinery expressed the critical, rationalistic, and empiricist views of the *philosophes* (see Figure 38.3). The practicality of science and knowledge in general was emphasized. One of the work's main messages was that almost anything could be discovered or understood or clarified through reason. An underlying current was criticism of the irrational and of whatever stood in the way of the Enlightenment, whether it was religious intolerance or traditional social institutions. The first volume appeared in 1751. Its threat to the status quo was recognized by governmental and Church authorities, who censored it, halted its publication, and harassed its editors. Thanks in great part to the persistence of Diderot, who fought the authorities and dealt with a difficult group of contributing authors, the project was completed with the publication of the final volume in 1772. The *Encyclopedia* sold well and played an important role in the penetration of Enlightenment ideas outside the major cities and courts.

By this time the Enlightenment was evolving to a different stage. The *philosophes* were becoming more quarrelsome among themselves. This argumentation reflected a greater acceptance of the fundamental philosophy of the Enlightenment, for the debates tended to center on how far Enlightenment concepts could be extended. Some *philosophes*, such as Baron d'Holbach (1723–1789), verged on atheism in attacks on organized religion. Others, such as Marie-Jean de Condorcet (1743–1794), were so optimistic that they almost made a religion out of progress itself. Enlightenment thinkers were also tending to specialize. Some laid the foundations for the development of the social sciences during the nineteenth century. For example, Cesare Beccaria (1738–1794) contributed works on modern criminology and penology, and Adam Smith (1723–1790) wrote what would turn into the fundamental text of classical economics. Finally, some Enlightenment thinkers took more challenging positions, often contradicting some of the ideas of the Enlightenment itself and providing a transition to the succeeding intellectual traditions. The most important example of these thinkers is Jean-Jacques Rousseau (1712–1778).

One of the most original thinkers and writers of all time, Rousseau crusaded for a return to nature—beautiful, pure, simple nature. The message struck home in a society weary of arbitrary and often corrupt governmental bureaucracy and an oppressively artificial and elaborate code of social etiquette. Rousseau was lionized. Great ladies, including the queen of France, began playing milkmaid. In his novel *La Nouvelle Heloise*, Rousseau extolled the beauties of free love and uninhibited emotion. In *Emile* he expounded the "natural" way of rearing and educating children. He would let children do what they like and teach them "practical" knowledge. Rousseau shared much with other *philosophes*, even contributing to the *Encyclopedia*, but after the 1750s he broke from them for personal as well as intellectual reasons. In *Origin of Inequality Among Men* (1753), Rousseau argued that civilization was not necessarily a progressive boon to humanity, that human beings had lost much since their exit from the state of nature. In *The Social Contract*, Rousseau became one of the few *philosophes* to make a fundamental contribution to political theory. Rousseau generally placed greater faith in emotion, feeling, and intuition than in reason. In this he was a forerunner of the romantic spirit and expounded its principles long before that movement reached its peak.

The *philosophes* had a self-conscious sense of a spirit of enlightenment. They felt that they were leading a mission of liberation, that by striking the match of reason the darkness of the past would be dispelled and humanity would quickly and easily liberate itself. By becoming thus enlightened, humanity could move from childhood to adulthood. They attacked war and the military values of the traditional aristocracy. They rejected artificial social distinctions. They lauded most forms of freedom, including freedom of the press, of speech, and of religious belief. They supported the application of science to economic activity, a view appealing to the middle class and liberal aristocracy. They believed that their eighteenth-century civilization was ready for enlightenment and the great progress that would result. Yet the optimism of most of the *philosophes* was not wild-eyed; indeed, there was an underlying current of pessimism in the works of thinkers such as Diderot, de Sade, Rousseau, and even Voltaire.

In characterizing the *philosophes*, historians have disagreed. Some view the *philosophes* as shallow, self-concerned dilettantes who had few deep or original ideas and who were afraid of real reform. Most historians, however, argue that the *philosophes* were thoughtful, sincere thinkers who performed an important service by laying the intellectual foundations for modern society.

FIGURE 38.3. The Encyclopedia This engraving from one of the many technical articles in the *Encyclopedia* shows workers preparing type for printing, with detail of materials used in the process. It reveals the optimistic faith in the ease and practicality of learning typical of Enlightenment thought. (French Embassy Press and Information Division)

3. WOMEN AND THE SOCIAL CONTEXT

There were several centers of Enlightenment thought in the cities and courts of Europe, particularly western Europe, but the heart of the Enlightenment was in Paris. Several regular gatherings were held in the salons of wealthy Parisian patrons, usually women of the aristocracy or upper middle class such as Madame du Deffaud or Madame Geoffrin. There the *philosophes* met with each other and members of the international upper middle class and aristocratic elite. They debated the ideas of the Enlightenment in an environment lush with art, music, and wealth. These gatherings facilitated the spread of Enlightenment ideas among social and intellectual elites and added much to the social respectability of intellectuals.

As patrons and as intellectual contributors to these gatherings, women played an important role in the Enlightenment. Women such as Madame Geoffrin provided essential financial support to several *philosophes*, particularly for the *Encyclopedia*. Other women corresponded by letter with leading intellectual, political, and social figures throughout Europe, using letter writing as an art just as conversation was an art in the salons. The salons were open to women with the right intellectual or social qualifications. The *philosophes* tended to support improving the education and position of women. The Enlightenment emphasis on individualism theoretically and in the long run led toward accepting the idea of political and social equality between men and women. Nevertheless, it cannot be said that the *philosophes* advocated equal rights for women in a modern sense nor that they challenged fundamental assumptions about the subordinate public roles appropriate for women. One of the few people to argue for real change in the condition of women in the eighteenth century was Mary Wollstonecraft (1759–1797). In 1792 she published *Vindication of the Rights of Women*, but generally her plea for equal rights for all human beings fell on deaf ears.

Meetings in Paris salons were paralleled by smaller meetings in other French and foreign cities as well as by less organized meetings in coffeehouses and homes of the liberal aristocracy. Enlightenment ideas were read and discussed in local academies, Freemason lodges, societies, libraries, and clubs.

4. ENLIGHTENMENT AND RELIGION

The Enlightenment was profoundly secular in character, but religion played an important role. Very few Enlightenment thinkers were either atheists or traditional Christians. Most were skeptics, influenced by the arguments of Pierre Bayle (1647–1706). Many believed in some form of deism. They believed that this wonderful mechanism called the universe could not have come into being by accident. Some infinite Divine Being must have created it and set it in motion. However, the finite mind of human beings cannot comprehend the infinite. Therefore, God is unknowable. Furthermore, God, having set his perfect mechanical laws in motion, will never tamper with them nor interfere in human affairs. God is impersonal.

It is readily apparent that the beliefs of the *philosophes* were diametrically opposed to the doctrines of the Christian churches—Roman Catholic, Protestant, and Orthodox alike. Christian theologians argued that God remained active in the universe, that God's ways are revealed through religious literature and institutions, and that faith constitutes a valid alternative to reason. Enlightenment thinkers and Christian leaders were soon engaged in debate, both spending much time and effort attacking each other. In countries such as France and Italy, where clerics were strongly entrenched in government, they censored the writings of the *philosophes* and sought to interrupt their work. In the long run, however, the ideas of the Enlightenment spread, and the Church probably lost more than it gained by so ardently attacking the *philosophes* and their ideas.

5. POLITICAL AND ECONOMIC ASPECTS OF THE ENLIGHTENMENT

Enlightenment thinkers devoted much thought to matters of government. If human beings are by nature rational and good, then surely, if given the opportunity, they can devise for themselves efficient and benevolent political institutions. Corrupt tyrannies were no longer tolerable. Of the numerous "enlightened" thinkers in the field of political science, three stand out above the others in influence: Locke, Montesquieu, and Rousseau.

Locke's most eloquent plea was for the natural rights of human beings, which are life, liberty, and property. He theorizes, in his *Two Treatises of Civil Government,* that to safeguard these rights individuals voluntarily contracted to surrender a certain amount of their sovereignty to government. The powers of the government, however, whether it be monarchical or popular, are strictly limited. No government may violate the individual's right to life, liberty, and property. If it does, the people who set it up can and should overthrow it. These ideas were fundamental in the thinking of the makers of both the French and the American revolutions. Jefferson wrote many of Locke's ideas into the Declaration of Independence, frequently using his exact words. They likewise appear in the United States Constitution and in numerous French declarations of liberty.

Baron de Montesquieu (1689–1755) was less a theorizer than a discerning student of history and shrewd analyst of political systems. His masterpiece is *The Spirit of the Laws.* Although a great admirer of the English government after the Glorious Revolution, Montesquieu came to the conclusion that different types of government are best suited to various conditions. For instance, absolute monarchy is best for countries of vast area, limited monarchy for countries of moderate size like France, and republics for small states like Venice or ancient Athens. Not only did he approve of Locke's doctrine of limited sovereignty, but he specified how it can best be secured—by a separation of powers and a system of checks and balances. The powers and functions of government should be equally divided among king, lords, and commons, each one being checked by the other two. This theory was probably Montesquieu's greatest practical contribution to the science of government. The principle was incorporated into the United States Constitution—kings, lords, and commons becoming executive, judicial, and legislative branches of government.

The real father of the theory of modern democracy was not Locke nor Montesquieu, both of whom distrusted rule by the masses, but Rousseau. This morbid, erratic genius based the conclusions in his *Social Contract* and in his *Second Discourse* upon pure imagination. People in the state of noble savagery were free, equal, and happy. It was only when some began marking off plots of ground saying "this is mine" that inequality began. In order to restore their lost freedom and happiness, people entered into a compact, each with all the others, surrendering their individual liberty to the whole. Since sovereignty is indivisible, the general will is all-powerful. Although Rousseau never made it clear just how the general will would actually operate in practice, he apparently assumed that the individual would be free by virtue of being part of the general will. Rousseau had great influence on the leaders of the second and more radical phase of the French Revolution.

Some of the eighteenth-century planners of the better life through reason turned their thoughts to economics. Since the late fifteenth century, mercantilism had been the dominant economic theory and practice in western Europe. This system of regulated nationalistic economy reached its peak in the seventeenth century. Only the Dutch Netherlands held out for free trade. But if, according to the fundamental assumptions of the Enlightenment, the universe is run by a few simple mechanical laws, why should there not be a similar natural order in the field of economics? A group of French Physiocrats, led by Quesnay, personal physician to Louis XV, began to teach that economics has its own set of natural laws, that the most basic of these laws is that of supply and demand, and that these laws operate best when commerce is freed from government regulation. This doctrine came to be known as *laissez faire* (or free trade and enterprise).

The chief developer of the theory of laissez faire was Adam Smith, a Scottish professor of philosophy who associated with the Physiocrats while sojourning in France. His *Wealth of Nations,* published in 1776, has remained the bible of laissez-faire economics ever since. The ideas of the French Physiocrats and Adam Smith strongly influenced the leaders of the American and French revolutions.

6. ENLIGHTENED DESPOTISM

While critical and combative, the *philosophes* were not political or social revolutionaries. They hoped for rather painless change from above rather than a revolutionary transfer of power to the still unenlightened masses. Many followed Voltaire in believing that enlightened despotism was the form of government that offered the greatest chances for enactment of enlightened reforms. By the middle of the eighteenth century several monarchs found these views attractive, styled themselves as enlightened monarchs, and attempted to enact reforms that at least appeared to fit with Enlightenment thought. These monarchs have been distinguished from their predecessors and termed "enlightened despots." To what extent this is a valid characterization of their rule remains to be seen.

The most sensational of the enlightened despots was Frederick the Great of Prussia (1740–1786). Frederick had from boyhood loved music, poetry, and philosophy. At the end of the Seven Years' War (1756–1763), the second of his two wars of aggression, he settled down as a model enlightened despot and attempted to apply the laws of reason to statecraft. Frederick was an avid reader of the French philosophers. He even invited Voltaire to visit him at Potsdam, but Prussia was not big enough to hold two such egos at once. The two quarreled and, after several years, parted.

Frederick made much of religious toleration. However, he continued to penalize the Jews and never ceased to ridicule Christians of all denominations. He was a strong advocate of public education, although he spent very little on it in comparison with what he spent on his army. The centralized Prussian bureaucracy became the most efficient government in Europe. True to the prevailing thought of the Enlightenment, however, he had no faith in popular self-government. Nor did he make a move to free the serfs or to end the feudal system in Prussia. Probably the most lasting of Frederick's contributions to Prussia were his codification of the law and improvements in the administration of justice. In the field of economics, Frederick was a mercantilist, although he did share the Physiocrats' appreciation of the importance of agriculture.

The most sincere of all the enlightened despots was Joseph II of Austria (1780–1790). Unfortunately, he lacked the practical sagacity of Frederick the Great. His well-meaning but ill-conceived efforts to centralize the administration of the far-flung Hapsburg territories, to replace the numerous languages of his subjects with German, to secularize the strongly entrenched Roman Catholic church, and to free the serfs in a society still based on feudalism, all backfired.

Other monarchs, such as those of Sweden, Sardinia, Spain, and Portugal, attempted or enacted reforms that could be seen as enlightened. Even in Russia, Catherine the Great made apparent efforts at enlightened reforms, but ultimately she did not put most of those reforms into practice.

Significantly, France alone of the great powers on the Continent failed to produce an even faintly enlightened despot. Upon attaining the French throne in 1774, the well-meaning Louis XVI appointed the Physiocrat Turgot as minister of finances. Turgot, a friend of Voltaire, initiated a program of sweeping reforms that might have forestalled the French Revolution. However, within two years' time the powerfully entrenched vested interests persuaded the weak-willed king to dismiss him.

Whether there was a phenomenon of enlightened despotism occurring during the eighteenth century remains a debated question among historians. If there was, it was usually a matter more of form than content. Several eighteenth-century monarchs acted in certain enlightened ways, believed themselves to be enlightened, admired some of the *philosophes*, and were admired in return. Several supported culture, favored a less religious and more rational justification for their rule, and consulted with *philosophes*. Yet most of their "enlightenment" was superficial. Many of the reforms they made were simply an update in the long process of making the central government more effective and powerful. Few tried to enact fundamental social, political, or economic reforms dictated by Enlightenment thought, and even those who tried, such as Joseph II, generally failed to effect those reforms.

7. CONCLUSION

Enlightenment thinkers applied and popularized a secular, rational, reformist way of thinking that undermined the intellectual foundations of traditional society. These thinkers, probably unknowingly, laid the intellectual foundations for the revolutions that swept Europe and America from the last quarter of the eighteenth century to the mid-nineteenth century. Moreover, their way of thinking and the ideas that arose from it would form the intellectual core of the liberal middle-class ideology that was ascendant during the nineteenth century and is still strong in the twentieth century.

SUGGESTED READING

General

C. Becker, *The Heavenly City of the Eighteenth-Century Philosophers* (1932). An influential, thought-provoking volume by a leading historian.

E. Cassirer, *The Philosophy of the Enlightenment* (1951). An important synthesis, but difficult.

P. Gay, *The Enlightenment: An Interpretation. Vol. I: The Rise of Modern Paganism. Vol. II: The Science of Freedom* (1969). Detailed treatment of a leading authority.

P. Hazard, *The European Mind, 1680–1715* (1963). Excellent on the early Enlightenment.

L. Krieger, *Kings and Philosophers, 1689–1789* (1970). A broad survey making connections between thought and politics.

H. Payne, *The Philosophes and the People* (1976). Focuses on the gap between the *philosophes* and the people.

The *Philosophes*

T. Bestermann, *Voltaire* (1969). A solid biography.

A. M. Wilson, *Diderot* (1972). An excellent biography.

Enlightened Despotism

J. Gagliardo, *Enlightened Despotism* (1967). A good introduction.

E. Wangermann, *The Austrian Achievement, 1700–1800* (1973). A good study of enlightened monarchs.

Sources

L. G. Crocker, ed., *The Age of Enlightenment* (1969). A good anthology.

P. Gay, ed., *The Enlightenment: A Comprehensive Anthology* (1973). A good selection of documents

RETROSPECT

The seventeenth and eighteenth centuries were the apogee of royal absolutism as a form of government in the Western world. The clearest example of royal absolutism arose in France, where under Henry IV, Richelieu, Mazarin, and Louis XIV, the Bourbon monarchy achieved a degree of control that was virtually complete and a position of dominance in Europe that has seldom been equaled. European history during the years 1661–1715 has been called the age of Louis XIV. Louis and his court were the envy of all other monarchs, who sought to emulate them. France possessed a military strength so great that the major states of western and central Europe working in combination held France in check only with difficulty.

The most noteworthy exceptions to royal absolutism in western Europe were found in England and the Dutch Netherlands, where constitutionalism prevailed. In England royal absolutism had reached its peak during the sixteenth century under the vigorous and politically crafty Tudor rulers. The Stuart kings, who came to the throne in 1603 when Elizabeth I died childless, were full of fine absolutist theories but were unable to carry them out smoothly. They soon found themselves in a running fight, mostly over money matters and power, with Parliament, a stronghold of the landed and commercial interests. In a showdown—the Puritan Revolution—the parliamentary forces, under the able leadership of Oliver Cromwell, triumphed. Before the century had ended, one Stuart king had been executed, another invited to the throne on terms, and a third driven out of the country. During the course of the seventeenth and eighteenth centuries England's parliamentary and cabinet system gradually took shape. Constitutionalism had prevailed over royal absolutism. The landed and commercial interests now in control of the English government, however, were no less aggressive in foreign and colonial affairs than had been the royal monarchs.

The Dutch Netherlands, while somewhat unique, also developed a political system emphasizing constitutionalism rather than royal absolutism. Lacking the military resources and potential of their larger neighbors, France and England, the Dutch nevertheless achieved a phenomenal commercial and financial dominance in the Western world. Their economic exploits were accompanied by a preeminence in the fields of painting and philosophy. The Dutch lived under a republican form of government and enjoyed a degree of individual freedom that could not be matched in Europe.

Royal absolutism dominated political forms in central and eastern Europe during the seventeenth and eighteenth centuries. There the most important political developments were the rise of two military despotisms—Prussia and Russia. The Hohenzollerns of Prussia, consistently pursuing the policies of royal absolutism, militarism, and territorial aggrandizement, more than doubled their territory and population and challenged Austria for the leadership of the German-speaking world. Russia, under two strong absolutist monarchs, Peter the Great and Catherine the Great, decisively defeated Sweden and the Ottoman Turks and gained valuable territory facing the West. Poland, failing to develop a strong central government, disappeared from the map, carved up by Russia, Prussia, and Austria.

While Prussia, Russia, and Austria were struggling for the mastery of central and eastern Europe, the French, the English, and the Dutch were competing for dominance in North America and Asia. In this contest the English emerged victorious in North America and India, and the Dutch in the East Indies. The English found it relatively easy to drive the Indians out of eastern North America and colonize the continent with Europeans. In Asia the English and the Dutch defeated the natives but were unable to Europeanize these people who had such firmly established societies, cultures, and religions.

The economy and society—rural, based on agriculture, and with a vast mass of peasantry dominated by the privileged aristocracy—changed only slowly for most of the period. Gradually the central governments, the growing cities, and the middle classes altered life within the traditional village. The pace of social change quickened in the mid–eighteenth century as population grew, agriculture was revolutionized, and cottage industry spread. Religious affiliations changed little; established Catholic and Protestant churches remained committed to the hierarchical social order and the dominant political systems of their states. Even the numerous pietist and quietist religious sects that arose during this period passively accepted, for the most part, the political authority of the established and usually absolutist governments.

The baroque and classical styles, which prevailed in literature and the arts in western Europe throughout most of the seventeenth and eighteenth centuries, generally harmonized with and often exalted the absolutist monarchs and their courts. These styles stressed a combination of grandeur, richness, and order that appealed to monarchs and the privileged orders, who so often were the patrons of the arts.

The seventeenth and eighteenth centuries spawned two developments that would eventually undermine the intellectual foundations of the traditional Christian Western society: the Scientific Revolution and the Enlightenment. The Scientific Revolution challenged the traditional, theological, earth-centered conception of the universe and offered a new perception of the universe as infinite, moving, and lawful, with the earth merely one of many bodies. Truth would no longer be based on custom, faith, or authority but, rather, on rigorous reasoning founded on observed facts and mathematical laws. In the process of this Scientific Revolution, the foundations for the modern natural sciences were established. The Enlightenment popularized and extended the Scientific Revolution. The main Enlightenment thinkers—the *philosophes*—used reason to criticize traditional customs and institutions. They optimistically believed that people could easily become enlightened and thereby progress to a new level of maturity. Their ideas would play an important role in the revolutions of the late eighteenth and the nineteenth centuries and would form a basis for the liberal ideology that would rise to dominance during the nineteenth and twentieth centuries.

Yet even these intellectual developments properly belong to the seventeenth and eighteenth centuries. They stressed order and power, which were so important to the period. They reflected the dynamic between royal absolutism and constitutionalism—particularly in the Enlightenment admiration for English political institutions and enlightened despotism. They remained limited to a small elite, just as the glamour, affluence, and power of the period remained limited almost entirely to the royalty, the aristocracy, and the small upper middle class. The lower classes, whose labor and blood made so much regal and military splendor possible, received few benefits and were unaware of the fundamental intellectual developments that were occurring. From the late eighteenth century on, much would change.

INDEX

Page references in *italic* refer to illustrations, maps, and their captions.